CHARTER OF THE UNITED NATIONS

CHARTER OF THE UNITED NATIONS

COMMENTARY AND DOCUMENTS

Third and Revised Edition

LELAND M. GOODRICH

EDVARD HAMBRO *and*

ANNE PATRICIA SIMONS

COLUMBIA UNIVERSITY PRESS

1969 NEW YORK *&* LONDON

Foreword

Leland Goodrich and I first met at the San Francisco Conference in 1945. He was a member of the Secretariat; I was on the Norwegian Delegation. The plan we had nourished in correspondence matured into fruitful collaboration resulting in *Charter of the United Nations: Commentary and Documents,* published by the World Peace Foundation in 1946. It was a simple, straightforward book which filled a need. A new and revised edition was published in 1949.

Our cooperation was always wholehearted and based on mutual confidence, but we lived on different continents, a circumstance which did not facilitate the task we had set ourselves. The main burden fell on Leland Goodrich because the book was published in the United States and he was immersed in academic life, while I was a secretary of the Norwegian Ministry of Foreign Affairs during the preparation of the first edition, and Registrar of the International Court of Justice at The Hague during the preparation of the second.

A French and later a Turkish edition were published, but we never seemed to find the time for a third and revised edition. Professor Goodrich moved to Columbia University and with increased fame and authority came new and heavier responsibilities, while I became a university teacher in Norway and later Member of Parliament. Yet whenever we met we discussed a new edition and, finally, agreed that it was needed even though we could not devote sufficient time to it. We were fortunate indeed in having the collaboration of Miss Anne Simons, who has worked with Leland Goodrich in the preparation of this edition. My contribution has been minimal, which is as it should be, since I am now the permanent representative of Norway at the United Nations, and any definite view put forward by me in such a book might conceivably cause some embarrassment. However, a short foreword has been deemed advisable despite the adage that a good book does not need a foreword and a bad one does not deserve it. I profit from this occasion to emphasize some of the changes which seem among the most important features of the development of the world organization during the past twenty years.

The United Nations remains the most important center of inter-

national politics twenty years after it was created. This fact has caused
the optimists deep disappointment, the realists grim satisfaction, and
the pessimists grudging recognition. From crisis to crisis it lives on,
and as any living organism it grows and changes. Each new crisis is
disturbing, but strengthens the determination to survive and succeed.

The atmosphere of international debates has changed dramatically
since the days when polished and elegant phrases were exchanged on
the shores of Lake Geneva. Courtesy and restraint seem to belong to
the past era of morning coats and top hats. The San Francisco Conference was in certain respects more reminiscent of the League of
Nations of the 1930s than the United Nations of the 1960s. Turtle Bay
is vastly different from Church House and even from Flushing
Meadows.

The great increase in the number of member states has inevitably
brought about major changes. The countries of Africa and Asia today
command a majority of the votes in the General Assembly. In its various organs, debates are largely dominated by representatives from
these states. This fact may cause alarm among other members claiming
that the numerical strength of these new states bears no relation to
their real weight in the world community. This argument seems to
gain strength from the development of the policy governing the admission of new members. The Charter as originally adopted contained
certain criteria for membership. States which were not considered to
live up to these standards were not admitted. They had to demonstrate to the member states both their willingness and their ability to
fulfill the obligations of membership before being admitted. This part
of the Charter is today a dead letter. Any territory which has been
granted independence is almost automatically admitted, and it would
be in contravention of international good manners to ask whether an
applicant could fulfill the obligations of membership. Brave indeed
would be the member state which had the temerity to speak and vote
against the admission of a territory which might be considered unable
to lead an unaided existence as a fully sovereign independent state.

As a consequence of this acceptance of the principle of universality
a pattern of groupings has developed within the United Nations.
These groups are sometimes the natural result of geographical
propinquity, sometimes the expression of common political interests
in the East–West or South–North constellation. They may tend to
destroy the cohesiveness of the organization, but simultaneously they
make for a smoother functioning of the machinery. Numerically
most important is the Afro–Asian group, followed by the Latin
American group, and the group called "Western Europe and others."
There are smaller but important groups such as the Arab group, the

Eastern group, the Northern group, the group of nonaligned states, and numerous subgroups of different kinds.

No realistic appraisal of the functioning of the United Nations is possible without taking these groups into consideration. Some of them function actively and are organized with a chairman and a steering committee; others have only a rotating chairman. Some make decisions binding on the members of the group; others deal only with elections and work on the principle of consensus. Delegates who are in a position to influence their colleagues behind the scenes at such group meetings may be more effective in their work than the brilliant speakers who are more in the public eye. An appraisal of these trends belongs, however, in works on the politics of the Organization and not in a book with the more modest aim of elucidating the manner in which the Charter has been interpreted and applied.

With the admission of so many new member states the voting in the General Assembly, and to a lesser extent in the other organs, may at times look less than realistic. Today large majorities can be obtained and valid resolutions passed without the participation of any of the major powers in the organization. A weighted vote has been suggested to counteract this tendency, but it is doubtful whether this would be necessary or sufficient. The fact remains that most decisions of the Assembly are merely recommendations which may have great moral or political effect without, as a rule, being legally binding. No state can ignore such decisions without running certain risks, yet it is quite clear that the authority of decisions varies according to the size and composition of the majority. A resolution adopted against the vote of all the permanent members of the Security Council would not be given the same weight as one supported by all these members. A vote recommending sanctions against a state would carry little weight if the trading partners of the same state made it clear that they would not accept such a recommendation—quite aside from the fact that it is for the Security Council and not for the Assembly to make such a decision.

One consideration which must be kept in mind when evaluating the work of the Organization is that action means more than words, that what is done by the United Nations is far more important than what is said. Public utterances are often at variance with events in the world of facts. A striking example is the complex and vital field of peace-keeping operations. No resolution of a general character has been adopted during the long and bitter debates of recent years, yet even during the worsening political crises the Security Council has voted in favor of continuing the operations in Cyprus, and of enlarging the scope of UNTSO in the Middle East.

Denunciations and accusations fill the air. Financial and political crises follow each other with frightening regularity. Dissatisfaction is ripe, voices of doom are heard. Yet far more important is the fact that year after year the leading statesmen of the world flock to New York because the United Nations continues to be the dominant world forum, the focal point of the hopes and longings of humanity, and the best machinery for peace devised in our world of today despite all setbacks and all disappointments. How the machinery is used will determine whether "we shall nobly save or meanly lose the last best hope on earth."

Edvard Hambro

January, 1969

Preface to the Third Edition

The first edition of the Commentary was prepared before the United Nations had been organized and had begun to function. It was intended to assist the reader to a better understanding of the Organization by acquainting him with its background and the discussions that had taken place at San Francisco in connection with the drafting of the Charter. The second edition, published in 1949, still placed great emphasis on the background and drafting of the Charter but also undertook an analysis of the practice of the first three years. Since the second edition was published, close to two decades have elapsed. During that period, the Organization has undergone important changes, many of them of a fundamental nature. And yet these changes have, with only minor exceptions of a structural nature, taken place within the framework of the original Charter. Its capacity for adaptation has been fully demonstrated.

Since the task which we have set for ourselves in the third edition is to show how through Charter interpretation this development has been possible, the principal emphasis is on the practice of the organs of the United Nations and on the attitudes and conduct of its members. Fortunately we have been saved the necessity of a detailed systematic examination of the records of the United Nations by the existence of certain aids which have made our task manageable. Had it not been for the availability of the *Repertory of Practice of United Nations Organs*, the *Repertoire of Practice of the Security Council*, and the *Yearbook of the United Nations*, it is doubtful that we could have accomplished what we set out to do. These excellent publications of the United Nations Secretariat have made it possible for us to take many shortcuts that have been time-saving and, we hope, not seriously detrimental to the end product. In fact our task has been to make available in one volume, larger to be sure than we had hoped it would be, materials that are to be found to a large extent in the numerous volumes that make up these valuable guides.

We have found it necessary to establish a cut-off date, January 1, 1966, in order to bring our task to a conclusion. Unfortunately the time required to bring the revision to that date has made this revision seem already outdated. Nevertheless, adherence to it, with few exceptions, has seemed justified as the first two decades of the Organization's existence seem a significant period, and for a work of this time a substantial time-lag is probably inevitable. In some instances we have carried the analysis beyond the cut-off date in order to complete what appears to be a particularly significant development.

This revision is not intended to be an historical account of the United Nations. In explaining how Charter provisions have been interpreted in the practice of organs and the behavior of members, no systematic attempt has been made to take account of the relevant scholarly literature that has appeared since the inception of the United Nations. Use has been made almost exclusively of official documents. The most obvious exception to this rule has been the frequent use and citation of Ruth Russell's *History of the United Nations Charter,* which up until the publication of Volume I of *Foreign Relations of the United States* for 1945 provided the only available access to important top-level discussions at San Francisco.

In the use of the documentary records of the United Nations to explain how the Charter has been interpreted and applied, we have encountered the difficulty of relating particular decisions and discussions to particular articles. Sometimes the relation to a particular article is clear, but more often there is no reference in a resolution adopted or statement made to the particular article of the Charter upon which it is based. Often in the course of discussions various reasons are advanced and different articles are cited with no clear indication in the end as to which considerations have been decisive in the final decision. The tendency in the United Nations to politicize issues and to seek accommodations makes the task of using United Nations practice for the purpose of showing how specific articles have been interpreted and to what extent these interpretations have been accepted an extremely difficult one. Very often one has to rely on what seems to be reasonable inferences.

The preparation of this revision of the Commentary would not have been possible without assistance from many sources and in many forms. The project would not have been undertaken in the first place without the promise of generous support from the World Peace Foundation, the Rockefeller Foundation and the Carnegie Endowment for International Peace. A special debt is owed to the trustees and officers of these bodies, and particularly to Joseph E. Johnson, Lawrence S. Finkelstein, and Kenneth W. Thompson for their encouragement and help. Schuyler C. Wallace and Andrew W. Cordier, successively deans of the School of International Affairs, have been generous in providing assistance. Mark Zacher and Aida Levin, while graduate students at Columbia, helped in preparing drafts and checking references. Not least in their contribution have been a succession of secretaries, especially Elizabeth Hyde (Mrs. H. Denman Scott), Carole Mack (Mrs. Donald N. Stone), and Dolores Libera who have done so efficiently and enthusiastically the work of typing drafts and redrafts. Mrs. Janet Duffy helped put much of the manuscript in better shape by her editorial assistance. Our indebtedness to Robert Tilley and Joan McQuary of the Columbia University Press for their cooperation and assistance in getting a difficult manuscript into printed form is indeed great.

Leland M. Goodrich
Anne Patricia Simons

NEW YORK AND WASHINGTON

Contents

CONTENTS

Abbreviations Used in the Footnotes

ECOSOC Res.

Economic and Social Council Resolution.

Executive Agreement Series No. 236

U.S. President, "Declaration by the United Nations," Executive Agreement Series No. 236. Washington D.C., Jan. 1, 1942.

GAOR/2d Sess., 1st Ctte./74th Mtg.

General Assembly Official Records, 2d Session, First Committee, 74th Meeting.

GA Res. 1871(XVII)

General Assembly Resolution No. 1871, 17th Session.

Hears/USS CFR/81C1/

Hearings, U.S. Senate, Committee on Foreign Relations, 81st Congress, 1st session.

H. Doc. 358/77C1/

"The Atlantic Charter," House of Representatives Document No. 358, 77th Congress, 1st session, Aug. 21, 1941 (Washington, Government Printing Office, 1941).

ICJ Reports

International Court of Justice, *Reports of Judgments, Advisory Opinions and Orders.* Leyden, Sitjhoff.

LNOJ

League of Nations Official Journal. Geneva.

LNTS

League of Nations Treaty Series. Geneva.

PCIJ

Permanent Court of International Justice. The Hague.

Report of the Executive Committee

Report of the Executive Committee to the Preparatory Commission of the United Nations. PC/EX/113/ Rev. 1.

Report of the Preparatory Commission

Report of the Preparatory Commission of the United Nations. PC/ 20/Dec. 23, 1945.

Repertoire of the Security Council — Repertoire of the Practice of the Security Council, 1948–1951. New York, United Nations Headquarters, 1954.

Supp. 1 — 1st Supplement, 1952–1955.

Supp. 2 — 2d Supplement, 1956–1958.

Supp. 3 — 3d Supplement, 1959–1963.

Repertory — Repertory of Practice of United Nations Organs. 5 vols. New York, United Nations headquarters, 1957.

Supp. 1 — 1st Supplement, 2 vols. 1957.

Supp. 2 — 2d Supplement. 3 vols. 1963–64.

SCOR/3d Yr./ 227th Mtg. — Security Council Official Records, 3d Year, 227th Meeting.

SC Res. — Security Council Resolution.

State Dept., American Foreign Policy 1950–1955. — U.S. Department of State. American Foreign Policy, 1950–1955. Publication No. 6446. Washington D.C., 1957.

State Dept., Cairo and Teheran. — U.S. Department of State. Foreign Relations of the United States: The Conferences at Cairo and Teheran, 1945. Publication No. 7187. Washington D. C., 1961.

State Dept., Foreign Relations of the United States, 1928. — U.S. Department of State. Foreign Relations of the United States, 1928. Secretary of State to Ambassador of France. Publication No. 1839. Washington D.C., 1942.

State Dept., Inter-American Conference. — U.S. Department of State. Report of the Delegation of the United States of America to the Inter-American Conference on Problems of War and Peace, Mexico City, Feb. 21–Mar. 8, 1945. Publication No. 2497. Washington D.C., 1946.

State Dept., International Aviation Conference. — U.S. Department of State. International Civil Aviation Conference, Chicago, Nov. 1–7, 1944. Final Act and Related Documents. Publication No. 2282. Washington D.C., 1945.

State Dept., International Court of Justice. — U.S. Department of State. The International Court of Justice: Se-

State Dept., *Malta and Yalta Documents*.

State Dept., *Post-War Foreign Policy Preparation, 1939–1945*.

State Dept., *Potsdam Conference Documents*.

State Dept., *Report to the President*.

State Dept., *Treaties and Other International Acts*.

State Dept., *UN Monetary and Financial Conference*.

State Dept., *The U.S. and the UN*.

State Dept., *U.S. Participation in the UN*.

lected Documents Relating to the Drafting of the Statute. Publication No. 2491. Washington D.C., 1946.

U.S. Department of State. *Foreign Relations of the United States: The Conferences at Malta and Yalta, 1945*. Publication No. 6199. Washington D.C., 1945.

U.S. Department of State. *Post-War Foreign Policy Preparation, 1939–1945*. Publication No. 3580. Washington D.C., 1950.

U.S. Department of State. *Foreign Relations of the United States: The Conference of Berlin, 1945*. Vol. II. Publication No. 7168. Washington D.C., 1960.

U.S. Department of State. *Charter of the United Nations: Report to the President on the Results of the San Francisco Conference*. Publication No. 2349. Washington D.C., 1945.

U.S. Department of State. *Treaties and Other International Acts Series, 1555*. Publication No. 2653. Washington D.C., 1947.

U.S. Department of State. *United Nations Monetary and Financial Conference*. Bretton Woods, New Hampshire, July 1-22, 1944. Final Act and Related Documents. Publication No. 2187, Conference Series 55. Washington D.C., 1944.

U.S. Department of State. *The United States and the United Nations: Report by the President to the Congress for the Year 1947*. Publication No. 3024. Washington D.C., 1948.

U.S. Department of State. *United States Participation in the United Nations: Report of the President to Congress for the Year 1961*. Publication No. 7413. Washington D.C., 1962.

TCOR	*Trusteeship Council Official Records.* New York.
TC Res.	Trusteeship Council Resolution.
UNCIO, *Documents.*	*Documents of the United Nations Conference on International Organzation.* 22 vols. New York and London, UN Information Organization, 1945.
UNTS	United Nations Treaty Series. New York.
Y.U.N.	*Yearbook of the United Nations.* New York, Columbia University Press, through in cooperation with the United Nations, through 1964; United Nations, Dept. of Public Information, 1965– .

CHARTER OF THE UNITED NATIONS

Introduction

The Charter of the United Nations, signed at San Francisco on June 26, 1945, was a document with roots in the past and possibilities for the future that could only be imagined. From one point of view, it represented a stage in the historical development of mankind's social organization. Its provisions were based largely on past experience and found substantial if not exact expression in earlier instruments. From another point of view, however, the Charter was a commitment to purposes and principles the realization of which in the light of the changing world conditions might require substantial adaptation of institutional and procedural arrangements.

It is necessary to think of the Charter not only as a treaty embodying the maximum limitations on a state's freedom of action, that nations at that stage of history and in the light of experience were prepared to accept as consistent with their national interests, but also as a constitutional document setting forth guidelines for future development. The exact nature of this development was to be determined not only by the Charter itself but also by the way in which the members of the United Nations interpreted these guidelines and made use of the Organization in dealing with the ever-changing problems of an ever-changing world. The Charter thus provided the constitutional basis for achieving international peace, security, and well-being, and pointed the way—but the ultimate verdict was to rest with the actors themselves.

The Need for a "General International Organization"

The idea of an international organization to keep the peace, worldwide in the scope of its activity, found its first practical expression in the League of Nations.

Back of the League, however, was a considerable experience with institutions and procedures of more limited scope which had as their purpose the prevention of war and the promotion of other common purposes by organized international cooperation.

At the end of World War I, the League of Nations was established, largely on the initiative and through the leadership of Woodrow Wilson. Wilson believed that the old system of balance of power had been discredited by the failure of diplomacy to prevent World War I and that the only dependable guarantee of peace was to be found in the willingness of peace-aspiring nations to use their combined forces to restrain aggression. We know that the League failed in its major purpose, but we do not know what would have happened if one of Wilson's major assumptions—that the United States would be an active member—had materialized. Without the United States as a member, the League was congenitally and fatally weak; although it achieved some useful results and demonstrated the need for organized international cooperation, it was not able to survive the holocaust of World War II.

It was a tribute to the validity of the League idea, however, that almost from the beginning of World War II, thought was given in responsible government circles to establishing an international organization to keep the peace once the war ended. In their Declaration of Principles, known as the Atlantic Charter, of August, 1941, President Roosevelt and Prime Minister Churchill expressed their hope "to see established a peace which will afford to all nations the means of dwelling in safety within their own boundaries, and which will afford assurance that all the men in all the lands may live out their lives in freedom from fear and want." [1] By adhering to the Declaration by United Nations of January 1, 1942, the states at war with the Axis Powers, including China, the Soviet Union, the United Kingdom, and the United States, subscribed to the purposes and principles set forth in the Atlantic Charter.[2] Early in 1942, the Advisory Committee on Post-War Foreign Policy was set up in the U.S. State Department to consider international problems that would confront the United States at the conclusion of hostilities. By June, attention was explicitly focused on the problem of a permanent international organization, which soon became a major concern of the committee, as well as of Secretary of State Hull and President Roosevelt.[3]

During 1942 and 1943, official thinking and policy formulation in Washington had so far developed that Secretary Hull was ready to take advantage of the meeting of Allied foreign ministers in Moscow in October, 1943, to secure a firm commitment to the idea of establishing

---

[1] H. Doc. 358/77C1/1941.   [2] Executive Agreement Series 236.
[3] State Dept., *Post-War Foreign Policy Preparation, 1939–1945*, pp. 270–300, 595–606.

an international organization to keep the peace.[4] By the Moscow Declaration of October 30, 1943, the governments of China, the Soviet Union, the United Kingdom, and the United States declared

that they recognize the necessity of establishing at the earliest practicable date a general international organization, based on the principle of the sovereign equality of all peace-loving states, and open to membership by all such states, large and small, for the maintenance of international peace and security.[5]

Preliminary Negotiations

The making of a charter to give effect to the Moscow commitment was a complex and lengthy process. In fact, the work of preparation began in the U.S. State Department as early as June, 1942, and continued into the summer of 1944. The Tentative Proposals, the product of this preparatory work, were accepted by the President and by congressional leaders of both parties as the basis for discussion in the Dumbarton Oaks Conversations of August 21–October 7, 1944. The draft which finally emerged reflected the thinking of many minds and had bipartisan support.[6]

It was considered essential to secure the preliminary agreement of the four major powers at the expert level on the proposals to be submitted to a conference of allied nations. The Dumbarton Oaks Conversations took place in two phases: the first, with representatives of the Soviet Union, the United Kingdom, and the United States participating, extended from August 21 to September 28; the second, to which the Republic of China, the United Kingdom, and the United States were parties, lasted from September 29 to October 7. These negotiations resulted in agreed-upon proposals which, though incomplete, represented substantial acceptance of United States suggestions, modified in some respects by the ideas of other participants.[7] Where unresolvable differences appeared in the course of negotiations, they were left for discussion and resolution at a higher political level.

The Dumbarton Oaks Proposals[8] did not cover such important questions as voting procedure in the Security Council and the role of the proposed international court. They did not deal with other matters of a technical nature—such as privileges and immunities, registration

---

[4] See Cordell Hull, *The Memoirs of Cordell Hull* (New York, Macmillan, 1948), II, 1274–1307.

[5] State Dept., *Bulletin*, IX, 308.

[6] For text, see *Post-War Foreign Policy Preparation, 1939–1945*, pp. 595–606.

[7] For details, see Ruth B. Russell, *A History of the United Nations Charter* (Washington, Brookings Institution, 1958), pp. 411–77.

[8] For text, see Appendix, pp. 664 ff.

of treaties, and arrangements for non-self-governing territories. The Proposals, however, gave a clear indication of the kind of organization the major powers had in mind and would presumably strongly support at the forthcoming conference. In many respects, it was to be an organization similar to the League of Nations it was to replace.

Following publication of the Dumbarton Oaks Proposals, further negotiations and discussions were necessary to fill some of the gaps left by the Proposals and to prepare the way for subsequent agreements. At the Crimea (Yalta) Conference of February 3–11, 1945,[9] the heads of government of the Soviet Union, the United Kingdom, and the United States agreed on the formula governing Security Council voting procedure, which was subsequently included in the proposals submitted to the governments invited to the San Francisco Conference. Accord was also reached on the basic principles governing the establishment of a trusteeship system. It was also decided to call a conference of the United Nations in San Francisco on April 25, 1945 "to prepare the Charter of such an organization, along the lines proposed in the informal conversations at Dumbarton Oaks," and that invitations should be extended by the United States on behalf of the Sponsoring Governments to those states that had declared war on Germany or Japan by March 1, 1945 and had signed the Declaration by United Nations.

Two other conferences held before San Francisco helped to lay the groundwork for the 1945 Charter. At the Mexico City Conference of the American Republics, February 2–March 8, 1945,[10] the United States gained support for the Dumbarton Oaks Proposals, and a hemispheric position on the question of regional security was formulated. The meeting of the United Nations Committee of Jurists, April 9–20, 1945,[11] prepared a draft statute of an international court of justice to serve as a basis for discussion at San Francisco.

San Francisco

The final stage in the making of the Charter was the United Nations Conference on International Organization (UNCIO) which met at San Francisco, April 25–June 26, 1945.[12] Invitations to the Conference were issued on March 5 by the government of the United States in the names of the four Sponsoring Governments, to the following: Australia, Belgium, Bolivia, Brazil, Canada, Chile, Colombia, Costa Rica, Cuba,

[9] See State Dept., *Malta and Yalta Documents,* pp. 975–77.
[10] State Dept., *Inter-American Conference,* pp. 72–75.
[11] State Dept., *International Court of Justice,* pp. 98–133.
[12] For official records, see UNCIO, *Documents.* See also, State Dept., *Report to the President.*

Czechoslovakia, Dominican Republic, Ecuador, Egypt, El Salvador, Ethiopia, France, Greece, Guatemala, Haiti, Honduras, India, Iran, Iraq, Lebanon, Liberia, Luxembourg, Mexico, the Netherlands, New Zealand, Nicaragua, Norway, Panama, Paraguay, Peru, the Philippines, Saudi Arabia, Syria, Turkey, Union of South Africa, Uruguay, Venezuela, and Yugoslavia. Poland, though a signatory of the Declaration by United Nations, was not invited because of the failure of the Sponsoring Governments to agree on the government to be recognized. In the invitation it was suggested that the Conference consider the Dumbarton Oaks Proposals "as affording a basis" for the proposed charter. It was also indicated that in the event that the invited governments desired "in advance of the Conference to present views or comments concerning the proposals," the government of the United States would "be pleased to transmit such views and comments to the other participating Governments."

The Conference convened at San Francisco on April 25, 1945, with all the sponsoring and invited states represented. Subsequently, Argentina, the Byelorussian Soviet Socialist Republic, Denmark, and the Ukrainian Soviet Socialist Republic sent representatives on invitation of the Conference, bringing the total number of participants to fifty.

The agenda of the Conference, approved at a meeting of the heads of delegations on April 27, 1945, included "the Dumbarton Oaks Proposals, as supplemented at the Crimea Conference, and by the Chinese proposals agreed to by the Sponsoring Governments, and the comments thereon submitted by the participating countries." [13] It was also agreed to set a time limit of one week for submission of proposed amendments and comments; this limit was not to apply, however, to trusteeship matters.[14]

The Conference was organized into general committees, commissions, and technical committees. The general committees included the Steering Committee, consisting of the chairmen of delegations; the Executive Committee, consisting of the chairmen of the delegations of the four Sponsoring Governments, France, and nine other governments; [15] the Coordination Committee, composed of a representative of each state represented on the Executive Committee; and the Credentials Committee.

[13] UNCIO, *Documents*, V, 81–97.

[14] Comments and proposed amendments were brought together by the Secretariat in a loose-leaf volume with the title *Comments and Proposed Amendments Concerning the Dumbarton Oaks Proposals, Submitted by the Delegations to the United Nations Conference on International Organization, May 7, 1945.* See UNCIO, *Documents*, III, 637–710.

[15] Australia, Brazil, Canada, Chile, Czechoslovakia, Iran, Mexico, the Netherlands, and Yugoslavia.

The commissions, consisting of delegates from all participating governments, were four in number: Commission I (General Provisions), Commission II (General Assembly), Commission III (Security Council), and Commission IV (Judicial Organization). Each commission had the tasks of developing general principles for the guidance of its technical committees, considering the recommendations of its technical committees and the relationship of these recommendations to those of other commissions, and of recommending to the Conference in plenary session "proposed texts as parts of the Charter." [16]

The technical committees were set up under the commissions to consider and formulate recommendations on the various parts of the agenda referred to them. Each committee consisted of a delegate from each government participating in the Conference. The committee structure and assignments, as related to the commissions, were as follows (the roman numeral indicating the commission to which the committee reported):

Committee I/1	Preamble, Purposes and Principles
Committee I/2	Membership, Amendment, and Secretariat
Committee II/1	Structure and Procedures
Committee II/2	Political and Security Functions
Committee II/3	Economic and Social Cooperation
Committee II/4	Trusteeship System
Committee III/1	Structure and Procedures
Committee III/2	Peaceful Settlement
Committee III/3	Enforcement Arrangements
Committee III/4	Regional Arrangements
Committee IV/1	International Court of Justice
Committee IV/2	Legal Problems

The technical committees followed no uniform procedure in the performance of their functions. In one committee, the work of examination and detailed consideration was turned over to a subcommittee whose recommendations were then discussed and acted upon by the full committee. Another committee considered and gave answers to general questions suggested by detailed proposals and comments, asked a drafting subcommittee to translate the general conclusions into specific texts, and then considered and acted upon the texts proposed. Still another committee considered the suggested amendments to the Dumbarton Oaks Proposals, indicated those it approved with respect to the general idea, and then asked a drafting subcommittee to prepare a text which was then submitted to the committee for final decision. Where committee assignments overlapped, the Steering Committee or

16 UNCIO, *Documents*, I, 401–5.

the Executive Committee decided which technical committee should consider the matter. This, however, did not prevent different committees from considering the same question; to avoid and resolve conflicts, various devices were resorted to, including the establishment of joint subcommittees and appeal to the Steering and Executive committees.

The texts recommended by the technical committees were submitted to the commissions for approval, usually a purely formal proceeding. They were also referred to the Coordination Committee, which, with the assistance of the Advisory Committee of Jurists, reviewed the texts with an eye to improving their phraseology, securing uniformity of terminology, eliminating contradictions and inconsistencies, and obtaining the best arrangement of the substance of the proposed charter. The Coordination Committee could, on its own responsibility, make no change of a substantive nature, though it might ask a technical committee to consider a proposal involving such a modification. In general, the function of the Coordination Committee was to put the pieces together into one document, without modifying the decisions of the technical committees, except with their consent. The draft of the Charter as thus prepared was then submitted to the Steering Committee for its approval, and finally to the Conference in plenary session. The signing of the Charter by the delegates on June 26, 1945, followed final approval by the Conference on the previous day.[17]

An Assessment of the San Francisco Proceedings

The procedure in the final drafting of the Charter at San Francisco offered ample opportunity for discussion and, more particularly, gave the delegates of those states not represented in the Dumbarton Oaks Conversations the opportunity to express their points of view. Furthermore, decisions were taken by a two-thirds vote of those present and voting. This process, of necessity, however, operated within a political context which gave to the major powers, because of their leading role in the conduct of the war and their indispensability to the success of the proposed organization, a measure of influence on the decisions that the smaller powers could not hope to equal. Thus, freedom of discussion, equality of voting power, and the possibility of decisions being taken by a modified majority did not in fact deprive the great powers of an effective veto. Faced with the possibility that a particular decision would be unacceptable to one of the major powers (more particularly, the United States or the Soviet Union) who might for that reason refrain from joining the Organization, members of the Conference were not prepared to force the issue. Effective control over important

[17] *Ibid.*, 612–32.

Conference decisions was achieved through informal consultations of the heads of the delegations of China, France, the Soviet Union, the United Kingdom, and the United States (the "Big Five") assisted by their chief advisers.[18]

Notwithstanding the effective "veto power" that a great power possessed, there were in fact fairly important questions on which the smaller nations were able to press their points of view with considerable success in the face of resistance by the major powers, especially if the latter were not in full agreement among themselves. This was especially true of questions relating to the role of the General Assembly and the responsibilities of the Organization in the economic and social fields. While it may be argued that concessions by the major powers were more apparent than real, it would seem to be a justified conclusion, particularly in the light of the subsequent development of the Charter, that the smaller powers did succeed in introducing important changes in the Dumbarton Oaks Proposals, even as modified by the amendments proposed by the Sponsoring Governments themselves.

While the organization and procedures of the Conference were reasonably effective in achieving full discussion and fair consideration of the many proposals submitted, they were not equally successful in producing a well-drafted document free of inconsistencies and ambiguities. In fact, the highly complex committee structure, the necessity of meeting deadlines, and the decision to have five official languages— English, French, Spanish, Russian, and Chinese—made the task of putting the decisions of the Conference into good technical form a herculean one. Thus, there was not time at the end for technical committees to reconsider decisions which, in the light of the total perspective of the Charter, appeared open to serious question. In addition the task of translating the Coordination Committee's final English draft into the other four languages was carried out under pressures hardly conducive to technical perfection.

Getting the Organization Started

The Charter was signed on June 26, 1945. Of necessity, an uncertain length of time was to elapse before the Charter would enter into force and the organs of the United Nations could be established and begin to function. It was recognized at San Francisco that a vast amount of preparatory work had to be done if the Organization was to function smoothly from the beginning. Consequently, at the time of the signing of the Charter, interim arrangements were agreed to that established a

[18] See Russell, pp. 641–42.

Preparatory Commission "for the purpose of making provisional arrangements for the first sessions of the General Assembly, the Security Council, the Economic and Social Council, and the Trusteeship Council, for the establishment of the Secretariat, and for the convening of the International Court of Justice." [19] The Commission was to consist of one representative of each government signatory to the Charter. When not in session, its functions and powers were to be exercised by an Executive Committee, composed of the representatives of those states that had constituted the Executive Committee of the Conference. The Commission was to be assisted by an executive secretary and such staff as might be required.

The Executive Committee, holding its first meeting in London on August 16, 1945, prepared a report, including drafts, that served as the basis of the Preparatory Commission's work. The final report of the Preparatory Commission,[20] adopted on December 23, 1945, included specific recommendations; draft proposals integrally connected with them, such as the draft provisional staff regulations and the provisional rules of procedure of the principal organs; a number of reports and memoranda setting forth the views of the Commission and of special expert bodies; and certain supplementary materials, including extracts from summary records of committee meetings.

The Charter entered into force on October 24, 1945, when instruments of ratification had been deposited by the Republic of China, France, the Soviet Union, the United Kingdom, and the United States, and by the majority of remaining signatories, as provided in Article 110. The General Assembly held its first meeting at Central Hall, Westminster, London, on January 10, 1946, with representatives of all fifty-one members present.[21] The Security Council initially convened on January 17, the nonpermanent members having been elected by the Assembly on January 12. The Economic and Social Council met for the first time on January 23. The Trusteeship Council was unable to meet until March 26, 1947, because of delay in the conclusion and Assembly approval of trusteeship agreements. The first session of the International Court of Justice was held on April 3, 1946. On February 1, Trygve Lie was appointed the first Secretary-General by the Assembly, on recommendation of the Security Council. Except for the Trusteeship Council, the United Nations was a going concern early in 1946, al-

[19] Interim Arrangements, Art. 1. See UNCIO, *Documents*, XV, 511–13.

[20] PC/20, Dec. 23, 1945. For report of the Executive Committee, see PC/EX/113/Rev. 1, Nov. 12, 1945.

[21] Poland had signed the Charter and deposited an instrument of ratification following agreement by the U.K., U.S., and the USSR on the government to be recognized.

though the final decision on the location of permanent headquarters was not made until December 14.

The United Nations and the League of Nations Compared

The new organization for which the Charter provided was in many respects like the League of Nations.[22] It was based on the principle of voluntary association of independent sovereign states for the achievement of common purposes. Like the League, it was composed initially of nations victorious in a world war, and while the effort was made to disassociate it to some extent from the peace settlements, there was no avoiding the conclusion that the peace it was expected to keep would, to a large extent, be the peace made by the victorious powers in the war about to end. The structure of the new organization was similar to that of the League: a deliberative organ including all members, quasi-executive organs, a court, and a secretariat. While the Charter provided for three councils instead of the Covenant's one, it must be borne in mind that the League Permanent Mandates Commission had functions similar to those of the Trusteeship Council, and that the Economic and Social Council for which the Charter provided was anticipated in the recommendations of the Bruce Committee in 1939.[23]

There were, however, important differences, at least in emphasis, between the organization provided for by the Charter and that of the Covenant. While both documents emphasized the maintenance of peace as a primary objective, the Charter gave much more recognition to the importance of international cooperation in dealing with economic and social problems, and to the need for safeguarding basic human rights if the world was to be spared another catastrophe. This new emphasis was quite understandable in the light of the role that economic and social dislocations had played in events leading to World War II, recognition of the increased responsibility of governments in the economic and social fields, and the extent to which the denial of human rights had been associated with aggressive regimes.

An even more striking difference, however, was the approach taken by the Charter to the problem of keeping the peace. Whereas the Covenant had emphasized the legal approach to the prevention of war by placing specific obligations upon members, the Charter approach was essentially political, since in the last analysis the measures to be taken and their effectiveness were made to depend on the readiness of

---

[22] For a detailed comparison, see Leland Goodrich, "From League of Nations to United Nations," *International Organization*, I (1947), 3–21.

[23] The Development of International Cooperation in Economic and Social Affairs (Bruce Report), LN Doc. A.23.1939.

the major military powers to cooperate in defense of common interests. Furthermore, unlike the Covenant, the Charter in effect recognized that the new organization could not be effective in keeping the peace if challenged by a great power. In that event, members would be thrown back on their own resources, supplemented by such cooperative arrangements as might be worked out in the name of collective self-defense.

The Charter also appeared to differ from the Covenant in its more detailed definition and sharper differentiation of functions and powers of the various organs. Whereas the Covenant had defined the functions and powers of the Assembly and Council in the same general terms though according specific duties to each, the Charter—on the assumption that the General Assembly was an organ of deliberation and the Security Council an organ of action—defined in considerable detail the functions and powers of each, emphasizing the primary responsibility of the Council for making specific decisions to maintain or restore peace and security, and the responsibility of the Assembly to develop and recommend general principles of cooperation for strengthening peace and security. To be sure, this differentiation of function appeared to be clearer under the Dumbarton Oaks Proposals than under the Charter as finally adopted. At San Francisco, certain provisions were accepted which blurred the distinction the Dumbarton Oaks conferees had sought to make, and which laid the basis for subsequent extensive development of the responsibilities and powers of the General Assembly in the maintenance of peace and security.

Another important difference between the Charter system and that of the League concerned the role accorded to the international organization in dealing with non-self-governing territories. Apart from a general assurance of just treatment to indigenous populations, the Covenant was concerned with those colonial territories which Germany and the Turkish empire had been forced to relinquish and which the victorious allied powers agreed to place under the League mandates system. In regard to these territories it was almost wholly concerned with eliminating abuses, and only in the case of Class A mandated territories was independence envisaged. The Charter approach is quite different. Members undertake to work for the political, economic, and social development of the inhabitants of all territories under their administration, and, in the case of territories under trusteeship, they assume strong obligations and agree to accept a larger measure of international supervision than under the League mandates system. Furthermore, by making the General Assembly responsible for performing United Nations supervisory functions, the Charter seeks to give assurance that members administering trust territories will not be allowed to escape their obligations. Recognition by members of "the principle of equal rights and self-determination of peoples" (Article 1[2]) is another peg upon which proponents of independence for non-self-governing people have been able to hang their case.

It is a great mistake, however, to attach decisive importance to the differences between the Covenant and the Charter. If the system of the Charter has met with considerable success and still after over two decades is a going concern—in contrast to the failure of the League in a shorter period of time—the principal explanation is not to be found in the technical superiority, or even in the superior validity, of the basic concepts of the Charter. Both the Covenant and the Charter were based on and gave expression to high purposes, and both contained provisions sufficiently general in form and elastic in content to permit members to do what might be necessary to give effect to these purposes. The important difference has been that, from the beginning, the League had to function without the participation and support of the one great power that had the means to make it effective, and never achieved at any one time the degree of universality of the United Nations. Furthermore, the League suffered from the excessive expectations of its friends, and from the failure of many of its leading supporters and members to recognize the price that had to be paid for peace. The United Nations, on the other hand, has functioned in an atmosphere of greater realism and has drawn vitality from the fact that even its most powerful members recognize its value in a world of competing ideas and political systems, and its indispensability to a world capable of instant self-destruction.

How the United Nations Has Developed

The Charter as signed at San Francisco and subsequently ratified by the original signatories was a treaty, an agreement entered into between states in accordance with customary procedures for so doing. The opening words of the Charter—"We the peoples of the United Nations . . ."—are misleading, although they convey a meaning that was in the minds of many people at the time. The concluding words of the preamble—"Accordingly, our respective Governments . . . have agreed to the present Charter of the United Nations and do hereby establish an international organization to be known as the United Nations"—are more accurately descriptive of the process of establishing the Organization and suggestive of the result. Further indication of the treaty-like character of the Charter is to be found in the San Francisco understanding with respect to withdrawal. While the document itself contains no explicit provision regarding withdrawal, the understanding embodied in the declaration accepted by the governments represented at San Francisco was that members might withdraw under certain circumstances.[24] While the declaration attempted to discourage withdrawal by stressing the obligation to cooperate for the purposes set forth in the Charter, it clearly recognized that, legally, the situation was analogous to the case of any multipartite agreement.

But, while the Charter clearly is a treaty, it is also the constitution of an organization. As a constitution it is not an ordinary treaty. The member states commit themselves not only to act in pursuance of its purposes and in conformity with its principles, but also to establish certain organs with defined powers and operating procedures to accomplish these purposes. In addition, they authorize the Organization to ensure that nonmembers as well as members act in accordance with the principles of the Charter, so far as may be necessary for the maintenance of international peace and security.[25]

The Charter as a constitution, and even as a treaty, is not a static thing. It and the Organization that it creates must be adapted to new and changing circumstances and to the desires and expectations of members. One method by which this may be done is formal amendment. The Charter provides for this by a process that reflects to some degree the basic treaty character of the instrument,[26] but it also suggests that this is no ordinary treaty. It provides a method of change which permits a special majority to decide that change shall take place. Nevertheless, the amendment process is difficult. For the major powers, a right of veto does exist. Thus far, the few amendments that have been adopted cannot be considered as affecting the fundamental nature of the Organization or the basic rights and duties of members.

It can generally be said of treaties and of constitutions that substantive changes and adaptations are more commonly achieved by a process of interpretation and application to situations as they arise than by formal amendment. Constitutions of international organizations frequently make explicit provision for a procedure to be used to obtain authoritative interpretations.[27] Such provisions do not substantially affect the responsibility that rests on members and organs to interpret provisions of the constitution in the course of day-to-day operations.

24 See commentary on ch. II.

25 See Benjamin Cohen, *The United Nations: Development, Growth, and Possibilities* (Cambridge, Harvard University Press, 1961) for development of the idea that the Charter is a constitution to be liberally interpreted.

26 See commentary on Arts. 108 and 109.

27 Art. 37(2) of the Constitution of the International Labour Organisation, for example, stipulates that any question or dispute relating to the interpretation of the Constitution shall be referred for decision to the International Court of Justice.

The question of the method of Charter interpretation was considered at some length at San Francisco. It was agreed that no provision of an explicit nature should be made in the Charter itself. Agreement was reached, however, on a statement included in the report of the technical committee dealing with the matter and approved by the Conference.

The statement was as follows:

In the course of the operations from day to day of the various organs of the Organization, it is inevitable that each organ will interpret such parts of the Charter as are applicable to its particular functions. This process is inherent in the functioning of any body which operates under an instrument defining its functions and powers. It will be manifested in the functioning of such a body as the General Assembly, the Security Council, or the International Court of Justice. Accordingly, it is not necessary to include in the Charter a provision either authorizing or approving the normal operation of this principle.

Difficulties may conceivably arise in the event that there should be a difference of opinion among the organs of the Organization concerning the correct interpretation of a provision of the Charter. Thus, two organs may conceivably hold and may express or even act upon different views. Under unitary forms of national government the final determination of such a question may be vested in the highest court or in some other national authority. However, the nature of the Organization and of its operation would not seem to be such as to invite the inclusion in the Charter of any provision of this nature. If two Member States are at variance concerning the correct interpretation of the Charter, they are of course free to submit the dispute to the International Court of Justice as in the case of any other treaty. Similarly, it would always be open to the General Assembly or the Security Council, in appropriate circumstances, to ask the International Court of Justice for an advisory opinion concerning the meaning of a provision of the Charter. Should the General Assembly or the Security Council prefer another course, an ad hoc committee of jurists might be set up to examine the question and report its views, or recourse might be had to a joint conference. In brief, the Members or the organs of the Organization might have recourse to various expedients in order to obtain an appropriate interpretation. It would appear neither necessary nor desirable to list or to describe in the Charter the various possible expedients.

It is to be understood, of course, that if an interpretation made by any organ of the Organization or by a committee of jurists is not generally acceptable it will be without binding force. In such circumstances, or in cases where it is desired to establish an authoritative interpretation as a precedent for the future, it may be necessary to embody the interpretation in an amendment to the Charter. This may always be accomplished by recourse to the procedure provided for amendment.[28]

[28] UNCIO, *Documents*, XIII, 709–10.

Clearly, this statement leaves matters in a rather untidy and uncertain situation for anyone interested in learning what the Charter means at any particular time. Apparently, it can mean different things to different organs and to different members. An interpretation accepted by the General Assembly, for example, may be unacceptable to the Security Council because of its different membership and voting procedure. An interpretation adopted by the Assembly by a two-thirds vote may not be accepted by a substantial minority of members. Can it be said that the Assembly has the power to make a binding decision with respect to its powers when in principle on substantive issues its power is limited under the Charter to making recommendations? The statement quoted above says that an interpretation made by an organ if "not generally acceptable" is without binding force. How many dissents are required to make it possible to say that an interpretation is "not generally acceptable"? In answering this question, is the importance of the dissenters to be considered as well as the number?

The statement envisages the possibility that questions of interpretation will be submitted to the Court. However, such procedure presents problems. If the Court is asked to give an advisory opinion by an organ competent to make such requests, the opinion is presumably not binding on the organ requesting it, although clearly entitled to great respect. For members of the Organization, the same can be said; and for them in particular, the binding force of the interpretation would depend on the extent of its acceptance by the requesting organ and the competence of that organ to impose its conclusions on members. If, however, members submit a dispute involving a question of Charter interpretation to the Court for judgment, that body's decision would be binding on the parties and on members intervening under Article 63 of the Statute. The decision would presumably not be binding on other members, and in any case would not be likely to concern a matter of great political importance.

We are faced then with a situation in which the responsibility for interpreting the Charter and adapting it to specified situations is shared widely and with very limited possibility of an authoritative interpretation. Furthermore, since the responsibility for interpretation is vested in organs and members alike, the process is more likely to be political than judicial. This means that the view taken of the meaning of the Charter in any particular situation is more often than not the result of a bargaining process or an exercise of power than an attempt to apply Charter provisions by a process of reasoning based on accepted principles of interpretation. Decisions tend to reflect the common interests of members in achieving certain results. Considering that the perceived interests of members change and that the voting alignments of members vary according to the issues presented, this politicizing of the interpretation process inevitably produces inconsistencies and confusion in the way the Charter is interpreted and applied.

There has, however, been one thread of continuity in the interpretation and application of the Charter to date. By and large, members, when they rely heavily on the United Nations for the advancement of their national interests and the support of their national policies, tend to take a liberal view with regard to the powers of organs and the capacity of the United Nations to act in furtherance of its purposes. Thus, on the one hand, non-Communist members under the leadership of the United States, during the first decade, took a liberal view of the power and responsibilities of the General Assembly to justify the use of that veto-free organ to support their policies and achieve their purposes in the "cold war." On the other hand, members, when they do not see the possibility of utilizing the United Nations to serve national interests (possibly because of their being in a minority position on important issues), tend to take a restrictive line in Charter interpretation. They take the view, well stated by Judge Winiarski in his dissenting opinion in the "Certain Expenses" case, that "[the] Charter, a multilateral treaty which was the result of prolonged and laborious negotiations, carefully created organs and determined their competence and means of action." [29] They do not accept the view that the powers of United Nations organs are to be interpreted liberally in the light of the purposes of the Organization. They would not agree that just because an action is appropriate for the fulfillment of a Charter purpose, the presumption is thereby created that the action is permissible.

For anyone interested in how a particular article of the Charter has been interpreted and applied, the fact that interpretation has been subordinated to such an extent to political considerations creates special difficulties. Quite apart from the inconsistencies and divergences which make generalization difficult, there has been a general tendency to avoid relating a particular decision or course of action to a particular Charter provision. This has been in no small measure the consequence of the bargaining involved in the creation of majorities necessary to the adoption of resolutions. References to specific provisions of the Charter as providing the basis for the proposed action are likely to be among the controversial points that can be sacrificed in the interest of wider agreement. Consequently, the scholar or practitioner interested in relating the development of the United Nations to Charter provisions must often draw inferences from the language used in the decisions of organs and in the statements of United Nations officials and members as to the specific Charter provisions being relied upon.

[29] *ICJ Reports,* 1962, p. 230.

The United Nations After Twenty Years

It is a truism to say that the United Nations after twenty years is quite different from the Organization described in the Charter. It is not the fact of difference that is significant but the degree. In many respects, the United Nations of today is hardly recognizable from a reading of Charter provisions. The extent of the gap is due fundamentally to the gap between the basic assumptions of the Charter and the conditions of the postwar world. Instead of great-power cooperation permitting the Security Council to function and discharge its responsibilities, there has been great-power conflict indirectly encouraging the use of the General Assembly and the right of collective self-defense under arrangements outside the framework of the United Nations. Instead of peace settlements providing the basis for the maintenance of international peace and security in the postwar period, after twenty years the principal military victors have failed to agree on the terms of peace with the principal enemy states. Instead of armaments being regulated on the basis of internationally guaranteed peace and security, national armaments have been maintained at highly competitive levels. Instead of peace being enforced and peaceful settlements being achieved, cease-fires and provisional arrangements have been concluded under United Nations auspices for limiting fighting, but little or no progress has been made in achieving peaceful settlement of the differences that produced the armed conflict. Instead of an organization clearly dominated by the great powers, we find one which in many areas of its activity is under the controlling influence of the smaller states. Instead of an organization primarily concerned, in its economic activities, with avoiding another "great depression," we have one focusing its activities on the economic and social development of underdeveloped states and territories. Instead of an organization concerned with respect for all human rights everywhere, we have one almost wholly preoccupied with the elimination of racial discrimination. Instead of an organization devoted to the orderly and progressive development of self-government in non-self-governing territories, we have one in which independence is regarded as an end to be achieved without regard to degree of readiness.

The listing of contrasts could be carried further, but is sufficient to indicate how much the spirit, dominant purposes, balance of forces, and activities of the Organization have changed. It is, however, significant and encouraging that while the League twenty years after its birth was in its death throes, the United Nations after an even longer period of time is still a living organization, a vital and constructive force in the life of our times.

Charter of the United Nations

[Preamble]

**WE THE PEOPLES OF THE UNITED NATIONS
DETERMINED**

to save succeeding generations from the scourge of war, which twice in our lifetime has brought untold sorrow to mankind, and

to reaffirm faith in fundamental human rights, in the dignity and worth of the human person, in the equal rights of men and women and of nations large and small, and

to establish conditions under which justice and respect for the obligations arising from treaties and other sources of international law can be maintained, and

to promote social progress and better standards of life in larger freedom,

AND FOR THESE ENDS

to practice tolerance and live together in peace with one another as good neighbors, and

to unite our strength to maintain international peace and security, and

to ensure, by the acceptance of principles and the institution of methods, that armed force shall not be used, save in the common interest, and

to employ international machinery for the promotion of the economic and social advancement of all peoples,

**HAVE RESOLVED TO COMBINE OUR EFFORTS TO
ACCOMPLISH THESE AIMS.**

Accordingly, our respective Governments, through representatives assembled in the city of San Francisco, who have exhibited their full powers found to be in good and due form, have agreed to the present Charter of the United Nations and do hereby establish an international organization to be known as the United Nations.

A preamble is a customary part of a treaty and serves the purpose of defining in general terms the purposes which the parties have in view and the considerations that have led them to agree. The Dumbarton Oaks Proposals did not contain a preamble. The first two chapters of the Proposals, dealing with "Purposes" and "Principles," contained provisions regarding motives and intent that are commonly found in a preamble. At San Francisco, several delegations expressed interest in having a preamble and, in the technical committee, a draft was proposed by Field Marshal Smuts of South Africa which became the basis of discussion. With considerable modification, more of form and style than of content, this draft became the preamble approved by the Conference.[1]

It was recognized in the committee discussion at San Francisco that it was difficult, if not impossible, to make a clear distinction as to function and value between the preamble, the statement of "Purposes" (Article 1), and the enumeration of governing "Principles" (Article 2). The technical committee attempted such a differentiation, however, as follows:

(a) The "Preamble" introduces the Charter and sets forth the declared common intentions which brought us together in this Conference and moved us to unite our will and efforts, and made us harmonize, regulate, and organize our international action to achieve our common ends.

(b) The "Purposes" constitute the *raison d'être* of the Organization. They are the aggregation of the common ends on which our minds met; hence, the cause and object of the Charter to which member states collectively and severally subscribe.

(c) The chapter on "Principles" sets, in the same order of ideas, the methods and regulating norms according to which the Organization and its members shall do their duty and endeavor to achieve the common ends. Their understandings should serve as actual standards of international conduct.[2]

The view of the technical committee was that all provisions of the Charter, "being in this case indivisible as in any other legal instrument, are equally valid and operative." Each, therefore, is to be construed and applied "in function of the others." [3] While the preamble is an integral part of the Charter, it does not define the basic obligations of members. It does have significance, however, as a statement of motivating ideas and purposes that the members of the Organization have in mind, and its words can be used, and are used, as evidence of these

---

[1] For further detail on Conference consideration, see Ruth B. Russell, *A History of the United Nations Charter* (Washington, Brookings Institution, 1958), pp. 910–19.

[2] UNCIO, *Documents*, VI, 446–47.   [3] *Ibid.*, p. 447.

ideas and purposes in any interpretation of the articles that follow.[4]

While the preamble was explained by its authors as a statement of "declared common intentions," in the discussions and decisions of United Nations organs relatively little use has been made of it. In a few instances, as in the case of the General Assembly resolution of December 18, 1962, on principles of international law concerning friendly relations and cooperation between states,[5] and in the discussion on the "Uniting for Peace" draft resolution,[6] one does find supporting references to the preamble or its specific language. More commonly, the ideas expressed in United Nations decisions, though contained in the preamble, are also set forth in subsequent articles of the Charter, and all that one can say with some certainty is that the preamble reinforces, without being essential to, the propositions being advanced. For example, the reference in the preamble to faith in "fundamental human rights" and "in the dignity and worth of the human person" gives support and emphasis to the provisions of Articles 1 and 55 in particular; these have been principally relied upon in efforts to eliminate racial discrimination.[7] The emphasis of the preamble on combining justice with respect for international obligations is in line with the authority given to the General Assembly under Article 14, implicitly rather than explicitly, to review and make recommendations with respect to the revision of international agreements in the interest of peace and justice.[8]

Use of the words "We the peoples of the United Nations" at the beginning of the Charter was proposed by the United States delegation at San Francisco. The purpose was to emphasize that the Charter was an expression of the wills of the peoples of the world. The proposal met with a restrained, if not cool, response on the part of other delegations, who saw certain practical difficulties as well as substantial unreality in its acceptance. Its adoption constituted a departure from past practice which had been, as in the case of the Covenant of the League of Nations, to refer only to states or their governments as interested parties. To meet objections, the conclusion of the preamble was modified to convey the idea that though the Charter purported to reflect the resolution of peoples, the actual agreement was between governments.[9]

[4] *Ibid.* See also State Dept., *Report to the President,* pp. 34–35. For example of use of preamble in interpreting an international instrument, see advisory opinion of Permanent Court of International Justice on competence of International Labour Organisation, PCIJ, Series B, No. 2, esp. pp. 25–27.

[5] GA Res. 1815(XVII), Dec. 18, 1962. See also GA Res. 109(II), Oct. 21, 1947 on the Balkan crisis.

[6] GAOR/5th Sess., 1st Ctte./362d Mtg./Oct. 13, 1950/para. 21; and 300th Plen. Mtg./Nov. 2, 1950/paras. 91–92.

[7] See commentary on Art. 55.   [8] See commentary on Art. 14.

[9] For detailed account of what happened at San Francisco, see Russell, pp. 913–15.

In the Dumbarton Oaks Proposals, it had been suggested that the new organization be given the name "The United Nations." The title had been suggested by President Roosevelt. The idea back of the suggestion was, first, that this name accurately described the kind of organization that was necessary to the achievement of common purposes, and second, that it had already been given recognition in the Declaration by United Nations of January 1, 1942.[10] The official British position was that the name affirmed both the fact that the Organization "is a result of the common effort which has saved civilization from the Nazi and Fascist attacks and the belief that such a close union will continue in the future." [11]

At San Francisco, some delegations felt that the name was unwise because it tended to perpetuate the idea of a military coalition formed for limited purposes under given historical circumstances. For them the name, being associated with military action against certain states, might impede progress toward universality of membership. Most of the delegations, however, found the name appropriate, and in the end, it was unanimously approved as a tribute to President Roosevelt by the technical committee and by the Conference.

[10] U.S. Executive Agreement Series 236.
[11] *British Parliamentary Papers,* Misc. No. 6 (1944), Cmd. 6571, para. 1.

CHAPTER I

Purposes and Principles

It was decided at the Dumbarton Oaks Conference to generalize the obligations of members of the proposed organization and to set them out in the two initial chapters of the Proposals under the headings "Purposes" and "Principles." This decision was related to the general conception held by members of the Conference regarding the kind of organization of peace and security that would be most effective.[1] The League Covenant had imposed on members the obligation "to respect and preserve against external aggression the territorial integrity and political independence of all members" (Article 10), and to apply "immediately" sweeping economic and financial sanctions against any member resorting to war in violation of its obligations (Article 16). At Dumbarton Oaks, the view prevailed that the effectiveness of a system for the maintenance of peace and security depended on the unity of purpose of the states possessing the greatest power, and that the co-operation of these states could best be achieved by a commitment to act in accordance with defined purposes and principles of a general nature. With the guiding principles and purposes established, the Security Council would be able to act promptly and effectively whenever conditions were determined to require it and by the means deemed most likely to be efficacious.

At San Francisco, proposals were made to modify the Dumbarton Oaks text by introducing additional and more precise definitions of standards to govern the conduct of members and of the Security Council in the maintenance of international peace and security.[2] In particular, it was proposed that justice and international law should be made criteria for collective measures taken to maintain or restore international peace and security, and that an obligation equivalent to that of Article 10 of the Covenant be added to the purposes and principles of the new organization. These proposals were successfully resisted; they would, argued the United States and British delegates, have the effect of depriving the United Nations system of collective security of the

[1] See Ruth B. Russell, A *History of the United Nations Charter* (Washington, Brookings Institution, 1958), pp. 455–57.
[2] *Ibid.*, pp. 655–57, 672–75.

desirable flexibility and selectivity in its actual operation. The role of
the purposes and principles set forth in the Charter, as conceived at
San Francisco by the major governments, was clearly described by
Lord Halifax, speaking for the United Kingdom, in Commission I:

Mr. President, the purposes and the principles in Chapters I and II [3]
seem to me and to my Delegation of the highest importance. I think they
introduce a new idea into international relations, for instead of trying to
govern the actions of the members and the organs of the United Nations
by precise and intricate codes of procedure, we have preferred to lay down
purposes and principles under which they are to act. And by that means,
we hope to insure that they act in conformity with the express desires of
the nations assembled here, while, at the same time, we give them freedom
to accommodate their actions to circumstances which today no man can
foresee.

We all want our Organization to have life. We want it to develop its own
codes of procedure. We want it to be free to deal with all the situations
that may arise in international relations. We do not want to lay down rules
which may, in the future, be the signpost for the guilty and a trap for the
innocent. And, so far as words can go, I venture to assert that the rights and
interests of all members are safeguarded in our purposes and principles,
while the power of action by the Security Council in the interest of all is
made easier. By that means, Mr. President, I, for one, hope that we may
succeed in creating an organic body which will have within itself the seeds
of a vigorous life, and so may grow into the great society of nations of
which, throughout the centuries, men and women have dreamed and which,
in our own time, please God, may bring healing and hope to a wounded
world. [4]

The purposes and principles of the Charter, or particular phrases in
them, have been repeatedly invoked in the preamble and operative
parts of resolutions and in statements of member representatives. [5] So
far as the Security Council is concerned, the purposes and principles,
formulated as they are in general terms, have contributed to the flexible and selective functioning of the Organization in the peace and
security field. In the case of the General Assembly, the purposes and
principles have served a somewhat different purpose. Taken together
with the broad definition of the Assembly powers of discussion and
recommendation in Articles 10, 11, 13 and 14, they have contributed to
an expansion of the Assembly's role. While it may be an exaggeration
to say that the purposes and principles alone have provided the "seeds

---

[3] Arts. 1 and 2 of the Charter.   [4] UNCIO, *Documents*, VI, 26.

[5] See *Repertory*, Vol. I; *Supp. 1*, Vol. I; and *Supp. 2*, Vol. I, for tabulation of
decisions of the General Assembly referring to purposes and principles as a whole;
and for tabulations of decisions referring to specific purposes and principles.

of a vigorous life" for the Organization, it is true that they have provided valuable guidelines for organs and members alike, and have improved the capacity of the Organization for adaptation and growth.

Article 1

The Purposes of the United Nations are:

1. To maintain international peace and security, and to that end: to take effective collective measures for the prevention and removal of threats to the peace, and for the suppression of acts of aggression or other breaches of the peace, and to bring about by peaceful means, and in conformity with the principles of justice and international law, adjustment or settlement of international disputes or situations which might lead to a breach of the peace;

2. To develop friendly relations among nations based on respect for the principle of equal rights and self-determination of peoples, and to take other appropriate measures to strengthen universal peace;

3. To achieve international cooperation in solving international problems of an economic, social, cultural, or humanitarian character, and in promoting and encouraging respect for human rights and for fundamental freedoms for all without distinction as to race, sex, language, or religion; and

4. To be a center for harmonizing the actions of nations in the attainment of these common ends.

Article 1 defines the objectives of the Organization. In his *Report to the President,* the Chairman of the United States Delegation to the San Francisco Conference declared that the "Purposes" here listed "are binding on the Organization, its organs, and its agencies, indicating the direction their activities should take and the limitations within which their activities should proceed." [6] This statement reflects the significance attached by the Conference to the inclusion of the statement of purposes in an article of the Charter instead of limiting it to the preamble.

As this article conclusively shows, the United Nations is conceived as a multipurpose organization. In fact, not all its purposes are listed here. The important objectives of the United Nations with respect to non-self-governing territories, which are set forth in some detail in Articles 73 and 76, are not included. Nor are United Nations objectives in the economic and social fields given the detailed and explicit definition they receive in subsequent articles. The order of listing, together with the content of subsequent Charter provisions, gives support to the view

[6] State Dept., *Report to the President,* p. 36.

that the maintenance of peace and security is the primary purpose of the Organization and takes priority over other purposes.[7]

The question of the order of priority of purposes is of practical importance, since they are clearly not consistent with each other in all respects. For example, implementation of the principle of self-determination (paragraph 2) may lead to results that some regard as inconsistent with the maintenance of peace and security (paragraph 1). Furthermore, emphasis on collective measures for maintaining or restoring international peace and security (paragraph 1) may lead to different results than stressing the importance of harmonizing the actions of members for the attainment of common ends (paragraph 4). The priorities members give to the different purposes of the United Nations have had an important influence in determining the matters with which the Organization is concerned at any particular time and the course of action that is followed.

In the development of the Organization, and more particularly in the growth of the functions and activities of its organs, great reliance has been placed on the "Purposes" as set forth in Article 1. This has been particularly true of the General Assembly, the responsibilities and powers of which are not defined as sharply or in as great detail as are those of the Councils, and which also has the advantage of a very broad power of discussion and recommendation, particularly under Article 10. Two examples of particular significance in the development of the Assembly's role may be cited: the Uniting for Peace resolution [8] by which the General Assembly assumed for itself a "residual responsibility" for discharging the functions set forth in Article 1(1) in case the Security Council, vested with primary responsibility for maintaining international peace and security by Article 24, was prevented from discharging it because of lack of unanimity among the permanent members; and the Declaration on Granting Independence to Colonial Countries and Peoples [9] by which the General Assembly, invoking inter alia Article 1(2), proclaimed "the right to self-determination" of all peoples and the corresponding obligation of all member states to transfer immediately all power to the peoples of non-self-governing territories.

Another example of the use made of Article 1 to justify the exercise of wide powers by the General Assembly is found in the advisory opinion of the International Court of Justice in the "Certain Expenses" case. In this opinion, the Court asserted that "[in] determining whether the actual expenditures authorized constitute 'expenses of the Organi-

---

[7] See, for example, separate opinion of Judge Sir Gerald Fitzmaurice in "Certain Expenses" case, *ICJ Reports*, 1962, especially pp. 213–15.
[8] GA Res. 377(V), Nov. 3, 1950.   [9] GA Res. 1514(XV), Dec. 14, 1960.

zation within the meaning of Article 17, paragraph 2, of the Charter',
. . . such expenditures must be tested by their relationship to the
purposes of the United Nations." [10] It added that, "when the Organization takes action which warrants the assertion that it was appropriate
for the fulfillment of one of the stated purposes of the United Nations,
the presumption is that such action is not *ultra vires* the Organization." [11]

The view that the purposes set forth in Article 1 can be used to
justify the exercise by United Nations organs of power not expressly
authorized by other provisions of the Charter has not gone without
challenge. The Soviet Union and other members have denied the authority claimed by the General Assembly, in the exercise of a "residual
responsibility" for the maintenance of international peace, to initiate
peace-keeping operations. In a dissenting opinion in the "Certain Expenses" case, Judge Winiarski stated the position quite succinctly in
these words:

The Charter has set forth the purposes of the United Nations in very
wide . . . terms. But . . . it does not follow, far from it, that the Organization is entitled to seek to achieve those purposes by no matter what
means. The fact that an organ of the United Nations is seeking to achieve
one of those purposes does not suffice to render its action lawful. The
Charter, a multilateral treaty which was the result of prolonged and laborious negotiations, carefully created organs and determined their competence
and means of actions.

The intention of those who drafted it was clearly to abandon the possibility of useful action rather than to sacrifice the balance of carefully established fields of competence, as can be seen, for example, in the case of the
voting in the Security Council. It is only by such procedures, which were
clearly defined, that the United Nations can seek to achieve its purposes.[12]

Maintenance of International Peace and Security

The Charter follows the Dumbarton Oaks Proposals in making the
maintenance of international peace and security the first purpose of the
United Nations. The peace to be maintained is "international peace";
the United Nations is concerned with internal disorder only to the
extent that it affects international peace.

Article 1(1) recognizes two paths to be followed in achieving international peace and security. One is the path to collective measures; the
other is that of peaceful settlement or accommodation. It is significant
that, at San Francisco, the major powers refused to accept an amendment requiring that collective measures be taken in accordance with

[10] *ICJ Reports*, 1962, p. 167.   [11] *Ibid.*, p. 168.   [12] *Ibid.*, p. 230.

international law and justice, on the grounds that this would tie the hands of the Security Council to an undesirable extent and that, in any case, the object of collective measures was to prevent or suppress the use of armed force, and not to achieve a settlement.[13] However, they were willing to accept an amendment to the Dumbarton Oaks text providing that adjustment or settlement of international disputes or situations should be "in conformity with the principles of international law and justice." It was intended thereby to provide a safeguard against the settlement of any dispute or the accommodation of any situation by the sacrifice of rights of small nations in the interest of a doubtful peace, as had been done at Munich in 1938.

Article 1(1) contains phraseology which differs in certain respects from that of subsequent articles concerned with the maintenance of international peace and security. In this paragraph, the words "effective collective measures" are used to describe the measures to be taken for the prevention and removal of threats to the peace, and the suppression of acts of aggression. Articles 39, 41, and 42 speak of "measures" to be taken by the Security Council. Article 2(7) refers to "enforcement measures"; Article 50 refers to "preventive or enforcement measures"; and Article 5 to "preventive or enforcement action." The words "effective collective measures" have been interpreted to have a broader connotation than the words describing the action taken by the Security Council under Chapter VII, and to justify the recommendation of collective measures by the General Assembly under its "residual responsibility" and the existence of an obligation on the part of members to take collective measures to defeat aggression. In the Uniting for Peace resolution, the General Assembly affirmed that failure of the Security Council to exercise its primary responsibility "does not relieve Member States of their obligations or the United Nations of its responsibility to maintain international peace and security." [14] Some delegates emphasized that the responsibility and powers of the General Assembly under Article 10 should be determined in light of Article 1(1), which contains the twofold injunction that measures be "collective" and "effective." [15]

The phraseology relating to peaceful settlement also differs from that of subsequent related articles in that it places more emphasis upon settlement in conformity with justice and international law than do the provisions of Article 2(3) and Chapter VI.

Detailed provision for implementation of the purposes set forth in

[13] UNCIO, *Documents*, VI, 453.   [14] GA Res. 377(V), Nov. 3, 1950.
[15] See statements by Belaunde (Peru), GAOR/5th Sess., 1st Ctte./356th Mtg./ Oct. 10, 1950/paras. 27–28; Rao (Brazil), *ibid.*, para. 51; and Padilla Nervo (Mexico), 360th Mtg./Oct. 12, 1950/para. 35.

Article 1(1) is made in subsequent articles of the Charter relating to obligations of members, the powers and responsibilities of organs, and the procedures to be followed.[16]

The Development of Friendly Relations on the Basis of Equal Rights and Self-Determination

Article 1(2) has special importance because of its recognition of the principle of self-determination. Except for the phrase "based on the principle of equal rights and self-determination of peoples," which was added at San Francisco, the paragraph does little more than state the obvious, since any organization to maintain international peace and security and promote international cooperation in economic and social relations must be concerned with the development of friendly relations as the basis of effective action. The phrase "to take appropriate measures to strengthen universal peace" is a kind of all-inclusive statement which covers specific methods, such as the regulation of armaments, not specifically mentioned in Article 1(1). It is of interest—though of no particular significance—that this paragraph refers to "universal" instead of "international" peace. There is no evidence that it was intended by this phraseology that the Organization should be concerned with domestic peace as such.

During World War I, the concept of self-determination was given explicit formulation by Woodrow Wilson in his Fourteen Points as a principle governing the determination of territorial boundaries in the peace treaties to be signed at the end of the war. Yet, this principle found no place in the Covenant of the League of Nations and its application was confined to Central and Eastern Europe.

On colonial matters Wilson demanded "[a] free, open-minded, and absolutely impartial adjustment of all colonial claims, based upon a strict observance of the principle that in determining all such questions of sovereignty the interests of the populations concerned *must* have equal weight with the equitable claims of the government whose title is to be determined."

In the interwar period, criticism of colonialism began to gather momentum and the outbreak of World War II greatly strengthened the belief that colonialism was dying. This was brought home to many, particularly in the United States, by the slight resistance with which the colonial peoples of South East Asia, with the exception of the Filipinos who had been promised independence, opposed the Japanese

---

[16] See, in particular, Arts. 2(3) and (4); Art. 24; and chs. vi, vii, and viii, and commentary.

invaders. Thus, the United States, in its wartime planning for the future international organization, gave considerable attention to proposals providing for a system of international supervision over all dependent peoples. The Atlantic Charter proclaimed the "right of all peoples to choose the form of government under which they will live"; [17] however, Prime Minister Churchill did not consider this statement applicable to colonial peoples.

The principle of equal rights and self-determination received no mention in the Dumbarton Oaks Proposals. The addition of the phrase "based on respect for the principle of equal rights and self-determination of peoples" to the second paragraph of Chapter I (Purposes) was proposed at the San Francisco Conference by the Sponsoring Governments at the suggestion of the Soviet Union. When the amendment was discussed in Committee I/1, two different viewpoints developed. On the one hand, "it was strongly emphasized . . . that this principle corresponded closely to the will and desires of peoples everywhere and should be clearly enunciated." On the other hand, "it was stated that the principle conformed to the purposes of the Charter only in so far as it implied the right of self-government of peoples and not the right of secession." [18] Controversy focused also on the use of the words "nations" and "peoples" rather than "the more usual reference throughout the Charter to relations among 'states.' " [19] In recommending the draft, the technical committee indicated its understanding that:

the principle of equal rights of peoples and that of self-determination are two complementary parts of one standard of conduct: that the respect of that principle is a basis for the development of friendly relations and is one of the measures to strengthen universal peace; that an essential element of the principle in question is a free and genuine expression of the will of the people.[20]

The text of the Sponsors' draft was ultimately approved. However, questions regarding the difference—if any—between the terms "nations," "peoples," and "states," the meaning of "self-determination," and whether one or two principles were involved, were left unresolved.[21]

One of the controversies that has arisen in the interpretation of the Charter concerns the nature of "self-determination." It has been maintained that self-determination is a legal right which gives rise to legal claims and legal obligations. Obversely, it has been asserted that it is a political principle applicable as circumstances permit, with due regard

[17] See message of President Roosevelt to Congress: H. Doc. 358/77C1/ Aug. 21, 1941.
[18] UNCIO, *Documents*, VI, 296.   [19] Russell, p. 811.
[20] UNCIO, *Documents*, VI, 455.   [21] See Russell, p. 813.

to geography, strategic unity, and economic and historical realities. Another issue that has arisen is the relationship of the Charter provision on self-determination to the domestic jurisdiction principle stated in Article 2(7). One view is that, inasmuch as the Charter proclaims the principle of self-determination in Articles 1(2) and 55, implementation of this principle is in no way limited by the provisions of Article 2(7) prohibiting United Nations intervention in "matters which are essentially within the domestic jurisdiction of any state." Another view holds that Article 2(7) has an overriding effect and applies to all the provisions of the Charter, with the sole exception of enforcement measures provided for in Chapter VII. Some member states have distinguished between minorities living within the boundaries of a state and the peoples of non-self-governing, noncontiguous territories, and have held that the exercise of self-determination by the latter is a question of international concern beyond the scope of domestic jurisdiction.

The practice of United Nations organs has been to regard self-determination as a "right," and to discuss matters involving issues of self-determination despite the claim of domestic jurisdiction by member states.

Despite the opposition of some members, the General Assembly in 1950 recognized that the right of peoples and nations to self-determination is a fundamental human right.[22] Subsequently it decided to include in the covenants on human rights an article on the right of self-determination.[23] In 1955, the following text was accepted in the Third Committee, over the opposition of many Western European countries, for inclusion in both draft covenants on human rights:

All peoples have the right of self-determination. By virtue of this right they freely determine their political status and freely pursue their economic, social and cultural development.

The peoples may, for their own ends, freely dispose of their natural wealth and resources without prejudice to any obligations arising out of international economic cooperation, based upon the principle of mutual benefit, and international law. In no case may a people be deprived of its own means of subsistence.[24]

In 1954, the General Assembly requested the Commission on Human Rights to make recommendations concerning the permanent sovereignty of peoples over their "natural wealth and resources, having due regard to the rights and duties of states under international law and to the importance of encouraging international cooperation in the economic development of underdeveloped countries." [25] Subsequently, in

[22] See GA Res. 421(V), Dec. 4, 1950.   [23] GA Res. 545(VI), Feb. 5, 1952.
[24] GAOR/10th Sess./1955/*Annexes*, agenda item 28-I (A/3077, para. 77).
[25] GA Res. 837(IX), Dec. 14, 1954.

1958, the General Assembly after "noting" that the right of peoples and nations to self-determination includes permanent sovereignty over their natural wealth and resources, decided to establish a Commission "to conduct a full survey of the status of this basic constituent element of the right of self-determination." [26] Based on the report of this Commission, the General Assembly in 1962 adopted a resolution in which it referred to the "inalienable right" of all states "freely to dispose of their natural wealth and resources." [27]

The situation involving the Algerian independence movement was submitted to the General Assembly as one that "obviously" involved the provisions of Article 1(2). France, for its part, denied the competence of the United Nations in the matter and refused to participate in the debate. During the discussions, many members held that it was the duty of the United Nations to enable the Algerian people to achieve self-determination. However, it was only after General de Gaulle, in his speech of September 16, 1959, gave the Algerians the opportunity to determine their own status, that the General Assembly made express reference to Article 1(2) in a resolution and recognized the "right of the Algerian people to self-determination." [28]

A similar situation existed in the case of Angola. The Portuguese government claimed that Angola was an integral part of Portugal and that the United Nations had no authority to deal with a condition of internal disorder in the territory. Other members, however, claimed that the situation endangered international peace and security and in addition invoked the right of the inhabitants to self-determination as justifying United Nations action. The principle was invoked successfully both in the Security Council and in the General Assembly. The Portuguese government was urged by the Assembly to undertake measures that would ensure the transfer of power to the people of Angola in accordance with the Declaration on the Granting of Independence to Colonial Countries and Peoples.[29]

The United Kingdom's claim of domestic jurisdiction with respect to the Cyprus question in 1957 gave rise to extensive discussions over the nature and scope of self-determination as well as the groups entitled to it. No mention of "self-determination" was made in the resolutions adopted by the Assembly on this dispute,[30] which was settled in direct negotiations between Greece, Turkey, and the United Kingdom

[26] GA Res. 1314(XIII), Dec. 12, 1958.
[27] GA Res. 1803(XVII), Dec. 14, 1962.
[28] GA Res. 1573(XV), Dec. 19, 1960. See previous resolutions, 1012(XI), Feb. 15, 1957; and 1184(XII), Dec. 10, 1957.
[29] See, as example of UN action, GA Res. 1819(XVII), Dec. 18, 1962.
[30] GA Res. 1013(XI), Feb. 26, 1957; and 1287(XIII), Dec. 5, 1958.

in 1959, resulting in the establishment of the Republic of Cyprus.

Although no express reference was made to self-determination in the resolutions adopted by the General Assembly on the Hungarian question, certain ones contained references to the right of the Hungarian people to a government responsive to their national aspirations, and to the holding of free elections in Hungary under United Nations auspices to enable the people of Hungary to determine for themselves the form of government they wished established.[31]

In the controversy concerning the future of West Irian (West New Guinea), the principle of self-determination was invoked by both sides to the dispute. Indonesia argued that the matter had been settled when the people of West Irian had taken part in the Indonesian independence movement and that Indonesia had the right to refuse the application of the principle of self-determination to what was an integral part of its territory. For its part, the Netherlands contended that to transfer the territory to Indonesia or to enter into negotiations regarding its future status without consulting the wishes of the inhabitants would violate their right to self-determination. The situation was discussed by the General Assembly at several sessions, but no resolutions were adopted. Ultimately, an agreement was reached by Indonesia and the Netherlands in 1962, calling for temporary United Nations administration of the territory, transfer of the administration to Indonesia as soon as possible after May 1, 1963, and exercise of the right of self-determination by the inhabitants of West Irian before the end of 1969.[32]

The principle of self-determination has played a key role in the concerted effort to end colonialism. On December 14, 1960, the General Assembly unanimously adopted the Declaration on the Granting of Independence to Colonial Countries and Peoples sponsored by forty-three Asian and African members. The General Assembly "[s]olemnly" proclaimed therein "the necessity of bringing to a speedy and unconditional end colonialism in all its forms and manifestations"; declared that "all peoples have the right to self-determination" and that immediate steps should be taken to transfer all powers to the peoples of all territories not yet independent without any conditions or reservations; and denied that inadequacy of preparation should ever be a pretext for delaying the exercise of the right of self-determination.[33]

At the following session, the Assembly established a special commit-

[31] See, for example, GA Res. 1004(ES-II), Nov. 4, 1956; 1005(ES-II), Nov. 9, 1956; 1131(XI), Dec. 12, 1956; 1133(XII), Sept. 14, 1957; and 1312(XIII), Dec. 12, 1958.
[32] UN Doc. S/5169, Sept. 21, 1962; and GA Res. 1752(XVII), Sept. 21, 1962.
[33] GA Res. 1514(XV), Dec. 14, 1960.

tee to examine the application of the Declaration and make suggestions and recommendations on the progress of its implementation. Subsequently, the Assembly invited the committee to propose specific measures for the speedy application of the Declaration and authorized it to bring to the attention of the Security Council any developments in the colonial sphere which might threaten international peace and security.[34]

The Declaration on the Granting of Independence to Colonial Countries and Peoples and the practice of the General Assembly and the special committee all suggest the following conclusions with respect to the principle of self-determination, status compatible with it, and groups to which it applies:

1. The principle has been applied to situations involving colonial rule of noncontiguous territories inhabited by people of a predominantly different culture.

2. There has been a very strong inclination on the part of a sizable majority of members to insist that independence is the only status compatible with the principle of self-determination, although there has been a growing awareness of the need for some flexibility in the case of dependencies which, because of the smallness of their territory and population, are hardly viable entities;

3. The principle of "self-determination of peoples" has been interpreted to mean that the inhabitants of a territory treated as an administrative unit by the colonial power should determine its political status on the basis of universal adult suffrage and by majority vote. Once the choice has been made, attempts at secession by disaffected minority groups have been held to be incompatible with the Charter.[35]

International Cooperation and Human Rights

The authors of the Charter recognized that the maintenance of international peace and security was not solely a matter of settling disputes or dealing with threats to the peace or acts of aggression. There was also the need to create conditions, other than purely political, favorable to the existence of peace. In addition, quite apart from their interest in peace and security, they recognized the need of international cooperation to promote human welfare in a world which no longer permits this objective to be adequately achieved by national action alone.

It is to be noted that the purpose here stated is "to achieve international cooperation in solving international problems" and in "promoting and encouraging respect for human rights and for fundamental freedoms." This emphasis on cooperation is consistent with the first

---

[34] GA Res. 1654(XVI), Nov. 27, 1961, and 1810(XVII), Dec. 17, 1962.
[35] See, for example, operative para. 6 of the Declaration.

principle set forth in Article 2, "the sovereign equality" of all members of the Organization. The United Nations was not intended to have the powers of a government in dealing with the economic and social problems here listed; rather, its function was conceived as that of serving as a means of promoting cooperation between states in finding solutions to common problems and of achieving maximum support from members for the work of the Organization. One reason for giving the principle of domestic jurisdiction contained in Article 2(7) a more general application than was originally provided in the Dumbarton Oaks Proposals was to provide assurance that the strengthening of the economic and social provisions of the Charter did not give the United Nations power to coerce states in respect to matters that had hitherto been regarded as falling within their exclusive domestic jurisdiction.

The issue of the extent to which Article 1(3) imposes obligations on members and provides the legal basis for United Nations action, particularly on the part of the General Assembly, has arisen especially with respect to proposals for promoting respect for human rights and fundamental freedoms.[36] On the one hand, the view has been expressed that Article 2(3) commits the Organization only to promoting cooperation between members; that no member is legally obligated to respect a particular right or freedom until it enters into an agreement recognizing the existence of the right and undertaking to respect it; and that until this is done, the Organization has no competence to concern itself with an alleged violation since the matter is "essentially within the domestic jurisdiction" of the member. On the other hand, it has been argued that, notwithstanding Article 2(7), Article 1(3), together with Articles 55 and 56 , places an obligation on members to respect human rights and fundamental freedoms, that the General Assembly may consider alleged violations of rights, such as the right not to be discriminated against on the basis of race, and that members are required to cooperate with the Assembly in carrying out its recommendations by the terms of Article 56.

Harmonizing the Actions of Nations

The text of Article 1(4) is taken from the Dumbarton Oaks Proposals with only one change; the substitution of "be" for "afford," was accepted at San Francisco without discussion. The emphasis of this paragraph is on the necessity of agreement as a basis for action, particularly agreement among the major powers.[37] Apart from those cases where reference has been made to the purposes and principles of the

[36] For details on UN implementation of purposes set forth in Art. 1(3), see chs. ix and x and commentary.
[37] See, for example, GA Res. 1495(XV), Oct. 17, 1960.

United Nations generally, there have been few specific references to this paragraph in the resolutions adopted by United Nations organs and in the statements of government representatives. And yet, the basic idea that there must be harmonization of the policies and actions of states if the Organization is to achieve practical results has underlaid all the activities of the Organization.

Thus it is one of the essential purposes of the Organization to help bring this about. Resolutions adopted by majority votes are not enough, though they may contribute to the desired result. What is needed for the Organization to succeed in its purposes is a broad working consensus of its members in support of decisions taken.

Article 2

The Organization and its Members, in pursuit of the Purposes stated in Article 1, shall act in accordance with the following Principles.

Article 2 is of fundamental importance in the total economy of the Charter. It lays down basic principles which the Organization, functioning through its various organs, and its members, must respect. Since the General Assembly, the Security Council, the Economic and Social Council, and the Trusteeship Council are composed of member states, it might be thought that—at least with respect to the activities of these organs—the inclusion of the word "Organization" is superfluous. This, of course, would not, in any case, be true of all the activities of the Organization, for example, those of the Secretariat and the Court. Furthermore, since the Organization has a separate personality and legal capacity from that of its members, its inclusion is justifiable for technical as well as more broadly political reasons. Frequent references to the "Principles of the Organization" as providing standards of conduct are to be found in the resolutions adopted by United Nations organs and in statements by members. Commonly, both principles and purposes are referred to in this connection.[38]

1. The Organization is based on the principle of the sovereign equality of all its Members.

The Moscow Four-Power Declaration of October 30, 1943, called for the establishment of an organization "based on the principle of the sovereign equality of all peace-loving states." [39] The Dumbarton Oaks Proposals listed this as the first of the principles of the new Organiza-

[38] See *Repertory*, I, 15–20; *Supp. 1*, I, 16; *Supp. 2*, I, 14–18.
[39] State Dept. *Bulletin*, IX, 308.

tion. At San Francisco, the principle was retained, but modified as to language by the substitution of "its Members" for "peace-loving states." [40]

The term "sovereign equality" is far from being self-explanatory. In fact, there are few precedents for its use in the literature and practice of international relations. It combines in one expression two distinct but closely related ideas, that of state sovereignty and that of the equality of states. According to the report of the technical committee which considered the matter at San Francisco, "sovereign equality" includes the following elements:

(1) that states are juridically equal;
(2) that each state enjoys the rights inherent in full sovereignty;
(3) that the personality of the state is respected, as well as its territorial integrity and political independence;
(4) that the state should, under international order, comply faithfully with its international duties and obligations. [41]

The principle of state equality has found frequent expression in the official statements of governments, the decisions of domestic and international tribunals, and the writings of jurists. It has been commonly interpreted to mean equality before the law. Thus defined, it is consistent with substantial inequality of participation and influence in international organizations. [42] In the United Nations, as in the League of Nations before it, states are given unequal rights of participation in the membership of organs and subsidiary organs; and in the United Nations Security Council, unequal legal effects are attached to their votes. The Charter gives to the votes of permanent members of the Security Council more decisive legal effects under certain circumstances than to the votes of nonpermanent members. But—and this is perhaps closer to impairment of the principle of juridical equality as traditionally understood—it also provides that the great majority (but not all) of the members may under certain circumstances be legally bound by decisions taken without their specific consent. [43] In a sense, the strong opposition on the part of the smaller states to the veto in the Security Council, and particularly to the extent of its use, has reflected a reluctance to accept an impairment of the principle of juridical equality.

The principle of state sovereignty is even more difficult to harmonize with participation in an international organization. Defined in its crudest and most extreme form, it is incompatible with the effec-

[40] Not all the participants in the San Francisco Conference were "states" in the sense of fully independent political entities. See commentary on Arts. 3 and 4.

[41] UNCIO, *Documents*, VI, 457.

[42] See Edwin D. Dickinson, *The Equality of States in International Law* (Cambridge, Harvard University Press, 1920).

[43] See Arts. 25 and 27, and commentary.

tive functioning of an international organization as it denies the possibility of limiting the freedom of action of the state. The Charter is based on the assumption, however, that states in the exercise of their sovereignty may accept legal limitations on their freedom of action, and they are not free to disregard these restrictions as long as they remain members. There is, however, the question of who decides what these limitations are and what are the powers and responsibilities of organs established by agreement of member states under the Charter. The principle of state sovereignty consequently has relevance to the question of Charter interpretation and also to the principle of a reserved domestic jurisdiction as set forth in Article 2(7).[44]

In actual United Nations practice, the principle of state sovereignty finds application not so much in direct explicit references to it as in assertions that actions of the Organization or of states constitute infringements of the sovereignty, independence, or freedom of action of states, or constitute improper intervention in matters essentially within the domestic jurisdiction of states. While Article 2(7) explicitly provides protection against intervention by the United Nations in domestic matters, the principle of state sovereignty extends this protection to intervention by another state or group of states.[45]

The principle of state sovereignty has been frequently invoked as a limitation on the United Nations and its members, ordinarily without any specific reference to Article 2(1). The principle has also been invoked in opposition to proposed United Nations resolutions for dealing with disputes or situations under Chapter VI. For example, when the Commission of Investigation, established under the Security Council resolution of December 19, 1946, to investigate border incidents along Greece's northern frontier, recommended the creation of a commission or commissions with powers of investigation and good offices, the representatives of Poland and the USSR held that such action constituted an infringement upon the sovereignty of the states concerned and that the real cause of the existing difficulties was foreign military intervention in the internal affairs of Greece.[46] A similar claim with respect to the establishment of a commission of inquiry was made by the government of Hungary in 1957.[47] Such claims have not received majority support.

In other instances, the principle has been invoked in support of United Nations action deemed necessary to preserve the independence

[44] See p. 12 and commentary on Art. 2(7).
[45] This is explicitly provided in Article 15 of the Charter of the Organization of American States and Article III of the Charter of the Organization of African Unity.
[46] SCOR/2d Yr./1947/*Special Supp.* 2, I, 156–57.
[47] UN Doc A/3493, Jan. 11, 1957.

of members against outside interference. Thus, in the Hungarian case, the General Assembly, by its resolution of December 12, 1956,[48] condemned "the violation of the Charter" by the USSR in depriving Hungary of its liberty and independence. In dealing with the situation in the Congo in 1960, the Security Council requested states to refrain from any action "which might undermine the territorial integrity and the political independence of the Republic of the Congo." [49] At its twentieth session, the General Assembly by a vote of 114 to 0, with 2 abstentions, adopted the Declaration on the Inadmissibility of Intervention in the Domestic Affairs of States and the Protection of their Independence and Sovereignty,[50] by which it "solemnly" declared that

1. No State has the right to intervene, directly or indirectly, for any reason whatever, in the internal or external affairs of any other State. Consequently, armed intervention and all other forms of interference or attempted threats against the personality of the state or against its political, economic and cultural elements, are condemned.

2. No State may use or encourage the use of economic, political or any other type of measures to coerce another State in order to obtain from it the subordination of the exercise of its sovereign rights or to secure from it advantages of any kind. Also, no State shall organize, assist, foment, finance, incite or tolerate subversive, terrorist or armed activities directed toward the violent overthrow of the regime of another State, or interfere in civil strife in another State.

When the General Assembly decided at its seventeenth session to study certain principles of international law concerning friendly relations and cooperation among states, it included the principle of sovereign equality.[51] The Special Committee, established at the Assembly's eighteenth session to prepare a report,[52] was able to reach agreement on the following "points of consensus":

1. All States enjoy sovereign equality. As subjects of international law they have equal rights and duties.

2. In particular, sovereign equality includes the following elements:

a) States are juridically equal.

b) Each State enjoys the rights inherent in full sovereignty.

c) Each State has the duty to respect the personality of other States.

d) The territorial integrity and the political independence of the State are inviolable.

[48] GA Res. 1131(XI), Dec. 12, 1956.
[49] SC Res. of July 22, 1960 (Doc. S/4405). A similar request was later made by the General Assembly. GA Res. 1474(ES-IV), Sept. 20, 1960. See also GA Res. 2077(XX), Dec. 18, 1965, on question of Cyprus.
[50] GA Res. 2131(XX), Dec. 21, 1965.
[51] GA Res. 1815(XVII), Dec. 18, 1962.
[52] GA Res. 1966(XVIII), Dec. 16, 1963.

e) Each State has the right freely to choose and develop its political, social, economic and cultural systems.

f) Each State has the duty to comply fully and in good faith with its international obligations, and to live in peace with other States.[53]

Among the points on which there was lack of agreement was whether a state has the right to dispose freely of its natural wealth and resources. Some maintained that an absolute right exists. Others felt that any statement to that effect should be balanced by a reference to the General Assembly's resolution of December 14, 1962,[54] which recognized the international law standard as governing compensation for expropriation of private property.

While members have found it possible to reach some agreement, in general or even fairly specific terms, on what the principle of sovereign equality entails, it nevertheless remains true that the principle lends itself in application to a wide variety of interpretations and is frequently used by members as a means of unduly restricting the United Nations and promoting selfish national interests. On the other hand, it does protect the independence of each member against infringement by other member states, and is a reminder that the Organization is one of limited powers based on the consent of its members.

2. All Members, in order to ensure to all of them the rights and benefits resulting from membership, shall fulfill in good faith the obligations assumed by them in accordance with the present Charter.

Although the principle stated in Article 2(2) would seem fundamental to the establishment of any international legal order, it was considered desirable to state it explicitly as one of the principles binding upon the Organization and its members. It was contained in the Dumbarton Oaks Proposals, though the words "in good faith" do not appear until San Francisco. The words were then inserted at the request of the delegation of Colombia, which thought it appropriate to state explicitly the idea of good faith as a *leit motif* of the new organization since good faith had so conspicuously been lacking from international relations in the preceding years.[55] The proposal was approved by unanimous vote.

One clear inference is that members who do not fulfill their obligations are not in a position to demand the benefits of membership. This idea finds detailed application in Articles 5, 6, and 19. It has been

---

[53] GAOR/20th Sess./1965/*Annexes*, agenda items 90 and 94, p. 134 (Doc. A/5746). At its twentieth session, the Assembly took note of the report and directed the Committee to submit a comprehensive report on all the principles listed in its 1962 resolution. GA Res. 2103(XX), Dec. 20, 1965.

[54] GA Res. 1803(XVII), Dec. 14, 1962.   [55] UNCIO, *Documents*, VI, 71–80.

suggested that "good faith" means "first, objectivity in the self-interpretation by States of accepted obligations, and secondly, self-restraint by States in the application of rules which, although not positively accepted by individual States, [follow] from custom and reason." [56] With regard to "obligations," diverse points of view have been expressed with respect to the nature of the obligations in question—whether moral obligations are included, the obligations excluded by the qualifying phrase "in accordance with the Charter," and the conditions under which obligations are terminated under the doctrine of *rebus sic stantibus*.[57]

3. All Members shall settle their international disputes by peaceful means in such a manner that international peace and security, and justice, are not endangered.

The principle expressed in Article 2(3) is the logical corollary of the principle set forth in Article 2(4) that members shall refrain from "the threat or use of force against the territorial integrity or political independence of any State, or in any other manner inconsistent with the Purposes of the United Nations." The Dumbarton Oaks Proposals included the principle but in a somewhat different form; the words "international" and "and justice" did not appear. The word "international" was inserted at San Francisco to make it clear that the obligation did not apply to domestic disputes. Article 2(7) achieves the same result by explicit exclusion. The inclusion of the words "and justice" was more controversial and clearly altered the scope of the principle. The Sponsoring Governments agreed at San Francisco to support a Chinese amendment to modify the Dumbarton Oaks text setting forth the purpose of peaceful settlement (Article 1[1]) by adding the words "with due regard for the principles of justice and international law," but they were opposed to changing the Dumbarton Oaks text of the principle of peaceful settlement by adding "and justice" on the ground that "it would add an imprecise element to an otherwise matter-of-fact statement." [58] They were overruled in committee, however, and finally agreed to accept the addition. The purpose of the change was to prevent appeasement at the expense of smaller states.

The principle that states should settle their disputes by peaceful means has found frequent expression in international agreements. The manner of formulation has varied widely. Under the League of Nations

[56] Tammes (Netherlands): GAOR/20th Sess., 6th Ctte./874th Mtg./Nov. 12, 1965/para. 12.

[57] See discussions, GAOR/20th Sess., 6th Ctte./on "Principles of International Law concerning Friendly Relations and Co-operation among States."

[58] Russell, p. 658.

Covenant, members undertook to submit to the Council any dispute "likely to lead to a rupture" that was not settled by diplomacy or by submission to arbitration or judicial settlement (Article 15). By the Paris Treaty for the Renunciation of War of August 27, 1928, the parties agreed that "the settlement or solution of all disputes or conflicts of whatever nature or of whatever origin they may be, which may arise among them, shall never be sought except by pacific means." [59] The Charter makes the maintenance of international peace and security through peaceful settlement one of the primary purposes of the Organization; imposes upon members "the obligation" to settle their international disputes by peaceful means, "in such a manner that international peace and security, and justice, are not endangered"; requires parties to any dispute "which is likely to endanger international peace and security" to seek "first of all" a solution by "peaceful means of their own choice";[60] and contains detailed provisions on the responsibilities and powers of United Nations organs in performing the function of peaceful settlement.[61] The language of this paragraph clearly indicates a primary concern with the maintenance of peace and security.

The principle of peaceful settlement has been accepted, often in the exact language of the Charter, in a number of multilateral treaties and declarations of a regional or limited-party nature.[62] Efforts to reach agreement on statements clarifying the interpretation and application of the principle in the light of other Charter provisions have thus far been unsuccessful. The principle was one of those which the General Assembly asked its Special Committee on Principles of International Law concerning Friendly Relations and Co-operation among States to consider with a view to "progressive development and codification." The Committee and the Assembly's Sixth Committee were unable to reach general agreement on the meaning of the principle, quite apart from its progressive development with a view to "more effective application." [63]

The principle as stated in Article 2(3) refers only to disputes. Article 1(1) refers to "situations," as do Articles 34, 35, and 36. Peaceful adjustment of "situations" is not explicitly declared to be a principle, except in so far as it may be inferred from the obligation of Article 2(4). There is also the question of when a "dispute" exists and who

[59] Art. 2. For text, see 94 LNTS, 57.   [60] See Art. 33 and commentary.

[61] See especially Articles 11, 14 and 24, and chs. VI, VII, VIII, and XIV.

[62] These have included the Pact of the League of Arab States (1945), the Inter-American Treaty of Reciprocal Assistance (1947), the Charter of the Organization of American States (1948), the North Atlantic Treaty (1949), the Warsaw Treaty (1955), the Bandung Declaration (1955), the Belgrade Declaration (1961), and the Charter of the Organization of African Unity (1963).

[63] See discussions in Sixth Committee of the eighteenth and twentieth sessions of the General Assembly, and Report of the Special Committee, GAOR/20th Sess./ *Annexes*, agenda items 90 and 94, pp. 104–15 (Doc. A/5746).

decides. Is a unilateral assertion of the existence of a dispute sufficient? The restriction of the principle to "international" disputes is consistent with the provision of Article 2(7), and presumably Article 33 is to be interpreted in the same way, even though the word "disputes" is not similarly qualified in that article. The question, however, still remains to be decided in each case whether a particular dispute is international or not; there has been no agreement on the criteria to be applied.[64]

Different views have been expressed regarding the obligation to settle disputes the continuance of which might endanger international peace. Some have taken the view that the Organization is concerned only with the more serious disputes and that members are under no obligation to seek the settlement of minor disputes. Others, citing references in the preamble to living in peace "as good neighbors" and in the purposes to the development of "friendly relations," take the view that members are under the obligation to settle by peaceful means their less serious disputes. The requirement that justice not be endangered has provided a basis for the contention that the obligation to seek a peaceful settlement is not satisfied unless the parties are willing to accept a just settlement. Since "justice" is a highly subjective standard, this can, and has, provided the excuse for not settling disputes that are obviously of a serious nature.

The obligation to settle international disputes by peaceful means does not include the obligation to settle particular kinds of disputes by particular means or to follow any particular order of priority in the choice of methods. The only exception to this general statement is that, under Article 52(2), members are required to "make every effort to achieve pacific settlement of local disputes" through regional arrangements or by regional agencies before referring them to the Security Council. It is also stated in Article 36(3) that in making recommendations to the parties, the Security Council should take into consideration that legal disputes should "as a general rule" be referred by the parties to the International Court of Justice. A member is not obligated, however, to submit a legal dispute to the Court except in those cases where it has agreed in advance to do so.[65]

4. All Members shall refrain in their international relations from the threat or use of force against the territorial integrity or political independence of any state, or in any manner inconsistent with the Purposes of the United Nations.

Article 2(4) lays down one of the basic principles of the United Nations. As an organization established to maintain international peace and security, the United Nations' success is obviously dependent on the

[64] See commentary on Art. 2(7).   [65] See commentary on Art. 92.

extent to which its members respect this basic principle, and the extent to which its organs are effective in discharging their responsibilities to that end.

The Covenant obligated members of the League "to respect and preserve against external aggression the territorial integrity and existing political independence of all Members," and placed on them the further obligation not "to resort to war" under specified conditions (Articles 12, 13, and 15). By the terms of the Locarno Treaty of Mutual Guarantee of October 16, 1925, Germany and Belgium and Germany and France mutually undertook that they would "in no case attack or invade each other or resort to war against each other." [66] The parties to the Paris Treaty for the Renunciation of War of August 27, 1928, solemnly declared that they condemned "recourse to war for the solution of international controversies" and renounced it "as an instrument of national policy in their relations with one another." [67] Attempts made in the interwar period to make the League system of collective security more effective by defining aggression more explicitly and by strengthening the obligation to take effective measures against the aggressor were unsuccessful.[68] At Dumbarton Oaks, the conferees had little hesitation in including in the principles of the new organization the obligation of members to refrain from "the use or threat of force in their international relations in any manner inconsistent with the purposes of the Organization." [69] The phraseology was intended to achieve not only a maximum commitment of members, but also and more particularly to give the Security Council guidance combined with wide discretion in the interpretation and application of its responsibilities for the maintenance of international peace and security.

At San Francisco, the phrasing of this principle was discussed along with that of the main purpose of the Organization to maintain international peace and security, the principles of "sovereign equality" and the peaceful settlement of disputes, and the responsibilities and powers of the Security Council and General Assembly in the area of peace and security.[70] There was strong resistance on the part of the major powers to the inclusion of any references to international law and justice as criteria for Council action in maintaining peace and to the inclusion of a definition of aggression or a commitment of members to come immediately to the assistance of the victim of aggression. The major powers did agree, however, to the inclusion of the words "against the territorial integrity or political independence of any state" in Article 2(4) in response to the demand of the smaller states that there should be some

[66] Art. 2. 54 LNTS, 289.   [67] Art. 1. 94 LNTS, 57.

[68] See Royal Institute of International Affairs, *International Sanctions* (London, 1938), pp. 177–87.

[69] *Dumbarton Oaks Proposals*, ch. II, para. 4.   [70] See Russell, esp. pp. 655–75.

assurance that force would not be used by the more powerful states at the expense of the weaker ones.[71] As the result of this decision, some of the phraseology of Article 10 of the League of Nations Covenant was included in the Charter. The resulting obligation of United Nations members is much more limited than that of the League members in that while the former are obliged "to respect," they are not obligated to "preserve as against external aggression" the political independence and territorial integrity of members.

The Relation of Article 2(4) to Other Charter Provisions

The phraseology of Article 2(4) would appear to be more adequate than that of the League Covenant for excluding the use of force or the threat of force in international relations. Nevertheless, no prohibition, no matter how wisely and clearly formulated, is self-operative. It requires interpretation and application to particular circumstances. Furthermore, its interpretation and application in practice do not take place in isolation, but rather in the total context of the purposes and principles of the Charter, the responsibilities and powers of organs, and the interests and particular concerns of members. It is therefore necessary, in examining how this paragraph has been interpreted and applied, to bear in mind other Charter provisions that have influenced decisions of United Nations organs and attitudes of members in situations where Article 2(4) has been invoked, or at least has appeared applicable.

Mention has been made earlier of the possible conflicts between different purposes and principles of the Organization. This has particular relevance to Article 2(4). Moreover, Article 1 proclaims the first purpose of the Organization to be the maintenance of international peace and security by the taking of effective collective measures to prevent or remove "threats to the peace" and to suppress "acts of aggression or other breaches of the peace." It does not use the words "force" or "threat of force." Qualification of the Organization's purpose to achieve peaceful settlement or accommodation by the words "in conformity with the principles of justice and international law" encourages the claim that, unless law and justice are served, recourse to force may be justified. In addition, the principle of self-determination in Article 1(2) has been used to support the claim that force can be used on behalf of independence movements.

Even more significant than possible conflicts between different purposes and principles is the failure of the Charter to relate closely those

[71] See UNCIO, *Documents*, VI, 342–46.

provisions concerning powers and responsibilities of organs to the principle of Article 2(4). While the Security Council is required to act in accordance with the principles as well as the purposes of the United Nations (Article 24[2]), it is specifically directed "to determine the existence of any threat to the peace, breach of the peace, or act of aggression" and to make recommendations or decide measures to restore international peace and security. The language used and the discretion vested in the Council have resulted in there being no necessary identity between what is legally prohibited under Article 2(4), and what the Council seeks to control in the discharge of its responsibilities.[72] The General Assembly, in the exercise of its wide-ranging powers under Articles 10, 11, and 14, has used the language of Articles 1(1) and 39 in defining the conditions under which it seeks to control the use of force.[73] The lack of necessary identity between the conduct prohibited by Article 2(4) and that which the Security Council and the General Assembly seek to control is, of course, a reflection of the essentially political character of the decisions taken by these organs and the attitudes adopted by members.

General Interpretation by United Nations Organs

The Security Council has not at any time sought to formulate a general and accepted interpretation of Article 2(4). This is, perhaps, not surprising—the Council's responsibility under the Charter is to deal with disputes and situations as they arise. The General Assembly, however, under Article 11, may "consider the general principles of cooperation in the maintenance of international peace and security" and make recommendations with respect thereto; and under Article 13, it has the responsibility to initiate studies and make recommendations for promoting international political cooperation and encouraging the development and codification of international law. Among the matters the Assembly has considered have been the essential conditions of peace, the definition of aggression, and the principles of international law concerning friendly relations and cooperation among states. In dealing with each of these matters, the Assembly has sought to achieve agreement upon a more detailed definition of the conduct covered by Article 2(4).

In 1949, the General Assembly, by a vote of 53 to 5 with 1 abstention, adopted the "Essentials of Peace" resolution,[74] containing twelve

---

[72] See Rosalyn Higgins, *The Development of International Law Through the Political Organs of the United Nations* (London, Oxford University Press, 1963), pp. 167–75.

[73] GA Res. 377(V), Nov. 3, 1950.   [74] GA Res. 290(IV), Dec. 1, 1949.

principles that members were called upon to respect. Of these the second was a repetition in substance of Article 2(4). The third was "to refrain from any threats or acts, direct or indirect, aimed at impairing the freedom, independence, or integrity of any State, or at fomenting civil strife and subverting the will of the people in any State." [75]

During its fifth session, the General Assembly considered the definition of aggression in connection with a Yugoslav proposal regarding the duties of states on the outbreak of hostilities. It referred a USSR proposal to the International Law Commission and requested that it report its conclusions.[76] The Commission reported that it was unable to reach a decision on a satisfactory definition of aggression.[77] In the Assembly discussions following the report, there were two basic points of disagreement: first, between those who believed a definition was neither possible nor desirable, and those who thought it was possible and would serve a useful purpose by providing an objective standard for determining aggression; and second, among those who held different views as to the proper definition of aggression.[78] The Assembly finally decided to postpone further consideration of the matter to a later session.

In 1962, the Assembly decided to undertake a study of "the principles of international law concerning friendly relations and co-operation among States in accordance with the Charter with a view to their progressive development and codification, so as to secure their more effective application." It listed the principle contained in Article 2(4) as one of four to be studied.[79] The following year, it established a special committee to make recommendations, account being taken of practice and observations of governments.[80] Members of the committee reached substantial agreement on a formulation with respect to Article 2(4) that included the following:

(a) Wars of aggression constitute international crimes against peace.
(b) Every State has the duty to refrain from organizing or encouraging the organization of irregular or volunteer forces or armed bands within its territory or any other territory for incursions into the territory of another State.
(c) Every State has the duty to refrain from instigating, assisting or organizing civil strife or committing terrorist acts in another State, or

[75] GAOR/4th Sess./261st Plen. Mtg./Dec. 1, 1949/p. 438. The vote on this paragraph was 54 to 0 with 5 abstentions.
[76] GA Res. 378(V), Nov. 9, 1950.
[77] GAOR/6th Sess./1951/*Supp. 9* (A/1858), pp. 8–10.
[78] For discussion, see GAOR/6th Sess., 6th Ctte./278th-295th Mtgs./Jan. 5–22, 1952; and *ibid.*, 268th Plen. Mtg./Jan. 31, 1952.
[79] GA Res. 1815(XVII), Dec. 18, 1962.
[80] GA Res. 1966(XVIII), Dec. 16, 1963.

from conniving at or acquiescing in organized activities directed towards such ends, when such acts involve a threat or use of force.

(d) Every State has the duty to refrain from the threat or use of force to violate the existing boundaries or another State, or as a means of solving its international disputes, including territorial disputes and problems concerning frontiers between States.[81]

In the subsequent Assembly discussion, it was apparent that there still remained important points on which no agreement was possible, and that even on the points covered by the consensus, reservations were entertained by some United Nations members.[82]

Interpretation and Application in United Nations Practice

In actual United Nations practice, a number of questions have arisen which may be grouped under the following headings: 1) the meaning of "threat or use of force"; 2) the limitation imposed by the words "in their international relations"; and 3) the conditions under which force may be used without violating the injunction of Article 2(4).

1. THE MEANING OF "THREAT OR USE OF FORCE." There has been extensive discussion but no general agreement among members regarding the kind of force referred to here. One view holds that "force" means "armed force" and does not include political and economic pressure. It is argued that this is the reasonable interpretation, that it is the interpretation supported by the record of discussions at San Francisco and other provisions of the Charter, and that broader interpretation would lead to practical difficulties in distinguishing between permissible and impermissible pressures. It is suggested that economic and political pressures can best be considered in the context of limitations placed on intervention by the principle of sovereign equality.

Another view counters that there is no legal reason why "force" should not be interpreted to include political and economic pressure; that, except in specific cases, the Charter does not make a sharp distinction between armed and other forms of force; that, quite apart from what may have been the intention of the authors of the Charter, its provisions must be interpreted in the light of present needs and developments; and that the use of political and economic coercion

---

[81] Report of the Special Committee on Principles of International Law concerning Friendly Relations and Co-operation among States. GAOR/20th Sess./1965/ *Annexes,* agenda items 90 and 94/pp. 83–104 (Doc. A/5746). In the Committee, the U.S. representative objected to the connotation of "violate" in (d), but later in the Sixth Committee, the objection was withdrawn on the assumption that "violate" did not encompass lawful use of force. GAOR/20th Sess., 6th Ctte./877th Mtg./Nov. 17, 1965/paras. 11–18.

[82] For discussion, see GAOR/20th Sess., 6th Ctte./871st Mtg./Nov. 8, 1965; and 875th–893d Mtgs./Nov. 15–Dec. 8, 1965.

could be as great a threat to the political independence of states under present conditions as military force.[83]

The General Assembly has adopted a number of resolutions on the conditions of peace in which it has called upon states to refrain from various forms of political and economic coercion.[84] Neither the Assembly nor the Security Council has, however, determined that use of such means of coercion constitutes the use of force under Article 2(4).

Claims to that effect have been dealt with in other terms. Thus, Egyptian restrictions on Israel's use of the Suez Canal were treated as a violation of the armistice agreement and freedom of navigation,[85] and consideration of the complaint of Cuba that the United States was committing economic aggression by reducing its sugar quota and refusing to refine Cuban crude oil was deferred pending a report from the Organization of American States.[86] From the practice of United Nations organs, it seems reasonable to conclude that, while various forms of economic and political coercion may be treated as threats to the peace, as contrary to certain of the declared purposes and principles of the Organization, or as violating agreements entered into or recognized principles of international law, they are not to be regarded as coming necessarily under the prohibition of Article 2(4), which is to be understood as directed against the use of armed force.

The prohibition of armed force in this paragraph is not limited to its actual use. The threat of its use is also prohibited. However, it is not easy to determine in any particular case what constitutes a threat. While there have been numerous charges made by members in United Nations organs of such threats, for example, that France and the United Kingdom by their military preparations were threatening to use force against Egypt over her nationalization of the Suez Canal,[87] there have been no decisions of United Nations organs that such a threat of force has been committed. Rather, the practice has been to treat such claims within the broader context of "threats to the peace," and thus avoid the determination that any member has been guilty of the prohibited action.[88]

[83] For summary of positions taken, see Report of Special Committee, GAOR/ 20th Sess./1965/*Annexes*, agenda items 90 and 94, pp. 87–90.

[84] See, for example, GA Res. 380(V) and 381(V), Nov. 17, 1950. The Declaration on the Granting of Independence to Colonial Countries and Peoples, GA Res. 1514(XV), Dec. 14, 1960, contains in para. 7 a general statement which can be interpreted to this effect.

[85] UN Doc. S/2322, Sept. 1, 1951 and SCOR/6th Yr./549th–558th Mtgs./July 26–Sept. 1, 1951.

[86] UN Doc. S/4395, July 19, 1960.

[87] See letters of USSR and Egyptian representatives, UN Docs. S/3649, Sept. 15, 1956 and S/3650, Sept. 17, 1956; and SCOR/11th Yr./734th–738th Mtgs./Sept. 26–Oct. 8, 1956.

[88] See commentary on Art. 39.

The threat or use of force may be indirect as well as direct. The report of the Special Committee on Principles of International Law Concerning Friendly Relations and Co-operation among States and the subsequent discussion in the General Assembly indicated the existence of a wide consensus that giving active assistance to the organization of civil strife in another state or encouraging the organization of armed bands for incursions into the territory of another state was a violation of Article 2(4).[89] The General Assembly and the Security Council have both, formally or by inference, registered their disapproval of such acts as being inconsistent with the purposes and principles of the United Nations. In its resolution of November 27, 1948, the Assembly "[considered] that the continued aid given by Albania, Bulgaria and Yugoslavia to the Greek guerrillas [was] inconsistent with the purposes and principles of the Charter of the United Nations."[90] The Security Council, in its resolution of June 11, 1958, on the charge of the Lebanese government that the United Arab Republic had incited and supported terrorism and rebellion against it, decided to dispatch an observation group "to ensure that there is no illegal infiltration of personnel or supply of arms or other *matériel* across the Lebanese border."[91] Later, the General Assembly, by unanimous resolution, called upon all members "to act strictly in accordance with the principles of mutual respect for each other's territorial integrity and sovereignty, of non-aggression, of strict non-interference in each other's internal affairs."[92]

2. THE SIGNIFICANCE OF "IN THEIR INTERNATIONAL RELATIONS." The obvious reason for including this phrase was to limit the application of the principle that force or threat of force should not be used to relations between states. Thus, the principle does not prevent a government from using force within its metropolitan area to put down a revolution or other disturbance. This conclusion is further supported by the provisions of Article 2(7). Nevertheless, the Security Council may find that the situation resulting from such use of force constitutes "a threat to the peace" under Article 39, justifying the taking of measures to maintain international peace and security.

The use of force to put down independence movements in colonial areas has been a frequent occasion for United Nations concern. In the Indonesian case, the Netherlands maintained that it was justified in using armed force to maintain its authority within a colonial territory and that the resulting situation was no proper concern of the United

89 See p. 53.
90 GA Res. 193(III). The resolution was adopted by a vote of 47 to 6 with no abstentions.
91 UN Doc. S/4023, June 11, 1958.
92 GA Res. 1237(ES-III), Aug. 21, 1958.

Nations.[93] The Security Council never explicitly decided the question of its competence, but, by its decision explicitly calling upon the parties "to cease hostilities forthwith," [94] it strongly implied that it found a threat to, or a breach of, international peace to exist. It thereby took the view that even a domestic use of force might have such international consequences as to justify appropriate measures of restraint.

By the terms of the Declaration on the Granting of Independence to Colonial Countries and Peoples, the General Assembly adopted the position that "[all] armed action or repressive measures of all kinds directed against dependent peoples shall cease in order to enable them to exercise peacefully and freely their right to complete independence, and the integrity of their national territory shall be respected." [95] While the provisions of Article 2(4) were not specifically invoked, the General Assembly sought by this Declaration to apply the same restraint to the use of force for putting down revolutionary disturbances in colonial areas that Article 2(4) places on the use of force in international relations.[96] In dealing with the situation in Angola, which Portugal claimed was an integral part of its metropolitan territory, both the Security Council and the General Assembly reaffirmed the provisions of the Declaration and called upon the Portuguese authorities to desist from repressive measures against "the people of Angola." [97]

3. CONDITIONS UNDER WHICH FORCE MAY BE USED IN INTERNATIONAL RELATIONS. The threat or use of force in international relations is prohibited if it is "against the territorial integrity or political independence of any state" or "in any other manner inconsistent with the Purposes of the United Nations." The interpretation of the first limiting phrase raises the same difficulties as occurred under Article 10 of the League of Nations Covenant. Is the prohibition violated if a member sends its armed forces into the territory of another state for "protective" purposes, with the declared intention of withdrawing them as soon as the threat to the weaker state has been removed? Is the territorial integrity of a state respected so long as none of its territory is taken from it? Or does respect for the territorial integrity of a state require respect for its territorial inviolability? The expression "political independence" would appear to lend itself to easier interpretation. Clearly, the political independence of a state is violated if the state is coerced through the threat or use of force into taking action it would not otherwise take. And yet fictions can be used to conceal the true situation. Consistency "with the Purposes of the United Nations" is a requirement that lends itself to a

[93] SCOR/2d Yr./171st Mtg./July 31, 1947/pp. 1639–48.
[94] UN Doc. S/459, Aug. 1, 1947.   [95] GA Res. 1514(XV), Dec. 14, 1960.
[96] See commentary on Art. 1(2).
[97] See UN Doc. S/4835, June 9, 1961; and GA Res. 1742(XVI), Jan. 30, 1962.

wide range of possible interpretations, depending upon whether one adopts a generous or restrictive view of what these purposes are.

There is general agreement that the use of force is legitimate provided it is authorized by a competent United Nations organ. This general statement, however, is not particularly helpful in determining the legitimacy of the use of force in a particular situation, since the question remains whether the United Nations organ that purports to authorize the use of force has acted in accordance with the Charter, and whether the member state is acting in conformity with a United Nations decision. The question has arisen in a number of cases. In 1950, the Security Council by its resolution of June 27, recommended that members of the United Nations "furnish such assistance to the Republic of Korea as may be necessary to repel the armed attack and to restore international peace and security in the area." [98] A number of members sent military forces to assist the Republic of Korea under the authority of this resolution. The Soviet Union contended that the armed forces—chiefly from the United States—assisting the Republic of Korea were guilty of aggressive action, that they were intervening in an internal conflict, and that the resolution of the Security Council was adopted in disregard of the voting requirement of Article 27(3). The overwhelming majority of members, however, regarded the Security Council resolution as legitimizing the use of force by members.

The competence of the General Assembly to legitimize the use of force by member states in the case of a breach of the peace or act of aggression, as the Uniting for Peace resolution purported to do, has been denied by the Soviet Union and some other members.[99] Their argument has been that, under the Charter, the Security Council is the only organ with responsibility for authorizing the use of armed force by members. Others have held, however, that the Assembly has a residual responsibility and may recommend military measures that members can in any event take in the exercise of the right of self-defense under Article 51.[100]

The question of the legitimacy of the use of force by military contingents placed by members at the disposition of the United Nations for peace-keeping operations arose in the Congo case. Their right to use force in self-defense had been generally admitted.[101] In the Congo situation, however, the use of force was authorized, as a last resort, to

[98] UN Doc. S/1511, June 27, 1950.
[99] See commentary on Arts. 10, 11, and 24.
[100] See, for example, statements by Younger (U.K.) and Urrutia (Colombia): GAOR/5th Sess., 1st Ctte./360th Mtg./Oct. 12, 1950/paras. 4, 71–73.
[101] See United Nations Emergency Force. Report of the Secretary-General. UN Doc. A/3943, Oct. 9, 1958, para. 179.

prevent civil war and to effect the expulsion of foreign mercenaries,[102] measures that were considered essential to ending a serious threat to the peace.

The Charter explicitly permits the use of force in the exercise of the inherent right of individual or collective self-defense if an armed attack occurs against a member of the United Nations.[103] There has been much discussion and little agreement on the extent of this right. It has, however, been widely invoked to legitimize bilateral and multilateral arrangements for collective self-defense, as well as the use of armed force by single states or groups of states without advance commitments, and under alleged emergency circumstances to meet direct or indirect aggression.

A closely related question is whether the sending of armed force by a member into the territory of another state, on the invitation of its government, to assist in maintaining order, putting down revolutionary movements, or protecting persons and property, is justified under Article 2(4). There have been a number of instances of such action. In 1956, the Soviet Union contended that its armed forces intervened in Hungary at the invitation of the properly constituted Hungarian government and that United Nations consideration would be in violation of Article 2(7).[104] In 1958, the United States sought to justify its military intervention in Lebanon on the ground that its military assistance had been requested by the Lebanese government in resisting "indirect aggression," and that it was acting under Article 51. Similar justification was claimed by the United Kingdom for its intervention in Jordan. While many members favored the General Assembly's calling for prompt withdrawal of these forces, the resolution, finally adopted by unanimous vote, requested the Secretary-General to make such "practical arrangements" as would "adequately help" in upholding the purposes and principles of the Charter and "facilitate the early withdrawal of the foreign troops." [105] United Nations practice would appear to support the sending of armed forces into the territory of another state at the invitation of its government if circumstances justify this as an exercise of the right of collective self-defense under Article 51. Many members have called attention to the dangers of possible abuse.

[102] UN Docs. S/4741, Feb. 20, 1961 and S/5002, Nov. 24, 1961.

[103] See commentary on Art. 51 for further elaboration.

[104] The General Assembly did not accept this justification and called upon the USSR to withdraw its forces without delay. GA Res. 1004(ES-II), Nov. 4, 1956 and 1005(ES-II), Nov. 9, 1956. The votes were 50 to 8 with 15 abstentions, and 48 to 11 with 16 abstentions.

[105] GA Res. 1237(ES-III), Aug. 21, 1958.

In a few cases, the claim has been made that the use of armed force is justified when taken under the authority of regional organizations or arrangements for the maintenance of international peace and security.[106] The claim was made in the case of armed assistance by the members of the Arab League to the Palestine Arabs in their resistance to the establishment of an independent state of Israel and in the case of the United States interdiction of the introduction of Soviet missiles into Cuba in 1962. That armed force may be used under the authority of a regional organization or arrangement is not open to question. The issue in controversy is whether such use of force is permissible except as authorized by the Security Council or in the exercise of the right of individual or collective self-defense against an armed attack.

Attempts have been made to justify the use of armed force on a number of other grounds that have in common a measure of support in earlier international law, or the broad purposes of the Organization. Thus, Egypt (later the UAR) sought to justify the restrictions placed on the passage of certain ships and cargoes through the Suez Canal on the ground that a state of war with Israel still existed permitting the exercise of belligerent rights.[107] The Security Council, however, took the position that since the armistice agreement had established a de facto state of peace intended to be permanent, the belligerent right of visit, search and seizure could not be legally exercised.[108] In principle, it would appear that the claim to the right to use force in the exercise of a belligerent right is in fundamental contradiction to the Charter, unless it can be established that the belligerent right has an independent justification under the Charter.

In a number of instances, claims have been made that the use of force is justified by the legitimate nature of the objectives sought. The argument is, in effect, that no other means are available for achieving desirable purposes. The plea of self-help is a somewhat legalistic statement of the same argument. In the Suez Canal case in 1956, the United Kingdom sought to justify its military intervention on the ground that the fighting between Israel and Egypt threatened freedom of navigation through the Canal, on which British economic life was dependent.[109] Members of the United Nations were overwhelmingly of the opinion, however, that the preferred procedure was to use the peaceful means provided by the Charter, and that "the use of force or armed

[106] For fuller discussion, see commentary on Arts. 52 and 53.

[107] See SCOR/6th Yr./550th Mtg./Aug. 1, 1951/p. 4; and 551st Mtg./Aug. 1, 1951/pp. 1–2.

[108] UN Doc. S/2322, Sept. 1, 1951.

[109] SCOR/11th Yr./749th Mtg./Oct. 30, 1956/p. 3; and 751st Mtg./Oct. 31, 1956/p. 7.

intervention to secure rights, even lawful rights, has been strictly prohibited unless ordered by the Security Council . . . No country may take the law into its own hands." [110]

The United States government sought to justify its military intervention in the Dominican Republic on April 28, 1965, on the ground that "the threat to the lives of its citizens, and a request for assistance from those Dominican authorities still struggling to maintain order" made necessary the dispatch of "security forces." [111] Much was also made of the alleged Communist attempt to seize power. The United States action was criticized in the Security Council by some members on the ground that it violated Article 2(4) and constituted, or ran the risk of becoming, unjustified armed intervention. The resolution adopted by the Council called for a "strict cease fire" and cooperation with a representative of the Secretary-General. [112]

A substantial number of members have held that the use of armed force is justified to terminate colonialism and to implement the principle of self-determination, provided the result is not achievable by peaceful means. The Indian use of armed force to end Portuguese control of Goa, Damao, and Diu in December, 1961, was justified by some members as a permitted means of ending colonialism when there was no possibility of doing so by negotiation; obversely, it was attacked by others as a violation of Article 2(4) and an illegal method of resolving a territorial dispute. A proposal that the Security Council deplore the Indian use of force and call for the withdrawal of Indian forces received 7 affirmative votes, against 4 negative votes, but was defeated by the negative vote of the Soviet Union. [113]

In later discussions on principles of international law concerning friendly relations and cooperation among states, a number of members took the view that armed force could be used by peoples in defense against colonialism, and some argued that armed force could be used by members in support of peoples seeking to end colonial rule. Others took an opposing view, pointing out that this would give a state freedom to use armed force provided it made the charge of colonial domination in so doing. [114]

[110] Delegate of Columbia: GAOR/1st Emergency Special Sess./562d Plen. Mtg./ Nov. 1, 1956/p. 15. The same position was taken by the Western powers with respect to Soviet blocade of Berlin. See Higgins, pp. 216–21 on this and related points.

[111] SCOR/20th Yr./1196th Mtg./May 3, 1965/p. 14.

[112] UN Doc. S/6355, May 14, 1965.

[113] See SCOR/16th Yr./987th and 988th Mtgs./Dec. 14 and 18, 1961.

[114] See Report of the Special Committee on Principles of International Law concerning Friendly Relations and Co-operation among States, GAOR/20th Sess./Annexes, agenda items 90 and 94/pp. 92–93 (Doc. A/5746).

5. All Members shall give the United Nations every assistance in any action it takes in accordance with the present Charter, and shall refrain from giving assistance to any state against which the United Nations is taking preventive or enforcement action.

The two principles set forth in Article 2(5) were separately stated in paragraphs 5 and 6 of Chapter II of the Dumbarton Oaks Proposals. At San Francisco, they were accepted unanimously in the technical committee. The French delegation proposed an amendment which would have expressly denied to any member the right to claim exemption from the two principles on the ground of its neutrality. It was agreed, however, that the amendment was unnecessary since the two principles by themselves had that effect.[115] It was subsequently decided to combine them into one paragraph since they were complementary to each other.

In his report to the President on the work of the Conference, the Chairman of the United States delegation (the Secretary of State) interpreted the paragraph as follows:

It means first of all that the Members will be obligated to give to the Organization any assistance which their obligations under the Charter require of them. . . . From this general obligation stem the other more specific obligations to give assistance on particular matters which are further elaborated in other provisions of the Charter. It means also the corollary of this obligation. It constitutes a general pledge not to strengthen the hand of a state which has violated its obligations under the Charter to the point where preventive or enforcement action has become necessary.[116]

Although the paragraph does not expressly so state, both obligations relate primarily to the maintenance of international peace and security, and have been so interpreted and applied. Articles 25, 39, 40, 41, 42, and 49 have special importance for this paragraph.

In practice, the two principles have been given a broader application than the words themselves or the report of the Secretary of State would indicate. They have been invoked in substance in support of General Assembly as well as Security Council decisions, and the decisions members have been called upon to support have not by any means been limited to those initiating "action" in the sense of Article 11(2), or to preventive or enforcement measures under Article 40, 41, and 42. In dealing with hostilities in Palestine, the Security Council called upon "Governments and authorities concerned" to refrain from certain acts which would have the effect of worsening the situation, and to give the

[115] UNCIO, *Documents*, VI, 459–60. It should be noted that although Switzerland has never applied for membership, Austria, also a neutralized state, has been admitted to membership without any objection based on this paragraph.
[116] State Dept., *Report to the President*, p. 42.

greatest possible assistance to the United Nations mediator.[117] In the Greek case, the General Assembly recommended that members refrain from action designed to assist those fighting against the Greek government.[118] In its resolution of February 1, 1951, the General Assembly called upon "all States and authorities to continue to lend every assistance to the United Nations action in Korea" and "to refrain from giving any assistance to the aggressors in Korea." [119] It should be noted that in this case, the "United Nations action" was initiated by a Security Council recommendation and not by a binding decision under Article 42.

The principles of this paragraph received a particularly broad application in the Congo case. After the Security Council had authorized the Secretary-General to provide military and technical assistance to the Republic of the Congo in the establishment of internal order and security,[120] it subsequently requested "all States to refrain from any action which might tend to impede the restoration of law and order," [121] and called upon "Member States, in accordance with Articles 25 and 49 of the Charter, to accept and carry out the decisions of the Security Council and to afford mutual assistance in carrying out measures decided upon by the Security Council." [122] The effectiveness of the United Nations program was shortly thereafter threatened by the political disintegration of the Congo and the rendering of direct assistance to competing factions and authorities by member governments. When the Security Council was unable to take a decision because of the failure of the permanent members to agree, the General Assembly, by a resolution adopted by vote of 70 to 0 with 11 abstentions, reiterated the previous requests of the Council, and in addition,

without prejudice to the sovereign rights of the Republic of the Congo, [called] upon all States to refrain from the direct and indirect provision of arms or other materials of war and military personnel and other assistance for military purposes in the Congo during the temporary period of military assistance through the United Nations, except upon the request of the United Nations through the Secretary-General for carrying out the purposes [of the Security Council and the General Assembly resolutions].[123]

In this case, the principles of Article 2(5) appear to have been utilized to gain support for a United Nations program of action under circumstances where it could not be said that a legal obligation to give support necessarily resulted from other Charter provisions.

In dealing with the situation in Angola and the practice of apartheid

[117] UN Doc. S/801, May 29, 1948.   [118] GA Res. 193(III), Nov. 27, 1948.
[119] GA Res. 498(V), Feb. 1, 1951.   [120] UN Doc. S/4387, July 13, 1960.
[121] UN Doc. S/4405, July 22, 1960.   [122] UN Doc. S/4426, Aug. 9, 1960.
[123] GA Res. 1474(ES-IV), Sept. 20, 1960.

in South Africa, both the General Assembly and the Security Council utilized the language of Article 2(5) to mobilize pressure against Portugal and the Republic of South Africa respectively.[124]

These are only a few of the many instances in which the principles of this paragraph have been invoked to solicit support for United Nations measures which members are not strictly speaking legally bound by Charter provisions to support. This use has been made by the General Assembly as well as the Security Council. In fact, one can say that the principles have been particularly useful to majorities in the General Assembly seeking to marshal support for resolutions which under the Charter are only recommendations.

6. The Organization shall ensure that states which are not Members of the United Nations act in accordance with these Principles so far as may be necessary for the maintenance of international peace and security.

Article 2(6) corresponds to the second section of paragraph 6 of Chapter II of the Dumbarton Oaks Proposals, which was accepted at San Francisco without substantive change. Its approach to the problem of the relations of a peace and security organization to nonmembers differs from that adopted in the League of Nations Covenant. Article 17 of that document provided that in the event of a dispute involving a state not a member of the League, the state should be invited "to accept the obligations of membership . . . for the purposes of such dispute" upon conditions deemed just by the Council. If the invitation was accepted, the provisions of Articles 12 to 16 inclusive would be applicable, with such modification as the Council might deem necessary. If a nonmember refused to accept the obligations of membership and resorted to war against a member, the sanctions provisions of the Covenant became applicable. If both parties were nonmembers and refused to accept the obligations of membership for the purposes of the dispute, the Council might take such measures and make such recommendations as would prevent hostilities and result in the settlement of the dispute.

The Charter adopts a more direct approach to the problem by placing on the United Nations itself, acting through those organs that have competence, the obligation to see that states which are not members act in accordance with the principles of Article 2 "so far as may be necessary for the maintenance of international peace and security."

---

[124] See, for example, on the situation in Angola, GA Res. 1742(XVI), Jan. 30, 1962 and 1819(XVII), Dec. 18, 1962; and UN Doc. S/5471, Dec. 4, 1963; and on the practice of apartheid, GA Res. 1663(XVI), Nov. 28, 1961; 1761(XVII), Nov. 6, 1962; and 1978A(XVIII), Dec. 16, 1963.

The Organization thereby assumes authority not based on the consent of the nonmember states themselves. Because of the recent experience with aggression by Japan and Germany when these states were not members of the League of Nations, and the decision at San Francisco not to include the enemy states as original members of the United Nations, it was agreed when the Charter was being written that some provision of this nature was desirable to provide basic authority for dealing with nonmember states.[125]

Article 2(6) establishes the principle that actions of nonmembers are a matter of concern to the United Nations. It is not the only Charter provision that deals with the relation of the Organization to nonmember states. Article 11(2) gives the General Assembly the power to discuss questions relating to the maintenance of international peace brought before it by nonmembers acting under Article 35. Article 32 makes provision for the participation of nonmember states in the discussions of the Security Council, which, according to Article 24, has "primary responsibility for the maintenance of international peace and security." Article 35(2) provides that a nonmember may bring its dispute to the Security Council or the General Assembly for peaceful settlement if it accepts in advance, for the purposes of the dispute, the obligations of pacific settlement contained in the Charter. Article 50 gives a nonmember the right to consult the Security Council on special economic problems arising from the carrying out of preventive or enforcement measures. Article 93(2) enables a nonmember to become a party to the Statute of the Court on conditions to be determined by the Assembly on recommendation of the Security Council. Chapter XVII on transitional security measures clearly envisages action to be taken against certain nonmember states, i.e., enemy states as defined in Article 53(2).

Neither the Security Council nor the General Assembly has adopted a resolution containing a specific reference to Article 2(6). The article has been referred to and invoked in support of particular positions in communications from members and in statements made during the consideration by the Council or Assembly of specific questions. In requesting the inclusion of the Spanish question in the agenda of the Security Council in 1946, Poland invoked the obligation of the United Nations under this article.[126] When the question was brought before the General Assembly, some members again made use of this article to support their contention that the United Nations had an obligation to act. The article was cited as one basis for action when the Security Council was considering the Greek and Corfu Channel questions. Dur-

---

[125] See State Dept., *Report to the President*, p. 42.
[126] SCOR/1st Yr., 1st Ser./1946/*Supp. 2*, p. 55.

ing the General Assembly consideration of the question of observance by Bulgaria and Hungary of human rights and fundamental freedoms, Article 2(6) was invoked by many delegations to emphasize the obligation of the United Nations to ensure respect for its principles by nonmember states as being essential to peace and security.[127] In a number of instances, the Security Council and the Assembly have adopted resolutions directed in effect to specific nonmember states recommending or requesting that specific action be taken in the interest of international peace and security. Thus, the Security Council, in its resolution of May 29, 1948,[128] called upon "Governments and authorities," including the provisional government of Israel, to adopt certain measures under threat of action under Chapter VII. By resolution of July 15, it ordered an "immediate and unconditional cease-fire," and decided that the truce should remain in force "until a peaceful adjustment of the future situation of Palestine is reached."[129] Later, on November 24, 1953, the Council adopted a resolution directed explicitly to Israel and Jordan.[130]

The General Assembly has adopted numerous resolutions invoking the general or specific principles of the Charter which have been directed to various addressees, including "all nations," "all States," "all Members and all other States," and "every State," the clear intention being that nonmembers as well as members should be guided by them.[131] No question has been raised regarding the propriety of such measures.

7. Nothing contained in the present Charter shall authorize the United Nations to intervene in matters which are essentially within the domestic jurisdiction of any state or shall require the Members to submit such matters to settlement under the present Charter; but the principle shall not prejudice the application of enforcement measures under Chapter VII.

It has not been uncommon to include in treaties for the peaceful settlement of international disputes provisions excluding matters solely within the domestic jurisdiction of the parties.[132] The Covenant of the

[127] See GAOR/3d Sess., 2d Part/1949/ad hoc Pol. Ctte./34th-41st Mtgs./and 189th-203d Plen. Mtgs.

[128] UN Doc. S/801, May 29, 1948.

[129] UN Doc. S/902, July 15, 1948. Israel did not become a member until May 11, 1949.

[130] UN Doc. S/3139/Rev. 2, Nov. 24, 1953. Jordan did not become a member until Dec. 14, 1955.

[131] See *Repertory*, Vol. I; *Supp. 1*, Vol. I; and *Supp. 2*, Vol. I, for examples of such resolutions.

[132] See Robert R. Wilson, "Reservation Clauses in Treaties of Obligatory Arbitration," in *American Journal of International Law*, XXIII (1929), pp. 68–93.

League of Nations contained a provision of a comparable nature, applicable only, however, to the Council and Assembly when performing conciliatory functions under Article 15. Paragraph 8 of that article read as follows:

If the dispute between the parties is claimed by one of them, and is found by the Council, to arise out of a matter which by international law is solely within the domestic jurisdiction of that party, the Council shall so report, and shall make no recommendation as to its settlement.

Paragraph 10 made this limitation applicable to the Assembly when exercising conciliatory powers on reference by the Council. The limitation imposed on the Council was invoked in only three cases: the Aaland Island case, the dispute between the United Kingdom and France concerning nationality decrees in Tunis and Morocco, and the dispute between Greece and Turkey concerning the expulsion of the Oecumenical Patriarch. The Permanent Court of International Justice in its advisory opinion in the Nationality Decrees case held that the limitation extended to matters which are not "in principle, regulated by international law" and with respect to which a state remains "sole judge," but, observed the Court, "[the] question whether a certain matter is or is not solely within the jurisdiction of a State is an essentially relative question; it depends upon the development of international relations." [133]

At the Dumbarton Oaks Conference, it was decided to include in the Proposals a paragraph to the effect that the provisions regarding the peaceful settlement of disputes by the Security Council should not apply to "situations or disputes arising out of matters which by international law are solely within the domestic jurisdiction of the state concerned." [134] This paragraph was the result largely of United States initiative and followed in most respects the League provision. It was considered a necessary safeguard, especially if a party to a dispute was not allowed to vote in its case. [135]

At San Francisco, the Sponsoring Governments proposed an amendment to the Proposals that involved substantial revision of the text of the domestic-jurisdiction limitation and its transfer from the section on "Pacific Settlement of Disputes" (Chapter VIII, section A) to the chapter on "Principles," with the result that it would become a governing principle for the Organization and its members. [136] The most significant textual changes proposed were the introduction of the concept of United Nations intervention, the substitution of "essentially" for "solely," and the elimination of any reference to an international law

[133] PCIJ, Series B, no. 4, p. 24.
[134] *Dumbarton Oaks Proposals*, ch. VIII, sec. A., para. 7.
[135] Russell, pp. 463–64.   [136] UNCIO, *Documents*, VI, 622–28.

standard. In the view of the Sponsoring Governments, this amendment was necessary because of the broadening of the Organization's functions, particularly in respect to economic, social, and cultural matters. One declared purpose was to require the Organization to deal with governments in carrying out its economic and social objectives, instead of allowing the Organization to "penetrate directly into the domestic life and social economy of the member states." [137] It was not intended to weaken the effectiveness of the United Nations in maintaining or restoring international peace and security. To make this clear, the new proposal contained a qualifying clause providing that "this principle shall not prejudice the application of Chapter VIII, section B." [138]

This proposed amendment of the Sponsoring Governments was critically received at San Francisco. Some delegations argued that it undermined the authority and influence of the United Nations, it weakened the role of law in the new Organization, and it opened the way to arbitrary acts based on considerations of expediency and national interest. Other delegations, notably the Australian, believed that the new proposal did not go far enough; while the permanent members of the Security Council, who would be in a position to exercise the veto, would be adequately safeguarded so far as Council decisions were concerned, the smaller states would not be sufficiently protected against pressure that might be brought to bear in connection with wholly domestic matters. To meet this objection in part, the Conference adopted an Australian proposal to amend the qualifying clause at the end of the amendment of the Sponsoring Governments to read "enforcement measures under" Chapter VIII, section B.

To understand the argument for this change, one must consider related provisions of the Dumbarton Oaks Proposals as presented to the Conference. Chapter VIII, section B, paragraph 2, of the Proposals authorized the Security Council, after determining the existence of a threat to the peace, breach of the peace, or act of aggression, to "make recommendations or decide upon the measures to be taken to maintain international peace and security." This could be interpreted to mean that the Security Council had the power to decide upon the terms of settlement of a dispute as well as upon the enforcement measures to be taken. An amendment to this paragraph did specify that the "measures" be taken in accordance with Articles 41 and 42.[139] Nevertheless, it still remained possible that the Security Council, when faced with a threat of force or an actual armed attack by one state over a matter

[137] *Ibid.*, pp. 507–8. See commentary on Art. 56.
[138] Entitled "Determination of Threats to the Peace or Acts of Aggression and Action with Respect Thereto."
[139] See commentary on those articles.

falling within the domestic jurisdiction of another, would make recommendations for settlement and would exercise strong pressure to secure their acceptance. In fact, it was argued that the proposed amendment of the Sponsoring Governments, without the Australian amendment, might actually place a premium on the threat or use of force.[140]

Article 2(7) is not concerned with the intervention of one state in matters falling within the domestic jurisdiction of another, but rather with the relations of the Organization and its members. At San Francisco it was considered necessary, in view of the assumption by the proposed organization of wide functions in the economic, social, and cultural fields, "to make sure that the United Nations under prevalent world conditions should not go beyond acceptable limits or exceed due limitations." Both the rule and the exception "can be looked upon as being really implicit in any organization which is genuinely international in character." [141]

In the course of the discussion at San Francisco, it was emphasized that this is not a "technical and legalistic formula." Proposals to include a reference to international law and to substitute "solely" for "essentially" were resisted. It was argued that the intention of the new paragraph was to establish a general principle, that international law was subject to constant change and was difficult to define, and that in the modern world it was not easy to find any matter that was "solely domestic." A special merit of the proposed text was that it was capable of evolutionary development "as the state of the world, the public opinion of the world, and the factual interdependence of the world makes it necessary and appropriate." [142] The point was also made that the inclusion of a reference to international law was unnecessary since the paragraph, being part of an international agreement, would be interpreted by reference to international law in any case.[143]

Interpretation: Authority and Procedure

Objections to the proposal of the Sponsoring Governments at San Francisco were based not only on its substance but also, and possibly to an even greater degree, on the absence of assurance that the principle as stated would not be interpreted arbitrarily and according to purely political requirements. Proposals were made that questions involving the interpretation of the paragraph be referred to the International Court of Justice. Various alternative suggestions were made to this end, including one that the compulsory jurisdiction of the Court

---

140 UNCIO, *Documents*, VI, 436–40.   141 *Ibid.*, p. 486.
142 *Ibid.*, pp. 507–8.   143 *Ibid.*, pp. 494–99.

over such questions be accepted. In opposition to conferring any special competence on the Court, it was argued that the principle of compulsory jurisdiction had been rejected,[144] and that there was no reason why the general understanding with respect to Charter interpretation should not apply to this paragraph as well.[145] Also, some pointed out that since the paragraph was not to be interpreted solely by legal standards, there was no reason for making the Court its sole, or even its principal, interpreter.

In practice, Article 2(7) has been interpreted by the same methods as other Charter provisions. Each organ has interpreted the paragraph as it is applicable to its particular functions, and, except when the organ has the authority to take a binding decision (as in the case of the exercise by the Court of its contentious jurisdiction), members have not necessarily considered themselves bound by such interpretations.

There have been a large number of cases in which Article 2(7) has been invoked in objecting to the competence of United Nations organs and in which there has been an extended discussion of the principle of domestic jurisdiction. In a number of other cases, objections have been raised but no discussion has occurred.[146] In addition, there have been a number of cases where, by implication, decisions have had some bearing on the interpretation of this article but where the article has not been explicitly referred to either in discussion or in the final decision taken.

In the majority of cases where Article 2(7) has been invoked before the political organs, no specific proposal has been submitted on the question of competence. Some who have invoked the article have stated that since the matter under consideration falls essentially within their domestic jurisdiction, they will not participate in the discussion. Others have participated in the debates, and have voiced their objections either before or after adoption of the agenda. In relatively few instances have there been proposals for dealing with the specific question of the applicability of Article 2(7).

During discussion on the adoption of the agenda at the seventh session of the General Assembly, a member moved that the Assembly was not competent to consider the question of race conflict in the Union of South Africa. The President ruled that under the Assembly Rules of Procedure, the proposal regarding competence had priority over the question of inclusion in the agenda. The ruling was challenged on the ground that the Assembly would be in a position to decide the

---

[144] See commentary on Art. 92.   [145] See "Introduction," p. 14.

[146] Cases in the first of these two categories are analyzed in detail in *Repertory*, Vol. I; *Supp. 1*, Vol. I; and *Supp. 2*, Vol. I. Cases in the second category are listed in an annex.

question of competence only after the item had been discussed. The Assembly reversed the President's ruling, and without pronouncing on the question of competence, included the item in the agenda.[147]

The Assembly has also been unwilling to decide the question of competence before discussing the substance of the matter.[148] Its Rules of Procedure provide, however, that any motion calling for a decision on its competence to adopt a particular proposal shall be put to a vote before the vote on the proposal itself.[149] In three instances, the Assembly has adopted motions specifically deciding that draft resolutions before it are within its competence under Article 2(7).[150] In the Indonesian case, the Security Council did not adopt an amendment offered by the United States to the effect that action on a proposed draft resolution was taken "without in any way deciding the juridical question concerning . . . competence" under Article 2(7).[151] The draft resolution as finally adopted on August 1, 1947 contained no reference to the question of competence.

In no case has a political organ of the United Nations asked the Court to give an advisory opinion on the interpretation of the paragraph. A South African proposal to ask the Court whether the matters covered by the Indian complaint over treatment accorded to persons of Indian origin were essentially within the domestic jurisdiction of South Africa was defeated by a vote of 31 to 21, with 2 abstentions.[152] A proposal of Belgium that the Court be asked to give an advisory opinion on whether the Security Council was competent to deal with the Indonesian question was defeated by a vote of 4 to 1, with 6 abstentions.[153] The major arguments advanced against requesting the Court's opinion included the following: that the political organ had responsibility, that the question had political as well as legal aspects, and that requesting an opinion would involve excessive delay. A practical difficulty in the way of asking the Court for an advisory opinion is that, the question of competence may be raised with respect to the consideration of a question or the adoption of any proposal. Considering the range and variety of proposals that can be submitted on any item, reference of each to the Court would not only involve extensive delays but also place a very heavy burden on the Court itself.

[147] GAOR/7th Sess./381st Plen. Mtg./Oct. 17, 1952/esp. para. 150.
[148] GAOR/3d Sess., 2d Part, 1st Ctte./263d Mtg./May 9, 1949/p. 253.
[149] Rule 81, UN Doc. A/520/Rev. 8, Mar. 1966.
[150] When considering the question of the treatment of people of Indian origin in the Union of South Africa at the third session and the question of threats to the political independence and territorial integrity of Greece at the third and fourth sessions.
[151] SCOR/2d Yr./173d Mtg./Aug. 1, 1947/pp. 1687–1702.
[152] GAOR/1st Sess., 2d Part/52d Plen. Mtg./Dec. 8, 1946/p. 1061.
[153] SCOR/2d Yr., No. 84/195th Mtg./Aug. 26, 1947/p. 2224.

The interpretation of Article 2(7) has been an issue before the Court in connection with cases submitted to it by the parties for decision and in relation to questions referred to it for advisory opinions.[154] The question has been raised in actual litigation, where the claim of compulsory jurisdiction has been advanced. In the Interhandel Case, for example, the Court held that the domestic-jurisdiction limitation of Article 2(7) did not apply if the interpretation and application of principles of international law were in question, but refused jurisdiction on other grounds.[155] In its advisory opinion on the interpretation of peace treaties with Bulgaria, Hungary, and Romania, the Court refused to accept the contention that the General Assembly under Article 2(7) was incompetent to request the opinion. The Court held that it was sufficient for its purposes that the Assembly justified its action under the terms of Articles 55 and 56.[156]

In the development and implementation of United Nations programs, the Secretary-General can play an important role in interpreting Article 2(7). Thus, in his report on the experience derived from the establishment and operation of UNEF, Secretary-General Hammarskjöld gave his interpretation of the limitation which the domestic-jurisdiction principle placed on the operations of the Force.[157] In his statement to the Security Council at the time of the initial consideration of the Congo question, he stated that the conduct of United Nations forces under the Council's resolution would be based on this interpretation.[158] The Council formally incorporated this view in its resolution of August 9, 1960, and in a later memorandum, the Secretary-General informed the Council of the interpretation which he proposed to adopt in the absence of guidance to the contrary.[159]

Interpretation of Article 2(7) in United Nations Practice

Efforts to elucidate the substantive meaning given to this paragraph in United Nations practice encounter difficulties common to efforts to interpret other Charter provisions, but in certain respects more serious.[160] These difficulties arise from the highly decentralized system of Charter interpretation which often produces uncertainty as to whether a particular interpetation has general acceptance, and the failure of United Nations organs to be explicit with respect to the Charter bases

[154] See Shabtai Rosenne, Law and Practice of the International Court of Justice (Leyden, Sitjhoff, 1965), I, 393–99 and II, 713–14.
[155] ICJ Reports, 1959, pp. 23–26.   [156] ICJ Reports, 1950, pp. 70–71.
[157] UN Doc. A/3943, Oct. 9, 1958.
[158] SCOR/15th Yr./873d Mtg./July 13, 1960/p. 5.
[159] UN Doc. S/4417/Add. 6, Aug. 12, 1960.
[160] For interpretation of this article in UN practice, see Repertory, Vol. I; Supp. 1, Vol. I; Supp. 2, Vol. I; Higgins, pp. 58–130; and M. S. Rajan, The United Nations and Domestic Jurisdiction (London, Longmans, 1958).

for their decisions. In order for the limitation of Article 2(7) to apply, it is necessary that the action constitute intervention, that the substantive matter be "essentially within the domestic jurisdiction" of a state, and that the application of enforcement measures not be in question.

There has been considerable discussion of what constitutes intervention. Two opposing views have found expression in United Nations discussions and in scholarly writings. One view holds that intervention means what it meant in traditional international law. According to this view,

Intervention is a technical term of, on the whole, unequivocal connotation. It signifies dictatoral interference in the sense of action amounting to denial of the independence of a state. It implies a peremptory demand for positive conduct or abstention—a demand which, if not complied with, involves a threat of or recourse to compulsion in some form.[161]

The other view is that intervention should not be interpreted in a narrow technical sense but rather in the sense understood by the layman to mean interference in any form. In support of this view, attention is called to the discussion at San Francisco, the clear intention to make the principle applicable to all organs, and the fact that the narrow interpretation would deprive the article of all meaning, since the exemption of enforcement action excludes from the limitation the only kind of Organization action that could be described as intervention under the traditional definition.[162]

United Nations organs have never given a clear preference to either view. Ambiguity results from the fact that a permissive view with respect to what the Organization *may* do can be the result either of a restrictive definition of intervention or a restrictive interpretation of "essentially within the domestic jurisdiction." United Nations practice is conclusive, however, on one point, namely, that placing a matter on the agenda for discussion does not constitute intervention.[163] With regard to discussion, the same would appear to be true, although some members have taken an opposing view.[164] The argument for not regarding discussion as intervention is that only after discussion can a decision be taken as to the competence of the organ. But in practice it is difficult, if not impossible, to prevent discussion of substance at this preliminary stage, and it has not generally been done. On the question

[161] H. Lauterpacht, "The International Protection of Human Rights," *Recueil des Cours,* LII (1947-I), 19. See also Rajan, pp. 66–83.

[162] See Lawrence Preuss, "Article 2, Paragraph 7 of the Charter of the United Nations and Matters of Domestic Jurisdiction," *Recueil des Cours,* LXXIV (1949-I), 553–653.

[163] See *Repertory,* Vol I; *Supp. 1,* Vol. I; *Supp. 2,* Vol. I, for references to cases; and Higgins, p. 69.

[164] See statement of delegate of Union of South Africa: GAOR/7th Sess., 1st Ctte./541st Mtg./Dec. 9, 1952/p. 226.

whether steps taken beyond discussion, such as establishing a commission of inquiry or making recommendations to the parties, constitute intervention, the record is not clear since the attitude adopted on this issue cannot usually be separated from the assessment made of the degree of international concern. It has been suggested, however, that a distinction can be made between a recommendation of a general nature addressed to all members and one that is directed to a particular state.[165]

Generally speaking, fears expressed at San Francisco that Article 2(7) would be a serious limitation on the work of the United Nations have not been justified in practice. Although the existence of the paragraph has provided a basis for arguments that a United Nations organ does not have competence, the general direction of United Nations practice has been to claim for the Organization the full measure of competence that a liberal interpretation of the positive grant of powers would justify. This general conclusion is supported by attitudes commonly expressed by members and decisions taken on a wide range of claims.[166]

The substitution of the word "essentially" for "solely," and the explanation given at San Francisco for so doing, led some to fear that the principle laid down by the Permanent Court of International Justice in the Tunis-Morocco Nationality Decrees opinion would be weakened. This has not proved to be the case. Claims that matters may be essentially within the domestic jurisdiction, even though subject to provisions of customary international law and treaties, have not been admitted. For instance, in connection with its treatment of persons of Indian origin, the Union of South Africa maintained that, even if the Capetown Agreement was regarded as a binding treaty, the matter of the treatment of one's nationals was "essentially" within a state's domestic jurisdiction.[167] The General Assembly repeatedly adopted resolutions that implicitly denied this claim. Likewise, in the case of the interpretation of the peace treaties with Bulgaria, Hungary, and Romania, the claim that the treatment of nationals was an "essentially" domestic matter was denied by the International Court of Justice in its opinion and by the General Assembly.[168]

Basically, the same issue is raised with respect to the competence of United Nations organs under the terms of the Charter. The question in this case is whether Charter provisions have the effect of transforming

[165] See discussion on question of race conflict in the Union of South Africa: GAOR/8th Sess., ad hoc Pol. Ctte./32d Mtg./Nov. 23, 1953/para. 40; 33d Mtg./ Nov. 24, 1953/para. 49.

[166] See Higgins, pp. 58–130 for scholarly discussion.

[167] GAOR/3d Sess., 2d Part, 1st Ctte./265th Mtg./May 10, 1949/p. 276.

[168] ICJ Reports, 1950, p. 601; GA Res. 272(III), Apr. 30, 1949.

matters otherwise within domestic jurisdiction into matters of legitimate international concern, or whether Article 2(7) has the effect of preventing such transformation from taking place.

In the Spanish case, the question was raised whether the character of a government could be treated as a matter of legitimate concern to the United Nations. International law had in the past recognized the right of a state to determine its form of government as one of the essential aspects of national sovereignty. The claim was made in this case, however, that the existence of the Franco regime endangered international peace and security, and the Security Council was asked to take appropriate measures. In opposition, it was argued that the nature of the political regime fell essentially within the domestic jurisdiction of the state.[169] The validity of this argument was not admitted either by the Security Council or the General Assembly, and the latter recommended collective measures to secure a change of government.[170] Although the United Nations action in this case may be regarded as the product of unique circumstances and not likely to be repeated, it does illustrate the willingness of United Nations organs to encroach on traditional concepts of domestic jurisdiction in the discharge of their responsibilities under the Charter, the limitation of Article 2(7) notwithstanding.

The Security Council and the General Assembly have been involved in a number of situations in which governments have engaged in the use of military force to put down independence movements in noncontiguous territories assertedly under their sovereign control. A variety of Charter-based claims have been advanced, including claims that international peace and security are endangered, that the right of self-determination is being denied, and that human rights are being violated. Metropolitan governments, however, have commonly invoked the principle of domestic jurisdiction, claiming that the territory in question is an integral part of the metropolitian area,[171] or that even if it is a non-self-governing territory under the terms of the Charter, its relations with the administering state are matters of domestic jurisdiction.[172]

The objections based on Article 2(7) have no doubt influenced decisions of United Nations organs. In some instances, they have been decisive in preventing resolutions from being adopted; in others, they have influenced the content of resolutions by making it seem advisable

[169] SCOR/1st Yr., 1st. Ser., No. 2/34th Mtg./Apr. 17, 1946/pp. 176–77; and 35th Mtg./Apr. 18, 1946/pp. 180–81.
[170] GA Res. 39(I), Dec. 12, 1946.
[171] French claim with respect to Algeria and Portuguese claim with respect to Angola.
[172] Cases of Indonesia, Tunisia, Morocco, and Cyprus.

or necessary to water down the proposal under consideration in order to achieve wide support. However, the great majority of members have supported the competence of the United Nations to discuss colonial conflicts and to adopt a wide variety of resolutions recommending with varying degrees of urgency that a settlement be reached that is consistent with United Nations purposes and principles.[173] Since the adoption of the Declaration on the Granting of Independence to Colonial Countries and Peoples by the General Assembly in 1960, there has been a tendency in the Assembly in particular, to consider that no aspect of "colonialism" should be treated as a matter falling "essentially" within the domestic jurisdiction of a state.

Under the terms of Article 73 of Chapter XI, members administering non-self-governing territories are required to transmit to the Secretary-General information on economic, social, and educational conditions in these territories. States administering such territories have invoked the domestic jurisdiction principle without success to prevent the General Assembly from using this information as the basis for discussing aspects of the administration of such territories and making recommendations of a general nature for the more effective attainment of Charter purposes.[174]

The establishment by the General Assembly in 1961 of a special committee to follow up the implementation of the 1960 Declaration had the practical result of bringing all non-self-governing territories under a form of international supervision comparable to that of the trusteeship system. While individual members might insist that the domestic jurisdiction principle had relevance to matters of this kind, there is no question that the overwhelming sentiment of the United Nations membership as expressed in Assembly resolutions has been to the contrary.[175]

The competence of the United Nations, and particularly the General Assembly, to deal with cases of alleged violation of human rights has been a subject of controversy from the beginning of the United Nations. The question has been debated most extensively (though not exclusively) in connection with South African policies of racial discrimination. The issue was first raised over South African treatment of its nationals of Indian origin; later, the focus of attention was South Africa's apartheid policies. No one questions the competence of the General Assembly to deal with the question of human rights in general terms by adopting the Universal Declaration and preparing draft covenants.[176] South Africa and some other members have challenged,

---

[173] For further discussion, see commentary on Art. 1(2). See also Higgins, esp. pp. 90–106.
[174] See commentary on Art. 73.
[175] See GA Res. 1514(XV), Dec. 14, 1960; and 1654(XVI), Nov. 27, 1961.
[176] See commentary on Art. 55.

however, the competence of the General Assembly to deal with alleged violations of human rights when the persons involved are nationals of the accused state. The argument has been that, in the absence of an international agreement by which a state agrees to respect specific human rights, the treatment a state accords its own nationals remains essentially within its domestic jurisdiction and outside United Nations competence. The General Assembly, it is argued, only has competence to promote voluntary cooperation between members in achieving respect for human rights. The Assembly, however, has not accepted this claim and has acted on the premise that it does have competence to deal with such situations on the ground that Charter provisions dealing with human rights are being violated.[177] In the case of treatment of South African nationals of Indian origin, the legal basis of General Assembly resolutions was somewhat ambiguous because of the alternative possibilities of basing Assembly action on violation of the Charter and the Capetown Agreement. In the case of apartheid, however, the General Assembly has been specific in charging violations of obligations under the Charter,[178] and by inference denying the applicability of Article 2(7) for that reason.

The interpretation and application of the domestic-jurisdiction limitation has been an issue in United Nations peace-keeping operations undertaken on the basis of the consent of the host state, particularly in the Congo. In proposing the course of action that the Security Council decided, on July 13, 1960,[179] to undertake, the Secretary-General emphasized by reference to his earlier report on the experience of UNEF that the United Nations must not be employed "in situations of an essentially internal nature" nor permitted "in any sense to be a party to internal conflicts." [180] Although the Secretary-General was under strong pressure from the Congolese government and some members of the United Nations to use United Nations forces to support the efforts of the central government to establish its authority in Katanga, he consistently took the view that the Force should not be used to influence the outcome of an internal conflict.[181] This interpretation was accepted by the Security Council.[182] With the disintegration of the central government and the national-security forces, the Secretary-General found it necessary to redefine the mission of the United Nations, but he still adhered to the concept of a neutral politi-

[177] See commentary on Arts. 55 and 56. For detailed discussion, see Higgins, pp. 118–30.

[178] See, for example, GA Res. 1663(XVI), Nov. 28, 1961.

[179] UN Doc. S/4387, July 13, 1960.

[180] UN Doc. A/3943, Oct. 9, 1958, para. 166.

[181] See Second Report by the Secretary-General, UN Doc. S/4417, Aug 6, 1960; and statement to Security Council, SCOR/15th Yr./884th Mtg./Aug. 8, 1960/pp. 2–7.

[182] UN Doc. S/4426, Aug. 9, 1960.

cal role, while accepting responsibility for rendering technical assistance.[183]

The Assembly, however, by its resolutions of September 20, 1960, undertook direct participation in the internal political struggle by requesting the Secretary-General "to assist the Central Government of the Congo in the restoration and maintenance of law and order throughout the territory of the Republic of the Congo and to safeguard its unity, territorial integrity and political independence in the interest of international peace and security" and appealed to the Congolese for the speedy solution of their internal conflicts with United Nations assistance.[184] To achieve these objectives, the United Nations actively assisted in the reconstruction of the Congolese national government. Later, the Security Council authorized "the use of force, if necessary, in the last resort" to prevent the occurrence of civil war, [185] and directed the Secretary-General "to take vigorous action, including the use of requisite measure of force, it necessary," for the apprehension and removal of foreign military and paramilitary personnel and political advisers not under United Nations command, and mercenaries.[186]

While the military action that put an end to the Katangese secession was justified on grounds of self-defense, this justification carried conviction only within the context of the above directives. It was never made clear whether these undoubted interventions in the internal affairs of the Congo were to be justified on the ground of the initial invitation of Congolese government that military assistance be given, or on the ground that the acts in question were necessary to the maintenance of international peace and security. If the second, there is the further query whether they came under the exception of enforcement action or must be justified as appropriate preventive measures. If the measures taken in the Congo are to be regarded as preventive measures under Article 40 of the Charter, the exception at the end of Article 2(7) obviously does not apply, and the conclusion would appear to follow that measures adopted in good faith to prevent the aggravation of a situation where a threat to international peace is found to exist are not to be regarded as intervention in matters essentially within the domestic jurisdiction of a state.[187]

[183] SCOR/15th Yr./887th Mtg./Aug. 21, 1960/pp. 10–12.
[184] GA Res. 1474(ES-IV), Sept. 20, 1960. For discussion, see GAOR/4th Emergency Special Sess., 858th–863d Plen. Mtgs./Sept. 17–20, 1960.
[185] UN Doc. S/4741, Feb. 21, 1961.   [186] UN Doc. S/5002, Nov. 24, 1961.
[187] See E. M. Miller, "Legal Aspects of UN Action in the Congo," *American Journal of International Law*, LV (1961), pp. 1–28; and Oscar Schachter, "Preventing the Internationalization of Internal Conflict: A Legal Analysis of the UN Congo Experience," *Proceedings of the American Society of International Law*, Apr. 25–27, 1963, pp. 216–24.

CHAPTER II

Membership

The basis for membership is fundamentally important to any organization. The significance of this issue for the United Nations was reflected in the high-level negotiations concerning its original membership and the careful consideration given at the San Francisco Conference to those articles of the Charter bearing upon United Nations membership. The significance of this matter is further underlined by the Charter requirement that decisions concerning admission, suspension, and expulsion of members must be approved not only by a two-thirds vote in the General Assembly (Article 18), but by the Security Council as well. In practice, this has meant that no decision on membership may be taken against the wishes of any of the five permanent members of the Security Council.

From the beginning, United Nations membership has been an intensely political issue. Few matters have prompted so bitter a debate over so extended a period, and decisions have been greatly influenced by political considerations. In an organization where so much emphasis has been placed upon voting, the composition of the organs, especially the General Assembly, inevitably becomes a matter of considerable importance to those charged with the direction of national policies.

Universality versus Limited Membership

For an international organization, the question of universal versus limited membership is of fundamental importance. A small group, dedicated to the same goals, and agreed as to how those goals should be pursued, has a number of obvious advantages over a larger, more diversified group. A closed organization can be strong and efficient but it may invite counter-alliances and become wrecked on the shoals of power politics. On the other hand, one may be forced to sacrifice so much to obtain universal membership—or a close approximation of it—that the organization becomes loose and ineffective. Nonetheless, the goals of the United Nations, as contained in the statement of purposes in Article 1 of the Charter, are of such a nature as virtually to require universal membership for their successful fulfillment.

The concept of a "universal" organization had considerable support in much of the early thinking about the kind of organization to be established to maintain postwar peace. There were, however, serious obstacles to achieving such an objective. As a point of principle, for instance, was it desirable, or even possible, to include as original members of the new organization states that had not indicated a desire to join or a willingness to accept the purposes and obligations of the organization? Of more practical significance was the fact that the United Nations had its origins in a wartime coalition which at the time had not yet completed the defeat of the Axis powers or agreed on the outlines of the new postwar order. Under these circumstances, "universality" could at the most be viewed as a future goal.

In the meetings of the major powers at Dumbarton Oaks and Yalta, it was agreed that membership in the Organization would be initially restricted, with the door left open for subsequent admission of "other peace-loving states." At San Francisco, there was considerable support for the principle of universality, particularly from the Latin American states,[1] but even the most ardent advocates of the principle recognized that it could not be attained under existing circumstances. Thus, original membership was drawn almost exclusively from those states that had supported the United Nations in the war against the Axis.[2]

The principle of universality was raised during the debate on other provisions of the Charter concerning membership. Its proponents sought to draft the provisions on the admission of new members in such a manner as to facilitate rather than delay the achievement of their goal. The desirability of a universal organization was a major argument in the unsuccessful efforts to exclude from the Charter any provision for the expulsion of members.[3] It was also a major factor in the spirited debate on whether members had the right to withdraw from the United Nations and whether the Charter should contain a specific provision either permitting or prohibiting withdrawal from the Organization.

Right of Withdrawal

Under the League Covenant, a member might withdraw after giving two years' notice (Article 1[3]).[4] The fact that the Dumbarton Oaks Proposals were silent on this subject was variously interpreted at San Francisco. Some delegates claimed that members had the right to with-

---

[1] See Ruth B. Russell, A History of the United Nations Charter (Washington, Brooking's Institution, 1958), pp. 843–44.

[2] See commentary of Art. 3.   [3] See commentary on Arts. 5 and 6.

[4] Withdrawal is expressly provided for in many of the constitutions of the specilized agencies.

draw if such action was not expressly forbidden. Others felt that, in the absence of express provision, there was no right of withdrawal. They argued that recognition of such a right would undermine the permanent character of the Organization and the principle of universality. It was initially agreed, in the committee concerned with membership questions, that the Charter should contain no formal clause either permitting or forbidding withdrawal. At the same time, the committee adopted an "interpretation" to the effect "that withdrawal or some other form of dissolution of the Organization would become inevitable if . . . the Organization was revealed to be unable to maintain peace or could do so only at the expense of law and justice." [5]

At a later stage of the Conference, the issue of withdrawal was raised in more acute form. Dissatisfied with the provisions governing Charter amendment,[6] many delegates changed their positions. There was considerable support for an explicit provision in the Charter permitting withdrawal. Others still felt this would weaken the Organization by encouraging withdrawals. As a consequence of this debate, the "interpretation" was redrafted [7] to emphasize that it was the "highest duty" of members "to continue their cooperation within the Organization for the preservation of international peace and security." It was not the purpose of the Organization, however, "to compel" a member to continue its membership if "because of exceptional circumstances," it felt "constrained to withdraw." [8]

By way of illustration, the declaration specified certain conditions under which withdrawal would be proper. These included the above-quoted statement concerning the possible failure of the United Nations to carry out its functions. A member might also be justified in withdrawing if its "rights and obligations" were changed by a Charter amendment with which it did not concur and was thus unable to accept. Another possible justifying circumstance would be if an amendment "duly accepted" by the necessary majority failed to secure the necessary number of ratifications. This provision was directed toward the possibility of a "desirable" amendment's being blocked by one or more permanent members.

Clearly, the committee did not intend that these reasons should be considered as exhausting the "exceptional" circumstances that justify withdrawal. Nor can a declaration adopted by the Conference be considered "binding" upon members to the same extent as a provision of the Charter itself. In the absence of any express provision regarding withdrawal, each member retains the right to withdraw at will. The purpose of the declaration apparently was to place upon the member

[5] UNCIO, *Documents*, VII, 123.   [6] See commentary on ch. xviii.
[7] UNCIO, *Documents*, VII, 262–67.   [8] *Ibid.*, Report of Ctte. I/2, p. 328.

the duty to justify its withdrawal in the eyes of the Organization and its members.

The issue of withdrawal did not come up within the United Nations until December 31, 1964, when the President of the General Assembly and the Office of the Secretary-General were notified that Indonesia was withdrawing from membership in the United Nations as a consequence of the election to the Security Council of Malaysia, a state which it did not recognize and with which it was involved in a bitter dispute. Appeals by the President of the Assembly and the Secretary-General were unavailing; on January 20, 1965, a formal letter was addressed to the latter stating that the only alternative left to Indonesia was withdrawal from the Organization. It was also withdrawing from some of the specialized agencies. Indonesia asked that its Permanent Mission be permitted to maintain its official status until March 1 in order to wind up its affairs and offered to accord the same privilege to the United Nations Office in Indonesia.

In his reply, the Secretary-General stated that the position Indonesia had taken gave rise to a situation for which no express provision had been made in the Charter. The letters were circulated to members of the Security Council and the General Assembly,[9] and a number of informal consultations were held, but the matter was not discussed by either organ.

"Universality" in the United Nations Debates

In debates in the General Assembly and the Security Council, there have been frequent references to universal membership as the desired goal of the Organization. These sentiments were voiced most vigorously during the ten-year period of deadlock over admission of new members.[10] A number of the resolutions adopted by the Assembly on this subject made specific reference to the "general sentiment in favor of universality." [11] The principle of universality has also been cited in other connections, for example, in warnings against any actions tending to force members out of the Organization, either by expulsion or by voluntary withdrawal.

Throughout these debates, a recurrent theme has been that the United Nations was not intended to be a "club" of "like-minded" states, and that there should be room within the Organization for states with widely differing ideologies and different economic and political sys-

[9] See UN Docs. S/6157, Jan. 21, 1965;/6166, Jan. 29, 1965; and/6206, Feb. 26, 1965.
[10] See commentary on Art. 4.
[11] GA Res. 197B(III), Dec. 8, 1948; and 817(IX), Nov. 23, 1954. See also 506(VI), Feb. 1, 1952; 718(VIII), Oct. 23, 1953; and 918(X), Dec. 8, 1955.

tems. Less frequently it has been pointed out that, under the Charter, membership in the Organization *is* based on the principle of "selectivity," not "universality." Members *are* required to be "like-minded," at least to the extent that all must support the purposes and principles of the Charter and fulfill their obligations thereunder.

As one study pointed out, "the choice between universality and selectively is intimately related to what the primary function of the United Nations is deemed to be." [12] For those who view the United Nations primarily as a "security" agency for collective resistance to aggression, "selectivity" and "like-mindedness" provide the basis for a more effective Organization. Obversely, the principle of universality appeals to those who emphasize the role of the United Nations as a "center for harmonizing the actions of nations" (Article 1[4]), and see peaceful settlement as its most important function.[13]

Since 1955, when the membership deadlock ended, the alacrity and near unanimity with which the United Nations has generally acted in admitting to membership the new states that have arisen in Asia, Africa, and the Caribbean, have reduced appeals to the principle of universality to the issue of representation of China.

Representation of Members

The Charter contains no provisions setting forth criteria or methods by which questions concerning representation in the United Nations should be decided. The General Assembly and the three Councils have each established rules for dealing with credentials of representatives; generally, the approval of credentials is routine.[14] A Secretariat memorandum written in early 1950 pointed out that "despite the fairly large number of revolutionary changes of government and the larger number of instances of breach of diplomatic relations among Members," there had not, up to that time, been a "single instance of a challenge" to the credentials of a representative.[15] In the decade and a half since then, the situation has been much the same. Normally, when one regime has been replaced by another, the credentials of the representatives designated by the new government have been accepted without challenge. There have been, however, a few instances when the United Nations has been faced with rival claims as in the case of China.[16]

[12] *Review of the United Nations Charter,* USS/83C2/1954, Staff Study 3, p. 80.

[13] The debate between these two schools was very lively in the early 1950s. See *ibid.,* pp. 79–82.

[14] See commentary on Arts. 9, 23, 61, and 86.

[15] "Legal Aspects of the Problems of Representation in the United Nations" SCOR/5th Yr./*Supp.* for Jan. 1–May 31, 1950, p. 21.

[16] For other instances, see commentary on Arts. 9 and 23.

Discussion of the Chinese question in 1950 revealed sharply divergent attitudes among members. It was generally recognized that each organ was free to decide for its own purposes any issues concerning representation. This, of course, could result in the development of a highly undesirable situation in which there would be no uniformity in representation on the various organs. Some members, principally the Latin American states, argued that any controversy over representation should be decided by the General Assembly, as the organ in which all members were represented. This approach was countered by the argument that each organ was sovereign within its sphere and that to entrust the decision to the Assembly would violate Article 7 of the Charter. The resolution adopted by the General Assembly recommended that "whenever more than one authority claims to be the government entitled to represent a Member State in the United Nations," the question should be considered by the General Assembly (or by the Interim Committee if the Assembly is not in session) and that "the attitude adopted" by that organ "should be taken into account in other organs of the United Nations and in the specialized agencies." [17] This resolution was adopted, however, only after the deletion of a paragraph setting forth "the factors to be taken into consideration in determining any such question." [18]

In first drawing attention to this problem in 1950, the Secretary-General stated that "the primary difficulty" was that the question of representation of members in the United Nations had been "linked up with the question of recognition" by member states. This linkage was, in his view, "unfortunate from the practical standpoint, and wrong from the standpoint of legal theory." He pointed out that lack of recognition, or lack of diplomatic relations, had not been considered as a valid reason for voting against a candidate for admission to the United Nations. Moreover, in United Nations practice, a member could "properly vote to accept a representative of a government which it did not recognize or with which it had no diplomatic relations" and "such a vote did not imply recognition or a readiness to assume diplomatic relations."

Recognition of new states or new governments was a "unilateral act," he pointed out, an "essentially" political decision made by each state in accordance "with its own free appreciation of the situation." On the

[17] GA Res. 396(V), Dec. 14, 1950.

[18] Another change was the substitution of the phrase "attitude adopted" for the stronger term "decisions reached" by the Assembly. See GAOR/5th Sess./*Annexes*, agenda item 61 (A/1578, Dec. 1, 1950). For the debate leading up to the adoption of the resolution, see *ibid.*, ad hoc Pol. Ctte./18th–24th Mtgs./Oct. 20–26, 1950; and 57th–60th Mtgs./Nov. 27–28, 1950/pp. 111–59, and 364–89; and 325th Plen. Mtg./Dec. 14, 1950/pp. 675–77.

other hand, membership of a state in the United Nations and representation of a member in its organs were "clearly determined by a collective act." In his opinion, any controversy over representation should be decided upon the basis of which claimant "in fact is in a position to employ the resources and direct the people of the State in fulfillment of the obligations of membership." The relevant criteria were whether the government exercised effective authority within the territory of the state and whether it was "habitually obeyed by the bulk of the population." [19]

Aside from the validity of the Secretary-General's arguments for divorcing the question of recognition by an individual state from that of representation in the United Nations, inevitably, the considerations that prompt one government to recognize another will have an influence upon attitudes on any question of representation in the Organization. Members, naturally, tend to vote for the admission of states they have recognized and to vote for the seating of representatives of governments they have recognized. Moreover, the General Assembly debate demonstrated that the positions taken by members were closely related to the general policies of their governments with regard to recognition. British policy, for example, is based upon the criterion of effective control over territory and population; recognition in no way implies "approval" of the regime being recognized. For others, "legitimacy" of the new government is of fundamental significance. For the United States, recognition is not an automatic act but a "privilege"; policy with respect to recognition is based "on objective considerations of national interest." [20] The divergent schools of thought were reflected in the proposals made during the 1950 General Assembly debate.

The British proposal followed the same lines as the essentially "objective" approach contained in the Secretary-General's memorandum. It stated that "the right of a government to represent" a member in the United Nations "should be recognized if that government exercises effective control and authority over all or nearly all the national territory, and has the obedience of the bulk of the population of that territory, in such a way that this control, authority and obedience appear to be of a permanent character." [21]

The other approach, which places greater emphasis on "subjective" considerations, was embodied in the Cuban draft resolution. It listed as criteria not only "effective authority over the national territory" but

[19] See "Legal Aspects of the Problems of Representation in the United Nations," SCOR/5th Yr./*Supp.* for Jan. 1–May 31, 1950/pp. 18–23. See also letter of protest by the representative of Nationalist China, *ibid.,* pp. 23–26.

[20] State Dept. *Bulletin,* Vol. XXXIX, No. 1002 (Sept. 8, 1958), p. 385.

[21] GAOR/5th Sess./1950/*Annexes,* agenda item 61, p. 8.

also the following: general consent of the population; respect for human rights and fundamental freedoms; and ability and willingness to achieve the purposes of the Charter, observe its principles, and fulfill the international obligations of the state.[22] Additional conditions were suggested by other members: that the government make an express declaration of its willingness to fulfill its international obligations; that the new government shall have been established "without the intervention of another state"; that it be "independent of foreign control"; that the general consent of the population be "expressed through freely conducted or internationally supervised or observed elections."[23] To many members, the application of such criteria would constitute a gross interference in the domestic affairs of member states.

In the end, as noted, the Assembly decided against including any specific criteria in its resolution, thus leaving future controversies to be considered, in the words of the resolution, "in the light of the purposes and principles of the Charter and the circumstances of each case."

Question of Succession

India was an original member of the United Nations, even though at the time it was not yet fully independent.[24] In 1947, with the transfer of sovereignty by the United Kingdom to India and Pakistan, the question was raised whether both should be considered original members of the Organization. It was finally decided that Pakistan should apply for admission in the usual manner. On the general issues involved in the case, the Sixth Committee of the General Assembly agreed that, when a new state is created, no matter how formed, it cannot claim the status of a member of the United Nations "unless it has been formally admitted as such in conformity with the provisions of the Charter."[25]

In this case, the United Nations was faced with "division" of a member state; the case of the United Arab Republic was just the opposite. Egypt and Syria were both original members of the United Nations. When the United Arab Republic was formed in February, 1958, their separate memberships in the United Nations ended, but the United Arab Republic was treated as a member by right of succession. In 1961, when Syria withdrew from the UAR, it resumed its original status. Both changes were effected without action by the United Na-

---

[22] *Ibid.*, p. 5.

[23] Amendments by Venezuela, Uruguay, and China, *ibid.*, pp. 7, 13, and 6.

[24] See commentary on Art. 3.

[25] GAOR/2d Sess., 6th Ctte./42d–43d Mtg./Oct. 6–7, 1947/pp. 37–43. For the full text of the relevant "Statement by the Rapporteur of the Sixth Committee," see *ibid.*, Annexes, pp. 306–8.

tions organs beyond the routine acceptance of new credentials for representatives on various United Nations bodies. The same was true when Tanganyika and Zanzibar, both United Nations members, joined to form the United Republic of Tanzania in 1964.[26] It is doubtful whether these instances should be considered as firm precedents, especially in any case where the fission or fusion process was not obviously and fully acceptable to both parties. Indeed, the above-mentioned agreement in the Sixth Committee stated that, "as a general rule" a state does not "cease" to be a member "simply because its constitution or its frontier have been subjected to changes," and that "the extinction" of a state "as a legal personality recognized in the international order must be shown before its rights and obligations can be considered thereby to have ceased to exist." [27]

Article 3

The original Members of the United Nations shall be the states which, having participated in the United Nations Conference on International Organization at San Francisco, or having previously signed the Declaration by United Nations of January 1, 1942, sign the present Charter and ratify it in accordance with Article 110.

The Charter establishes two categories of members of the United Nations: the "original" members designated in Article 3, and those subsequently admitted to membership in accordance with Article 4. The distinction, however, is purely formal and does not in any way imply a difference in status between the two groups.[28]

The Declaration by United Nations

There was never any question that those states that had joined in the war against the Axis powers would provide the core of the proposed postwar peace organization. When the question of membership was first discussed during the Dumbarton Oaks Conversations, the Soviet Union proposed that initially the Organization should be composed exclusively of those states that had signed the Declaration by United Nations of January 1, 1942. The original twenty-six signers of the Declaration included China, the Soviet Union, the United Kingdom, the United States, all members of the Commonwealth, most states of Cen-

[26] See, for example, the action taken in the Trusteeship Council, TCOR/21st Sess./88th Mtg./March 7, 1958/p. 23.
[27] See "Statement by the Rapporteur of the Sixth Committee," GAOR/2d Sess., 6th Ctte./1947/*Annexes*, p. 307.
[28] See UNCIO, *Documents*, VII, 325.

tral America, and representatives of those European countries with established governments-in-exile. By the time of the Dumbarton Oaks Conversations, nine additional states had adhered to the Declaration. There remained, however, a number of states, mainly Latin American, that had not signed the Declaration but had, nevertheless, broken relations with the Axis and given assistance to the Allied cause. The United States wished to include these "associated" states among the original members of the Organization. The issue was not resolved at Dumbarton Oaks; indeed, it became enmeshed with the Soviet request that each of the sixteen Soviet republics be included as original members.[29]

Table 1
ORIGINAL MEMBERS OF THE UNITED NATIONS
(*With Date of Adherence to "Declaration by United Nations"*)

** Argentina		Lebanon	Mar. 1, 1945
* Australia	Jan. 1, 1942	Liberia	Feb. 26, 1944
* Belgium	Jan. 1, 1942	* Luxembourg	Jan. 1, 1942
Bolivia	Apr. 27, 1943	Mexico	June 5, 1942
Brazil	Feb. 8, 1943	* Netherlands	Jan. 1, 1942
** Byelorussian SSR		* New Zealand	Jan. 1, 1942
* Canada	Jan. 1, 1942	* Nicaragua	Jan. 1, 1942
Chile	Feb. 12, 1945	* Norway	Jan. 1, 1942
* China	Jan. 1, 1942	* Panama	Jan. 1, 1942
Colombia	Dec. 22, 1943	Paraguay	Feb. 12, 1945
* Costa Rica	Jan. 1, 1942	Peru	Feb. 11, 1945
* Cuba	Jan. 1, 1942	Philippines	June 10, 1942
* Czechoslovakia	Jan. 1, 1942	*** Poland	Jan. 1, 1942
** Denmark		Saudi Arabia	Mar. 1, 1945
* Dominican Republic	Jan. 1, 1942	Syria	Mar. 1, 1945
Ecuador	Feb. 7, 1945	Turkey	Feb. 24, 1945
Egypt	Feb. 27, 1945	** Ukrainian SSR	
* El Salvador	Jan. 1, 1942	* Union of South	
Ethiopia	July 28, 1942	Africa	Jan. 1, 1942
France	Dec. 26, 1944	* Union of Soviet	
* Greece	Jan. 1, 1942	Socialist Republics	Jan. 1, 1942
* Guatemala	Jan. 1, 1942	* United Kingdom	Jan. 1, 1942
* Haiti	Jan. 1, 1942	* United States	Jan. 1, 1942
* Honduras	Jan. 1, 1942	Uruguay	Feb. 23, 1945
* India	Jan. 1, 1942	Venezuela	Feb. 16, 1945
Iran	Sept. 10, 1942	* Yugoslavia	Jan. 1, 1942
Iraq	Jan. 16, 1943		

  * Original signers of the "Declaration."
  ** Not signatories to the "Declaration," but invited after the San Francisco Conference convened.
  *** Original signer of the "Declaration," but did not participate in the Conference.

Agreement was finally reached at the Yalta Conference that invitations to attend the forthcoming conference to establish the new organization would be extended to those states that had already signed the

29 On the Dumbarton Oaks Conversations, see Russell, pp. 433–37 and 506–9.

Declaration by United Nations, and also "such of the Associated Nations as have declared war on the common enemy" by March 1, 1945.[30] None of the former enemy states was to be included. The United States had reservations regarding Argentina; the British raised a similar reservation regarding Ireland. It was, however, agreed that Denmark, once liberated, should be given the opportunity to join the new Organization.[31] Meanwhile, the original Soviet proposal for separate membership for each of the Soviet republics had undergone modification. In the end, it was agreed that, when the conference for establishing the Organization was held, the United Kingdom and the United States would "support a proposal to admit to original membership two Soviet Socialist Republics, i.e., the Ukraine and White Russia." [32]

Under pressure from the United States, all six Latin American "associated" states signed the Declaration by United Nations before the expiration of the deadline set at Yalta.[33] In addition, five Middle Eastern countries also signified their adherence to the Declaration.[34] On December 26, 1944, even before the Yalta Conference, France had announced its adherence to the Declaration, the actual signing taking place on January 1, 1945.

Participation in the San Francisco Conference

At the time of the San Francisco Conference, forty-seven countries had met the qualifications agreed upon at Yalta. Unfortunately, it proved impossible to extend an invitation to Poland, one of the original signers of the Declaration, because the major powers remained divided over the establishment of a provisional Polish government. It was decided at the Conference, however, that as soon as a government was agreed upon, Poland would be given the opportunity to sign the Charter and become an original member.[35]

As soon as the San Francisco Conference convened, it immediately faced two critical issues concerning participation that were practically, though not in principle, interconnected. The Soviet Union now insisted that the Byelorussian SSR and the Ukrainian SSR should not only be

[30] See State Dept., *Malta and Yalta Documents,* p. 976.

[31] For an account of this discussion, see *ibid.,* pp. 771 ff., and Russell, pp. 533 and 537 ff.

[32] State Dept., *Malta and Yalta Documents,* p. 976.

[33] See Russell, pp. 506 ff. and 556.

[34] In some cases (Lebanon, Saudi Arabia, and Syria), the actual signing of the Declaration did not take place until after the deadline. See State Dept. *Bulletin,* Vol. XII, No. 303 (Apr. 15, 1945), pp. 681–82. For decisions on these states and those on Iceland, Denmark, and Italy, see Russell, pp. 626–28.

[35] UNCIO, *Documents,* V, 93 ff. See also Russell, pp. 628–31, and 636–37.

included as original members of the Organization but also be invited to take part in the Conference. After some maneuvering, the Soviet proposal was accepted unanimously, if not enthusiastically, by the conferees.[36]

The second issue, the extension of an invitation to Argentina, provoked a more spirited debate. In negotiations with the other American republics preceding the San Francisco Conference, the United States had agreed, with some reluctance, to support Argentina for membership in the United Nations provided that that country demonstrated its acceptance of the principles agreed upon by the United States and the other Latin American states at the Mexico City Conference of February–March 1945.[37] After Argentina declared war on the Axis on March 27, the United States was willing to resume diplomatic relations but was still unwilling to sponsor Argentina's signature to the Declaration by United Nations. But, eventually, the United States joined with the Latin American states in proposing that Argentina be invited to attend the San Francisco Conference. Despite vocal Soviet opposition, this invitation was extended.[38]

There was one additional participant. During the opening phase of the Conference, Denmark was represented by an "observer." Subsequently, after the withdrawal of German forces and the establishment of a government, Denmark was invited (June 5, 1945) to participate fully in the San Francisco proceedings.

As can be seen from the above, the "arithmetic" of Article 3 is rather complicated. In brief, there were forty-seven signers of the Declaration by United Nations. Forty-six of these (all but Poland) "participated" in the San Francisco Conference from the outset. Subsequent invitations to Argentina, Byelorussia, Ukraine, and Denmark raised the number of participants to fifty. On October 15, Poland finally signed the Charter. Thus, there were fifty-one countries that signed and ratified the Charter [39] and therefore qualified as "original" members of the Organization in accordance with Article 3.

The Meaning of the Term "States"

Although Article 3 designates the original members of the United Nations as "states," clearly the word was not intended to have the meaning usually given to it in international law. It is sometimes diffi-

---

[36] UNCIO, *Documents,* I, 344, and V, 90–93 and 155. See also Russell, pp. 636–39.

[37] See Russell, ch. xxii.

[38] UNCIO, *Documents,* I, 344–59, and V, 155–56 and 376–81. See also Russell, 632–33 and 637–39.

[39] On ratification, see commentary on Art. 110.

cult to draw a firm distinction between "states" and other international entities, such as protectorates. The membership provision of the League Covenant (Article 1) used the phrase "any fully self-governing State, Dominion or Colony." Obviously, two original members of the United Nations—Byelorussia and the Ukraine—were not "states" in any sense of the word as used in international affairs. At San Francisco, there were other participants that did not enjoy that degree of independence usually associated with the term "state." The Philippines did not become fully independent until July 4, 1946; the final transfer of sovereignty by the British in India did not occur until August 15, 1947. Moreover, there was some ambiguity as to the status of Syria and Lebanon. Both had been mandates under the League system, and their independence had been declared and generally accepted, but final arrangements with France (the mandatory power) had not been completed at the time the two countries became original members of the United Nations.

The problem raised by the fact that some of the contemplated original members were not yet fully independent was recognized at San Francisco. Various drafting changes were suggested as a consequence, including the elimination of the word "states" from Article 3 and the substitution of "nations" for "states" in relevant provisions of the Charter. Finally, it was decided to use the term "states" with the understanding that, regardless of their status, all participants in the conference that signed and ratified the Charter would be "original members" of the Organization.[40]

Article 4

1. Membership in the United Nations is open to all other peace-loving states which accept the obligations contained in the present Charter and, in the judgment of the Organization, are able and willing to carry out these obligations.

2. The admission of any such state to membership in the United Nations will be effected by a decision of the General Assembly upon the recommendation of the Security Council.

One of the most remarkable phenomena of the postwar era has been the expansion of the number of independent sovereign states. In this development the United Nations has played an important role; at the same time, this revolutionary change in the character of the international community has had a profound effect upon the Organization itself. By the end of 1965, the United Nations had grown from the fifty-

40 Russell, pp. 927 ff.

one original members to 117 members, and further additions were anticipated.

Expansion of Membership

The path to achieving this great expansion of United Nations membership was not smooth. Differences among the major powers precluded the admission of all but a handful of new members during the first decade of the Organization's history. The Security Council and the General Assembly readily agreed in 1946 to the admission of four states that had been neutral during World War II—Afghanistan, Iceland, Sweden, and Thailand (Siam).[41] Yemen was admitted in 1947 and that same year, after the subdivision of the Indian subcontinent and the transfer of sovereignty from the United Kingdom, Pakistan also became a member. Burma was admitted in 1949. Israel's application was approved in May, 1949. After the formal transfer of sovereignty from the Netherlands, Indonesia joined the Organization in 1950. Thus, in five years, nine new members were admitted to the United Nations, but during that same period nearly twice as many applications were turned down.

The Western powers refused to support the five Soviet-backed candidates—Albania, Bulgaria, Hungary, Mongolia, and Romania. Their applications, consequently, failed to receive the necessary seven votes in the Security Council. In turn, the Soviet Union used its veto to block the admission of the other applicants. From 1950 to 1955, the issue of the admission of new members remained completely deadlocked.[42]

As the list of candidates continued to grow, pressure for a solution to the impasse mounted, and was particularly apparent in the annual debates in the General Assembly. When the tenth session convened (1955), it seemed possible that agreement might be reached on approving all pending applications, except for those from the "divided" countries of Korea and Vietnam. The Assembly asked the Council to give prompt consideration to this possibility.[43] Hopes for the admission of these eighteen applicants received a setback when China used its veto in the Council to block the admission of the Mongolian People's Republic. The Soviet Union then withdrew its support from the arrangement. The next day, however, the USSR introduced a new proposal that excluded not only the two divided countries but also

[41] This application was delayed for a short time until difficulties with France were straightened out.

[42] For discussion on the development of the deadlock and the efforts to break it, see below pp. 94–96.

[43] GA Res. 918(X), Dec. 8, 1955.

Mongolia and Japan. This was approved by the Council and subsequently by the Assembly. Thus, on December 14, 1955, the impasse on membership was finally broken with the admission of Albania, Austria, Bulgaria, Cambodia, Ceylon, Finland, Hungary, Ireland, Italy, Jordan, Laos, Libya, Nepal, Portugal, Romaina, and Spain.[44]

Table 2
MEMBERS ADMITTED TO THE UNITED NATIONS, 1946–1965

Afghanistan	Nov. 19, 1946	Libya	Dec. 14, 1955
Albania	Dec. 14, 1955	Madagascar	Sept. 20, 1960
Algeria	Oct. 8, 1962	Malawi	Dec. 1, 1964
Austria	Dec. 14, 1955	* Malaysia	Sept. 17, 1957
Bulgaria	Dec. 14, 1955	Maldive Islands	Sept. 21, 1965
Burma	Apr. 19, 1948	Mali	Sept. 29, 1960
Burundi	Sept. 18, 1962	Malta	Dec. 1, 1964
Cambodia	Dec. 14, 1955	Mauritania	Oct. 27, 1961
Cameroon	Sept. 20, 1960	Mongolia	Oct. 27, 1961
Central African Rep.	Sept. 20, 1960	Morocco	Nov. 12, 1956
Ceylon	Dec. 14, 1955	Nepal	Dec. 14, 1955
Chad	Sept. 20, 1960	Niger	Sept. 20, 1960
Congo (Brazzaville)	Sept. 20, 1960	Nigeria	Oct. 7, 1960
Congo (Leopoldville)	Sept. 20, 1960	Pakistan	Sept. 30, 1947
Cyprus	Sept. 20, 1960	Portugal	Dec. 14, 1955
Dahomey	Sept. 20, 1960	Romania	Dec. 14, 1955
Finland	Dec. 14, 1955	Rwanda	Sept. 18, 1962
Gabon	Sept. 20, 1960	Senegal	Sept. 28, 1960
The Gambia	Sept. 21, 1965	Sierra Leone	Sept. 27, 1961
Ghana	Mar. 8, 1957	Singapore	Sept. 21, 1965
Guinea	Dec. 12, 1958	Somalia	Sept. 20, 1960
Hungary	Dec. 14, 1955	Spain	Dec. 14, 1955
Iceland	Nov. 19, 1946	Sudan	Nov. 12, 1956
Indonesia	Sept. 28, 1950	Sweden	Nov. 19, 1946
Ireland	Dec. 14, 1955	** Tanganyika	Dec. 14, 1961
Israel	May 11, 1949	Thailand	Dec. 16, 1946
Italy	Dec. 14, 1955	Togo	Sept. 20, 1960
Ivory Coast	Sept. 20, 1960	Trinidad & Tobago	Sept. 18, 1962
Jamaica	Sept. 18, 1962	Tunisia	Nov. 12, 1956
Japan	Dec. 18, 1956	Uganda	Oct. 25, 1962
Jordan	Dec. 14, 1955	Upper Volta	Sept. 20, 1960
Kenya	Dec. 16, 1963	Yemen	Sept. 30, 1947
Kuwait	May 14, 1963	Zambia	Dec. 1, 1964
Laos	Dec. 14, 1955	** Zanzibar	Dec. 16, 1963

* Originally admitted as the Federation of Malaya.
** Became a single member as United Republic of Tanganyika and Zanzibar on April 26, 1964, changing its name to the United Republic of Tanzania on November 1, 1964.

[44] GA Res. 995(X), Dec. 14, 1955. For the debate, see GAOR/10th Sess., ad hoc Pol. Ctte./25th–32d Mtgs./Dec. 1–7, 1955/pp. 107–54; 552d and 555th–556th Plen. Mtgs./Dec. 8 and 14–15, 1955/pp. 409–20 and 433–35; SCOR/10th Yr./701st–705th Mtgs./Dec. 10–14, 1955.

This action did not end all controversy over the admission of new members. There were still occasions when the veto was used to block applications, but the main obstacle to the expansion of the Organization's membership had been removed.

The divided countries of Germany, Korea, and Vietnam remain outside the Organization. Switzerland has chosen not to join the United Nations, partly for fear of jeopardizing its cherished neutrality. Nevertheless, the United Nations has become a "universal" organization to an extent far beyond that of the essentially European-oriented League of Nations, and at a pace far more rapid than even the most far-sighted of the drafters of the Charter could have dreamed.

Criteria for Membership

The idea that membership in the United Nations should be limited to "peace-loving" states first found expression in the Moscow Declaration of October 30, 1943, in which China, the United Kingdom, the Soviet Union, and the United States agreed to the establishment of a general international organization to maintain international peace and security. The phrase was incorporated in the Dumbarton Oaks Proposals, which declared that membership in the Organization should be open to all "peace-loving states." At the San Francisco Conference, it was generally agreed that the Dumbarton Oaks text was inadequate and that "adherence to the principles of the Charter and complete acceptance of the obligations arising therefrom were essential conditions to participation by States in the Organization." [45] Various additional criteria were suggested, including one that members should have "democratic institutions." [46] It was decided, however, that any attempt to evaluate the character and policies of governments would raise difficulties and might indeed be "a breach of the principle of non-intervention" in the affairs of sovereign states. The decision against enumeration of additional elements was not intended to imply that "considerations of all kinds" could not be taken into account "in passing upon the admission of a new member." [47] When, subsequently, the International Court of Justice, at the request of the General Assembly, rendered an advisory opinion upon the conditions for the admission of new members, it took a more restrictive view.[48]

As pointed out in the discussion of original membership in the United Nations,[49] the term "state" is not used in the Charter in any

---

[45] UNCIO, *Documents*, VII, 326.
[47] UNCIO, *Documents*, VII, 326.
[49] See pp. 84–85.

[46] See Russell, p. 844.
[48] *ICJ Reports*, 1948, p. 65.

narrow legal sense. During the debates on the admission of new members, there have been numerous instances, especially in the Security Council, in which questions have been raised as to whether an applicant was a truly sovereign, independent state.[50]

On the one hand, doubt about the status of Outer Mongolia was a major factor in the initial failure of the Council to approve that country's application. On the other hand, the Soviet Union asserted that states such as Ceylon, Jordan, and Nepal, which had formerly been under British jurisdiction, could not be considered independent states because of the nature of their continuing ties with London. In 1952, the Soviet Union similarly judged as unqualified for United Nations membership the "Associated States" of Indochina—Cambodia, Laos, and Vietnam—which, in the Soviet view, were not sovereign states but "French puppets." At the same time, France charged that the Democratic Republic of Vietnam was so completely lacking in the necessary qualifications that its application for membership should not even be considered. The applications of the Republic of Korea and the Peoples Democratic Republic of Korea prompted a similar series of charges concerning their status.

Applications have been opposed because of legal claims by members against the territories concerned. As a result of Soviet backing of Iraq's claims, Kuwait was initially denied United Nations membership.[51] Although Mauritania's initial application was also vetoed by the Soviet Union in support of Moroccan claims,[52] it was accepted the next year. The controversial status of Israel, including the hotly disputed issue of the extent of its borders, was one of the major reasons why Israel's initial application failed to gain majority support in the Council, although following the cessation of hostilities with its Arab neighbors, the application was approved.[53] In so far as the interpretation of the term "state" has been raised in discussions on new members, remarks have tended to reflect attitudes of a political nature rather than concern with whether the applicant meets legal requirements.[54]

Initially, the phrase "peace-loving state" tended to be used to describe a country that had joined in the fight against the Axis. At the

---

[50] See *Repertoire of the Security Council*, 1946–1951, pp. 272–73, for considerations that have been raised in connection with statehood of applicants.

[51] SCOR/16th Yr./985th Mtg./Nov. 30, 1961.

[52] SCOR/15th Yr./911th Mtg./Dec. 4, 1960/p. 44; and 16th Yr./971st Mtg./Oct. 25, 1961/p. 13; and GA Res. 1602(XV), Oct. 27, 1961.

[53] SCOR/3d Yr., No. 130/386th Mtg./Dec. 17, 1948/p. 37; 4th Yr., No. 17/414th Mtg./Mar. 4, 1949/p. 14; and GA Res. 273 (III), May 11, 1949.

[54] There was, however, considerable discussion of legal issues in connection with Irsael's application for membership. See in particular the analysis presented by the U.S. representative. SCOR/3d Yr., No. 128/383d Mtg./Dec. 2, 1948/pp. 8–14.

least, a "peace-loving state" had to be anti-fascist (or at the very least non-fascist) in character. The San Francisco Conference agreed on an interpretative commentary which declared ineligible for admission to membership "states whose regimes have been established with the help of military forces belonging to the countries which have waged war against the United Nations," as long as those regimes are in power.[55] This statement, directed particularly against the Franco government in Spain, was reaffirmed by the Potsdam Declaration of August 2, 1945. The United Kingdom, the Soviet Union, and the United States stated that they did not "favour any application for membership" from the Franco regime which, "having been founded with the support of the Axis powers," did not "in view of its origins, its nature, its record and its close association with the aggressor States, possess the qualifications necessary to justify" membership in the United Nations.[56] Both statements were subsequently endorsed by the General Assembly in 1946.[57]

At Potsdam, the three governments also agreed to support the admission of states that had remained neutral during the war, so long as they met the qualifications set down in the Charter. Thus, they accepted the principle that active participation in the war against the Axis was not a precondition to a state's being considered "peace-loving." Nonetheless, the wartime activities of applicants continued to be a factor in debates on admission. The relations of Ireland and Portugal with the Axis powers and Franco Spain were cited by the Soviet Union in opposition to their admission to membership. Greece opposed Albania's application partly on the ground of its activities during World War II.

The Potsdam Conference opened the way for the reentry of some of the former enemy states into the international community. Britain, the Soviet Union, and the United States declared that the conclusion of peace treaties with "recognized democratic" governments in Bulgaria, Finland, Hungary, Italy, and Romania would enable them to support applications for the membership of these countries in the United Nations.[58] It was not until 1955 that these states were finally admitted. The Western powers protested over the way governments were established in Bulgaria, Hungary, and Romania, and subsequently charged these governments with failure to live up to the terms of the peace treaties. The Soviet Union blocked the admission of Italy and Finland as long as the three Eastern European states were not admitted to the United Nations.

[55] UNCIO, *Documents*, I, 615–16.
[56] State Dept., *Potsdam Conference Documents*, II, 1493.
[57] GA Res. 32(I), Feb. 9, 1946. In 1955, Spain was admitted to the UN with a minimum amount of opposition. GA Res. 995(X), Dec. 14, 1955.
[58] State Dept., *Potsdam Conference Documents*, II, 1492.

Adverse "findings" by United Nations organs and disregard of United Nations resolutions have been frequently cited as grounds that applicants could not be considered "peace-loving." For example, reasons for members' unwillingness to support Albania's application included: 1) the finding by the International Court as to Albania's responsibility for damage to British ships in the Corfu Channel; 2) its refusal to carry out the Court's award in that case; 3) other indications of Albania's unwillingness to carry out its international obligations; 4) the findings concerning the support given by Albania to rebel forces in Greece; and 5) Albania's refusal to cooperate with United Nations efforts to bring about a settlement of that situation. The last two points were also raised in connection with Bulgaria's application. The defiance of United Nations resolutions by the North Koreans was cited among the reasons for denying that regime admission to membership. One may also note that the approval of Israel's application for membership was preceded by extensive questioning in the Assembly, as to Israel's attitude toward various United Nations resolutions.[59]

Article 4 requires that applicants "accept" the obligations contained in the Charter. Under the rules of the Security Council and the General Assembly, an application for membership must contain "a declaration made in a formal instrument that it accepts" these obligations.[60]

While it is for the applicant to declare its acceptance of Charter obligations, it is for the Organization itself to pass "judgment" on whether the applicant is "able and willing" to carry out those obligations. Discussions concerning the "ability" of states to carry out their obligations have been closely connected with arguments as to whether the applicant is an independent sovereign state and is "peace-loving."

At San Francisco, the question was raised whether a state could become a member of the United Nations and still retain a permanent "neutral" status. The answer was negative. It was pointed out that the Security Council decisions that a member would be obligated to carry out might involve participation in economic or military sanctions, which would be incompatible with a "neutral" status.[61] In this connection, it should be noted that obligations under the Charter take precedence over obligations under any other international agreement.[62]

Concern for its neutral status has been a major reason for Switzer-

[59] GAOR/3d Sess., 2d Part, ad hoc Pol. Ctte./45th–51st Mtgs./May 5–9, 1949/ pp. 227–355.

[60] SC Provisional Rules of Procedure, Rule 58; and GA Rules of Procedure, Rule 135. Originally, a separate declaration was filed after the applicant had been admitted.

[61] UNCIO, *Documents*, VII, 327.

[62] See commentary on Art. 103.

land's not joining the United Nations.[63] The incompatibility between "neutrality" and the obligation to participate in United Nations enforcement measures was the subject of extensive debate in Japan prior to that country's admission to the United Nations because of the clauses in the Japanese Constitution renouncing war and precluding the maintenance of military forces.[64] These provisions were in the end not considered as an impediment to United Nations membership. The matter was not even discussed by the Security Council or the General Assembly in connection with Japan's application. Nor was there any discussion in connection with Austria's application of the fact that as part of the arrangements for ending the postwar occupation of that country, Austria's "permanent neutrality" had been guaranteed.

The two issues most stressed in discussions on the "willingness" of an applicant to carry out the obligations of the Charter have been the candidate's record in fulfilling in good faith its obligations under other international instruments and in cooperating with United Nations efforts to promote the purposes of the Organization. The previously mentioned discussions concerning the "peace-loving" nature of applicants are relevant here. The discussion on the admission of Bulgaria, Hungary, and Romania is of interest. Among the reasons put forward for refusing to support their applications were that the three countries had failed to carry out their obligations under the peace treaties regarding the observance of human rights and fundamental freedoms, and that they had refused to comply with their treaty obligations for the settlement of disputes over these issues, despite an advisory opinion by the International Court and resolutions adopted by the United Nations General Assembly.

Differences among members as to whether a candidate met the qualifications set out in Article 4 contributed to the long deadlock on the admission of new members, but the central issue was the denial of membership to applicants for reasons unrelated to the conditions set forth in Article 4(1). The Soviet Union took the position that it would block all applications for admission so long as Soviet-supported candidates were excluded from the Organization.

This situation prompted the General Assembly to request an advisory opinion from the International Court on the conditions for admission of members to the United Nations. The Court gave a negative answer to the Assembly's question whether a member was "juridically entitled to make its consent to the admission dependent on conditions

[63] Jacqueline Belin, *La Suisse et Les Nations Unies* (New York, Carnegie Endowment for International Peace, 1956), pp. 71 ff.

[64] Japanese Association of International Law, *Japan and the United Nations* (New York, Carnegie Endowment for International Peace, 1958), especially pp. 197–217.

not expressly provided" by Article 4(1). In the Court's opinion, the conditions listed in that article "constitute an exhaustive enumeration"; they are "not merely stated by way of guidance or example." In answer to a second question, the Court stated that "in particular" a member cannot "subject its affirmative vote to the additional condition that other States be admitted to membership." [65] This opinion was supported by a majority (nine) of the judges. In general, the dissenting judges took the position that a state may, in making determinations under Article 4, be guided by political considerations, and that so long as it is acting in good faith in accordance with the purposes and principles of the Organization, its determinations cannot be questioned.

Process of Admission: The Roles of the Security Council and General Assembly

In requiring that an applicant for membership in the United Nations must be approved by both the General Assembly and the Security Council, the Charter departs from the League Covenant, under which admission of new members was a function of the Assembly alone. At San Francisco, there was considerable support for continuing the League system. On the other hand, it was emphasized that the primary purpose of the Charter was "to provide security against a repetition" of World War II, and that therefore "the Security Council should assume the initial responsibility of suggesting new participating states." [66]

An application for membership is submitted to the Secretary-General and must contain "in a formal instrument" a declaration accepting the obligations contained in the Charter.[67] In accordance with the Provisional Rules of Procedure of the Council, the letter of application is placed upon the provisional agenda and the Council decides whether or not to consider it.[68] The Rules state that, unless the Council decides otherwise, the application is to be referred to the Committee on the Admission of New Members, a body composed of all the members of the Council. The Committee is charged with examining the applications and reporting to the Council thereon. It may, if it so desires, require information from the applicants.[69] For several years, applica-

---

[65] *ICJ Reports,* 1948, p. 65.   [66] UNCIO, *Documents,* VII, 451.

[67] SC, Provisional Rules of Procedure, Rule 58; GA, Rules of Procedure, Rule 135.

[68] The Secretary-General must place any application for membership before the members of the Council (see Rules 7 and 59). Normally, applications are automatically placed on the agenda. The application from the Democratic Republic of Vietnam, first made in November, 1948, was not discussed by the Council until 1952. See SCOR/7th Yr./600th and 603d Mtgs./Sept. 16 and 19, 1952.

[69] SC, Provisional Rules of Procedure, Rule 59.

tions have been discussed directly by the Council without reference to Committee.[70]

After the members of the Council and invited members (if any) have expressed their views, the Council customarily proceeds to vote upon a simple draft resolution stating that the Council has "examined the application" and "recommends to the General Assembly" that the applicant "be admitted to membership in the United Nations." The concurring votes of the permanent members of the Council are required for the adoption of the resolution. If the application is approved, the Council's recommendation, together with "a complete record of the discussion," is forwarded to the Assembly. If the Council does not recommend the applicant for admission, or if it postpones consideration of the application, it is required to submit a "special report" to the Assembly, together with a complete record of the discussion. Under this rule,[71] the Council is required to make its recommendations well in advance of an Assembly session. It is not always possible for the Council to do so, since its actions are to some extent dependent upon the timing of the submission of applications. Generally, when an application has been received after an Assembly session has started, the Council has considered the application, and has submitted its recommendation to the Assembly as quickly as possible.

During the first ten years a large number of applications failed to receive the necessary majority support in the Security Council or the necessary unanimous support of the permanent members. The situation was seriously aggravated by the position that the Soviet Union adopted in making its support of certain applications conditional upon the "simultaneous" admission of candidates that had Soviet, but not Western, backing.

The search for ways to end the deadlock that developed over admission of new members took various forms. Efforts were made to minimize or circumvent the role of the Security Council. Australia introduced suggestions in both the Council and the General Assembly emphasizing the primary and final responsibility of the Assembly on membership questions.[72] Australia had played a leading part in the efforts at San Francisco to restrict the Council's role by proposing that the Council be associated with the process only in the case of the

[70] For discussion on this point, see SCOR/7th Yr./598th–599th Mtgs./Sept. 10 and 12, 1952.

[71] Rule 60 of the Provisional Rules of Procedure. The wording of this rule was the result of negotiations in 1947 between the Council's Committee of Experts and a committee of the Assembly; the latter organ being concerned about the bottling up of applications by the Council. See *Repertoire of the Security Council,* 1946–1951, pp. 260–62.

[72] SCOR/1st Yr., 1st Ser., No. 2/41st Mtg./May 16, 1946/pp. 261–66; GAOR/ 1st Sess., 2d Part, 1st Ctte./1946/*Annexes,* p. 318.

admission of ex-enemy states,[73] but was no more successful in the United Nations than at San Francisco in securing acceptance of its suggestions.

Argentina put forward an even more radical thesis concerning the process of admission. While conceding that the Charter gives the Council the power to recommend admission of new members, the Argentine position was that the Assembly should proceed to decide on applications regardless of the Council's action. When asked by the Assembly for an advisory opinion on this matter, the International Court rejected this interpretation:

The admission of a State to membership in the United Nations, pursuant to paragraph 2 of Article 4 of the Charter, cannot be effected by a decision of the General Assembly when the Security Council has made no recommendation for admission by reason of the candidate failing to obtain the requisite majority or of the negative vote of a permanent Member upon a resolution so to recommend.[74]

The second line of attack was against the use of the veto in the Security Council on membership questions. Apprehension about the use of the veto in this connection had been voiced at the San Francisco Conference. Some Council members have contended that the veto should not be considered applicable to the admission of new members,[75] and the Assembly itself has recommended that the decision should be made by any seven members of the Council.[76] These efforts were unsuccessful, as were the Assembly's related efforts to put pressure on the Security Council by adopting various resolutions concerning those applications that had failed, for one reason or another, to get approval by the Council.

In these resolutions the General Assembly adopted several different approaches: it requested the Council to reexamine pending applications [77] and, in the cases of those applicants barred because of the Soviet veto, it adopted resolutions declaring that in the Assembly's judgment they fully met the conditions set forth in Article 4(1), and should therefore be admitted to membership.[78] On two occasions, as mentioned, the Assembly sought the advice of the International

[73] UNCIO, *Documents*, VIII, 296 and 299.   [74] *ICJ Reports*, 1950, p. 10.

[75] See, for example, statements by Argentina and Cuba. SCOR/3d Yr./279th Mtg./Apr. 10, 1948/p. 8; 12th Yr./790th Mtg./Sept. 9, 1957/pp. 3 and 10.

[76] GA Res. 176(III), Apr. 14, 1949. See also GA Res. 296K(IV), Nov. 22, 1949, which specifically requests the permanent members to refrain from using the veto in connection with recommendations for membership.

[77] GA Res. 35(I), Nov. 19, 1946; 495(V), Dec. 4, 1950; 506(VI), Feb. 1, 1952; and 620A(VII), Dec. 21, 1952.

[78] GA Res. 113C-H(II), Nov. 17, 1947; 197C-I(III), Dec. 8, 1948; 296B-J(IV), Nov. 22, 1949; and 620B-G(VII), Dec. 21, 1952.

Court.[79] Subsequently, it established a "special" committee to make a detailed study of the question.[80]

With the failure of attempts to put pressure on the Council, efforts were made to find some acceptable compromise solution. The Assembly itself established a "committee of good offices" to consult with the members of the Council with the object of "exploring the possibilities of reaching an understanding which might facilitate the admission of new members." [81] Finally, at the tenth session of the Assembly in 1955, agreement was reached on the "simultaneous admission" of applicants with Soviet and Western backing.[82]

Article 5

A Member of the United Nations against which preventive or enforcement action has been taken by the Security Council may be suspended from the exercise of the rights and privileges of membership by the General Assembly upon the recommendation of the Security Council. The exercise of these rights and privileges may be restored by the Security Council.

The initiative for inclusion of a provision for suspension of members came from the United States and was based upon the belief that this course was preferable to the expulsion of members from the Organization. The concept of suspension was accepted at Dumbarton Oaks, although the Soviet Union insisted that the Charter should provide for expulsion as well.

At San Francisco, a substantial majority favored deleting the provision concerning expulsion, while at the same time broadening the conditions for suspension to cover not only members against which the Council was taking action but also members that "violated the principles of the Charter in a grave or persistent fashion." [83] This amendment to the provision for suspension was subsequently dropped when the Conference finally accepted the provision for expulsion.

The exercise of rights and privileges of a member can be suspended only if the Security Council has already decided to take "preventive or enforcement action" against that member. Clearly, Article 5 would be applicable if the Council decided to take the measures open to it under Articles 41 and 42. It is doubtful whether suspension would be considered appropriate under any other circumstances. The records of

79 GA Res. 113B(II), Nov. 17, 1947; and 296(IV), Nov. 22, 1949.
80 GA Res. 620A(VII), Dec. 21, 1952.
81 GA Res. 718(VIII), Oct. 23, 1953, and 817(IX), Nov. 23, 1954.
82 For details on the action taken, see above pp. 86–87.
83 UNCIO, *Documents*, VII, 115.

the United Nations throw no light on this point, since the question of suspending a member has never been raised in either the General Assembly or the Security Council, partially because the Council has never taken action against a member that has been clearly labeled as "preventive or enforcement."

It should be noted that the suspension of a member's rights and privileges does not follow automatically from a decision by the Security Council to take preventive or enforcement action. Initially, the Security Council must recommend suspension and the concurrence of the permanent members is required. To become effective, the recommendation of the Council must then be approved by two-thirds of the members present and voting in the General Assembly (Article 18). Suspension is thus a joint action of the two organs. However, under Article 5, restoration of rights and privileges is left to the Security Council alone. This is in part a reflection of the primary responsibility of the Council for the maintenance of international peace and security. A move at San Francisco to associate the Assembly with this decision was defeated, mainly on the ground that the Council, being in continuous session, could take this action speedily, while reference to the Assembly might entail undesirable delay.

The Charter does not delineate the rights and privileges that would be affected by suspension. This matter was not considered during the discussions on the drafting of the Charter, nor has it ever been discussed in the United Nations itself. Clearly, the suspended member would lose its right to be represented (and to vote) in the General Assembly. It would not be eligible for election to any of the three Councils; and if elected previously, it could not continue to serve on them. On a number of other points, the effect of suspension is less clear.

Because Article 5 specifically refers to the rights and privileges of *members,* it can be argued that the status of a suspended member would be analogous to that of a nonmember of the United Nations.[84] The suspended member would then retain the right to bring to the attention of the General Assembly or the Security Council any dispute to which it was a party and to participate in the Council's discussion of that dispute (Article 35[2] and 32). By the same line of reasoning, suspension would not necessarily deprive the member of all rights of access to the International Court of Justice, since under certain circumstances the Court is "open" to states not members of the United Nations.[85] Given the general interest of the United Nations in promoting

[84] For a contrary view, see Hans Kelsen, *The Law of the United Nations* (London, Stevens, 1950), p. 713.
[85] See commentary on Art. 93.

the fullest utilization of procedures of peaceful settlement, there would be good reasons for considering that a suspended member should be accorded the same rights and privileges of access as those permitted to nonmember states.

Finally, it should be noted that membership in the United Nations has not been considered as a prerequisite for a state's being designated an administering authority of a trust territory. By analogy, a suspended member could continue to administer a trust territory but its right to participate in the work of the Trusteeship Council (especially its right to vote) would no doubt be restricted. This matter was touched upon at San Francisco, but no conclusions were reached. In reply to questions concerning what would happen if a state administering a trust territory committed aggression or withdrew from the Organization, the position of the United Kingdom and the United States was that the action to be taken in such a case could only be decided "in the light of all the circumstances prevailing at the time." [86]

Suspension of a member's rights and privileges can be viewed from two angles: one, as a step to preclude the member from hindering in any way the preventive and enforcement action being carried out by the Security Council; and two, as a means of applying additional pressure upon the state to comply with the Council's directives. While the need for the Organization to take effective measures for the prevention or suppression of threats to, or breaches of, the peace would be paramount, it may be assumed that, in so far as is possible, the other purposes of the United Nations—promotion of peaceful settlement and international economic and social cooperation—would not be unduly jeopardized.

Article 6

A Member of the United Nations which has persistently violated the Principles contained in the present Charter may be expelled from the Organization by the General Assembly upon the recommendation of the Security Council.

The Soviet Union proposed such a provision during the Dumbarton Oaks Conversations [87] and forcefully defended its proposal at the San Francisco Conference. Many members considered that "suspension" was preferable to "expulsion" as a means for dealing with recalcitrant members. A suspended member would be deprived of rights and privileges but would still be bound by its obligation under the Charter. They argued that expulsion "would entail more drawbacks for the

[86] UNCIO, *Documents*, X, 620–21.   [87] See Russell, pp. 438–39.

Organization itself than for the state concerned" [88] and that it was likely to "close the door to subsequent reconciliation." Proponents of inclusion of the provision for expulsion argued that the principal purpose of the Organization was the maintenance of peace and security, not universality; that expulsion would not necessarily bar subsequent readmission, if such a step were justified; and that the Organization should be able to oust members that were "admittedly incorrigible." The Conference delegates eventually decided to provide in the Charter for the expulsion of members that "persistently" violated the principles of the Charter. The "Principles" referred to in Article 6 are presumably those set forth in Article 2.

The language of the article suggests that expulsion is a measure of last resort, to be taken only if a member persists in ignoring its obligations. By contrast, the League Covenant (Article 16 [4]) provided that any member violating "any covenant of the League" might be declared to be no longer a member. In fact, however, this provision was invoked only once—against the Soviet Union after its attack upon Finland in 1939.

Considering the seriousness of the action, the grounds for expulsion from the United Nations seem rather imprecisely worded. Yet it should be noted that expulsion is not an automatic action, but one to be decided upon by the two major political organs of the United Nations. As in the cases of admission and suspension, a majority of two-thirds of those present and voting is required in the General Assembly for expulsion of a member and this step can be taken only upon recommendation of the Security Council by a nonprocedural vote. Thus, the permanent members, and indeed any member supported by any one of them, are safeguarded against expulsion. Under the Covenant, the power of explusion was vested solely in the Council and, if the member concerned was represented on the Council, its vote was not counted.

In the United Nations, despite occasional statements made in the heat of debate that this or that member "ought" to be expelled, this step has never been taken. Growing hostility among the United Nations membership to the racial policies of the Republic of South Africa and its refusal to comply with United Nations wishes regarding the former mandated territory of South West Africa, has, however, led to discussion in the Assembly of the possible expulsion of that state from the Organization. At the sixteenth session in 1961, a group of African states proposed that the Assembly, among other things, draw the "attention" of the Security Council to Article 6 of the Charter with a view to an "early discussion of the continued membership" of South Africa in the United Nations. Although approved in committee, this proposal

[88] For divergent views on this subject, see UNCIO, *Documents,* VII, 330–31.

failed to obtain a two-thirds vote in plenary, as did a substitute proposal that the Security Council consider "what measures should be taken" against South Africa for its "persistent violations of the Charter." [89] At the next session, however, the Afro-Asian group mustered sufficient support for a resolution that included a request to the Security Council to take "appropriate measures, including sanctions . . . and, if necessary to consider action under Article 6 of the Charter." [90]

Some doubts have been raised, primarily by Latin American representatives, as to the propriety of the Assembly's action on the ground that under the Charter the initiative for expulsion should come from the Security Council, not the Assembly. However, as is usual in the United Nations, the debate has centered on the political wisdom, rather than the legal basis, of the proposed steps.

The principal arguments against the move to expel South Africa closely parallel the original opposition to the inclusion of Article 6 in the Charter: by expelling South Africa, the United Nations would be taking a "purely negative step"; expulsion would isolate South Africa and relieve it of its Charter obligations; and it would undermine the forces working for reform within the country and cut off all avenues of United Nations influence.

The 1961 and 1962 resolutions of the General Assembly "strongly" deprecate South Africa's "continued and total disregard . . . of its Charter obligations." South Africa's policies had been found "inconsistent" with the Charter and "incompatible" with United Nations membership.[91] Although the Assembly, over the years, has variously phrased its condemnation, it has not made a specific finding that South Africa has "persistently violated the Principles" of the Charter, the specific criterion for expulsion set down in Article 6 of the Charter.

[89] For the proposals, see GAOR/16th Sess., Special Pol. Ctte./1961/*Annexes,* agenda item 76 (A/4968, Nov. 14, 1961). For the debate, see *ibid.*, Special Pol. Ctte./267th–288th Mtgs./Oct. 23–Nov. 14, 1961/pp. 37–148, and 1067th Plen. Mtg./Nov. 28, 1961/pp. 882–90.

[90] GA Res. 1761(XVII), Nov. 6, 1962. For the debate, see GAOR/17th Sess., Special Pol. Ctte./327th–342d Mtgs./Oct. 8–Nov. 2, 1962/pp. 5–91; 1164th Plen. Mtg./Nov. 6, 1962/pp. 659–75.

[91] GA Res. 616(VII), Dec. 5, 1952, and 1248(XIII), Oct. 30, 1958. At its 1962 session, the Assembly adopted similar declarations concerning Portugal's attitude toward its overseas territories, Angola in particular: GA Res. 1807(XVII), Dec. 14, 1962, and 1819(XVII), Dec. 18, 1962.

CHAPTER III

Organs

Article 7

1. There are established as the principal organs of the United Nations: a General Assembly, a Security Council, an Economic and Social Council, a Trusteeship Council, an International Court of Justice, and a Secretariat.

2. Such subsidiary organs as may be found necessary may be established in accordance with the present Charter.

Principal Organs

The Charter lists six "principal" organs of the United Nations. The General Assembly, as the organ with broad authority on which all members are represented, and the Security Council, as the organ primarily responsible for the maintenance of international peace and security, are, naturally, principal organs of the Organization. The Covenant did not list the principal organs of the League; it merely stated that "the action of the League . . . shall be effected through the instrumentality of an Assembly and of a Council, with a permanent Secretariat" (Article 2). Raising the Secretariat's status in the United Nations to that of a principal organ reflects the responsibilities assigned to it and especially the political role of the Secretary-General which, under the Charter, is of much greater significance than was that of the Secretary-General of the League.

The International Court of Justice is a principal organ, and indeed the "principal judicial organ" of the United Nations (Article 92). Its predecessor, the Permanent Court of International Justice, was not formally accorded the same status, although for practical purposes the position of the Court has been much the same in the two systems. The inclusion of the Economic and Social Council (ECOSOC) and the Trusteeship Council among the principal organs of the United Nations underlines the importance attached to the activities of the United Nations in these fields. The decision to establish these two additional Councils, however, stemmed also from the belief that, at the Council

level, responsibilities in the economic and social field and in the supervision of the administration of trust territories should be separated
from responsibility for the maintenance of international peace and
security in which, it was recognized, the major military powers have a
special interest.

These six bodies, although listed as "principal organs," differ in the
degree of their independence. The General Assembly occupies a special position because of its control over the budgetary and administrative aspects of the Organization (Articles 17 and 101) and its role in
determining the composition of the other organs (Articles 23, 61, 86, 97
and Article 4 of the Statute of the International Court of Justice). Also,
the Assembly is authorized to discuss and make recommendations relating to the "powers and functions of any organs" provided for in the
Charter (Article 10). Furthermore, ECOSOC and the Trusteeship
Council both operate "under the authority of the General Assembly"
(Articles 60 and 85). In contrast, the Charter attempts to guard the
Security Council from encroachments upon its prerogatives by the
Assembly (Article 12).

Subsidiary Organs

Changes in the list of principal organs, including the creation of new
"principal" organs, would require amendment of the Charter. Article
7(2) makes it clear that there is no such limitation on the establishment of "subsidiary" organs. Both the Security Council and the General
Assembly are specifically authorized to establish "such subsidiary organs" as they deem "necessary for the performance" of their functions
(Articles 22 and 29). ECOSOC is instructed to set up commissions in
various fields of its activities (Article 68). In practice, all the principal
United Nations organs have from time to time established subsidiary
bodies of one type or another to assist them in their work.

As the *Repertory of United Nations Practice* points out, the term
"subsidiary organ" has not been defined by any organ of the United
Nations; in the practice of the Organization, "such expressions as 'commissions,' 'committees,' 'subsidiary organs,' 'subsidiary bodies,' and
'subordinate bodies' have been used interchangeably." [1] These have
varied greatly "as regards origin, composition, structure, function and
duration of existence." [2] Nonetheless, the *Repertory* lists the following
as "some features common to all subsidiary organs":

[1] *Repertory*, I, 224.
[2] For further discussion on this point, see the Secretariat study "Constitutional
Questions relating to Agencies within the Framework of the United Nations,"
GAOR/9th Sess./1954/*Annexes*, agenda item 67.

(a) A subsidiary organ is created by, or under the authority of, a principal organ of the United Nations;

(b) The membership, structure and terms of reference of a subsidiary organ are determined, and may be modified by, or under the authority of, a principal organ;

(c) A subsidiary organ may be terminated by, or under the authority of, a principal organ.[3]

Characteristically, a subsidiary organ has been established to carry out a specific task assigned to it by one of the principal organs and has gone out of existence when that task has been completed. Some, such as the United Nations Children's Fund, the Office of the United Nations High Commissioner for Refugees, and the United Nations Relief and Works Agency for Palestine Refugees in the Near East, are "operating agencies," functioning on a "continuing" basis. Others, such as the Advisory Committee on Administrative and Budgetary Questions, the International Law Commission, and the commissions of ECOSOC, have been established on a more or less "permanent" basis. Subsidiary organs in the United Nations system generally tend to be long-lived. There are exceptions, most notably subsidiary organs engaged in preparatory work, appointed to investigate particular situations, or asked to study and report on some aspect of the Organization's activities.

Although most subsidiary organs function under the direction of, and report to, the principal organ that created them, there have been numerous deviations from this pattern. The Atomic Energy Commission, for example, was established by the General Assembly but was to submit its reports and recommendations in the first instance to the Security Council; in matters concerning peace and security it was also accountable to the Council, which was authorized to issue directions to the Commission.[4] The Office of United Nations Mediator for Palestine was also created by the General Assembly,[5] but in fact the Mediator's main task was to work with the Security Council to bring about an armistice in Palestine.

In the economic and social fields, even more than in the political field, there has been a tendency to establish subsidiary bodies that operate under both ECOSOC and the General Assembly. In this connection, it should be noted that there are a few "special bodies" which, although they come within the United Nations framework, have a special relationship to that system. Most notable of these are the organs responsible for the international control of narcotic drugs. A distinctive feature of these organs is that their structure and terms of reference are

[3] *Repertory*, I, 228.   [4] GA Res. 1(I), Jan. 24, 1946.
[5] GA Res. 186(S-2), May 14, 1948.

established not by resolution of a principal organ of the United Nations but by international treaty.

In general, United Nations organs have followed a pragmatic approach to the creation of additional machinery. There has been a wide variety in the kinds of subsidiary and special organs established, with the details of composition, terms of reference, and methods of operation being adapted to the special requirements of the particular task to be undertaken.

Article 8

The United Nations shall place no restrictions on the eligibility of men and women to participate in any capacity and under conditions of equality in its principal and subsidiary organs.

The need for including a specific statement of this kind in the Charter was seriously questioned at the San Francisco Conference.[6] Many of the delegates, while not opposed in principle, believed that a specific reference was superfluous, since the principle of nondiscrimination was implicit throughout the Charter. It finds explicit expression in the Preamble, and in Articles 1(3), 55(c), and 76(c). Because some delegates attached considerable importance to having the principle expressly stated, it was finally decided to do so. Article 8 was placed in Chapter III of the Charter in order to emphasize that the principle of equality applied not only to the Secretariat but to all principal and subsidiary organs of the United Nations.

Drafting a suitable provision applicable to all United Nations organs proved difficult,[7] for the delegates wished to avoid impinging in any way upon the freedom of members to select their delegations. Article 7 of the League Covenant had stipulated that "all positions under or in connection with the League, including the Secretariat, shall be open equally to men and women." In contrast, Article 8 of the Charter is phrased in a negative form. It does not provide for equality, but merely prohibits any restrictions by the United Nations on the right of men and women "to participate . . . under conditions of equality."

The application of this article, not surprisingly, has been of special interest to the United Nations Commission on the Status of Women, which on numerous occasions has considered the participation of women in the work of the Organization.

With respect to positions in the Secretariat, the original staff regulations stated that men and women were equally eligible for all posts

---

[6] The Dumbarton Oaks Proposals contained no such provision.

[7] UNCIO, *Documents*, VII, 334–35.

(Staff Regulation 10). Subsequently, this regulation was replaced by a more comprehensive statement to the effect that, "in accordance with the principles of the Charter, selection of staff members shall be made without distinction as to race, sex, or religion (Staff Rule 53)." At each of its sessions from 1948 through 1955, the Commission on the Status of Women requested reports from the Secretary-General on the subject of the employment of women in the Secretariat and urged him to assure equal opportunity to women therein. The Commission has also repeatedly called attention to the desirability of appointing more women to senior posts within the Secretariat. Although the major emphasis has been upon the appointment and promotion of women, the Commission has also been concerned that there be no discrimination against women staff members concerning conditions of employment.

The Commission has repeatedly expressed the view that more governments should appoint women to posts on their delegations and asked the Secretary-General to supply data on this subject. ECOSOC, acting on the basis of the Commission's reports and recommendations, recommended that member states "consider women equally with men in appointing delegations to organs and agencies of the United Nations and to international bodies and conferences," [8] and endorsed the appointment of women to serve on visiting missions to trust territories.[9] In general, however, it has been felt that this is a matter to be decided by the governments themselves.

[8] ECOSOC Res. 154B(VII), Aug. 20, 1948.
[9] ECOSOC Res. 385E(XIII), Aug. 27, 1951.

CHAPTER IV

The General Assembly

As the one United Nations organ in which all members participate on an equal basis, the General Assembly performs the functions customarily assigned to a plenary body. These include elective functions in relation to the other principal organs; overall supervision of the financial and administrative affairs of the Organization; and constituent functions, exercised jointly with the Security Council, on such matters as membership and Charter amendments.[1]

In these respects the position of the General Assembly is similar to that of its predecessor, the League Assembly. With regard to the distribution of functions and powers between the General Assembly and the three Councils, however, the Charter system differs markedly from that of the League.

The Dumbarton Oaks Proposals clearly and avowedly adopted the principle that a distinction should be made between the functions and powers of the General Assembly and those of the Security Council in the maintenance of international peace and security in order to avoid the overlapping and alleged confusion that attended the granting of wide and undifferentiated powers to the Assembly and Council of the League. To this end, the drafters of the Charter attempted to state with some precision the nature and scope of the Assembly's powers. Its functions were to discuss, to consider, and to recommend, but not to take action. This was to be the prerogative of the Security Council. Furthermore, as the detailed provisions regarding the powers and procedures of the Security Council in dealing with disputes and situations suggested,[2] that organ was to have the primary responsibility for dealing with disputes and situations which endangered international peace and security.

At San Francisco, this allocation of powers came in for considerable

---

[1] The Assembly's powers, functions, and procedures as set out in ch. IV are supplemented by numerous provisions throughout the Charter regarding its role in specific areas. For elective functions, see Arts. 23, 61, 86, and 97 of the Charter and Arts. 4 to 12 of the Statute of the International Court; for financial and administrative affairs, see Arts. 17, 19, and 101; and for constituent functions, see chs. II and XVIII.

[2] Chs. VI and VIII of the Dumbarton Oaks Proposals.

criticism, and numerous proposals were made for increasing the powers of the General Assembly. These efforts met with a measure of success and as a result the Charter as finally drafted left the definition of the respective powers and responsibilities of the two organs somewhat unclear, thus opening the way to subsequent controversy and a substantial expansion in practice of the Assembly's powers and influence in the peace and security field.

In respect to economic and social matters and the problem of non-self-governing territories, the relation of the General Assembly to the Councils, in comparison with that under the League system, was initially conceived as favoring the more representative organ. Whereas the League Council had important independent responsibilities in these areas, the Economic and Social Council and the Trusteeship Council, while being given specific functions and powers, were expected to discharge their responsibilities "under the authority of the General Assembly." In practice the Assembly has chosen to exercise this authority to the full, with the result that the Councils have come to resemble more closely subsidiary organs than principal organs of the United Nations which the Charter declares them to be.

The General Assembly operates through plenary meetings, seven main committees, two sessional committees, and occasional ad hoc committees to expedite the work of the session.[3] Also the Assembly has a large number of subsidiary bodies of various types that function independently of sessions to implement Assembly resolutions or prepare matters for its further consideration. These are discussed in the commentary on Article 22.

At regular Assembly sessions the principal discussions and the preparation of most draft resolutions take place in the "main committees."[4] As in the plenary, all members are represented in these committees; their procedures, however, are less formal. Originally, there were six main committees:

Committee I	Political and Security
Committee II	Economic and Financial
Committee III	Social, Humanitarian, and Cultural
Committee IV	Trusteeship (including Non-Self-Governing Territories)
Committee V	Administrative and Budgetary
Committee VI	Legal

[3] The organization and procedures of the Assembly are discussed extensively in Sydney Bailey, *The General Assembly of the UN* (New York, Praeger, 1960).

[4] Except when the Assembly is meeting in emergency special session. See commentary on Art. 20.

Because of its heavy workload in the political field, the Assembly found it necessary to establish an additional committee. From 1947 through 1955, an ad hoc political committee was created at each session.[5] In 1956 the Special Political Committee was established on a permanent basis.

The Assembly's two "sessional" committees are the Credentials Committee and the General Committee.[6] The latter, presided over by the President and composed of the Vice-Presidents and the chairmen of the main committees, was intended as the "steering" committee for Assembly sessions. At the outset of each session it examines the items proposed for the agenda and makes recommendations thereon and on other matters for expediting the business of the session, including the setting of a target date for completion.

COMPOSITION

Article 9

1. The General Assembly shall consist of all the Members of the United Nations

2. Each Member shall have not more than five representatives in the General Assembly.

Composition of Delegations

One purpose of Article 9(2) was to protect smaller states which might not be able to send large delegations to the Assembly and might consequently be placed at a disadvantage unless the size of a delegation was limited.

At Dumbarton Oaks, it was agreed to limit the number of representatives, but no precise figure was set.[7] At San Francisco, there were those who preferred that no limits be set in the Charter, while others supported a limit of three representatives, which had been the number under the League Covenant (Article 3[4]). It was finally agreed that a maximum of five would provide for "a proper distribution of the work" of the Assembly.[8]

In addition to five representatives, each member under the Assem-

---

[5] The 1947 committee, the ad hoc committee on the Palestinian Question, dealt only with this one subject.

[6] See commentary on Art. 9.

[7] Ruth B. Russell, *A History of the United Nations Charter* (Washington, Brookings Institution, 1958), p. 425.

[8] UNCIO, *Documents,* VIII, 295 and 481.

bly's Rules of Procedure may appoint five alternate representatives and as many advisers, technical advisers, experts, and persons of similar status as may be required (Rule 25). Upon designation by the delegation chairman, an "alternate" may act as a representative (Rule 26). Advisers, experts, and persons of similar status may serve as representatives on Assembly committees but are not eligible to act as officers or to represent their country in plenary meetings (Rule 103).

Credentials

Under the Rules of Procedure, the credentials of representatives and the names of members of a delegation are to be submitted to the Secretary-General "if possible no less than one week before the date fixed for the opening of the session." They may be issued by "either the Head of State or Government or by the Minister for Foreign Affairs" (Rule 27). Telegraphed credentials are accepted provisionally. In the event of an objection regarding the credentials of any representative, he may sit "provisionally with the same rights as other representatives, until the Credentials Committee has reported and the General Assembly has given its decision" (Rule 29).

The Credentials Committee (consisting of nine members) is appointed at the beginning of each session on the proposal of the Acting President. Its task is to examine the credentials of representatives and report to the Assembly thereon "without delay" (Rules 49–51). For the first four years, the Committee had no difficulties in certifying that credentials were in proper form. Since 1950, objection has been raised on a number of occasions that the issuing authority was not legally entitled to act on behalf of the member state concerned. As a result, Assembly approval of the Credentials Committee's report has become one of the last rather than one of the first items of business to be considered at a session.

Disputes over Credentials and Representation

The question of representation in the Assembly was first considered in 1950 in connection with the Republic of China.[9] It has been considered on a number of subsequent occasions, chiefly in relation to China.

At its fifth session, the Assembly rejected an Indian proposal that the Central Government of the People's Republic of China was entitled to represent China in the Assembly. From 1951 through 1960,

[9] This gave rise to a general debate on the "Recognition by the United Nations of the Representation of a Member State." See commentary on ch. II.

a direct vote, and indeed a full discussion on this issue, was avoided through a decision either to "postpone" consideration or "not to consider" the matter. At each session, challenges to the credentials of the Nationalist government were raised in the Credentials Committee but were overruled. At its sixteenth session, the Assembly decided to include in its agenda the item "Restoration of the lawful rights of the People's Republic of China in the United Nations." A Soviet proposal to "remove" the representatives of the Nationalist government and invite the Central government of the People's Republic to send its representatives to participate in the work of the United Nations and all its organs was rejected.[10]

When the situation arising out of the Hungarian revolt was brought before an emergency special session of the Assembly in November, 1956, the situation was confused and the Hungarian Permanent Mission to the United Nations informed the Secretary-General that it had not been "authorized to take part" in the discussion. The Assembly decided to take no action on the Hungarian credentials.[11] Similar Assembly actions at each subsequent session through 1962 can be viewed as a form of protest as to the manner in which the revolt was put down.

When the Congo was admitted to membership at the opening of the fifteenth session, no delegation was seated because the "constitutional and political position in that country" was far from clear.[12] The Security Council reached an impasse on whether to seat the delegation authorized by Congolese President Kasavubu or the representative bearing credentials issued by Prime Minister Lumumba. Subsequently, a group of African and Asian members proposed that the Lumumba delegation be seated. At this point, the Congolese president arrived to address the Assembly.[13] In his statement, the president listed the members of the Congolese delegation with himself as head. Although the Assembly had decided to adjourn its discussion on the situation in the Congo, it proceeded after a bitter debate to accept the credentials issued by the head of state.[14]

Following the revolt in the Yemen in 1962, credentials were submitted by both the minister of foreign affairs of the Kingdom of the Yemen and by the president of the Yemen Arab Republic. The royalist

10 The Assembly decided that "any proposal to change the representation of China" was an "important question" and would therefore require the support of two-thirds of the members present and voting. GA Res. 1668(XVI), Dec. 15, 1961. This decision was reaffirmed in GA Res. 2025(XX), Nov. 17, 1965.

11 GA Res. 996(ES-I and II), Nov. 9, 1956.

12 Statement by the President. GAOR/15th Sess. 864th Mtg./Sept. 20, 1960/p. 6.

13 By tradition no credentials are required for Chiefs of State, although there is no rule to that effect.

14 GA Res. 1498(XV), Nov. 22, 1960.

delegation was seated provisionally in the Assembly but subsequently the credentials issued by the president of the Republic were accepted.[15]

In short, problems over the acceptance of credentials have arisen in some cases where the situation in the country concerned is unclear and in others where the members are divided on policy grounds as to which of conflicting sets of credentials should be accepted. Refusal to accept credentials has also been a form of protest, as in the Hungarian case and the Assembly decision in 1965 to take no action on the credentials of the South African delegation.[16]

FUNCTIONS AND POWERS

Article 10

The General Assembly may discuss any questions or any matters within the scope of the present Charter or relating to the powers and functions of any organs provided for in the present Charter, and, except as provided in Article 12, may make recommendations to the Members of the United Nations or to the Security Council or to both on any such questions or matters.

Article 10 states the General Assembly's powers of discussion and recommendation in their broadest form. Its place as the initial article in the enumeration of the Assembly's powers and functions indicates its importance. "The range of questions or matters which it authorizes the Assembly to discuss is as wide as the scope of the Charter itself." [17] The subsequent Charter provisions are in effect particularizations of these broad powers. Article 11(4), in establishing the Assembly's role in the maintenance of international peace and security, specifically states that its terms "shall not limit the general scope of Article 10."

The drafting of Article 10 provoked one of the gravest crises at the San Francisco Conference and was resolved only after direct, high-level exchanges between Washington and Moscow. In practice, it has been the principal basis for the expansion of the Assembly's role beyond that envisaged when the Charter was adopted.

The Dumbarton Oaks Proposals contained no such grant of authority and indeed one of the most widespread criticisms of the Proposals was that they gave the Assembly no real power in the political field. The result was a plethora of amendments submitted before and during the San Francisco Conference seeking a larger role for the Assembly. Most

[15] GA Res. 1871(XVII), Dec. 20, 1962.
[16] GA Res. 213A(XX), Dec. 21, 1965.   [17] *Repertory*, I, 257.

of these concerned its specific powers regarding the maintenance of international peace and security in relation to those of the Security Council,[18] but many were directed toward the inclusion in the Charter of some more general reference to the Assembly's freedom of discussion.

At an early stage in the committee debates at San Francisco, a decision was taken that the Assembly should have the power "to discuss and make recommendations in respect of any matters within the sphere of international relations" and that this power should be interpreted as broadly as possible.[19]

The desire of most members to include a specific provision to this effect ran into difficulties when the Soviet Union first objected and then insisted upon a qualifying clause limiting the Assembly's power of discussion to "any matter within the sphere of international relations *which affects the maintenance of international peace and security.*" [20] This proposal was rejected. When the Soviet Union later sought to reverse the committee's action and indicated that it would not sign the Charter unless the language was changed to meet its desires, the Conference found itself at one of the most critical points in its proceedings.

The rigidity of the Soviet position made compromise very difficult, for many other delegations were strongly opposed to any attempt to limit the Assembly's freedom of discussion, particularly in the light of the Soviet effort to restrict discussion in the Security Council by extending the scope of the permanent member's veto.[21] Only after the United States ambassador took the matter up directly with the Soviet foreign minister, emphasizing the seriousness of the situation, was agreement on an acceptable wording of Article 10 finally reached. This debate should be viewed in the context of the struggle by the smaller, especially the middle-sized, powers to protect their interests by broadening the powers of the one United Nations organ on which they would be fully represented.

The Assembly has seldom cited Article 10 in its resolutions. In few instances would it be possible to determine whether the Assembly was exercising its powers under Articles 10, 11, 14, or some combination thereof. As a practical matter this is of no significance, considering the similarity of its powers under all three articles.

[18] See commentary on Arts. 11 and 12.

[19] Subject only to the restriction on the Assembly's right to make recommendations when the Council was dealing with a particular question. See UNCIO, *Documents,* IX, 60.

[20] *Ibid.* For a full account of the complicated drafting history of Art. 10 and its relationship to action on other articles, see Russell, pp. 761–64 and 770–75.

[21] See commentary on Art. 27(3).

Article 10, however, has played a basic role in the Assembly's proceedings. This is best summarized in the following:

The "general scope" of this Article and the breadth of the powers of discussion which it confers on the Assembly have been referred to many times in committee and in plenary meeting by representatives who wished to stress the over-all responsibility of the Assembly as a world forum for the consideration of international problems and its role in the Organization as the only principal organ on which all States Members are represented. References of this type have not been confined to the discussion of political matters alone; they have also occurred in connexion with the consideration of questions relating to the Assembly's activities in the economic, social, and humanitarian spheres, questions concerning Non-Self-Governing and Trust Territories, and frequently also questions of an internal character affecting the methods and procedures of the General Assembly in the conduct of its business. In short, there is scarcely any field in which the Assembly has taken an interest where reference has not been made, at one time or another, to the provisions of Article 10.[22]

"Within the Scope" of the Charter

Almost invariably, Article 10 has been cited together with other articles that define the powers of the Assembly in more specific terms, such as Articles 11, 13, and 14. It has usually been referred to as an additional, rather than the principal, basis for the Assembly's actions.

The broad scope of Article 10 has been most frequently emphasized in replies to objections that the Assembly in considering a particular question or taking a particular course of action would be intervening in the domestic affairs of states in violation of the injunction contained in Article 2(7).[23] Along with Article 10, Articles 1, 2, 55, and 56 have been frequently mentioned as justification for Assembly action in connection with the treatment of persons of Indian origin in South Africa and in connection with the apartheid policies of that country. It has been argued that the broad powers of the Assembly under Article 10, together with the Charter provisions on human rights, enable it to act even when the states concerned are not members of the United Nations, as in the cases of Tibet and the observance of human rights and fundamental freedoms in Bulgaria, Hungary, and Romania.

On various matters related to non-self-governing territories, Article 10 and Article 73(c) have been linked, as in the early discussions on Cyprus. The purposes and principles of the Charter and the right of members to bring matters before the Assembly in accordance with Article 35 have also been linked to Article 10 in this manner.

[22] *Repertory,* I, 257.
[23] It has also been cited in reply to objections based on Art. 107.

"Powers and Functions" of United Nations Organs

While the Assembly may discuss "any matters . . . related to the powers and functions of any organs provided for in the present Charter," Article 10 specifically authorizes it to make recommendations to members and to the Security Council. The lack of reference to the other two Councils is explained by the fact that they operate under the Assembly's authority and their relationships are governed by other Charter articles.[24] Thus, this section of Article 10, although referred to in various contexts, has been primarily relevant to the kinds of recommendations the Assembly may make with respect to the powers and functions of the Security Council.

Many Assembly resolutions have had a bearing on the Council's powers and functions, but most have been in exercise of powers under other articles of the Charter; for example, specific and general recommendations on the admission of new members (Article 4), and on disarmament and various measures relating to the maintenance of international peace and security (Article 11). Article 10 was cited as the basis for the Assembly's recommendations concerning voting procedure in the Security Council.[25] Together with Articles 11 and 13, it was also cited in the Assembly resolution recommending that the Security Council examine the utility and desirability of appointing a rapporteur or conciliator at the initial stage of any dispute.[26]

The relationship between the overall responsibilities of the Assembly and the right of other organs to determine their own procedures was raised in connection with these resolutions as well as in many other instances. Objections based on the autonomy of other organs were made, for example, to the Assembly's resolution on the "Recognition by the United Nations of the Representation of a Member State"[27] which stated that other organs and the specialized agencies should take into account the "attitude" adopted by the Assembly when one or more authorities claimed the right to represent a member state in the United Nations.

Article 11

1. The General Assembly may consider the general principles of cooperation in the maintenance of international peace and security, including the principles governing disarmament and the regulation of

---

[24] See, in particular, commentary on Arts. 60 and 85.

[25] GA Res. 117(II), Nov. 21, 1947; and 267(III), Apr. 14, 1949. See also GA Res. 40(I), Dec. 13, 1946.

[26] GA Res. 268B(III), Apr. 28, 1949.   [27] GA Res. 396(V), Dec. 14, 1950.

armaments, and may make recommendations with regard to such principles to the Members or to the Security Council or to both.

2. The General Assembly may discuss any questions relating to the maintenance of international peace and security brought before it by any Member of the United Nations, or by the Security Council, or by a state which is not a Member of the United Nations in accordance with Article 35, paragraph 2, and, except as provided in Article 12, may make recommendations with regard to any such questions to the state or states concerned or to the Security Council or to both. Any such question on which action is necessary shall be referred to the Security Council by the General Assembly either before or after discussion.

3. The General Assembly may call the attention of the Security Council to situations which are likely to endanger international peace and security.

4. The powers of the General Assembly set forth in this Article shall not limit the general scope of Article 10.

The significance of Article 11 cannot be overstressed. Although only infrequently cited, it has been the basis for many of the Assembly's most important actions. By specifically authorizing the Assembly to discuss and make recommendations on questions related to the maintenance of international peace and security, Article 11 provides the basis for the assertion of the Assembly's right to deal with "threats to the peace, breaches of the peace, and acts of aggression" whenever the Security Council is unable to discharge its primary responsibility for maintaining peace and security.[28]

The principle of the Council's "primary responsibility" was accepted by most of the delegations at San Francisco, many of whom were nonetheless reluctant to have the Assembly assigned such a subordinate role as was envisaged in the Dumbarton Oaks Proposals. To give the smaller countries some voice in the application of enforcement measures, various amendments were introduced to associate the Assembly more directly with these decisions, by requiring its concurrence in the application of such measures, except in cases of extreme urgency, or by providing for subsequent review by the Assembly of the Council's decisions.[29] The major powers, however, were unwilling to accept such encroachments upon the Council's primary responsibility, but it was agreed that nonmembers of the Council would participate in any decisions where their armed forces would be involved (Article 44). At the same time, the provisions for Assembly review of the Council's activities were somewhat clarified (Article 15).

[28] See pp. 122–25.   [29] See Russell, pp. 750–51.

The provision in the Dumbarton Oaks Proposals concerning the Assembly's authority to consider and make recommendations on both "general principles" and "any questions" related to the maintenance of international peace and security was split into separate paragraphs to emphasize the importance of the latter. In addition the Assembly was authorized to call the Council's attention to "any situation likely to endanger international peace and security" (Article 11[3]). Although the major powers were unwilling to remove the restriction on recommendations by the Assembly on disputes or situations being dealt with by the Council, the relevant Charter provisions on this point were clarified.[30]

General Principles of Cooperation

In contrast to the controversy during the drafting of the Charter over the Assembly's powers in connection with "questions [i.e., specific questions] relating to the maintenance of international peace and security," the appropriateness of authorizing it to consider and make recommendations on "general principles of cooperation" in this field was never questioned. Moreover, in this area the Assembly's actions are not subject to the injunction of Article 12.

The Assembly's functions in this respect must be viewed in conjunction with its broader authority under Article 13, especially its mandate to "initiate studies and make recommendations for . . . promoting international cooperation in the political field." In establishing the Interim Committee, the Assembly conferred on it the function of considering and reporting "on methods to be adopted to give effect" to both these Charter provisions.[31] Recommendations adopted pursuant to the Uniting for Peace resolution, largely on the basis of the work of the Collective Measures Committee, have also concerned "methods" that might be used to maintain and strengthen international peace and security.[32]

An enumeration of all the resolutions that could be considered as coming within the scope of Article 11(1) is not attempted here.[33] Rather examples of different types will be given.

Occasionally, the Assembly has included in its resolutions on particu-

30 See commentary on Art. 12.

31 GA Res. 111(II), Nov. 13, 1947. See also GA Res. 196(III), Dec. 3, 1948; and 295(IV), Nov. 21, 1949.

32 GA Res. 377(V), Nov. 5, 1950; 503(VI), Jan. 12, 1952; and 703(VII), Mar. 17, 1953.

33 For resolutions adopted through 1958, see the tabulations in *Repertory*, I, 334–54; *Supp. 1*, I, 132–36; *Supp. 2*, II, 92–102.

lar disputes and situations provisions that might be called "general principles." [34] A number of resolutions such as the "Appeal to the Great Powers" have been directed toward cooperation among the permanent members of the Security Council.[35] Some have dealt with very narrow subjects,[36] while others have been exceedingly broad in scope, as for example the endorsement of Secretary-General Lie's plan for peace through the United Nations.[37] In short, the Assembly has adopted many resolutions that might be considered as incorporating "general principles of international cooperation," but few can be considered as being exclusively exercises by the Assembly of its functions under this part of Article 11.

During the first few years of the United Nations Assembly, discussions on "general principles" of cooperation were tied in with the question of disarmament and the Soviet "peace offensive." They covered such matters as condemnation of "war propaganda," and omnibus proposals for "averting a new world war" and strengthening "peace and friendship among nations." These proposals by the Soviet Union and its allies were often met by equally broad counterproposals by the Western powers, as were embodied in the "Essentials of Peace" and "Peace through Deeds" resolutions.[38] As the intensity of the cold war subsided, the emphasis shifted to measures for "relieving international tension and developing international cooperation," and later to "peaceful coexistence." [39]

These discussions have at various times taken on a legal coloration and merged with the Assembly's responsibilities in developing international law. Assembly consideration of "the promotion of international law concerning friendly relations and cooperation among States" is a good example.

All of these discussions have tended to have heavy ideological overtones, as well as a direct bearing upon specific current political issues. They have rarely, if ever, produced any noticeable effect upon the operations of the Organization or the conduct of its members.

[34] See, for example, the reminder to members of their Charter obligations included in the resolution on South Africa's racial policies. GA Res. 616B(VII), Dec. 5, 1952.

[35] GA Res. 190(III), Nov. 3, 1948.

[36] For example, the "Duties of States on the Outbreak of Hostilities," GA Res. 378(V), Nov. 17, 1950.

[37] GA Res. 494(V), Nov. 20, 1950.

[38] GA Res. 290(IV), Dec. 1, 1949; and 380(V), Nov. 17, 1950.

[39] See, for example, GA Res. 914(X), Dec. 16, 1955; and 1236(XII), Dec. 14, 1957.

Disarmament and the Regulation of Armaments

The contrast between the major emphasis in the League Covenant on disarmament and the paucity of provisions on this subject in the United Nations Charter is commented upon elsewhere in this study.[40] In one respect the Charter follows the League approach in according a role to both the General Assembly and the Security Council. The latter is directed to draw up plans for the regulation of armaments (Article 26), while the Assembly is empowered to consider the principles governing disarmament and the regulation of armaments, and it may make recommendations in this regard "to the Members or to the Security Council or to both."

The inclusion of a specific mention of the Assembly's role resulted from a Soviet initiative at Dumbarton Oaks. Both the United Kingdom and the United States considered that the general grant of authority to the Assembly was broad enough to cover matters of this kind and that no specific grant was necessary. They also pointed out that it would be difficult to distinguish between the responsibilities of the Council and the Assembly during the planning stages,[41] and of the Assembly and a general conference that might be called to negotiate a disarmament agreement.[42] Nonetheless, the United States and the United Kingdom accepted the Soviet proposal, which was later adopted at San Francisco without opposition.

Article 11(1) refers to both "disarmament" and the "regulation of armaments." At Dumbarton Oaks, the British and American representatives agreed with reluctance to include the term "disarmament," which the Soviet Union insisted upon.[43] Article 47, which establishes the terms of reference of the Military Staff Committee, also refers to "the regulation of armaments and possible disarmament," but there is no mention of "disarmament" in Article 26.

The terminology employed in the United Nations has been quite confusing. The Soviet Union has tended to use the term "disarmament," even in connection with proposals that called for no reduction of arms. The Western powers initially showed a preference for "regulation and reduction of armaments" and later for "regulation, limitation, and balanced reduction of armaments."[44] It was not until 1952 that

40 See commentary on Art. 26.

41 Recommendations by the General Assembly under Art. 11(1) are not subject to the injunctions laid down in Art. 12.

42 Russell, pp. 476–77.   43 *Ibid.*, p. 442.

44 See Bernard G. Bechhoefer, *Postwar Negotiations for Arms Control* (Washington, Brookings Institution, 1961), pp. 7, 22–23.

the word "disarmament" appeared in the terms of reference of subsidiary organs established to deal with this subject.[45]

Under the Charter, the competence of the Assembly in the field of disarmament is permissive and confined to the formulation of general principles, whereas that of the Security Council is mandatory and directed toward the formulation of specific plans. That the Assembly rather than the Council has been the principal forum for disarmament discussions has been due to a number of factors. To begin with, it was the first organ to consider the subject. Second, after the Council reached an impasse over the reports of the Atomic Energy Commission and the Commission for Conventional Armaments, discussion on disarmament virtually ceased in that organ. Moreover, without discounting the amount of technical discussion that has taken place, disarmament discussions have contained an unusually large element of propaganda, and it would appear that, in general, states have preferred to utilize the broad forum of the Assembly to advance their positions. Furthermore, although the discussions have centered on the armaments of the major powers, disarmament has been a matter of great concern to the membership of the Organization as a whole.

At the beginning of its first session, the General Assembly took a major step when, on the initiative of the five permanent members of the Security Council and Canada, it established the United Nations Atomic Energy Commission.[46] Although established by the Assembly, the Commission was to report to the Council and was accountable to and subject to directives from that organ with respect to security matters.[47]

At the second part of its first session, the Assembly unanimously adopted a resolution on the "principles governing the general regulation and reduction of armaments." [48] The responsibilities of the Security Council for formulating plans for the establishment of a system of arms regulation and its primary responsibility for the maintenance of international peace and security were recognized in that the Assembly's recommendations were largely addressed to the Council. In accordance with these recommendations, the Council established its Commission for Conventional Armaments.

The discussions in the two commissions and the Council discussions on their reports revealed a deep split between the Soviet Union on the

45 GA Res. 502(VI), Jan. 11, 1952, establishing the Disarmament Commission.
46 GA Res. 1(I), Jan. 24, 1946.
47 These provisions resulted primarily from suggestions by the Soviet Union. See Richard G. Hewlitt and Oscar E. Anderson Jr., *The New World 1939–1946* (University Park, Pennsylvania State University Press, 1962), I, 476.
48 GA Res. 41(I), Dec. 14, 1946. At the same time it also adopted GA Res. 42(I) concerning information on armed forces.

one hand and the Anglo–American-led majority on the other. By 1950, negotiations had come to a complete halt. They were revived again in 1952, when the two commissions were abolished and a single disarmament commission was established.[49]

This commission was established "under the Security Council"; it was to "formulate plans for the establishment within the framework of the Security Council" of international control machinery to ensure implementation of a disarmament agreement. It was to report to both the Assembly and the Council, but in practice its work was never discussed in the Council.

For the next few years, the Disarmament Commission, and more especially its subcommittee, were the major forums for disarmament negotiations. At each Assembly session disarmament was a major topic of debate, largely on the basis of the Commission's reports.

In 1957, after an impasse had been reached in the Disarmament Commission, the Soviet Union proposed that it be enlarged to include the entire United Nations membership. This proposal was rejected, although the size of the Commission was increased. The Soviet Union announced that it would not take part in the Commission's work. This stand was later reversed when the Assembly decided to include all members. But from 1957 on, the major negotiations on general disarmament have taken place not in the organs of the United Nations but in ad hoc bodies established by agreement of the major powers, in particular the Eighteen Nation Disarmament Committee.[50] These bodies have had only a tenuous connection with the United Nations. They have, at the invitation of the Assembly, utilized the facilities of the United Nations and the services of the Secretariat. At the request of the Assembly, they have submitted reports to the United Nations. The annual discussions on disarmament in the Assembly have taken place largely on the basis of these reports.

There are few, if any, subjects on which the General Assembly has passed more resolutions than on disarmament.[51] A number of the resolutions have been related to "principles," for example, its initial resolution on the "principles governing the regulation and reduction of

[49] GA Res. 502(VI), Jan. 11, 1952. This resolution followed the recommendations of the Committee of Twelve, which the Assembly had established at its previous session to explore the possibilities of merging the two commissions. GA Res. 496(V), Dec. 13, 1950.

[50] The ENDC was established at the end of 1961 to replace the Ten Nation Disarmament Committee which had been composed of five NATO and five Warsaw Pact countries. The membership of ENDC is as follows: Canada, France (which does not participate), Italy, United Kingdom, United States, Bulgaria, Czechoslovakia, Poland, Romania, Soviet Union, Brazil, Burma, Ethiopia, India, Mexico, Nigeria, Sweden, and the United Arab Republic.

[51] A listing of the relevant resolution for the period 1946–59 is given in *Repertory*, I, 355–61; *Supp. 1*, I, 137; *Supp. 2*, II, 103–5.

armaments" and its endorsement of the Soviet–United States "Joint Statement of Agreed Principles for Disarmament Negotiations." [52] On occasion, the Assembly has gone beyond principles, as for example when it approved the "majority plan" developed in the Atomic Energy Commission for an international control system.[53]

Table 3
UNITED NATIONS SUBSIDIARY ORGANS CONCERNED
WITH DISARMAMENT

Name	*Method of Establishment*	*Membership*
Atomic Energy Commission (AEC)	GA Res. I(1), Jan. 24, 1946	Security Council members plus Canada
Subcommittee	Pursuant to GA Res. 191(III), Nov. 4, 1949	Canada, China, France, Soviet Union, U.K., U.S.
Commission for Conventional Armaments	SC Res. of Feb. 13, 1947, pursuant to GA Res. 41(I), Dec. 14, 1946	Security Council members
Committee of Twelve	GA Res. 496(V), Dec. 13, 1950	Same as AEC
Disarmament Commission (i)	GA Res. 502(VI), Jan. 11, 1952	Same as AEC
Subcommittee	Pursuant to GA Res. 715(VIII), Nov. 28, 1953	Canada, France, Soviet Union, U.K., U.S.
Disarmament Commission (ii)	GA Res. 1150(XII), Nov. 19, 1957	Same as AEC plus Argentina, Australia, Belgium, Brazil, Burma, Czechoslovakia, Egypt, India, Italy, Mexico, Norway, Poland, Tunisia, Yugoslavia
Disarmament Commission (iii)	GA Res. 1252(XIII), Nov. 4, 1958	All members of the UN

For the most part, however, the Assembly resolutions have been concerned primarily with establishing machinery for the negotiation of disarmament agreements and with attempts to work out a basis for agreement between the Soviet Union and the Western powers. Its major contribution has probably been the constant pressure it has exerted on those powers to continue their negotiations.

Strengthening the Assembly Machinery

THE INTERIM COMMITTEE. The Interim Committee, on which all members were to be represented, was established in 1947 to function

[52] GA Res. 41(I), Dec. 14, 1946; GA Res. 1722(XVI), Dec. 20, 1961.
[53] GA Res. 191(III), Nov. 4, 1948.

between Assembly sessions to assist in discharging its functions in the field of peace and security. Included within its mandate,[54] were studies and recommendations for international political cooperation in accordance with Articles 11(1) and 13(1a); consideration of specific matters referred to it by the Assembly; and consideration of disputes or situations proposed for the next Assembly session. The principal purpose in creating the Committee, largely unstated, was to have in being an organ that could investigate serious situations and summon a special Assembly session when necessary, particularly if the Security Council was paralyzed by the veto.

The Soviet Union protested that the establishment of the Committee was a violation of the Charter and that the purpose was to create a new organ "to weaken, circumvent, and act as a substitute for the Security Council, on which the Charter placed primary responsibility for maintaining peace and security." [55] After the Committee was established, the Soviet Union and its allies refused to participate in its work. The Commission never played the important role expected of it and, although still in being, ceased to meet after March 17, 1951.[56]

THE UNITING FOR PEACE RESOLUTION. The second major step in building up the role of the Assembly in the peace and security field was the adoption of the Uniting for Peace resolution in 1950. Just as the immediate stimulus for the creation of the Interim Committee was the deteriorating situation in Greece, this effort to strengthen the Assembly stemmed from the realization that the initial United Nations response to the attack on the Republic of Korea had been possible only because the Soviet Union had been absent from the Security Council and that this circumstance was unlikely to recur.

In proposing the resolution, the United States sought to provide the United Nations with what it considered to be the following "essential elements of a collective security system":

the means of determining aggression, an organism to put collective measures into operation, military forces in readiness to carry out those measures, and some apparatus to perfect the methods for co-ordinating collective action.[57]

The key provision in the resolution is the following:

. . . if the Security Council, because of lack of unanimity of the permanent members, fails to exercise its primary responsibility for the maintenance

[54] GA Res. 111(II), Nov. 13, 1947.
[55] GAOR/2d Sess., 1st Ctte./74th Mtg./Oct. 14, 1947/p. 129–39. For the complete debate see *ibid.*, 74th–78th Mtgs./Oct. 14–18, 1947; 94th–97th Mtgs./Nov. 5–6, 1947; and 110th–111th Plen. Mtgs./Nov. 13, 1947.
[56] For resolutions reestablishing the Committee, see GA Res. 196(III), Dec. 3, 1948; and 295(IV), Nov. 21, 1949.
[57] Harding F. Bancroft, "Can the U.N. Become a Collective Security Organization?" State Dept. *Bulletin*, Vol. XXIV, No. 619 (May 14, 1951), p. 772.

of international peace and security in any case where there appears to be a threat to the peace, breach of the peace, or act of aggression, the General Assembly shall consider the matter immediately with a view to making appropriate recommendations to Members for collective measures, including in the case of a breach of the peace or act of aggression the use of armed force when necessary, to maintain or restore international peace and security.[58]

To ensure that the Assembly could act promptly, the resolution provides for the calling of emergency special sessions in such situations on twenty-four hours notice either by the vote of any seven members of the Security Council or by a majority of United Nations members.[59] The Assembly Rules of Procedure were amended to facilitate speedy action at such sessions.

The resolution also contained the recommendation that members maintain within their national armed forces "elements so trained, organized, and equipped that they could promptly be made available . . . for service as a United Nations unit or units, upon recommendation by the Security Council or the General Assembly." [60] Members were also invited to survey their resources "in order to determine the nature and scope of the assistance" they might be in a position "to render in support of any recommendations of the Security Council or of the General Assembly for the restoration of international peace and security."

Under the resolution, the Collective Measures Committee was established [61] "to study and make a report to the Security Council and the General Assembly" on methods "which might be used to maintain and strengthen international peace and security." The Committee was expected to consider in detail the methods for giving effect to any recommendations for the application of collective measures.

In adopting the Uniting for Peace resolution, the Assembly was in effect asserting its right to make a determination of the kind described in Article 39 and to recommend "collective measures" to deal with the situation in any case where the Council fails to act because the per-

58 Note that recommendations for the use of force are not applicable to a "threat to the peace."

59 With the ratification of the Charter amendments concerning composition and voting procedure in the Security Council, the number of votes now required is 9 rather than 7.

60 To assist members in carrying out this provision the resolution further provides for the appointment of a "panel of military experts" who could supply "technical advice regarding the organization, training, and equipment" of such units.

61 The resolution also established the Peace Observation Commission to observe and report "on the situation in any area where there exists international tension the continuance of which is likely to endanger the maintenance of international peace and security."

members are in disagreement.[62] The preamble to the resolu-
cognizes the Council's "primary responsibility for the main-
of international peace and security" but declares that the
Council's failure to discharge that responsibility "does not relieve
Member States of their obligations or the United Nations of its responsibility" and in particular "does not deprive the General Assembly of its
rights or relieve it of its responsibility under the Charter." As the
supporters of the resolution repeatedly pointed out, the Council's
responsibility is "primary" but not exclusive.

The Uniting for Peace resolution provided one of the most extensive
debates on the Charter that has ever taken place.[63] The basis cited for
the resolution was the Assembly's power under Articles 10 and 11. In
the Soviet view, the resolution was in violation of the "primary responsibility" of the Security Council and the principle of great power
unanimity. It argued that the kinds of measures contemplated in the
resolution fell within the Council's exclusive jurisdiction, citing in particular the stipulation in Article 11(2) that any question "on which
action is necessary shall be referred to the Security Council by the
General Assembly either before or after discussion." In reply, the point
was stressed that the Assembly would take up a matter under the
Uniting for Peace plan only after the Council had had an opportunity
to take action and failed to do so. It was further argued that the term
"action" should be interpreted as "enforcement action" of the kind the
Council alone could take under Articles 41 and 42 of the Charter, that
is, "decisions" as to collective measures members were legally bound to
carry out, and not "recommendations" for such measures.

In effect, the Uniting for Peace resolution proclaimed the paramountcy of the purpose of the United Nations as stated in Article
1(1): "To maintain international peace and security, and to that end:
to take effective collective measures for the prevention and removal of
threats to the peace, and for the suppression of acts of aggression or
other breaches of the peace." In the view of the large majority of
United Nations members, the implementation of this purpose took
precedence over those Charter provisions (largely in Chapter VII)
concerning the specific methods and procedures by which threats to
the peace, breaches of the peace, and acts of aggression were to be
handled.

Whether fully within the terms of the Charter or not, the resolution
provided a system quite different from that which the drafters of the

---

[62] The resolution is so worded that the disagreement does not necessarily have
to involve the use of the veto, although that is clearly what the sponsors had in
mind.

[63] See GAOR/5th Sess., 1st Ctte./354th–371st Mtgs./Oct. 9–21, 1950; and
299th and 302d Plen. Mtgs./Nov. 1–3, 1950.

Charter had intended, one more closely resembling the "decentralized system" of the League of Nations than the "centralized system" set out in Chapter VII of the Charter.[64] Instead of "decisions" by the Security Council, which members are obligated to carry out, collective action is to be based upon recommendations by the Assembly which, while they may carry great political or moral weight, are not legally binding upon members.

The provisions for calling emergency special sessions contribute to the Assembly's effective handling of certain serious situations, such as the Suez crisis of 1956 and the Middle East crisis of 1958. The Uniting for Peace resolution may also have had a psychological effect in broadening members' attitudes toward the kinds of measures the Assembly may take. The Assembly has never called for collective military measures as envisaged in the resolution and as elaborated in the reports of the Collective Measures Committee.[65] It has, however, authorized the establishment of United Nations peace-keeping forces composed of military units voluntarily contributed by members "to secure and supervise the cessation of hostilities" agreed to by the parties involved.[66]

"Recommendations" under Article 11(2)

The Assembly is authorized to consider any question related to the maintenance of international peace and security brought by any member, by the Security Council, or by a nonmember under the special circumstances stated in Article 35(2). No questions have ever been brought by nonmembers, although some have been brought on their behalf. Except in those cases where it has called for a special or emergency special session of the Assembly, the Council has never brought a question to the Assembly under Article 11.[67]

Members have tended to favor a broad interpretation as to what questions are related to the maintenance of peace and security, especially in connection with human rights and the treatment of non-self-governing territories. As pointed out in the commentary on Article 10, seldom do the terms of Assembly resolutions or the debates leading up to their adoption provide a basis for concluding that the Assembly is acting under a particular Charter provision. It should also be noted that in contrast to the Charter provisions concerning the operations of

[64] Geoffrey L. Goodwin, *Britain and the United Nations* (New York, Carnegie Endowment for International Peace, 1958), p. 246.

[65] These reports deal in great detail with the application of both economic and military measures. See GAOR, 6th Sess., *Supp. 13;* and 7th Sess., *Supp. 17.*

[66] GA Res. 1000(ES-1), Nov. 5, 1956; and 1001(ES-1), Nov. 7, 1956.

[67] See commentary on Arts. 12 and 20.

the Security Council under Chapters VI and VIII, the Assembly's authority to discuss and make recommendations is stated in very general terms.

Like those adopted under Articles 10 and 14, resolutions under Article 11(2) are "recommendations," regardless of how they are worded. The Assembly has taken a very broad view as to the kinds of resolutions it may adopt. It has frequently appealed for, endorsed, recommended, or called for negotiations between the parties concerned. It has endorsed other procedures of pacific settlement, such as recourse to regional organizations, good offices, mediation, conciliation, and occasionally judicial settlement or arbitration. It has expressed its view, sometimes in great detail, as to the terms upon which a matter should be settled. It has established subsidiary organs to assist the parties in reaching a settlement and has requested the Secretary-General, the Assembly President, and other prominent individuals to perform functions of this kind.

It has called upon states directly concerned to take various kinds of measures, including the cessation of hostilities, withdrawal of troops, release of political prisoners, cessation of repressive acts, the holding of elections, and the granting of amnesties. It has established subsidiary organs to assist in and observe compliance with such measures, including the creation of peace-keeping forces. It has called upon all states, other United Nations organs, and other organizations to assist in carrying out its resolutions, either in general or by taking specific steps or refraining from certain actions.

The Assembly has been generally unmoved by arguments tending to restrict the area of its competence. It has been far less sensitive than the Security Council to objections that it is intervening in the domestic affairs of states in contravention to Article 2(7). The restrictions imposed by Article 12 have also been narrowly interpreted,[68] as has the injunction in Article 11(2) requiring reference to the Security Council of any question on which "action" is necessary.

As pointed out in the preceding section, the Soviet Union and some other states objected to the interpretation given to the term "action" in connection with the Uniting for Peace resolution. Similar objections were raised when the Assembly asserted its authority to brand the People's Republic of China as an aggressor for its intervention in the Korean conflict and recommended the application of an embargo on the shipment of various kinds of strategic materials to that country.[69] In other cases, the Assembly has considered itself justified in calling for the application of economic sanctions, i.e., against South Africa and

[68] See commentary on Art. 12.
[69] GA Res. 498(V), Feb. 1, 1951; and 500(V), May 18, 1951.

Portugal, but it has also sought to invoke the Council's powers to apply such measures under Chapter VII, as will be noted in the next section.

Objections that the measures taken by the Assembly in connection with the United Nations Emergency Force established during the Suez crisis of 1956 were improper and encroachments upon the Security Council's primary responsibility have been the basis for refusal by the Soviet Union and others to contribute their share of the costs as determined by the General Assembly. In its advisory opinion, however, the International Court of Justice upheld a broad interpretation of the Assembly's powers. It stated that "the kind of action referred to in Article 11(2) is coercive or enforcement action." The term "action" must mean "such action as is solely within the province of the Security Council." The last sentence of Article 11(2) "has no application where the necessary action is not enforcement action." [70]

Reference to the Security Council

Under Article 11, there are three ways for the Assembly to bring a matter to the Security Council: under paragraph 3, it may "call the attention" of the Council to situations "which are likely to endanger international peace and security"; under paragraph 2, it may make "recommendations" to the Council on questions related to the maintenance of peace and security; and it is obligated to refer to the Council any such question on which "action" is necessary.

The kinds of resolutions the Assembly has adopted in its efforts to invoke the Council's jurisdiction have been varied. In its 1961 resolution on South Africa's apartheid policies, for example, the Assemby merely drew the Council's attention to the provisions of Article 11(3).[71] Generally, in resolutions of this kind, the Assembly has expressed its own view as to the gravity of the situation. In first calling the Council's attention to the situation in Southwest Africa, the Assembly stated that its continuance would "endanger international peace and security." [72] In subsequently bringing the situation again to the Council's attention, it characterized it as a "serious threat to the peace." [73] Similar findings were indicated in its resolutions directing the Council's attention to the problem of apartheid, and the situations in Rhodesia, Angola, and other territories under Portuguese administration.[74]

[70] *ICJ Reports,* 1962, pp. 164–65.   [71] GA Res. 1663(XVI), Nov. 28, 1961.
[72] GA Res. 1596(XV), Apr. 7, 1961.
[73] GA Res. 1899(XVIII), Nov. 13, 1963; and 2074(XX), Dec. 17, 1965.
[74] See respectively, GA Res. 1761(XVII), Nov. 6, 1962; 2054(XX), Dec. 15, 1965; 2022(XX), Nov. 5, 1965; 1742(XVI), Jan. 30, 1962; and 2107(XX), Dec. 21, 1965.

While in some cases, the Assembly has merely brought a matter to the Council's attention, it has sometimes specifically asked the Council "to keep the matter under constant review," to keep "watch" over the situation, or to consider the situation as a "matter of urgency." [75]

In some of its resolutions, the Assembly has indicated the action it wished the Council to take. The original Assembly resolution on Spain recommended that the Council consider "the adequate measures to be taken in order to remedy the situation," if a government deriving its authority "from the consent of the governed" were not established "within a reasonable time." [76] In connection with territories under Portuguese administration, the Assembly asked the Council to take the "necessary" and "appropriate" measures to secure compliance with United Nations resolutions on this subject. [77]

In its resolution on the partition of Palestine, the Assembly was more specific as to the course of action it wished the Council to follow. The Council was requested to "determine as a threat to the peace, breach of the peace or act of aggression . . . any attempt to alter by force the settlement" envisaged in the resolution. If it decided that such a threat existed, the Council was to "supplement the authorization of the General Assembly by taking measures, under Articles 39 and 41 of the Charter," to empower the United Nations Palestine Commission to exercise "the functions" assigned to it under the resolution. [78] The Assembly has similarly sought to invoke the Council's powers under Chapter VII to obtain compliance with resolutions on the situation in Angola and in South Africa. It has called for the application of economic sanctions against Portugal and South Africa, [79] and has asked the Council to consider, if necessary, action under Article 6 to expel South Africa from the Organization.

The Assembly attempts to obtain from the Security Council the kinds of action it considered necessary to deal with these situations have not been very successful. Some of its resolutions, such as those on Spain and Southwest Africa, were not considered by the Council. The Council has been unwilling to accept the Assembly's characterizations of certain situations as "threats" to international peace. It has made its own determination as to the nature of the situation and the course of action it would follow. It has generally been reluctant to utilize its

[75] Angola, GA Res. 1742(XVI), Jan. 30, 1962; South West Africa, GA Res. 2074(XX), Dec. 17, 1965; Rhodesia, GA Res. 2024(XX), Nov. 11, 1965. See also GA Res. 1913(XVIII), Dec. 3, 1963 on the Portuguese territories.
[76] GA Res. 39(I), Dec. 12, 1946.
[77] GA Res. 1913(XVIII), Dec. 3, 1963; and 2107(XX), Dec. 21, 1965.
[78] GA Res. 181(II), Nov. 29, 1947.
[79] GA Res. 1761(XVII), Nov. 6, 1962; 2054(XX), Dec. 15, 1965; and 1819(XVII), Dec. 18, 1962.

powers under Chapter VII to secure compliance with Assembly (or even its own) resolutions.[80]

Article 12

1. While the Security Council is exercising in respect of any dispute or situation the functions assigned to it in the present Charter, the General Assembly shall not make any recommendation with regard to that dispute or situation unless the Security Council so requests.

2. The Secretary-General, with the consent of the Security Council, shall notify the General Assembly at each session of any matters relative to the maintenance of international peace and security which are being dealt with by the Security Council and shall similarly notify the General Assembly, or the Members of the United Nations if the General Assembly is not in session, immediately the Security Council ceases to deal with such matters.

The purpose of Article 12 is to protect the Security Council's primary responsibility for the maintenance of international peace and security by excluding Assembly interference with its operations. The drafters of the Charter sought to avoid the situation that had obtained under the League Covenant where there was no differentiation of the jurisdictions of the Council and the Assembly. Article 12(1) was intended to avoid the possibility of conflicting actions by the two organs.

At San Francisco, the small and middle-sized powers argued against any restrictions on the Assembly's power of recommendation, even on matters before the Security Council. They opposed the provision in the Dumbarton Oaks draft which stipulated: "The General Assembly should not on its own initiative make recommendations on any matter relating to the maintenance of international peace and security which is being dealt with by the Security Council."

While the major powers stressed the need to avoid jurisdictional conflicts, the other delegates were concerned lest a matter become "frozen" in the Security Council.[81] Many considered that the Assembly should be able, by a two-thirds vote, to declare that the Council was no longer "exercising its function" with respect to a particular dispute or situation.[82] This proposal was unacceptable to the major powers, but as a result of these discussions, a number of modifications were made in the Dumbarton Oaks draft. In particular, a paragraph was added requiring the Secretary-General to keep the Assembly informed of the status of questions being considered by the Council.[83]

[80] See commentary on Arts. 39 and 41.   [81] Russell, pp. 760–61.
[82] UNCIO, *Documents*, VIII, 512.
[83] At the same time, the right of the Assembly to call the Council's attention to dangerous situations was affirmed. See commentary on Art. 11(3).

Extent of the Limitation

The restriction imposed by Article 12(1) is limited. It applies only to the Assembly's "recommendatory," not to its "deliberative," powers. The right of the Assembly "to discuss, consider, and debate any questions relating to the maintenance of international peace and security is absolute." [84]

The restriction does not apply to all matters being considered by the Council, but only to "disputes and situations." It does not constitute a limitation on the Assembly's right to make recommendations relating to the "general principles of cooperation in the maintenance of international peace and security." [85]

The Assembly has not considered that Article 12(1) precludes it from adopting *any* resolution relating to a dispute or situation before the Council. For example, at its fourth session, the Assembly adopted a resolution on the Indonesian question, even though the Council was actively dealing with the dispute. The resolution did not, however, deal with the substance of the issues involved. In fact, at the time, the Assembly decided it was not competent to adopt another proposal on the ground that it was in the nature of a "recommendation" and therefore came within the limitations of Article 12(1).[86]

"While the Security Council Is Exercising" Its Functions

During the early years of the United Nations, a very broad interpretation was given to this phrase. Its meaning was first considered in connection with the Spanish question. When division among the permanent members resulted in a deadlock, the Council decided to keep the situation under, "continuous observation" and maintain it upon "the list of matters" of which the Council was "seized." An Australian proposal that this action would not "in any way prejudice the rights of the General Assembly" was vetoed.[87] To free the Assembly from the restrictions imposed by Article 12(1), the Council subsequently removed the question from the list of items of which it was seized,[88] an action not subject to the veto.

This narrow interpretation that the Assembly could not make recommendations on any dispute or situation on the "list of matters of

[84] *The Charter of the United Nations,* Hears./USS CFR/79C1/1945/p. 246.
[85] There is a specific reference to Art. 12 in Arts. 10, 14, and 11(2) of the Charter but not in Art. 11(1) or Art. 13.
[86] GAOR/4th Sess./272d Plen. Mtg./Dec. 7, 1949/p. 564.
[87] SCOR/1st Yr., 1st Ser./49th Mtg./June 26, 1946, pp. 441 ff.
[88] *Ibid.,* 79th Mtg./Nov. 4, 1946/p. 498.

which the Security Council seized" was challenged at the time and on numerous subsequent occasions. It has been frequently argued that for the Council to be "exercising" its functions, it must be actively dealing with the matter.[89] In practice, this initial effort to impose a broad restriction upon the Assembly's powers has not been sustained.

The Secretary-General's Notification

The "notification" the Secretary-General is required to submit to the Assembly under Article 12(2) includes all disputes and situations the Council has placed on its agenda that have not subsequently been disposed of and is in this respect identical with the above-mentioned "list of matters of which the Security Council is seized." The difficulty is that the Council has been liberal in placing matters on its agenda, but it has seldom removed them. Thus the notification contains items the Council has not discussed for more than twenty years.[90] In a few instances, the Council has specifically removed items from "the list of matters" to free the Assembly's hands. Its action on the Spanish question has already been mentioned. It took similar action with respect to the Greek frontier incidents question and the complaint of aggression against Korea.[91] In these cases the Council had reached an impasse and the action was taken to make sure that there would be no question as to the competence of the Assembly to act.

Council Requests to the General Assembly

The Council has never specifically requested the Assembly to make recommendations with respect to a dispute or situation before it. The two proposals to apply this provision of Article 12(1) were vetoed.[92]

When, however, the Council itself has called a special or emergency special session of the General Assembly to deal with a particular dispute or situation, the Assembly may make recommendations, even though the matter remains on the Council's agenda. This is only logical

[89] See, for example, the debate as to whether the Assembly was precluded from dealing with the problem of West Irian since the Council remained seized of the "Indonesian" question. GAOR/9th Sess., Gen. Ctte./92d Mtg./Sept. 22, 1954; and 477th Plen. Mtg./Sept. 24, 1954.

[90] Since 1951, the notification has been divided into two parts: one listing the items the Council has dealt with during the preceeding year, and the other those items that it has not considered during that time.

[91] SCOR/2d Yr./202d Mtg./Sept. 15, 1947/p. 2405; 6th Yr./531st Mtg./Jan. 31, 1951/p. 12.

[92] In connection with the Spanish question, SCOR/1st Yr., 1st Ser./47th Mtg./June 18, 1946/p. 379; and in connection with the Greek frontier incidents question, SCOR/2d Yr./202d Mtg./Sept. 15, 1947/p. 2405.

since there would be no point in calling the Assembly into session merely to discuss an issue.

The first time the Council called a special Assembly session was for the purpose of considering "further the question of the future government of Palestine." [93] In convoking emergency special sessions to deal with the Suez crisis of 1956, the Hungarian revolt of 1956, the Middle East crisis of 1958, and the situation in the Congo in 1960, the Council did not indicate the particular purpose in calling the session.[94] In each case, the Council had reached the point where it could not act because of disagreement among the permanent members, thus satisfying the condition listed in the Uniting for Peace resolution for calling emergency special sessions.[95]

Other Aspects of Application

Instances in which items have been considered by the General Assembly when the same, or substantially the same, matters remained on the Council's "agenda" are too numerous to list. One area where the application of Article 12 has been particularly confused is in cases where a question has been considered first by the Assembly and has subsequently been brought before the Council.

In adopting the Palestine partition plan, for example, the Assembly asked the Security Council to take certain steps for its implementation. When the Council found itself unable to do so, it called a special Assembly session, while at the same time intensifying its efforts to bring about a cessation of hostilities. Both organs continued to be actively engaged in handling the question. It could be argued that each was dealing with a different aspect of the problem, but this distinction gets blurred at times and is even more obscure in other cases such as the Korean question.

The General Assembly had been dealing with the problem of the independence of Korea for a number of years before the Security Council became involved following the attack upon South Korea in June, 1950. At its next session, the Assembly resumed consideration of the problem, while the Council continued its efforts. Following the intervention of the People's Republic of China in the conflict, the Council found itself unable to act, and this aspect of the matter was

[93] SCOR/3d Yr./277th Mtg./Apr. 1, 1948/pp. 34–35.
[94] SCOR/11th Yr./751st Mtg./Oct. 31, 1956/para. 147; 754th Mtg./Nov. 4, 1956/para. 75; 13th Yr./838th Mtg./Aug. 7, 1958/para. 225; 15th Yr./906th Mtg./Sept. 17, 1960/paras. 195–96.
[95] See commentary on Art. 20. A special session was also called to consider the Franco–Tunisian dispute after the Council became deadlocked but was not called by the Council. Nonetheless, the Assembly proceeded to make recommendations even though the matter remained on the Council's agenda.

placed on the Assembly's agenda. The Korean complaint, as previously mentioned, was then removed from the Council's agenda to permit the Assembly to act.

Also of interest are the actions taken by the General Assembly and the Security Council on certain African questions. The racial situation in South Africa, the situation in Rhodesia, and Portuguese actions in its African territories were considered first by the Assembly, the Council becoming involved partly as the result of pressures by the Assembly. These questions, as well as the situation in the Congo, moved back and forth between the two organs with little concern over the application of Article 12.

Article 12(1) has become somewhat of a dead letter in so far as strict adherence to its language is concerned. Nonetheless, the Assembly has for the most part respected the intent of the article by not interfering, when the Council was making active efforts to bring about a satisfactory solution. Paradoxically, the intended purpose of avoiding conflicting action by the two organs has found occasional acceptance in the Council, when it has refused to deal with certain matters on the ground that by doing so it would interfere with decisions taken by the Assembly.[96]

Article 13

1. The General Assembly shall initiate studies and make recommendations for the purpose of:
   a. promoting international cooperation in the political field and encouraging the progressive development of international law and its codification;
   b. promoting international cooperation in the economic, social, cultural, educational, and health fields, and assisting in the realization of human rights and fundamental freedoms for all without distinction as to race, sex, language, or religion.
2. The further responsibilities, functions, and powers of the General Assembly with respect to matters mentioned in paragraph 1(b) above are set forth in Chapters IX and X.

Article 13, except for the part relating to the progressive development and codification of international law, adds little to what other articles of the Charter provide.[97] The Dumbarton Oaks Proposals provided that "[the] General Assembly should initiate studies and make

---

[96] See, for example, the Council's refusal to include on its agenda "Noncompliance by the United Kingdom, France and Israel" with Assembly resolutions on the Suez crisis. SCOR/11th Yr./755th Mtg./Nov. 5, 1956.

[97] Notably Arts. 1(3), 10, 11, 14, and 35; and chs. ix and x.

recommendations for the purpose of promoting international cooperation in political, economic, and social fields and of adjusting situations
likely to impair the general welfare." [98] At San Francisco, the insistence on greater emphasis on law as the basis of the Organization and
as providing the desired standard of conduct in international relations
led to the inclusion of references to international law in Article 1(1)
and of a provision explicitly directing the General Assembly to encourage its progressive development and codification. On the other hand,
the interest of the United States delegation, under the influence of
Senator Vandenberg, in strengthening the General Assembly's authority as an organ of peaceful revision led to the introduction of a new
article dealing exclusively with the Assembly's powers of "peaceful
adjustment" of situations, including those "likely to impair the general
welfare." [99]

Article 13 does not state who may request the General Assembly to
initiate studies or to whom the recommendations may be made. In
practice, studies have been requested by other principal organs and by
subsidiary organs, by specialized agencies, and by member states.
Recommendations have been addressed to members, states, and particular groups of states; to principal and subsidiary organs; to specialized agencies and other intergovernmental organizations; and to
nongovernmental organizations. A few recommendations have been in
the form of general statements or addressed to private persons. Generally, recommendations under paragraph 1(a) have been addressed to
governments and to other organs and subsidiary organs with responsibilities in the relevant areas, while recommendations under paragraph
1(b) have had a wider range of addressees.

Promoting International Cooperation in the Political Field

The General Assembly specifically invoked its authority under this
article in establishing the Interim Committee in 1947.[100] One of the
duties of the Committee was to consider and make recommendations
to the General Assembly on how best to promote international cooperation in the political field. At its first session the Interim Committee requested the Secretariat to prepare a study on Article 11(1) and
13(1a) with a view to illuminating their special significance. According
to the conclusions of this study:

Article 13, paragraph 1, may be regarded as a transition from the functions
of the General Assembly dealing with the maintenance of peace and se-

[98] Ch. v, sec. B, para. 6.   [99] See Art. 14 and commentary.
[100] GA Res. 111(II), Nov. 13, 1947.

curity, to its functions, more nearly legislative in character, dealing with constructive efforts to secure cooperation between states in the field of "peaceful change" with which Article 14 deals. The word "political" is given no explanation, but it is set off as against legal development in the same clause, and as against economic, social, and other fields, which were transferred to the following clause. In all fields, political or not, an opportunity is afforded to the General Assembly to diminish the causes of war by securing agreement and cooperation among states which might otherwise resort to war. [101]

Among the recommendations made by the Interim Committee and approved by the General Assembly were that the Secretary-General be asked to prepare a revised text of the General Act of September 26, 1928, for the pacific settlement of international disputes, that the Security Council adopt the procedure of appointing a rapporteur or conciliator for any dispute or situation brought to its attention, and that a panel for inquiry and conciliation be established.[102] Largely because of nonparticipation of some members in its work, the Interim Committee failed to become an effective instrument for promoting political cooperation.

The General Assembly has adopted a number of resolutions setting forth general principles which members, and particularly the major powers, are asked to respect in order to strengthen peace and friendship among nations.[103] During the first decade of the United Nations such resolutions were commonly by-products of the propaganda phase of the cold war and were not taken seriously as constructive peace efforts.[104] Furthermore these resolutions did not specifically refer to Article 13(1) as their Charter base, and may be regarded more properly as efforts to formulate general principles of cooperation in the maintenance of international peace and security under Article 11(1).[105] In like manner, the General Assembly resolution calling for the study of "the principles of international law concerning friendly relations and cooperation among States," though using the language of Article 13(1) with respect to the progressive development of international law, invoked the authority of the General Assembly under Article 11(1) "to consider the general principles of cooperation in the maintenance of international peace and security." [106]

[101] UN Doc. A/AC.18/33/Feb. 27, 1948/p. 9.
[102] GA Res. 268A, B, and D(III), Apr. 28, 1949.
[103] For example, GA Res. 290(IV), Dec. 1, 1949, entitled "Essentials of Peace."
[104] See, for example, statement of delegate of New Zealand, GAOR/4th Sess., 1st Ctte./328th Mtg./Nov. 15, 1949/p. 279.
[105] See Art. 11(1) and commentary.
[106] GA Res. 1815(XVII), Dec. 18, 1962.

Progressive Development of International Law
and Its Codification

Various methods have been used to encourage the progressive development of international law and its codification. On occasion the Secretary-General has been charged with preparing studies which have served as the basis for later General Assembly resolutions on legal principles. Thus in connection with a survey conducted by a United Nations commission, the Secretariat was requested to prepare a study concerning the status of "the permanent sovereignty of peoples and nations over their natural wealth and resources" as a basic constituent of the right of self-determination. This study together with the commission's report provided the basis for the General Assembly's eight-point declaration concerning the permanent sovereignty of peoples and nations over their natural resources.[107]

On several occasions the General Assembly has established special committees for the purpose of studying and making recommendations or drafting legal instruments on various topics. The procedure followed in an endeavor to formulate the principles of international law concerning friendly relations and cooperation among states is the most recent example of this technique. In 1962 the General Assembly listed seven principles deserving study: abstention from the threat or use of force, peaceful settlement of disputes, noninterference by states in matters within the domestic jurisdiction of another, sovereign equality, equal rights and self-determination, duty of states to cooperate with one another, and good faith in the fulfillment of obligations.[108] At its next session the General Assembly established a special committee and instructed it to draw up a report containing the conclusions and recommendations on the first four principles referred to above,[109] and in 1965, after examining the committee's report, the Assembly requested it to "complete the consideration and elaboration" of all seven principles in 1966. The special committee was only able to reach a consensus on the principle of sovereign equality.[110]

Another method of implementing Article 13(1a) has been the use of the Sixth Committee of the General Assembly to draft a convention which is then recommended to member states. This procedure was followed in the case of the Genocide Convention.[111] It should be noted, however, that draft conventions on this subject had previously been prepared by the Secretary-General and an ad hoc committee

[107] GA Res. 1803(XVII), Dec. 18, 1962.
[108] GA Res. 1815(XVII), Dec. 18, 1962.
[109] GA Res. 1966(XVIII), Dec. 16, 1963.
[110] UN Doc. 5746, Nov. 16, 1964.   [111] GA Res. 266A(III), Dec. 9, 1948.

established by the Economic and Social Council. The Genocide Convention is the only case of a convention being drafted by the Sixth Committee.

In addition to making use of the above methods to carry out the provisions of Article 13(1a), the General Assembly in 1947, on the basis of a study made by the Committee on the Progressive Development of International Law and Its Codification, established the International Law Commission, and approved its Statute.[112] The members of the Commission are elected by the General Assembly and are to be "persons of recognized competence in international law" representing "the main forms of civilization" and "the principal legal systems of the world." [113] The provisions of the Statute reflect a clear intention to assimilate the qualifications of members of the Commission to those of judges of the International Court of Justice (Articles 2 and 9). The members are elected for five-year terms and may be reelected (Article 10). As a result of increases in United Nations membership after 1955 the membership of the Commission was increased from fifteen to twenty-one in 1956 and to twenty-five in 1961.[114] Although members are selected to serve as individual legal experts rather than representatives of their government, the basic requirement that they be persons of recognized competence in international law "has on occasion been minimized in the preoccupation with political and geographical factors." [115]

Functions of the International Law Commission

The main function of the Commission is to promote the progressive development and codification of international law. Article 15 of the Commission's Statute states that " 'progressive development of international law' is used for convenience as meaning the preparation of draft conventions on subjects which have not yet been regulated by international law or in regard to which the law has not yet been sufficiently developed in the practice of States," while " 'codification of international law' is used for convenience as meaning the more precise formulation and systematization of rules of international law in fields where there already has been extensive State practice, precedent, and doctrine."

Consistent with this distinction between "progressive development"

[112] GA Res. 174(II), Nov. 21, 1947. For text of the revised Statute see United Nations Office of Public Information, *The Work of the International Law Commission*, pp. 55–60.

[113] Arts. 2 and 8 of the Statute.

[114] GA Res. 1103(XI), Dec. 18, 1956; and 1647(XVI), Nov. 6, 1961.

[115] Herbert W. Briggs, *The International Law Commission* (Ithaca, Cornell University Press, 1965), p. 42.

and "codification" the Commission's Statute sets forth different procedures applicable to each. Article 18, which provides that "the Commission shall survey the whole field of international law with a view to selecting topics for codification," has been interpreted as giving the Commission the right to initiate projects in this area. The Commission, however, must "give priority to requests of the General Assembly to deal with any question." When a draft is considered to be satisfactory the Commission requests the Secretary-General to issue it as a Commission document, and governments are requested to submit comments on it (Article 21). Taking these comments into consideration, the Commission prepares a final draft in the form of articles and an explanatory report which are submitted with its recommendations to the General Assembly through the Secretary-General (Articles 20 and 22). The Commission may recommend that the General Assembly take no action, the report having already been published; take note of or adopt the report by resolution; recommend the draft to members with a view to the conclusion of a convention; or convoke a conference to conclude a convention.

With regard to the development of international law, the Commission does not have the right to choose the topics to be studied. The initiative must come from the General Assembly, the principal organs of the United Nations other than the General Assembly, specialized agencies, official bodies established by inter-governmental agreement, or member states (Articles 16 and 17). In dealing with proposals of the General Assembly for the progressive development of international law, the Commission appoints a rapporteur, formulates a plan of work, circulates a questionnaire to governments, and may consult with scientific institutions and individual experts. The drafts of the Commission are issued by the Secretary-General as Commission documents, and governments are invited to submit their comments. Such comments are taken into consideration in the preparation of the final draft which is submitted to the General Assembly together with the Commission's recommendations (Article 16).

With respect to proposals submitted by member states or bodies other than the General Assembly, the Commission, if it deems appropriate to proceed with the study of such proposals, formulates a plan of work and circulates a questionnaire to all United Nations members and to the organs, specialized agencies or official bodies concerned with the question. Subsequently, the Commission submits a report and its recommendations to the General Assembly, but before doing so, it may, if it deems desirable, make an interim report to the organ or agency that submitted the proposal. If the General Assembly invites the Commission to proceed with its work in accordance with a suggested plan, then the procedure applicable to proposals originating in the Assembly is to be followed.[116]

The distinction between progressive development and codification of international law was made because the Soviet member of the Committee on the Progressive Development of International Law and Its Codification insisted that all the work of the Commission should be submitted to the General Assembly in the form of international conventions. Since some felt that the convention method would present disadvantages when the task before the Commission was to ascertain and declare law which already existed rather than to develop new law, a compromise was struck. The Soviet representative's views were met in the Statute "as to progressive development, but he was induced to agree to scientific restatements among other methods, for codification." [117] The Committee on the Progressive Development of International Law and Its Codification, however, recognized that "no clear cut distinction between the formulation of the law as it is and the law as it ought to be could be rigidly maintained in practice" and "that in any work of codification, the codifier inevitably has to fill in gaps and amend law in the light of new developments." [118] The Commission has, in practice, followed essentially the same procedure in both cases. It has generally considered that its drafts constitute both codification and progressive development of international law in the sense in which these terms are used in the Statute, and has found it impractical to determine in which category particular provisions fall.[119]

In addition to its functions relating to the progressive development of international law and its codification, the Commission has been charged with considering "ways and means for making the evidence of customary international law more readily available, such as the collection and publication of documents concerning State practice and of the decisions of national and international courts on questions of international law" (Article 24). Pursuant to this provision, the Commission has made various recommendations with reference to the preparation and distribution of publications concerning international law and the General Assembly has taken steps to comply with the Commission's suggestions.[120]

[116] Art. 17. The only projects that have been submitted under this provision have been two requests of ECOSOC concerning the nationality of married women and the elimination or reduction of statelessness.

[117] Briggs, p. 139.   [118] UN Doc. A/AC.10/51, June 17, 1947, para. 10.

[119] United Nations Office of Public Information, *The Work of the International Law Commission*, p. 12.

[120] See, for example, GA Res. 487(V), Dec. 12, 1950; 602(VI), Feb. 1, 1952; 686(VII), Dec. 5, 1952; 987(X), Dec. 3, 1955; 1291(XIII), Dec. 5, 1958; 1451(XIV), Dec. 7, 1959; 1506(XV), Dec. 12, 1960; and 1814(XVII), Dec. 18, 1962.

The drafting of the "Law of the Sea" by the International Law Commission provides a good illustration of the Commission in action. In 1949 the regime of the high seas was selected by the Commission as a subject for codification. Subsequently, the Commission, pursuant to a recommendation by the General Assembly,[121] decided to initiate work on the regime of the territorial sea. In 1953 the Commission completed some draft articles on the continental shelf and fisheries which were submitted to the General Assembly for its consideration. The Assembly, however, decided not to deal with any aspect of the regime of the high seas or of that of the territorial sea until the Commission had studied and reported on the whole subject.[122] Pursuant to the General Assembly decision, the Commission in 1956 consolidated in a single report all the rules adopted with respect to the high seas, territorial seas, the contiguous zone, continental shelf, and fisheries and the protection of the living resources of the sea. On the basis of these draft articles the United Nations Conference on the Law of the Sea, which met in Geneva in 1958, adopted four conventions: on the territorial sea, the high seas, the continental shelf, and fishing and conservation of the living resources of the high seas.

Although, as will be seen below, the Commission recognized that some aspects of its work fell within the category of progressive development, no questionnaires to governments were circulated as stipulated in Article 16(c) of the Commission's Statute. The Commission did submit its draft articles to governments for their comment and took them into account in drafting the final text and making its recommendations. On some questions, such as the problem of delimiting the territorial sea of two adjacent states, the Commission consulted with experts to seek clarification on technical aspects.

During the period 1949 to 1966, the Commission completed the following drafts, which were submitted to the General Assembly: Draft Declaration on Rights and Duties of States, Principles of International Law Recognized in the Charter of the Nüremberg Tribunal and in the Judgment of the Tribunal, Draft Code of Offenses against the Peace and Security of Mankind, Draft Conventions on the Elimination of Future Statelessness, Draft Articles on the Law of the Sea, Model Rules on Arbitral Procedure, Draft Articles on Diplomatic Intercourse and Immunities, Draft Articles on Consular Relations, and Draft Articles on the Law of Treaties. Multilateral conventions based on Commission drafts, were concluded under the auspices of the United Nations on the Law of the Sea, Diplomatic Relations, Reduction of Statelessness, and

[121] GA Res. 374(IV), Dec. 6, 1949.
[122] GA Res. 798(VIII), Dec. 7, 1953; and 899(IX), Dec. 14, 1954.

Consular Relations.[123] A conference for the conclusion of a convention on the Law of Treaties was envisaged.[124]

Promoting International Cooperation in the Economic and Social Fields

Paragraphs 1b and 2 of Article 13 set forth, in part directly and in part by reference to chapters IX and X, the functions and powers of the General Assembly in the fields of economic and social activity and of human rights. Apart from slight differences in wording, the objectives set forth in paragraph 1b are the same as those defined in Article 55. However, the latter article contains a more specific description of the particular areas in which international cooperation is to be promoted. Consequently the substance of the activity covered by this article is treated in connection with Article 55. With respect to types of action taken by the Assembly, the general comments above on kinds of action taken to implement Article 13 apply to this paragraph. This aspect is also considered in the commentary on Article 55. Frequent use has been made by the General Assembly of its powers under this article.[125]

Article 14

Subject to the provisions of Article 12, the General Assembly may recommend measures for the peaceful adjustment of any situation, regardless of origin, which it deems likely to impair the general welfare or friendly relations among nations, including situations resulting from a violation of the provisions of the present Charter setting forth the Purposes and Principles of the United Nations.

The powers of discussion and recommendation accorded to the General Assembly under Article 14 are a particularization of its broad powers under Article 10, and are subject to the same limitations. In this sense, Article 14 is similar to Article 11. While the latter article specifically empowers the Assembly to discuss and make recommendations on questions relating to the maintenance of international peace and security, Article 14 makes it clear that the Assembly may also recommend

---

[123] For texts of drafts and conventions listed above, see United Nations Office of Public Information, *The Work of the International Law Commission;* see also *Official Records of the United Nations Conference on Consular Relations, Vienna, Mar. 4–Apr. 22, 1963,* Vol. II.

[124] GA Res. 2166(XXI), Dec. 5, 1966.

[125] For the tabulation of studies initiated by the General Assembly under Article 13(1b), see *Repertory,* I, 446–61; *Supp. 1,* I, 163–68; *Supp. 2,* II, 133–43.

measures for the peaceful adjustment of other types of situations which are not necessarily of the character covered by Article 11.

There was no provision similar to Article 14 in the Dumbarton Oaks Proposals, although they did authorize the General Assembly to "initiate studies and make recommendations for the purpose . . . of adjusting situations likely to impair the general welfare." [126] The impetus for including Article 14 as a separate article in the Charter stemmed largely from the desires of some delegates to give the Assembly powers similar to those entrusted to the League Assembly. Under Article 19 of the Covenant the Assembly was authorized to "advise the reconsideration by Members of the League of treaties which have become inapplicable." It was a desire not to tie the new world organization to any wartime agreements that prompted Senator Vandenberg to take the lead in proposing the inclusion in the Charter of a specific provision for treaty revision.[127]

On the other hand, there were those who sought to include in the Charter a specific reference to the sanctity of treaties and who objected that any reference to treaty revision would weaken the nature of international contractual obligations which provide the basis for orderly relations among the nations of the world. It was also argued that such a provision would virtually invite enemy states to seek revision of the peace treaties concluded at the end of World War II.

In the end a compromise was reached. A reference was added to the preamble of the Charter concerning the establishment of "conditions under which justice and respect for the obligations arising from treaties and other sources of international law can be maintained." No mention of treaty revision was included in Article 14 on the ground that it was unnecessary, since "regardless of origin" was broad enough to cover such situations.[128]

As the report of the United States Secretary of State explained:

explicit reference to the revision of treaties would throw the weight of the Organization too heavily on the side of revision and encourage change beyond the needs of situations requiring it. It was argued that it is not possible to launch an international organization based on international integrity and at the same time intimate any lack of respect for treaties, which are the principal instruments through which international integrity functions. Indeed, consideration of the general welfare and friendly relations

[126] This phrase was included in the provision that eventually became Art. 13 of the Charter.

[127] He later accepted and championed the broader phraseology eventually used in Art. 14. See Arthur H. Vandenberg, *The Private Papers of Senator Vandenberg* (Boston, Houghton Mifflin, 1952), pp. 96, 122, 162–63, 168, 183–84.

[128] See Russell, pp. 755–56, 759, and 764–69; and UNCIO, *Documents*, IX, 126–30, 138–42, 149–52, 200, and 347.

might call for a recommendation that a treaty should be respected by its signatories rather than that it should be revised. The thousands of treaties in operation as the bond of orderly relations among the nations of the world should not be weakened by raising doubts about their value or permanence.

The report concluded that the "broad powers entrusted to the General Assembly will enable it to render effective aid in the difficult process of 'peaceful change'." [129]

The General Assembly has indeed played an important role in bringing about changes in the postwar world, although in many cases the process has been far from "peaceful." The importance of the Assembly's role in this respect has been less in its efforts to bring about the revision of formal treaties between members than in its championship of the principle of "equal rights and self-determination of peoples."

Article 14 has been frequently invoked by members in bringing questions to the General Assembly, usually together with Article 10 and sometimes with reference to Article 35 and to the purposes and principles of the Charter. It has also been frequently cited in the debates in the Assembly to justify the right of the Assembly to consider and make recommendations on particular questions.[130] In connection with a number of questions involving the former enemy states, the broad powers of the Assembly to consider situations, "regardless of origin," have been invoked to counter arguments by the Soviet bloc that Article 107 precluded any action by the Assembly.[131] More often, the application of Article 14 has been discussed in connection with alleged violations of the purposes and principles of the Charter, especially those concerning human rights and self-determination. Article 14 has been invoked to justify action by the Assembly in these cases in the face of arguments that the questions being dealt with are matters of domestic jurisdiction.

In considering the apartheid policies of South Africa, for example, the General Assembly asked its Special Commission to study the situation in relation "to the provisions of the Charter and, in particular, to Article 14." [132] In its report, the commission gave the following interpretation of the scope of the article:

[129] State Dept., *Report to the President*, p. 58.
[130] For citations of incidental references to Art. 14, see *Repertory*, I, 468, n. 6; *Supp. 1*, I, 170, n.2; and *Supp. 2*, II, 146, n.1.
[131] See in particular the debate on "Suggestions" regarding revisions of the Italian peace treaty. GAOR/2d Sess., Gen. Ctte./37th–38th Mtgs./Sept. 21, 1947/pp. 15–17; and 90th and 91st Plen. Mtgs./Sept. 23, 1947/pp. 277–92.
[132] GA Res. 721(VIII), Dec. 8, 1953.

It is clear that by the inclusion of Article 14 in the Charter it was intended also to make provision for cases (regardless of origin) which, though not directly threatening peace and security, were likely to bring interests into conflict with one another, to impair friendly relations among nations, and to prejudice the "general welfare." . . . The Charter makes particular mention in this Article of the fact that the situations in question include those "resulting from a violation of the provisions of the present Charter setting forth the Purposes and Principles of the United Nations."

This last passage of Article 14 recognizes explicitly and clearly that any violation of the Purposes and Principles of the Charter, the Organization's *raison d'être,* is prejudicial to the "general welfare" and might impair "friendly relations among nations." [133]

The relation of Article 14 to the principle of self-determination was also discussed at some length in connection with a proposal that the Assembly establish a commission to examine any situation resulting from alleged denial or inadequate realization of the right of self-determination.[134]

As in the case of Articles 10 and 11, "the General Assembly under Article 14 can only make recommendations," [135] and does so subject to the injunction contained in Article 12.[136]

As previously pointed out, it is not customary for the General Assembly to refer in its resolutions to the specific article of the Charter under which it is acting and whether a particular resolution constitutes an exercise by the Assembly of its powers under Article 14 or under Articles 10 or 11 is of no practical significance. The Assembly did specifically refer to its responsibilities under Article 14 in calling upon Portugal to submit information on its non-self-governing territories.[137] In a number of other cases the Assembly has used the language of Article 14 without referring to it. In its initial resolution regarding the treatment of persons of Indian origin in South Africa, for example, the Assembly stated that "friendly relations between the two Member States have been impaired," [138] and in the preamble to its 1947 Palestine resolution the Assembly stated that the "present situation in Palestine is one which is likely to impair the general welfare and friendly relations among nations." [139]

[133] GAOR/8th Sess./*Supp. 16*/para. 114.
[134] For citations to these discussions, see *Repertory, Supp. 1,* 173, n.11.
[135] Unlike Arts. 10 and 11, Art. 14 does not indicate to whom "recommendations" are to be addressed.
[136] For one view of the relationship between Art. 14 and Arts. 11(2) and 12, see "Certain Expenses of the United Nations," *ICJ Reports,* 1962, pp. 163 and 172.
[137] GA Res. 1542(XV), Dec. 14, 1960.   [138] GA Res. 41(I), Dec. 8, 1946.
[139] GA Res. 181(II), Nov. 29, 1947. For other examples, see GA Res. 427(V), Dec. 14, 1950; 509(VI), Dec. 14, 1951; and 1497(XV), Oct. 31, 1960.

Article 15

1. The General Assembly shall receive and consider annual and special reports from the Security Council; these reports shall include an account of the measures that the Security Council has decided upon or taken to maintain international peace and security.

2. The General Assembly shall receive and consider reports from the other organs of the United Nations.

By authorizing the General Assembly to "receive and consider" reports from the other organs of the United Nations, the Charter entrusts the Assembly with the function of overall review of the work of the Organization. That this role should be exercised by the Assembly, as the one organ in which all members are represented, was readily accepted by the drafters of the Charter. There was, however, considerable discussion at the San Francisco Conference concerning the kinds of action the Assembly might take upon receipt of the reports of the Security Council.[140]

Reports of the Security Council

The special emphasis in Article 15 upon reports from the Security Council, as well as the inclusion in Article 24(3) of a specific provision obligating the Council to submit reports to the Assembly, stemmed from the desire to assure that those members not represented on the Council would be fully informed of its activities. At San Francisco, a proposal requiring the Council to give reasons for all its actions and decisions was defeated, but it was decided to add to the Dumbarton Oaks text a specific statement to the effect that the Council's report should include "an account of the measures" it had "decided upon or taken to maintain international peace and security."

While it was agreed that the Security Council, through the General Assembly, owed world public opinion an account of how it had performed its functions, the delegates were divided on the question of whether the Assembly should be empowered to pass judgment upon the Council's actions. The disagreement on this point was part of the general division between those who sought to associate the Assembly more closely with the actions of the Council in maintaining peace and security and those who sought to prevent any interference by the Assembly with the functioning of the Council. There was considerable

[140] For the principal discussion at San Francisco, see UNCIO, *Documents,* IX, 86–88, 93–94, 182–86, 411–13, 427–29, and 433–37.

support for empowering the Assembly "to approve or disapprove in whole or in part" the Council's reports and to make "recommendations" or "decisions" thereon. Eventually, it was decided merely to state that the Assembly "shall receive and consider" the reports. Although it would not have the right to approve, or make recommendations on, the reports themselves, it would have the right to discuss any question arising from matters contained in the reports and, subject to the limitations imposed by Article 12, to make recommendations thereon.[141]

In practice, the annual report of the Security Council is hardly ever discussed by the General Assembly.[142] It consists of a summary of the Council's debates and decisions, and is included on the agenda of each regular Assembly session. During the first years the report was referred to one of the political committees, but the practice soon developed of dealing with it directly in plenary where the Assembly, usually without formal vote, adopts a resolution "taking note" of the report.

With regard to "special reports" by the Security Council, neither Article 15(1) nor Article 24(2) makes it clear whether they are to be submitted on the initiative of the Council or at the request of the Assembly. In accordance with its Provisional Rules of Procedure, the Council has submitted several special reports to the Assembly concerning the admission of new members to the United Nations. Especially during the long deadlock over admissions, these reports were fully discussed in the Assembly, which in several instances made recommendations to the Security Council on the subject matter.[143]

The Council has on occasion transmitted documentation to the Assembly. When, for example, the Council decided to remove from its agenda the questions of Franco Spain and the Greek frontier incidents to permit the Assembly to make recommendations thereon, it also instructed the Secretary-General to place at the Assembly's disposal the records of the Council's discussions on the two questions. Similarly, the Council instructed the Secretary-General to transmit to the Assembly the reports of the Atomic Energy Commission and the Commission for Conventional Armaments, together with the records of the Council's discussions on these reports.

Reports from Other United Nations Organs

The Rules of Procedure of the Assembly provide that the provisional agenda of each regular session shall include the report of the Secretary-General on the work of the Organization; and reports from the Secu-

[141] *Ibid.*, pp. 94, 412, 186; and XI, 184.
[142] For the few instances in which criticism or reservations have been made, see *Repertory*, I, 488–89.
[143] See commentary on Art. 4.

rity Council, the Economic and Social Council, the Trusteeship Council, and the International Court of Justice.[144]

The International Court has never submitted an annual report to the General Assembly. Neither the Statute of the Court nor the Charter articles concerning the Court makes any mention of reports to the General Assembly.

The Secretary-General, on the other hand, is specifically required by Article 98 to "make an annual report to the General Assembly on the work of the Organization." These reports, which are essentially factual summaries of the various activities of the Organization, are circulated well in advance of the Assembly session. The first Secretary-General often supplemented his annual reports with an additional statement of his views, either in writing or orally during the opening general debate in the Assembly. The second Secretary-General, preferring not to take part in the general debate, developed the practice of submitting his annual report in two parts, a summary of the work of the Organization and a separate "introduction," presenting his views concerning the role of the United Nations; this was circulated shortly before the opening of each session.

Although the Secretary-General's reports on specific agenda items— made either at the Assembly's request or on his own initiative—play an important part in the Assembly discussions, the annual report on the work of the Organization has never been the subject of discussion; nor does the Assembly even formally "take note" of the report.

Though the Charter contains no provision expressly requiring it, both ECOSOC and the Trusteeship Council submit annual reports to the General Assembly. It should be noted that both operate "under the authority of the General Assembly," [145] which has principal responsibility in these fields. As a result, the annual reports of ECOSOC and the Trusteeship Council are handled by the Assembly quite differently from the reports of other United Nations organs.

The report of the Trusteeship Council is referred to the Fourth Committee of the General Assembly. Various parts of the report are discussed by the Committee in relation to items on its agenda. In addition to the adoption of resolutions on specific subjects, including recommendations concerning the operation of the Trusteeship Council, it has become the practice of the Assembly to adopt a general resolution taking note of the Council's report and recommending that it take into account the comments and suggestions made during the discussion.

[144] Rule 13. The rule also covers reports from subsidiary organs and from the specialized agencies. See commentary on Arts. 22 and 57.
[145] See commentary on Arts. 60 and 85.

ECOSOC's report is handled in much the same way. Those parts of the report dealing with economic matters are referred to the Second Committee; those relating to social questions, including human rights, are taken up by the Third Committee. During the early years, parts of the report were considered by a Joint Second and Third Committee (with the Fifth Committee sometimes included). On the basis of the Joint Committee's report, the Assembly generally adopted a resolution taking note of the ECOSOC's report. This practice has been abandoned, however, and in general, the Assembly at one of its plenary meetings takes note of the report without adopting a formal resolution on the matter.

Article 16

The General Assembly shall perform such functions with respect to the international trusteeship system as are assigned to it under Chapters XII and XIII, including the approval of the trusteeship agreements for areas not designated as strategic.

The Charter assigns to the General Assembly overall responsibility for the operations of the trusteeship system, except that "strategic" trusteeships come under the authority of the Security Council.[146] The powers and functions of the Assembly are spelled out in Chapters XII and XIII.[147]

Article 17

1. The General Assembly shall consider and approve the budget of the Organization.
2. The expenses of the Organization shall be borne by the Members as apportioned by the General Assembly.
3. The General Assembly shall consider and approve any financial and budgetary arrangements with specialized agencies referred to in Article 57 and shall examine the administrative budgets of such specialized agencies with a view to making recommendations to the agencies concerned.

Article 17 is the only one in the Charter that deals exclusively with the finances of the Organization.[148] Its importance is obvious since it is

[146] See commentary on Arts. 82 and 83.
[147] See especially commentary on Arts. 76, 79, and 85 to 88.
[148] Arts. 33 and 35(3) of the Statute of the Court deal with the financing of that organ.

a well-recognized principle that financial control carries with it the means of exercising important, if not decisive, influence over substantive policies and activities.

Article 6(5) of the Covenant of the League of Nations originally provided that: "The expenses of the Secretariat shall be borne by Members of the League in accordance with the apportionment of the expenses of the International Bureau of the Universal Postal Union."

This provision was found in practice to be too narrow in scope and unsatisfactory in operation. By an amendment which entered into force on August 13, 1924, the following text was substituted: "The expenses of the League shall be borne by the Members of the League in the proportion decided by the Assembly."

The Covenant contained no provision explicitly dealing with the authorization of expenditures and the review of financial operations. In practice, the Council initially assumed the function of approving the budget as prepared by the Secretary-General, but the Assembly early asserted and established its exclusive right of approval. Furthermore, by 1928 the Supervisory Commission, initially appointed by the Council to assist in the review of budget estimates and the supervision of financial administration, came under the exclusive control of the General Assembly and its Fourth Committee (Finance).[149]

The United States Tentative Proposals gave the General Assembly the power "to approve the budget of the organs and agencies of the Organization," and "to determine a provisional and a continuing basis of apportionment of expenses of the Organization among the Member States, together with the procedure of apportionment." In taking decisions with respect to these matters, however, each member state was to have voting power "in proportion to its contribution to the expenses of the Organization." Decisions were to be taken by two-thirds vote.[150] These proposals, with the exception of that for weighted voting, were in substance incorporated into the Dumbarton Oaks Proposals.[151]

At the San Francisco Conference, there was complete agreement that the General Assembly should have the power to approve the budget and apportion expenses. The only issue discussed at any length was whether the Charter should specify the method of apportionment and the procedures of budgetary preparation and examination. It was decided that the General Assembly should be left free to decide these

---

[149] See J. David Singer, "The Finances of the League of Nations," *International Organization*, XIII (1959), 255–73, and Felix Morley, *The Society of Nations* (Washington, Brookings Institution, 1932), pp. 500–44; and Regulations for the Financial Administration of the League of Nations, LN Doc. C.614.M.191, 1928 X.

[150] State Dept., *Post-War Foreign Policy Preparation, 1939–1945*, pp. 597–98.

[151] See especially ch. v, sec. B(5), and sec. C(2).

matters. The text finally approved was drafted to make clear the obligation of each member to pay its share of the expenses.[152]

The matter of budgetary and financial arrangements was given detailed consideration by the Preparatory Commission and its Executive Committee, and the recommendations of the Commission were in substance adopted by the General Assembly in its first session.[153]

Article 17(3) has a different history. It was developed in the context of concern to achieve coordination of the policies and activities of the United Nations and the specialized agencies. The Dumbarton Oaks Proposals gave the Economic and Social Council the power "to examine the administrative budgets of such specialized organizations or agencies" as might be brought into relationship with the Organization "with a view to making recommendations to the organizations or agencies concerned." [154] At San Francisco, it was decided to give this power to the General Assembly, as well as the related power to approve financial arrangements with the agencies.[155]

The Budgetary Power

The power "to consider and approve the budget" is the basis of the General Assembly's control over the expenditures of the Organization. This control extends to determining the manner in which estimates are presented, the procedure by which they are considered, the authorization of expenses, and the method of accounting.[156]

The extent of the General Assembly's control over expenditures is indicated by the following provisions of the Financial Regulations.

Regulation 13.1: No council, commission or other competent body shall take a decision regarding expenditures unless it has before it a report from the Secretary-General on the administrative and financial implications of the proposal.

Regulation 13.2: Where in the opinion of the Secretary-General, the proposed expenditure cannot be made from the existing appropriations, it shall not be incurred until the General Assembly has made the necessary appropriation, unless the Secretary-General certifies that provision can be made under the conditions of the resolution of the General Assembly relating to unforeseen and extraordinary expenses.

The Economic and Social Council, the Trusteeship Council, and the regional economic commissions have incorporated, into their Rules of

---

[152] See Russell, pp. 862–63.

[153] See *Report of the Preparatory Commission*, pp. 104–13; GA Res. 68(I) and 69(I), Dec. 14, 1946; and 80(I), Dec. 11, 1946.

[154] Ch. ix, sec. c(d).   [155] Russell, p. 803.

[156] Financial regulations were adopted by the General Assembly at its fifth session, Res. 456(V), Nov. 16, 1950; and amended at its tenth session, Res. 950(X), Nov. 3, 1955; and 973B(X), Dec. 15, 1955.

Procedure, rules giving effect to Financial Regulation 13.1. The Provisional Rules of Procedure of the Security Council do not contain any such provision. Financial provision for implementation of Security Council decisions has in fact been made by the General Assembly as the organ empowered to appropriate funds. In those cases where the Council has taken a decision at a time when the General Assembly is not in session, the Secretary-General has incurred the necessary expenditure under the provisions of the annual resolution on unforeseen and extraordinary expenses.[157] In only two or three instances has the Council directly concerned itself with the financial aspects of resolutions adopted by it.[158]

The power of the General Assembly to consider and approve the budget and to authorize expenditures is subject to Charter provisions governing the functions and powers of the United Nations and its organs.[159] The International Court of Justice has suggested, however, that an expense incurred by an organ in excess of its powers may be an expense of the Organization under Article 17(2).[160]

The Assembly's control over expenditures is limited in another respect: it may not be free to disapprove a particular expenditure proposed to it. In the case of certain awards of compensation made by the United Nations Administrative Tribunal to United States nationals who had been terminated or dismissed from the United Nations Secretariat, the United States representative argued that the General Assembly's power to consider and approve the budget extended to reviewing awards and refusing to authorize payment of those found unsound.[161] In its opinion, given at the request of the Assembly and accepted by it, the International Court of Justice observed that

the function of approving the budget does not mean that the General Assembly has an absolute power to approve or disapprove the expenditure proposed to it; for some part of that expenditure arises out of obligations already incurred by the Organization, and to this extent the General Assembly has no alternative but to honour these engagements.[162]

Similarly, the Court has observed that obligations may be incurred by the Secretary-General, acting under the authority of the Security Council or the General Assembly, and that the Assembly "has no alternative but to honour these engagements." [163] Obligations incurred

157 *ICJ Pleadings*, 1962, "Certain Expenses of the United Nations (Article 17, paragraph 2 of the Charter)," pp. 45–47.
158 See *ibid.*, pp. 47–48.
159 The question of Charter limitations is extensively discussed in connection with the financing of peace-keeping operations; see below, pp. 157–65.
160 *ICJ Reports*, 1962, p. 169.
161 GAOR/8th Sess., 5th Ctte./420th Mtg./Dec. 3, 1953/paras. 23–70.
162 *ICJ Reports*, 1954, p. 58.   163 *ICJ Reports*, 1962, p. 169.

by the United Nations under bonds issued by the Secretary-General under General Assembly authority are a case in point.[164]

Budgetary Procedure

The regular budget of the Organization is prepared, considered, and approved on an annual basis, the financial year being the calendar year. The estimates prepared by the Secretary-General must be submitted to the Advisory Committee on Administrative Budgetary Questions at least twelve weeks prior to the opening of the regular annual session of the General Assembly.[165] Together with the report of the Advisory Committee, they must be transmitted to members at least five weeks before the opening of the annual session. They are considered by the Fifth Committee, whose decisions are taken by simple majority. The Committee's decisions are incorporated into a draft resolution, which must be approved by the General Assembly in plenary session by a two-thirds majority.[166] Revised estimates are prepared and considered in a similar way, and when approved are incorporated into the annual appropriation resolution.

The annual appropriation resolution is not the only means by which the General Assembly authorizes expenditures. Each year, the Assembly adopts a resolution on unforeseen and extraordinary expenses which authorizes the Secretary-General, under certain conditions, to incur obligations and expenditures for which no provision has been made in the budget. "Unforeseen expenses" cover additional obligations and expenditures arising in connection with the implementation of approved programs provided for in the budget. "Extraordinary expenses" cover obligations and expenditures arising as the result of the approval by a council, commission, or other competent United Nations body of new programs and activities not contemplated when the budget was approved.[167]

As the result of the extraordinary financial demands of peace-keeping operations in the Middle East (UNEF) and the Congo (ONUC), the conditions under which the Secretary-General can authorize expenditures under the resolution on unforeseen and extraordinary expenses were reexamined by the General Assembly.

[164] See GA Res. 1739(XVI), Dec. 20, 1961.

[165] For parts and sections into which the budget is divided see, for example, Budget Estimates for the Fiscal Year 1966 and Information Annexes, GAOR/20th Sess./1965/*Supp. 5* (A/6005).

[166] For details see Financial Regulations and Rules of the United Nations, esp. Regulations 3.1 to 3.7, and Rules of Procedure of the General Assembly, UN Doc. A/4700, Feb., 1961.

[167] *ICJ Pleadings*, "Certain Expenses of the United Nations (Article 17, paragraph 2 of the Charter)," p. 42.

Under the terms of resolutions adopted up to 1960, the Secretary-General, with the prior concurrence of the Advisory Committee on Administrative and Budgetary Questions, had practically unlimited authority to incur expenses for duly authorized activities. Since then, his authority has been more closely defined. The General Assembly limited to $2 million the commitments the Secretary-General could enter into for fiscal year 1963 in the maintenance of peace without the concurrence of the Advisory Committee on Administrative and Budgetary Questions, and further provided that, if as a result of a decision by the Security Council, commitments relating to the maintenance of peace and security should arise in an estimated total exceeding $10 million before the eighteenth session, a special session of the General Assembly "shall be convened by the Secretary-General to consider the matter." [168]

In addition to authorizations under the regular budget resolution and the resolution relating to unforeseen and extraordinary expenses, the General Assembly may authorize expenditures by special resolutions. In the case of peace-keeping operations which have necessitated exceptionally large expenditures, special accounts have been established and special authorizations have been voted by the General Assembly following submission of estimates by the Secretary-General, and examination and recommendation by the Advisory Committee on Administrative and Budgetary Questions.[169]

Appropriations approved by the General Assembly on the basis of the annual budget estimates submitted by the Secretary-General have progressively increased over the years in response to increased membership, increasing needs, and higher price levels. Proposals to establish budget ceilings, either for the whole budget or for the administrative budget as distinguished from the operational, have not been accepted.[170] Since 1956, special appropriations have been made for UNEF and ONUC. The following table gives the amounts appropriated under the annual appropriation resolutions for the years 1946–1966, expenses for UNEF and ONUC not being included:

1946	$19,390,000	1950	49,641,773
1947	27,740,000	1951	47,798,600
1948	34,825,195	1952	48,096,780
1949	43,487,128	1953	48,327,700

168 GA Res. 1862(XVII), Dec. 20, 1962. The same limitation was imposed for subsequent years. See GA Res. 2126(XX), Dec. 21, 1965.

169 See, for example, GA Res. 1090(XI), Feb. 27, 1951; 1864(XVII), Dec. 20, 1962, on UNEF; and 1590(XV), Dec. 20, 1960, and 1865(XVII), Dec. 20, 1962, on ONUC.

170 The Assembly in 1959 asked the Secretary-General to limit the public information expenditure for 1960 to "about $5 million." GA Res. 1405(XIV), Dec. 1, 1959.

1954	47,827,110	1961	72,969,300
1955	46,963,800	1962	82,144,740
1956	48,556,350	1963	93,911,050
1957	48,807,650	1964	101,327,600
1958	55,062,850	1965	108,472,800
1959	60,802,120	1966	121,567,420
1960	63,149,700		

Apportionment of Expenses

Article 17(2) is the logical corollary to 17(1). In the discussions at San Francisco, there was general agreement that this paragraph gives the General Assembly power to apportion expenses of the Organization among members and places upon them the obligation to pay the amounts thus determined. In United Nations practice, disagreements that have arisen have related principally to the interpretation and application of this paragraph with respect to expenses incurred in connection with operations involving the use of armed forces.[171]

After some preliminary discussion, it was decided at San Francisco to leave the details regarding the method of apportionment to the future determination of the General Assembly. The Preparatory Commission recommended that an expert committee be established to prepare a detailed scheme of apportionment, and that expenses should be apportioned "broadly according to capacity to pay." [172] The Committee also recommended the establishment of a Working Capital Fund to cover initial expenses and to insure means of financing future contingencies, the Fund to be established by advances from members determined broadly on the basis of capacity to pay.[173] In the San Francisco discussions and in the Preparatory Commission, the problem of providing necessary funds appears to have been viewed in terms of meeting the requirements of the regular budget.

Circumstances of the postwar period have not only produced a great expansion of United Nations activities in response to a variety of political, economic, and social needs, but have also encouraged the adoption of a variety of devices to permit states to take action without the possibility of obstruction by those states opposed or uncooperative. This has been particularly true of operations in the economic and social field. In the field of peace and security, the failure of members to implement key features of the peace and security system has opened the way to the development of new approaches to the maintenance of peace and security that have placed unforeseen financial demands upon the Organization.[174] The magnitude of these demands and the

---

[171] For further discussion, see pp. 157–65.
[172] Report of the Preparatory Commission, pp. 107–8.
[173] Ibid., pp. 109–10.   [174] See commentary on Arts. 42 and 43.

failure of members to agree on the manner of meeting them has created a serious financial crisis for the Organization.

For purposes of analysis, the problem of meeting expenses will be discussed under three headings: 1) expenses included in the regular budget; 2) expenses in the field of economic and social cooperation not included in the regular budget (largely operational and excluding the expenses included in the budgets of the specialized agencies); and 3) expenses of peace-keeping operations.

Expenses Included in the Regular Budget

After allowance is made for other sources of income,[175] these are apportioned among members by decision of the General Assembly in accordance with a scale based on the recommendation of the Committee on Contributions.[176] Under its initial terms of reference, the Committee was directed to apportion the expenses of the Organization "broadly according to capacity to pay." The Committee was told that "comparative estimates of national income would appear prima facie to be the fairest guide," but to prevent possible anomalies, the Committee was instructed also to take into account comparative per capita income, temporary economic dislocations resulting from the war, and ability of members to obtain foreign currencies.[177] According to the Assembly's Rules of Procedure, "the scale of assessments, when once fixed by the General Assembly, shall not be subject to a general revision for at least three years, unless it is clear that there have been substantial changes in relative capacities to pay" (Rule 161).

The Assembly decided in its eleventh session, on the recommendation of the Committee on Contributions, that the per capita contributions of no member should exceed that of the member bearing the highest assessment.[178] In 1957, the Assembly decided that "in principle" the maximum contribution of any one member should not exceed 30 percent of the total.[179] The minimum contribution is .04 percent of the total.

Inequalities of contributions under the approved scales of assessment

---

[175] For 1963, the following items other than assessments of members were listed in the Budget Estimates: staff assessments, income from extra-budgetary funds, general income, sale of UN postage stamps, sale of publications and services to visitors, and catering services. GAOR/20th Sess./1965, *Supp. 5*, p. 199.

[176] This is an expert committee consisting of ten members elected by the General Assembly and advising it concerning apportionment of expenses. Rules of Procedure of the General Assembly, Rules 160–61. For scale of assessments approved by the General Assembly for 1964, see *Y.U.N.*, 1963, pp. 551–52.

[177] GA Res. 14A(I), Feb. 13, 1946.

[178] GAOR/11th Sess./1955/*Supp. 10* (A/3121), paras. 12–15.

[179] GA Res. 1137(XII), Oct. 14, 1957.

are very great. Under the scale adopted by the General Assembly for 1965 to 1967,[180] eighteen members out of 117 were assessed for 86.21 percent of the total net expenditure of the Organization under the regular budget. These included:

Argentina	.92	Italy	2.54
Australia	1.58	Japan	2.77
Belgium	1.15	Netherlands	1.11
Brazil	.95	Poland	1.45
Canada	3.17	Sweden	1.26
China	4.25	Ukrainian SSR	1.97
Czechoslovakia	1.11	USSR	14.92
France	6.09	U.K.	7.21
India	1.85	U.S.	31.91

Four members contributed 60.13 percent of the total. Fifty-one members each contributed the minimum of .04 percent or a total of 2.04 percent.

*Expenses in the Field of Economic and
Social Cooperation*

Apart from administrative costs and those of technical programs included in the regular budget, operational expenses in the economic, social, and humanitarian fields have been met by voluntary contributions. This permits greater flexibility in the establishment and implementation of programs. Although it may be inferred from the opinion of the International Court of Justice in the "Certain Expenses" case that costs of economic and field operations may be considered expenses of the Organization and therefore subject to binding apportionment by the General Assembly,[181] that organ has not seen fit to treat the costs of such major operations in this manner. To do so would unquestionably create additional obstacles to their establishment; it would lead to large-scale refusals to contribute, and would limit the possibilities of participation by nonmember states.[182]

Special accounts are established by General Assembly resolution, and the funds are administered in accordance with the Financial Rules and Regulations of the United Nations. Among operations financed by voluntary contributions have been the Expanded Program for Technical Assistance (EPTA), the Special Fund, the United Nations

[180] GA Res. 2118(XX), Dec. 21, 1965.   [181] *ICJ Reports*, 1962, p. 168.

[182] Part V of the regular budget makes modest provision ($6.4 million in 1963) for technical programs. The expenditure for these programs is apportioned according to the regular scale. The Soviet Union regards this practice as contrary to the Charter and does not consider itself obligated to contribute to these programs. See statement by Soviet representative. GAOR/18th Sess., 5th Ctte./1022d Mtg./Oct. 22, 1963/para. 6.

Children's Fund, the United Nations Relief and Work Agency for Palestine Refugees in the Near East (UNRWA), and the programs administered by the Office of the United Nations High Commissioner for Refugees.[183]

Contributions by members to these special accounts differ markedly from those made to the regular budget in accordance with the scale prescribed by the General Assembly. In all cases, substantial contributions are made by nonmembers, especially the Federal Republic of Germany and Switzerland. The number of contributions varies greatly. For 1965, the number of contributors to the voluntary accounts ranged from thirty-seven in the case of the programs of the Office of the High Commissioner for Refugees to 114 for UNICEF. Also, there is wide variation in the percentages contributed by particular countries. The United States contribution, for example, to UNRWA for 1965 was 70 percent of the total, while its contributions to EPTA and the Special Fund were 40 percent. These percentages are to be compared with its 31.91 percent share of the regular budget.

Expenses of Peace-Keeping Operations

The question of the manner of financing peace-keeping operations did not arise until the establishment of the United Nations Emergency Force (UNEF) in 1950 and became critical with the establishment of the United Nations Force in the Congo (ONUC) in 1960. It would seem that this question had not arisen in the minds of the drafters of the Charter. They had presumably anticipated that the costs of military enforcement measures under Article 42 would be borne by the contributors of military contingents according to agreements concluded under Article 43, and that the great powers would bear the major part of the costs. Failure to conclude agreements under Article 43 and inability of the permanent members to agree on the use of military forces precluded the financing of such programs as the authors of the Charter apparently intended.

The conception of United Nations peace-keeping operations was developed to meet the needs of a special situation where an international military force could help to improve the chances for peaceful settlement without engaging in coercive action against a state and where the acceptability and effectiveness of the force would be improved by the nonparticipation of major-power contingents. This entailed special arrangements with respect to financing, since the smaller states contributing military contingents could not be expected

[183] For summary, see *ICJ Pleadings*, "Certain Expenses of the United Nations (Article 17, paragraph 2 of the Charter)," pp. 37–89.

to bear the whole cost of the operation. In the case of UNEF, the General Assembly adopted the policy of treating as expenses to be borne by the Organization "all extra and extraordinary costs which a government is obliged to incur in making forces available," [184] the costs of equipment and salaries that would exist in any case being borne by the contributing governments. A similar policy was followed in the case of ONUC.

UNEF and ONUC costs assumed by the United Nations under this policy exceeded by far the costs of comparable activities in which the Organization had engaged in the past, and in fact exceeded the amount of the regular United Nations budget. In earlier operations, such as the United Nations Truce Supervision Organization in Palestine (UNTSO) and the United Nations Military Observer Group in India and Pakistan (UNMOGIP), the costs had amounted to less than $3 million and had been included in the regular budget. In the cases of UNEF and ONUC, separate accounts were set up with special expense authorizations by the General Assembly, but with clear affirmations by the Secretary-General and the Assembly that these expenditures were to be treated as "expenses of the Organization" to "be borne by the Members as apportioned by the General Assembly." [185] In its efforts to provide funds to meet the expenses of UNEF and ONUC, the General Assembly relied initially on a combination of voluntary contributions and compulsory assessments. [186]

Because of failure of some members of the United Nations—including major contributors to the regular budget—to pay their apportioned shares of the expenses of these operations, a serious financial as well as constitutional crisis developed during the period 1960–66. The question of how United Nations peace-keeping operations might be financed to avoid such a crisis in the future, along with the question of how to eliminate the deficit that had arisen as the result of failure of members to pay, was the central concern of United Nations members during this time.

Broadly speaking, three positions have been taken. One group of members, including the United States and a number of Western members, has maintained that peace-keeping operations may be initiated by the General Assembly in case the Security Council is unable to act in the discharge of its primary responsibility; that the expenses of peace-keeping operations are expenses of the Organization; [187] that the Gen-

[184] Report of the Secretary-General, UN Doc. A/3694, Oct. 9, 1957.

[185] See UN Doc. A/3302, Nov. 6, 1956; and GA Res. 1001(ES-1), Nov. 7, 1956; 1089(XI), Dec. 21, 1956; and 1583(XV), Dec. 20, 1960.

[186] See GA Res. 1122(XI), Nov. 26, 1956; 1089(XI), Feb. 27, 1957, for UNEF; 1583(XV), Dec. 20, 1960, and 1619(XV), Apr. 12, 1961, for ONUC.

[187] This position, many times stated in discussions of the General Assembly, the Fifth Committee, and its special committee, was fully developed in the oral

eral Assembly has the power to apportion these expenses and in doing so to determine the amounts members are obligated to pay; and that in apportioning expenses the Assembly may use the same scale as in the regular budget or a modified scale, although it may decide to rely in whole or in part on contributions. The essence of this position has been that the principle of collective financial responsibility should be respected, that all members should pay something, and that no member should pay a disproportionate share.[188]

A second group, including the Soviet Union, other socialist states, and generally France, has taken an opposite position: it denies the right of the General Assembly to initiate operations involving the use of armed forces; denies that expenses of these operations are expenses of the Organization under Article 17(2); asserts that "expenses of the Organization" are expenses covered by the regular budget and are strictly administrative in nature; and claims for the Security Council the exclusive authority to allocate expenses of peace-keeping operations on a binding basis. The Soviet Union and other socialist members would place the major burden of payment on those responsible for the situation requiring the use of armed forces.[189] Until 1963, the Soviet Union and other socialist members had paid in full their contributions under the regular budget which included the costs of the Truce Supervisory Organization in Palestine, the United Nations Commission for the Unification and Rehabilitation of Korea, and the United Nations Field Service. In 1963, these members announced that they would not contribute to these costs and the costs of the United Nations bond issue even though included in the regular budget. They took the position that they were not bound to pay contributions under the regular budget to the extent that expenses resulting from the use of military forces were included in it.[190]

A third position, taken by many Latin American, African, and Asian members (sometimes in modified form), is that the General Assembly

statements of Mr. Abraham Chayes before the ICJ. *ICJ Pleadings*, "Certain Expenses of the United Nations (Article 17, paragraph 2 of the Charter)," pp. 397–412. It was supported by the Court in its advisory opinion. *ICJ Reports*, 1962, p. 151.

188 See U.S. memorandum of Oct. 8, 1964, UN Doc. A/5739. For summary of this and other positions, see "Report of the Working Group on the Examination of the Administrative and Budgetary Procedures of the United Nations," UN Doc. A/5407, Mar. 29, 1963.

189 See memoranda submitted by the Soviet Union, July 10 and Sept. 11, 1964. UN Docs. A/5721 and A/5729. See statement by the Permanent Representative of France in the Working Group, Oct. 16, 1964, UN Doc. A/AC.113/47, for a modified version of this position.

190 See Statement of Soviet representative, Oct. 22, 1963. GAOR/18th Sess., 5th Ctte./1022d Mtg./paras. 1–5. Compare with later statement of the U.S. representative in the Special Committee on Peace-Keeping Operations, Aug. 16, 1965. See below, pp. 163–64.

has the power to initiate peace-keeping operations if the Security Council fails to act; that the expenses of such operations may be apportioned by the Assembly but should not be regarded as "normal expenses" to be financed in the same manner as the regular budget; that these expenses should be apportioned in accordance with special criteria which would recognize the special responsibilities of certain members of the Council; and that other members should only be expected to make contributions of a symbolic character as a token of international solidarity.[191]

In order for any draft proposal to obtain the necessary two-thirds majority in the General Assembly, it has been necessary for those members taking the first position to make concessions to the third group with respect to criteria to be applied. Thus in the fifteenth Assembly, the resolution finally approved for the financing of ONUC for the period January 1 to October 31, 1961, recognized in its preamble that the "extraordinary expenses" of the Congo operation were "different in nature" from the expenses of the regular budget. Although it provided for the apportionment of expenses up to $100 million in accordance with the scale of regular budget, "pending the establishment of a different scale of assessment," it specified reductions of 50 to 80 percent for certain members based on their low contributions to the regular budget and receipt of technical assistance. In addition, all members were urged to make voluntary contributions, permanent members of the Security Council were urged to make "sizable additional contributions," and Belgium, "a State directly concerned," was called upon to make "a substantial contribution." [192]

This resolution obtained the necessary two-thirds majority,[193] but provided no solution to the financial problem because of the refusal of some members to be bound by it. In an effort to find a generally satisfactory solution, the Assembly established a Working Group to consider methods for covering the costs of peace-keeping operations and the relation between such methods and existing administrative and budgetary methods.[194] This body in its report to the sixteenth session

[191] See statements made by Latin American delegates in the Fifth Committee of the fifteenth Assembly, especially that of the Venezuelan delegate at the 826th meeting, Mar. 28, 1961. The Mexican delegate on the basis of the *procès verbaux* of the San Francisco Conference argued that the expenses of peace-keeping operations were not "expenses of the Organization" under Art. 17(2), but he did not deny the Assembly's power to apportion. UN Doc. A/C.5/862, Apr. 14, 1961.

[192] GA Res. 1619(XV), Apr. 21, 1961. GA Res. 1633(XVI), Oct. 30, 1961, authorizing expenditures to cover the period Nov. 1, 1961, to June 30, 1962, contained similar provisions as did GA Res. 1733(XVI), Dec. 20, 1961, for financing UNEF.

[193] The vote was 54 to 15 with 23 abstentions.

[194] GA Res. 1620(XV), Apr. 21, 1961. The group was subsequently referred to as the Working Group on the Examination of the Administrative and Budgetary Procedures of the United Nations.

of the Assembly was not able to identify principles for the financing of peace-keeping operations that would meet with general acceptance.[195]

As for the moot question whether expenses of UNEF and ONUC as authorized by the General Assembly were "expenses of the Organization," the Assembly decided, at its sixteenth session, to ask the International Court for an advisory opinion.[196] On July 20, 1962, the Court gave its opinion, by a vote of 9 to 5, that the expenditures in question "constitute 'expenses of the Organization' within the meaning of Article 17, paragraph 2, of the Charter of the United Nations." [197] In reaching this conclusion, the Court took the position that "expenditures must be tested by their relationship to the purposes of the United Nations," and did not exclude the possibility that expenses incurred by organs in excess of their competence were to be regarded as expenses of the Organization.[198] The Assembly, in its seventeenth session, by a vote of 75 to 17 with 14 abstentions, decided to accept the Court's opinion.[199] Discussion in the Fifth Committee indicated a wide range of views on the proper action to take. Some favored accepting the opinion, others favored taking note of it, and others indicated their total dissent. Even those in favor attached different meanings to the action of acceptance.[200]

On the day the Assembly accepted the opinion of the Court, it adopted a second resolution reestablishing the 1961 Working Group, with its membership increased from fifteen to twenty-one, "to study . . . special methods for 'financing peace-keeping operations' of the United Nations involving heavy expenditures, such as those for the Congo and the Middle East, including a possible special scale of assessments." [201] Further, the Assembly recognized "the necessity of establishing at the earliest possible opportunity different financing methods from those applied to the regular budget to cover, in the future," such United Nations operations. It requested the Working Group to take into account the criteria for sharing the costs of peace-keeping operations mentioned in previous resolutions of the Assembly, and to give particular attention to:

(a) The references to a special financial responsibility of members of the Security Council as indicated in General Assembly resolutions 1619(XV) of 21 April 1961 and 1732 (XVI) of 20 December 1961;
(b) Such special factors relating to a particular peace-keeping operation as might be relevant to a variation of the sharing of the costs of the operation;

195 UN Doc. A/4971, Nov. 15, 1961.   196 GA Res. 1731(XVI), Dec. 20, 1961.
197 *ICJ Reports*, 1962, p. 151.   198 *Ibid.*, pp. 167–68.
199 GA Res. 1854A(XVII), Dec. 19, 1962.
200 For further discussion, see comment on Art. 96.
201 GA Res. 1854B(XVII), Dec. 19, 1962.

(c) The degree of economic development of each Member State and whether or not a developing State is in receipt of technical assistance from the United Nations;

(d) The collective financial responsibility of the Members of the United Nations.

The report of the Working Group was considered by the General Assembly in a special session in 1963. On the basis of the report of the Fifth Committee,[202] the Assembly, by a vote of 92 to 11 with 3 abstentions, adopted a resolution which affirmed

that the following principles, *inter alia*, shall serve as guide lines for the equitable sharing, by assessed or voluntary contributions or a combination thereof, of the costs of peace-keeping operations involving heavy expenditures that may be initiated in the future:

(a) The financing of such operations is the collective responsibility of all States Members of the United Nations;

(b) Whereas the economically more developed countries are in a position to make relatively larger contributions, the economically less developed countries [203] have a relatively limited capacity to contribute towards peace-keeping operations involving heavy expenditures;

(c) Without prejudice to the principle of collective responsibility, every effort should be made to encourage voluntary contributions from Member States;

(d) The special responsibilities of the permanent members of the Security Council for the maintenance of peace and security should be borne in mind in connexion with their contributions to the financing of peace and security operations;

(e) Where circumstances warrant, the General Assembly should give special consideration to the situation of any Member States which are victims of, and those which are otherwise involved in, the events or actions leading to a peace-keeping operation.[204]

These principles were not acceptable to the Soviet Union and France, and those members that had joined with them in the second position described above.[205] Discussions in the Working Group were continued in an effort to find a basis of general agreement. In a working paper submitted in September, 1964, the United States, while accepting the basic ideas of the Assembly resolution and preserving the

202 UN Doc. A/5438, June 26, 1963.

203 In resolutions for the financing of UNEF and ONUC for the period July 1 to Dec. 31, 1963, the Assembly determined by a process of exclusion who were to be considered "economically less developed countries." GA Res. 1875(S-IV), June 27, 1963.

204 GA Res. 1874(S-IV), June 27, 1963. For discussion on the report of the Working Group and the financing of UNEF and ONUC, see GAOR/4th Special Sess./5th Ctte./984th–1005th Mtgs./May 15–June 26, 1963.

205 See above, p. 159.

right of the General Assembly to initiate peace-keeping operations in case of the Security Council's inability to act, suggested a procedure for initiating and financing such operations that would give to the permanent members of the Security Council greater influence in such decisions—without, however, giving any one of them the veto.[206] This proposal was not acceptable to the Soviet Union.

The nineteenth session of the Assembly, unable to proceed with its normal operations because of the unwillingness of members to face the consequences of a confrontation over the applicability of Article 19,[207] did, however, adopt a resolution by "no objection procedure" establishing a special committee on peace-keeping operations (the "Committee of Thirty-Three") to undertake "a comprehensive review of the whole question of peace-keeping operations in all their aspects, including ways of overcoming the present financial difficulties of the Organization" and to report not later than June 15, 1965.[208] The President of the Assembly, who served as chairman of the committee, and the Secretary-General, in a report to the committee on consultations with members, suggested certain "broad guidelines" as "possibly useful and practical." [209] These proposed guidelines were not acceptable, however, to all members of the committee. In its report to the Assembly, the committee stated that more time was required to complete the consideration of the matter before it, and requested that all members submit before August 1 their views on the proposed guidelines.[210] Members were reported to be in agreement, however, "that the United Nations should be strengthened through a cooperative effort and that the General Assembly, when it reconvenes, should conduct its work according to the normal procedure established by its rules of procedure."

On August 16, at a meeting of the special committee, the permanent representative of the United States stated that while maintaining its position regarding the authority of the General Assembly to apportion the expenses of peace-keeping operations, the obligations of members to pay, and the applicability of Article 19, the United States recognized that the General Assembly was not prepared to carry out the relevant provisions of the Charter in the context of the present situation, and consequently would not seek to frustrate the consensus of the membership that the General Assembly should proceed normally. But, he added, the United States "must make it crystal clear that if any Member can insist on making an exception to the principle of collective

206 UN Doc. A/AC. 113/30, Sept. 14, 1964.   207 See commentary on Art. 19.
208 GA Res. 2006(XIX), Feb. 18, 1965.
209 See UN Doc. A/AC.121/4, May 31, 1965.
210 UN Doc. A/5915, June 15, 1965; for views expressed, see UN Doc. A/5915/Add. 1, *Annex II.*

financial responsibility with respect to certain activities of the Organization, the United States reserves the same option to make exceptions if, in our view, strong and compelling reasons exist for doing so." [211]

At its meeting on August 31, 1965, the chairman of the committee stated the consensus of the committee: that the Assembly should carry out its work normally in accordance with its rules of procedure, that the question of the applicability of Article 19 should not be raised, and that the financial difficulties of the Organization should be solved through voluntary contributions by members, with highly developed countries making substantial contributions.[212]

At its twentieth session, the General Assembly, after further extended discussion, adopted two resolutions dealing with the conduct and financing of peace-keeping operations, neither of which set forth any general agreement on the basic issues. In one resolution, the Assembly requested the Special Committee on Peace-Keeping Operations to continue its work, taking into account the debates in the Special Political Committee, and to report to the Assembly in its next session. In the other, the Assembly referred to the committee the proposal made by the Irish delegation for "its careful consideration." [213]

While the question of financing peace-keeping operations was being considered by the General Assembly, the United Nations was called upon to consider the financing of particular peace-keeping operations on an ad hoc basis. In each case, the mode of financing was determined at the time of the decision to establish the force. Under the General Assembly resolution confirming the agreement of August 15, 1962, between the Netherlands and Indonesia,[214] the two states shared on an equal basis the costs to the United Nations of the United Nations Temporary Executive Authority (UNTEA) and the United Nations Security Force, which were to administer and maintain order in West Irian pending transfer of the territory to Indonesia.

In the Yemen case, the Secretary-General reported to the Security Council that Saudi Arabia and the United Arab Republic had accepted identical terms of disengagement and had agreed to share equally the costs to the United Nations of stationing observers along each side of the agreed demilitarized zone. The Soviet Union, while holding to its view that the cost of aggression should be borne by the aggressor, indicated its willingness to accept the arrangement. The Council, noting that the parties had agreed "to defray the expenses over a period of

[211] UN Doc. A/AC.121/PV.16, Aug. 16, 1965.

[212] Second Report of the Special Committee on Peace-Keeping Operations. UN Doc. A/5916, Aug. 31, 1965.

[213] GA Res. 2053A and B(XX), Dec. 15, 1965. The Irish proposal had been before committee as a nine-power proposal. UN Doc. A/SPC/L.121/Rev. 1.

[214] GA Res. 1752(XVII), Sept. 21, 1962.

two months," requested the Secretary-General to establish the observation function as he had defined it.[215] The United States took the position that this did not prejudice financing for a longer period under the General Assembly resolution on unforeseen and extraordinary expenses. France and the Soviet Union maintained that extension would require a Security Council decision. Subsequent extensions were made on the basis of informal consultations by the Secretary-General.

In the Cyprus case, the Security Council resolution of March 4, 1964,[216] recommended that the peace-keeping force be established by the Secretary-General, in consultation with the governments of Cyprus, Greece, Turkey, and the United Kingdom for a three-month period and that "all costs pertaining to it" be met in a manner to be agreed upon by them, by the governments providing the contingents, and by the Government of Cyprus. The Secretary-General was also authorized to accept voluntary contributions. The Council also recommended the appointment of a United Nations Mediator and requested that the expenses of the Mediator and his staff be provided "from funds of the United Nations, as appropriate." The same arrangements for financing were made when the force was extended in subsequent Council resolutions.

Financial Authority with Respect to Specialized Agencies

The League of Nations budget covered the activities of the technical organizations (the Economic and Financial Organization, the Communications and Transit Organization, and the Intellectual Cooperation Organization) and the two autonomous organizations (the International Labour Organisation and the Permanent Court of International Justice). The Covenant provided that international bureaus already established and bureaus and commissions that might be established in the future should be placed under the direction of the League and that their expenses might be included in expenses of the League Secretariat (Article 24). Though this was never achieved to any great extent, the principle upon which the League was initially founded was that of central control over the financing of international activities.

The principle of the United Nations system is a different one, namely, that various organizations set up to meet particular needs in the economic, social, and humanitarian fields should have substantial autonomy in the choice of programs and the means of carrying them out, subject to coordination by United Nations organs, which would have powers of discussion and recommendation.[217] Article 17(3) is a

[215] UN Doc. S/5331, June 11, 1963.   [216] UN Doc. S/5575, Mar. 4, 1964.
[217] On development of official U.S. thinking, see Russell, pp. 303–25.

particular application of this principle. It gives the General Assembly the power to approve financial and budgetary arrangements with the specialized agencies and to examine the administrative budgets of these agencies and make recommendations with respect thereto to the agencies in question.

When the initial agreements between the United Nations and the specialized agencies envisaged in Articles 57 and 63 of the Charter were being negotiated, the specialized-agency representatives took the position that the General Assembly, in strict conformity with the letter of Article 17, should have the right to examine budgets and make recommendations, but that it should not have any control over expenditures because that would limit the autonomy of the agencies in determining their own programs. The Negotiating Committee of the Economic and Social Council argued in favor of acceptance of the principle of budgetary consolidation.[218] The language finally adopted in all agreements falls short of acceptance of that principle.[219] Most of the agreements contain a clause recognizing the desirability of establishing close budgetary and financial relationships,[220] in order that the administrative operations of the United Nations and the agency may be carried on in the most efficient and economical manner possible and that the maximum measure of coordination and uniformity may be obtained. These agreements also contain a clause providing for consultation concerning the desirability of the inclusion of the agency budget in that of the United Nations.[221] The agreements list specific forms of cooperation to be undertaken, including consultation in the preparation of budgets, transmission of the annual agency budget to the United Nations, participation of a representative of the agency without vote in the deliberations of the General Assembly on the budget, collection of contributions of members of the agency who are members of the United Nations in accordance with subsequent agreements, studies of other financial and fiscal matters of common interest with a view to common services and uniformity, and acceptance by the agency "as far as may be practical" of standard practices and forms recommended by the United Nations.[222]

The agreements with the Universal Postal Union and the International Telecommunication Union simply provide for the transmission

---

[218] See Walter A. Sharp, "The Specialized Agencies and the United Nations: Progress Report I," *International Organization*, I (1947), 464–65.

[219] For analysis of agreements, see *Repertory*, II, paras. 8–14. See also comment on Art. 63.

[220] The agreements with the IBRD, IMF, IDA, IFC, UPU, and ITU are exceptions.

[221] The agreement with IAEA does not contain this clause.

[222] See, for example, Art. 14 of the agreement between the UN and FAO. UN Doc. A/78, Sept. 30, 1946.

of the agency budgets to the United Nations and for recommendations by the General Assembly to the agencies. The agreements with the financial and monetary agencies provide that annual reports and quarterly financial statements will be furnished, but specifically obligate the United Nations to take into consideration that the agencies do not rely for their annual budgets upon contributions from their members, and that the appropriate authorities enjoy "full autonomy" in deciding the form and content of the budget.[223]

In performing its functions under Article 17(3), the General Assembly is assisted by the Advisory Committee on Administrative and Budgetary Questions which, according to the Assembly's Rules of Procedure, "shall also examine in behalf of the General Assembly the administrative budgets of specialized agencies and proposals for financial and budgetary arrangements with such agencies" (Rule 158). Although Article 17(3) refers only to "administrative budgets," the agreements provide for transmittal of the entire budgets; the General Assembly has examined the budgets in their entirety as a means to the coordination of policies and activities provided for in Article 58.[224]

Examination of the administrative budgets and recommendations by the Assembly have produced uneven results. Many of the agencies have adopted financial regulations generally in line with those of the United Nations. Likewise, most have modeled their staff regulations on those of the United Nations.[225] The majority have agreed on a joint audit procedure.[226] Efforts to develop a common form of budget have been unsuccessful, as have explorations of the possibility of establishing a consolidated budget.[227] Most of the agencies have become members of the United Nations Joint Staff Pension Fund and a measure of uniformity in social security systems has been achieved. Substantial progress has been made in the coordination of budgetary procedures in relation to technical assistance and other extra-budgetary programs.[228] The Administrative Committee on Coordination has been an important instrument in implementing recommendations for the coordination of administrative and budgetary practices.

[223] See, for example, Art. X(3) of the agreement between the UN and the IBRD.
[224] For example, see UN Docs. A/2835, Dec. 6, 1954; and A/2861, Dec. 11, 1954; and GA Res. 884(IX), Dec. 14, 1954. See commentary on Art. 58.
[225] See *Repertory*, I, 550.   [226] *Ibid.*, pp. 551–52.
[227] *Ibid.*, pp. 547–48 and 552–53.
[228] *Ibid.*, pp. 549–58; *Supp. 1*, I, 191; *Supp. 2*, II, 185–87.

VOTING

Article 18

1. Each member of the General Assembly shall have one vote.

2. Decisions of the General Assembly on important questions shall be made by a two-thirds majority of the members present and voting. These questions shall include: recommendations with respect to the maintenance of international peace and security, the election of the non-permanent members of the Security Council, the election of the members of the Economic and Social Council, the election of members of the Trusteeship Council in accordance with paragraph 1(c) of Article 86, the admission of new Members to the United Nations, the suspension of the rights and privileges of membership, the expulsion of Members, questions relating to the operation of the trusteeship system, and budgetary questions.

3. Decisions on other questions, including the determination of additional categories of questions to be decided by a two-thirds majority, shall be made by a majority of the members present and voting.

Previous to the establishment of the United Nations, the commonly prescribed rule of international conferences and organizations of a political nature had been that substantive decisions should be taken by unanimous vote. This was the rule of the League of Nations as set forth in Article 5 of the Covenant, subject to some minor exceptions. It was based on the principle of state sovereignty. In the practice of the League Assembly, however, the distinction was made between decisions taken by unanimous vote and *voeux*, expressions of opinion as to what was desirable, which could be adopted by a majority vote.

In the drafting of the United Nations Charter, there was general agreement to move in the direction of some form of majority voting for all decisions of the General Assembly. The provisions of the Dumbarton Oaks Proposals were to this effect and, with textual changes and some extension to cover decisions in connection with the trusteeship system, became Article 18 of the Charter. The significance of this new approach was considerably qualified by the fact that on most substantive questions the General Assembly was only given the power to recommend.

"Each Member . . . One Vote"

This provision was accepted at San Francisco without discussion. It is consistent not only with the past practice of international assemblies of a similar nature but also with the principle of sovereign equality set forth in Article 2.[229] In contrast to the three Councils which have limited membership, the Assembly is composed of the total membership of the Organization and provides an equal opportunity for all members to take part in discussions and to vote. In spite of obvious inequalities of members in respect to such factors as area, population, and wealth, no consideration was given at San Francisco to introducing a system of weighted voting, and though these inequalities have become even more manifest in recent years as the result of the large number of small states admitted to membership, no proposals have been made in the United Nations for changing the rule of Article 18(1) that each member has one vote. The Main Committees, composed of all members of the General Assembly, follow the same rule.[230]

The Decision-Making Process

The Charter uses a wide variety of language in describing actions that the General Assembly may take. In articles dealing with the matter in its broadest terms,[231] the power of the General Assembly is defined as that of discussion and recommendation. In other articles relating to specific actions, the words "approve," "establish," "adopt," and "elect" are used, suggesting final conclusive action.[232] The term "decision," as used in Article 18 is inclusive, referring to all types of action which the General Assembly takes while performing its functions under the Charter.

The Charter specifies the majorities by which decisions of the Assembly shall be made, but does not prescribe the particular procedure to be followed for determining that the majorities exist. The assumption would appear to be that normally decisions will be taken by voting. Rule 89 of the Rules of Procedure provides that the Assembly "shall normally vote by show of hands or by standing but any representative may request a roll-call." The Rules prescribe the manner

---

[229] A member may, however, lose its right to vote as the result of suspension (Art. 4), expulsion (Art. 5), or being two years in arrears in the payment of financial contributions (Art. 19). On the last point, see commentary on Art. 19.

[230] *Rules of Procedure of the General Assembly*, UN Doc. A/520/Rev. 8, Mar. 1966, Rule 125.

[231] Arts. 10, 11, 13, and 14.   [232] See, for example, Arts. 17, 21, 22, and 23.

in which voting is to be conducted, how questions are to be voted upon, and the manner of conducting elections.[233] In practice, however, many decisions are taken without formal voting, on the basis of a consensus established by the President. Thus states have been admitted to membership in the United Nations by "acclamation," and procedural matters have usually been decided on the suggestion of the President by the tacit consent of members.

The provisions of Article 18(2) and (3) do not apply to the Main Committees and other committees of the General Assembly. The Rules of Procedure of the Assembly determine the procedure by which committees conduct their business. They provide that all decisions "shall be made by a majority of the members present and voting" (Rule 126). Consequently, a Main Committee may approve and recommend a proposal that is unable to obtain the two-thirds majority necessary for its adoption by the Assembly.

At the nineteenth session, to avoid a confrontation over the application of Article 19, the Assembly agreed to follow a special "no objection" procedure. This involved the conduct of business in plenary meetings of the Assembly by methods other than those specifically provided in the Rules of Procedure. The "no objection" procedure involved consultations by the President or the Secretary-General with members for the purpose of establishing that the necessary agreement existed. In announcing the decision in plenary, the President would state that such consultation had taken place, that the indicated agreement appeared to exist, and that it was so decided.[234] This procedure was employed not only in cases where there was unanimity on the substantive question, but also in some cases of disagreement. In such cases, the President's statement of the decision was based on a vote or consultation taken informally and outside the Assembly chamber showing the necessary majority support.[235] When the Albanian delegate introduced a proposal that the Assembly resume business under its established Rules of Procedure, the President ruled that he was bound by the previous decision of the Assembly, taken under "no objection" procedure, to conclude the consideration of remaining urgent items by the same procedure.[236] The President's ruling was upheld by a roll call vote, the only one taken before the Assembly adjourned.

[233] Rules 89–97. A secret ballot is required in all elections (Rule 94).

[234] See, for example, GAOR/19th Sess./1286th Plen. Mtg./Dec. 1, 1964; 1312th and 1313th Plen. Mtgs./Dec. 29, 1964; and 1314th Plen. Mtg./Dec. 30, 1964.

[235] The President's consultation, for example, in filling a vacancy in the Board of Auditors showed that two candidates received support. The candidate receiving a majority was declared elected under "no objection" procedure. GAOR/19th Sess./1328th Plen. Mtg./Feb. 16, 1965/paras. 9–10.

[236] GAOR/19th Sess./1330th Plen. Mtg./Feb. 18, 1965/para. 25. For earlier decision, see *ibid.*, 1327th Plen. Mtg./Feb. 8, 1965/paras. 7–10, 41.

Article 18 clearly states that the required majority is determined on the basis of "members present and voting." The Rules of Procedure specify that this means members "casting an affirmative or negative vote." Members that abstain are not considered as voting (Rule 88). This provision permits decisions to be taken by less than a majority of the total membership.[237]

The Two-Thirds Majority Requirement for Important Questions

In defining voting procedure in the Security Council, the Charter distinguishes between decisions on procedural matters and decisions on all other matters, the latter requiring concurrence of the permanent members.[238] At San Francisco, the future permanent members of the Council agreed on a statement which sought to clarify the distinction and indicated that in case of doubt the decision as to which voting procedure was applicable would be taken by a nonprocedural vote.[239] No similar questions were raised with respect to the proposal of the Sponsoring Governments on General Assembly voting, though the Dumbarton Oaks text was modified in certain respects.[240] The categories of important matters were extended to include the election of members of the Trusteeship Council and questions relating to the operation of the trusteeship system. Whereas the Dumbarton Oaks text used the term "important decisions," the Charter refers to "decisions . . . on important questions." There is no evidence from the proceedings of the Conference regarding the reasons for the change.

It is not clear from the phrasing of Article 18(2) whether the listing of "important questions" was intended to be exhaustive. Taking the text by itself, one might reasonably conclude that the enumeration is not exhaustive, and that there may be other questions in addition to those enumerated in the second sentence that are to be treated as important without a determination under paragraph 3. On the other hand, the phrasing of paragraph 3 would suggest that the categories listed in paragraph 2 exhaust the content of "important questions" unless the General Assembly determines that other categories are to be added.

The decision whether a question is "important" can be of critical importance in determining the fate of a proposal. Members of the

[237] Compare provisions of Arts. 108 and 109, which require approval by majority or two-thirds majority of the members of the General Assembly. See commentary on these articles. Art. 10 of the Statute of the International Court of Justice prescribes "an absolute majority of votes in the General Assembly" for the election of a judge. This phrase is interpreted "to mean the smallest number greater than half the potential voters," regardless of whether they are present, vote, or abstain. Shabtai Rosenne, *The Law and Practice of the International Court of Justice* (Leyden, Sitjhoff, 1965), I, 178.

[238] See Art. 27 and commentary.   [239] See pp. 217–20.   [240] Ch. v, sec. c.

Assembly who constitute a majority in support of a particular proposal may use their voting strength to determine that the two-thirds majority rule does not apply, thereby making it possible for a decision to be taken by a smaller majority. Members may, however, be influenced by legal and other considerations to vote for the application of the two-thirds rule even though this may prevent the taking of a decision favored by them.[241]

At the twentieth session of the General Assembly, a draft resolution was introduced by twenty-three members dealing with the implementation of the Declaration on Granting Independence to Colonial Countries and Peoples.[242] This draft contained provisions which some members viewed as recommendations with respect to the maintenance of international peace and security, and therefore as requiring a two-thirds majority for adoption.[243] A motion that the proposal required only a simple majority was, however, adopted by a roll call vote of 59 to 45. The draft resolution was finally approved, by a vote of 74 to 6 with 27 abstentions,[244] but in the voting on disputed paragraphs, one paragraph calling for the dismantling of military bases in colonial territories failed to receive a two-thirds majority as would have been necessary for its adoption if it had been considered as dealing with an important question. By contrast, the General Assembly in its sixteenth session decided by a majority vote that a decision on a Czechoslovak proposal with respect to the work of the United Nations Scientific Committee on the Effects of Atomic Radiation must be taken by a two-thirds majority vote and thereby prevented adoption of the proposal since the vote on the merits was 37 in favor and 20 against with 27 abstentions.[245]

A review of the proceedings of the General Assembly reveals that the vast majority of Assembly decisions have been unanimous or made by at least a two-thirds majority.[246] Most decisions have been taken without any indication that members considered that the voting procedure for "important questions" applied. In only a very small number of cases has there been any reference in the course of discussion to the application of the rule regarding "important questions."[247]

[241] For comparison of Security Council procedure, see Art. 27 and commentary.
[242] UN Doc. A/L. 476/Rev. 1/Add. 1, Dec. 15, 1965.
[243] For debate and voting, see GAOR/20th Sess./1336th, 1385th–1390th, 1398th, 1400th, 1405th and 1407th–1408th Plen. Mtgs.
[244] GA Res. 2105(XX), Dec. 20, 1965.
[245] See GAOR/16th Sess./1043d Plen. Mtg./Oct. 27, 1961/pp. 505–7.
[246] During the first thirteen regular sessions, for example, of approximately 1,365 resolutions adopted, all but 18 were adopted by a two-thirds vote or more. See *Repertory*, Vol. II; *Supp. 1*, Vol. I; *Supp. 2*, Vol. II.
[247] During the first thirteen regular sessions, there was reference to the application of the rule in connection with less than 40 of the resolutions adopted.

Only in a few instances has the Assembly taken a decision that a particular draft resolution concerned an "important question" or that a two-thirds majority was necessary for its adoption. Even less often has the General Assembly decided that a simple majority would suffice for the taking of a decision. Sometimes the President announces before the vote that the two-thirds vote requirement applies. He may also announce that a proposal has been adopted when it has received a majority but not a two-thirds majority, or conversely, that it has been rejected even though it has received a majority, but not a two-thirds majority. Such rulings by the President can be overruled, but it is seldom that they are even debated. Only occasionally has the President stated the grounds upon which his actions are based.

Thus there has been little discussion in the Assembly of what constitutes an "important question" and on what basis a two-thirds majority is required. Even when such a discussion has taken place, members are commonly divided on the criteria to be applied. The Assembly decision consequently reflects a variety of considerations, many of which are basically of a political nature. Agreement exists only on the end result.

A variety of considerations have been advanced in the course of Assembly discussions as being relevant to the determination that a question is important in the sense of Article 18(2) and therefore requires an application of the two-thirds majority rule. Among these have been the following:

1. Whether one or more paragraphs of a draft resolution relates to an important question. This, for example, was the argument advanced in the General Assembly's sixth session with respect to a draft resolution on Libya, which contained a paragraph recommending Libya's admission to the United Nations,[248] and with respect to certain paragraphs of the 1965 draft resolution on the implementation of the Declaration on Granting Independence to Colonial Countries and Peoples.

2. Whether or not the question comes within one of the categories listed in Article 18(2). Those who have invoked this particular consideration take the view that the enumeration in Article 18(2) is exclusive and that consequently a question that cannot be brought within one of these categories cannot be an important question unless so determined under Article 18(3). This argument has been advanced particularly with respect to colonial questions, exclusive of those relating to "the operation of the trusteeship system." [249]

[248] GAOR/6th Sess./370th Plen. Mtg./Feb. 1, 1952, p. 473.

[249] See debate on the question of South West Africa. GAOR/2d Sess./104th and 105th Plen. Mtgs./Nov. 1, 1947/pp. 573–648. On setting up a special committee to examine information from non-self-governing territories, see GAOR/2d Sess./108th Plen. Mtg./Nov. 3, 1947/pp. 735–44.

3. Whether the intrinsic importance of the question justifies determining that a two-thirds majority is required even though the question is not included in the Article 18(2) enumeration. The intrinsic importance of the question may be evidenced by its similarity to questions listed as important (colonial questions, for instance); its involving Charter interpretation; or its political importance.[250]

4. Whether the effects of the resolution are important. The effects referred to may be the legal effects as in the case of a draft resolution which if adopted would effect the rights and obligations of a member under the Charter; financial effects, as in the case of resolutions requiring the additional expenditure of money; or effects on the working of the Organization.[251]

5. Whether a proposal that is procedural in form deals with an important subject matter. Unlike Article 27, Article 18 does not make the vote required for a decision dependent on whether a matter is procedural or nonprocedural. Nevertheless, there has been a tendency to treat procedural questions as falling in the category of questions that can be decided by a simple majority. However, it has been argued successfully that if the terms of reference of a proposed committee involve interpretation of the Charter, or if a proposal to seat delegates in a case of contested representation has important political consequences, the question should be considered important.[252]

The Charter does not clearly specify whether the term "decisions . . . on important questions" refers only to final decisions, or whether it also applies to decisions made prior to the adoption of final decisions, such as decisions on the approval of paragraphs which are parts of draft resolutions or amendments thereto offered in plenary. The matter was considered by the Assembly at an early stage and at its request the Secretary-General made a report on the matter.[253] The

[250] For Charter interpretation, see debate on question of treatment of persons of Indian origin in the Union of South Africa where it was argued that two-thirds majority requirement should apply to proposal because it related to Charter obligations of a member. GAOR/1st Sess., 2d Part/52d Plen. Mtg./Dec. 8, 1946/pp. 1048–60. For political importance, see, for example, debate in the sixteenth session of the Assembly on the U.S. proposal to determine the question of Chinese representation an important question, especially statements of representatives of Australia. GAOR/16th Sess./1072d Plen. Mtg./Dec. 6, 1961/pp. 639–40; Canada, *ibid.*/1074th Plen. Mtg./Dec. 8, 1961/p. 962; United Kingdom, *ibid.*/1079th Plen. Mtg./Dec. 14, 1961/p. 1045; and U.S., *ibid.*/p. 1046.

[251] Considerable stress was placed on this last point in the debate on the China question, referred to above.

[252] See debate and Assembly decision in the eleventh session on a request that a draft resolution to set up a committee to study the application of the provisions of ch. xi to new members be considered an important question. GAOR/11th Sess./656th and 657th Mtgs./Feb. 20, 1957/pp. 1153–66. See debate on China question, referred to above.

[253] GAOR/5th Sess.; *Annexes,* agenda item 49; UN Doc. A/1356, especially paras. 22, 24–26.

Assembly decided to include in its Rules of Procedure a rule to the effect that decisions on amendments to proposals relating to important questions and on parts of such proposals put to a vote separately shall be made by the two-thirds majority prescribed in Article 18(2).[254]

In those cases where members of the General Assembly have expressed themselves on the question whether the two-thirds majority rule should be followed and a decision has been taken, the Assembly would appear to have adopted the position that the enumeration of categories in Article 18(2) is not exclusive, and that for the purpose of requiring a two-thirds majority on the basis of the importance of the question, it is not necessary either to determine that it falls within one of the enumerated categories or in a special category established under Article 18(3). While the accepted criteria of importance are not easy to determine, it would appear that members of the Assembly in most cases recognize the desirability of a larger consensus than is represented by a simple majority on questions that are intrinsically important from the point of view of the particular interests of members and the development of the Organization.

The Determination of Additional Categories

Article 18(3) has been referred to in General Assembly discussions in two principal respects: to support the view that the enumeration of categories in paragraph 2 is exhaustive; and to provide a possible basis for the determination that a question not included in one of these categories is important. The argument has been advanced in connection with certain colonial questions that the procedure of this paragraph should be followed if the Assembly is to treat such questions as important for the purposes of Article 18. However, the Assembly has not followed this course.

The General Assembly has in one instance made an explicit determination that a particular category of questions should be treated as important and decided in accordance with Article 18(2) by a two-thirds majority. This was the effect of the Assembly's resolution of October 11, 1954, laying down special rules to govern its consideration of reports of the Committee on South West Africa.[255] Special Rule F provided that decisions of the General Assembly on questions relating to reports and petitions concerning the territory should be regarded as "important questions within the meaning of Article 18, paragraph 2." It should also be noted that the General Assembly, without any explicit reference to Article 18(3), has provided in its Rules of Procedure that

[254] Rule 86, adopted Nov. 1, 1950, GA Res. 475(V). Before this time the practice of the Assembly on amendments had not been consistent.
[255] GA Res. 844(IX), Oct. 11, 1954.

questions relating to the inclusion of additional items in its agenda and the reconsideration of proposals shall be decided by a two-thirds majority.[256]

Article 19

A Member of the United Nations which is in arrears in the payment of its financial contributions to the Organization shall have no vote in the General Assembly if the amount of its arrears equals or exceeds the amount of the contributions due from it for the preceding two full years. The General Assembly may, nevertheless, permit such a Member to vote if it is satisfied that the failure to pay is due to conditions beyond the control of the Member.

The Covenant of the League of Nations contained no comparable provision. The Financial Regulations of the League stipulated that the Secretary-General was to notify members of sums due and request payment or notification as to when payment might be expected. He was to make requests for payment at three-month intervals. At meetings of the Council following these requests, he was to report on the financial situation and steps taken. A similar statement was to be made annually to the Assembly, which should "take such action as it may deem proper." [257] No agreement was ever reached on sanctions to be applied against a delinquent. Diplomatic measures were fully utilized to obtain payment, but no measures were taken that seriously risked withdrawal of the delinquent member.[258] In spite of relatively high percentages of payments in successive years, the situation was never regarded as wholly satisfactory.[259]

The Dumbarton Oaks Proposals did not make any provision for sanctions in case of delinquency. Article 19 had its origin in amendments proposed by various governments which had the League experience in mind.[260] In the technical committee dealing with this matter at San Francisco, agreement was easily reached on a text embodying these proposals; this was subsequently approved by the Conference as Article 19 "with the overwhelming support of the representatives of

[256] See Rules 15, 19, and 83.

[257] Regulations for the Financial Administration of the League of Nations, LN Doc. C.614. M191, 1928, X, Art. XXI.

[258] See Singer, pp. 267–68; and Seymour Jacklin, "The Finances of the League," *International Affairs*, XIII (1934), 702.

[259] During the period 1919–41, 91.26 percent of assessments were collected, but only 76.36 percent within the years due. C. Wilfred Jenks, "Some Legal Aspects of the Financing of International Institutions," *Transactions of the Grotius Society*, XXVIII (1943), 89–90.

[260] See comment of Norwegian Government, UNCIO, *Documents*, III, 356.

nations large and small." [261] During the technical committee's consideration of the matter, an amendment was proposed by Australia that would have specifically provided that a member should have no vote if it had not carried out its obligations under what is now Article 43 of the Charter.[262] The committee decided to postpone consideration of this proposal until the competent technical committee had considered the matter of special agreements to provide military assistance and had made its recommendation.[263] The Australian delegate subsequently withdrew his proposal. This bit of history was recalled in 1960 by the Mexican delegate in the Fifth Committee of the General Assembly to support his view that the penalty of Article 19 was not intended to apply to failure to contribute to expenses resulting from military operations, and that consequently the expenses of the Congo operation were not to be regarded as expenses of the Organization under Article 17(2).[264]

The Preparatory Commission recommended that the Committee on Contributions, whose establishment it proposed, should have among its functions that of considering, and reporting to the General Assembly on "the action to be taken if Members fall into default with their contributions," and in this connection, "that it should advise the Assembly in regard to the application of Article 19 of the Charter." [265] The recommendation was incorporated into the General Assembly resolution establishing the Committee.[266] Rule 161 of the Assembly's Rules of Procedure provides that the Committee shall advise the General Assembly "on action to be taken with regard to the application of Article 19 of the Charter." At each Assembly session, the Committee on Contributions has considered a report by the Secretary-General on the collection of contributions that has included a detailed statement of the amounts due from each member. At its fifth session, the Assembly adopted the following financial regulation to serve as a guide in the interpretation of Article 19:

Contributions and advances shall be considered as due and payable in full within thirty days of the receipt of the communication of the Secretary-General referred to in regulation 5.3 above, or as of the first day of the financial year to which they relate, whichever is the later. As of 1 January of the following financial year, the unpaid balance of such contributions and advances shall be considered to be one year in arrears.[267]

261 State Dept., *Report to the President,* p. 60.
262 UNCIO, *Documents,* VIII, 470.
263 *Ibid.,* p. 365.
264 UN Doc. A/C.5/862, Apr. 14, 1961, pp. 6–13.
265 *Report of the Preparatory Commission,* p. 108.
266 GA Res. 14A(I), Feb. 13, 1946.
267 Regulation 5.4 of the *Financial Regulations and Rules of the United Nations.*

The Secretary-General has interpreted this regulation to mean that no member is in arrears within the terms of Article 19 unless the arrears equal or exceed the amount of the contributions due for the preceding two full years, not counting the current year.[268] In 1958, 1960, and 1963, there were instances of members being reported in arrears to the extent specified in Article 19, but payments were received which reduced the arrears below the critical level, before any occasion arose for applying the article.

When the General Assembly met in its fourth special session in May, 1963, the Secretary-General reported in a letter to the President that Haiti was in arrears in the payment of its financial contributions "within the terms of Article 19." He stated that contributions due from Haiti exceeded by $22,400 "the amount of the contributions due from it for the preceding two full years," and that "a payment exceeding that amount would be necessary in order to reduce the arrears below the limit specified in Article 19." [269] In reply, the President (Zafrulla Khan) stated that he "would have made an announcement drawing the attention of the Assembly to the loss of voting rights in the Assembly" of Haiti "had a formal count of votes taken place in the presence of a representative of that State at the opening plenary meeting." The President also stated that he was transmitting a copy of the Secretary-General's letter and of his reply to the Chairman of the Fifth Committee "so that he may be informed of the situation which will give rise to the loss of voting rights in the Fifth Committee of the Member concerned, if the situation is not previously rectified." [270] He thus indicated that Article 19 applied to voting not only in plenary but also in the main committees of the Assembly.[271] Subsequently, before the occasion of a formal vote arose, a payment was made by Haiti, making the first sentence of Article 19 inapplicable.

In a subsequent letter to the Secretary-General, the permanent representative of the Soviet Union stated that the position of his government was that since Article 19 concerned a basic right of a member state—the right to vote in the General Assembly which is a manifestation of the principle of sovereign equality—the article must be applied in strict conformity with the provisions of the Charter which, in Article 18(2), lays down the procedure for taking decisions regarding the suspension of the rights of member states. He therefore contended that the question whether a particular member should retain its right to vote could only be decided by the General Assembly itself by a two-thirds majority of members present and voting. He denied that there

---

[268] UN Doc. A/C.5/588, pp. 4–6.   [269] Letter of May 14, 1963.
[270] Letter of May 15, 1963.
[271] It has not been considered applicable in subsidiary Assembly bodies.

was any basis in the Charter for "any automatic deprivation of the Member State's right to vote," and that it was "impossible to recognize as having legal force," an approach to the question that would consist of the President's declaring, without the Assembly having considered and decided the matter, that a member had lost its right to vote.[272]

The question of the interpretation and application of Article 19 became critical at the nineteenth session of the General Assembly as a result of the failure of members to pay their apportioned shares of the expenses of UNEF and ONUC. As of October 4, 1964, ten members, including the Soviet Union, were in arrears in their contributions in amounts equal to or in excess of their assessed contributions for 1962 and 1963, if assessments for UNEF and ONUC were included. If these assessments were not included, only one member (Paraguay) was delinquent.[273] By February 3, 1965, thirteen members, including the Soviet Union and France, were two years in arrears, on the assumption that UNEF and ONUC expenses were included.[274]

The Soviet position, supported in substance by France, was that the arrears to which Article 19 applies are arrears in the payment of expenses under Article 17, which do not include expenditures for the maintenance of United Nations armed forces, because only the Security Council has the power to make such assessments; and that the question of suspension of a member's right to vote could only be decided by a two-thirds vote of the Assembly.[275]

The United States argued that the provisions of Article 19 were simple and clear, leaving no discretion to the General Assembly except with respect to a claim that failure of a member to pay is due to conditions beyond its control. If this claim is not made, the Charter "does not say that the General Assembly shall vote as to whether the delinquent shall have no vote; it simply says that the delinquent shall have no vote." On the question whether expenses of UNEF and ONUC should be included in the determination of delinquency, the United States held that the General Assembly, on the basis of an advisory opinion of the Court, had already decided this question affirmatively.[276]

[272] UN Doc. A/5431, June 11, 1963. This was the position taken by Maurice Viaud of the Committee on Contributions in a separate opinion included in the 1964 Report of the Committee. GAOR/19th Sess./1964/*Supp. 10* (A/5810), p. 12; and by Sosa Rodriguez, President of the eighteenth session, who let it be known that, unlike Zafrulla Khan, he did not consider Art. 19 automatic and mandatory.

[273] "Report of the Committee on Contributions," GAOR/19th Sess./1964/*Supp. 10* (A/5810), p. 10.

[274] UN Docs. A/5847, Rev. 1, Jan. 29, 1965 and Rev. 1/Add. 1, Feb. 2, 1965; and Doc. A/5871, Feb. 3, 1965.

[275] UN Docs. A/5729, Sept. 11, 1964, and A/5431, June 11, 1963.

[276] UN Doc. A/5739, Oct. 8, 1964.

To avoid confrontation over the applicability of Article 19, and in the light of the reluctance of members to apply the sanction of Article 19 to those members allegedly two years in arrears, agreement was reached among members before the opening of the nineteenth session of the General Assembly on December 1, 1964, that issues other than those that could be disposed of without objection would not be raised during the general debate.[277] Following the conclusion of the general debate, the Secretary-General stated that he and the President of the Assembly had had further consultations with members, and that to his knowledge a consensus existed to continue to avoid a confrontation on the applicability of Article 19 by avoiding votes and proceeding on the basis of no voting. When the Albanian delegate later demanded that the Assembly return to its normal procedure and demanded a role call vote on his proposal, the President ruled that the Assembly had decided to continue the procedure of no voting. In explaining his government's position on the Albanian appeal from the President's ruling, the United States delegate stated that:

Inasmuch as the procedural vote for which the President has called on his ruling deals only with the issue of whether the Assembly should or should not continue to proceed on a non-voting basis and not with the substantive business of the Assembly, the United States considers that such a vote would not involve or prejudice the question of the applicability of Article 19 and that the question can in no way be affected by it.[278]

The agreement that the General Assembly should conduct its business during the nineteenth session on a no-voting basis to avoid a confrontation over the applicability of Article 19 was in part based on the hope that agreement would be reached between the major protagonists on the methods of conducting future peace-keeping operations and coping with the financial difficulties of the Organization. Faced with the failure of the Special Committee on Peace-Keeping Operations to find a basis for agreement, and with pressure from members to break the deadlock and thus enable the Assembly to resume its normal procedures at its twentieth session, the United States representative announced at a meeting of the Special Committee on August 16 that, without abandoning positions previously taken on the financing of peace-keeping operations and the applicability of Article 19, and without abandoning positions and precedents established by the General Assembly by numerous resolutions adopted "by overwhelming majori-

[277] For account of the background and proceedings of the 19th session of the GA, see *Y.U.N.*, 1964, pp. 3–60.
[278] State Dept. *Bulletin*, LII (Mar. 8, 1965), 354; GAOR/19th Sess./1330th Plen. Mtg./Feb. 18, 1965/para. 101.

ties," his government would not seek "to frustrate" the consensus of the membership "that the Assembly should proceed normally." [279]

It is of some significance that throughout the debate over the applicability of Article 19, no one challenged the principle of Article 19 that its sanction should be applied to a member two years or more in arrears in its contributions. The controversy was entirely over the question of which expenses could be regarded as expenses of the Organization, which members must pay and which could properly be included in calculations of the existence of arrears. The denial by some members that the General Assembly had the power to decide this question and the unwillingness of some members to apply the sanction of Article 19 against a major power had the effect of substantially lessening, if not destroying, the practical significance of the article.

PROCEDURE

Article 20

The General Assembly shall meet in regular annual sessions and in such special sessions as occasion may require. Special sessions shall be convoked by the Secretary-General at the request of the Security Council or of a majority of the Members of the United Nations.

Regular Sessions

The General Assembly is the only principal organ of the United Nations required under the Charter to meet in "regular annual sessions." Under Rule 1 of the Assembly's Rules of Procedure, sessions convene on the third Tuesday in September, although on occasion the opening has for various reasons been postponed.

It was originally thought that the General Assembly would be able to complete its work in a five- or six-week session. These hopes were soon dashed, partly as a result of the Assembly's growing involvement in the handling of matters relating to the maintenance of international peace and security. Various methods have been suggested for curtailing the length of Assembly sessions, but with little success.

Under its own rules, the Assembly is required at the beginning of each session to fix a closing date, but often has failed to finish its work within the prescribed time and has recessed, taking up at a resumed

[279] UN Doc. A/AC.121/PV.16, Aug. 16, 1965.

session those agenda items still not acted upon. The drafters of the Charter certainly did not intend that the General Assembly should be, like the Security Council, in "continuous session." [280] There is, however, nothing in the Charter or in the Assembly's Rules of Procedure to prevent one session of the Assembly from continuing until the next, and this has occasionally happened. The fifth, seventh, and eighth sessions were prolonged to enable the Assembly to deal speedily with any developments that might occur during the Korean conflict. The eleventh session was extended because of the Suez and Hungarian crises. The nineteenth session adjourned on February 18, 1965, until September of that year when it had its final meeting to receive the report of the Special Committee on Peace-Keeping Operations.

Special Sessions

The Charter provides for the convocation of special sessions of the Assembly at the request of the Security Council or a majority of United Nations members. Aside from the manner of convocation, the Charter does not distinguish between "regular" and "special" sessions. The latter, however, operate under slightly streamlined rules of procedure: the various time limits for calling special sessions are shorter than for regular sessions.[281] Moreover, the provisional agenda of a special session consists "only of those items proposed for consideration in the request for the holding of the session." Supplementary or additional items may be added by a two-thirds majority of those present and voting, as compared with the simple majority required at a regular session.[282]

It has generally been accepted that a special session should be concerned only with the matter that prompted the calling of the session. For example, the first special session was convoked for the specific purpose of constituting a committee to prepare for the consideration of the Palestine question at the next regular session. Nonetheless, the agenda of some special sessions (and emergency special sessions) have been expanded to deal with noncontroversial matters, in particular the approval of pending applications for membership.

The rules concerning time limits and agenda are even more stringent in the case of emergency special sessions, provided for in the Uniting for Peace resolution of November 3, 1950. The resolution contained the following provision:

[280] This was one of the principal Soviet objections to the establishment of the Interim Committee; see commentary on Art. 22.

[281] Compare Rules 5, 12, and 16 with Rules 10, 13, and 18.

[282] Rules 17, 18, and 19.

If the Security Council, because of lack of unanimity of the permanent members, fails to exercise its primary responsibility for the maintenance of international peace and security in any case where there appears to be a threat to the peace, breach of the peace, or act of aggression, the General Assembly shall consider the matter immediately with a view to making recommendations to Members. . . . If not in session at the time, the General Assembly may meet in emergency special session within twenty-four hours of the request therefor. Such emergency special sessions shall be called if requested by the Security Council on the vote of any seven members, or by a majority of Members of the United Nations.[283]

The Rules of Procedure of the Assembly were revised to enable it to meet on twenty-four hours' notice and to bypass a number of the usual procedures.[284] The president and vice-president for these sessions are the chiefs of delegations of the members whose nationals occupied those posts at the previous regular session; the matter that has prompted the calling of the session is discussed directly in plenary unless the Assembly decides otherwise, and the agenda is restricted to subjects covered by the Uniting for Peace resolution.

Although the idea of emergency special sessions was generally accepted, the Soviet Union argued that a decision by the Security Council to call a special session was not a matter of procedure and that the concurring votes of the permanent members were therefore required.[285] The Assembly, however, had already gone on record that this was a procedural matter.[286] The first emergency special session was convoked by the Security Council despite the negative votes of France and the United Kingdom, and the second and fourth emergency special sessions despite Soviet opposition.[287]

Of the eight special or emergency special sessions of the Assembly, all but three have been convoked as a result of resolutions adopted by the Security Council.

Under the Assembly's Rules of Procedure, any member may request that the Secretary-General summon a special session. The request is immediately communicated to all members and if a majority concur within thirty days a special session is called (Rule 9); this was the method by which the first and third special sessions were convoked.

---

[283] GA Res. 377(V), Nov. 3, 1950. In accordance with the amendment of Art. 27, the Assembly's rules were changed by GA Res. 2046 (XX), Dec. 8, 1965, to require the vote of any nine members of the Council for requesting an emergency special session.

[284] See changes in Rules 8, 9, 10, 16, and 19 and 65.

[285] GAOR/5th Sess., 1st Ctte./357th Mtg./Oct. 10, 1950/para. 42.

[286] GA Res. 267(III), Apr. 14, 1949.

[287] In the last instance, the Soviet representative stated that any resolution to call the session that did not have the approval of all the permanent members would be illegal. He did not, however, challenge the President's ruling that the resolution had been adopted; in fact, the USSR participated in the session.

Other attempts to utilize this procedure have failed. The General Assembly itself may also "fix a date for a special session" (Rule 11). The fourth special session was convoked in this manner when at the end of the seventeenth session, the Assembly decided to convene a special session prior to June, 1963, to consider the report of its working group regarding the financial situation of the Organization.[288]

The question arises as to the vote required for the calling of a special session. Normally, the Assembly operates on the basis of a simple or two-thirds majority of those present and voting (see Art. 18). In accordance with Article 20 of the Charter, however, it would seem that at least one half the entire membership of the Organization would have to give approval before a special session could be convoked.[289]

Article 21

The General Assembly shall adopt its own rules of procedure. It shall elect its President for each session.

During its first session, the General Assembly operated under a set of provisional rules of procedure drawn up by the Preparatory Commission and modified in some respects during the course of the session. After thorough review, the Assembly at its second session adopted its permanent Rules of Procedure.[290] In contrast to the rules of procedure of other United Nations organs which have been infrequently changed, the Assembly's rules have been amended repeatedly, especially during the first ten years.[291] The most important of these amendments were the revisions made in accordance with the Uniting for Peace resolution to enable the Assembly to meet in emergency special session; [292] the special rules adopted by the Assembly to enable it to discharge its responsibilities in connection with the territory of South West Africa; [293] and the revisions required by the amendments to Articles 23, 27, and 61 of the Charter.[294]

[288] GA Res. 1866(XVII), Dec. 20, 1962. See also GA Res. 1985(XVIII), Dec. 17, 1963, which provided for the calling of a special session "if as a result of a decision of the Security Council, commitments relating to the maintenance of international peace and security should arise in an estimated total exceeding $10 million."

[289] A similar question could arise if a special session were convoked by the Interim Committee, as provided for in the Uniting for Peace resolution.

[290] GA Res. 173(II), Nov. 17, 1947. For more detailed comment on the rules and their application, see *Repertory*, I, *Supp. 1*, I, and *Supp. 2*, II.

[291] For a list of changes through 1957, see Bailey, p. 275.

[292] See commentary on Art. 20.

[293] These special rules contained in Annex III to the Rules of Procedure were adopted pursuant to an advisory opinion by the International Court of Justice. See commentary on Art. 80.

[294] GA Res. 2046(XX), Dec. 8, 1965.

Most of the other changes have resulted from efforts to make the Assembly a more effective and efficient organ, and especially to cut down on the duration of Assembly sessions. This subject has been considered at some length at various times by the Assembly, either on the initiative of a member, or on the basis of reports from the Secretary-General or special committees of the Assembly.

Certain suggestions developed by the Special Committee on Methods and Procedures [295] were incorporated in an annex to the Rules in the form of general guiding principles.[296] A second annex concerns suggestions on methods and procedures for dealing with legal and drafting questions.[297] It cannot be said, however, that these various suggestions have had much effect upon the work of the Assembly.

The President

One of the first orders of business is the election of the President by secret ballot and without nominations.[298] Until the President is elected, the Chairman of the delegation that held the office at the previous session presides. The practice has grown up whereby the permanent members are excluded from the presidency and the office rotates among the major groupings of states within the United Nations.[299] The President during his tenancy has no vote and is generally considered an officer of the United Nations rather than a representative of his government. It is generally agreed that the President should serve until his successor is elected. Thus, he or the head of his country's delegation presides over any special or emergency special sessions that may be convoked during his year in office.

Vice-Presidents

The Charter makes no mention of General Assembly Vice-Presidents; they are provided for, however, under its Rules of Procedure. Originally there were seven (Rule 31); at the eleventh session the number was raised to eight.[300] A ninth Vice-President was elected at the beginning of the twelfth session, and at the end of the session the number was raised to thirteen.[301] At the same time, the Assembly

[295] For the Committee's report, see GAOR/4th Sess./1948/*Supp. 12.*
[296] GA Res. 362(IV), Oct. 22, 1949.   [297] GA Res. 684(VII), Nov. 6, 1952.
[298] Because of the impasse over the application of Art. 19 (see commentary), the nineteenth session refrained from voting, and the president was chosen by acclamation.
[299] The major exception has been that in the first twenty years no President was chosen from members of the Eastern European bloc.
[300] GA Res. 1104(XI), Dec. 18, 1956.
[301] GA Res. 1192(XII), Dec. 12, 1957.

decided that Vice-Presidents should be elected as follows: the five permanent members of the Security Council, four members from Asian and African states, two from Latin America, two from Western Europe and "other states," and one from Eastern Europe. The number is reduced by one for that group from which the President is chosen. The Vice-Presidents preside, generally in rotation, over plenary sessions of the Assembly whenever the President is absent. They are also members of the General Committee.[302]

Article 22

The General Assembly may establish such subsidiary organs as it deems necessary for the performance of its functions.

Any organ of the size of the General Assembly, with such multiple and varied responsibilities, must necessarily depend upon a large number of subsidiary organs to assist it in the performance of its functions.[303] During the course of its history, the Assembly has established over two hundred committees, commissions, panels, special representatives, boards, and agencies. As of the end of 1965, forty-nine "subsidiary, ad hoc, and related" bodies established by the Assembly were in existence.[304]

Functions and Characteristics of Subsidiary Organs

The Assembly has assigned a wide variety of functions to its subsidiary organs. They have been established in all the areas of the Assembly's responsibilities.[305] A great many have been established to assist the Assembly in carrying out its responsibilities in the administrative and financial field. From time to time the Assembly has established committees to examine a particular problem (e.g., the Special Committee on Peace-Keeping Operations), but a high percentage of the subsidiary organs in the administrative and budgetary field have what might be termed a "permanent" status (e.g., the Advisory Committee on Administrative and Budgetary Questions, the Committee on Contributions, and the Board of Auditors). Since most of these bodies operate in areas where the Secretary-General also has responsibilities, they often have a special relationship to him. For example, the mem-

[302] See above, p. 108.
[303] On the definition of "subsidiary" organ, see commentary on Art. 7.
[304] See *Y.U.N.*, 1965, pp. 824–39.
[305] For a classified tabulation of the subsidiary organs established by the Assembly up to Aug. 31, 1959, see *Repertory*, I, 703–33; *Supp. 1*, II, 228–39; *Supp. 2*, II, 246–74.

bers of the Investments Committee are appointed by the Secretary-General, subject to confirmation by the Assembly. Some of these subsidiary organs are also of special interest to the United Nations staff and the specialized agencies and this is often reflected in the method for selecting members. The Joint Staff Pension Board, for example, includes members representing the General Assembly, the Secretary-General, the staff, and the specialized agencies.

Many of the more important subsidiary organs established by the General Assembly can be described as "operating" agencies created to administer a variety of relief, rehabilitation, and assistance programs in the field, as for instance, the Relief and Works Agency for Palestine Refugees in the Near East, the Office of the High Commissioner for Refugees, and the Development Programme. Most of these operations are financed by voluntary contributions, have special staffs, and more complex organizational arrangements than the usual subsidiary organs of the Assembly.

Many of them, as well as others such as the Conference on Trade and Development (UNCTAD), have a special relationship with ECOSOC, often reporting to or through that organ and sometimes receiving directives from it. A number of ad hoc committees established to examine particular problems in the economic and social field have had a similar relationship to ECOSOC (e.g., the Committee on a Capital Development Fund).

Most of the subsidiary organs established by the Assembly in the trusteeship field, such as the various commissions and commissioners charged with observing and/or assisting in the carrying out of plebiscites and elections, have had a similar relationship to the Trusteeship Council.

Both ECOSOC and the Trusteeship Council operate "under the authority" of the Assembly.[306] The Security Council, however, has the primary responsibility for the maintenance of international peace and security and the Assembly has generally sought to take this into account when establishing subsidiary organs in this area. Subsidiary organs charged with responsibilities in the disarmament field, for example, have reported to both the Assembly and the Council and occasionally have been subject to directives from the latter organ (e.g., the Atomic Energy Commission).[307] The Palestine Commission was another example of a body established by the Assembly but subject to instructions from the Security Council.

In the peace and security field, the Assembly has entrusted a wide variety of responsibilities to subsidiary organs it has created. Some

[306] See commentary on Arts. 60 and 85.
[307] See commentary on Arts. 11 and 26.

have been in the nature of permanent organs to serve where they might be useful (e.g., the Peace Observation Commission and the Panel for Inquiry and Conciliation). But most have been established to deal with particular situations. Many have been investigatory organs, such as the Special Committee on Palestine, the Eritrean Commission and the Special Committee on Hungary. Others have been established for the purpose of "observing" a situation (e.g., the Special Committee on the Balkans) or a particular event (e.g., the Temporary Commission for Korea whose primary function was to observe elections in that country).

A number of bodies have been charged with functions of mediation, conciliation and good offices (e.g., the Conciliation Commission for Palestine and the Good Offices Commission on the Question of Treatment of People of Indian Origin in the Union of South Africa). Subsidiary organs have also been established by the Assembly to assist in the formation of new governments (e.g., the Commissioner for Libya) or new governmental arrangements (e.g., the Temporary Executive Authority charged with administering the territory of West Irian). Also considered as subsidiary organs of the Assembly are military forces such as UNEF, which was established to supervise the cessation of hostilities in the Middle East in 1956 and the Security Force responsible for maintaining law and order in West Irian during the transitional period prior to Indonesia's assuming responsibility for the territory.

In addition to the subsidiary organs created to carry out functions in a particular area, there have been a number of committees and commissions established to undertake studies of a general character, such as the Collective Measures Committee and the various committees to consider a definition of aggression. Many of these committees have been charged with studying problems in which the Assembly has had a continuing or long-term interest. The International Law Commission, for example, assists the Assembly in discharging its responsibility for "encouraging the progressive development of international law and its codification." [308]

From the above, it can be seen that subsidiary organs of the General Assembly have varied greatly with respect to their powers, functions and relationships to the Assembly and other United Nation organs. They have also differed in such particulars as size, method of establishment, composition and duration.

Subsidiary organs of the Assembly have varied in size, from commit-

[308] See commentary on Art. 13. Other examples are the Special Committee on the Situation with Respect to the Implementation of the Declaration on the Granting of Independence to Colonial Nations and Peoples and the Committee on the Peaceful Uses of Outer Space.

tees on which all members are represented (e.g., the Disarmament Commission and UNCTAD), to a single individual (e.g., the Special Representative for Hungary, and the Mediator for Palestine). In most cases, the resolution establishing the subsidiary organ lists the states that are to be represented on it, although occasionally the selection is left to the President of the General Assembly (e.g., the Special Committee on Peace-Keeping Operations) or to the Secretary-General (e.g., the Special Representative in Jordan). In some cases specific criteria are laid down in the resolution with respect to composition (e.g., the stipulation that the committees on information from non-self-governing territories be composed of an equal number of administering and nonadministering states and the regulations regarding membership in the subsidiary organs of UNCTAD).

Most subsidiary organs have been composed of representatives of member states, although some have been composed of experts serving in their individual capacities. "Experts" have been used most often in examining and/or advising on problems requiring a high degree of "technical" or specialized knowledge. The International Law Commission, for example, is composed of individuals elected by the General Assembly. The members of the Investments Committee are individuals appointed by the Secretary-General. A rather high number of the ad hoc and standing bodies in the administrative and budgetary field are composed of individual experts (e.g., the Administrative Tribunal and the 1961 Committee of Experts on the Review of the Activities and Organization of the Secretariat). Other examples of persons serving in their individual capacities, as distinct from representatives of states, are the heads of the various "operating agencies" and the individuals appointed to carry out specific tasks in the political and trusteeship fields.

Many subsidiary organs have been terminated when the task for which they were created has been completed. In some cases, because of the persistence of the problem, the organ has continued in existence for a considerable period of time (e.g., the Conciliation Commission for Palestine). As already pointed out, many of the subsidiary organs in the administrative and budgetary field, as well as most of the "operating" agencies, have assumed a permanent character. They are, of course, subject to an Assembly decision to terminate or modify their functions, as for example the decision to merge the activities of the Special Fund and the various organs in the technical assistance field and the decisions to entrust the Special Committee on Colonialism with various functions previously performed by other special committees.

Powers of the Assembly

Although the power of the General Assembly to establish subsidiary organs is clearly stated in the Charter, there have been a number of occasions when the objection has been raised that in creating a particular subsidiary organ to carry out particular functions the Assembly would be exceeding its powers under the Charter. Article 2(7) has been frequently cited in arguments that the creation of a subsidiary organ would be in violation of the injunction against intervention in matters essentially within the domestic jurisdiction of a state.[309]

Closely related to the arguments based on Article 2(7) were the objections raised by some of the members administering non-self-governing territories against the Assembly's decision to establish special committees to examine the information submitted on those territories in accordance with Article 73(e). Arguments that the Assembly had no power to establish supervisory machinery in this area, and that for it to do so would be tantamount to a modification of the Charter, were rejected.[310]

It appears to be generally accepted that a subsidiary organ established by the General Assembly cannot operate in the territory of a state without that state's consent. This was made clear in the terms of reference of the Interim Committee and the Peace Observation Commission.[311] The element of "consent" was of crucial importance in establishing the United Nations Emergency Force (UNEF) following the Suez invasion in 1956.[312]

The competence of the Assembly has also been challenged on the ground that in establishing certain subsidiary organs it was encroaching upon the responsibilities assigned to the Security Council under the Charter. The Soviet Union, and some other states, raised this objection in connection with the Interim Committee, the Collective Measures Committee, the Panel of Military Experts, the Panel of Field Observers, and UNEF, all of which, it was alleged, were attempts by the Assembly to arrogate to itself powers that legally belonged to the

[309] For further discussion, see commentary on Art. 2(7).

[310] See commentary on Art. 73(e).

[311] GA Res. 111(II), Nov. 13, 1947 and 377(V), Nov. 3, 1950.

[312] See GA Res. 998(ES–I), Nov. 4, 1956 and the report of the Secretary-General setting forth the guiding principles for the organization and functioning of the Force. GAOR/ES–I/*Annexes*, agenda item 5. See also the Secretary-General's report on the UNEF experience. GAOR/12th Sess./1958/*Annexes*, agenda item 65 (A/3943). There have been numerous instances where subsidiary organs of the General Assembly have been unable to discharge their functions fully because of the refusal of one or more of the parties to allow them access to their territories (e.g., the committees to investigate or observe developments in Korea, the Balkans, Hungary).

Security Council. These objections were overridden, most members stressing the broad powers of the Assembly under Article 10 of the Charter and its "residual" responsibility for the maintenance of international peace and security under Article 11.[313]

The question of endowing subsidiary organs with functions beyond those specifically assigned to the Assembly by the Charter has been raised in a number of instances. In implementation of the Palestine partition plan, the Assembly established the United Nations Palestine Commission. A number of states argued, unsuccessfully, that the Assembly was conferring on the Commission executive, legislative, and administrative powers that the Assembly itself did not possess.[314] Somewhat similar arguments were raised in connection with abortive proposals to establish an international criminal court.[315]

In connection with the United Nations Administrative Tribunal, some controversy arose over the kinds of powers and functions the Assembly could confer upon a subsidiary organ, especially whether a subsidiary organ could take decisions binding upon the Assembly itself. On this point, the International Court gave its opinion that the Assembly could establish a tribunal competent to render judgments binding on itself.[316]

The question of its competence to confer powers was also raised in connection with the Assembly's establishment of the Interim Committee. The Soviet Union, and others opposed to the creation of the Committee, argued that it could not properly be considered as a "subsidiary" organ in view of its composition, the fact that it was to function continuously, and the broad range of powers to be conferred upon it, but these arguments were rejected by the great majority of members.[317]

[313] See commentary on Art. 11.

[314] GAOR/2d Sess./124th–126th Plen. Mtgs./Nov. 26 and 28, 1947/pp. 1324–79; and ad hoc. Ctte. on the Palestinian Question/24th–31st Mtgs./Nov. 20, 21, 22, 24 and 25, 1947/pp. 147–95.

[315] See Report of the Committee on International Criminal Jurisdiction, GAOR/9th Sess./*Supp. 12.* See also the previous report and the debate thereon, GAOR/7th Sess./*Supp. 11;* and 6th Ctte./321st–328th Mtgs./Nov. 7, 8, 10, 11, 12, 14 and 17, 1952/pp. 95–139.

[316] Advisory Opinion of July 1, 1954. *ICJ Reports,* 1954, pp. 56–57.

[317] GAOR/2d Sess./110th–111th Plen. Mtgs./Nov. 13, 1947/pp. 753–822; and 1st Ctte./74th–78th Mtgs./Oct. 14–18, 1947 and 94th–97th Mtgs./Nov. 5–6, 1947/pp. 129–79 and 307–36.

CHAPTER V

The Security Council

COMPOSITION

Article 23

1. The Security Council shall consist of *fifteen* [1] Members of the United Nations. The Republic of China, France, the Union of Soviet Socialist Republics, the United Kingdom of Great Britain and Northern Ireland, and the United States of America shall be permanent members of the Security Council. The General Assembly shall elect *ten* other Members of the United Nations to be non-permanent members of the Security Council, due regard being specially paid, in the first instance to the contribution of Members of the United Nations to the maintenance of international peace and security and to the other purposes of the Organization, and also to equitable geographical distribution.

2. The non-permanent members of the Security Council shall be elected for a term of two years. In the first election of the non-permanent members *after the increase of the membership of the Security Council from eleven to fifteen, two of the four additional members* shall be chosen for a term of one year. A retiring member shall not be eligible for immediate re-election.

3. Each member of the Security Council shall have one representative.

From the time the first plans were drawn up for an organization to maintain the postwar peace, it was clear that those countries primarily responsible for the conduct of the war against the Axis would occupy a "special" position within the new organization. It came to be realized, however, that any plan concentrating the power to maintain peace exclusively in their hands was unlikely to prove attractive to other nations. As a result, it was decided that the Security Council, the body primarily responsible for maintaining international peace and security,

---

[1] The Charter originally provided for eleven members, five permanent and six elected (for original text, see p. 680). Italics indicate amendment that entered into force Aug. 31, 1965.

should include a number of elected nonpermanent members representing the interest of all states in the preservation of peace.

At the same time, the "Big Three"—the Soviet Union, the United Kingdom, and the United States—were expanded to the "Big Five." Although skeptical of Roosevelt's views of China's ability to play a major role in the postwar world, Churchill and Stalin accepted the inclusion of China as one of the states that was to have a special position in the new Organization. Churchill's insistence upon including France among this small elite group was accepted with somewhat similar skepticism by Roosevelt and Stalin as to the postwar position of France.

When the delegates assembled at San Francisco to adopt the Charter of the United Nations, they were faced with an agreement among the major powers that the Security Council of the new Organization should be composed of five permanent members and six members to be elected by the General Assembly. Although various proposals were made to modify the provisions regarding the composition of the Council, only one—concerning criteria for the election of nonpermanent members—was adopted. Thus, Article 23 as originally adopted corresponded almost exactly with the provisions agreed upon during the Dumbarton Oaks Conversations.

Permanent Members

The Charter lists the permanent members of the Security Council as the "Republic of China, France, the Union of Soviet Socialist Republics, the United Kingdom of Great Britain and Northern Ireland, and the United States of America." At the San Francisco Conference, it was suggested that a phrase be added identifying the permanent members as those "having the greatest responsibility for the maintenance of peace" to justify the special position accorded them, but this suggestion was rejected.[2]

The Covenant of the League of Nations (Article 4) had provided for permanent representation on the Council of the "Principal Allied and Associated Powers" (France, Italy, Japan, the United Kingdom, and the United States). But the Covenant also permitted the Council, with the approval of the majority of the Assembly, to designate "additional" permanent members. The Charter of the United Nations contains no such provision. Any change in the list of permanent members, whether by deletion or addition, can be accomplished only by amending the Charter itself.

The Charter also effectively blocks the development of a class of

2 UNCIO, *Documents*, XI, 289.

semi- or quasi-permanent Council members by declaring that no retiring member is eligible for reelection to the Security Council. Under the Covenant, the Assembly (by a two-thirds majority) could establish the conditions of reeligibility for election to the Council. In part because of the frictions that developed in the League over this matter, it was decided to include in the United Nations Charter a specific prohibition against reelection.

The guarantee of continuous membership in the Security Council is only one of the prerogatives accorded to the "permanent members" under the Charter. The concurrence of all five of them is, with few exceptions, needed before the Security Council can make any substantive decision (Article 27). No amendment to the Charter can become effective unless ratified by all the permanent members (Articles 108 and 109). Indeed, the Charter itself could not come into force until all five had deposited their instruments of ratification (Article 110).

The special position of the permanent members with regard to the maintenance of international peace and security is further emphasized in other articles. They alone are members of the Military Staff Committee (Article 47). As a "transitional" arrangement (Article 106), these five powers were to "consult" with a "view to joint action on behalf of the Organization" for maintaining peace until the time when the entry into force of arrangements under Article 43 enabled the Security Council to exercise its responsibilities under Article 42.

Size of the Council

There was general agreement at Dumbarton Oaks that the size of the Security Council should be set at eleven members. What was wanted was a body large enough to provide for the representation of various interests, yet small enough to act efficiently. In an eleven-member Council, the nonpermanent members had a slight majority, but since seven votes were required for any decision, neither the permanent nor the nonpermanent members as a group could make a decision without assistance from the other. A great many proposals were introduced at San Francisco to increase the number of nonpermanent members on the Council, but the major powers successfully resisted these pressures.[3]

Under the Covenant, the number of nonpermanent members of the Council was set at four but eventually rose to eleven through the exercise of the power granted to the Council to increase the number of members with the approval of a majority of the Assembly. The idea of

---

[3] UNCIO, *Documents*, XI, 763–64.

including in the Charter a provision for possible increase in the number of nonpermanent members was abandoned at Dumbarton Oaks.[4]

The first proposal to increase the size of the Council by amending Article 23 was introduced by a group of Latin American states at the 1956 session of the General Assembly. It called for raising the number of nonpermanent members from six to eight. The distribution of seats on the Council had long been a source of dissatisfaction, and with the rapid increase in the membership of the United Nations after 1955, pressures mounted for increasing its size. However, the Soviet Union was opposed on the ground that the Charter could not be amended so long as China was not represented in the United Nations by the Peiping regime; and, of course, no amendment could come into effect without the ratification of all of the permanent members of the Security Council. When the proposal came to a vote in the General Assembly in 1960, it was defeated in large part because of the insistence of a group of Asian and African states that the approval of the amendment be linked with a call for an immediate redistribution of Council seats.[5] In 1963, agreement was finally reached to increase the number of elected members from six to ten; this amendment came into force on September 1, 1965.[6]

Term of Office

The two-year term for the elected members of the Council was a compromise reached at Dumbarton Oaks. The United States favored annual elections so that more members of the Organization would have a chance to serve on the Council; the British, stressing the need for continuity and experience, proposed a three-year term.[7] In the interest of continuity, it was also decided to stagger the terms of the nonpermanent members, with half of them being elected each year. To accomplish this, it was necessary to employ a special procedure for the first elections. The Assembly, by the required two-thirds vote elected the six nonpermanent members; by a simple majority, it was decided that Australia and Brazil would serve a full two-year term; the tie vote for the third full term was broken when Poland was chosen by lot. The other three members (Egypt, Mexico, and the Netherlands) were thus elected, in accordance with Article 23, for a one-year term.[8] In some-

[4] Ruth B. Russell, *A History of the United Nations Charter* (Washington, Brookings Institution, 1958), p. 442.

[5] For discussion on the distribution of seats on the Council, see below.

[6] GA Res. 1991(XVIII), Dec. 17, 1963; for further comment, see commentary on Art. 108.

[7] Russell, p. 443.

[8] GAOR/1st Sess., 1st Part/4th and 5th Plen. Mtgs./Jan. 12, 1946/pp. 72 ff.

what similar fashion, the amendment to Article 23 provided that of the four additional members, two should be initially chosen for one-year terms.[9]

Under the Assembly's Rules of Procedure, the elected members of the Council take office on January 1 following their election (Rule 140). Should any of them cease to be a member of the Council, the Rules provide for the election of another member to fill out the unexpired term (Rule 141). Through 1955, all elected members served two-year terms. At the tenth session of the Assembly, the deadlock that developed over the election of one nonpermanent member was eventually resolved by splitting the term. Yugoslavia was elected on the understanding that at the end of the year it would resign and the Philippines would be elected to serve out the second year of the term. Some doubts were raised about the legality of this arrangement and some representatives reserved their position, but the compromise was accepted.[10] Similar compromises were agreed upon to break the deadlocks that developed in subsequent elections.[11]

Criteria for the Election of Nonpermanent Members

Initially, the United States opposed the inclusion in the Charter of any statement of criteria for the election of the nonpermanent members of the Security Council. When the matter was discussed at Dumbarton Oaks, the Chinese representative proposed that certain general principles should be established to insure that the Council was adequately representative of the international community. Britain proposed that in the elections, "due regard" should be paid to the "contributions" of states to the objectives of the Organization. The United States, however, still favored leaving the General Assembly unrestricted in electing the nonpermanent members.[12]

At the San Francisco Conference there was widespread interest in criteria for selecting the nonpermanent members of the Security Council.[13] The Latin American states, almost without exception, sought to assure the adequate representation of their region either through a "permanent" seat or a definite allocation of the nonpermanent seats. Others, such as Egypt and the Philippines, also favored some form of regional representation. Still others, some of the Western European states and some of the Commonwealth Members, sought to protect the position of the so-called "middle powers" by linking the distribution of

---

[9] GA Res. 1991(XVIII), Dec. 17, 1963.
[10] GAOR/10th Sess./559th Plen. Mtg./Dec. 16, 1955/pp. 494 ff.
[11] At the 14th, 15th, 16th, and 18th Assembly sessions; see Table 4.
[12] Russell, p. 444.   [13] UNCIO, *Documents*, III, 658–60.

Council seats to the contributions of states to the maintenance of peace. Possible criteria considered during the discussions at San Francisco included the following:

geographical distribution, rotation, contribution of the Members of the Organization towards the maintenance of international peace and security and towards the other purposes of the Organization, guaranties concerning the active defense of international order and means to participate substantially in it, combinations of elements including population, industrial and economic capacity, future contributions in armed forces and assistance pledged by each member state, contributions rendered in the second World War, and so on; also special assignment of non-permanent seats to certain groups of nations.[14]

After extended discussion,[15] agreement was reached on a compromise solution, embodied in the first paragraph of Article 23. This was not meant to be a rigid or automatic formula, but rather an indication of the factors the Assembly is expected to take into account in electing the nonpermanent members of the Council.

In the first election, the criteria of "contributions" and "geographical distribution" were neatly balanced. In subsequent years, the "middle powers" were elected to the Council with greater frequency than the small powers, but, as a glance at Table 4 indicates, geographical distribution has come to be the predominant factor.

Distribution of Nonpermanent Seats

The pattern established at the first session of the General Assembly for the distribution of nonpermanent seats in the Security Council was as follows: two for Latin America and one each for the Commonwealth, Western Europe, the Middle East, and Eastern Europe. This distribution was in part the result of a "gentleman's agreement," the exact nature of which has been the subject of controversy.[16] Even during this first election, there were some protests over backstage maneuvering.[17] Insistence, particularly by the Soviet Union, that the same arrangements should prevail in subsequent elections raised much stronger objections.[18] Nevertheless, despite some bitterly contested elections, the general pattern established at the first session for the distribution of the nonpermanent seats on the Council prevailed through the first decade. It eventually broke down before the demands

[14] UNCIO, *Documents*, XI, 676–77.   [15] Russell, pp. 648–49.
[16] See below, p. 199.
[17] See statement by New Zealand. GAOR/1st Sess., 1st Part/4th Plen. Mtg./Jan. 12, 1946/p. 76.
[18] See, for example, statement by India. GAOR/2d Sess./109th Plen. Mtg./Nov. 3, 1947/p. 750.

of the increasingly numerous Asian and African members of the Organization for greater representation.

Table 4

ELECTED MEMBERS OF THE SECURITY COUNCIL, 1946–1966

1946 *	1952–53	1959–60
Mexico	Chile	Argentina
Egypt	Pakistan	Tunisia
Netherlands	Greece	Italy

1946–47	1953–54	1961–62
Brazil	Colombia	Chile
Australia	Lebanon	United Arab Republic
Poland	Denmark	Liberia (1961) **
		Ireland (1962) **

1947–48	1954–55	1962–63
Colombia	Brazil	Venezuela
Syria	New Zealand	Ghana
Belgium	Turkey	Romania (1962) **
		Philippines (1963) **

1948–49	1955–56	1963–64
Argentina	Peru	Brazil
Canada	Iran	Morocco
Ukrainian SSR	Belgium	Norway

1949–50	1956–57	1964–65
Cuba	Cuba	Bolivia
Egypt	Australia	Ivory Coast
Norway	Yugoslavia (1956) **	Czechoslovakia (1964) **
	Philippines (1957) **	Malaysia (1965) **

1950–51	1957–58	1965–66
Ecuador	Colombia	Uruguay
India	Iraq	Netherlands
Yugoslavia	Sweden	Jordan (1965) ***
		Mali (1966) ***

1951–52	1958–59
Brazil	Panama
Turkey	Canada
Netherlands	Japan

    * Elected for a one-year term only.
   ** Term split by agreement.
  *** Term split by agreement with understanding that if the amendment to Article 23 entered into force during 1965, both Jordan and Mali would serve two-year terms.

Largely to meet this demand, it was decided to increase the number of nonpermanent members from six to ten. In its resolution approving this amendment to the Charter, the General Assembly decided that the seats should be allocated as follows: five for Africa and Asia; one for

Eastern Europe; two for Latin America; and two for Western European and "other States." [19] On December 10, 1965, the General Assembly held its first elections under the amended Article 23. It chose Argentina, Bulgaria, Japan, Mali, and Nigeria for two-year terms, and New Zealand and Uganda for one-year terms.

There has been a tendency on the part of many members to interpret the term "geographical distribution" as meaning "regional representation." As early as the first session, the Assembly was warned that "there were states which belong to a given region but not necessarily to a particular group in that region." If it were interpreted that "any vacancy . . . should always be filled by another Member of the same group or region," the consequence would be that some states "would always be excluded from obtaining a place on the Council." This would "obviously be . . . detrimental to the best interests of the Organization." [20]

Nevertheless, the states elected to the Council are generally those whose candidacies have the backing of other states in the group with which they are associated. There have been few contests in the election of states from Latin America, Western Europe, and the Middle East. From 1949 through 1960, each time the Soviet-backed candidate was defeated for election, the Soviet representative protested that the Assembly had violated the Charter and the "gentleman's agreement" on the distribution of Council seats. The existence of any agreement permitting the Soviet bloc to designate the Eastern European member of the Council was denied by the United States, although others, including Britain, considered that the candidate put forward by the group concerned should generally receive support. [21]

Representation and Credentials

Article 23 provides that "each Member of the Security Council shall have one representative." This is similar to the provisions for representation in the other two Councils and contrasts with the five representatives each member is allowed in the General Assembly. [22] The Council's Provisional Rules of Procedure require that the credentials of a representative be communicated to the Secretary-General "not less than twenty-four hours" before the representative takes his seat on the

[19] GA Res. 1991(XVIII), Dec. 17, 1963. "Other states" is the term used to cover such members as Australia, Canada, Israel, New Zealand, and South Africa.
[20] Statement by China. GAOR/1st Sess., 1st Part/5th Plen. Mtg./Jan. 12, 1946/pp. 88–89.
[21] See Geoffrey L. Goodwin, Britain and the United Nations (New York, Carnegie Endowment for International Peace, 1958), pp. 240–41.
[22] Arts. 9(2), 61(3), and 86(2).

Council. An exception is made for heads of government and ministers of foreign affairs, who may sit on the Council without having submitted credentials. In 1950 the Rules were revised to add a requirement that "credentials shall be issued either by the Head of the State or of the Government concerned or by its Minister of Foreign Affairs" (Rule 15).

The credentials are examined by the Secretary-General who is called upon under the Rules to submit a report to the Council for approval.[23] Initially, the Secretary-General's reports were placed on the Council's agenda and formally approved by it. Since 1948, however, it has been the practice merely to submit the report to the members, and then, in the absence of any request for consideration by the Council, the report is considered as having been approved without objection.[24]

"Pending approval" of his credentials, a representative is seated "provisionally" with the same rights as other representatives. Similarly, if any objection is raised concerning the credentials of a representative, he "shall continue to sit with the same rights as other representatives until the Security Council has decided the matter" (Rules 16 and 17).

For the most part, approval of credentials of representatives on the Security Council has been routine. There have, in fact, been only two cases where they have been challenged. The first was the question of representation of China, an issue which since 1950 has been raised in all of the United Nations organs. The second case, involving Iraq, an elected member of the Council, presented a relatively simple problem. The government of a nonpermanent member of the Security Council had been overthrown and a new regime established. After watching developments for a few weeks, the Council accepted the credentials of the representative of the new government.[25]

The question of China's representation was more complicated. By the end of 1949, the People's Republic of China had extended its control over all of mainland China. The Nationalist government, however, remained in existence on Taiwan, and its representative continued to sit in the organs of the United Nations. At the first meeting of the Council in January, 1950, the Soviet representative proposed that the Security Council decide "not to recognize the credentials of the representative" of the Nationalist government. At its next meeting, the Council rejected this proposal by a vote of 3 to 6 with 2 abstentions;

[23] On the question whether the matter of representation is one to which the veto is applicable, see commentary on Art. 27.

[24] *Repertoire of the Security Council*, pp. 11 ff.

[25] See SCOR/13th Yr./827th Mtg./July 15, 1958/pp. 1 ff.; 834th Mtg./July 18, 1958/pp. 1–7; and 838th Mtg./Aug. 7, 1958/pp. 1 ff. See also *Supp.* for July, Aug., and Sept., 1958, pp. 54–56, and 124–25.

thereupon, the Soviet representative withdrew in protest from the Council.[26]

When the Soviet representative returned to exercise the presidency of the Council in August, 1950, his first act was to "rule" that "the representative of the Kuomintang group seated in the Council does not represent China and cannot therefore take part in the meetings of the Security Council." The President was overruled. After a long, involved, and bitter debate, the Council also rejected the Soviet proposal to include on the agenda an item entitled "recognition of the representative of the Central People's Government of the People's Republic of China as the representative of China." [27]

Soviet representatives in the Security Council have consistently refused to recognize the representatives of Nationalist China, referring to them when unavoidable by their personal names. However, in contrast to the other organs of the United Nations where the question of Chinese representation has been debated almost annually, there has been no real discussion in the Security Council on this issue since 1950. In January, 1955, when the Council considered the question of hostilities in the Formosa straits, the Soviet representative proposed that the Council decide "not to admit the Kuomintang representative to participate in the consideration" of the matter. The Council instead adopted a United States proposal not "to consider any proposals to exclude the representative of the Government of the Republic of China, or to seat representatives" of the People's Republic of China.[28]

During the Security Council's discussion in January, 1950, the Indian representative proposed that the Council adopt the following additional rule of procedure:

Where the right of any person to represent, or to continue to represent, a State on the Security Council, or at a meeting of the Security Council, is called in question on the ground that he does not represent, or has ceased to represent, the recognized government of that State, the President of the Council shall, before submitting the question to the decision of the Council, ascertain . . . and place before the Council, so far as available, the views of the Governments of all the other States Members of the United Nations on the matter.[29]

[26] SCOR/5th Yr./459th Mtg./Jan. 10, 1950/p. 1; and 460th Mtg./Jan. 12, 1950/p. 9.

[27] *Ibid.*, 480th Mtg./Aug. 1, 1950/p. 9; and 482d Mtg./Aug. 3, 1950/p. 22.

[28] SCOR/10th Yr./689th Mtg./Jan. 31, 1955/pp. 1 ff. Note also Soviet protests when China assumed the presidency of the Council. See, for example, *ibid.*, 700th Mtg./Sept. 8, 1955/p. 1.

[29] SCOR/5th Yr./462d Mtg./Jan. 17, 1950/p. 11. See also *ibid.*, 460th Mtg./Jan. 12, 1950/p. 7.

The proposal was referred to the Council's Committee of Experts, which later reported that, whereas members were agreed that some uniform procedure should be established, the majority were of the opinion that the General Assembly was the more appropriate organ for taking action on this matter.[30] The issue was subsequently considered by the Assembly and a resolution was adopted recommending that on any issue involving rival claims to representation, the "attitude" adopted by the Assembly "should be taken into account by other organs of the United Nations." [31]

FUNCTIONS AND POWERS

Article 24

1. In order to ensure prompt and effective action by the United Nations, its Members confer on the Security Council primary responsibility for the maintenance of international peace and security, and agree that in carrying out its duties under this responsibility the Security Council acts on their behalf.

2. In discharging these duties the Security Council shall act in accordance with the Purposes and Principles of the United Nations. The specific powers granted to the Security Council for the discharge of these duties are laid down in Chapters VI, VII, VIII, and XII.

3. The Security Council shall submit annual and, when necessary, special reports to the General Assembly for its consideration.

Article 24 establishes the basic principle of the "primary responsibility" of the Security Council for the maintenance of international peace and security. By the terms of this article, members not only "confer" this responsibility on the Council but agree that in carrying out its duties the Council "acts on their behalf." Any decisions of the Security Council taken in discharge of its responsibilities must, therefore, be considered as action taken by the Organization as a whole. All members share in any responsibilities the Council assumes and all are subject to any obligation it imposes. Decisions of the Council apply equally to those voting in favor and those voting against, as well as to those members which, not being represented on the Council, have no opportunity to vote at all.[32] This point has been of special concern to

[30] *Ibid.*, 468th Mtg./Feb. 28, 1950/pp. 10–11.

[31] GA Res. 396(V), Dec. 14, 1950. For discussion on this resolution and the debates concerning the "criteria" upon which a decision should be based, see commentary on ch. II.

[32] This is further emphasized by the obligations assumed by members under Art. 25 of the Charter. See commentary on that article.

some of the nonpermanent Council members. One of the grounds upon which Australia objected to the Council's assuming certain responsibilities for the Free Territory of Trieste was that it would impose obligations on members not then represented on the Council.[33] On other occasions, however, nonpermanent members have specifically stated that they felt themselves bound by decisions taken by the Council prior to the time they became members of the Council.[34]

The Council's Primary Responsibility

In placing the "primary responsibility" for the maintenance of international peace and security upon the Security Council, the founders of the Organization recognized that organ as best fitted, by virtue of size and composition, to insure "prompt and effective action." This effort to associate responsibility with power was viewed by many as one of the major advances of the Charter of the United Nations over the League system, in which the powers of the Council and the Assembly were largely identical. At the San Francisco Conference, numerous attempts were made to diminish the primacy of the Security Council, principally through enlarging the powers and responsibilities of the General Assembly [35] and regional organizations.[36] In both respects, provisions were added to the Charter spelling out these responsibilities in greater detail, but the primary position of the Council, particularly with regard to enforcement measures, remained intact. The text of Article 24 corresponds to the Dumbarton Oaks draft with the single addition of a paragraph requiring the Council to submit reports for the consideration of the Assembly.

In the Security Council, the phraseology of Article 24 has been most often used in statements to the effect that, if the Council did not act or did not take a particular action, it would be failing to discharge the responsibility conferred upon it under the Charter. Closely related are the frequent statements that it is the Security Council, rather than some other organ or agency, which should act. This point has been raised in connection with actions by regional organizations, subsidiary bodies, the Secretary-General, and most especially the General Assembly.

[33] See SCOR/2d Yr./89th Mtg./Jan. 7, 1947/pp. 5 ff.; and 91st Mtg./Jan. 10, 1947/pp. 57–58.

[34] See, for example, statement of Colombia regarding the Council's resolution calling for the lifting of restrictions on passage through the Suez Canal. SCOR/9th Yr./664th Mtg./Mar. 29, 1954/p. 5; and statement by Denmark, *ibid.*, 663d Mtg./Mar. 25, 1954/p. 3.

[35] For specific proposals for amending Art. 24 in this respect, see UNCIO, *Documents*, XI, 767–78. See also commentary on Arts. 10–12.

[36] See commentary on ch. viii.

From the beginning, it was recognized that the necessary condition for the satisfactory discharge by the Council of its responsibilities was the ability and willingness of the permanent members to agree. With the failure of this agreement to materialize, the move began, under the leadership of the United States, to increase the role of the General Assembly in the maintenance of international peace and security. In the view of some members, especially the Soviet Union, these measures were clearly contrary to the Charter provisions conferring "primary responsibility" upon the Security Council. Those favoring the measures pointed out that the Council's responsibility is "primary" but not "exclusive," and that under the Charter, the General Assembly has important responsibilities of its own for the maintenance of international peace and security.[37]

General Powers

Article 24(2) states that "specific powers granted to the Security Council" are laid down in chapters VI, VII, VIII, and XII of the Charter. This statement raises the question whether the Council has these powers only or whether it may exercise such other powers, consistent with the purposes and principles of the Charter, as are necessary for it to discharge its responsibilities. The latter, more liberal interpretation has been generally accepted.

The issue of the general powers of the Security Council came up the first time the Council was called upon to consider a matter relating to the maintenance of international peace and security. The specific question was whether the Council could retain on its agenda the complaint by Iran against the Soviet Union despite a request by Iran that it be removed. The restricted interpretation of the Council's powers, as most fully developed in a memorandum by the Secretary-General,[38] was that the Council could not retain its jurisdiction over the question in the absence of a specific exercise by the Council of its powers under Chapter VI. The majority of the Council members took a much broader view. The representative of Mexico, for example, held that Article 24 "invests the Council with implied powers wider in scope than the specific powers" enumerated in paragraph 2 of that article.[39]

When the Security Council in early 1947 considered a request by the Council of Foreign Ministers that it assume certain responsibilities for the Free Territory of Trieste, the discussion centered more directly

[37] For further discussion, see commentary on Art. 11.
[38] SCOR/1st Yr., 1st Ser., No. 2/33d Mtg./Apr. 16, 1940/pp. 143–45.
[39] *Ibid.*, 36th Mtg./Apr. 23, 1946/p. 210. See also discussion at the 33d Mtg./Apr. 10, 1946/pp. 143–44; and report of the Committee of Experts, *ibid.*, Supp. 2, pp. 47–50.

upon the interpretation of Article 24. The representative of Australia objected that the Council had no authority under the Charter to accept these responsibilities. Most of the Council members, however, seemed to share the opinion given by the Secretary-General that Article 24 constituted "a grant of power sufficiently wide" to enable the Security Council to accept the responsibilities in question. According to this view, members of the United Nations had "conferred upon the Security Council powers commensurate with its responsibility for the maintenance of peace and security." [40]

These and other decisions taken by the Security Council during the first years of its operations established the general practice of interpreting the authority of the Council in a broad and flexible manner. Although it is generally accepted that the Council, in the discharge of its responsibilities, can exercise powers beyond those specifically listed in Article 24(2), this does not mean that these powers are considered unlimited.

Limitations on Powers

The first sentence of Article 24(2) states that the Security Council "shall act in accordance with the Purposes and Principles of the Charter." The reference here is to the specific provisions of Articles 1 and 2 of the Charter.

At the San Francisco Conference, various attempts were made to restrict the powers of the Council even further. Norway sought to alter the terms of Article 24(2) so as to require the Council to act not only in accordance with "the purposes and principles of the Charter" but also in accordance with the "provisions of the Charter, and the consideration that no solution should be imposed upon a State of a nature to impair its confidence in its future security or welfare." This proposal was defeated,[41] as were more indirect efforts to limit the powers of the Council, such as the introduction of a definition of aggression,[42] and the proposed alteration of Article 1(1), which would have made the phrase "in conformity with the principles of justice and international law" apply not only to the functions of pacific settlement but also to any action taken with regard to threats to the peace, breaches of the peace, and acts of aggression.[43]

Generally, when the competence of the Security Council has been challenged, the discussion has centered on the powers of the Council

[40] See discussion in SCOR/2d Yr./89th Mtg./Jan. 7, 1947/pp. 4 ff.; and 91st Mtg./Jan. 10, 1947/pp. 44 ff.
[41] UNCIO, *Documents*, XI, 378–80.   [42] See commentary on Art. 39.
[43] See commentary on Art. 1(1).

under Chapters VI and VII of the Charter. Occasionally, Article 24 has been invoked in connection with arguments that nowhere in the Charter is the Security Council authorized to take the kind of action under consideration. Relevant in this connection is Egypt's position with regard to the Council's resolution calling for the removal of restrictions on the passage of ships through the Suez Canal. While supporting the position that the functions and powers of the Council were not limited to the specific powers listed in Article 24(2), the Egyptian representative pointed out that those functions and powers were nonetheless limited and "should be strictly regulated and governed by the fundamental principles and purposes" of the Charter. In his view, the Council's resolution was not "in accordance with the . . . Charter" and his government was therefore under no obligation to accept and carry it out.[44] This position, however, received little support from other members of the Council.

Also, relevant is the initial discussion in the Security Council on the question of Angola, which focused on a proposal calling for the implementation of various decisions of the General Assembly. Portugal took the position that the competence of the Security Council was "specifically limited to the matters referred to in Chapters VI, VII, VIII, and XII of the Charter," [45] a restrictive interpretation which, as pointed out above, had been specifically rejected by the Council in its early years.

While taking a broader view of the competence of the United Nations in this matter, the United Kingdom's representative contended that the proposed resolution seemed "to invite the Security Council wholly to ignore the limitations placed on its jurisdiction by Article 24 of the Charter." For the Council, in the absence of any danger to international peace, to take up the question of what effect a state ought to give to a resolution of the General Assembly was, in his view, "a wholly new interpretation" of the Charter which would mean "stretching the functions of the Security Council in such a manner as to blunt the edge of its major task, namely the maintenance of international peace and security." [46] The Council took no action at that time, although it did so later when the situation in the Portuguese territories had further deteriorated.

Apprehension over the efforts, primarily of the African members, to involve the Security Council in the whole range of "colonial" questions

----

[44] The reference here is to the terms of Article 25; see commentary on that article. For the Egyptian position, see SCOR/6th Yr./553d Mtg./Aug. 16, 1951/pp. 22–23; and 558th Mtg./Aug. 27, 1951/pp. 16–17. See also 9th Yr./664th Mtg./Mar. 29, 1954/p. 23.

[45] SCOR/16th Yr./944th Mtg./Mar. 10, 1961/pp. 6 ff.

[46] *Ibid.*, 946th Mtg./Mar. 15, 1961/p. 13.

has often been voiced. Statements similar to those by the United Kingdom, quoted in the preceding paragraph, have been frequent, although the specific invocation of Article 24 is less common.[47] In general, however, the majority of the members of the Council have taken a broad view of the kinds of questions with which the Council may concern itself.

Reports to the General Assembly

While the Security Council has the primary responsibility for the maintenance of international peace and security, it is obligated to render an account to the General Assembly of the measures it takes in this regard. The Dumbarton Oaks Proposals recognized the right of the Assembly to receive such reports. At the San Francisco Conference, the statement of this function of the Assembly was expanded and the obligation of the Security Council reiterated by the addition of paragraph 3 to Article 24.

The annual reports of the Security Council merely summarize the activities of the Council and in practice are not even discussed by the Assembly.[48] It is not clear whether "special reports" are to be submitted when considered "necessary" by the Security Council or by the General Assembly. The only special reports the Council has submitted have been in connection with the admission of new members. Even when the Council has considered a matter at the instigation of the General Assembly, it has not considered it necessary to render a special accounting to the Assembly, although on occasion it has requested the Secretary-General to transmit to the Assembly the records of its discussions.

Article 25

The Members of the United Nations agree to accept and carry out the decisions of the Security Council in accordance with the present Charter.

The obligations assumed by members of the United Nations under Article 25 are the direct consequence of the authority conferred on the Security Council under Article 24. If members agree that the Security Council, in discharging its "primary responsibility" for the maintenance of international peace and security, acts on their behalf, it is logical that they should also agree to accept and carry out decisions taken by

[47] See, for example, the statement of the U.K. on the question of Southern Rhodesia. SCOR/18th Yr./1066th Mtg./Sept. 10, 1963/para. 61.
[48] See Art. 15 and commentary.

the Council in discharge of that responsibility. The extent of the obligations of members under Article 25, however, has never been made clear.

At San Francisco, Belgium sought to limit the obligations of members to those decisions taken by the Security Council in exercise of its powers under Chapters VI, VII, and VIII of the Charter. Considered unduly restrictive by some delegates, this proposal failed to obtain the necessary two-thirds majority vote.[49] During the debate in the Security Council on the Statute for the Free Territory of Trieste, the Security-General cited the rejection of the Belgian amendment to support the conclusion that members were obligated to accept and carry out decisions of the Council, whether taken in accordance with its general or specific powers.[50]

The obligations of members under Article 25 are limited, however, to decisions taken "in accordance with the present Charter." The Dumbarton Oaks draft of this provision prompted questions at the San Francisco Conference as to whether this phrase was intended to define the manner in which members were to accept and carry out decisions or the manner in which the Security Council was to make decisions. The text was therefore redrafted to make it clear that members were obligated to carry out only those decisions of the Council that were legally mandatory.[51]

As the prefatory note in the *Repertory of United Nations Practice* points out, Article 25 "contains no precise delimitation of the range of decisions to which it relates," and the Security Council "has on no occasion found it necessary to define the scope of the obligation incurred by Members of the United Nations under Article 25." [52] There have been frequent statements in the Security Council to the effect that a member was under an obligation to comply with the terms of a particular resolution. From the discussions in the Council, however, it is difficult to discern much of a consensus as to what "decisions" members are obligated to accept and carry out.

Obviously, the Charter does not impose any obligation on members to accept and carry out "recommendations" that the Security Council might make, for example, under Article 36 or 37. It was made clear at San Francisco that such recommendations have no binding force and there have been repeated statements to that effect in the Security Council. The status of a Council resolution calling upon the parties to a dispute to settle it by peaceful means in accordance with Article 33 of the Charter is slightly different in that, in this case, the Council is in

[49] UNCIO, *Documents*, XI, 395.
[50] SCOR/2d Yr./91st Mtg./Jan. 10, 1947/p. 45. See also commentary on Art. 24.
[51] Russell, p. 665.   [52] *Repertory*, II, 39.

effect bringing to the attention of the parties an obligation they have already accepted in paragraph 1 of that article.[53]

With regard to the Security Council's functions of pacific settlement, one point of difference that has arisen is whether states are obligated to cooperate in any investigation the Council may decide to undertake. This matter was discussed at some length in connection with the question of the Greek frontier incidents. In the view of the Soviet Union, "all decisions taken under Chapter VI, including decisions to conduct an investigation, are in the nature of recommendations . . ." and states are therefore under no obligation (other than a moral one) to accept such resolutions.[54] Other members drew a distinction between "recommendations" under Articles 36 and 37 and "decisions" to investigate. While conceding that under Chapter VI the Security Council had no power of "sanctions" or "enforcement," the United States representative nevertheless argued that the Security Council could take "decisions" under Chapter VI and that under Article 25 members had a "duty . . . to conform to those decisions." [55]

There is certainly room for argument whether there are any decisions the Security Council may take in the field of pacific settlement that are binding upon members. But clearly, when the Council exercises its authority under Chapter VII, it can make decisions that members are obligated to accept and carry out. "Recommendations" by the Council under Article 39 are no more binding than recommendations under Chapter VI; but members are obligated to accept and carry out decisions by the Council calling for nonmilitary or military measures in accordance with Articles 41 and 42.

The situation with regard to Article 40 is less clear, but the preponderant opinion appears to be that the Council has the authority to obligate members to comply with provisional measures. This point has been made on numerous occasions during the discussion of the conflicts between Israel and the Arab states. Both members of the Council and the parties concerned have generally considered Article 25 applicable to those resolutions of the Council directed toward maintaining the cease-fire and armistice agreements between the parties.[56]

[53] For further discussion, see commentary on ch. vi, especially p. 261.

[54] SCOR/2d Yr./167th Mtg./July 25, 1947/p. 1541.

[55] Ibid. For other statements on this point, see ibid., 166th–168th Mtgs./July 24–28, 1947/pp. 1519–60. The relationship of Art. 25 to an investigation by the Council had been previously discussed in connection with this same question. See ibid., 134th–137th Mtgs./May 16–22, 1947/pp. 842 ff. See also commentary on Art. 34.

[56] Note, however, Egypt's contention that it was under no obligation to carry out the Council's resolution concerning restrictions on passage through the Suez Canal on the ground that the resolution was not "in accordance with the present Charter." See commentary on Art. 24.

The cease-fire in this case had been specifically ordered by the Security Council under Article 40 of the Charter. In other cases, such as the Indonesian question, the Council has been less specific and there has been some disagreement concerning the applicability of Article 25. In the view of many members of the Council, the Netherlands was, in accordance with Article 25, under an obligation to comply with certain of the Council's resolutions calling for a cease-fire and other measures. This position was contested by other members on the grounds that the Council had omitted any reference to Article 40 from its resolutions and, indeed, had never formally declared that there was a threat to the peace, breach of the peace, or act of aggression in accordance with Article 39 of the Charter.[57]

The lack of any formal determination under Article 39, however, did not hinder the Security Council from taking decisions considered binding upon members in connection with the Congo situation. Originally, the Council called upon Belgium to withdraw its troops and requested all states to refrain from any actions which "might tend to impede the restoration of law and order" or "undermine the territorial integrity and the political independence of the Republic of the Congo."[58] Then, shortly after the adoption of this resolution, the Secretary-General drew the Council's attention to the obligations of members under Articles 25 and 49.[59] The resolution adopted by the Council on August 9, 1960, called upon all members "in accordance with Articles 25 and 49 of the Charter of the United Nations, to accept and carry out the decisions of the Security Council and to afford mutual assistance in carrying out measures decided upon by the Council."[60] Neither the resolution nor the discussions leading up to its adoption made clear exactly what specific measures the members (other than Belgium) were obligated to undertake.

Subsequently, on September 20, the General Assembly also adopted a resolution invoking Articles 25 and 49. This section of the resolution was in the form of a "request" to all member states to accept and carry out the decisions of the Security Council and to afford mutual assistance in carrying out measures decided upon by the Security Council. Again, there was no discussion of the extent of the obligations of members, but the resolution did call upon all states to refrain from supply-

57 SCOR/3d Yr./389th Mtg./Dec. 22, 1948/p. 49; 4th Yr./397th Mtg./Jan. 7, 1949/pp. 27–28; 398th Mtg./Jan. 11, 1949/pp. 3, 5, and 11; and 417th–420th Mtgs./Mar. 11–21, 1949. See also commentary on Arts. 39 and 40.

58 SC Res. of July 22, 1960. SCOR/15th Yr./Supp. for July, Aug., and Sept., 1960/p. 34. See also SC Res. of July 14, ibid., p. 16.

59 SCOR/15th Yr./884th Mtg./Aug. 8, 1960/p. 4.

60 Ibid., 886th Mtg./Aug. 8 and 9, 1960/p. 52.

ing the Congo with arms, material, or military personnel except through United Nations channels.[61]

Both resolutions were reaffirmed by the Security Council in its resolution of February 21, 1961, which also called upon all states "to take immediate and energetic measures" to prevent the infiltration of unauthorized personnel into the Congo.[62] Following the adoption of this resolution, the Secretary-General addressed a note to all members calling attention to the "legal character" of the resolution "which, like the other resolutions on the Congo, must be regarded as a mandatory decision that all Members of the United Nations are legally bound to accept and carry out in accordance with Article 25 of the Charter." [63]

From the invocation by the Council and the Assembly of Article 49, it would appear that members considered that the action taken with regard to the Congo came within the framework of Chapter VII, even though none of the resolutions ever cited Article 39, 40, 41, or 42. Despite the lack of any discussion in either organ concerning the relationship between the decisions taken with regard to the Congo and the terms of Articles 25 and 49, there appears to have been a consensus that those decisions did impose obligations upon member states.[64]

Article 26

In order to promote the establishment and maintenance of international peace and security with the least diversion for armaments of the world's human and economic resources, the Security Council shall be responsible for formulating, with the assistance of the Military Staff Committee referred to in Article 47, plans to be submitted to the Members of the United Nations for the establishment of a system for the regulation of armaments.

One of the major, and most obvious, differences between the United Nations Charter and the Covenant of the League of Nations lies in the significance attached to the question of disarmament. In the League system, there was far greater emphasis upon disarmament as an independent approach to peace. Under the Covenant (Article 8[1]), members recognized that the maintenance of peace required "the reduction of national armaments." There is no such provision in the Charter.

[61] GA Res. 1474(ES–IV), Sept. 20, 1960.

[62] SCOR/16th Yr./*Supp.* for Jan., Feb., and Mar., 1961/p. 147.

[63] *Ibid.*, pp. 182–83. See also letter to Belgium invoking Art. 25, *ibid.*, pp. 178–79.

[64] For statements by the Secretary-General concerning the obligations of members, see commentary on Arts. 40 and 49.

Indeed, disarmament or the regulation of armaments is not even mentioned in the statement of the Organization's objectives (Article 1). The Covenant also set forth the criteria that national armaments should be reduced "to the lowest point consistent with national safety and the enforcement by common action of international obligations." At Dumbarton Oaks, a British suggestion that the Charter include a similar statement was rejected. The principles on which a regulatory system was to be based "were left entirely to future determination." [65]

Under the Covenant (Article 8[6]), members also agreed "to interchange full and frank information as to the scale of their armaments, their military, naval, and air programs, and the condition of such of their industries as are adaptable to warlike purposes." No comparable obligation is placed upon the Members of the United Nations.[66] In brief, while the Covenant sought to establish a legal basis for disarmament, the Charter confines itself to establishing machinery by which "principles" and "plans" for the regulation of armaments can be worked out at some future time.

There are a number of reasons for the differences between the two approaches. The Covenant was drafted at the end of a world war which many believed was brought on, in part at least, by the unbridled arms race that preceded it. By contrast, there was a widespread feeling that World War II might have been avoided if the major Western democracies had maintained adequate military strength. In addition, unlike the Covenant, the Charter was drafted at a time when the war was in full progress. Under the circumstances, planning a system of arms regulation and reduction might have seemed premature.

In the Atlantic Charter and the Moscow Declaration, the allies had committed themselves to the establishment of a system of arms regulation, but there was little discussion on details at any of the high-level meetings among the major allies. Similarly, the matter received little attention at Dumbarton Oaks or San Francisco.

The disarmament of the Axis powers was taken as axiomatic. It was apparently felt that the smaller states should remain virtually unarmed, relying for their security upon the joint action of the major powers working in accordance with the United Nations Charter. Given the nature of modern weapons, they could contribute little by way of military force to any United Nations enforcement action. Moreover, the desire to minimize the economic burdens of armaments was viewed as particularly relevant to the smaller states.

With respect to the major military powers, the dangers of an arms

[65] Russell, p. 477.
[66] Nor does the Charter deal with the private manufacture of arms, a problem to which the League devoted considerable time.

race were recognized but at the same time the need for sufficient forces to maintain the postwar peace was also emphasized. There appears to have been some agreement, at least within United States circles, that the maintenance of peace would require establishing a floor for national armaments as well as fixing a ceiling. For this reason, the United States proposals for the Charter used the term "regulation of armaments" rather than "disarmament." [67]

This approach of establishing minimum as well as maximum levels was later reflected in almost all the early United Nations resolutions which linked the reduction of armaments with the conclusion of agreements under Article 43 of the Charter for supplying the Security Council with armed forces.[68] With the failure of the major powers to agree on the principles governing such forces,[69] the collective security system envisaged in the Charter could not be brought into effect and could not thus provide the framework within which a system for the regulation of armaments could operate.

It is clear that the drafters of the Charter accorded a fairly low priority to the establishment of a system for regulating armaments; it would come in time with the conclusion of security arrangements. The principal reason why the United Nations became so urgently involved with this matter in the first year of its existence was the explosion of the atomic bomb and the United States decision to seek at once an international agreement to control this new force. As a result, the General Assembly at its very first session established the United Nations Atomic Energy Commission. While the Soviet proposal that the Commission be established by the Security Council was not accepted, it was agreed that the Commission would submit its reports and recommendations to the Council and would be accountable to it, and subject to directives from it, in matters "affecting security." [70] The fact that the Commission was to be concerned with all aspects of the development of atomic energy was the apparent justification for working through the Assembly, although the initiative might be viewed as an encroachment upon the special responsibility of the Security Council and the Military Staff Committee under Article 26.

The responsibilities of the Security Council were more fully recognized in the Assembly's subsequent resolution on the "principles governing the general regulation and reduction of armaments." [71] The

[67] For the inclusion of the term "disarmament" in the Charter, see commentary on Art. 11.
[68] Both the Soviet Union and the U.S. proposals of 1962 for general and complete disarmament also recognize the link between disarmament and supplying forces to the U.N.
[69] See commentary on Art. 43.   [70] GA Res. 1(I), Jan. 24, 1946.
[71] GA Res. 41(I), Dec. 14, 1946. For further comment on the relationship between the Assembly and the Council in this area, see commentary on Art. 11.

Assembly's "recommendations" to the Council led it to establish the Commission for Conventional Armaments.[72]

For the next few years, the major discussions on plans for the regulation of armaments took place in these two commissions. The Military Staff Committee played no part in these efforts, despite the fact that both Articles 26 and 47 envisage an advisory role for it in this connection. The United States effort to obtain Security Council approval of the findings and recommendations in the three reports of the Atomic Energy Commission was vetoed by the Soviet Union in June, 1948; however, the Assembly at its next session gave them its endorsement.[73] As for the discussion in the Commission for Conventional Armaments, the unbridgeable gap between the positions of the Soviet Union and the Western powers was apparent from the beginning. The Assembly repeatedly urged continuation of negotiations, but the lack of any basis for agreement had become obvious long before the two commissions ceased to function, following the Soviet boycott in early 1950 over the issue of Chinese representation.

From that time on the Security Council ceased to play any role in the efforts to work out agreements for the regulation of armaments. It did become involved in a few issues that might be considered as measures of "arms control," such as the United States proposal in 1958 for an international inspection system in the Artic region to guard against surprise attack and the Soviet proposal in 1952 for an appeal for accessions to the Geneva Protocol of 1925 concerning the prohibition on the use of bacterial weapons. But nothing came of either of these initiatives.[74]

The lack of agreement between the permanent members in the Security Council made it impossible for that organ to carry out its responsibilities under Article 26. As a result the principal forums for the discussion on disarmament and arms control became first the General Assembly and the Disarmament Commission[75] and later ad hoc bodies established by agreement between the United States and the Soviet Union.

Although the Security Council since 1950 has played no part in negotiating agreements, there continued to be indications that the

[72] SCOR/2d Yr., No. 13/105th Mtg./Feb. 13, 1947/p. 274.

[73] SCOR/3d Yr., No. 88/325th Mtg./June 22, 1948/pp. 11–12; GA Res. 191(III), Nov. 4, 1948.

[74] Following the breakdown of the summit conference in 1960, the Council adopted a resolution which, *inter alia*, requested governments to continue their efforts to achieve a constructive solution to the question of general and complete disarmament under effective international control. SCOR/15th Yr./863d Mtg./May 27, 1960/pp. 7–8.

[75] This commission, which in 1952 took over the work of the Atomic Energy Commission and the Commission for Conventional Armaments, submits reports to the Council, but they have never been discussed in that organ.

Council might have some role in the implementation of such agreements. During earlier periods nearly all proposals for regulating armaments envisaged a system "within the framework of the Security Council." Subsequently the broader phrase "within the framework of the United Nations" became more common, but a role for the Council was not ruled out. The Soviet proposal for general and complete disarmament, for example, gives the Council responsibilities for dealing with infringements of the treaty.[76] The exercise of such responsibility however, would not be in application of Article 26 but of the Council's powers under other articles of the Charter.

VOTING

Article 27

1. Each member of the Security Council shall have one vote.

2. Decisions of the Security Council on procedural matters shall be made by an affirmative vote of *nine* members.[77]

3. Decisions of the Security Council on all other matters shall be made by an affirmative vote of *nine* members including the concurring votes of the permanent members; provided that, in decisions under Chapter VI, and under paragraph 3 of Article 52, a party to a dispute shall abstain from voting.

The provision that each member of the Security Council shall have one vote is a usual one and has not been the occasion of any controversy. The special interest of Article 27 and its highly controversial nature arise from the provisions of paragraphs 2 and 3 which determine voting procedure and provide that in votes on nonprocedural matters, different consequences attach to the votes of permanent and nonpermanent members. Any one of the permanent members can prevent a decision from being taken on a nonprocedural matter, subject only to the qualification that a party to a dispute must abstain from voting.[78]

[76] UN Doc. A/C.1/867, Sept. 24, 1962.

[77] The amendments increasing the number of elected members of the Security Council from six to ten and the number of affirmative votes required for a decision from seven to nine (indicated by italics) did not enter into force until August 31, 1965, and elections under it did not occur until December, 1965, elected members taking office January 1, 1966. Consequently, in the analysis of practice for the period down to the end of 1965, "seven" will be used to indicate the number of affirmative votes required. For original text, see p. 681.

[78] The word "veto" is used in the subsequent discussion to indicate a negative vote of a permanent member which has the effect of preventing the adoption of a proposal that has received the necessary number of affirmative votes.

The effect of the voting procedure prescribed by Article 27 is to introduce a form of weighted voting for decisions on nonprocedural matters. It is significant that the Security Council is the only principal organ of the United Nations where this occurs. The justification for it at the time the Charter was adopted was the special responsibility assumed by and placed upon the major military powers for the maintenance of international peace and security. Efforts to reduce the special voting privileges of the permanent members at San Francisco failed because the major military powers made these the firm condition of their participation in the United Nations.

History

The voting procedure of the Security Council was one of the few questions upon which the Dumbarton Oaks conferees were unable to reach agreement. There was no sentiment in favor of requiring unanimity of all members for decisions on substantive questions as the League Covenant had done. Nor was there any willingness to accept the principle of majority or special majority vote for substantive decisions, without some qualification protecting the interests of the states that were to be permanent members of the Council. There was agreement in principle on the requirement of concurrence of the permanent members for all decisions on questions of substance, but there was lack of agreement on whether an exception should be made in the case of a permanent member party to a dispute when the Council was performing its function of pacific settlement, on the ground that no party should be a judge in it own case.[79] At the Crimea Conference in February, 1945, President Roosevelt proposed a formula to govern Security Council voting which was accepted by Marshal Stalin and Prime Minister Churchill.[80] This came to be known as the Yalta Formula and was incorporated into the Dumbarton Oaks Proposals submitted by the Sponsoring Governments to the other participants in the San Francisco Conference.[81]

At San Francisco, serious criticism was directed against the Sponsoring Governments' proposal, particularly the third paragraph requiring great power unanimity for substantive decisions. Numerous amendments were proposed by other governments participating in the Conference which had as their purpose to restrict the so-called "veto power" of a permanent member.[82] During the initial discussion in the

[79] See Russell, pp. 445–50.

[80] State Dept., *Malta and Yalta Documents*, pp. 661–67, 711–12. On the Yalta discussions, see Russell, pp. 531–40.

[81] Ch. VI, sec. C. For text, see Appendix.   [82] UNCIO, *Documents*, XI, 774–78.

technical committee on voting procedure, the representatives of the Sponsoring Governments were asked to interpret their proposal. When it became clear that there were differences among them, a subcommittee consisting of the Sponsoring States and a limited number of other Conference participants was established to seek clarification.[83] A list of questions was prepared by representatives of members of the subcommittee other than the Sponsoring States, and was submitted to the latter for their answers.[84] Their discussion extended over a two-week period.[85] A direct appeal to Marshal Stalin in Moscow was necessary before agreement was reached that the veto would not apply to a decision to consider and discuss a dispute or situation. The Soviet Union insisted firmly that the requirement of concurrence of the permanent members should apply to the preliminary question whether a decision was on a procedural or nonprocedural matter. The four-power agreement took the form of a statement by the Sponsoring Governments with which France associated itself. It did not address itself directly to the specific questions that had been raised by the other delegates. The agreed statement was presented to the subcommittee by the United States delegate on June 8, 1945. The text of what has come to be known as the "San Francisco Statement" is as follows:

Statement by the Delegations of the
Four Sponsoring Governments on Voting Procedure
in the Security Council

Specific questions covering the voting procedure in the Security Council have been submitted by a Sub-Committee of the Conference Committee on Structure and Procedures of the Security Council to the Delegations of the four Governments sponsoring the Conference—The United States of America, the United Kingdom of Great Britain and Northern Ireland, the Union of Soviet Socialist Republics, and the Republic of China. In dealing with these questions, the four Delegations desire to make the following statement of their general attitude towards the whole question of unanimity of permanent members in the decisions of the Security Council.

I

1. The Yalta voting formula recognizes that the Security Council, in discharging its responsibilities for the maintenance of international peace and security, will have two broad groups of functions. Under Chapter VIII, the Council will have to make decisions which involve its taking direct measures in connection with settlement of disputes, adjustment of situations likely to lead to disputes, determination of threats to the peace, removal of threats to the peace, and suppression of breaches of the peace. It will also have to make decisions which do not involve the taking of such measures.

[83] *Ibid.*, 817–18.   [84] *Ibid.*, 699–709.
[85] For details of discussions leading up to agreement, see Russell, pp. 716–35.

The Yalta formula provides that the second of these two groups of decisions will be governed by a procedural vote—that is, the vote of any seven members. The first group of decisions will be governed by a qualified vote— that is, the vote of seven members, including the concurring votes of the five permanent members, subject to the proviso that in decisions under Section A and a part of Section C of Chapter VIII parties to a dispute shall abstain from voting.

2. For example, under the Yalta Formula a procedural vote will govern the decisions made under the entire Section D of Chapter VI. This means that the Council will, by a vote of any seven of its members, adopt or alter its rules of procedure; determine the method of selecting its President; organize itself in such a way as to be able to function continuously; select the times and places of its regular and special meetings; establish such bodies or agencies as it may deem necessary for the performance of its functions; invite a Member of the Organization not represented on the Council to participate in its discussions when that Member's interests are specially affected; and invite any state when it is a party to a dispute being considered by the Council to participate in the discussion relating to that dispute.

3. Further, no individual member of the Council can alone prevent consideration and discussion by the Council of a dispute or situation brought to its attention under paragraph 2, Section A, Chapter VIII. Nor can parties to such dispute be prevented by these means from being heard by the Council. Likewise, the requirement for unanimity of the permanent members cannot prevent any member of the Council from reminding the Members of the Organization of their general obligations assumed under the Charter as regards peaceful settlement of international disputes.

4. Beyond this point, decisions and actions by the Security Council may well have major political consequences and may even initiate a chain of events which might, in the end, require the Council under its responsibilities to invoke measures of enforcement under Section B, Chapter VIII. This chain of events begins when the Council decides to make an investigation, or determines that the time has come to call upon states to settle their differences, or make recommendations to the parties. It is to such decisions and actions that unanimity of the permanent members applies, with the important proviso, referred to above, for abstention from voting by parties to a dispute.

5. To illustrate: in ordering an investigation, the Council has to consider whether the investigation—which may involve calling for reports, hearing witnesses, dispatching a commission of inquiry, or other means—might not further aggravate the situation. After investigation, the Council must determine whether the continuance of the situation or dispute would be likely to endanger international peace and security. If it so determines, the Council would be under obligation to take further steps. Similarly, the decision to make recommendations, even when all parties request it to do so, or to call upon parties to a dispute to fulfill their obligations under the Charter, might be the first step on a course of action from which the Security Council could withdraw only at the risk of failing to discharge its responsibilities.

6. In appraising the significance of the vote required to take such decisions or actions, it is useful to make comparison with the requirements of the League Covenant with reference to decisions of the League Council. Substantive decisions of the League of Nations Council could be taken only by the unanimous vote of all its members, whether permanent or not, with the exception of parties to a dispute under Article XV of the League Covenant. Under Article XI, under which most of the disputes brought before the League were dealt with and decisions to make investigations taken, the unanimity rule was invariably interpreted to include even the votes of the parties to a dispute.

7. The Yalta voting formula substitutes for the rule of complete unanimity of the League Council a system of qualified majority voting in the Security Council. Under this system non-permanent members of the Security Council individually would have no "veto." As regards the permanent members, there is no question under the Yalta formula of investing them with a new right, namely, the right to veto, a right which the permanent members of the League Council always had. The formula proposed for the taking of action in the Security Council by a majority of seven would make the operation of the Council less subject to obstruction than was the case under the League of Nations rule of complete unanimity.

8. It should also be remembered that under the Yalta formula the five major powers could not act by themselves, since even under the unanimity requirement any decisions of the Council would have to include the concurring votes of at least two of the non-permanent members. In other words, it would be possible for five non-permanent members as a group to exercise a "veto." It is not to be assumed, however, that the permanent members, any more than the non-permanent members, would use their "veto" power wilfully to obstruct the operation of the Council.

9. In view of the primary responsibilities of the permanent members, they could not be expected, in the present condition of the world, to assume the obligation to act in so serious a matter as the maintenance of international peace and security in consequence of a decision in which they had not concurred. Therefore, if a majority voting in the Security Council is to be made possible, the only practicable method is to provide, in respect of non-procedural decisions, for unanimity of the permanent members plus the concurring votes of at least two of the non-permanent members.

10. For all these reasons, the four Sponsoring Governments agreed on the Yalta formula and have presented it to this Conference as essential if an international organization is to be created through which all peace-loving nations can effectively discharge their common responsibilities for the maintenance of international peace and security.

II

In the light of the considerations set forth in Part I of this statement, it is clear what the answers to the questions submitted by the Subcommittee should be, with the exception of Question 19. The answer to that question is as follows:

1. In the opinion of the Delegations of the Sponsoring Governments,

the Draft Charter itself contains an indication of the application of the voting procedures to the various functions of the Council.

2. In this case, it will be unlikely that there will arise in the future any matters of great importance on which a decision will have to be made as to whether a procedural vote would apply. Should, however, such a matter arise, the decision regarding the preliminary question as to whether or not such a matter is procedural must be taken by a vote of seven members of the Security Council, including the concurring votes of the permanent members.[86]

When the technical committee again considered the question of Security Council voting procedure, along with the report of the subcommittee, the proposal of the Sponsoring Governments and their statement of interpretation were severely criticized on the grounds that important questions were left unanswered; that they were unduly restrictive in the scope they allowed for the use of the procedural vote, particularly when the Council was performing its function of peaceful settlement; that they violated the principle of "sovereign equality"; and that they created the likelihood that the Security Council would be unable to take decisions in the discharge of its responsibility.[87] The delegates of the Sponsoring Governments and France stressed the need of great-power unity if the Security Council was to discharge its duties, emphasized that the proposed text and statement of interpretation were as far as their governments were prepared to go, and called attention to the serious consequences that would result from rejection of the proposed text.[88]

That any decision relating to enforcement action should require the concurring votes of the permanent members was generally accepted at San Francisco as justifiable or at least realistic. The issue chiefly pressed in committee discussion concerned the appropriate procedure when the Council was performing its peaceful settlement function. The position of the Sponsoring Governments was that unanimity of the permanent members was necessary, except on the admittedly procedural questions of putting matters on the Council's agenda and giving states the opportunity to be heard, since a decision to carry out an investigation or make a recommendation of procedures or terms of peaceful settlement might have major political consequences and might even initiate a chain of events which would lead to enforcement action by the Council. Against this view, it was argued that when the Council was acting in a purely conciliatory capacity, without any

[86] UNCIO, *Documents*, XI, 710–14. For the text of the Dumbarton Oaks Proposals to which references are made throughout the statement, see Appendix.

[87] See, for example, Australian memorandum, UNCIO, *Documents*, XI, 438–40; and statement of Australian delegate in Commission III, *ibid.*, 124–27.

[88] For summary of discussion, see Russell, pp. 735–39.

power to bind interested parties and solely with a view to peaceful settlement or adjustment, no one state should be in the position to block a decision supported by the necessary majority. It was agreed in committee to settle this issue by voting on an Australian amendment to add the following at the end of Chapter VI, Section C, paragraph 2 of the Dumbarton Oaks Proposals: "Decisions made by the Security Council in the exercise of any of its duties, functions and powers under Chapter VIII, Section A [Chapter VI of the Charter], shall be deemed to be decisions on procedural matters." [89] The amendment was defeated by a vote of 10 affirmative votes, 20 negative votes, and 15 abstentions.

The proposal of the Sponsoring Governments was finally approved by the technical committee on a paragraph by paragraph vote. On the controversial paragraph 3 the vote was 30 in favor, 2 against, with 15 abstentions and 3 absences. The statement of the four Sponsoring Governments and France giving their agreed interpretation of the proposal was not formally endorsed by the technical committee, by Commission III, or by the Conference. It was included in the records of the technical committee and made an annex to the rapporteur's report.[90]

How Decisions Are Taken

Article 27 originally provided that decisions of the Security Council shall be taken by "an affirmative vote of seven members." This differed from the requirement for General Assembly decisions of a majority or two-thirds majority of the members present and voting, and for decisions of the Economic and Social Council and the Trusteeship Council of a simple majority of those present and voting. The Security Council requirement was introduced originally to insure that the support of at least two nonpermanent members would be necessary to a decision. With the increase in the size of the Council, the support of at least four nonpermanent members becomes necessary.

The requirement of a specific number of affirmative votes, instead of a majority or two-thirds majority of those present and voting, has made it possible for members to defeat a proposal by abstaining. There have been many instances where the number of affirmative votes has constituted a majority of the members present and voting,[91] or even a two-thirds majority without, however, equaling the number required for a decision.

Not all decisions of the Security Council are taken by the votes

[89] UNCIO, *Documents*, XI, 492.   [90] UNCIO, *Documents*, XI, 711–14.
[91] Assuming that the General Assembly rule is followed that "present and voting" includes only those casting affirmative and negative votes.

specified in Article 27. When the Council participates with the General Assembly in fixing the date and place of meeting of a General Conference to review the Charter, it takes its decision by a vote of any seven members.[92] According to Council precedents, this would not be considered a procedural question and the vote prescribed must be regarded as an exception to the requirements of Article 27. A second exception occurs in connection with the election of judges of the International Court of Justice. When the Council is performing that function, along with the General Assembly, "an absolute majority of votes" is required for election.[93] Furthermore, it is specifically stated that no distinction is to be made between permanent and nonpermanent members.[94] The number of votes required to constitute an "absolute majority" has not thus far been in doubt as voting has always taken place with all members of the Council present. It would appear to be consistent with the interpretation given to the phrase at San Francisco to require an absolute majority of the total membership.[95]

Not all decisions of the Security Council are taken by formal voting. The President may declare that a decision has been taken in the absence of objection, or state what he interprets to be the consensus. According to the *Repertory of United Nations Practice,* during the period 1946 to August 20, 1959, the Council took approximately 1,206 decisions, of which 835 were by voting. For the period, the figures indicate a tendency towards greater reliance on nonvoting.

Procedural and Other Matters

In the majority of cases in which the Security Council has voted, there is no indication of the attitude of the Council regarding the procedural or nonprocedural character of the matter voted on. Where the vote is unanimous, or the required number of affirmative votes include the votes of all the permanent members, the vote itelf gives no indication as to how the matter is viewed. The same is true when a proposal fails to receive the required number of affirmative votes. Only in two situations is the vote indicative: if there are seven (now nine) or more affirmative votes and a permanent member casts a negative vote; and if the Council decides explicitly that a matter is procedural or nonprocedural.

[92] Art. 109. To conform with the amendment to Art. 27 increasing the number of affirmative votes to nine, an amendment to Art. 109(1) was adopted by the Assembly on Dec. 20, 1965, GA Res. 2101(XX), and entered into force on June 20, 1968.

[93] Art. 10(1) of the Statute of the Court.   [94] Art. 10(2).

[95] Shabtai Rosenne, *The Law and Practice of the International Court of Justice* (Leyden Sijthoff, 1965), I, 180–81.

The view has been expressed on several occasions by members and accepted by the Council that matters coming under those articles of the Charter that are designated as concerned with Council procedure (Articles 28 to 32) are to be treated as procedural.[96] This interpretation finds support in the San Francisco Statement. From the limited number of cases that give some conclusive evidence of the Council's attitude and from statements made by members, it would appear that the following matters at the least are considered procedural: inclusion of items in the agenda; the order of items on the agenda; deferment of consideration of items on the agenda; removal of items from list of matters of which the Security Council is seized; rulings of the President; [97] suspension or adjournment of a meeting; invitation to participate in the proceedings under Articles 31 and 32 and Rule 39; conduct of business; and convocation of an emergency special session under the "Uniting for Peace" resolution of November 3, 1950.[98]

Matters treated by the Security Council as falling within the category of "other matters" have included those relating to the discharge of its responsibility for the maintenance of international peace and security, the admission of new members, and recommendations to the General Assembly on the appointment of the Secretary-General.[99] In most cases there has been general agreement in the Council as to whether the concurring votes of the permanent members are required for a decision. However, the distinction between "procedural" and "other" matters has not always been obvious and has occasionally been the subject of extended controversy. Practice has not been wholly consistent. There has been significant discussion on two issues: whether "procedural" refers only to the internal procedure of the Council; and whether a proposal to establish a subsidiary organ to carry out an investigation or inquiry is a procedural matter under Article 29 or substantive under Chapter VI.

The first issue was considered in connection with a United States proposal to request the General Assembly pursuant to Article 12, to consider and make recommendations with regard to the question of

[96] See discussion on proposal to invite Canada to participate in consideration of first Report of Atomic Energy Commission, SCOR/1st Yr./50th Mtg./July 10, 1946; and on proposal to invite a representative of People's Republic of China to attend a meeting of Council while the complaint of armed invasion of Taiwan was being considered, SCOR/5th Yr./506th Mtg./Sept. 29, 1950.

[97] See commentary on Art. 30.

[98] For cases in which the vote indicated the procedural character of the matter, see *Repertoire of the Security Council*, pp. 144–47; *Supp. 1*, pp. 63–65; *Supp. 2*, pp. 61–62; *Supp. 3*, pp. 89–90. See also *Repertory*, II, 88–91; *Supp. 1*, I, 272–73; *Supp. 2*, II, 311.

[99] For cases, see *Repertoire of the Security Council*, pp. 147–50; *Supp. 1*, pp. 65–67; *Supp., 2*, pp. 62–64; and *Supp. 3*, pp. 90–91. See also, *Repertory*, II, 92–96; *Supp. 1*, I, 274–75; and *Supp. 2*, II, 312–13.

Greek frontier incidents. It was argued that this was a procedural matter as it related to the internal procedure of the United Nations and relations between its organs. On the other hand, the contention was advanced that "procedural" related only to the internal procedure of the Council and that the proposal was therefore of political importance. The Council by vote decided that the matter was not procedural.[100] Indicative of a somewhat different view of the matter has been the acceptance of the provision of the "Uniting for Peace" Resolution by which the Security Council may call an emergency session of the General Assembly by seven (now nine) affirmative votes. It is to be noted that though in the debate preceding the adoption of the resolution, the Soviet Union objected to this provision on the ground that the nonprocedural vote requirement applied,[101] it did not challenge the President's ruling at the time of the calling of the first emergency session that a procedural vote was sufficient and participated in the session.

On the question of the nature of a decision to establish a subcommittee to carry out an investigation or inquiry, the practice of the Council has not been consistent. In 1948 in the Czechoslovak case a proposal was made to appoint a subcommittee "to receive or to hear such evidence, statements, and testimonies and to report to the Security Council." The Soviet representative requested that the Council take a vote to determine whether the matter was procedural. The proposal that the matter was procedural was put to a vote. There were 8 votes in favor, 2 against (one being that of a permanent member), and 1 abstention. The President (France) ruled that the proposal had been rejected, and when his ruling was challenged, he put the following question to a vote: "Will those who object to my interpretation raise their hands?" There were 6 in favor, 2 against, and 3 abstentions. Consequently, his ruling was upheld. When the Council voted on the original proposal, it was defeated by the negative vote of a permanent member.[102]

Later in 1959, in the Laos case, a proposal to appoint a subcommittee "to examine the statement made before the Security Council concerning Laos, to receive further statements and documents, and to conduct such inquiries as it may determine necessary and to report to the Security Council" was determined to be procedural on a ruling by the President. The Soviet representative protested, declaring the resolution to be illegal.[103] The issue involved in such cases is whether the

[100] SCOR/2d Yr./202d Mtg./Sept. 15, 1947/p. 2400.

[101] GAOR/5th Sess., 1st Ctte./557th Mtg./Oct. 10, 1950/para. 42; see commentary on Art. 20.

[102] See SCOR/3d Yr./288th Mtg./Apr. 29, 1948; and 303d Mtg./May 24, 1948.

[103] UN Doc. S/4214, Sept. 7, 1959; and SCOR/14th Yr./847th and 848th Mtg./Sept. 7, 1959.

matter is to be treated as procedural because the Council is acting under Article 29 of the Charter and Rule 28 of its Provisional Rules of Procedure or as nonprocedural because the subcommittee is authorized to make an "investigation" which, according to the San Francisco Statement, is when the chain of events begins which might require the Council "in the end" "to invoke measures of enforcement." How the issue is decided by the Council may depend on the procedure followed in determining the preliminary question.

The Procedure for Determining the Preliminary Question

One of the questions put to the Sponsoring Governments at San Francisco related to the manner of determining the voting procedure to be followed in a particular matter. Their answer was to the effect that the Charter contains an indication of the procedure to be followed, but that should a matter arise where there is doubt, "the decision regarding the preliminary question . . . must be taken by a vote of seven members of the Security Council, including the concurring votes of the permanent members."[104] The impression that the statement would seem to seek to convey that the question of method to be used in determining the applicable vote would rarely arise, and that the method of determining the issue when it did arise was an uncomplicated one has been belied by experience. Three issues have received particular attention: the extent to which the Security Council or its permanent members are bound by the San Francisco Statement; whether the determination of the nature of the matter for voting purposes should be made before or after the vote on the main proposal; and whether Rule 30 of the Provisional Rules of Procedure has use in the determination of the procedural or nonprocedural nature of a matter, and if so, how it is to be applied.

The permanent members of the Security Council have on a number of occasions indicated that they consider themselves bound by the San Francisco Statement, while adopting a less definite attitude with respect to the obligation of the nonpermanent members.[105] In those instances where permanent members have objected to the applicability of the "double veto" procedure, they have done so on the ground that the nature of the matter under consideration is clearly determined as procedural by specific provisions of the Charter and of the San Fran-

[104] See above, p. 220.
[105] See statements by representatives of the USSR: SCOR/1st Yr./57th Mtg./ Aug. 29, 1946/pp. 130, 132–33; 2d Yr./202d Mtg./Sept. 15, 1947/pp. 2397–98; U.S.: *ibid.*, 114th Mtg./Feb. 27, 1947/p. 430; 202d Mtg./Sept. 15, 1947/p. 2401; U.K.: *ibid.*, p. 2398; and France: 3d Yr./303d Mtg./May 24, 1948/pp. 19–20.

cisco Statement.[106] Until the enlargement of the Security Council, the affirmative vote of at least two permanent members was necessary to any decision. Since then, the possibility exists of a procedural decision by the Council without any permanent member casting an affirmative vote. This gives greater importance to the attitudes of nonmembers. A number of them in the past have explicitly denied that the San Francisco Statement binds the Council or them as individual members.[107] On three occasions when stating that the concurring votes of the permanent members were necessary to decide whether or not a matter was procedural, the President expressly invoked the San Francisco Statement as the basis for his decision.[108]

Council practice on the order in which the main proposal and the question whether it is a procedural matter should be put to a vote has not been uniform. In some cases the Council has voted on the main proposal first, and thereafter on the question whether the proposal was procedural.[109] In other cases, the Council has followed the reverse order.[110] The view that the preliminary question should be decided first has been based on the grounds that the San Francisco Statement so specifies and that the vote on the main proposal cannot be taken with full awareness of its consequences without knowing whether it is a matter of procedure or not. The opposing view has rested mainly on the contention that the necessity of deciding the preliminary question arises only when a proposal receives the required number of affirmative votes and one or more negative votes of permanent members.[111]

The issue with respect to the President's ruling arises in connection with the application of Rule 30 of the Council's Provisional Rules of Procedure. This provides that if a representative raises a point of order, the President shall state his ruling, and if it is challenged, he shall submit his ruling to the Council and "it shall stand unless overruled." Statements by the President that the matter is procedural or nonprocedural have at times preceded the vote on the main question and at

[106] See, for example, statement of the U.S. representative in the Czechoslovak case. SCOR/3d Yr./288th Mtg./May 29, 1948.

[107] For example, statements by representatives of Australia. SCOR/1st Yr./49th Mtg./June 26, 1946/p. 425; and 2d Yr./202d Mtg./Sept. 15, 1947/p. 2400. For references to other instances, see *Repertory*, II, para. 38.

[108] When the President was the representative of: Poland, SCOR/1st Yr., 2d Ser., No. 5/57th Mtg./pp. 127, 131, and 132; the USSR, 2d Yr./202d Mtg./pp. 2397–2401; and France, 3d Yr./303d Mtg./May 24, 1948/pp. 19–20.

[109] Practice followed, for example, in connection with proposals concerning Spanish question in 1946, Greek frontier question in 1947, and complaint of armed invasion of Taiwan in 1950.

[110] Proposals in connection with consideration of Albanian and Mongolian membership applications in 1946, Czechoslovak question in 1948, and Laotian question in 1959.

[111] See discussion on Greek frontier question. SCOR/2d Yr./202d Mtg./Sept. 15, 1947.

times have assumed the form of interpretations of the vote taken on the main question. Such statements have at times been accepted without dissent but on other occasions, the President's right to make them has been challenged, and the application of Rule 30 has been an issue.[112] Those members who insist on the rigorous application of Part II of the San Francisco Statement deny the right of the President to determine the question of the procedural nature of a vote by a ruling and insist that the question can only be decided by the Council by a positive decision registered by a vote in which the permanent members concur.[113]

Members who seek to restrict the application of the so-called "double veto" stress the applicability of Rule 30 and argue that if the President rules that a particular vote is procedural, his ruling stands unless overruled by a procedural vote.[114] Following the vote on the proposal to invite a representative of the People's Republic of China to take part in the discussion of the complaint of armed invasion of Taiwan, the President declared the proposal adopted even though a permanent member voted against it. After the representative of the Republic of China invoked the San Francisco Statement, the President asked the Council to vote on the question whether the vote taken was procedural. The vote was 9 to 1 (China) with one abstention in favor of the procedural nature of the proposal. The President declared the proposal adopted and then, interpreting the Chinese representative's statement as a challenge to his ruling, he put the challenge to a vote under Rule 30. There were no votes in favor, no votes against, and no abstentions. The President then declared that his decision stood.[115]

The Use of the "Veto"

The "veto," described as the use of a negative vote by a permanent member to prevent the adoption of a proposal which has received the required number of affirmative votes, was used 108 times up to the end of 1965.[116] This number includes 50 vetoes of membership applications and 2 of nominations for the office of Secretary-General. The vetoes of membership applications explain the relatively large number of vetoes during the first ten years (79) and include a considerable number of repeated vetoes of applications from the same state. The

[112] For details, see *Repertoire of the Security Council,* pp. 154–62.

[113] See statement of Soviet representative in Greek frontier incident case. SCOR/1st Yr./57th Mtg./Aug. 29, 1946/pp. 130–31.

[114] See statement by the Netherlands representative in the Greek frontier incidents case. *Ibid.,* pp. 130, 132–35.

[115] See SCOR/5th Yr./507th Mtg./Sept. 29, 1950.

[116] For list of vetoes, see Sydney D. Bailey, "Veto in the Security Council," *International Conciliation,* No. 566 (January, 1968).

remaining 56 vetoes have been of proposals falling broadly within the field of the Council's responsibility for the maintenance of international peace and security.

The large number of vetoes in the early years (23 during the first two years) led to allegations by some members that the right of veto was being abused. The question was discussed by the General Assembly in its first and second sessions. Reference was made to the sentence in the San Francisco Statement to the effect that it was not to be assumed that the permanent members "would use their 'veto' power wilfully to obstruct the operation of the Council," and the implicit assurance that the "veto" would only be used to protect important interests. On the other hand, it was argued that the "veto" had been introduced to assure great power unity and had been used only to protect the interests of a permanent member when the effort was being made to override those interests by a majority vote.

In its first session the General Assembly adopted a resolution urging the permanent members of the Council "to make every effort, in consultation with one another and with fellow members" to ensure that the use of the special voting privilege did not impede the Council in reaching decisions promptly; in its second session, on a United States initiative, the Assembly requested the Interim Committee to consider the problem and report.[117] The Committee's report to the General Assembly contained conclusions on the voting procedure applicable to four categories of decisions: decisions which under the Statute of the Court are taken by an absolute majority; decisions which under the Statute of the Court or the Charter are taken by the affirmative votes of any seven members; decisions which are procedural within the meaning of Article 27(2); and decisions that the Committee recommended should be taken by the affirmative votes of any seven members.[118] The fourth category included among others, admission of new members, decisions under Chapter VI (Pacific Settlement of Disputes), and decisions on the preliminary question whether the matter was procedural. The Committee suggested that its conclusions might be implemented by interpretation, by agreement among the permanent members, or by amendment of the Charter. After considering the Committee's report, the General Assembly in its third session adopted a resolution recommending that members of the Security Council consider as "procedural" those decisions so designated in the Interim Committee's report and that they "conduct their business accordingly." [119] It also recommended that the permanent members "seek agreement among themselves upon what possible decisions by the Security Council they might

---

117 GA Res. 40(I), Dec. 13, 1946; GA Res. 117(II), Nov. 21, 1947.
118 UN Doc. A/578, July 15, 1948.   119 GA Res. 267(III), Apr. 14, 1949.

forbear to exercise their veto," giving favorable consideration to the Interim Committee's list.

These efforts by the General Assembly to achieve greater restraint by permanent members in the use of the veto did not achieve their purpose. Such relaxation of the veto as has been achieved has been principally through the practice that has developed with respect to voluntary abstention.

Abstentions and Absences

The Charter makes explicit provision for abstention only in the case of Security Council decisions under Chapter VI and Article 52(3), when a party to the dispute must abstain from voting. Neither the Charter nor the Council's Provisional Rules of Procedure contain any provisions explicitly defining the effect to be given to an abstention or an absence in Security Council voting. At San Francisco, when the question was raised as to the effect of compulsory abstention the United States delegate explained that such abstention could not be used to prevent a decision since it was clearly an exception to the rule of unanimity.[120] No statement was made regarding the effect of a voluntary abstention, though the conclusion was permissible from the text of paragraph 3 and the importance attached by representatives of the Sponsoring Governments to the unity of the permanent members that an abstention was the equivalent of a veto. In the informal consultation of the delegations of the Sponsoring Governments and France there was agreement, with only France initially dissenting, that a voluntary abstention should be regarded as a negative vote.[121]

The requirement of abstention under Article 27(3) has not been rigorously interpreted and applied by the Council. Rather it has been treated as a guide to members in their voting. It has had possible influence on the choice of grounds for bringing matters to the attention of the Security Council.[122] Particularly during the early years there was some discussion of issues involved in the application of the compulsory abstention rule. The application of the abstention requirement has particular significance for permanent members because of their special voting privileges.

Apart from the question of the effect of a compulsory abstention, the following issues are involved in the interpretation and application of the clause: who decides and by what vote whether a Council member

---

[120] UNCIO, *Documents*, XI, p. 513.

[121] See *Foreign Relations of the United States, 1945*, I, 1258–1260.

[122] In 1948, for example, a rigid application of the provision would have made it difficult for any proposal to get seven affirmative votes if the U.S., the U.K., and France had brought their Berlin complaint under ch. VI.

is a party to a dispute and consequently must abstain from voting; when does a dispute exist as distinct from a situation; when is the Council exercising its powers under Chapter VI or Article 52(3); and what constitutes being a party. The Council has refrained from taking formal decisions on these issues, being more concerned with achieving practical results in the matters before it than in clarifying issues closely related to the highly controversial question of the scope of the veto.[123] Since one effect of the prohibition contained in Article 27(3) is to prevent a permanent member from exercising a veto in a dispute to which it is a party, occasionally a member of the Council, in a case in which a permanent member contends that the matter is nonprocedural, has used the argument that the interested permanent member is a party to the dispute and consequently cannot prevent a decision from being taken since it is required to abstain.[124] On the other hand, it has been argued that the Council should decide by a nonprocedural vote whether it is dealing with a dispute under Chapter VI, and consequently that the permanent member's concurrence is essential to a decision that it is obligated as a party to a dispute to refrain from voting.[125] In the absence of formal decisions by the Council, individual members have on a number of occasions abstained from voting on matters in which they were directly involved,[126] sometimes indicating that they were doing so in compliance with the obligation stated in Article 27(3).

While permanent members have shown a certain reluctance to relinquish the right to decide in each case as it arises whether they are obligated to abstain from voting, they have frequently abstained voluntarily in the voting where no obligation to abstain exists, and have been willing that this abstention should not be interpreted as a lack of concurrence, or as constituting a "veto." This is the principal procedural device that has been developed in practice for achieving a limited relaxation of the rule requiring unanimity of the permanent members on nonprocedural questions.[127] While there have been isolated

[123] For details on cases before Council and references to discussion, see *Repertoire of the Security Council*, pp. 167–70.

[124] See statements of the representative of Australia on Iranian question, SCOR/1st Yr./3d Mtg./Jan. 28, 1946/p. 44; Egypt on Syrian and Lebanese question, *ibid.*, 19th Mtg./Feb. 14, 1946/pp. 273–74.

[125] See statement by the Soviet representative on the Syrian and Lebanese question. SCOR/1st Yr./19th Mtg./Feb. 14, 1946/pp. 278–79, 280–81.

[126] For example, U.K. (Corfu Channel, 1946, and dispute with Egypt, 1947), Egypt (Palestine, 1950), and India (dispute with Pakistan, 1950–1951). For details and references, see *Repertoire of the Security Council*, pp. 166–67.

[127] For list of cases in which permanent members have abstained otherwise than in accordance with Art. 27(3), see *Repertoire of the Security Council*, pp. 170–73; *Supp 1*, pp. 67–68; *Supp. 2*, p. 64; *Supp. 3*, pp. 95–96. See also *Repertory*, II,

instances of doubt being expressed regarding the strict legality of this procedure, the result has generally been welcomed, and members of the Council generally, and in particular the permanent members, have accepted the practice of not regarding a voluntary abstention as a veto as being an established part of the law of the Charter.[128]

With respect to absences, there would appear to be less unanimity. The Council has adopted a number of decisions in the absence of a permanent member. This occurred in 1946 when the Soviet representative withdrew in protest against the Council's decision to keep the Iranian complaint on its agenda and in 1950 when the Soviet representative was absent for a period of seven months in protest against the seating of the representative of Nationalist China. During the first period, the decisions taken by the Council were not so clearly of a nonprocedural character as to constitute firm precedents, and, furthermore, it could be that, even if present, the Soviet Union would have been obligated as a party to the dispute to abstain. During the second period, however, a number of important decisions were taken by the Security Council in respect to the complaint of aggression against the Republic of Korea that were indubitably nonprocedural and came under the provisions of Chapter VII. The great majority of United Nations members viewed these as valid decisions and thereby treated an absence, like an abstention, as not constituting a veto.

The position taken by the Soviet Union was that the Security Council does not act legally as constituted by the Charter when it takes decisions in the absence of a permanent member.[129] Other members have argued that a permanent member by absenting itself abandons its special voting privilege, that an absence is similar to an abstention in its effects, and that a permanent member, by failure to discharge its responsibility of attendance at meetings, forfeits its right to participate in decisions taken.[130]

97–103; *Supp. 1,* I, 276; *Supp. 2,* II, 314. Through 1966 permanent members abstained voluntarily in relation to the whole or part of some 95 nonprocedural decisions of the Council, involving at least 87 of a total of 232 resolutions of the Council. Constantin A. Stavropoulos, "The Practice of Voluntary Abstentions by Permanent Members of the Security Council under Article 27, paragraph 3, of the Charter of the United Nations," *American Journal of International Law,* LXI (July, 1967), p. 744.

[128] See statements and references in *Repertoire of the Security Council,* pp. 173–75.

[129] SCOR/5th Yr./480th Mtg./Aug. 1, 1950/pp. 15–16, 20.

[130] See cases cited and statements quoted in *Repertoire of the Security Council,* pp. 175–78. See also commentary on Art. 28.

PROCEDURE

Article 28

1. The Security Council shall be so organized as to be able to function continuously. Each member of the Security Council shall for this purpose be represented at all times at the seat of the Organization.

2. The Security Council shall hold periodic meetings at which each of its members may, if it so desires, be represented by a member of the government or by some other specially designated representative.

3. The Security Council may hold meetings at such places other than the seat of the Organization as in its judgment will best facilitate its work.

Continuous Functioning

The idea that the Security Council should "function continuously" marks an important departure from the normal practice of international organizations. It was intended to assure that the Security Council would be able to deal promptly with any situation that might arise. By contrast, the other principal organs of the United Nations meet in regular periodic sessions, and in such special sessions as may be required.

Under the Provisional Rules of Procedure, the President is responsible for calling Security Council meetings. He is required to do so if requested by any member of the Council; if a dispute or situation is brought to the attention of the Council under Article 35 or 11(3); if the General Assembly makes recommendations or refers a question to the Council under Article 11(2); or if the Secretary-General brings a matter to the attention of the Council under Article 99 (see Rules 2 and 3). A request by a member of the Council or by the Secretary-General is invariably acted upon immediately; in other circumstances, the President exercises more discretion in scheduling meetings.

The Rules also state that "the interval between meetings shall not exceed fourteen days" (Rule 1), but this requirement has frequently been set aside. Usually, the President consults informally with members as to whether there is any objection to waiving the rule. Throughout 1959, for example, the Council held only five meetings.

Council meetings are generally scheduled at members' convenience, but this is a matter of courtesy and not a recognition of the right of a member to prevent or delay a meeting. Each member is responsible for its representation at meetings. For this reason, the Charter requires that members of the Council be represented "at all times at the seat of the Organization." Only once has the Council postponed deliberations because of the inability of representatives to attend, and then under very special circumstances. During the last part of 1948, the Council held its meetings in Paris, where the General Assembly was in session. In mid-December, the Dutch initiated hostilities in Indonesia. An immediate meeting of the Council was requested despite the fact that two days earlier the Council had held what was intended to be its last meeting before reconvening in New York. Since three members were unable to attend, the discussion was postponed for three days, at which time discussion proceeded despite the absence of one member. The Charter provision that the Council should be "so organized as to be able to function continuously" was cited in this instance to support the position that the Council should carry on its functions even if a member was unable to attend.[131]

Article 28 was invoked in the Council again early in 1950 when the Soviet Union walked out of the Council chamber in protest against the continued seating of the representative of the Nationalist Government of China in the Council. This was not the first Soviet walk-out; as early as 1946, the Soviet representative had taken a similar step in protest against the Council's refusal to postpone discussion of the complaint Iran had made concerning the continued presence of Soviet troops in northern Iran.[132] In the earlier case, the boycott applied only to the meetings on Iran's complaint and lasted only a short time. The 1950 boycott, however, was total and lasted from January until the beginning of August. In announcing its boycott, the Soviet Union declared that it would consider as illegal all proceedings of the Council taking place during its absence.[133] The protest against this position was led by the United States representative, who drew attention to the Charter requirement that the Council should be "so organized as to be able to function continuously." No single member, he went on, could prevent the Council from carrying on its proceedings.[134] This view was generally accepted by the other members, and during the period of the Soviet boycott the Council continued to meet and to take decisions. Subsequent Soviet protests that these decisions were invalid found no support by other Council members.

131 SCOR/3d Yr., No. 131/387th Mtg./Dec. 20, 1948.
132 SCOR/1st Yr., 1st Ser., No. 2/27th Mtg./Mar. 27, 1946/p. 58.
133 SCOR/5th Yr., No. 3/461st Mtg./Jan. 13, 1950/pp. 9–10.
134 Ibid., pp. 13–15.

Periodic Meetings

While the original United States proposal that the Security Council be "so organized as to be able to function continuously" was readily accepted at Dumbarton Oaks and at San Francisco, the British feared that this arrangement might sacrifice one of the most useful functions performed by the Council of the League of Nations. With the Security Council in continuous session, it was inevitable that members would be represented by second-level officials. A valuable attribute of the periodic meetings of the League Council was that they provided the foreign ministers of the members with the opportunity to meet and consider matters of common concern. The inclusion of Article 28(2) in the Charter was designed to meet this situation.[135] Although the article does not specifically refer to "foreign ministers," it was obviously intended that the "periodic" meetings would be attended by persons qualified to enter into discussions at the highest policy level.

After some discussion as to how often these meetings should occur, the Security Council decided to stipulate in its Provisional Rules of Procedure that periodic meetings should be held "twice a year, at such times as the Security Council may decide" (Rule 4).[136] Thus far, this rule, and the Charter provision itself, have remained a dead letter: no "periodic" meetings have ever been held.

One reason during the early years was that the foreign ministers of the major powers were in frequent contact through the meetings of the Council of Foreign Ministers. The first attempt to revitalize the concept of periodic meetings was made by Secretary-General Trygve Lie early in 1950. As the first of the ten points in his twenty-year program for peace through the United Nations, the Secretary-General proposed the inauguration of periodic meetings of the Security Council to be attended by foreign ministers, or heads or other members of the government. He favored semi-annual meetings, away from United Nations Headquarters, for a general review "at a high level of outstanding issues," particularly those that divided the great powers. Nothing came of this idea,[137] nor from a subsequent General Assembly resolution recommending the convening of a periodic meeting of the Council.[138]

135 See Russell, p. 445.
136 See SCOR/1st Yr., 1st Ser., No. 1/31st Mtg./Apr. 9, 1946/pp. 103–7.
137 See GAOR/5th Sess./308th Plen. Mtg./Nov. 17, 1950/p. 437. See also Trygve Lie, *In the Cause of Peace* (New York, Macmillan, 1954), chs. xvi and xvii.
138 GA Res. 503B(VI), Jan. 12, 1952. Note also GA Res. 817(IX), Nov. 23, 1954, suggesting a periodic meeting to help resolve the deadlock over admission of new members.

The possibility of periodic meetings was raised again by Secretary-General Hammarskjöld in 1953, when he expressed concern that so many important problems were being dealt with by ad hoc conferences rather than through the United Nations.[139] But the suggestion for periodic meetings was ignored.

The closest the Security Council has ever come to holding a periodic meeting was in the midst of the Middle East crisis of 1958. To counter a Soviet proposal for a "summit" meeting, the United Kingdom and the United States suggested a special meeting of the Security Council, at which members could be represented by heads of government or other specially designated representatives. Although there was tentative agreement on holding such a meeting, the idea was subsequently abandoned.[140] Instead, the issue was referred to an emergency special session of the General Assembly.

Place of Meeting

The Charter authorizes the Security Council to "hold meetings at such places other than the seat of the Organization as in its judgment will best facilitate its work." All Council meetings have been held at United Nations Headquarters except that from October through December, 1948, and from November, 1951, to February, 1952, meetings were held in Paris, since during these two periods the General Assembly sessions were held there.

The Provisional Rules of Procedure permit the Secretary-General or any member of the Security Council to propose that the Council meet at another place (Rule 5). Proposals to this effect were introduced in connection with the Congo. On September 8, 1960, the Prime Minister of the Republic of the Congo urged that the Council hold its next meeting on this matter in Leopoldville so that the members of the Security Council could "see for themselves the situation existing in the Republic of the Congo as a result of the United Nations authorities' interference in the Congo's domestic problems." [141] The Soviet Union submitted a formal proposal to this effect in the Security Council that was voted down for various reasons, including the fear that the adoption of the proposal might be interpreted as acceptance of the Prime Minister's contentions and thus constitute a rebuff to the Secretary-General.[142]

139 GAOR/10th Sess./1955/*Supp. 1*, pp. xi–xii.

140 For the exchange of communications, see SCOR/13th Yr./*Supp.* for July, Aug., and Sept., 1958/pp. 56–64, 65–78, and 97–124.

141 SCOR/15th Yr./*Supp.* for July, Aug., and Sept., 1960/p. 145.

142 *Ibid.*, 889th Mtg./Sept. 9 and 10, 1960/pp. 2–14. See also the Liberian proposal of Feb. 20, 1961, that the Council hold its next meeting either in or

Article 29

The Security Council may establish such subsidiary organs as it deems necessary for the performance of its functions.

To assist it in the "performance of its functions," the Security Council has established a wide variety of committees, commissions, and other subsidiary bodies.[143] These have differed so substantially in character that it is difficult to classify them.[144] The *Repertory of United Nations Practice* divides them into the three following groups:

(a) standing commissions or committees which deal with certain questions of a recurring nature and which meet at the seat of the Organization . . .

(b) commissions or committees which deal with particular questions in the field . . .

(c) drafting and other *ad hoc* committees and sub-committees which deal with a single specific problem and which meet at the place of meeting of the Council.[145]

Differences have arisen in respect to such matters as composition, terms of reference, methods of operation, and relations to the Security Council. One of the most controversial issues has been the voting requirement for establishing such organs.[146]

Standing Commissions or Committees

The subsidiary bodies classified as standing committees of the Council have certain common features: [147] they are composed of representatives of all members of the Council; they meet exclusively at headquarters; and they function as continuing bodies to assist the Council in a particular aspect of its work.

The Committee of Experts was established at the first meeting of the Security Council for the immediate purpose of examining the Council's Provisional Rules of Procedure.[148] Apparently, it was originally in-

---

near the Congo "with a view to establishing the United Nations' prestige and authority as well as reaching some point of reconciliation in that turbulent country." SCOR/16th Yr./941st Mtg./Feb. 20, 1961/p. 5.

[143] For a listing see *Repertory*, II, 123 ff.

[144] For detail on these points, see *Repertoire of the Security Council* and *Supplements*, ch. v.

[145] *Repertory*, II, 115.   [146] See commentary on Art. 27.

[147] The Military Staff Committee is also a standing committee of the Security Council, but it is of quite a different character as its establishment is provided for in the Charter itself. See commentary on Art. 47.

[148] SCOR/1st Yr., 1st Ser., No. 1/1st Mtg./Jan. 17, 1946/p. 11.

tended that the Committee would assist the Council by examining matters of a procedural or legal nature. Few questions of importance have, however, been referred to it. In April, 1946, it was asked to examine a memorandum by the Secretary-General concerning the Council's authority to deal with the Iranian complaint against the Soviet Union.[149] Other questions referred to the Committee have concerned narrow procedural issues and none has been referred to it since 1950.[150]

The Committee on the Admission of New Members was established in May, 1946, to carry out a preliminary examination of applications for United Nations membership.[151] This practice was followed with some regularity for three years. Since 1949, the Committee has been bypassed, the Council preferring to deal directly with admission of new members.

The Commission on Conventional Armaments was established by the Security Council in February, 1947, pursuant to the initial resolution of the General Assembly on the regulation and reduction of armaments.[152] During the next few years, it discussed and reported on various aspects of the subject. At the beginning of 1952, the Commission was dissolved as a result of a decision by the General Assembly that its work should be taken over by the Disarmament Commission.[153]

It should be noted that the General Assembly has, on occasion, recognized that the activities of "standing" commissions it has established are directly related to the functions of the Security Council. Thus, although the United Nations Atomic Energy Commission was established by the General Assembly, its composition was that of the Security Council (plus Canada); it was to submit its reports and recommendations to the Council; and in matters of security, it was to receive directions from, and be accountable to, the Security Council.[154] When the Assembly decided later that the work of the Atomic Energy Commission and the Commission for Conventional Armaments should be merged, it established the Disarmament Commission, specifically stated to be "under the Security Council." [155] It was to report

---

149 *Ibid.*, 33d Mtg./Apr. 16, 1946/p. 145.   150 See *Repertory*, II, 117–18.
151 SCOR/1st Yr., 1st Ser., No. 2/42d Mtg./May 17, 1946/p. 285.
152 SCOR/2d Yr./105th Mtg./Feb. 13, 1947/p. 274; GA Res. 41(I), Dec. 14, 1946.
153 SCOR/7th Yr./571st Mtg./Jan. 30, 1952/paras. 2–4. See also GA Res. 502(VI), Jan. 11, 1952.
154 GA Res. 1(I), Jan. 24, 1946. On the relations between the Council and the Commission see commentary on Art. 26.
155 GA Res. 502(VI), Jan. 11, 1952. Originally, the Disarmament Commission had the same composition as the Atomic Energy Commission. Later it was expanded to include the entire UN membership.

to the Assembly and to the Council; the latter has never, in fact, discussed any of its reports. Finally, in establishing the Peace Observation Commission under its "Uniting for Peace" resolution, the Assembly provided that the Commission could be utilized by either the Assembly or the Council.[156]

Subsidiary Organs Operating in the Field

Much of the important work of the Security Council has been carried on by commissions or committees dispatched by the Council to troubled areas. Some have been purely investigatory bodies, such as the Greek Frontier Commission and the fact-finding committee sent to Laos in 1959.[157] The principal function of others has been mediation, as in the case of the various subsidiary organs established to deal with the Indonesian question and the dispute between India and Pakistan.[158] Most subsidiary organs operating in the field have been assigned the task of observing, and assisting in, the implementation of Security Council resolutions.

These subsidiary organs have varied in size and in method of selection. Generally, the Council designates in its resolution those members to be represented on the commission or committee. But this is not always the case. In some instances individuals are designated: for example, the United Nations Representative for India and Pakistan. Sometimes these subsidiary organs are given detailed instructions by the Security Council, but for the most part, they are left free to carry out their missions in the light of developments in the area.

The role of the Secretary-General is to be noted since there has been an increasing tendency to place the detailed arrangements for these field operations in his hands. In connection with the Lebanese complaint of interference in its internal affairs, the Security Council took the basic decision "to dispatch urgently an observation group" to the area but the Secretary-General was authorized "to take the necessary steps to that end." [159] The United Nations operation in the Congo was similarly initiated by a Security Council resolution authorizing the Secretary-General to "take the necessary steps" to provide the necessary military and technical assistance to the Congolese Government.[160]

[156] GA Res. 377(V), Nov. 3, 1950.

[157] For further discussion on fact-finding commissions and committees, see Leland M. Goodrich and Anne P. Simons, *The United Nations and the Maintenance of International Peace and Security* (Washington, Brookings Institution, 1955), ch. VIII.

[158] See *ibid.*, ch. XII.   [159] SCOR/13th Yr./1158th Mtg./June 11, 1958/p. 17.

[160] SCOR/15th Yr./873d Mtg./July 13 and 14, 1960/p. 42.

In recommending a United Nations peace-keeping force for Cyprus, the Security Council provided that the size and composition of the force should be established by the Secretary-General, in consultation with the governments concerned. He was to appoint the commander of the force and also, in consultation with the governments concerned, a mediator.[161] The role of the Secretary-General in connection with the observation mission sent to Yemen was even more direct since only after arrangements were made was the question considered by the Security Council, which merely noted with satisfaction the Secretary-General's initiative and requested him to establish the observation arrangements as he had defined them.[162]

Finally, as in the case of "standing" commissions, there have been subsidiary organs of the General Assembly operating in the field that have been directly related to Security Council activities. Most important of these was the United Nations Mediator in Palestine. Although appointed by the General Assembly,[163] his principal task was to bring about a cessation of hostilities between Israel and the Arab states, in accordance with various resolutions of the Security Council. Other examples are the General Assembly's Special Committee on Apartheid and its Subcommittee on Angola, each of which supplied information to the Security Council.

Other Ad Hoc Committees

Of the ad hoc committees established by the Security Council, the most important have been charged with examining or collecting information for the Council such as the Subcommittee on the Spanish question and the Subcommittee on the Corfu Channel question. Most of the others have had very limited terms of reference and have discharged their tasks after a few meetings. During the early years, subcommittees were frequently appointed in an effort to work out an agreed resolution. In later years, this approach has seldom been used; efforts to work out agreements among Council members are usually conducted through informal methods.

Article 30

The Security Council shall adopt its own rules of procedure, including the method of selecting its President.

[161] SCOR/19th Yr./1102d Mtg./Mar. 4, 1964/p. 5.
[162] SCOR/18th Yr./1039th Mtg./June 11, 1963/p. 2.
[163] GA Res. 186(S-2), May 14, 1948.

Provisional Rules of Procedure

At its first meeting on January 17, 1946, the Security Council had before it a set of provisional rules formulated by the Preparatory Commission. These rules represented a compromise between those members who held that the Commission should draw up a complete set of rules and those who believed the entire matter should be left to the Security Council itself. The Council adopted the rules provisionally and at the same time established the Committee of Experts (composed of representatives of all the Council members) to consider the rules further.[164]

In a series of meetings during the spring of 1946, the Council adopted, with some slight modifications, the provisional rules recommended by the Committee of Experts.[165] It has operated under these provisional rules ever since.[166] Only three changes have been made. Because of confusion that arose during the first election of judges to the International Court of Justice, the Council added a new rule regarding the method of election (Rule 61).[167] As a result of conversations between a subcommittee of the Committee of Experts and a special committee of the General Assembly, certain additions were made to the Council's Rules concerning procedure for considering applications for membership in the United Nations (Rule 60[2] and [3]).[168] In 1950, the Council added to its Rules a requirement that credentials of representatives be issued by the Head of State or the Minister of Foreign Affairs (Rule 13). A proposal to add a new rule stipulating procedure to be followed in the event of controversy over representation in the Council was, however, not adopted.[169]

The Charter leaves to the Security Council the adoption of its rules of procedure. The General Assembly, however, is authorized under Article 10 to discuss and to make recommendations on any question or matter "relating to the powers and functions of any organs" of the United Nations. The General Assembly on a number of occasions, particularly during the first few years, discussed at length the opera-

[164] SCOR/1st Yr., 1st Ser., No. 1/1st Mtg./Jan. 17, 1946/p. 11. For the Rules, see "Extract from the Report of the Preparatory Commission," *ibid.*, *Supp. 1*, pp. 1 ff.

[165] For report of the Committee, see *ibid.*, *Supp. 2*, pp. 1–43. See also, *ibid.*, 31st Mtg./Apr. 9, 1946/pp. 100–19; 41st–42d Mtgs./May 16–17, 1946/pp. 253–77; 44th Mtg./June 6, 1946/pp. 310–11; and 48th Mtg./June 24, 1946/p. 91.

[166] For rules presently in force, see *Provisional Rules of Procedure of the Security Council*, Doc.S/96/Rev.4, July 29, 1952.

[167] SCOR/2d Yr., No. 43/138th Mtg./June 4, 1947/pp. 949 ff.

[168] *Ibid.*, No. 85/197th Mtg./Aug. 27, 1947/p. 2266.

[169] See commentary on Art. 23.

tions of the Security Council and made a number of specific recommendations for changes, especially regarding voting procedure in the Council.[170] They have had little effect, however, upon the Council's proceedings.

The *Repertoire of the Practice of the Security Council* contains a detailed commentary on the adoption and application of the Provisional Rules of Procedure. Only one aspect of the Council's proceedings, the role of the President, will be dealt with here.

The Presidency

The presidency of the Security Council rotates among member states in alphabetical (English) order.[171] Each President holds office for one calendar month. In proposing this rule, the Executive Committee of the Preparatory Commission stated that this method would "occasion least controversy" and would permit each member to hold office.[172]

The Committee also stated that it was essential "that the office of President be deemed to attach to the member state concerned and not to the person of its representative." [173] In this respect, the position of the person acting as President of the Security Council differs from that of the presidents of other United Nations organs. If the representative of the member state serving as President of the Council is absent, another member of his delegation takes over the duties of the office; in other organs, if the president is for any reason unable to preside, a vice-president (also an elected officer) takes his place.

Moreover, the person performing the duties of the President of the Security Council wears two hats: one as the presiding officer and the other as the spokesman for his own country. In the Assembly, and generally in the other two Councils, the President has no vote and whatever positions his government may advocate are put forward by someone else who sits as the representative of that country. Ordinarily, Security Council presidents have made a genuine effort to distinguish between their two roles, making it clear when they are acting in their official capacity and when they are speaking on behalf of their governments. But despite the best of intentions, lines are apt to blur. A deliberate effort by a President to exploit the powers at his disposal for the benefit of his government's position can, as the members of the Council discovered in August, 1950, create chaos.

The Rules provide a means for easing the problem of conflicting interests (Rule 20). Whenever the President "deems" that he should

[170] See commentary on Art. 27.

[171] Rule 18. The Security Council is thus the only UN organ not presided over by an "elected" official. Cf. Arts. 21, 72, and 90.

[172] *Report by the Executive Committee*, p. 44.   [173] *Ibid.*, p. 45.

not preside over the consideration of a particular question, "the presidential chair" for the purpose of that discussion "devolves" upon the representative of the member next in line for the presidency. Under this Rule, the President does not yield all his powers, but only the function of presiding over that particular discussion. The Rule has been infrequently invoked. The United States representative, for instance, yielded the chair to the representative of Argentina for the discussion of the Berlin crisis (October, 1948); China yielded to Cuba for the discussion of China's representation in the Security Council (January, 1950);[174] India yielded the chair during the discussion of the India–Pakistan question. Lebanon turned over the presidency during discussion of a dispute between Syria and Israel. But in general, representatives of the Arab states in the Security Council have not considered that they should refrain from presiding over discussions on various aspects of the Palestine question. Likewise, the French representative did not consider it necessary to yield the chair when the Security Council in October, 1956, was discussing the Anglo–French–Israeli invasion of Suez.

Under Rule 20, the representative himself decides whether or not he will preside. At one point during the discussion of a Soviet complaint concerning actions of United States aircraft, the Soviet representative raised the question of the applicability of Rule 20; the United States representative drew attention to the discretionary nature of the Rule and stated that he did not consider it necessary to vacate the chair.[175] On a later occasion, the Soviet representative replied in similar vein when the United States "requested" that he disqualify himself from presiding over a meeting called to consider Soviet charges regarding operations in the Congo.[176]

The presidents of the Security Council have from time to time, either on their own initiative or at the request of the Council, made valuable contributions to the handling of disputes before the Council. The most outstanding example is the role various presidents have played at different stages in the handling of the India–Pakistan question.[177] Because of the monthly rotation of the office, the presidents have been unable to play a role comparable in importance to their counterparts in the League, or indeed comparable to the role often played by the presidents of the General Assembly.

---

[174] At the same time the Council rejected a Yugoslav proposal to suspend Rule 18 in the light of the controversy over representation and to allow Cuba to act as President for the month. SCOR/5th Yr., No. 4/462d Mtg./Jan. 17, 1950/p. 15.

[175] SCOR/13th Yr./814th Mtg./Apr. 29, 1958/p. 3.

[176] SCOR/15th Yr./912d Mtg./Dec. 7, 1960.

[177] See *Repertoire of the Security Council*, pp. 20–21; and SCOR/12th Yr./774th Mtg./Feb. 21, 1957/p. 13.

The President's responsibilities under the Rules are as follows: he calls meetings of the Council (Rules 1–3); he approves the provisional agenda for each meeting (Rule 7); he signs the "official record" of the meeting and notes whether any "corrections" requested by members are of sufficient importance to submit to the Council itself (Rules 52 and 53); he represents the Council in its "capacity" as a United Nations organ (Rule 19); and he "presides" over meetings of the Council. As presiding officer, the President calls upon representatives in the order in which they signify their desire to speak (Rule 22); decides whether to give precedence to a rapporteur appointed by the Council (Rule 25); rules on the order in which amendments shall be voted upon (Rule 36); and rules on any point of order raised during discussion (Rule 30). There have been extended discussions in the Council concerning presidential rulings, especially on the right of the President to rule on certain matters.[178]

Article 31

Any Member of the United Nations which is not a member of the Security Council may participate, without vote, in the discussion of any question brought before the Security Council whenever the latter considers that the interests of that Member are specially affected.

Articles 31 and 32 of the Charter provide for participation in Security Council discussions of states not members of the Council. These articles recognize the principle that interested parties should be given an opportunity to present their views before any decision is taken that might affect their interests. Moreover, the hearing of interested parties provides the Council with an important means of obtaining information on which to base its decisions.

There are significant distinctions between these two articles. The application of Article 32 is confined to participation of states that are parties to a dispute under consideration by the Security Council. It applies equally to members and nonmembers of the United Nations. Invitations under Article 31 may be extended only to members of the Organization. However, a member may be invited to participate in the discussion of any question, if the Council considers that the member's interests are "specially affected." Another difference is that Article 32 places the Council under obligation to invite parties to a dispute. On the other hand, Article 31 is "permissive." The Council "may" invite

[178] See, for example, the debate on the President's invitation to Israel to participate in the Council's discussions. SCOR/3d Yr., No. 93/330th Mtg./July 7, 1948. See also SCOR/5th Yr., Nos. 22–35/480th–493d Mtgs./Aug. 1–31, 1950, in which there was an extended debate on rulings, challenges to rulings, overrulings, and refusals to rule.

members to participate and it is for the Council itself to decide whether the member's interests are "specially affected."

In practice, the distinction between Articles 31 and 32 has been considerably blurred in so far as participation of United Nations members has been concerned. In invitations to members to take part in the Council's discussions, Article 32 has seldom been cited. Article 31 may be referred to, but more frequently, invitations are issued without specific reference to either article. The reason is that the Council has always been reluctant to decide, especially at the outset of its discussions, that any question before it is a "dispute," since such a decision might have important implications, particularly for the application of Article 27.[179] The Council's failure to specify whether it is acting under Article 31 or 32 has caused little difficulty, primarily because no distinction has been made in the position of those invited under either article.[180] Moreover, the Council has given a very liberal interpretation to the phrase "specially affected." The mere request by a member has almost always been considered sufficient ground for an invitation.

Under the Provisional Rules of Procedure, the Council must invite participation of any member bringing a matter to its attention in accordance with Article 35(1) of the Charter (Rule 37). Members against which charges have been leveled are also invited. Another basis upon which invitations have been extended is geographic propinquity. Members, at their request, have frequently taken part in discussions on the admission of neighboring states to membership in the Organization.

The first extensive application of Article 31 occurred in March, 1947, when the Council, at the request of New Zealand, extended invitations to all members of the Far Eastern Commission to take part in the discussion on the strategic trusteeship agreement for the former Japanese mandated islands.[181] This decision was subsequently cited by the Philippines in its request to participate in the discussion of the Indonesian question on the ground of its vital interest in the maintenance of peace in that area. This request was turned down initially, some members of the Council expressing doubts whether the interests of the Philippines were "specially affected" within the meaning of Article 31. Shortly thereafter, the Council reversed its decision.[182] Not only the

---

[179] The matter of deciding that a question is a "dispute" before hearing the parties was discussed at length in connection with the Syria-Lebanon question. See SCOR/1st Yr., 1st Ser., No. 1/19th Mtg./Feb. 14, 1946/pp. 271–82. See also discussion on the Greek Frontier Incidents question, *ibid.*, 2d Ser., Nos. 24 and 26/82d and 84th Mtgs./Dec. 10 and 16, 1946/pp. 530–59, and 607 ff.

[180] For restrictions on invited representatives, see commentary on Art. 32.

[181] SCOR/2d Yr./118th Mtg./Mar. 12, 1947/p. 515.

[182] *Ibid.*, 178th and 184th Mtgs./Aug. 7 and 14, 1947/pp. 1839 and 1980.

Philippines but later a number of other countries from Southeast Asia were invited to be party to the discussion. The high point in the extension of invitations to participate in the Council's discussions came during the consideration of the Congo situation. At one meeting, twenty-three representatives of United Nations members were invited to the Council table.[183] Most were African states, but a number were non-African members that had supplied armed forces for the Congo operations.

The involvement of members in the work of subsidiary bodies has been the basis for a number of invitations. Canada, for example, was invited to participate in the discussions on the reports of the United Nations Atomic Energy Commission. Because of their membership on the Security Council's Committee of Good Offices, Australia and Belgium were both invited to join in discussions on the Indonesian question.

Most Security Council invitations have been extended as the result of a request from a United Nations member. Occasionally, the Council has acted on its own initiative. When it was considering the communist coup in Czechoslovakia, it invited that government to participate in its discussions. The invitation was declined, however, on the ground that the matter was outside the Council's jurisdiction.[184] Generally, members have been most anxious to take part in any discussion that might affect them. In 1963, however, the Council discussed the arrangements between Saudi Arabia and the United Arab Republic regarding Yemen without the participation of any one of the three governments concerned.[185] Another variation occurred when thirty-two members from Africa brought to the Council complaints against Portugal and South Africa and four of their number were specifically chosen to present the cases in the Council.[186]

Invitations are extended by the President of the Council. If there are objections, the matter is put to the vote. At an early date, it was established that this was a procedural matter.[187] Invitations are generally extended immediately after the Council has decided to place a matter on its agenda. Sometimes a request is not received until later in the proceedings, and occasionally the Council has deferred action on a request. Once a member has been invited to participate in discussion of

[183] SCOR/16th Yr./942d Mtg./Feb. 20–21, 1961/p. 2.

[184] SCOR/3d Yr./Supp. for April, 1948/p. 6. See also the refusal of South Africa to take part in the Council's discussion, S/PV 1050, July 31, 1963, pp. 6 ff.

[185] SCOR/18th Yr./1038th Mtg./June 11, 1963.

[186] Ibid., 1040th Mtg./June 22, 1963.

[187] Despite the negative vote of the Soviet Union, Canada was invited to take part in the Council's discussion on the rules of procedure of the UN Atomic Energy Commission. SCOR/1st Yr., 2d Ser., No. 1/50th Mtg./July 10, 1946/pp. 1–7.

a question, it is the normal practice for the President to invite the representative of that member to take his place at the Council table whenever that question is subsequently discussed.

There is one major exception to the Security Council's very liberal policy in connection with participation of members in its discussions. From the outset, it has held that adoption of the agenda is a matter to be discussed by Council members alone. Only after the Council has decided to place a matter on the agenda has it been considered appropriate for other states to take part in discussions.[188] This restriction caused little difficulty during the first years of the Council's operations for the simple reason that, with minor exceptions, that body almost invariably decided, with relatively little debate, in favor of discussing every matter a United Nations member chose to bring before it. When the Council in later years adopted a more restrictive attitude toward the questions it would discuss, there was considerable dissatisfaction with the policy of barring nonmembers of the Council from taking part in the often-lengthy debates on adoption of the agenda. In 1952, for example, the Council decided against placing the Tunisian question on its agenda and also refused to invite members that had joined in bringing the question to the Council's attention to take part in the preliminary discussion on the inclusion of this item on the agenda.[189] The next year, the Council followed the same course in connection with the question of Morocco.[190]

The same policy has been followed with regard to invitations to members against which complaints have been directed, as evidenced by the refusal of the Council to grant requests of Iran, Portugal, and South Africa that they be given an opportunity to present their views concerning inclusion on the agenda of the Anglo–Iranian dispute, the Angolan question, and the racial situation in South Africa, respectively. Once the Council decided to consider these questions, of course, the three members were invited to join in the discussions. This restriction on participation of nonmembers of the Council has been applied not only when the Council initially decides whether to consider a question, but also on subsequent occasions when the adoption of the agenda for a particular meeting has been discussed.[191]

[188] As an "exception," India and Pakistan were on one occasion permitted to present their views on the wording of the agenda. SCOR/3d Yr., Nos. 1–15/231st Mtg./Jan. 22, 1948/p. 144.

[189] One of those submitting the question, Pakistan, was a member of the Council. For the discussion, see SCOR/7th Yr./574th–576th Mtgs./Apr. 4–14, 1952.

[190] SCOR/8th Yr./619th–624th Mtgs./Aug. 26–Sept. 3, 1953.

[191] See action taken on request of Guatemala that the Council resume discussion of its complaint. SCOR/9th Yr./776th Mtg./June 25, 1954/pp. 1–34. See also rejection of a similar request of Cuba. SCOR/17th Yr./991st Mtg./Feb. 27, 1962/pp. 1–28.

Acceptance of the practice of restricting discussion on the adoption of the agenda has been by no means unanimous. The Soviet Union has consistently opposed this limitation, and many other members have indicated by their votes in the Council their reluctance to support this restriction. Those favoring the practice have stressed that adoption of the agenda is a "private" matter of business to be discussed and decided upon by members of the Council, that in discussing this point the Council is not considering the "substance" of the question before it, and that it would not be appropriate for other states to participate in these discussions.

One of the rare occasions when the Council sought to restrict participation of other members in its discussion of agenda items occurred in connection with the Anglo–French complaint over Egypt's action in nationalizing the Suez Canal. When Israel first asked to participate in these discussions, the Council postponed action on the request. Subsequently, similar requests were received from several members of the Arab League and again action was postponed. Eventually, the Council decided it would not be "convenient" to hear the representatives of these governments at that stage in the proceedings but invited them to submit their views in writing.[192] These written statements were subsequently circulated as Security Council documents. This was an exceptional procedure.

Article 32

Any Member of the United Nations which is not a member of the Security Council or any state which is not a Member of the United Nations, if it is a party to a dispute under consideration by the Security Council, shall be invited to participate, without vote, in the discussion relating to the dispute. The Security Council shall lay down such conditions as it deems just for the participation of a state which is not a Member of the United Nations.

As mentioned in the commentary on the preceding article, the Security Council has tended to avoid citing Article 32 when inviting other United Nations members to take part in its discussions. Among the few exceptions were the invitation to Iran in connection with Council's consideration of the Anglo–Iranian Oil question and the invitation to Honduras, Nicaragua, and Guatemala when the Council was considering Guatemala's complaint of interference in its affairs.[193]

[192] SCOR/11th Yr./734th Mtg./Sept. 26, 1956/pp. 20–21; 735th Mtg./Oct. 5, 1956/p. 2; 742d Mtg./Oct. 13, 1956/pp. 1–2.
[193] See SCOR/6th Yr./559th Mtg./Oct. 10, 1951/pp. 10–11; and 9th Yr./675th Mtg./June 20, 1954/p. 1.

Avoiding reference to Article 32 in invitations to nonmembers of the United Nations, however, has posed a more difficult problem, since this is the only article in the Charter applicable to such invitations. Nonetheless, the Council has in most instances avoided specifically invoking Article 32. In some cases, the Council in its invitations has cited Rule 39 of its Provisional Rules of Procedure which provides that: "The Security Council may invite members of the Secretariat or other persons, whom it considers competent for the purpose, to supply it with information or to give other assistance in examining matters within its competence." More often, invitations have been issued without reference either to Article 32 or Rule 39.

It should be noted that Rule 39 has been cited in connection with invitations to representatives of other organs or subsidiary bodies of the United Nations,[194] and also in connection with invitations to persons in their individual capacities or as representatives of groups or organizations. For example, invitations were extended to the former Czech representative in connection with the Czechoslovak question, to Nawab Moin Nawaz Jung in connection with the Hyderabad question, to the representatives of the Jewish Agency for Palestine and the Arab Higher Committee in connection with the Palestine question, to a representative of the Turkish Cypriote community in connection with the Cyprus question, and to representatives of the two contending factions during the 1965 crisis in the Dominican Republic.[195]

The procedures of the Security Council in extending invitations to nonmembers of the United Nations are much the same as those already described with regard to members of the Organization.[196] Generally, invitations are extended as the result of a request, although the Council has occasionally acted on its own initiative. Most requests have been granted. An invitation to a nonmember is considered a "procedural" matter and thus not subject to veto. Invitations are extended after adoption of the agenda, usually at the outset of discussion.[197] The Council has recognized that the parties directly concerned should be given the earliest opportunity to present their views, and has occasionally deferred discussion until they were in position to do so. But it has not considered that the inability (or refusal) of a party to attend a Council meeting should prevent or necessarily even delay its discussions.

[194] See *Repertoire of the Security Council*, pp. 103–5.
[195] SCOR/3d Yr./272d Mtg./Mar. 22, 1948/pp. 173–75; 360th Mtg./Sept. 28, 1948/pp. 3–13; 253d Mtg./Feb. 24, 1948/p. 257; 282d Mtg./Apr. 14, 1948, pp. 1–2; 19th Yr./1098th Mtg./Feb. 27, 1964/p. 10; and 20th Yr./1212th Mtg./May 19, 1965/p. 666.
[196] See commentary on Art. 31.
[197] See rejection of the Soviet proposal to link the decision on invitations to adoption of the agenda. SCOR/5th Yr./492d Mtg./Aug. 29, 1950/p. 21.

While granting requests of United Nations members has become almost routine, invitations to nonmembers have been subject to much more extensive debate. This is primarily because the Council is obligated to extend an invitation to a nonmember but only if the various criteria set out in Article 32 are met. Under the terms of that article, the nonmember must be a "state"; the Council must be considering a "dispute" and the nonmember must be a "party" to that dispute; and the nonmember must accept the "conditions" laid down by the Council.

Meaning of the Term "State"

The first and most extensive discussion on the interpretation to be given to the term "state" for the purpose of applying Article 32 occurred in August, 1947, concerning a proposal to invite the Republic of Indonesia to participate in the discussion of the Indonesian question.[198] Some members stated that they could not vote for the invitation because their governments had not recognized the Republic. Others drew attention to the de facto recognition accorded to the Republic by the Netherlands and other United Nations members. It was argued that the primary intent of Article 32 was to give both parties to a dispute the opportunity to present their views, and that application of the article did not require that a party possess all the attributes of sovereignty. The President of the Council announced that he was putting the proposed invitation to the vote "without any definition or determination of the sovereignty of that Republic" and with the understanding that every state retained "complete liberty either to recognize or not to recognize the sovereignty or independence" of the Indonesian Republic.[199] The President's statement has been cited frequently, both in the Council and the Assembly in support of the position that an invitation by either organ does not imply any "recognition" of sovereignty or of the representational claims of those invited to take part in the discussions.

On most subsequent occasions, the liberal policy the Council adopted in inviting Indonesia has been followed. One example was the invitation to the representative of Hyderabad to take part in the initial discussions on the Hyderabad question.[200] Another was the invitation

[198] For use of the term "state" in Arts. 3 and 4, see commentary on those articles.

[199] SCOR/2d Yr., No. 74/181st Mtg./Aug. 12, 1947/p. 1940. For the debate see also *ibid.*, No. 67/171st Mtg./July 31, 1947/pp. 1618 ff.

[200] SCOR/3d Yr./357th Mtg./Sept. 16, 1948/p. 11. Because of doubts about the status of Hyderabad and the validity of his credentials, this representative did not participate in the later discussion on this question. See *ibid.*, 360th Mtg./Sept. 28, 1948/p. 13.

extended in July, 1948, to representatives of the "Provisional Government of Israel," who had previously taken part in the Council's discussions as representatives of the Jewish Agency for Palestine. Despite some questions concerning the status of the "Provisional Government," this change in designation was sustained.[201]

Discussions in the Security Council on issues directly or indirectly related to the Korean conflict raised a number of questions concerning the status of representatives to be invited to take part in the discussions. When the Korean question was first considered, the President, citing Rule 39 of the Provisional Rules of Procedure, invited the representative of the Republic of Korea to participate in the discussion. A proposal by Yugoslavia that the government of North Korea be invited to state its case before the Council was rejected.[202] Subsequently, the Council's actions were challenged by the Soviet delegate, who insisted that Article 32 had been violated and that both North and South Korea should be heard. After an acrimonious, month-long debate, the representative of the Republic of Korea was again invited to take his place at the Council table and the Soviet proposal was rejected.[203] One basis for opposition to the Soviet proposal was that the General Assembly had declared that the Republic of Korea was the only lawfully established government in Korea,[204] and had repeatedly refused to permit the People's Republic of Korea to participate in its debates on the problem of Korea.

The question of invitations to the People's Republic of China posed even more complicated issues. The Soviet Union introduced a number of proposals to invite representatives of the Peiping regime "to attend the meetings of the Security Council" in connection with the consideration of the Korean conflict; the complaint concerning United States action regarding Formosa; the complaint of United States bombing of Chinese territory; and the request for an investigation of alleged bacterial warfare in Korea. During the discussions on these proposals, the Soviet Union cited Article 32 and maintained that the Council was under obligation to extend the invitations. Others countered that Article 32 was in no ways applicable, since the People's Republic of China could scarcely be considered "a state which is not a member of the United Nations." China was one of the original members of the Organization and the right of the Nationalist government to represent

---

[201] Ibid., 330th Mtg./July 7, 1948/pp. 2–9.
[202] SCOR/5th Yr./473 Mtg./June 25, 1950/pp. 4 and 18; and 474th Mtg./June 27, 1950/p. 7.
[203] Ibid., 494th Mtg./Sept. 1, 1950/pp. 2 and 21. For the debate, see ibid., 483d–490th Mtg./Aug. 4–25, 1950.
[204] GA Res. 195(III), Dec. 12, 1948.

China had been upheld by the Security Council.[205] The Soviet proposals were defeated.[206]

In connection with the complaint concerning United States action regarding Formosa, a complaint raised originally by the People's Republic of China, the Council did eventually decide to invite a representative of that regime to attend its discussions. The preamble to the resolution noted "the divergence of opinion" regarding the representation of China and stated that "without prejudice" to this matter the Council could "in accordance with rule 39" invite a representative of the People's Republic of China "to provide it with information or assist it in the consideration" of the complaint.[207] Also, following receipt of the special report of the United Nations Command concerning Chinese intervention in the Korean conflict, the Council, again citing Rule 39, decided to invite a representative of the People's Republic of China "to be present during the discussion" of the special report.[208] A representative of the Peiping regime subsequently participated in the Council's discussion to the extent of making a statement on the Formosa issue but refused the restricted invitation to take part in the consideration of the report of the United Nations Command.

The majority of members of the Security Council were generally sympathetic with the view that the People's Republic of China should be given an opportunity to take part in the Council's discussions. While its unique status presented some problems, the fact remained that the People's Republic of China was actively opposing United Nations action in Korea. A few years later, an invitation to participate in Council discussions on the hostilities in the Formosa straits was extended to the People's Republic almost without debate.[209]

Controversy has also arisen over the application of Article 32 to North and South Vietnam. An invitation to the Republic of Vietnam to participate in the Council's debate on the complaint by Cambodia against the Republic and the United States was objected to by the Soviet and Czech representatives on the ground that the regime was "illegal." [210] Subsequently, when the Council considered the United States complaint against North Vietnam, the Soviet Union insisted that it was the Council's "duty" under Article 32 to invite the government of

[205] See commentary on Art. 23.

[206] For the Soviet proposals, see SCOR/5th Yr./492d Mtg./Aug. 29, 1950/p. 21; 496th Mtg./Sept. 6, 1950/p. 21; 499th Mtg./Sept. 11, 1950/p. 19; 505th Mtg./Sept. 28, 1950/p. 21; 520th Mtg./Nov. 8, 1950/p. 5; and 7th Yr./585th Mtg./July 1, 1952.

[207] SCOR/5th Yr./506th Mtg./Sept. 29, 1950/pp. 3–5.

[208] *Ibid.*, 520th Mtg./Nov. 8, 1950/p. 8.

[209] SCOR/10th Yr./690th Mtg./Jan. 31, 1955/p. 22.

[210] SCOR/19th Yr./1118th Mtg./May 19, 1964/pp. 2–3.

North Vietnam to participate. No vote was taken on the matter; instead, the President informed both North and South Vietnam that the Council would "welcome" any information they wished to make available either through participation in the discussions or by other means.[211] South Vietnam furnished some information, but North Vietnam contested the competence of the Security Council to consider the matter.

Existence of a "Dispute"

With the notable exception of the Soviet Union, the Security Council members have generally agreed that Article 32 applies only when the Council is considering a "dispute" and that the Council itself should decide when the question before it is of such character. In its first debate on participation by nonmembers of the United Nations, the Security Council had to face the problem that the Charter does not provide for such participation in the consideration of a "situation." In September, 1946, the Council began consideration of a complaint by the Ukrainian SSR concerning the situation in Greece; both members were invited to participate in the discussion on the basis of Article 31. Albania, citing Article 32, also asked to present its views. There was general agreement that, since the matter had not been classified as a dispute, Article 32 was not applicable. The suggestion that an invitation be issued on the basis of Rule 39 of the Provisional Rules of Procedure also met with opposition. In the end, the Council decided to invite Albania "to make a factual statement," the President stating that this did not "imply the right to participate in the discussion." [212]

At the end of the year, a similar problem arose when the Council decided to consider the question of the Greek frontier incidents, which had been submitted to the Council by Greece as a "situation." There was a lengthy debate whether the Council should extend invitations "to participate" in the discussion not only to Greece and Yugoslavia but also to the two nonmember states, Albania and Bulgaria. It was decided that the two states would be invited "to participate," while initially the two nonmembers would be "invited to enable the Security Council to hear such declarations as they may wish to make." Having heard the initial statements by the parties, the Council agreed that all four states should be invited "to participate" in the discussion.[213]

[211] Ibid., 1141st Mtg./Aug. 7, 1964/p. 4.

[212] SCOR/1st Yr., 2d Ser., Nos. 8–10/60th Mtg./Sept. 4, 1946/p. 201; 61st and 62d Mtgs./Sept. 9, 1946/pp. 214 and 225–56; and 64th Mtg./Sept. 9, 1946/p. 267.

[213] Ibid., No. 24/82d Mtg./Dec. 10, 1946/p. 559; and No. 26/84th Mtg./Dec. 16, 1946/p. 613.

These two debates on the relevance of the distinction between a "dispute" and a "situation" for the purpose of applying Article 32 took place during the first year of the Council's operations when members were especially concerned about the precedents being established. Since then, the Council has seldom found it necessary to discuss this distinction.[214] A closely related point, however, was raised during the discussions on the Korean question. When the Soviet Union charged that the Council was violating Article 32 by not inviting the North Koreans to participate in the discussions, some opponents of the Soviet view argued that the Council was under no obligation to issue the invitation because the question under consideration was not a "dispute" but a "breach of peace," and therefore the article did not apply.[215]

It should be noted that the application of Article 32 requires not only that the question under consideration be a "dispute" but also that the state to be invited must be a party to the dispute. This requirement has seldom been mentioned. But proposals that East Indonesia and Borneo be invited to take part in the discussion of the Indonesia question were rejected largely on the ground that they, unlike the Republic of Indonesia, were not parties to the dispute under consideration by the Council.[216]

Conditions for the Participation of Nonmembers

Article 32 leaves it to the Security Council to "lay down such conditions as it deems just for the participation" of nonmembers in its discussions. In those cases where the Council has applied this provision, it has sought to place members and nonmembers on an "equal footing" by requiring that the latter "accept . . . for the purposes of the dispute, the obligations of pacific settlement" provided for in the Charter. This language is drawn from Article 35(2), which authorizes nonmembers in certain circumstances to bring disputes to the attention of the Security Council. Although various members of the Council have from time to time made statements concerning the extent of these obligations, the Council has been reluctant to specify just what they entail.

The Council first decided to use this formula when it agreed to invite

214 For one of the few discussions, see the arguments against inviting the People's Republic of China to take part in the discussion of the complaint of bombing of Chinese territory. SCOR/5th Yr./499th Mtg./Sept. 11, 1950/pp. 3, 12–15.

215 *Ibid.*, 488th Mtg./Aug. 17, 1950/pp. 2, 15–16; and 494th Mtg./Sept. 1, 1950/pp. 15–22.

216 SCOR/2d Yr./184th Mtg./Aug. 14, 1947/p. 1922; and 193d Mtg./Aug. 22, 1947/p. 2172.

Albania and Bulgaria "to participate" in the discussion on the Greek frontier incidents question.[217] The same conditions were attached to the invitation to Albania to participate in the discussion of the Corfu Channel question.[218] In some instances, nonmembers have indicated their acceptance of these obligations in advance, often in their requests to take part in the discussions or in communications bringing a dispute to the Council's attention.[219] It should be noted that the Council has not sought to attach any such conditions to invitations extended under Rule 39. No attempt, for example, was made to require the Republic of Korea or the People's Republic of China to accept any obligations of pacific settlement when invitations were extended to them.

Only once has the question been raised whether an invited state had in fact accepted the Charter obligations of pacific settlement. In May, 1954, after the Security Council had heard an initial statement by the representative of Jordan (not then a member of the United Nations) concerning its complaint against Israel, the representative of the latter government inquired whether Jordan had accepted the obligations of the Charter with regard to the pacific settlement of the dispute. The representative of Jordan subsequently notified the Council that he was not empowered "to take part" in the Council's discussions and no further consideration was given to the complaint by the Council.[220]

Position of Invited Representatives

Throughout the Security Council's discussions on Articles 31 and 32, it has been frequently asserted that the purpose of the articles is to place the parties on the same footing regardless of whether they are members of the Council or even of the United Nations. The Charter does not go so far in this regard as did the Covenant of the League of Nations. Any member not represented on the League Council was invited "to send a Representative to sit as a member at any meeting of the Council during the consideration of matters specifically affecting" their interests (Article 4[5]). Under the Charter, those invited to take part in the Council's discussions do not sit as "members" of the Council but as "invited" representatives and as such they do not enjoy all the privileges of Council members.

The most significant limitation on invited representatives is that, in

[217] See above, p. 252.

[218] SCOR/2d Yr., No. 16/95th Mtg./Jan. 20, 1947/p. 123.

[219] See communications from the Republic of Indonesia, Hyderabad, Jordan, and Kuwait. Ibid., No. 74/181st Mtg./Aug. 12, 1947/p. 191; 3d Yr. Supp. for Sept., 1948/p. 5; 5th Yr./511th Mtg./Oct. 10, 1950/p. 2; and 16th Yr./Supp. for July, Aug., and Sept., 1961/p. 3.

[220] See SCOR/9th Yr./670th Mtg./May 4, 1954/pp. 27 ff.; and 671st Mtg./May 12, 1954. See also Doc. S/3219, May 26, 1954.

accordance with Articles 31 and 32, they do not have the right to vote.[221] The Charter also requires a Council member which is a "party" to a dispute to abstain from voting on recommendations for the settlement of that dispute (Article 27[3]), but this provision only partially offsets the disparity between Council members and invited representatives.

A second limitation is set down in Rule 38, under which any member of the United Nations invited to participate in the Council's discussions "may submit proposals and draft resolutions" but these are put to the vote only at the request of a Council member.[222] There is no mention of the position of states that are not members of the United Nations or of representatives invited under Rule 39; however, any member of the Council is always free to ask for a vote on any proposal or draft resolution.[223]

While there have been numerous statements in the Security Council concerning the limited rights of those invited under Rule 39, in practice there does not seem to have been any difference in the position of those invited under this rule or Articles 31 and 32. Sometimes, of course, limitations upon the extent of participation have been incorporated in the terms of the invitations themselves, for example, in those cases where representatives have merely been given the opportunity to "make a statement" or present their views on a particular aspect of the question before the Council.

Aside from the above-mentioned limitations, a number of customary practices have grown up in the Council that differentiate between the position of invited representatives and Council members; for example, the latter are generally given priority in the order of speaking.

More significant restrictions have stemmed from the often-stated thesis that an invitation to participate in the Council's discussion of a question does not entitle invited representatives to take a part in certain discussions related to the conduct of Council business. As already noted, the Council has consistently held that adoption of the agenda is a matter to be decided by Council members alone, and all proposals that others be permitted to take part in discussions on this point have been rejected. The Council has also decided that its discussion of a request from a subsidiary organ of the Council for a clarification of its

221 For discussion on the position of members invited under Art. 44 of the Charter, see commentary on that article.

222 For further discussion on the submission of proposals, see *Repertoire of the Security Council*, 1946–1951, pp. 134 ff. Note the problems that this Rule has raised with regard to priority in the order of voting.

223 Note the vote on a draft originally submitted by the People's Republic of China and later sponsored by the Soviet Union. SCOR/5th Yr./530th Mtg./Nov. 30, 1950/p. 22.

mandate should be restricted to members.[224] In September, 1960, the Council took the same position when considering rival claims to represent the Congo before the Security Council.[225]

Objections have also been raised to the participation of invited representatives in discussion of such matters as removal of a question from the Council's agenda; adjournment or postponement of a meeting; and the manner in which the Council's voting is to be conducted. The rights of invited representatives to raise points of order and to speak after a vote has been taken have also been challenged.

[224] SCOR/2d Yr., No. 10/100th Mtg./Feb. 10, 1947/pp. 173 ff.
[225] SCOR/15th Yr./899th and 900th Mtgs./Sept. 14, 1960.

CHAPTER VI

Pacific Settlement of Disputes

The provisions concerning pacific settlement had "the doubtful distinction of being regarded as one of the most poorly drafted sections" of the Dumbarton Oaks Proposals.[1] This was due in large part to failure to reach agreement at Dumbarton Oaks on voting procedure in the Security Council. While the conferees were agreed that a decision on "enforcement measures" would require the unanimous consent of the permanent members of the Security Council, they were not in agreement on the appropriate voting procedures with respect to decisions on pacific settlement, being divided on the question whether the party to a dispute should be allowed to vote. If the principle of great power unanimity were to be applied without qualification, there would be no danger, in so far as the major powers were concerned, in authorizing the Council to decide on the merits of a dispute or even to enforce its decision. It was recognized, however, that other members, not protected by the veto, might not find such a system attractive.[2] On the other hand, if a permanent member was required to abstain when a party to a dispute and consequently was deprived of the use of the veto, such wide powers for the Council would be unacceptable to the major powers, the United States included.

A second source of confusion was failure to clarify the nature of the Security Council's task in performing the function of peaceful settlement. Those in the State Department who had been mainly responsible for the preparatory work on the United States proposals had taken the view that settling disputes was the responsibility of the parties themselves, not the Council. The proper role for the Council, they believed, was to see that these disputes did not endanger international peace and security. The Council should act as a "policeman" not a "judge."[3] This view was not fully accepted by others who regarded settlement as a desirable function of the Council.

At the San Francisco Conference numerous amendments were proposed to the Dumbarton Oaks provisions on pacific settlement. Again,

[1] Report of the New Zealand Delegation on the San Francisco Conference, quoted in Ruth B. Russell, *A History of the United Nations Charter* (Washington, Brookings Institution, 1958), p. 657.
[2] *Ibid.*, pp. 458 ff.   [3] *Ibid.*, p. 599.

the reconciling of differing views was impeded by extended controversy over voting procedure. By the time it became clear what the scope of the permanent members' right of veto would be, there was inadequate time left for a careful consideration of provisions on peaceful settlement. In particular, the present text is unsatisfactory in its treatment of "situations" and the powers of the Security Council in respect to them.[4]

The principal changes in the Dumbarton Oaks Proposals made at San Francisco were:

1. Rearrangement of the provisions to give pride of place to the obligation of parties to seek a solution of their disputes by peaceful means.[5]

2. Broadening of the Council's powers, especially by authorizing it to make recommendations on "situations" as well as "disputes" and to recommend "terms" as well as "procedures" for settlement.[6]

3. More explicit distinction between the actions of the Council in the field of pacific settlement and those taken to deal with "threats to the peace, breaches of the peace, and acts of aggression."

With respect to this last point, what had been two parts of one section in the Dumbarton Oaks Proposals (section VIIIA and B) became separate chapters of the Charter (Chapters VI and VII). Moreover, the provision in the Proposals linking the Council's actions in these two areas was deleted. The initial paragraph of section VIIIB of the Proposals would have empowered the Council "to take any measures necessary for the maintenance of international peace and security," should it decide that a "threat to the peace" had resulted from the failure of the parties to settle their disputes, either by peaceful means of their own choice or in accordance with the Council's recommendations.[7] This provision was open to the interpretation that the Council could, under the circumstances stated, "impose" a settlement upon the parties, a situation unacceptable to many delegates. The solution finally reached was to delete the specific reference to the possibility that failure to settle a dispute might be deemed a threat to the peace.[8]

Chapter VI of the Charter establishes with some precision the rights (Article 35) and obligations (Articles 33[1] and 37[1]) of states. It in-

[4] See Leland M. Goodrich, "The United Nations: Pacific Settlement of Disputes," *American Political Science Review*, XXXIX, 968; and Russell, pp. 657–68.

[5] See commentary on Art. 33.   [6] See commentary on Arts. 36 and 37.

[7] Under U.S. proposals at Dumbarton Oaks, this provision would have been the last paragraph of sec. A, but at the suggestion of the Soviet Union it became the first paragraph of sec. B. The determination of the threat to the peace would be the first step toward enforcement action rather than the last step in pacific settlement. Thus the principle of unanimity would apply to the determination, even if one of the permanent members was directly involved. Russell, p. 462.

[8] See commentary on Art. 39.

dicates the kinds of questions with which the Council should concern itself and the ways in which it should deal with them. But the Council is given considerable discretion in these respects. Although the Charter lays down guidelines, it does not set out the detailed procedures the Council is to follow in discharging its functions in the field of pacific settlement. In this respect the Charter differs from other endeavors to establish machinery for the pacific settlement of disputes, most of which attempt to impose far greater restrictions upon the way in which the system is to operate.[9]

In practice, the Council has taken a broad view of its proper role in peaceful settlement. It has dealt with a far wider range of questions than was originally expected. Its approach has been flexible, pragmatic, and essentially political rather than legal. It has not based its actions on specific Charter provisions but rather on its general powers and responsibilities. For these reasons, an analysis of the application of the provisions of Chapter VI provides a very incomplete picture of the Council's activities in the field of pacific settlement.[10]

Article 33

1. The parties to any dispute, the continuance of which is likely to endanger the maintenance of international peace and security, shall, first of all, seek a solution by negotiation, enquiry, mediation, conciliation, arbitration, judicial settlement, resort to regional agencies or arrangements, or other peaceful means of their own choice.

2. The Security Council shall, when it deems necessary, call upon the parties to settle their dispute by such means.

By placing Article 33 at the beginning of Chapter VI, the San Francisco Conference sought to emphasize the responsibility of the parties themselves to settle their disputes. The arrangement in the corresponding section of the Dumbarton Oaks Proposals was more logical. It began by authorizing the Security Council to carry out an investigation to determine whether the continuance of a dispute or situation was "likely to endanger the maintenance of international peace and security." The provision obligating the parties to seek a solution of such disputes by peaceful means and obligating the Council to call upon them to do so came after the authorization to the Council to deter-

[9] For example, the Hague Conventions, the League Covenant, and the Pact of Bogota.

[10] For a fuller account through 1954, see Leland M. Goodrich and Anne P. Simons, *The United Nations and the Maintenance of International Peace and Security* (Washington, Brookings Institution, 1955), Part III, and ch. VIII of the *Repertoire of the Security Council* and its *Supplements*.

mine whether the continuance of the dispute was likely to endanger international peace and security. The reversal of the positions of the two provisions causes some confusion of responsibility. Under Article 33, the parties are under an obligation to seek a settlement to disputes of a certain character before bringing them to the Security Council, but under Article 34 the Council has the responsibility for deciding whether the dispute is of that nature.

Moreover, changing the order of the two articles leads to the implication that the Council may call upon the parties to carry out their obligations under Article 33(1) without first determining under Article 34 that the continuance of the dispute is likely to endanger peace and security. In practice, however, the rather illogical arrangement of Chapter VI has not caused problems.

Obligations of Parties

Article 33(1) is a more detailed formulation of the general obligation of members stated in Article 2(3) to "settle their international disputes by peaceful means in such a manner that international peace and security, and justice, are not endangered." The obligation of members under Article 33(1) is limited; it applies only to disputes "the continuance of which is likely to endanger the maintenance of international peace and security." Efforts to broaden this obligation at the San Francisco Conference were unsuccessful.[11]

If a dispute is of the nature described in Article 33, the parties are obligated to seek a solution by the peaceful means listed in that article before referring the matter to the Security Council. They are not required to apply all the procedures enumerated therein, but they are expected to make a real effort to reach an agreed solution before coming to the Council. Generally, in their initial submissions, states bringing questions to the Council's attention have described in some detail their attempts to resolve the matter and the reasons why further efforts are impossible, or unlikely to be frutiful without the Council's intervention.

Although Article 33 applies specifically to "disputes," states have often followed the same practice when bringing "situations" to the Council's attention and even when the matter is characterized as a "threat to the peace." In bringing the Berlin question to the Council in 1948, for example, France, the United Kingdom, and the United States stated that they had "made every effort to resolve their differences directly with the Soviet Government" and that that government bore

11 Russell, p. 667.

the "sole responsibility for creating a situation in which further recourse to the means of settlement prescribed in Article 33" was "in existing circumstances" impossible.[12]

Very often the other party has challenged the description of prior efforts at settlement, has denied that further efforts are impossible, or has asserted that no real effort has been made. Such arguments have seldom dissuaded the Council from considering a dispute, although they have sometimes influenced its course of action.

It has often been argued that the Council should not consider a particular question because the possibilities of settlement under Article 33(1) have not been exhausted. This was the principal basis of the Council's decision in 1952 not to include on its agenda a complaint concerning the relations between France and Tunisia. During the debate there were a number of statements to the effect that the possibilities for settlement had not been exhausted, that the Council should not intervene since the two parties were in the process of negotiating their differences, and that a Council debate might impede their success.[13] This was an exceptional case, for the Council seldom declines to consider any matter brought to its attention.

The intent of Article 33 was to establish an obligation that was to be fulfilled by the parties *prior* to their enlisting the Council's assistance. This obligation has, however, been considered as a *continuing* one. In both the Security Council and the General Assembly, the point has been frequently made that even after the United Nations concerns itself with a controversy, the primary responsibility for settlement remains with the parties themselves. This continuing responsibility has been repeatedly emphasized in discussions on the India-Pakistan question and conflicts between Israel and the Arab states.

Procedures of Pacific Settlement

Article 33 enumerates various procedures for the pacific settlement of disputes.

Negotiation is the normal process by which states settle their differences; it is the method most frequently urged upon the parties by the Security Council and the General Assembly.

Enquiry is not strictly speaking a method of settlement but rather a means for finding a basis for a settlement. The value of an impartial body ascertaining the "facts" of a dispute has long been recognized, as

[12] SCOR/3d Yr./*Supp.* for Oct., 1948/p. 45. For other examples, see *Repertoire of the Security Council* and *Supplements*, ch. x, Part I.
[13] SCOR/7th Yr./574th–576th Mtgs./Apr. 4, 10, and 14, 1952.

evidenced in numerous treaties providing for commissions of enquiry in the event of a dispute.[14] In practice, such commissions have played a significant role in inducing states to agree upon terms for settling their disputes.

Mediation and conciliation are procedures by which third parties seek to assist the disputants in reaching a settlement. Mediation implies an effort by an outside party to bring the parties together and assist them in reaching a solution. Conciliation has generally been considered as a process instituted by the parties who agree to submit their dispute to a specially constituted organ for investigation and efforts to effect a settlement. In the debates and decisions of UN organs, the terms "mediation," "conciliation," and "good offices" have been used with little regard to subtle distinctions as to their meaning. The Security Council and the General Assembly have frequently established committees and commissions to perform functions of this kind. On a number of occasions, the Secretary-General, the President of the Security Council or the General Assembly, or some other designated individual has been asked to undertake similar responsibilities. Both organs have occasionally refrained from taking any action on a dispute in the light of outside efforts to bring about a solution through such procedures.

Arbitration is a method of pacific settlement in which the parties obligate themselves in advance to accept the decision of an arbitrator or arbitral tribunal. The rules to be applied are usually determined by a *compromis* or agreement between the parties. The tribunal to which the dispute is submitted may be specially created or provided for in an arbitration treaty. During the early years of the twentieth century, treaties of arbitration enjoyed a certain vogue, although practical results in terms of actual settlements through arbitration were less impressive. Since World War II, acceptance of the principle and use of the procedure of arbitration for settling international disputes have for various reasons suffered a noticeable decline.[15] Within the United Nations, there have been very few cases where resort to arbitration has been suggested.[16]

Judicial settlement has come to be identified with the submission of

14 See, in particular, the Hague Conventions for the Pacific Settlement of International Disputes of 1899 and 1907.

15 See Goodrich and Simons, ch. XIII.

16 The initial Security Council resolution on the Indonesian question called upon the parties to settle their disputes by "arbitration or other peaceful means" but the Netherlands rejected resort to arbitration. See SCOR/2d Yr./173d Mtg./Aug. 1, 1947/p. 1703; and 193d Mtg./Aug. 22, 1947/pp. 2144–47. India likewise rejected suggestions for arbitration in connection with its dispute with Pakistan. SCOR/4th Yr./*Special Supp.* 7, pp. 35–36 and 143–47; and SC Res. S/2017/Rev. 1, Mar. 21, 1951.

disputes to the principal judicial organ of the United Nations—the International Court of Justice. Up to 1966 the Court had delivered judgments in over twenty disputes submitted to it. There have been few instances in which the Security Council or the General Assembly have considered resort to the Court as the appropriate procedure for dealing with a dispute.[17]

"Resort to regional agencies or arrangements" was included in Article 33 largely in response to Latin American efforts at San Francisco to enhance the position of regional arrangements within the United Nations system. It is not a distinct "procedure" for pacific settlement but rather a general method for dealing with "local" disputes.[18]

The listing of various procedures for pacific settlement in Article 33 was not intended to be restrictive in any way. By specifically stating that the parties may resort to "other peaceful means of their own choice," the article makes it clear that they may have recourse to any conceivable means which may lead to a "peaceful" settlement of their dispute.

Action by the Security Council

Article 33(2) states that the Security Council "shall, when it deems necessary" call upon the parties to seek a settlement of their dispute by the peaceful means enumerated in paragraph 1. At the San Francisco Conference, there was some discussion as to whether the verb "may" or "shall" should be used. Those favoring "may" wished to emphasize that the Council's intervention was a matter within its own discretion and was in no way dependent upon the actions of the parties. Those favoring "shall" sought to underline the Council's duty to call upon the parties to fulfill their obligations. The final text was a compromise. The Council at its discretion decides whether the dispute is of such a character that it is necessary to call upon the parties to seek a solution. Once it decides that this necessity exists, it is incumbent upon the Council to issue such a call.

Article 33 contains the phrase "call upon" which is a stronger term than "recommend," the verb used in Articles 36, 37, and 38. This, and other distinctions between these articles, have had no practical significance, since the Council seldom bases its action on a particular article.

The Council has only once specifically referred to Article 33 in a resolution,[19] but in its debates the "spirit" of the article has been frequently invoked. Clearly the Council's activities have been greatly

---

[17] See commentary on Art. 36(2) and ch. xiv.
[18] See commentary on ch. viii, especially Art. 52.
[19] Res. 211, Sept. 29, 1965, on the India-Pakistan question.

influenced by the concept embodied in it. In most cases, the Council has directed its efforts towards inducing the parties themselves to enter into negotiations or to resolve their differences by other peaceful means. Whenever it has appeared that a settlement might be reached by such means, the Council has kept its intervention to a minimum.

In the first case considered by the Council, Iran's complaint of Soviet interference in its internal affairs, both parties indicated their willingness to seek a solution through direct negotiations. The Council, therefore, confined itself to noting these statements and requesting that it be informed of the results of the negotiations.[20] Shortly thereafter, an attempt to deal in the same way with a complaint by Syria and Lebanon against France and the United Kingdom was defeated. The Soviet Union vetoed the draft resolution on the ground that it did not go far enough in supporting the Syrian–Lebanese position.[21]

This was the first example of a situation the Council has repeatedly faced. Even when both parties have been willing to enter into negotiations, one or both have sought to stipulate the conditions under which the negotiations must take place or the basis upon which a settlement must be concluded. In these circumstances, the Council has often found it impossible to devise a formula that reconciles conflicting positions, and it has thus been frequently unable to adopt a resolution because of either a veto or the failure of any proposal to gain sufficient support. This was particularly true during the first ten years of the Council's history.[22] This obstacle has been somewhat overcome by the development of a practice dispensing with the necessity of a vote. If the discussion in the Council indicates that the parties are willing to enter into direct negotiations, or to seek a solution through regional arrangements or the good offices of another state, the President of the Council makes a statement noting the positions taken by the parties and the Council adjourns its consideration of the matter,[23] resuming its discussion if these efforts fail.

Article 33 is open to the interpretation that the Council is restricted to calling upon the parties to seek a solution through peaceful means of their own choice, and that it may not call upon them to resort to a particular procedure.[24] The idea that the parties themselves should choose the appropriate procedure was apparently the reason

---

[20] SCOR/1st Yr., 1st Ser./5th Mtg./Jan. 31, 1946/p. 70.

[21] *Ibid.*, 23d Mtg./Feb. 16, 1946/p. 368.

[22] For examples, see Goodrich and Simons, ch. XI.

[23] See, for example, the handling of the disputes between France and Tunisia. SCOR/13th Yr./821st Mtg./June 4, 1958; between Lebanon and the United Arab Republic, *ibid.*, 818th and 822d Mtgs., May 27 and June 5, 1958; and between Panama and the U.S., SCOR/19th Yr./1086th Mtg./Jan. 10, 1964.

[24] There is no bar to the Council recommending a particular procedure under Art. 36.

why the Council's initial resolution on the Indonesian question called upon the parties to "settle their disputes by arbitration or by other peaceful means." [25]

This interpretation of Article 33 has also been raised in the General Assembly. The Arab states objected to a draft resolution which cited Article 33 and urged direct negotiation with Israel. The singling out of "direct negotiations," it was argued, was contrary to Article 33 which left the choice of procedures to the parties involved. Although this argument was not accepted by the majority of members, the draft resolution still failed to get the necessary two-thirds support. [26]

Somewhat the same argument was raised at one point when the Security Council was considering a draft resolution urging India and Pakistan "to enter into negotiations" in accordance with Article 33. India's principal objection to the proposal, however, was to the inclusion of any suggestion as to the basis upon which a settlement should be sought. India also argued that Article 33 was not applicable, since the case before the Council was not a "dispute" but a "situation" created by Pakistan's "aggression." This draft resolution was vetoed by the Soviet Union. [27] Subsequently, however, when hostilities broke out between the two governments, the Council did call upon them "to utilize all peaceful means, including those listed in Article 33" to settle their differences. [28]

It should be noted that the Council has not considered that Article 33 is only applicable to "disputes." The "spirit" of that article has been frequently invoked under various circumstances to emphasize the general obligation of states to seek peaceful solutions to their problems. [29]

Article 34

The Security Council may investigate any dispute, or any situation which might lead to international friction or give rise to a dispute, in order to determine whether the continuance of the dispute or situation is likely to endanger the maintenance of international peace and security.

At Dumbarton Oaks and at San Francisco, Article 34 was regarded as basic to the Charter scheme for the pacific settlement of disputes,

[25] The original draft resolution mentioned only "arbitration." See SCOR/2d Yr./173d Mtg./Aug. 1, 1947/p. 1710.
[26] GAOR/7th Sess./406th Plen. Mtg./Dec. 18, 1952/para. 73.
[27] SCOR/17th Yr./1016th Mtg./June 22, 1962/para. 92.
[28] SC Res. 211, Sept. 29, 1965.
[29] See, for example, the resolution adopted by the Council following the breakdown of the "summit" conference in 1960. SCOR/15th Yr./863d Mtg./May 27, 1960/para. 48.

both from the point of view of the procedure to be followed and the special responsibilities and powers of the Security Council. It reflects the intention of those who drafted the Charter that the Security Council should deal only with the more serious disputes and situations.

The Council's authority under Article 34 is permissive. There is no obligation to carry out an investigation; it is for the Council to decide whether it will do so. Moreover, the Council itself may take the initiative; its decision to investigate is not dependent upon a request from any of the parties directly concerned.[30]

In a sense the Council begins its "investigation" when it decides to place a matter on its agenda and hear the views of the parties concerned. However, from the discussion at the San Francisco Conference, it would seem that the major powers at least envisaged that the Council would take a specific decision to undertake an investigation after a preliminary discussion of the dispute or situation. Under the "chain-of-events" thesis which they propounded in their statement on voting procedure in the Security Council, the principle of unanimity of the permanent members was not to apply to the decision to consider a matter and to hear the parties but would become applicable when the Council decided "to make an investigation." [31]

During its first year the Council tended to follow this approach; after an initial discussion the Council would decide whether it wished to undertake a formal investigation as a preliminary to making recommendations. For instance, the Council, after a preliminary discussion, in effect dismissed the Soviet complaint concerning British troops in Greece. It took similar action on the Ukrainian complaint concerning the situation in Indonesia after the majority of members rejected the proposition that the situation warranted an on-the-spot inquiry. On the other hand, in the Iranian case, the majority of members refused to accept the position that the Council could no longer deal with the case unless it decided to undertake an investigation under Article 34 or make the necessary determination that the dispute was of such a nature as to justify action by the Council under Article 33, 36, or 37.[32]

[30] For comment on the citation of Art. 34 in communications bringing disputes and situations to the Security Council's attention and on the phrase "any situation which might lead to friction or give rise to a dispute," see commentary on Art. 35.

[31] See commentary on Art. 27.

[32] See the memorandum of the Secretary-General, SCOR/1st Yr., 1st Ser./33d Mtg./Apr. 16, 1946/pp. 143–45; and the Report of the Committee of Experts, ibid., Supp. 2, Annex 29, pp. 47–50.

Powers of Investigation

Discussion in the Council concerning the application of Article 34 has centered on the establishment of subsidiary organs to carry out fact-finding functions for the Council. The first of these was established in connection with the Spanish question in April, 1946. In this instance the question of the application of Article 34 was finessed. The original Australian proposal contained a specific reference to the article and asked the proposed subcommittee to address itself to the question whether the situation "was likely to endanger the maintenance of international peace and security." These provisions were deleted from the resolution as adopted which merely provided for the appointment of a subcommittee to examine the statements that had been made, receive further statements and documents, and conduct such inquiries as it deemed necessary.[33]

Article 34 was specifically invoked later that year when the Security Council decided to establish a commission of investigation "to ascertain the facts relating to the alleged border violations along the frontier between Greece on the one hand and Albania, Bulgaria, and Yugoslavia on the other." [34] The only other time the Council has specifically invoked Article 34 was when it conferred on the India–Pakistan Commission the function of investigating "the facts pursuant to" that article.[35]

During the early years, some confusion arose from the fact that the Charter does not specifically confer a general power of investigation upon the Council. The only reference is in Article 34 which concerns an investigation for the limited purpose of determining whether the continuance of a dispute or situation is likely to endanger the maintenance of peace and security. Thus, for example, in the Greek frontier case the question was raised whether the Council could continue its investigation after having made such a determination.[36] It was generally agreed that the Council's investigatory powers were not confined to the situation described in Article 34.

The Council has established various kinds of committees and commissions for the purpose of "investigation," "observation," or the "elu-

[33] Cf. SCOR/1st Yr., 1st Ser./35th Mtg./Apr. 18, 1946/p. 198; and 39th Mtg./Apr. 29, 1946/p. 245.
[34] SCOR/1st Yr., 2d Ser./87th Mtg./Dec. 19, 1946/p. 701. An earlier proposal by the U.S. for an investigation under Art. 34 on this question had been vetoed by the Soviet Union. *Ibid.*, 70th Mtg./Sept. 20, 1946/p. 412.
[35] SCOR/3d Yr./230th Mtg./Jan. 20, 1948/p. 143.
[36] See SCOR/2d Yr./162d Mtg./July 22, 1947/pp. 1423 ff.

cidation" of facts, often with the express understanding that Article 34 is not being invoked.[37] A major controversy has arisen, however, over the distinction between a commission of "investigation" and a subsidiary body with more limited fact-finding functions. The debate does not involve the powers of the Council, but rather the applicable voting procedure in establishing subsidiary organs of the latter type.[38]

Although the competence of the Security Council to undertake an investigation has been accepted, there have been differences of opinion as to whether members are under an obligation "to accept and carry out" any decision to undertake an investigation. The Soviet Union has taken the position that such a "decision" is a "recommendation" and cannot have a "compulsory character." The United States, and many other members, have taken the contrary view. They have drawn a distinction between the Council's powers of recommendation under Articles 36 and 37 of the Charter and its powers to undertake an investigation which, they assert, would be binding upon members under Article 25.

Practice regarding Determination

From a reading of Chapter VI, it would seem clear that, to exercise its powers under Article 33(2), 36, or 37, the Council must first determine whether the continuance of a dispute or situation "is likely to endanger the maintenance of international peace and security." In practice the Council has seldom made such a finding.

There are a number of reasons why it has not done so. First, the original concept that the Council should concern itself only with disputes and situations where there is a clear danger to the maintenance of peace and security was discarded almost from the beginning. This development did not go unchallenged. During the early years there was considerable discussion as to whether the Council should confine itself to handling only those matters where the menace to peace was clear and the possibilities of settlement by other means exhausted.[39] In general, members have favored a broad interpretation of the Council's proper role. There has been a reluctance to dismiss any dispute or situation even when the danger to peace, or indeed the international character of the question, has seemed highly doubtful. On the whole, members have considered that any effort by the Council to resolve a

[37] See Goodrich and Simons, ch. viii.   [38] See commentary on Art. 27.

[39] Two of the best statements supporting a restricted interpretation of the Council's role were made by the representative of Brazil. See SCOR/2d Yr., No. 32/125th Mtg./Apr. 3, 1947/pp. 686–88; and No. 80/189th Mtg./Aug. 20, 1947/pp. 2105 ff.

dispute or ease a situation is a legitimate exercise of its powers. The case of the Israeli abduction of Adolf Eichmann from Argentina, for example, was hardly the kind of matter that the Council was intended to handle. Nonetheless, it considered Argentina's complaint and adopted a resolution declaring that such acts "cause international friction" and if repeated might "endanger international peace and security." [40]

A second factor that has mitigated against the Council's making a formal determination under Article 34 is that in most cases one of the parties involved has contended that the matter is not of such a serious nature. Under these circumstances, the Council has refrained from making a finding in order not to prejudice the possibilities of obtaining cooperation of that party in its efforts to achieve a solution.

Only once during the first ten years of its operations did the Security Council make a specific finding that a dispute was "likely to endanger the maintenance of international peace and security." This was at an early stage in the handling of the India–Pakistan question. [41] In 1956, the Council made a similar finding with respect to the breakdown of the Arab–Israeli armistice agreements. [42]

Another reason why the Council has sometimes avoided making a finding under Article 34 has been that in a number of cases disagreements have arisen as to whether the Council should take action under Chapter VI or VII. In the Indonesian case, for example, differences on this point resulted in the Council's adopting resolutions without making a finding under either Article 34 or 39 and without referring to the specific chapter of the Charter under which it was acting.

In later years, the Council did formally determine that various situations in Africa were likely to endanger the maintenance of international peace and security. [43] In 1960, it found that the situation arising from the racial policies of South Africa had led to "international friction, and if continued, might endanger the maintenance of international peace and security." [44] With regard to Angola, the Council

[40] SCOR/15th Yr./*Supp.* for Apr.–June 1960, p. 35.

[41] SCOR/3d Yr., No. 61/286th Mtg./Apr. 21, 1948/p. 40. The veto prevented adoption of resolutions on Spain and the Greek frontier case which contained similar findings.

[42] Resolution of Apr. 4, 1956 (Doc. S/3575). SCOR/11th Yr./*Supp.* for Apr., May, and June, 1956, pp. 1–2.

[43] It also characterized the situation in Cyprus as "likely to threaten international peace and security." Resolution 186, Mar. 4, 1964.

[44] SCOR/15th Yr./856th Mtg./Apr. 1, 1960/p. 14. See also subsequent resolutions that the situation in South Africa was "seriously disturbing international peace and security." SC Res. 181, Aug. 7, 1963; 182, Dec. 4, 1963; and 191, June 18, 1964.

found that the "continuance of the situation is an actual and potential cause of international friction and is likely to endanger the maintenance of international peace and security." [45] In its initial resolution on the situation in Rhodesia, the Council included a finding that "its continuance in time constitutes a threat to international peace and security." [46]

Formal findings of this kind were made in these cases largely because of disagreements among the members as to the type of action the Council should take. Many members, including most of the African states, considered that these situations were threats to the peace under Article 39 and that the Council should call for mandatory sanctions under Chapter VII. Others were unwilling to go so far. For them the purpose of the findings was to make it clear that whatever resolutions the Council adopted were in the nature of "recommendations," not binding upon members.

Article 35

1. Any Member of the United Nations may bring any dispute, or any situation of the nature referred to in Article 34, to the attention of the Security Council or of the General Assembly.

2. A state which is not a Member of the United Nations may bring to the attention of the Security Council or of the General Assembly any dispute to which it is a party if it accepts in advance, for the purposes of the dispute, the obligations of pacific settlement provided in the present Charter.

3. The proceedings of the General Assembly in respect of matters brought to its attention under this Article will be subject to the provisions of Articles 11 and 12.

Article 35 establishes the basic right of United Nations members to bring disputes or situations likely to lead to international friction to the attention of the Security Council or the General Assembly. It accords a more limited right to states that are not members of the Organization. Under Article 35, a state has a choice of bringing a matter to the Council or the Assembly. The action of the latter organ is, however, subject to the limitations imposed by Articles 11 and 12. When submitting questions of the kind covered by Chapter VI to the General As-

[45] SCOR/16th Yr./956th Mtg./June 9, 1961/pp. 29–30; and SC Res. 163, June 9, 1961. See also the Council's finding that the situation in Portugal's African territories was "seriously disturbing peace and security in Africa." SC Res. 180, July 31, 1963.

[46] SCOR/20th Yr./1258th Mtg./Nov. 12, 1965/p. 7; SC Res. 216, Nov. 12, 1965.

sembly, it is more usual for states to refer to the Assembly's broad powers under Articles 10, 11, and 14 of the Charter, although Article 35 has also been cited on occasion.[47]

Types of Disputes and Situations

Although the Charter places no restrictions on the kinds of disputes which may be brought to the attention of the Security Council,[48] the wording of Chapter VI indicates that, except in the special circumstances mentioned in Article 38, the Council is expected to take action only on those disputes the continuance of which is likely to endanger the maintenance of international peace and security.[49] The Assembly, however, is not under any such limitation.

With regard to "situations" which may be bought to the attention of the Council, Article 35 does stipulate that they must be "of the nature referred to in Article 34," that is, a situation which might "lead to international friction or give rise to a dispute." [50]

The scope of this limitation was first discussed when the Soviet Union, citing Articles 34 and 35, asked the Council to consider the question of the presence of Allied troops in non-ex-enemy territories. The discussion centered on whether this matter could be considered a "situation" within the meaning of these two articles. The Australian representative contended that a situation of the kind described in Article 34 was a "particular," not a "general world situation," and that the Soviet statement contained no "indication of where and between whom the friction is likely to arise and where and between whom the possible dispute may be occasioned." [51] Others disagreed with this "excessively narrow" interpretation of the Charter; [52] the Council, nevertheless, decided not to include the matter on its agenda. This discussion took place in the fall of 1946 before the Security Council had fully worked out its procedures. Subsequently, the Council included on its agenda a

[47] The only discussion of Art. 35 in the Assembly occurred in the debate as to whether the Interim Committee should be authorized to consider and report on questions submitted to the Assembly under that article. The Committee was given that authority but never had occasion to use it. See GA Res. 111(II), Nov. 21, 1947; and 196(III), Dec. 3, 1948.

[48] States may, of course, agree among themselves that certain disputes or categories of disputes will not be submitted to the Council. See, in this regard, the obligations of the members of OAS, commented upon under Art. 52.

[49] But see commentary on Art. 34.

[50] The phrase "international friction" was added at Dumbarton Oaks largely to insure that the Council could consider situations which might arise from the provisions of the peace treaties. Russell, pp. 459–60.

[51] SCOR/1st Yr., 2d Ser., Nos. 17–18/71st–72d Mtgs./Sept. 23–24, 1946/pp. 425, 454.

[52] See, for example, statement by France, ibid., p. 445.

number of issues fully as general in scope as the item unsuccessfully brought by the Soviet Union.

Submissions to the Security Council

If a state wishes to have a dispute or situation considered by the Security Council, the usual practice is to address a request to the President of the Council or the Secretary-General.[53] During the first ten years of the Council's operations, it was the normal practice to refer specifically to Article 35 in these communications. In later years, such references have become less frequent.[54] Generally, the submitting state gives its views as to the seriousness of the question, sometimes citing, or using the terminology of Article 34 or 39 of the Charter. Occasionally, there are also references to the efforts that have been made to comply with the obligation to seek a solution in accordance with Article 33. The submitting state may or may not indicate the action that it wishes the Council to take.[55]

Inclusion in the Agenda

Under the Council's Provisional Rules of Procedure, the President is required to call a meeting "if a dispute or situation is brought to the attention of the Security Council under Article 35" (Rule 3). The first item of business is the adoption of the agenda. In accordance with the Council's rules, the provisional agenda for each meeting is drawn up by the Secretary-General and approved by the President (Rule 7).

Not all matters that states bring to the attention of the Council are included on the provisional agenda. In some cases, a state may merely wish that its communication be circulated as a Council document. A state may address a protest or complaint to the Council without, however, requesting the Council to take action thereon. If the communication indicates that Council action is desired, the question is placed on the provisional agenda.[56]

[53] For a fuller account of the practice of submission, see Goodrich and Simons, ch. IV.

[54] Compare the "Tabulation of questions submitted to the Security Council" in *Repertory*, II, 267–70 with the tabulations in *Supp. 1*, I, 313 and *Supp. 2*, II, 374–77.

[55] A convenient analysis of the content of letters of submission can be found in the "Tabulations" cited in the preceding footnote.

[56] From reading the documents, it is not always clear why some questions have been placed on the provisional agenda while others have not. If there is any doubt as to whether consideration by the Council is desired, the matter is clarified through consultations between the President or the Secretary-General and the state concerned.

In adopting its agenda, the Council in effect decides that it will consider the matters listed thereon. This decision has been clearly established as "procedural" and consequently, no permanent member can exercise a veto. The reluctance of the Soviet Union to accept this position provoked a grave crisis at the San Francisco Conference. Most of the other delegations, particularly the United States, were adamant on this point, and the Soviet Union eventually acquiesced.[57]

While Article 35 gives a member the right to bring a dispute or situation to the attention of the Security Council, the Council itself decides whether to consider it. There have been numerous references to the "duty" of the Council to consider any matter brought to its attention by a member. Some representatives have gone so far as to argue that any such matter should be "automatically included on the agenda" and that the adoption of the agenda should be purely a matter of routine.[58]

This thesis has not been accepted by the Council, although there has been a reluctance to deny any member the right to present its complaint. During the first years, the Council seldom refused to include on its agenda a question brought to its attention by a member, although the politics of the cold war was responsible for the Council's refusal to consider a few items brought by the Soviet Union.[59] Of more significance were the Council's actions in relation to the efforts of certain African and Asian members to utilize the Council to put pressure on France to grant independence to its North African territories. Among the relatively few issues the Council has refused to consider were Tunisia (1952), Morocco (1953), and Algeria (1956).[60]

The arguments against inclusion of particular disputes or situations in the Council's agenda have varied.[61] The most frequent has been the contention that the matter referred to is "essentially within the domestic jurisdiction" of a state and that therefore its consideration by the Council would violate Article 2(7) of the Charter. This was the argument raised, for example, against consideration of the Czech coup of 1948, the Hungarian crisis of 1956, race relations in South Africa in

---

[57] See Russell, pp. 728–34.

[58] See for example, statement by Belgium in connection with the Berlin question: SCOR/3d Yr., No. 113/361st Mtg./Oct. 4, 1948/p. 16; statement by Chile on the Tunisian question: SCOR/7th Yr./574th Mtg./Apr. 5, 1952/paras. 39–51; and statement by Ghana in connection with the question of Southern Rhodesia: SCOR/18th Yr./1064th Mtg./Sept. 9, 1963/p. 4.

[59] For a listing, see Goodrich and Simons, p. 111.

[60] SCOR/7th Yr./576th Mtg./Apr. 14, 1952/paras. 121–22; 8th Yr./624th Mtg./Sept. 3, 1953/para. 45; and 11th Yr./730th Mtg./Sept. 26, 1956/para. 85.

[61] They are summarized in *Repertoire of the Security Council* under the heading "Requirements for the inclusion of an item in the agenda." See pp. 71–75, *Supp. 1*, pp. 22–25, and *Supp. 2*, pp. 30–34. They are also discussed at some length in Goodrich and Simons, pp. 113 ff.

1963, and various "colonial" questions including the above-mentioned issues concerning France's North African territories. Closely related has been the argument that no possible danger to international peace and security is involved.[62] It has also been argued that the complaint submitted to the Council is totally without foundation.

Another major ground for objections to the inclusion of items on the Council's agenda has been that a solution of the issue is being sought, or should be sought, through other procedures and that consideration of the matter by the Council would be "untimely" or "unfruitful." The Council rejected the Soviet argument that the Berlin question fell within the provenance of the Council of Foreign Ministers and that by reason of Article 107, the Council was not competent to consider it.[63] On the other hand, the desire not to interfere with negotiations was one of the arguments put forward for not considering the Tunisian question.[64] The Council has also sought to avoid any interference with the work of the General Assembly by refusing to consider certain matters being discussed by that body or reopening issues upon which the Assembly has reached a decision.[65] While all the above considerations have had an influence, it is impossible to state categorically in any particular case the specific grounds upon which the Council reached a decision not to consider a question.

The counter-arguments to the objections raised against the inclusion of a particular question on the Council's agenda have followed two lines. First, the substance of the objections has been denied; in particular states have argued that the matter is of sufficient international concern to justify consideration by the Council. Second, it has been argued that the Council should first place the item on its agenda, and then consider the various views concerning the nature of the question and whether or not any action should be taken thereon. This latter view has generally prevailed, for members have been reluctant to abridge in any way the right of members to bring matters to the attention of the Council.[66]

[62] See, for example, the discussion on the inclusion of the question of Morocco. SCOR/7th Yr./619th–624th Mtgs./Aug. 26–Sept. 3, 1953.

[63] SCOR/3d Yr., Nos. 113–14/361st and 362d Mtgs./Oct. 4–5, 1948.

[64] SCOR/7th Yr./574th–576th Mtgs./Apr. 4, 10, and 14, 1952.

[65] See, for example, the refusal to consider a USSR item concerning the non-compliance of France and the U.K. with UN resolutions on Suez: SCOR/11th Yr./758th Mtg./Nov. 5, 1956/para. 27; and refusal to consider Cuba's request regarding decisions taken at the Punta del Este Conference: SCOR/17th Yr./991st Mtg./Feb. 27, 1962/para. 144.

[66] The equitableness of this position is enhanced by the fact that only members of the Council take part in the discussion on the agenda (see commentary on Art. 32) and thus a refusal to include an item could have the effect of denying a state the right to present its case.

Consequences of the Decision

In general, the members of the Council have taken the position that in deciding to include a matter on its agenda it is not passing upon the question of its competence or upon the merits of the complaint. What then is the effect of the Council's decision? It is not a guarantee that the Council will take any action, nor does it necessarily mean that a full scale debate will take place. There is a presumption, however, that the states directly concerned will be given the opportunity to present their cases fully.

Once a question is included on the Council's agenda it is automatically included in the "Summary Statement of Matters of which the Security Council is Seized" and remains on that list until removed by the Council itself. This has consequences for the General Assembly by reason of Article 12.[67]

At an early stage the Council established that once a matter is included on its agenda, it becomes the "property" of the Council.[68] A state may indicate that it wishes to withdraw its complaint, but the Council itself decides whether the question will be taken off the agenda. In the Iranian case, the Council decided not to do so, but in the Lebanese case, it agreed to the request for removal.[69]

Submissions by Nonmembers

The Dumbarton Oaks Proposals made no distinction between the rights of members and nonmembers to bring matters to the attention of the Council or the Assembly. At San Francisco, however, there were strong objections to placing members and nonmembers on an equal basis. It was feared that a nonmember interested in discrediting the United Nations might bring questions before the Council or the Assembly with that object solely in view. Thus, it was decided to restrict the rights of nonmembers: they may bring to the attention of the Council or the Assembly only disputes to which they are parties and only if they accept in advance the obligations of pacific settlement for the purposes of the dispute.

Another cause of concern over the provisions in the Dumbarton Oaks Proposals was that the enemy states might take advantage of the right of nonmembers to seek redress through the Council or the Assembly for alleged wrongs having their origin in World War II and the

[67] See commentary on Art. 12.

[68] See discussion on the Iranian question. SCOR/1st Yr., 1st Ser./32d, 33d, and 36th Mtgs./Apr. 15, 16, and 23, 1946.

[69] SCOR/13th Yr./840th Mtg./Nov. 25, 1958.

peace settlements. The Conference decided against stating in the Charter that the enemy states would not have the right of recourse to the two organs before the peace treaties became effective. It was agreed, however, to include in the report of the committee a statement that the enemy states would not have this right until the Security Council accorded it to them.[70]

Article 35(2) has not played a very significant role in the operations of the Security Council nor has it played any role in the General Assembly. One reason is that many issues in which nonmembers have been directly involved (including ex-enemy states) have been brought to the Council or the Assembly on the initiative of member states.

In a few instances when Article 35(2) has been invoked, the question of the status of the nonmember has been raised. Iraq unsuccessfully challenged the right of Kuwait to bring a dispute before the Council on the ground that Kuwait was not a "state" as required by Article 35(2).[71] The interpretation of the term "state" was considered at length in the case of Hyderabad. Citing Article 35(2), Hyderabad in August–September, 1948, asked the Council to consider its dispute with India. In circulating this correspondence, the Secretary-General added a prefatory note to the effect that, not being in a position to determine whether the circulation of the documents was required under the Council's rules, he was bringing them to the attention of the Council for such action as it might desire to take. Despite numerous doubts about the status of Hyderabad, the question was placed on the Council's agenda.[72] Hyderabad's right to bring a matter to the Council was later contested at length by India.

A further attempt to invoke the provisions of Article 35(2) occurred in January, 1952, when the Prime Minister of Tunisia asked the Council to consider Tunisia's dispute with France. The question was not put on the provisional agenda of the Council, however, until some months later when a group of member states sought unsuccessfully to get the Council to consider the question.[73]

In each of the above instances, the communication bringing the matter to the attention of the Security Council contained a statement, in accordance with the requirements of Article 35(2), accepting for the purposes of the dispute the obligations of pacific settlement provided in the Charter.[74] The extent of these obligations has been considered

---

[70] UNCIO, *Documents*, XII, 547, 559–60.

[71] SCOR/16th Yr./957th Mtg./July 2, 1961/para. 55.

[72] SCOR/3d Yr./*Supp.* for Sept., 1948/pp. 5, 6; 357th Mtg./Sept. 16, 1948/p. 11.

[73] SCOR/7th Yr./*Supp.* for Apr.–June, 1952, pp. 9–15.

[74] See also request by Siam (Thailand) for consideration of its dispute with France. UN Doc. S/106, July 15, 1946.

by the Security Council primarily in connection with the participation of nonmembers in its discussions,[75] rather than within the context of the submission of questions by nonmembers.

One final point concerning the submission of questions by nonmembers that deserves mention is the unique position of the People's Republic of China. In the fall of 1950, the Security Council placed on its agenda two complaints by that government against the United States. In neither case was there any reference to Article 35(2) nor was there a specific acceptance of the obligations of pacific settlement. This is not surprising in view of Peiping's claims to represent China in the United Nations. The representative of Nationalist China disputed the right of the Peiping regime to bring a matter before the Council, but his arguments were overridden.[76]

Article 36

1. The Security Council may, at any stage of a dispute of the nature referred to in Article 33 or of a situation of like nature, recommend appropriate procedures or methods of adjustment.

2. The Security Council should take into consideration any procedures for the settlement of the dispute which have already been adopted by the parties.

3. In making recommendations under this Article the Security Council should also take into consideration that legal disputes should as a general rule be referred by the parties to the International Court of Justice in accordance with the provisions of the Statute of the Court.

The provisions of Article 36 were adopted at the San Francisco Conference with little debate. The three major changes made in the Dumbarton Oaks Proposals were empowering the Council to make recommendations on "situations" as well as "disputes"; the addition of the guideline incorporated in Article 36(2); and a more precise statement of the recommended procedure for handling "legal" disputes.

Under Article 36 the Council may make its recommendations "at any stage of a dispute" or "situation" the continuance of which is likely to endanger the maintenance of international peace and security. The Council itself decides when its intervention may serve a useful purpose. It need not await a request from any of the parties involved. Nonetheless, Article 36(2), as well as Article 33, implies that the Council should

[75] See commentary on Art. 32. Also see the debate on whether Jordan (then a nonmember) had accepted the obligations of pacific settlement in relation to a complaint that had been placed on the agenda by Lebanon in its behalf. SCOR/9th Yr./670th–671st Mtgs./May 4 and 12, 1954.

[76] SCOR/5th Yr./503d Mtg./Sept. 26, 1950/p. 29; and 506th Mtg./Sept. 29, 1950/p. 4.

not intervene prematurely, if reasonable progress toward settlement is being made.

As already pointed out, it is not the Council's practice to cite the specific article upon which it is basing its action or to employ the specific language of any article. Nor has the Council considered that it can only make recommendations when it has found that the continuance of the dispute or situation is "likely to endanger the maintenance of international peace and security." [77] Article 36 uses the term "recommend," but many of the Council's resolutions that could be considered as coming within the scope of the article have employed quite different verbs: "calls upon," "invites," "requests," "appeals," and even "demands."

"Appropriate Procedures and Methods of Adjustment"

Under Article 36(1), the Council may make recommendations with regard to both disputes and situations, the latter term having been added at the San Francisco Conference.[78] At that time no attempt was made to define "appropriate procedures and methods of adjustment," nor do the decisions and discussions in the Council shed much light on the meaning of the phrase.

There have been many instances where members have disagreed as to whether the Council was acting, should be acting, or had acted under Chapter VI rather than Chapter VII, but rarely have these statements referred specifically to Article 36. Nor have Council members sought to distinguish between the kinds of action the Council may take under Article 33, 36 or 37.[79] Therefore, an analysis of the kinds of resolutions the Council has adopted and the debates on them contributes little to an understanding of the interpretation and application of Article 36.

The Security Council has frequently recommended to states the procedures it considered appropriate in a given dispute or situation. It has often established machinery for implementing those procedures—commissions of good offices, mediation, conciliation, observation and peace-keeping forces. It has also entrusted the Secretary-General, the President of the Council, or other persons or groups of persons with functions of this nature.

The Council has considered that its powers under Chapter VI are sufficiently broad for it to request states to carry out provisional measures of the kind it may "call upon" them to take under Article 40. As one representative put it during the debate that followed Egypt's na-

[77] See commentary on Art. 34.   [78] Russell, p. 622.
[79] On the distinction between Arts. 36 and 37, see commentary on the latter article.

tionalization of the Suez Canal, there is "no legal problem about applying" the concept of provisional measures "from Chapter VII to the matters referred to in Chapter VI." [80] Members have also considered it appropriate for the Council under Chapter VI to call for measures similar to those listed in Article 41.[81]

Consideration of Procedures Already Adopted

Article 36(2) is another of the provisions added to the Charter at San Francisco on the initiative of the smaller powers. Their purpose was to guard against two contingencies: premature intervention by the Security Council when other procedures showed prospects of effecting a settlement; and possible attempts by states to evade their obligations under treaties for pacific settlement by invoking the Council's intervention.

Article 36(2) does not impose any restrictions upon the Council but merely states that it "should take into consideration" the procedures adopted by the parties. It does not state that the Council must be guided in its actions by this consideration. By permitting a certain degree of discretion, the flexibility of the Council's operations is maintained.

There are two points for the Council to take into consideration under Article 36(2): one is the existence of any agreements between the parties for the pacific settlement of their disputes, and the other is what procedures, if any, have already been utilized in seeking a settlement.

Seldom is any dispute brought before the Council without some effort having been made to settle it. Normally, the Council's intervention is sought on the ground that these procedures have failed or are not making satisfactory progress. In most cases, the Council's efforts have been directed toward getting the parties to resume their negotiations. Thus, for example, when the Council considered Iran's complaint against the Soviet Union in 1946, it initially confined itself to noting the "readiness" of the parties to resume negotiations.[82] To cite another case, in 1958 the Council adjourned its consideration of complaints by France and Tunisia after it was announced that the two parties had accepted the good office of the United Kingdom and the United States. Subsequently, discussions were again postponed to permit a direct exchange between the parties from which an agreement emerged.[83]

The clearest manifestations of concern for "procedures . . . al-

[80] See statement by Belgium: SCOR/11th Yr./743d Mtg./Oct. 13, 1956/paras. 62–65; and statements by Peru: *ibid.*, paras. 86–89; and the U.S., para. 12.

[81] See commentary on that article.

[82] SCOR/1st Yr., 1st Ser., No. 1/5th Mtg./Jan. 30, 1946/pp. 70, 71.

[83] SCOR/13th Yr./811th Mtg./Feb. 18, 1958/p. 9; 821st Mtg./June 4, 1958/p. 12; and 14th Yr./926th Mtg./June 18, 1959/p. 3.

ready . . . adopted" have occurred in connection with the operations of regional agencies. This is in accordance with the place the Charter assigns to the pacific settlement of local disputes through such agencies and also reflects the obligations members themselves have assumed under regional agreements. Members of the Council have generally been reluctant to intervene in any way with the procedures of regional organizations, even when one of the parties concerned has so requested.[84] But the Council has not considered that it must refrain from acting because of the existence of agreements among the parties.

The dispute between the Netherlands and Indonesia provides a good illustration of the complexity of the relationship between action by the Council and procedures agreed to by the parties. The original draft resolution before the Council called upon the parties to settle their dispute by arbitration in accordance with the Linggadjati agreement which they had concluded some months previously. In part because the Netherlands insisted that arbitration under the circumstances would be unsuitable, the resolution was broadened to call for settlement "by arbitration or by other peaceful means." Subsequent efforts to refer the issues in dispute to arbitration failed. The Netherlands opposed arbitration and many members considered that the Council could not "impose" a particular procedure on the parties, even in the light of a previous agreement between them. The dispute was therefore handled not by arbitration but through a Committee of Good Offices to which the parties agreed.[85]

The importance which the Security Council has attached to any agreements reached under its own auspices was demonstrated at a later stage in this dispute when the Council sought to uphold the status of agreements concluded by the parties through the efforts of the Council's Committee of Good Offices. A similar concern has been repeatedly shown for the agreements between India and Pakistan that were likewise concluded under the auspices of the Council and its agents. The most striking illustration is the consistent effort the Council has made to uphold the armistice agreements concluded between Israel and its Arab neighbors on orders from the Council. The Council has avoided any action that might undermine the position of the Truce Supervision Organization, refusing in some instances to act on complaints which it felt should be handled through the machinery established in the armistice agreements.

The Security Council has shown a similar respect for agreements worked out by the parties with the assistance of the Secretary-General.

[84] See commentary on Art. 52.
[85] See SCOR/2d Yr./171st Mtg./July 31, 1947/p. 1626; 173d Mtg./Aug. 1, 1947/p. 1839; 193d Mtg./Aug. 22, 1947/p. 2174; and 194th Mtg./Aug. 25, 1947/pp. 2203–4, 2209.

In connection with the Suez Canal question, for example, the Council approved the principles which the Secretary-General had worked out with Egypt on the one hand, and Britain and France on the other.[86] In the case of the arrangements for handling the situation in Yemen in 1963, the Council in fact merely gave its endorsement to arrangements worked out by the Secretary-General with the parties before the matter was brought to the Council.[87] In taking into consideration procedures or agreements already accepted by the parties, the Council has acted in accordance with the generally accepted view that its primary duty is to assist the parties themselves to reach agreement.

"Legal" Disputes

A second guideline for the Security Council to take into consideration in making recommendations for the pacific settlement of disputes is laid down in Article 36(3), which states that "legal disputes should as a general rule be referred by the parties to the International Court of Justice." The attempt to draw a distinction between "legal" and other kinds of disputes is as old as the effort to establish international machinery for pacific settlement. Generally "legal" disputes have been considered as those in which the parties are in dispute over conflicting claims of legal right; their solution is to be sought in the established rules of international law. In the case of other disputes, sometimes referred to as "political," the disagreement relates not to the application of international law but rather to the adequacy of the existing legal order. The disagreement arises from dissatisfaction with the applicable rules of law. The factors of "justice" and "expediency," rather than law, govern the search for a solution.

The distinction between the two categories of disputes is less emphasized in the Charter than it was in the Covenant of the League of Nations. Under the Covenant, members of the League agreed that, whenever any dispute suitable for arbitration or judicial settlement should arise between them which they were unable to settle by diplomacy, they would submit "the whole subject-matter" to arbitration or judicial settlement. Certain categories of disputes were declared to be "generally suitable" for settlement by these procedures.[88] The Charter does not contain a comparable provision.

Although many of the early United States plans for a postwar organization empowered the Council under certain circumstances to refer

[86] SCOR/11th Yr./*Supp.* for Oct.–Dec., 1956, pp. 47–48.

[87] SCOR/18th Yr./1038th Mtg./June 11, 1953/p. 9; and 1039th Mtg./June 11, 1963/p. 2.

[88] See Art. 13(2), which uses the same terms as Art. 36 of the Statute of the Court employs regarding the compulsory jurisdiction of the Court.

disputes to the Court,[89] this approach was later abandoned. The Dumbarton Oaks Proposals merely stated that "justiciable disputes should normally be referred to the international court of justice." [90]

At the San Francisco Conference, an effort was made to require the Council to refer justiciable disputes to the Court, but this move was unsuccessful, as was a related attempt to make the Court's jurisdiction compulsory.[91] Indeed, the Dumbarton Oaks text was revised to make it absolutely clear that the Council could not itself refer a dispute to the Court but could only recommend this procedure to the parties.[92]

That the Council under Article 36(3) can do no more than make a recommendation which the parties are free to accept or reject was made clear in the Corfu Channel dispute. The case was brought to the Council by the United Kingdom. Albania (a nonmember of the United Nations), in accepting an invitation to participate in the discussion, agreed to accept for the purposes of the dispute the Charter "obligations of pacific settlement." [93] After the Council recommended that the parties "immediately refer the dispute" to the International Court, the United Kingdom argued that the Council's resolution had established the Court's jurisdiction. Although the Court itself found it unnecessary to rule on this point, seven of the judges stated that it was "improper" to accept an interpretation according to which Article 36(3) introduced a new case of compulsory jurisdiction.[94]

The Corfu Channel case is the only instance in which the Council has recommended that a dispute be referred to the Court, and it did so only after the Soviet Union had vetoed a draft resolution recommending that the parties settle the dispute on the basis of a finding by the Council as to Albania's liability.[95]

Proposals that the Council recommend the reference of a dispute to the International Court have been made on two other occasions.[96] A proposal by Belgium recommending that the parties refer to the Court any dispute over the validity of the Anglo–Egyptian Treaty of 1936 failed to get majority support.[97] The Soviet Union vetoed a United States proposal that complaints concerning the violation of Soviet airspace by American aircraft be resolved either through a fact-finding

[89] See Russell, pp. 284, 289, and 296–97.   [90] Ch. VIII, sec. A.7.

[91] See commentary on ch. XIV.

[92] See Russell, pp. 604–5 and 661; and UNCIO, *Documents*, XII, 161. Note also that the term "justiciable" was changed to "legal."

[93] See commentary on Art. 32.

[94] See SCOR/2d Yr., No. 34/127th Mtg./Apr. 9, 1947/p. 727; Corfu Channel case, "Judgment on Preliminary Objection," *ICJ Reports*, 1948, pp. 31, 32; and *ICJ Yearbook*, 1947–48, pp. 55–60.

[95] SCOR/2d Yr., No. 29/122d Mtg./Mar. 25, 1947/p. 609.

[96] See also the Colombian proposal for possible use of the Court in connection with the dispute between India and Pakistan. SCOR/12th Yr./771st Mtg./Feb. 18, 1957/p. 3; and 773d Mtg./Feb. 20, 1957/pp. 28–29.

[97] SCOR/2d Yr., No. 86/198th Mtg./Aug. 28, 1947/p. 2302.

commission or through reference to the International Court for impartial adjudication.[98]

That the Council has so seldom considered recommending the reference of disputes to the International Court is due to a number of factors,[99] including the nature of the disputes submitted to it and the fact that in few instances have the parties directly concerned accepted the jurisdiction of the Court. The general reluctance of the Council to adopt a legal as opposed to a political approach to the problems submitted to it is further reflected in its failure to exercise its right to request advisory opinions from the Court on legal questions.[100]

Article 37

1. Should the parties to a dispute of the nature referred to in Article 33 fail to settle it by the means indicated in that Article, they shall refer it to the Security Council.

2. If the Security Council deems that the continuance of the dispute is in fact likely to endanger the maintenance of international peace and security, it shall decide whether to take action under Article 36 or to recommend such terms of settlement as it may consider appropriate.

The obligations of states under Article 33 and the powers of the Security Council under Article 36 of the Charter are further extended by the terms of Article 37. Paragraph 1 of that article is the only provision in the Charter that requires a member to submit an issue to the Security Council for settlement, and it applies to a limited range of questions.[101] States are obligated to refer to the Council "disputes" to which they are parties but only if the continuance of the dispute is "likely to endanger the maintenance of international peace and security" and only if efforts to settle it by the peaceful means listed in Article 33 have failed.

The obligation set forth in Article 37(1) was included in the Dumbarton Oaks Proposals and was accepted without opposition at the San Francisco Conference. The question was raised, however, whether both sides had to agree to submit the dispute to the Council. It was agreed that, if one party failed to discharge its obligations, this would not affect the right of the other party to seize the Council of the dispute.[102]

The decision at San Francisco to empower the Security Council to

[98] SCOR/15th Yr./883d Mtg./July 26, 1960/p. 39.
[99] On the general question of the role of judicial settlement see ch. xiv.
[100] See commentary on Art. 96.
[101] Cf. Arts. 12, 13, and 15 of the League Covenant.
[102] UNCIO, *Documents*, XII, 47.

recommend terms of settlement represented an extension of the Council's role in the pacific settlement process. The Dumbarton Oaks Proposals contained no specific provision for the Council to make recommendations of this kind.[103] The Proposals did provide that, if the Council deemed that the failure to settle a dispute constituted "a threat to the maintenance of international peace and security, it should take any measures necessary for the maintenance of international peace and security in accordance with the purposes and principles of the Organization." [104] This power was certainly broad enough to encompass "terms of settlement." Those opposing this provision wished to make it absolutely clear that the Council could not under any circumstances impose a settlement on the parties. Others considered that the Council's authority in the field of pacific settlement should not be restricted to recommending procedures of settlement but should, under certain circumstances, be extended to include terms of settlement as well.[105]

As a result of consultations with other Commonwealth countries prior to the San Francisco Conference, the British delegation pressed for broadening the authority of the Security Council in the field of pacific settlement to include recommendations of terms of settlement.[106] Within the United States delegation, those who opposed this move argued that the appropriate function of the Council was maintaining peace, and that settling of disputes should remain the responsibility of the parties concerned. They maintained that the Council should confine itself to encouraging the parties to reach agreement unless a threat to the peace developed, and that it should not recommend terms which it could not enforce.[107] This view was not pressed, however, partly because of the realization that the British proposal had broad support among the smaller powers. The proposal was accepted by the Sponsoring Powers and subsequently by the Conference as a whole.

Under the terms of Article 37(2), the Security Council has the choice of taking "action under Article 36" or of recommending "such terms of settlement as it may consider appropriate." One distinction between Articles 36 and 37 is that under the former the Council "may" make recommendations, while in the circumstances described in Article 37(1) it is required to do so. In practice this distinction has not been of significance. Moreover, the position of the parties is the same in either case in that the Council's recommendations have no binding effect.

[103] See, however, earlier U.S. plans that gave the Council authority in this regard. Russell, pp. 287 and 293.

[104] Ch. VIII, sec. B.1.   [105] See Russell, pp. 600–4.

[106] See also below on the inclusion of Art. 38 in the Charter.

[107] See Russell, pp. 662–65.

It is difficult to assess what effect, if any, Article 37 has had upon the Council's operations. It has never been cited in any of the Council's resolutions. In no case has the discussion indicated a consensus that the Council was exercising, or should be exercising, its authority under Article 37, although in some instances the opinion has been expressed that the point has not yet been reached for the application of Article 37. Thus, for example, in opposing a proposal calling for the withdrawal of French forces from Tunisia at the time of the Bizerte crisis, the United States representative expressed the view that the Council's proper role at that stage was to recommend appropriate procedures of adjustment in accordance with Article 36, "rather than to move prematurely to recommend terms of settlement under Article 37." [108]

The question arises whether the Security Council may exercise its authority under Article 37 unless it is seized of a matter in accordance with paragraph 1. Despite the categorical language in which the obligation of states is set forth in Article 37(1), only rarely has this article been cited by a state in bringing a matter to the Council's attention.[109] Frequently, however, one party has claimed that the dispute is likely to endanger the maintenance of international peace and security and that the efforts to settle it by peaceful means have failed, claims usually challenged by the other party. It would not appear that the Council's actions have been much influenced by either the explicit or implicit reference to Article 37 by one of the parties. More specifically, the manner in which a question has been brought to the Council has had no apparent bearing upon the actions it has taken. On more than one occasion, members of the Council have asserted that it is for the Council itself to judge its competence and that it can on its own initiative use the powers bestowed upon it by Article 37.[110]

The wording of Article 37 leads to the conclusion that for the Council to exercise its authority under this article, the members must be satisfied that the efforts of the parties to settle the dispute by peaceful means have failed and that the continuance of the dispute is "in fact" likely to endanger the maintenance of international peace and security. Generally, the Council has been very reluctant to reach either of these conclusions.

When the Council has expressed its opinion as to the basis upon which a dispute should be settled, it has at the same time urged the parties to continue their negotiations, either directly or under UN auspices. Moreover, the adoption of a resolution indicating the basis for

[108] SCOR/16th Yr./963d Mtg./July 22, 1961/p. 13.

[109] One example was the submission by Egypt of its dispute with the United Kingdom. SCOR/2d Yr./159th Mtg./July 17, 1947/pp. 1343–45.

[110] See, for example, statement by Peru. SCOR/11th Yr./737th Mtg./Oct. 8, 1956/paras. 26–34.

settlement is usually preceded by extensive efforts, generally informal, to get the parties to agree. For example, at an early stage in the handling of the India–Pakistan question, when the President reported on his conversations with the parties, the question was raised whether in view of the inability of the parties to agree, the Council had reached the point where it was obligated to recommend terms of settlement under Article 37.[111] The conversations were continued and before the Council adopted its comprehensive resolution of April 21, 1948, the President reported that the parties had been informed that in the event of their failure to agree the matter would be placed before the Council with recommendations concerning "articles of settlement." [112]

The adoption of this resolution is one of the few instances where the Council has made a formal determination that the continuation of a dispute was "likely to endanger international peace and security." [113] In 1957, the representative of Pakistan, after reviewing the long history of unsuccessful efforts to settle the controversy and concluding that all the processes for peaceful settlement had been exhausted, asked the Security Council to exercise its authority under Article 37(2) and spell out the measures the parties should take in order to bring about a solution.[114] In opposition to this course of action, the Indian representative pointed out that his government had originally brought the question as a "situation" and that the Council's resolution labeling it a "dispute" had been adopted over India's objections.[115] The Council in this instance did not endorse a specific proposal to which India objected, but it did continue in its resolutions to refer to the question as a "dispute."

Article 37 does not refer to "situations" but only to "disputes," and indeed to only a limited category of disputes. In practice, these distinctions do not seem to have had a significant effect upon the kinds of resolutions the Council has adopted. Following the second Dutch police action in Indonesia, for example, the Council in its resolution of January 28, 1949, dealt in considerable detail with the basis upon which it considered the matter should be settled. The Council had previously characterized the question as a "dispute" but had never found that it was "likely to endanger the maintenance of international peace and security." On a number of other occasions the Council has been asked to endorse a particular basis for settlement for a question

[111] SCOR/3d Yr./236th Mtg./Jan. 28, 1948/pp. 278–79.
[112] Ibid., 286th Mtg./Apr. 21, 1948/p. 3; and 284th Mtg./Apr. 17, 1948/p. 3.
[113] SCOR/3d Yr., No. 61/286th Mtg./Apr. 21, 1948/p. 40. Note the language used is that of Art. 34 not Art. 37, i.e., the phrase "in fact" was not included.
[114] SCOR/12th Yr./761st Mtg./Jan. 16, 1957/para. 112.
[115] Ibid., 762d Mtg./Jan. 23, 1957/para. 11.

which has been submitted as a "situation" and which the Council has never characterized as a "dispute." [116]

It should be noted that in no case has the Security Council ever declared that it was recommending "terms of settlement." In introducing the April 21, 1948, resolution on the India–Pakistan question, the President of the Council referred to the proposed recommendations as "articles of settlement," [117] but this term was not used in the resolution recommending "measures" which in the Council's opinion were "appropriate" to bring about a solution of the controversy. The Council's resolution of January 28, 1949, on the Indonesian question recommended in detail the "basis" on which a settlement should be negotiated.[118] Similarly, in the Suez case the Council agreed upon a set of "requirements" that should be met for "any settlement" of the question.[119]

In general, the members of the Council have not found it necessary to distinguish whether a proposal it was considering should be construed as a recommendation of "appropriate procedures" or "terms of settlement." In practice, the distinction is not likely to be clear cut. Nor has there been much discussion of the range of measures that it would be appropriate for the Council to recommend under Article 37.

In recommending or urging the parties to adopt a particular procedure, the Council has felt free to express its opinion on the substantive issues of the dispute but in general it has been reluctant to pass judgment on the merits of differing positions taken by the parties, preferring to emphasize the need for the parties themselves to reach agreement.

Article 38

Without prejudice to the provisions of Articles 33 to 37, the Security Council may, if all the parties to any dispute so request, make recommendations to the parties with a view to a pacific settlement of the dispute.

Article 38 is another of the provisions added to the Charter at the San Francisco Conference with a view to enlarging the range of activities of the Security Council in the field of pacific settlement. It was included in the Charter on the initiative of the Commonwealth coun-

---

[116] See, for example, the Anglo-French proposal of Oct. 13, 1956, on the Suez Canal. SCOR/11th Yr./*Supp.* for Oct.–Dec., 1956, pp. 19–20.

[117] SCOR/3d Yr., No. 59/286th Mtg./Apr. 21, 1948/p. 3.

[118] SCOR/4th Yr./*Supp.* for Feb., 1949/p. 2–3.

[119] SCOR/11th Yr./*Supp.* for Oct.–Dec., 1956/pp. 47–48.

tries.[120] This article differs from the other provisions of Chapter VI in that it authorizes the Council to make recommendations for the pacific settlement of a dispute, regardless of whether its continuance is likely to endanger the maintenance of international peace and security. In further contrast to other provisions of Chapter VI, Article 38 places no restrictions on the kinds of recommendations the Security Council may make. Thus, Article 38 constitutes a departure from the original concept of the Security Council as a body which should concern itself only with serious dangers to the peace; it represents another concession to the view that the Council should be available to render whatever assistance it can in ironing out differences among states. It should be noted, however, that the Council itself decides what, if any, action it will take; it may make recommendations but is under no obligation to do so.

The Charter stipulates that for the Council to make recommendations under Article 38 it must be requested to do so by all of the parties concerned. There has never been a case where all parties have joined in bringing a dispute before the Council, although there have been a number of instances where each party separately has sought to enlist its support. Both India and Pakistan, for example, brought charges against each other before the Council. This fact, as well as the fact that the Council acted originally upon the basis of conversations between the President and the two parties, prompted some references to Article 38 during the debate.[121] In the Indonesian case the United States representative expressed the view that since both parties had accepted the Council's offer of good offices, the dispute fell "under Article 38" of the Charter, and the Council therefore had the same authority as it would have had if the parties themselves had submitted a request to it.[122]

While it was undoubtedly intended that the Council should act under Article 38 only on the basis of a specific request from the parties, the above interpretation by the United States is in line with the Council's general approach of searching out and building upon areas of agreement between the parties. Since action by the Council under Article 38 is based upon agreement, it offers a means for by-passing the sticky question of domestic jurisdiction, for it should be noted that it contains no reference to the "international" character of the dispute.

Article 38 refers only to "recommendations." Nonetheless, it has been viewed as a means by which the Council might act in an arbitral

<hr>

[120] See Russell, pp. 662–63.

[121] See SCOR/3d Yr., Nos. 16–35/245th Mtg./Feb. 11, 1948/pp. 115, 116 (Colombia); and No. 74/304th Mtg./May 26, 1948/p. 21 (U.S.).

[122] SCOR/3d Yr., Nos. 16–35/251st Mtg./Feb. 21, 1948/p. 212.

capacity, that is, the parties might agree in advance not only to refer the dispute to the Council but also to be bound by its recommendations. The possibility that the Council could act under Article 38 in ways not normally open to it was raised during the discussion in the Interim Committee of the General Assembly on means for improving procedures of pacific settlement. It was pointed out that states are free to make arrangements among themselves to confer specific powers on the Security Council and it was suggested that in doing so, states consider the possibility of agreeing in advance to accept recommendations supported by a majority of Council members, even if the particular proposal was vetoed.[123]

Article 38 offers numerous opportunities for expanding the role of the Council in the pacific settlement of disputes. Thus far in the practice of the Council, however, these opportunities have remained unexplored.

[123] Suggestion by Belgium. See UN Doc. A/AC.18/54, Mar. 20, 1948.

CHAPTER VII

Action with Respect to Threats to the Peace, Breaches of the Peace, and Acts of Aggression

Paramount in the minds of the drafters of the Charter was the establishment of a system for the maintenance of peace and security that would be more effective than the League system had been. Under the Covenant, members of the League were obligated to "respect and preserve as against external aggression the territorial integrity and existing political independence" of all other members and to take "immediately" certain economic and financial measures against any member resorting to war in violation of its obligations under the Covenant.[1] These obligations were considerably weakened by subsequent "interpretations" and in practice sanctions were never fully applied.

The Charter enjoins members from "the threat or use of force against the territorial integrity or political independence of any state,"[2] but they are under no obligation to take action against a state violating this commitment unless the Security Council has taken a decision to that effect.

In contrast to the decentralized League system, the drafters of the Charter sought to concentrate the decision-making power in the Security Council. It would decide whether a threat to the peace, breach of the peace, or act of aggression had occurred and would also decide on the measures that should be taken to maintain or restore international peace and security. Members were obligated to accept and carry out these decisions and to make armed forces available to the Council in accordance with special agreements to be concluded once the Charter came into effect.[3] The ability to take military enforcement measures was viewed as a substantial advance over the League system.

---

[1] Arts. 10 and 16. They were not, however, obligated to take military measures.
[2] See commentary on Art. 2(4).   [3] See commentary on Art. 43.

The importance attached to the Council's power to order military measures did not stem from expectations that it would often be necessary to do so. The threat of military action, it was felt, would be a powerful inducement to states to comply with whatever measures the Council considered necessary to maintain or restore international peace and security. It would also serve to deter states from aggressive acts and would be an added incentive to settle disputes by peaceful means.

Another essential difference between the League and United Nations systems lay in the special position accorded to the major powers. The rule of unanimity that prevailed under the Covenant was discarded, but concurrence of the five permanent members was required for any decision by the Council under Chapter VII of the Charter.[4] Thus, the Council could not take action against any of the major powers. These powers were also free from commitment to take enforcement measures to which they had not given express consent, a point of particular importance to the United States. The requirement of great power unity was not, however, viewed solely as a protection for the major powers. It was also looked upon as a means of assuring their unity and of protecting other states, and the Organization itself from becoming involved in a conflict between them. In short, the drafters of the Charter recognized that it was unrealistic to attempt to establish a system of United Nations enforcement action which would be effective in the event a major power violated the peace. Indeed, most felt that the United Nations should not attempt to take action if those powers were not in agreement.

The Discussion at San Francisco

Although smaller states at the San Francisco Conference could accept the basic elements of this system for maintaining peace and security, they had certain apprehensions about the concentration of power in a body so dominated by the great powers. They feared that their interests might not be adequately protected, that the Council might fail to discharge its responsibilities, or that the great powers might attempt to impose their political solutions without due regard to the concerns of other states.

To achieve wider participation in the decisions of the Council or, alternatively, to limit the amount of discretionary power vested in an organ under the dominant influence of the major powers, a number of amendments were proposed to the Dumbarton Oaks text. These had as specific objectives increasing the size of the Council, allowing members of the Organization not members of the Council to participate in its

[4] See commentary on Art. 27(3).

discussions and decisions under certain circumstances, defining aggression, and giving greater assurance that Council decisions would not be arbitrary in nature.

These proposals for the most part were successfully resisted by the Sponsoring Governments and France. A concession was made with respect to participation in decisions regarding the use of armed force by a member "not represented" on the Council.[5] Furthermore, the Dumbarton Oaks text was revised to eliminate the provision expressly permitting the Security Council to determine that a failure to settle a dispute under Chapter VI was a threat to international peace and security, and assurance was given that recommendations for settlement under Chapter VI were not binding. Although the proposal to define aggression received considerable support, the view in the end prevailed that an exhaustive listing of acts of aggression was not possible, and that a partial listing would be more harmful than useful.[6] It was also emphasized that the Council should not be expected to discharge its responsibilities in an arbitrary manner since under the terms of Article 24 it was required to act "in accordance with the Purposes and Principles of the United Nations."

Relationship to Article 2(7)

Under the Dumbarton Oaks Proposals, the "domestic jurisdiction" clause was included in the provisions for the pacific settlement of disputes. At San Francisco it was decided to transfer this provision to the chapter on purposes and principles to make it clear that the injunction against intervention in domestic matters applied to the whole range of the Organization's activities.[7] This necessitated the inclusion of an exception to the effect that the principle "shall not prejudice the application of enforcement measures under Chapter VII." Thus, the Council's actions under Articles 41 and 42 are exempt from the "domestic jurisdiction" clause, but this exception does not extend to all actions by the Council under Chapter VII.

Obviously, any situation which the Council finds to be a "threat to the peace, breach of the peace, or act of aggression," could scarely be considered a "matter within the domestic jurisdiction" of any state regardless of the source of danger. It is so patently a matter of international concern that the Council is under an obligation to take the necessary measures to maintain or restore international peace and security. Nonetheless, there is a question as to the extent to which the domestic jurisdiction clause limits the actions, short of enforcement

[5] See commentary on Art. 44.   [6] See commentary on Art. 39.
[7] See commentary on Art. 2(7).

measures, that the Council make take.[8] In practice, claims based upon Article 2(7) have had very limited effect upon the Council's actions, and their persuasiveness tends to diminish as the gravity of the situation increases.

Article 39

The Security Council shall determine the existence of any threat to the peace, breach of the peace, or act of aggression and shall make recommendations, or decide what measures shall be taken in accordance with Articles 41 and 42, to maintain or restore international peace and security.

"If any single provision of the Charter has more substance than the others," stated the United States Secretary of State shortly after the Charter was adopted, "it is this one sentence." [9] The Secretary was giving expression to the hopes that the powers and responsibilities vested in the Security Council under Article 39 would provide an effective basis for maintaining international peace and security.

The responsibilities of the Council under this article are twofold: first, to determine the existence of a threat to the peace, breach of the peace, or act of aggression; and second, to make recommendations and decide on measures to maintain or restore international peace and security.

Responsibility for Making a Determination

Article 39 states that the Council "shall" make the determination called for in that article. There have been numerous statements that the Council has a duty to make such a determination whenever the circumstances so indicate, and that this is a responsibility it cannot evade. Admittedly, a measure of discretion is always involved in evaluating the facts of a situation, and the lack of any definition or consensus concerning the meaning of the terms used in Article 39 leaves considerable room for subjective political judgments.

It has, moreover, been argued that regardless of the circumstances, the Council should not make a determination under Article 39 unless members are prepared to apply the additional measures listed in Chapter VII. This point was raised during the early handling of the Palestine question, when members were particularly concerned over the fact that the Council did not have at its disposal the armed forces that were

[8] This has arisen principally in connection with "provisional measures." See commentary on Art. 40.

[9] State Dept., *Report to the President*, p. 90.

to be made available to it under Article 43. On the other hand, it was argued that the Council had no discretion in the matter but had a duty to make the required determination.[10] While this issue was not raised so directly in later discussions, it is clear that the reluctance of members to make a determination under Article 39 has been frequently affected by their unwillingness to embark upon a course that might require the application of enforcement measures. This has been particularly apparent in relation to certain African questions, such as South Africa, Angola, and Rhodesia.[11]

It has been frequently stated that the Council has the sole responsibility for making a determination under Article 39. During the discussion on the Greek frontier incidents, the Soviet Union, for example, argued that this responsibility could not be delegated to a commission of the Council, and that a subsidiary body could not be authorized to make a finding which would bind the Council in any way. It was also argued that the Council had to make its determination in the light of the particular circumstances of the situation and could not bind itself in advance to consider some act as a threat to the peace, breach of the peace, or act of aggression.[12]

Although many members in bringing complaints to the Security Council have alleged the existence of a situation of the nature described in Article 39, these claims do not appear to have had any effect upon the way in which the Council has proceeded to deal with the question. The Council has taken the same attitude toward findings by the General Assembly. It is accepted that such findings are not binding upon the Council, which must make its own determination as to the nature of the situation.

In adopting the Palestine partition resolution, the Assembly requested the Council to consider whether the situation in Palestine during the transitional period (if circumstances required) constituted a "threat to the peace" and, if so, to take the measures necessary under Articles 39 and 41 to empower the United Nations Palestine Commission to carry out its mandate. It further asked the Council to determine as a threat to the peace, breach of the peace, or act of aggression, any attempt to alter by force the settlement envisaged in the resolution.[13] The Commission later reported that it was impossible to implement the resolution unless the Council took measures, including the use of force

[10] See in particular statements in SCOR/3d Yr./296th Mtg./May 19, 1948/p. 6 (U.S.); 298th Mtg./May 20, 1948/pp. 15–20 (France); and 309th Mtg./May 20, 1948/pp. 13–15 (Belgium) and pp. 10–13 (U.K.).
[11] See commentary on Arts. 34 and 36.
[12] SCOR/2d Yr./159th Mtg./July 17, 1947/p. 1353 (Poland); and 160th Mtg./July 17, 1947/pp. 1377–78 (USSR).
[13] GA Res. 181A(II), Nov. 29, 1947.

if necessary, to maintain order and security in the area. The Council first considered whether it would be justified in finding a "threat to the peace." It was argued that the Council had the authority to prevent the use of force to obstruct the carrying out of the settlement but that it had no authority to enforce a political settlement.[14] The Council did not make the determination the Assembly requested, but subsequently, when the problem of containing hostilities in the area became more acute, the Council made its own determination that the situation constituted a "threat to the peace." [15] In other circumstances where the Assembly has drawn the Council's attention to a situation which it deemed a "threat to the peace," [16] the Council has not accepted the Assembly's characterization of the situation.

Although Article 39 states that the Security Council shall determine the existence of a threat to the peace, breach of the peace, or act of aggression, the Assembly has considered that it also has a right to make such a determination. As mentioned above, it has done so in calling matters to the Council's attention and in attempting to induce that organ to apply sanctions. It has also made such findings as a basis for its own recommendations as to the measures that should be taken to deal with the situation.[17] Under the Uniting for Peace resolution,[18] the Assembly asserted its authority to recommend collective measures in the event of a breach of the peace or act of aggression whenever the Council failed to exercise its primary responsibility because of disagreement among the permanent members. Thus, for example, the Assembly made a finding of aggression in the case of Communist Chinese military intervention in Korea after the Council found itself unable to act.[19]

Threats to the Peace

The Charter does not define a threat to the peace, breach of the peace, or act of aggression. No definition of these terms was accepted at San Francisco, and the effort to define them in the United Nations has been unfruitful. The distinctions between these three terms have not, however, been as much a source of controversy as the distinction

[14] SCOR/3d Yr./253d Mtg./Feb. 24, 1948/pp. 264–69 (U.S.).

[15] UN Doc. S/902, July 15, 1948.

[16] See, for example, its resolution on South West Africa: GA Res. 1899(XVIII), Nov. 13, 1963 and 2074(XX), Dec. 17, 1965; on South Africa: GA Res. 2054(XX), Dec. 15, 1965; on Rhodesia: GA Res. 2022(XX), Nov. 5, 1965; on the Portuguese territories: GA Res. 1742(XVI), Jan. 30, 1963.

[17] In addition to the cases mentioned in the preceding footnote, see, for example, its resolution on Algeria: GA Res. 1573(XV), Dec. 19, 1960.

[18] GA Res. 377(V), Nov. 3, 1950.

[19] GA Res. 498(V), Feb. 1, 1951.

between a "threat to the peace" under Article 39 and a dispute or situation the continuance of which is "likely to endanger the maintenance of international peace and security," the language used in Article 34.

The issue first arose in connection with the Spanish question where the difference of view centered on how immediate a threat the Franco regime posed. While some members favored the application of Articles 39 and 41, the majority considered that the Franco regime was only a "potential" threat to the peace and that the Council should deal with the matter under Chapter VI as a situation of the nature described in Article 34.[20] The proposal supported by the majority was vetoed, and a proposal under Chapter VII failed to receive sufficient votes for adoption.

The Council was similarly unable to take action on the Greek frontier incidents question, although in this case the majority of members approved the finding that support of the kind Albania, Bulgaria, and Yugoslavia were giving to guerrilla bands operating in Greece constituted a "threat to the peace" within the meaning of the Charter.[21]

The question of what constitutes a "threat to the peace" was discussed at length during the early handling of the Palestine situation. As already mentioned, the Council did not make the determination the Assembly requested. During the debate the United Kingdom stressed that any threat to the peace must be a threat to international peace. The United States, however, contended that internal disorders and incursions by armed bands could constitute a threat to the peace and pointed out that Article 39 did not specify a threat to "international" peace.[22] The initial attempt to invoke Article 39 failed to secure the necessary number of votes, and it was not until efforts to bring about a permanent cease-fire between Israel and the Arab states had failed that the Council declared that the situation constituted a "threat to the peace." [23]

For the next several years, the Council had few occasions to concern itself with the definition of a "threat to the peace." When the African and Asian states began to bring pressure upon the Council to apply Chapter VII to various situations in southern Africa, the debate was resumed. The Western powers were unwilling to consider that the racial policies of South Africa, no matter how deplorable, could be

[20] See, in particular, the report of the Council's subcommittee. SCOR/1st Yr., 1st Ser./*Special Supp.*, 1946; and the debate thereon, 45th–48th Mtgs./June 13, 17, and 24, 1946.

[21] SCOR/2d Yr./170th Mtg./July 29, 1947; and 188th Mtg./Aug. 19, 1947.

[22] See SCOR/3d Yr./296th and 298th Mtgs./May 19 and 20, 1948.

[23] *Ibid.*, 302d Mtg./May 22, 1948/p. 54; 388th Mtg./July 15, 1948/p. 66.

considered as a "threat to the peace." They were similarly disinclined to view the actions taken by the Rhodesian government [24] or by Portugal in its African colonies in this light. The African and Asian members, backed by the Soviet Union, emphasized the serious effects these policies were having on Africa as a whole and considered the application of sanctions against them essential for maintaining the peace of the continent. The Western powers were unwilling, however, to back resolutions that went beyond the scope of Chapter VI.[25] In connection with the situation in the Congo the Council adopted a finding that international peace and security were threatened.[26]

Breaches of the Peace

Various kinds of acts could be considered as constituting breaches of the peace. At the least, it would seem logical that any resort to armed force would come within the scope of the phrase. As one representative on the Security Council put it: "If military operations by one country against another cannot be called a breach of international peace, then I am at a loss to know what could be called a breach of the peace." [27]

Even when there has been no doubt that the use of armed force has gone beyond local skirmishes, the Council members have been reluctant to make a formal finding of a breach of peace. Disagreement among the members, especially the permanent members, as to the respective responsibilities of the parties involved has been a major reason for the Council's inaction.

In the case of the hostilities in Indonesia, Australia sought to get around this problem by proposing that the Council declare a "breach of the peace" without, however, assessing responsibility. A "breach of the peace," it was stated, signified a situation where "hostilities" were occurring but where it was "not alleged that one particular party" was the "aggressor" or had "committed an act of aggression." [28] This concept was not however accepted.

With respect to Korea, the one case where the Council has declared the existence of a breach of the peace, its resolution included a statement "noting with grave concern the armed attack upon the Republic of Korea by forces from North Korea." [29] Presumably, in this case it

[24] In 1966 the Council decided that the situation in Rhodesia constituted a "threat to the peace." SC Res. 232, Dec. 16, 1966.

[25] See commentary on Arts. 34 and 36.   [26] UN Doc. S/4741, Feb. 21, 1961.

[27] The Soviet Union on the Indonesian question. SCOR/2d Yr./173d Mtg./Aug. 1, 1947/p. 1692.

[28] Ibid., 171st Mtg./July 31, 1947/p. 1623.

[29] UN Doc. S/1501, June 25, 1960.

was felt that an attempt to label the "attack" as an act of aggression might cause undue delay, in view of the greater seriousness of such a charge.

From the Council's discussions, it would appear to be generally accepted that a determination of a breach of the peace is less serious than a finding of aggression, in so far as the positions of the parties are concerned, but more serious than a determination of a "threat to the peace" in terms of implications for further Council action.

In ordering a cease-fire in Palestine, for example, the Council declared that failure of the parties to comply "would demonstrate a breach of the peace within the meaning of Article 39 . . . requiring immediate consideration . . . with a view to . . . further action under Chapter VII." [30] In other instances it has been suggested that failure to comply with provisional measures the Council has called for should be considered as a breach of the peace.[31]

Acts of Aggression

This phrase was included in the Charter as the result of a Soviet proposal at Dumbarton Oaks. The United States considered that the term "breach of the peace" was broad enough to cover aggression. Both the United States and the United Kingdom accepted the Soviet proposal, although at the time the United Kingdom argued against any attempt to define the term.[32]

The attempt to define aggression has a long history. The League devoted considerable time to this exercise, and the issue also arose in connection with various agreements concluded during that era. The Soviet Union was one of the leading advocates of defining the term. The United States took the position, as stated in connection with the Kellogg-Briand Pact of 1928, that a definition was impracticable since it could not be all-inclusive and would make it possible for a would-be aggressor to use the definition for its own purposes.[33]

At the San Francisco Conference, many delegations proposed the inclusion of a definition of aggression in the Charter. The Sponsoring Governments successfully resisted this move for the reasons stated above but also on the ground that the determination should be made by the Security Council as the need arose. Any definition might hamper its freedom of action by forcing premature application of sanctions

---

[30] UN Doc. S/902, July 15, 1948.   [31] See commentary on Art. 40.

[32] Ruth B. Russell, A History of the United Nations Charter (Washington, Brookings Institution, 1958), pp. 464–65.

[33] See, in general, Julius Stone, Aggression and World Order (Los Angeles, University of California Press, 1958), ch. 2.

or by establishing standards that might not be easily applied in a particular case.[34]

The decision taken at San Francisco by no means ended the debate over the definition of aggression. In the United Nations, the issue has been discussed in the International Law Commission, in the General Assembly, in special committees established to study the question, and in other United Nations bodies.[35]

These discussions have been marked by a division between those who oppose a definition and those who consider that it would provide useful guidance to the United Nations organs and to members. Within the latter group, however, there has been considerable disagreement as to what actions should be included in the definition. The problem of "indirect aggression" has proved particularly troublesome. At one point, the Assembly, by a very close vote, went on record that it would be "possible and desirable" to define aggression "by reference to the elements which constitute it," [36] but no definition has ever been agreed upon.

Charges of aggression have been frequently made in the Security Council and in the General Assembly. Neither the decisions or the discussions in either organ indicate any consensus as to what constitutes "aggression." The Council has never made such a finding and indeed there have been relatively few proposals that it do so.[37]

Following the intervention of the People's Republic of China in the Korean conflict, however, the Assembly found that the government, "by giving direct aid and assistance to those who were already committing aggression in Korea and by engaging in hostilities against United Nations forces," was "itself engaged in aggression in Korea." [38] In the discussion preceding the adoption of this resolution, some members, while not disagreeing with the facts of the situation, questioned the political wisdom of making such a finding which might close the door to efforts to bring about a satisfactory agreed solution. On the other hand, the finding was considered necessary as a preliminary to the Assembly's subsequent action in recommending the application of collective economic measures against the Peiping regime. The debate illustrates that, while members may be willing to use the words "aggres-

[34] Russell, pp. 670 ff. For the position of the U.S. which led the fight against a definition, see *The Charter of the United Nations*, Hears./USS CFR/79C1/1945, p. 286; and State Dept., *Report to the President*, p. 91.

[35] See Stone, ch. 3.

[36] GA Res. 599(VI), Jan. 31, 1952. The vote was 29 to 24 with 2 abstentions.

[37] See, for example, rejection of Soviet proposals finding the U.S. guilty of aggressive acts against the People's Republic of China and in the U-2 incident and its proposals branding Belgium an aggressor in the Congo. UN Docs. S/1757, Sept. 2, 1950; S/4321, May 23, 1960; S/4386, July 13, 1960; and S/4402, July 20, 1960.

[38] GA Res. 498(V), Feb. 1, 1951.

sion" and "aggressive" quite freely in their statements, they are cautious about including them in formal findings.

"Recommendations" and "Decisions"

Once the Council has determined the existence of a threat to the peace, breach of the peace, or act of aggression, there are various courses of action it may take. The Dumbarton Oaks Proposals provided that in these circumstances, the Council "should make recommendations or decide upon the measures to be taken to maintain or restore peace and security." The breadth of this language, taken together with the previously mentioned provision linking the failure to settle a dispute with the determination of a threat to the peace, gave rise to fears that the Council could impose a political settlement upon the parties. At the San Francisco Conference it was agreed that the Council's powers to take "decisions" should be limited to "measures" taken "in accordance with Articles 41 and 42."

At the same time, various assurances were given regarding the Council's power to make "recommendations" with respect to threats to the peace, breaches of the peace, and acts of aggression. It was stated that the term "recommendations" in this provision had the same meaning as in the provisions regarding the pacific settlement of disputes; only the "situation" differed, and the recommendations were not mandatory in either case.[39]

The rapporteur's report, unanimously approved by the committee, included the following statement:

In using the word "recommendations" in Section B [Art. 39], as already found in paragraph 5, Section A [Art. 37(2)], the Committee has intended to show that the action of the Council so far as it relates to the peaceful settlement of a dispute or to situations giving rise to a threat of war, a breach of the peace or aggression, should be considered as governed by the provisions contained in Section A [Chapter VI]. Under such an hypothesis, the Council would in reality pursue simultaneously two distinct actions, one having for its object the settlement of the dispute or the difficulty, and the other, the enforcement of provisional measures, each of which is governed by an appropriate section in Chapter VIII [Chapters VI, VII, and VIII of the Charter].[40]

It was also made clear during the discussions that the Council did not have to chose between making recommendations or applying sanctions. It could do either or both, consecutively or simultaneously. In the case of "flagrant aggression," however, it was intended that enforcement measures should be fully applied without delay, although at the

[39] Russell, pp. 669–70.   [40] UNCIO, *Documents*, XII, 507.

same time the Council might "endeavour to persuade the aggressor to abandon its venture" by means of recommendations for pacific settlement and "by prescribing conservatory measures." Thus, when the Council makes a determination under Article 39, it may make "recommendations" in accordance with Article 39; call for "provisional measures" under Article 40; call upon members to apply nonmilitary enforcement measures under Article 41; and/or take such military action in accordance with Article 42 as it deems necessary to maintain or restore international peace and security.

The decisions and discussions of the Security Council with respect to "provisional" and "enforcement" measures are considered in the commentaries on Articles 40, 41, and 42. As for "recommendations" under Article 39, there is little in the Council's records that bears upon the exercise of its powers in this connection.

The only time the Security Council has specifically made a "recommendation" with respect to a threat to the peace, breach of the peace, or act of aggression was in connection with the attack on South Korea. After determining that the attack constituted a "breach of the peace," the Council "recommended" that members "furnish such assistance" to South Korea "as may be necessary to repel the armed attack and restore international peace and security in the area." Subsequently, it "recommended" that members make "military forces and other assistance . . . available to a unified command under the United States." [41]

These were scarcely the kinds of "recommendations" the drafters of the Charter had in mind when they adopted Article 39. This innovation was a means whereby a response could be carried out under United Nations auspices despite the fact that the Council did not have at its disposal the armed forces as originally intended under Article 43. At the time, this concept of military measures on the basis of a Council "recommendation" was accepted by a great majority of members, with the major exception of the Soviet bloc.

In the few instances that the Council has acted, or has appeared to have been acting, under Chapter VII of the Charter, it has been primarily concerned with averting or ending hostilities. Even when addressing itself to nonmilitary aspects of these situations, the Council has generally cast its resolutions in the form of calling for provisional measures rather than recommendations for settlement. During the short period that the Council was dealing with the Korean question, it directed its attention to the grave military situation. The search for a "political" solution was left to the General Assembly, which had in any event been dealing with the problem of the independence of Korea

[41] UN Docs. S/1511, June 27, 1950; and S/1588, July 7, 1950. Neither resolution specifically cited Art. 39.

since 1947. In connection with the Palestine question, the Council also focused its efforts on obtaining a cessation of hostilities and then on the maintenance of the armistice agreements. In so far as a search for a "pacific" settlement of the underlying disputes was concerned, this remained in the hands of the Assembly which had been originally responsible for working out a political solution.

With respect to the Congo, the Council's resolutions were directed toward the restoration of law and order and the maintenance of the political independence and territorial integrity of the Congo. For the most part, its actions were in the nature of provisional measures designed to prevent the aggravation of the situation, although some of the provisions in its resolutions could be regarded as "recommendations" e.g., those concerning the restoration of parliamentary institutions and the reorganization of the Congolese army. Even these were designed to create a climate in which a settlement would be possible.[42]

There is some difference of view as to whether the Council's actions in the Indonesian question came within the scope of Chapter VII. Its approach in this case, however, illustrates the original Charter concept of combining measures for the restoration of peace with efforts to work out a peaceful settlement of the dispute. The Council's resolution of January 28, 1949, for example, which called for the "immediate discontinuance of military operations" also "recommended" the basis for a permanent settlement.[43]

Article 40

In order to prevent an aggravation of the situation, the Security Council may, before making the recommendations or deciding upon the measures provided for in Article 39, call upon the parties concerned to comply with such provisional measures as it deems necessary or desirable. Such provisional measures shall be without prejudice to the rights, claims, or position of the parties concerned. The Security Council shall duly take account of failure to comply with such provisional measures.

Article 40 was added to the Charter at San Francisco on the initiative of the Republic of China. There was no corresponding provision in

[42] UN Doc. S/4741, Feb. 21, 1961. The General Assembly became more involved with the political, as opposed to the strictly military aspects of the situation.

[43] UN Doc. S/1234, Jan. 28, 1949. The Council took a similar approach in the dispute between India and Pakistan, but this case was handled under ch. vi rather than vii.

the Dumbarton Oaks Proposals.[44] The addition was part of the substantial revision made at San Francisco of provisions relating to the initial actions of the Security Council in dealing with threats to the peace, breaches of the peace, and acts of aggression (Article 39).

That the Council should be authorized to call for the application of provisional measures before making recommendations or taking decisions under Article 39 was readily accepted. There was some concern that recommendations under Article 39 and provisional measures under Article 40 might delay the application of enforcement measures in situations where they might be urgently needed.[45] The inclusion of Article 40 in the Charter was approved on the understanding that the Council was not required to follow any fixed order and could, if necessary, call for the immediate application of enforcement measures.

The primary intent of Article 40 was to empower the Council to take measures to prevent a threat to the peace from developing into an actual breach. As stated at San Francisco, the Council's authority to call upon the parties "to consent to certain conservatory measures refers above all to the presumption of a threat of war." [46]

Although there have been many proposals that the Security Council exercise its authority under Article 40, it has only twice cited that article in any of its resolutions. Nonetheless, the basic concept has been repeatedly applied. Whenever the Council has been faced with a situation where hostilities seemed imminent, or had actually broken out, it has given priority to attempts to avert or end the use of force, by calling upon the parties to take measures of a provisional nature.[47]

Relationship to Article 39

It is clear from the Charter that the Council may invoke Article 40 before making recommendations or taking decisions under Article 39. It is less clear whether it may do so without first making a determination under the latter article that a threat to the peace, breach of peace, or act of aggression exists. The practice of the Security Council provides no firm answer.

In the one case where Article 40 was specifically invoked the Council did make such a finding. After repeated efforts to bring about a truce in Palestine during the spring of 1948, the Council found that a "threat

[44] The U.S. Tentative Proposals had, however, contained a somewhat similar provision in sec. VI.B.1. State Dept., *Postwar Foreign Policy Preparation, 1939–1945*, p. 601.

[45] Russell, p. 676.   [46] UNCIO, *Documents*, XII, 507.

[47] The General Assembly has often followed a similar approach, e.g., in the Suez crisis of 1956.

to the peace" existed under Article 39 and ordered the governments and authorities concerned "pursuant to Article 40 . . . to desist from further military action" and to "issue cease-fire orders to their military and para-military forces." [48] This action implied that the Council's previous resolutions calling upon governments and authorities to take certain steps were adopted under Chapter VI rather than Chapter VII of the Charter. Subsequently when fighting broke out, the Council again invoked Article 40 in calling upon the parties "as a further provisional measure" to seek agreement with a view to establishing an armistice.[49] Since that time, the Council has repeatedly called upon Israel and the Arab states to take provisional measures of various kinds without however specifically citing Article 40. But in many instances it has referred to or reaffirmed the resolutions quoted above.

Most proposals that the Security Council act under Article 40 have been coupled with a formal finding under Article 39,[50] although occasionally it has been proposed that the Council invoke Article 40 without making such a finding.[51]

In the Korean case, the Council applied Articles 39 and 40 without citing them. Its initial resolution contained a determination that the attack on the Republic of Korea constituted "a breach of the peace" and called for the "immediate cessation of hostilities" and the "withdrawal" of North Korean troops.[52]

In other cases it has been less evident that the Council was acting under Article 40. The initial Australian draft resolution on the Indonesia question, for example, included a finding that the fighting between Indonesia and the Netherlands constituted a "breach of the peace under Article 39" and called upon the parties "under Article 40" to cease hostilities and seek a solution through arbitration.[53] The resolution as adopted, however, omitted any reference to Article 40 as well as a specific finding under Article 39.[54] During subsequent discussions, there were repeated statements that the Council's action was in effect taken under these two articles, a contention that the Netherlands disputed.

In dealing with the situation in the Congo, the Security Council

[48] Resolution of July 15, 1948. SCOR/3d Yr./*Supp.* for July, 1948/pp. 76–77.
[49] Resolution of Nov. 14, 1948. SCOR/3d Yr./*Supp.* for Nov., 1948/pp. 13–14.
[50] See, for example, the Australian proposal on the Greek frontier incidents question: UN Doc. S/471, Aug. 6, 1947; the U.S. proposal on the Cuban missile crisis: UN Doc. S/5182, Oct. 22, 1962; and the Cuban proposal concerning the decisions of the Punta del Este Meeting of Consultation, Jan. 22–31, 1962: UN Doc. S/5086, Mar. 8, 1962.
[51] See, for example, the six-power draft resolution on the Berlin crisis of 1948. UN Doc. S/1048, Oct. 22, 1948.
[52] UN Doc. S/1501, June, 25, 1950.   [53] UN Doc. S/454, July 31, 1947.
[54] UN Doc. S/459, Aug. 1, 1947.

adopted a number of resolutions calling for measures of the kind indicated in Article 40, including the withdrawal of Belgian troops. That article was never specifically cited and indeed it was not until February, 1961, several months after its initial actions, that the Council made a formal finding that the situation "threatened international peace and security." [55] In the view of the Secretary-General, however, the Council's resolutions could be considered "as implicitly taken under Article 40, and, in that sense, as based on an implicit finding under Article 39." [56]

In dealing with such questions as the Guatemalan complaint in 1954, the Franco–Tunisian dispute in 1961, the Yemini complaint against the United Kingdom in 1964, and the Dominican crisis of 1965, the Council's initial action was to call upon the parties concerned to take certain steps, including usually a cease-fire, to calm the situation and to refrain from any actions that might aggravate it.[57] None of these resolutions cited Article 40 or contained a determination of the nature called for under Article 39.

With respect to Cyprus, the Council's action in calling for measures of this kind was coupled with a finding that the situation was "likely to threaten international peace and security." [58] Throughout its consideration of the relations between India and Pakistan, the Council frequently called upon the parties to take various types of provisional measures without citing Article 40 and without a finding under Article 39. At an early stage it did decide that the continuance of the dispute "was likely to endanger the maintenance of international peace and security," the language of Article 34.[59]

It would seem to be generally accepted that the Council may call for provisional measures in connection with its efforts to settle disputes under Chapter VI. The Council's powers to recommend "appropriate procedures and methods of adjustment" can be interpreted to include such measures.[60] The failure of the Council to indicate under which chapter it is acting does, however, raise questions as to the extent of the obligations of the parties to comply with these resolutions.

[55] UN Doc. S/4741, Feb. 21, 1961.

[56] SCOR/15th Yr./920th Mtg./Dec. 13–14, 1960/pp. 14–25. See also his letter to Belgium that UN forces were taking over certain bases and property "as a provisional measure under Article 40 of the Charter." SCOR/16th Yr./*Supp.* for Jan., Feb., Mar., 1961/p. 71.

[57] See UN Docs. S/3237, June 20, 1954; S/4882, July 22, 1961; SC Res. 188, Apr. 9, 1964; and SC Res. 203, May 14, 1965.

[58] SC Res. 186, May 4, 1964.   [59] UN Doc. S/726, Apr. 21, 1948.

[60] See commentary on Art. 36.

Legal Effects of Provisional Measures

The legal effects of Security Council resolutions calling for the application of provisional measures are by no means clear. It can be argued that, in exercising its powers under Article 40, the Council is doing no more than making recommendations to the parties concerned. This would seem to have been the initial United States attitude, as evidenced by the following statement: "The measures envisaged in this Article are measures which the disputing parties will be asked to undertake themselves upon recommendation of the Council, and are therefore not to be regarded as preliminary sanctions." [61]

The fact that the term "calls upon" is used would suggest, however, that resolutions adopted under Article 40 are more than "recommendations." [62] The same verb is used in Article 33 authorizing the Council to call the attention of members to their obligations of peaceful settlement. Moreover, under Article 41, the Council may "call upon" members to apply non-military measures which they are obligated to "accept and carry out."

"Provisional measures" are not "enforcement measures" and do not therefore fall under the specific exception stated in Article 2(7). It is not clear whether they come within the scope of "preventive" action, thus providing grounds for suspension in the event of noncompliance (Article 5) and requiring members to refrain from giving assistance to states that refuse to carry out the Council's resolutions (Article 2[5]).

An analysis of the decisions and discussions of the Security Council contributes little to resolving these ambiguities. Seldom can a resolution calling for provisional measures be considered as an unequivocal exercise of the Council's powers under Article 40. Nor do the debates leading up to the adoption of such resolutions usually indicate a consensus within the Council as to the Charter basis for the action taken.

There would appear to be considerable agreement that the parties concerned are obligated to comply with resolutions specifically adopted under Article 40, that other members are obligated to assist in carrying out such resolutions, and that the Council can adopt any measures it deems necessary to ensure compliance with such resolutions, subject to the general limitations of the Charter.

There is considerable less agreement as to whether these obligations are applicable, if the Council fails to cite Article 40 and/or fails to make a formal determination under Article 39 that a threat to the peace, breach of the peace, or act of aggression exists. The Council's

[61] State Dept., *Report to the President*, p. 92.
[62] Note, however, that the French text of the Charter uses the verb "inviter."

failure to take either of these actions was the basis for the refusal of the Netherlands to consider itself obligated to comply with the Council's resolutions on the Indonesian question.

On the other hand, the Council's resolutions on the Congo situation were considered binding upon the parties concerned and United Nations members in general, even though neither the debates in the Council nor its resolutions indicated that the Council was acting under Article 40 or 41.[63] It was repeatedly stressed that the United Nations was not taking "enforcement measures." There would appear to have been an assumption, however, at least by the Secretary-General, that the measures were to be considered as "preventive action" requiring the support of all members. At the same time, it was stressed that the United Nations actions were in full conformity with Article 2(7) of the Charter since the Organization was not intervening in the domestic political affairs of the Congo.

The "force" the Council intends to give to its resolutions is sometimes reflected in the terms it uses. The Council has at times "appealed," "called upon," "recommended," and "urged" or "requested" provisional measures. On other occasions it has "insisted," "demanded," or "ordered." In dealing with the Palestine question, for example, the Council first "appealed" to the governments and peoples to take all possible action to prevent or reduce disorder in that area. Subsequently, it "called" for a cessation of acts of force and conclusion of a truce, and threatened that refusal to comply with its resolutions would require consideration of action under Chapter VII.[64] By the time the Council reached the point of explicitly applying Chapter VII, the term "calls upon" had been so debased that the Council felt it necessary to "order" a cessation of military action.[65] Later, the Council reverted to the use of the term "calls upon" in its attempts to obtain and maintain the armistice agreements between Israel and the Arab states. It has been frequently asserted that the parties are under an obligation to comply with these measures since the agreements themselves were concluded pursuant to a Council resolution invoking Article 40.

When the Council considered the outbreak of hostilities between India and Pakistan in 1965, it also began by "calling upon" the parties to cease hostilities, and subsequently "demanded" that they do so.[66]

Whatever the "legal" situation, the fact that Article 40 states that the Council "shall duly take account of failure to comply with such provi-

[63] See commentary on Arts. 25 and 49.
[64] UN Docs. S/691, Mar. 5, 1948; S/714, Apr. 1, 1948; S/773, May 22, 1948; and S/801, May 29, 1948.
[65] UN Doc. S/902, July 15, 1948.
[66] See SC Res. 209, Sept. 4, 1965; SC Res. 210, Sept. 6, 1965; SC Res. 211, Sept. 20, 1965; SC Res. 214, Sept. 27, 1965; and SC Res. 215, Nov. 5, 1965.

sional measures" would indicate that they have a different status than mere recommendations.

Nature of Provisional Measures

The Charter does not specifically indicate the kinds of provisional measures the parties may be called upon to undertake. The Council has complete freedom to determine what measures are "necessary or desirable . . . in order to prevent an aggravation of the situation."

Article 40 does stipulate that provisional measures are to be "without prejudice to the rights, claims, or positions of the parties." This would imply that the Council cannot impose a political settlement on the parties, but must direct its efforts toward maintaining or restoring international peace and security, although in practice it could be difficult to apply provisional measures without affecting the parties' positions. This became particularly evident during the United Nations operations in the Congo when actions taken could not avoid affecting the positions of the parties.

The Council included the "without prejudice" clause in one of its resolutions invoking Article 40 [67] and also in other resolutions which were adopted under Chapter VI.[68] There has been some discussion concerning the intent of the phrase and whether it precluded the Council from calling for certain types of measures. The point has been made that it was not intended to limit the Council's actions in taking provisional measures but was designed to prevent such measures from adversely affecting the substantive rights of the parties.[69] In general, it cannot be said that the phrase has had much effect upon the Council's actions.

The Council has followed a variety of practices in calling for measures that might be deemed "provisional." It has issued general appeals and called for specific actions. Although Article 40 specifically refers to the "parties concerned," the Council has addressed its resolutions to "peoples," "governments," "authorities," "communities," specific states, and the United Nations membership as a whole. The Council has called for cease-fires, cessations of hostilities, withdrawal of troops and para-military personnel, the conclusions of truces or armistices, and various measures to maintain such agreements.

[67] UN Doc. S/1021, Nov. 4, 1948. See also its resolution on the Indonesian question. UN Doc. S/1234, Jan. 28, 1949.

[68] See the Council's resolution on the Palestine question. UN Docs. S/723, Apr. 17, 1948; S/733, May 22, 1948; and S/3538, Jan. 19, 1956. For discussion on the appropriateness of including this phrase in a resolution adopted under ch. VI, see SCOR/8th Yr./631st Mtg./Oct. 27, 1953.

[69] See SCOR/2d. Yr./207th Mtg./Oct. 3, 1947; 209th Mtg./Oct. 9, 1947; and 215th Mtg./Oct. 29, 1947.

It would appear that members have considered that the Council, in calling for provisional measures, may call upon the parties to enter into negotiations not only for implementing those measures but also on the underlying causes of the conflict,[70] although there have been some objections that this is inconsistent with the "without prejudice" clause. The Council has also called for the release of prisoners, the ending of acts of repression, and other measures of a political rather than a military nature, although it is not clear that all these were meant to be "provisional measures" in the Charter sense.

Compliance with Provisional Measures

The Security Council has taken various kinds of steps to ensure compliance. It has established commissions and designated special representatives to assist the parties in reaching agreements. It has occasionally entrusted the Secretary-General or one of his representatives with similar tasks. It has set deadlines. It has created machinery for observing a truce or armistice, such as the Truce Supervision Organization in Palestine and the Military Observer Group for India and Pakistan. It has established peace-keeping forces, such as those that operated in the Congo and in Cyprus. It has, moreover, often made clear its intention to keep the situation under review with a view to further action.

Article 40 states that the Council "shall duly take account of failure to comply" with provisional measures. In the Palestine case, the Council coupled its call for a truce with a threat that if its call were rejected or if the truce were subsequently repudiated or violated, the situation would be "reconsidered with a view to action under Chapter VII of the Charter." Later, in ordering a cease-fire, the Council stated that failure to comply "would demonstrate the existence of a breach of the peace" requiring immediate consideration with a view to further action under that chapter. Finally, when hostilities again broke out, the Council appointed a committee to study as a matter of urgency the further measures it would be appropriate to take under Chapter VII, if the parties failed to comply with the provisional measures indicated by the Council.[71] In this case, these threats of further action appear to have had some effect. In others it is more doubtful.

[70] The Council followed this approach in connection with the Indonesian and India-Pakistan questions. See also proposals on the Greek frontier incidents question: UN Docs. S/471, Aug. 6, 1947; and S/486, Aug. 12, 1947; Berlin: UN Doc. S/1048, Oct. 22, 1948; and the Franco-Tunisian dispute: UN Doc. S/4878, July 22, 1961; and S/4905, July 29, 1961.

[71] UN Docs. S/801, May 29, 1948; S/902, July 15, 1948; S/1070, Nov. 4, 1948. See also UN Doc. S/3538, Jan. 19, 1956, which contains a similar threat,

In complaining of France's failure to abide by the Council's resolution calling for an immediate cease-fire and return of armed forces to their previous positions,[72] Tunisia asked the Council "in accordance with Article 40" to take into account the French refusal to abide by its Charter obligations and to take vigorous action under subsequent articles of the Charter to enforce its decisions.[73] The Council was unable, however, to take further action.

In calling on India and Pakistan to cease hostilities and withdraw their armed personnel to previous positions, the Council indicated that it would keep the matter under "urgent and continuous review" so that it might "determine what further steps may be necessary to secure peace and security in the area." [74] Subsequently, the Secretary-General, in reporting on his unsuccessful efforts to obtain an effective cease-fire, suggested that the Council invoke Article 40, order the two governments to desist from further military action, and declare that their failure to comply would demonstrate a breach of the peace within the meaning of Article 39.[75] In this case an agreement was finally reached without the need of invoking Chapter VII.

The strongest action taken by the Council to obtain compliance with its measures was in connection with the situation in the Congo. In its initial resolution calling for the withdrawal of Belgian troops, the Council authorized the Secretary-General to provide the Congolese government "with such military assistance" as might be necessary.[76] This led to the creation of the United Nations Congo Force which was followed by a number of resolutions calling on Belgium, the government and other authorities in the Congo, and on all United Nations members to undertake various kinds of measures, many of which could be considered as coming within the scope of Article 40. Finally at the height of the crisis over Katanga, the Council urged "the United Nations to take immediately all appropriate measures to prevent the occurrence of civil war in the Congo, including . . . the use of force, if necessary, in the last resort." [77]

---

although the proposed references to a breach of the peace and action under ch. vii were not included in the resolution as adopted.

[72] UN Doc. S/4882, July 22, 1961.

[73] SCOR/16th Yr./964th Mtg./July 28, 1961/para. 80.

[74] SC Res. 210, Sept. 6, 1965.   [75] UN Doc. S/6686, Sept. 16, 1965.

[76] UN Doc. S/4387, July 14, 1960.

[77] UN Doc. S/4741, Feb. 20–21, 1961. See also the authorization of the use of force to carry out the Council's repeated resolutions for the removal of mercenaries and foreign military, paramilitary, and political advisory personnel, not under the UN command. UN Doc. S/5002, Nov. 24, 1961.

Article 41

The Security Council may decide what measures not involving the use of armed force are to be employed to give effect to its decisions, and it may call upon the Members of the United Nations to apply such measures. These may include complete or partial interruption of economic relations and of rail, sea, air, postal, telegraphic, radio, and other means of communication, and the severance of diplomatic relations.

The idea that the members of the international community can, by applying collectively measures short of the use of armed force, bring sufficient pressure to bear upon a state to induce it to live up to its international obligations is a recurrent theme in international organizations.

Under Article 16 of the Covenant, the members of the League of Nations assumed the obligation to sever "all trade and financial" relations with any member that resorted to war in disregard of its obligations under the Covenant. When the members of the League actually applied sanctions against Italy following its invasion of Ethiopia, they failed for various reasons to accomplish their objective.

The drafters of the Charter sought to establish a stronger system by centralizing the decision-making power in the Security Council. Despite their obligations under the Covenant, members were in effect free to decide for themselves what, if any, measures they would take, whereas under the Charter they are obligated to carry out whatever measures the Council decides should be "employed to give effect to its decisions." Nonmilitary enforcement measures are applicable to a broader range of situations under the Charter, for example, threats to the peace, breaches of the peace, and acts of aggression, than were economic sanctions under the Covenant. Moreover, the Charter seeks to enhance the effectiveness of nonmilitary measures by requiring United Nation members to comply with the Council's decisions on military measures, an obligation that the members of the League were not required to assume. The Council is free to decide what measures are to be applied, but there is an implication that "military" measures will be taken if nonmilitary measures prove to be inadequate.

During the Dumbarton Oaks Conversations, there was complete agreement that the Council should have the right to call upon members to apply measures short of the use of armed force. The enumeration of measures in Article 41 resulted from a Soviet proposal which the United Kingdom and the United States accepted, although they feared that such a listing might tend to limit the Council's freedom of action. The text is, however, phrased in permissive terms and cannot be considered as limiting the Council's powers. It does not exclude the possibility of resort to other measures not enumerated in Article 41 so long as they fall within the category of "measures not involving the use of armed force." The text approved at Dumbarton Oaks was accepted at San Francisco virtually without debate.[78]

During the twenty-year period 1946 to 1966, the Security Council never specifically invoked Article 41, although there were a number of cases where such action was proposed.[79]

Article 41 was first discussed in the Council in connection with a Polish proposal calling upon members to sever diplomatic relations with Franco Spain. The majority of the Council members, however, opposed the application of Chapter VII in this case and favored a request by the Council to the General Assembly that it adopt a recommendation to that effect. This proposal was vetoed, both France and the Soviet Union voting against it,[80] but the Assembly eventually recommended the withdrawal of ambassadors from Spain.[81]

The application of Article 41 was also seriously considered during 1948 when the Council was attempting to bring about a cessation of hostilities between Israel and its Arab neighbors. China and the United Kingdom at one point proposed the appointment of a committee "to examine . . . the measures which it would be appropriate to take under Article 41" if the parties failed to comply within a reasonable time with the Council's call for the withdrawal of military forces.[82] No enforcement measures were, however, ever decided upon.

The Council rejected the Soviet proposal for the application of sanctions against Belgium in connection with the situation in the Congo.[83] At various times, however, the Council called upon member states to take certain measures and refrain from certain actions that might impede United Nations efforts to restore law and order in the Congo or undermine the territorial integrity or political independence of that country.[84] These resolutions were considered as legally binding upon

[78] Russell, pp. 466, 676.

[79] It did so for the first time in December, 1966, when it called for the application of various economic and financial measures against Southern Rhodesia. SC Res. 232, Dec. 16, 1966.

[80] SCOR/1st Yr., 1st Ser./34th Mtg./Apr. 17, 1946; and 48th Mtg./June 24, 1946. See also the report of the Council's subcommittee, *ibid., Special Supp.*

[81] GA Res. 39(I), Dec. 12, 1946.

[82] The resolution as adopted referred to ch. vii in general rather than Art. 41. SCOR/3d Yr./*Supp.* for Oct., 1948/p. 72.

[83] SCOR/16th Yr./942d Mtg./Feb. 20, 1961.

[84] For other examples of resolutions of this kind adopted by the Security Council of the General Assembly, see commentary on Art. 2(5).

members even though they contained no specific reference to Article 41.[85]

The Council has on a number of occasions called for the application of the kinds of measures listed in Article 41 without citing that article and indeed without determining that the situation was of the nature requiring action under Chapter VII. In connection with the situation in South Africa, for example, the Council called upon all states to boycott South African goods, to refrain from exporting strategic materials to that country, and to cease "the sale and shipment of arms, ammunition, and all types of military vehicles." The latter injunction was expanded in a subsequent resolution.[86] The Council also requested all states to "to take all measures to prevent the sale and supply of arms and military equipment" to Portugal or to assist that country in any way in its continued "repression of the peoples" in its African territories. It later called for a broader embargo on militarily significant materials.[87]

Following Southern Rhodesia's unilateral declaration of independence, the Council called upon all states not to recognize "this illegal authority"; not to entertain "any diplomatic or other relations" with it; to refrain from any action to assist the regime; to desist from providing it with arms, equipment, and military material; and "to do their utmost . . . to break all economic relations with Southern Rhodesia, including an embargo on oil and petroleum products." [88]

In all these cases, some members felt that the Council should specifically invoke Chapter VII, but in none of the resolutions is there a reference to Article 41 or any other provision of Chapter VII.[89] Indeed, in some instances members stated their understanding that the Council was acting under Chapter VI and that consequently members were not legally obligated to apply the measures called for in the Council's resolutions.[90]

In most of these cases, the Council acted after repeated urgings by the General Assembly for the application of sanctions[91] and in some cases the Assembly itself has requested members to take measures of the type covered in Article 41.[92] After condemning the People's Republic of China for its aggression in Korea, for example, the Assembly

---

[85] See commentary on Arts. 25 and 49.
[86] SCOR/18th Yr./1056th Mtg./Aug. 7, 1963; and 1078th Mtg./Dec. 4, 1963.
[87] *Ibid.*, 1049th Mtg./July 31, 1963; and 20th Yr./1268th Mtg./Nov. 23, 1965.
[88] SC Res. 217, Nov. 20, 1965. See also the Council's previous Resolution 216, Nov. 12, 1965.
[89] With the exception noted in footnote 79.
[90] See, for example, statements by the U.S. and the U.K. in connection with the resolutions on South Africa. SCOR/18th Yr./1056th Mtg./Aug. 7, 1963/pp. 2–13; and 1078th Mtg./Dec. 4, 1963/pp. 11–16.
[91] See commentary on Art. 11.
[92] See for example, GA Res. 1761(XVII), Nov. 6, 1962, on South Africa; 1819(XVII), Dec. 18, 1962, on Angola.

recommended an embargo on supplying that country with various items that might contribute to its military power.[93]

The Soviet Union and some other states have at various times contended that the Security Council has a monopoly on the application of enforcement measures and that measures of the kind enumerated in Article 41 can only be taken in accordance with a decision by that organ. In reply to this argument, it has been pointed out that states may on their own initiative take measures such as breaking off diplomatic, economic, and financial relations with another state and that nothing in the Charter precludes them from taking such action collectively in response to a resolution by the General Assembly or a regional organization.[94] This is the basic thesis of the Uniting for Peace resolution,[95] which provides for the application of collective political and economic measures on the recommendation of the General Assembly in situations where the Council has failed to deal with a "threat to or breach of the peace, or an act of aggression."

Article 42

Should the Security Council consider that measures provided for in Article 41 would be inadequate or have proved to be inadequate, it may take such action by air, sea, or land forces as may be necessary to maintain or restore international peace and security. Such action may include demonstrations, blockade, and other operations by air, sea, or land forces of Members of the United Nations.

The Charter leaves to the Security Council a wide measure of discretion in deciding whether a particular situation calls for the application of military enforcement measures. It may do so if it considers "that measures provided for in Article 41 . . . have proved to be inadequate," but the Council need not wait for such proof. As was unanimously agreed at the San Francisco Conference, "in the case of flagrant aggression imperiling the existence of a member of the Organization, enforcement measures should be taken without delay, and to the full extent required by the circumstances." [96]

[93] GA Res. 500(V), May 18, 1951.

[94] On the question of regional agencies and enforcement measures, see commentary on Art. 53.

[95] GA Res. 377(V), Nov. 3, 1950. The Collective Measures Committee established under this resolution undertook an extensive study of the problems involved in applying nonmilitary measures regardless of whether they were taken in response to an Assembly recommendation or a Council decision. See GAOR/6th Sess./Supp. 13, 1951; 7th Sess./Supp. 17, 1952; and 8th Sess., Annexes, agenda item 19, 1953.

[96] UNCIO, Documents, XII, 507.

The Council also has discretion as to the kinds of military measures to be taken and what contributions various members shall be required to make.[97] Article 42 lists some of the measures the Council may take, i.e., "demonstrations, blockade, and other operations by air, sea, or land forces of Members of the United Nations." This listing, which was not intended to be inclusive, resulted from a Soviet proposal at Dumbarton Oaks.[98]

In empowering the Security Council to take military enforcement decisions that all members are obligated to accept and carry out, the Charter goes far beyond the system established under the League of Nations Covenant. Although the Covenant imposed upon members a specific obligation to apply nonmilitary sanctions, they were not required to carry out any military measures that the League Council might consider desirable. That organ could only recommend military measures under Articles 10 and 16. Moreover, such a recommendation required a unanimous vote in the League Council, whereas under the Charter members may be bound without their consent, except for the five permanent members each of whom can veto any decision to apply Article 42.

Article 42 has never been applied by the Security Council. The permanent members failed to agree on the armed forces that were to be made available to the Security Council and they have been equally unable to agree on joint action in the particular situations the Council has faced.[99] Thus, whatever measures have been taken by the United Nations, or under its auspices, that have required the use of armed force have been based on the concept of voluntary contributions.

Only once has the application of Article 42 been formally proposed. During the Suez crisis in 1956, the Soviet Union cited that article in proposing that the Security Council authorize all members and specifically the Soviet Union and the United States to send "naval and air forces, military units, volunteers, military instructors, and other forms of assistance" to Egypt to enforce compliance with the United Nations resolutions for a cessation of military action and the withdrawal of troops.[100]

Not all military operations authorized by the Security Council necessarily fall under Article 42. The Korean action was taken on the basis of a "recommendation" by the Council under Article 39.[101] The United Nations forces established by the Council in such situations as the

[97] See commentary on Art. 49.
[98] The Soviet list also included "air raids on military objectives." See Russell, p. 466.
[99] See commentary on Arts. 43 and 106.
[100] SCOR/11th Yr./755th Mtg./Nov. 5, 1956/pp. 4–14.
[101] SCOR/5th Yr./473d–474th Mtgs./June 25 and 27, 1950.

Congo, Yemen, and Cyprus were generally regarded as "peace-keeping" operations. They were not intended to implement enforcement measures. Although the Congo force was authorized to use force in certain circumstances,[102] the Secretary-General, as well as a number of members, stressed that in this case the Council's decisions, while binding upon members, were not taken under Article 42.[103]

Article 42 by itself does not specify the sources of the "air, sea, or land forces" for implementing military enforcement measures. The drafters of the Charter clearly expected that the forces would be made available to the Security Council in accordance with the "special agreements" to be concluded under Article 43. The link between the two articles is specifically indicated in Article 106, which envisages possible joint action by the permanent members "pending the coming into force of such special agreements referred to in Article 43 as in the opinion of the Security Council enable it to begin the exercise of its responsibility under Article 42."

Moreover, at San Francisco, it was agreed that members were not obligated to furnish the Council with armed forces or other forms of assistance in excess of those provided for in their special agreements.[104] This leads to the inference that a member is under no obligation to take military action under Article 42 until it has concluded a special agreement under Article 43.

At an early stage in the Council's history, the United States took the position that until those agreements had been concluded and entered into force, the Council would be unable to fulfill its responsibilities as the enforcement agency of the United Nations and that the provisions of Chapter VII relating to military enforcement measures would "remain inoperative." [105]

It is difficult to harmonize such a conclusion with the language of Articles 2(5), 25, 39, 42, and 49. Members are under the obligation to "accept and carry out" the Council's decisions and to afford "mutual assistance in carrying out the measures" the Council decides upon. From the attitudes expressed in the United Nations, however, it seems generally accepted that in the absence of the Article 43 agreements, the legal obligations of members do not extend to supplying the Council with armed forces on other than a voluntary basis.

---

[102] SC Res. S/4741, Feb. 21, 1961; and S/5002, Nov. 24, 1961.

[103] See, for example, statements by the Secretary-General in SCOR/15th Yr./920th Mtg./Dec. 13–14, 1960/paras. 72–77; and 16th Yr./942d Mtg./Feb. 20–21, 1961/paras. 19–21. See also E. M. Miller, "Legal Aspects of the UN Action in the Congo," *American Journal of International Law*, Vol. LV, No. 1 (Jan., 1961), pp. 1–28.

[104] UNCIO, *Documents*, XII, p. 508.

[105] SCOR/2d Yr./138th Mtg./June 4, 1947/p. 53.

The successes that the United Nations has had with voluntary peace-keeping forces established under the auspices of the Council and the General Assembly do not compensate for the fact that Article 42 has become a dead letter. The knowledge that the Council had armed forces at its disposal and the expectation that they would be used, if necessary, was intended to make it easier for the Council to handle conflicts without having to resort to armed force. Thus, the inability to apply Article 42 has weakened the essential foundation of the whole United Nations system for maintaining peace and security, including its provisions for the pacific settlement of dispute.

Article 43

1. All Members of the United Nations, in order to contribute to the maintenance of international peace and security, undertake to make available to the Security Council, on its call and in accordance with a special agreement or agreements, armed forces, assistance, and facilities, including rights of passage, necessary for the purpose of maintaining international peace and security.

2. Such agreement or agreements shall govern the numbers and types of forces, their degree of readiness and general location, and the nature of the facilities and assistance to be provided.

3. The agreement or agreements shall be negotiated as soon as possible on the initiative of the Security Council. They shall be concluded between the Security Council and Members or between the Security Council and groups of Members and shall be subject to ratification by the signatory states in accordance with their respective constitutional processes.

In considering the means of supplying the Security Council with the armed forces necessary for carrying out its decisions, the architects of the Charter faced three broad alternatives. The first and most radical was to establish a truly international force which would be over and above national armies and indeed might at some time replace them. There is a long history of proposals for such a force. The idea had been rejected at the time the League of Nations was founded, as it was later rejected at San Francisco. The advantages of having a standing force under control of the Organization were outweighed, it was held, by the political difficulties involved. Such an encroachment on national sovereignty was likely to be unacceptable to many, including the United States Congress.[106]

[106] For discussion among U.S. planners on an international force, see Russell, pp. 235–36, 254, and 257–58. See also commentary on Art. 45.

The second alternative was to leave the enforcement of Council decisions to an ad hoc coalition of national forces acting under some form of overall international direction; this was substantially the system envisaged in the League Covenant. The League experience gave little assurance for the effectiveness of such an approach, and indicated the need for a more specific commitment by members to supply the forces required for the maintenance of peace.[107]

The third alternative also relied upon a system of national contingents, but with advance agreement by the members as to the forces and other forms of assistance to be supplied. This system was proposed at the Dumbarton Oaks Conference by the United States and was accepted by the other three governments, with the important and additional stipulation that the agreements had to be approved by the Security Council.[108] The Soviet Union also sought to include specific reference to the obligation of members to furnish bases, but both the United States and the United Kingdom strongly objected on the ground that this would be an infringement of the sovereign rights of members.

The concept of advance agreements for making armed forces and other assistance available to the Security Council was accepted by all the delegates at the San Francisco Conference. The only modifications of the Dumbarton Oaks draft proposed were amendments submitted by France to include in the Charter more detailed provisions concerning matters to be covered by special agreements, and by New Zealand and Australia to strengthen the position of the Security Council in negotiating the special agreements.

Among the additions the French sought were the specific inclusion of "rights of passage" in the assistance to be rendered to the Council; and a provision that the special agreements should govern not only the numbers and types of forces but also the period within which they would be available to the Council, the zone in which they would normally be stationed, and the facilities, assistance, and means of communications to be provided. There were objections to inclusion in the Charter of so much detail on the content of the future agreements. Eventually, an agreement was reached on inclusion of reference to "rights of passage" in Article 43(1), partly on the ground that the Covenant contained such a provision, and on the understanding that the mention of this specific matter was not "intended to exclude the grant of other facilities." The statement that the special agreements would cover the "degree of readiness and general location" of the forces was also added to Article 43(2).[109]

107 See Russell, p. 235.   108 Ibid., pp. 252–64, 467.
109 UNCIO, Documents, XII, 509–10 and 432–33.

Under the Dumbarton Oaks Proposals, the special agreements were to be "concluded" among the members subject to "approval" by the Security Council. This provision was criticized at San Francisco on the ground that it allowed "excessive latitude" to member states.[110] To remedy this defect, a proposal by Australia and New Zealand was accepted whereby agreements would be negotiated on the initiative of the Security Council, and be concluded between the Security Council and members or groups of members.

Article 43 refers to a "special agreement or agreements," thus leaving open for future decision whether it would be best to conclude one all-inclusive agreement, a series of limited agreements, or some combination of the two. The significance of the inclusion of the phrase "groups of members" in Article 43 is twofold: it was intended to facilitate negotiations between the Security Council and states such as Australia and New Zealand, which had already entered into mutual agreements on joint security and defense arrangements; it also covered the possibility of an agreement between the Council and the permanent members, which were expected to provide the bulk of the forces and were also charged with special responsibilities for the transitional period until the agreements under Article 43 came into force. In this connection, it should be noted that the discussions at San Francisco on "transitional security arrangements" made it clear that it was not necessary for all the agreements to be concluded before the system envisaged in Chapter VII could begin to operate. It was left to the Security Council to decide when progress in this respect had reached the point where it could begin to exercise its responsibilities.[111]

Report of the Military Staff Committee

Article 43(3) calls for the special agreements to be negotiated "as soon as possible." The first step in this regard was taken by the Security Council on February 16, 1946, when it directed the Military Staff Committee to examine Article 43 "from a military point of view" and report to the Council thereon.[112] The urgency with which the conclusion of the agreements was viewed was underlined by the General Assembly's resolution of December, 1946, on the general regulation and reduction of armaments, which recommended that the Security Council "accelerate as much as possible the placing at its disposal of the armed forces mentioned in Article 43 of the Charter." [113] The Council subsequently, on February 13, 1947, requested the Military Staff Committee to

110 *Ibid.*, p. 510.   111 See commentary on Art. 106.
112 SCOR/1st Yr., 1st Ser., No. 2/23d Mtg./Feb. 16, 1946/p. 369.
113 GA Res. 41(I), Dec. 14, 1946.

submit, "as soon as possible and as a matter of urgency," the recommendations the Council had asked for in February, 1946, and, as a first step, to submit to the Council not later than April 30, 1947, its recommendations regarding the basic principles which should govern the organization of United Nations armed forces.[114]

The Committee's report consisted of forty-one draft articles, twenty-five of which had been accepted unanimously.[115] Most of the points of disagreement—certainly the important ones—were between the Soviet Union on the one hand and the other permanent members on the other. With a few exceptions, China, the United Kingdom, and the United States were agreed on all aspects of the report, with France taking an independent middle position on some points.

AREAS OF AGREEMENT. It was agreed that the armed forces made available to the Security Council should be composed of land, sea, and air units normally maintained as components of the armed forces of the member nations. They should be of sufficient strength to enable the Security Council to take prompt action in any part of the world for the maintenance or restoration of international peace and security (Articles 3 and 5). It was recognized that the size of the forces required would be directly influenced by the great "moral weight and potential power" behind any Council decision to employ forces for enforcement action (Article 5).

All members should have the opportunity, as well as the obligation, to place forces, facilities, and other assistance at the disposal of the Security Council, but none should be encouraged to increase the strength of its forces or to create a particular component for the specific purpose of making a contribution (Articles 9 and 13). To facilitate the early establishment of armed forces, it was agreed that the permanent members should "contribute initially the major portion of these forces." Contributions from other members would be added as they became available; these contributions did not necessarily have to be in the form of armed forces, for the other members might fulfill their obligations by providing other kinds of assistance (Articles 10 and 14).

The forces were to be employed, in whole or in part, only on the decision of the Security Council and only for the period necessary for the fulfillment of the tasks envisaged in Article 42 of the Charter.[116] The report emphasized the need for the Security Council to be able to act promptly and the corresponding necessity for members to maintain

---

[114] SCOR/2d Yr./1947/*Supp. 5/Annex 13*, S/268/Rev. 1, pp. 58–59. For debate and vote, see *ibid.*, 2d Yr., No. 13/105th Mtg./Feb. 13, 1947.

[115] SCOR/2d Yr./1947/*Special Supp. 1*.

[116] Art. 18. China and France supported a statement that members would have the right to make use of their own forces in cases of self-defense and of national emergencies, but this was not approved by the other members. Art. 17.

the forces at the required degree of readiness. They were, moreover, to provide for necessary replacements in personnel and equipment and for this purpose to maintain specified levels of reserves (Articles 19, 22, 24, 29, and 30).

With regard to "strategic direction and command," it was agreed that the forces should be under the exclusive command of the respective contributing nations, except when operating under the Security Council. Then they would come under the control of the Council, be based as directed by the Council, and be under the strategic direction of the Military Staff Committee (Articles 36, 37, and 38). The Security Council might appoint an overall or supreme commander (or commanders) on the advice of the Military Staff Committee (Article 41). The contingents, however, would retain their national character and be subject to the discipline and regulations in force in their own national armed forces. The command of the national contingents would be exercised by commanders appointed by the respective member nations who would be entitled to communicate directly with the authorities of their own countries on all matters (Articles 39 and 40).

AREAS OF DISAGREEMENT. A basic point of disagreement between the Soviet Union and the other members concerned the strength and composition of the contributions to be made by the permanent members.[117] China, France, the United Kingdom, and the United States took the position that the initial contributions of all the permanent members should be "comparable," but that, "in view of the differences in size and composition of the national forces of each permanent member and in order to further the ability of the Security Council to constitute balanced and effective combat forces for operations," these contributions might differ widely as to the strength of the separate components of land, sea, and air forces. The United States contended that in order to have a force of the mobility and striking power required, one utilizing the latest techniques and developments, it was necessary for each member to provide those armaments it was best able to contribute.[118] The Soviet Union, however, insisted that the contributions of the permament members should be equal both in overall strength and in composition. Except by "special decision" of the Security Council, no permanent members should be allowed to contribute any forces of a type not made available by each of the others or to include in its contingents any component larger than, or different in composition from, the component contributed by any other permanent member.

Other major points upon which the Soviet Union and the other

[117] Art. 11. Disagreement on this point was responsible for the lack of agreement on a number of other articles in the report, such as Arts. 7, 8, 31, and 28.
[118] SCOR/2d Yr., No. 43/138th Mtg./June 4, 1947/p. 956.

members disagreed concerned the provision of bases, the location of forces, and their withdrawal following completion of their assignment.[119] China, the United Kingdom, and the United States considered that the special agreements should include a general guarantee covering rights of passage and the use of whatever bases might be required, as well as specific provisions covering details of the bases and other facilities to be made available to the Security Council. The Soviet Union objected especially to the provisions concerning bases, pointing out that there was no mention of this point in Article 43 of the Charter and claimed that the provision on bases might "be utilized by some states as a means of exerting political pressure" on other members.[120]

As for the location of forces, it was agreed that when engaged in action, they would be based as directed by the Security Council. The Soviet Union insisted that, when they were not so employed, the forces should be kept within the frontiers or territorial waters of the contributing nations, with the sole exception of forces engaged in the occupation of the former enemy countries. China, the United Kingdom, and the United States, on the other hand, held that within the terms of the special agreements, the forces might be based at the discretion of member nations in any territory or waters to which they had legal rights of access. France took a slightly different position, considering that the locations should be defined more specifically. The Soviet Union also objected to the provision that the forces should be so distributed geographically as to enable the Security Council to take prompt action in any part of the world.[121]

The Soviet Union favored strict provisions for the withdrawal of forces. Under its proposal, the forces would be withdrawn to their own territory or territorial waters within thirty to ninety days after they had completed their mission. Any extension of the time limit would require specific authorization by the Security Council. While favoring prompt withdrawal, the other members considered that the timing should be decided upon by the Council. Under the Soviet plan, any one of the permanent members could in effect force a premature withdrawal. The Soviet Union objected that the four-power formula might be "used as a pretext for the continued presence of foreign troops in the territory of another state." [122]

[119] For disagreement on the implementation of Art. 45 of the Charter, see commentary on that article.

[120] France took a middle position. SCOR/2d Yr./1947/*Special Supp. 1*/pp. 20–22. See also the Soviet statement in SCOR/2d Yr., No. 44/139th Mtg./June 6, 1947/pp. 970–71. Note also the divergent position taken on this point at the Dumbarton Oaks Conference, see above, p. 318.

[121] See SCOR/2d Yr./1947/*Special Supp. 1*/pp. 26–30.

[122] See *ibid.*, pp. 17–19. See also Soviet statement in SCOR/2d Yr., No. 44/139th Mtg./June 16, 1947/p. 975.

At first glance, these differences may not seem sufficiently grave to rule out the possibility of eventual agreement. But the problem, as the Soviet representative pointed out, was primarily political rather than technical.[123] Disagreements over the details of the articles in the report of the Military Staff Committee reflected growing distrust, especially between the Soviet Union and the United States. These two nations were obviously in fundamental disagreement as to the kind of force the Security Council should have at its disposal.

In the United States view, the problem facing the United Nations was that of enforcing peace "in all parts of the world." To do so, the Organization needed, "first of all, a mobile force able to strike quickly at long range and to bring to bear, upon any given point in the world where trouble may occur, the maximum armed force in the minimum time." [124] The Soviet delegate's position was that "it would be sufficient for the Security Council to have at its disposal relatively small armed forces"; in this connection, he drew attention to the fact that the former enemy states were "under the control of the Allies," and that the United Nations had already gone on record in favor of the general regulation and reduction of armaments. There was thus no need for "excessively numerous armed forces." [125] The Soviet view derives a measure of support from the assumption—quite generally made from the beginning—that the forces made available to the Security Council would not, by virtue of Article 27(3), be used against a permanent member, nor indeed in any case where the five permanent members were not in agreement. The United States appeared unwilling to concede this point,[126] and Soviet apprehensions as to the possible future use of these forces may have been increased further by the following statement by the United Kingdom representative:

If any one of the permanent members, guilty of a breach of the peace or of an act of aggression, were to call a halt to the United Nations force, the remainder of the United Nations would be entitled [under Article 51] to take action against that Member. Their forces, already made available to the Security Council, could legitimately be jointly employed to that end for so long as the Security Council failed to take the measures necessary to maintain international peace and security.[127]

Soviet suspicions were undoubtedly further enhanced by the provisional estimates the United States submitted regarding the overall strength and composition of the forces to be made available to the

[123] SCOR/2d Yr., No. 50/146th Mtg./June 25, 1947/p. 1099.
[124] Ibid., 138th Mtg./June 4, 1947/p. 956.
[125] Ibid., No. 44/139th Mtg./June 6, 1947/p. 968.
[126] See, for example, ibid., 142d Mtg./June 18, 1947/p. 1026.
[127] Ibid., No. 45/140th Mtg./June 10, 1947/p. 995.

Security Council. It should be noted that, on this point, the estimates of the other permanent members were much closer to those of the Soviet Union than to those of the United States.

The United States envisaged a large force with heavy emphasis on mobility and striking power. With regard to ground forces, the United States proposed twenty divisions; the French, sixteen; the Soviet Union, twelve; and Britain and China, eight to twelve. It was the estimates for air and naval forces, however, that strikingly revealed the differences between the United States and the other members regarding the kind of forces the Security Council would require. The United States proposed an air force more than three times as large as that favored by any of the other permanent members. Its naval estimates included over three times as many destroyers, over seven times as many submarines, and in addition called for battleships, aircraft carriers, and assault craft; none of these were mentioned in the Soviet figures.[128]

Although discussion of the report of the Military Staff Committee in June–July, 1947, resulted in some clarifications and minor drafting changes, it proved impossible to reconcile the differences among the permanent members. Discussions continued in the Military Staff Committee for another year or so. Since then, the committee has continued to meet, but only as a matter of form.

Subsequent Developments

The failure of the negotiations on special agreements called for in Article 43 was accompanied by a growing realization that fundamental disagreement among the major powers all but precluded their joint action "on behalf of the Organization" as envisaged under the transitional security arrangements set forth in Chapter XVII.[129] In consequence, there were numerous proposals over the years for other ways of providing the United Nations with the military forces needed for maintaining international peace and security.

The first of these was a very modest proposal by Secretary-General Trygve Lie. Drawing upon United Nations experience, especially in Palestine, he suggested the creation of a United Nations Guard Force to be recruited by the Secretary-General and placed at the disposal of the Security Council and the General Assembly. He stressed that the force "would not be used as a substitute for the forces contemplated in

---

[128] For the estimates, see *Y.U.N.*, 1947–48, p. 495. The United States subsequently revised its estimates downward. See State Dept., *The United States and the United Nations, 1947*, p. 108.

[129] See commentary on Art. 106.

Articles 42 and 43" of the Charter.[130] The Soviet Union, however, attacked the proposal as contrary to the Charter, and other members showed little enthusiasm for it.[131]

A much more far-reaching plan for making forces available to the United Nations was incorporated in the Uniting for Peace resolution, adopted by the General Assembly in November, 1950. Among its provisions was a recommendation that each member "maintain within its national armed forces elements so trained, organized, and equipped that they could promptly be made available . . . for service as a United Nations unit or units." The plan was designed to provide for possible future actions by the United Nations similar to that then being undertaken in Korea. At the same time, the Assembly, on the initiative of the Soviet Union, recommended that the Security Council "devise measures for the earliest application of Articles 43, 45, 46, and 47 of the Charter." [132] It is unlikely that anyone at that time considered that a new effort to conclude the special agreements called for in Article 43 would meet with success. The recommendation can more logically be viewed as reflecting the reluctance of many members to abandon completely the original concept of a collective security system based on great-power unity.

Although most members, except for the Soviet group, voted for the Uniting for Peace resolution, there was little positive response to the recommendation for earmarking forces for possible use by the United Nations; [133] this indicated the general reluctance of members to make advance commitments. They had been willing to do so when they originally accepted the Charter, but with the understanding that their commitments would be limited under the special agreements and that they would not be called upon to implement their pledges in any situation in which the major powers were not agreed. Even though the Uniting for Peace resolution envisaged action on the basis of "recommendations" which members would not be legally obligated to accept and carry out, members were still wary of committing themselves in any way.

Dislike for advance commitments, however, does not appear in most

[130] See GAOR/3d Sess./1948/*Supp. 1*/pp. xvii–xviii.

[131] Trygve Lie's later suggestions for an International Brigade in Korea and for a UN Legion in connection with the Uniting for Peace resolution met with a similarly cool reception. For an account of his initiatives, see Stephen M. Schweibel, "A United Nations 'Legion,'" in William R. Frye, *A United Nations Peace Force* (New York, Oceana, 1957).

[132] GA Res. 377A and B(V), Nov. 3, 1950.

[133] For the initial responses, see *Report of the Collective Measures Committee,* GAOR/6th Sess./1951/*Supp. 13*(A/1891), pp. 37–43. See also Leland M. Goodrich and Anne P. Simons, *The United Nations and the Maintenance of International Peace and Security* (Washington, Brookings Institution, 1955), pp. 408 ff.

cases to have deterred members from responding positively to requests from the Secretary-General, under General Assembly and Security Council resolutions, for military forces to carry out peace-keeping functions in specific situations. Various proposals have been made from time to time to utilize the United Nations experience with these ad hoc arrangements as a basis for the creation of a standing United Nations peace force, but there has been little enthusiasm for this with the exception of the United States.[134] Secretary-General Hammarskjöld, in particular, considered that a standing United Nations force was unnecessary and impractical.[135]

Article 44

When the Security Council has decided to use force it shall, before calling upon a Member not represented on it to provide armed forces in fulfillment of the obligations assumed under Article 43, invite that Member, if the Member so desires, to participate in the decisions of the Security Council concerning the employment of contingents of that Member's armed forces.

Article 44 is one of the additions to the Dumbarton Oaks Proposals agreed upon at the San Francisco Conference to provide greater protection for the interests of the smaller, and especially the middle-sized, powers. Many of these states viewed with alarm the absence of any provision assuring them of the opportunity to present their views in the Security Council before they were called upon to supply armed forces for the carrying out of a Council decision. The permanent members of the Council, it was pointed out, by reason of their veto power, reserved to themselves "the right not to participate in any action with which they did not agree." At least, the other members of the Organization should be assured of not being called upon to go to war without even being consulted; there should be "no military action with out representation," as one delegate put it.[136] The decision of the San Francisco Conference on this point, it was warned, was likely to affect the obligations members would be willing to accept when the time came for negotiating the "special agreements" called for under Article 43.

[134] For the U.S. position, see, for example, statements by President Eisenhower and Secretary Dulles at the time of the crisis over Lebanon. GAOR/3d Emer. Spec. Sess./733d Plen. Mtg./Aug. 13, 1958/paras. 28 ff.; and 13th Sess./749th Plen. Mtg./Sept. 18, 1958/paras. 48 ff. See also *United Nations Emergency Force.* Hears./HR CFR Subcommittee on International Organizations and Movements/85C2/1958.

[135] GAOR/15th Sess./1960/*Supp. 1A*/p. 4. See also his report on the experience derived from UNEF. GAOR/18th Sess./1958/*Annexes*, agenda item 65(A/3943, Oct. 9, 1958).

[136] UNCIO, *Documents*, XII, 303, 316.

The text finally agreed upon was based on a Canadian proposal, modified slightly during the debate. Under it, the Council is required to invite a member not represented on it to "participate" before calling upon that member to provide armed forces, if the member so requests. However, participation under Article 44 applies only when the Council is taking a decision "concerning the employment of contingents of . . . armed forces." A move led by Egypt to expand the scope of the article to grant the same privileges to any member called upon to provide "facilities and assistance" was defeated on the grounds that this would unduly hamper the work of the Council and that the position of these members was adequately protected by other articles of the Charter, in particular Articles 31, 43, and 47(2).

It should be noted that Article 44 differs from other articles concerning participation in the work of the Security Council. Those invited to participate in the Council's discussions in accordance with Articles 31 and 32 of the Charter are specifically denied the right to vote. Under Article 44, an invited member is entitled to participate in the "decisions," not merely the "discussions," of the Council. It was intended that these members should have the right to vote on any proposals concerning the employment of the armed forces they agreed to put at the disposal of the Security Council,[137] but it was made clear that an invited member would be entitled to participate only in those decisions concerning its own armed forces.

Since the "special agreements" called for in Article 43 have never been concluded, there has been no occasion for the application of Article 44. When members have supplied armed forces for carrying out United Nations resolutions, they have done so on a voluntary basis and the way in which these forces have been employed has been primarily a subject of negotiation rather than decision by the Security Council. Thus, in general, members supplying such forces have not considered it necessary to participate in the Council's discussions.[138]

Article 45

In order to enable the United Nations to take urgent military measures, Members shall hold immediately available national air-force contingents for combined international enforcement action. The strength and degree of readiness of these contingents and plans for their combined action shall be determined, within the limits laid down in the special agreement or agreements referred to in Article 43,

[137] See State Dept., *Report to the President*, p. 94.
[138] Many of the members supplying forces for UN operations in the Congo, however, did take part in the Council's discussions.

by the Security Council with the assistance of the Military Staff Committee.

This provision for national air force contingents to be immediately available for urgent military measures stemmed from a Soviet proposal at Dumbarton Oaks that the Security Council should have at its command an "international air-force corps" for emergency use. At an earlier stage, United States planners had considered the possibility of establishing an international air force, but had concluded that the political problems involved were insolvable.[139] When the Soviet proposal was discussed at Dumbarton Oaks, the United States made clear its opposition to any "international" forces, and even opposed a British suggestion for an examination of their practicability.[140] Thus, Article 45 provides for national air force contingents to be immediately available for "combined international enforcement action."

At the San Francisco Conference, the wisdom of giving a unique place to air-force contingents was questioned by some delegates. Both France and Australia proposed that contingents from all services be held immediately available. These proposals were withdrawn, partly as the result of the decision to specify in Article 43 that the special agreements making forces available to the Security Council would cover not only the number and types of forces but also "their degree of readiness and general location." Moreover, it was agreed that the mention of air-force contingents was "solely for the purpose of supplementary precision" and would not "in any way" restrict the "general scope" of Article 43.[141]

When the Military Staff Committee subsequently considered the principles governing the organization of armed forces to be made available to the Security Council, the implementation of Article 45 was one of the points of disagreement. The Soviet Union took the view that the implementation of this article could take place only after the conclusion of the special agreements, when the Security Council, with the assistance of the Military Staff Committee, would determine what portion of the "overall numbers of national air force contingents made available to the Security Council under the agreements should be held immediately available for the taking of urgent military measures in case of necessity." [142] The other four members felt that the strength, com-

[139] Russell, pp. 235–36. See also the proposal for a small air force composed of earmarked national contingents, *ibid.*, p. 254.

[140] *Ibid.*, pp. 470–72.

[141] France, however, announced that it was not relinquishing its "future advocacy of the principle that international forces of all categories" should be at the disposal of the Council. UNCIO, *Documents,* XII, 432–33, 511.

[142] SCOR/2d Yr./1947/*Special Supp. 1*/p. 13.

position, and readiness of the national air-force contingents to be made available under the Article 43 agreements should be determined in part by the special obligations arising from Article 45. This difference was not considered as crucial as other disagreements within the Military Staff Committee; the Soviet Union referred to it as a difference over "time rather than principle." [143]

Article 46

Plans for the application of armed force shall be made by the Security Council with the assistance of the Military Staff Committee.

The Military Staff Committee was intended to serve as a general staff responsible to the Security Council for overall strategic planning and technical advice on military matters.[144] This concept evolved out of the experience of World War II. As the United States Secretary of State explained, what was done "was simply to take the idea of the Combined Chiefs of Staff which played such a significant role in Anglo-American strategic planning and direction and adjust it to the needs of the new Organization." [145]

There are many historical examples of the importance of advance planning for joint military operations. In the League of Nations, France persistently stressed the need for such planning to assure the effectiveness of whatever joint military action might be taken under the Covenant. There are, however, rather severe limitations upon the amount of useful advance planning any body such as the Military Staff Committee can undertake. A national military staff can consider a range of possibilities and draw up plans to meet them. Within a coalition, agreement may be more difficult but planning is not impossible. In an organization such as the United Nations, however, advance planning can be of only the most general kind, because of the impossibility of identifying the possible "enemy" in advance.

Article 47

1. There shall be established a Military Staff Committee to advise and assist the Security Council on all questions relating to the Security Council's military requirements for the maintenance of international peace and security, the employment and command of forces

---

[143] SCOR/2d Yr., No. 44/139th Mtg./June 6, 1947/p. 979. See also comment by Australia, *ibid.*, p. 1016.

[144] For the organization and functions of the Military Staff Committee, see commentary on Art. 47.

[145] See State Dept., *Report to the President,* p. 98.

placed at its disposal, the regulation of armaments, and possible disarmament.

2. The Military Staff Committee shall consist of the Chiefs of Staff of the permanent members of the Security Council or their representatives. Any Member of the United Nations not permanently represented on the Committee shall be invited by the Committee to be associated with it when the efficient discharge of the Committee's responsibilities requires the participation of that Member in its work.

3. The Military Staff Committee shall be responsible under the Security Council for the strategic direction of any armed forces placed at the disposal of the Security Council. Questions relating to the command of such forces shall be worked out subsequently.

4. The Military Staff Committee, with the authorization of the Security Council and after consultation with appropriate regional agencies, may establish regional subcommittees.

The position of the Military Staff Committee as a subsidiary organ within the United Nations system is unique in that its establishment, composition, and terms of reference are provided for in the Charter itself. The need for an organ to carry out the functions listed in Article 47 was readily agreed upon at Dumbarton Oaks, and the text proposed by the Sponsoring Governments was accepted by the San Francisco Conference virtually without change. Only two issues—the composition of the Committee and the establishment of regional subcommittees—provoked any extended debate.

Composition

The restriction of the membership of the Military Staff Committee to the five permanent members of the Security Council was highly distasteful to many of the other powers. Considerable pressure was exerted at San Francisco to secure wider representation upon the Committee. The two main proposals were that the Committee be composed of the chiefs of staff of all the members of the Council, and that some provision be made for "regional" representation on the Committee.

The principal argument against enlargement was that, because of the nature of its functions, the Committee had to be small and had to have continuity of membership. Moreover, it was felt that the interests of other members were adequately safeguarded by other provisions of the Charter. It was pointed out that Article 47(2) provides that, when appropriate, members not represented on the Committee should be invited to be associated with its work, and that there was no question but that the Committee would consult any member whose forces were to be used. In addition, members would be invited under Article 44 to participate in the decisions of the Security Council itself before they were called upon to provide armed forces.[146] In the light of these explanations, the Conference accepted the Dumbarton Oaks text. "Concern for efficiency, for permanency of membership, and for apportioning military responsibility according to military capacity, dictated leaving the membership unchanged." [147]

This restricted membership caused some difficulty in the relationship between the Military Staff Committee and the Security Council, or, more precisely, the nonpermanent members of the Council. The problem is made more difficult by certain decisions the Committee has taken concerning its methods of operation. Its meetings have been strictly private; its records have been available only to the members of the Committee; and even its secretariat was for some time quite separate from the general Secretariat of the Organization. This situation was strongly criticized, especially by the Australian representative on the Security Council. He stressed the right of any member of the Council to ask the Committee for interpretations, explanations, or assistance, pointing out that it was the function of the Committee to advise the Security Council as a whole.[148]

Regional Subcommittees

The second aspect of Article 47 discussed at San Francisco was the provision enabling the Military Staff Committee, "with the authorization of the Security Council," to establish "regional subcommittees." [149] To protect the position of the regional organizations, it was proposed that subcommittees be established only "in agreement with regional organizations." When this was objected to, a compromise was reached whereby the subcommittees would be established "after consultation" with the appropriate regional agencies. It

[146] See UNCIO, *Documents*, XII, 381–82.

[147] State Dept., *Report to the President*, p. 97.

[148] See SCOR/2d Yr., No. 44/139th Mtg./June 6, 1947/pp. 983 ff.; and No. 49/145th Mtg./June 24, 1947/p. 1090. On the right of any member to address questions to the Committee, see also the exchange between the Netherlands and the U.K. during the discussion of Art. 47 at San Francisco. UNCIO, *Documents*, XII, 388.

[149] Under the Dumbarton Oaks Proposals, this matter was included as part of the authorization to the Security Council to establish subsidiary organs, but the sponsoring powers subsequently proposed transferring this function to the Military Staff Committee.

was made clear, however, that it was "definitely intended to leave to the Military Staff Committee the final decision as to the establishment of such subcommittees." [150]

This provision was obviously intended to facilitate the utilization of regional agencies for enforcement action as envisaged in Article 53 of the Charter. The subcommittees could also make a useful contribution to the proper integration of the plans and activities of regional agencies and the Security Council. No action has ever been taken to implement this provision of the Charter. It was not even mentioned in the Military Staff Committee's report on principles governing the organization of the armed forces to be placed at the disposal of the Security Council.[151]

Functions

The functions of the Military Staff Committee as laid down in Article 47 are threefold. First, it is to advise and assist the Security Council on all questions relating to the Council's military requirements for the maintenance of international peace and security; its second category of functions relates to the employment and command of forces placed at the disposal of the Council; and lastly, the Committee is to advise and assist on questions relating to the regulation of armaments and possible disarmament.

The only task the Military Staff Committee has undertaken has been the preparation for the Security Council of a report on the "General Principles Governing the Organization of the Armed Forces Made Available to the Security Council by Member Nations of the United Nations." As pointed out in the commentary on Article 43, this report revealed a fundamental disagreement among the members of the Committee. Following the failure to break this deadlock, the Military Staff Committee, for all practical purposes, ceased to function.

As to the functions of the Military Staff Committee with regard to the "employment and command" of forces placed at the disposal of the Security Council, Article 47(3) makes it clear that the Committee was expected to exercise "strategic direction" rather than tactical command. Questions of command arrangements were left for subsequent consideration. The Military Staff Committee devoted one chapter of its

---

[150] UNCIO, *Documents*, XII, 548. See also Russell, p. 678.

[151] See statement by Belgium on this point. SCOR/2d Yr., No. 43/138th Mtg./ June 4, 1947/pp. 960–61. Various military advisory committees have been set up by the parties to regional security arrangements, but these have no relations with the Military Staff Committee of the UN.

above-mentioned report to questions of "Strategic Direction and Command." This was one area in which all the members were in basic agreement, but the failure to conclude the agreements called for in Article 43 has meant that the Military Staff Committee has had no role to play in any of the situations in which the United Nations has employed armed forces.

In the Korean conflict, pursuant to recommendations by the Security Council, direction of the forces contributed by member states fell to the United States, functioning as the "Unified Command." After studying this experience, the Collective Measures Committee concluded that in any future collective action of this kind, an "executive military authority" should be designated and made responsible for the "coordination, strategic direction, and control of military operations." [152] In peace-keeping operations, such as UNEF and the Congo force, the functions of planning and direction have been entrusted to the Secretary-General, acting with the assistance of advisory committees and within the broad framework of resolutions by the General Assembly and the Security Council. In challenging the legality of these operations, the Soviet Union has cited Article 47 and the by-passing of the Military Staff Committee.

The third category of functions of the Military Staff Committee as listed in Article 47(1) is to advise and assist the Security Council on questions relating to "the regulation of armaments and possible disarmament." The counterpart to this provision is Article 26 of the Charter, which makes the Security Council "responsible for formulating, with the assistance of the Military Staff Committee . . . plans . . . for the establishment of a system for the regulation of armaments." As pointed out in the commentary on Article 26, the Security Council has not since 1949 played an active part in the United Nations discussions on disarmament. Even during the initial period when the Council was concerned with this subject, it did not ask for advice or assistance from the Military Staff Committee. When the Council established the Commission for Conventional Armaments, it did instruct the Commission to "make such proposals as it may deem advisable concerning the studies which the Military Staff Committee . . . might be asked to undertake," but the Commission made no such proposals. Thus, the Committee has played no role in the disarmament discussions.[153]

---

[152] GAOR/6th Sess./1951/*Supp. 13*(A/1891), p. 32.

[153] Both the Security Council and the General Assembly, however, recognized the significant relationship between arms reduction and the Committee's responsibilities with regard to the Art. 43 agreements. See SCOR/2d Yr./*Supp. 5/Annex 13*(S/268/Rev. 1), pp. 58–59; and GA Res. 41(I), Dec. 14, 1946.

Article 48

1. The action required to carry out the decisions of the Security Council for the maintenance of international peace and security shall be taken by all the Members of the United Nations or by some of them, as the Security Council may determine.

2. Such decisions shall be carried out by the Members of the United Nations directly and through their action in the appropriate international agencies of which they are members.

Article 48 restates and amplifies the obligations of members to carry out the decisions of the Security Council for the maintenance of international peace and security. The initial paragraph serves a dual purpose. First, it emphasizes the obligations of all members of the United Nations to take action. Second, it introduces an element of flexibility into the Charter arrangements by giving the Security Council discretionary authority to decide which members shall be called upon to take action. Article 48(2) recognizes that, in addition to the United Nations itself, there are other international agencies which may be in a position to make a contribution to the maintenance of peace, and that the obligations of members extend to their actions in these agencies.

Selective Participation

Implicit in Article 48 is the authority of the Security Council to direct some members of the United Nations to take certain kinds of action, while others may be required to take other kinds of measures. The Council, for example, might decide that military action should be taken by the members of a regional organization or by those situated in a particular geographic area, while others might be required to apply political or economic measures only. As the United States Secretary of State pointed out in his report on the San Francisco Conference, "while security and world peace are of universal concern, the realities of geography must also be considered." Moreover, he continued, "one must also recognize a distinction between the world-wide responsibilities of the great powers and the more restricted scope of activities of the lesser states" whose "military effectiveness in areas remote from their home territories is likely to be slight." [154] Here again is a manifestation of the original assumption that the bulk of the forces for any military action decided upon by the Security Council would be supplied by the five permanent members. This assumption was further supported by

[154] State Dept., *Report to the President*, p. 98.

the conclusion of the Military Staff Committee that the obligations of other members under Article 43 might be fulfilled by the furnishing of facilities and other assistance rather than armed forces.[155]

In practice, the situation has been virtually the reverse. For the most part, whatever forces the United Nations has required have been contributed by members other than the permanent members of the Security Council. The plans the Secretary-General drew up for the organization of UNEF and the United Nations force in the Congo specifically excluded contribution of forces by the permanent members. That the Secretary-General decided which members would be asked to contribute forces was one of the grounds upon which the Soviet Union challenged the legality of these operations. The Soviet Union charged that the original Security Council resolution on the Congo was implemented in violation of the Charter, under which the Council alone determines which states are to participate in any action undertaken for the maintenance of international peace and security.[156] This argument was rejected by the International Court of Justice. Drawing attention to the repeated confirmation of the Secretary-General's actions by the Security Council and the General Assembly, the Court in its advisory opinion stated that "it is impossible to reach the conclusion that the operations in question usurped or impinged upon the prerogatives conferred by the Charter on the Security Council." [157]

Role of the Specialized Agencies

The Charter recognizes that international agencies other than the United Nations can play a role in the maintenance of international peace and security. The role of regional agencies is dealt with specifically in Chapter VIII. Less specifically stated is the relationship of the specialized agencies to the Charter system for the maintenance of international peace and security. The Charter does not provide for a direct link between the Security Council and these agencies. The organ principally responsible for relations with them is ECOSOC, which in turn is obligated to assist the Security Council upon request.[158] However, as Article 48 recognizes, one of the best guarantees of adequate coordination is the pursuit by members, in the various agencies, of policies consistent with their obligations under the Charter.

All the agreements between the United Nations and the specialized agencies provide that the latter will render assistance to the United

[155] SCOR/2d Yr./1947/*Special Supp. 1*/p. 3.
[156] See, for example, GAOR/16th Sess./1961/*Annexes*, agenda items 49, 50.
[157] "Certain Expenses of the United Nations," *ICJ Reports*, 1962, pp. 175–77.
[158] See commentary on Arts. 63 and 65.

Nations. The extent of the commitment to support action by the Security Council, however, varies from agency to agency. Thus, the International Bank and the International Fund agree to provide the Security Council with information. Their agreements also take note of the "obligations" assumed by members under Article 48(2) and state that the two agencies will "have due regard for decisions of the Security Council under Articles 41 and 42." The agreements with ILO, FAO, UNESCO, and ICAO, on the other hand, contain more explicit provisions by which the agencies agree "to cooperate" with ECOSOC "in furnishing such information and rendering such assistance to the Security Council as that Council may request, including assistance in carrying out decisions for the maintenance or restoration of international peace and security."

On two occasions, the Security Council has addressed requests to the specialized agencies for assistance. At an early stage in the Korean conflict, the Council asked the agencies to provide assistance to the Unified Command for the relief and support of the civilian population in Korea.[159] Shortly after the United Nations became involved in the situation in the Congo, the Council, following a request by the Secretary-General, invited the specialized agencies to render such assistance as might be required.[160]

The most extensive discussion of the role the specialized agencies might play in the maintenance of international peace and security occurred in connection with the Uniting for Peace resolution. As a consequence of that resolution, ECOSOC asked the Secretary-General "to consult with the specialized agencies as to the specific arrangements they might most appropriately make in order to provide for the furnishing by them of such information and for the rendering of such assistance in the maintenance or restoration of international peace and security as may be requested by the Security Council or the General Assembly." [161] In response to this initiative, a number of the agencies adopted resolutions pledging their cooperation in any measures taken under the Uniting for Peace resolution.

The possible role of the specialized agencies was examined in considerable detail by the Collective Measures Committee, which was charged by the Assembly with studying methods "which might be used to maintain and strengthen international peace and security." On the basis of the Committee's first report, the General Assembly recommended that members belonging to other international bodies or

159 SCOR/5th Yr., No. 21/479th Mtg./July 31, 1950/p. 3.
160 SCOR/15th Yr./877th Mtg./July 20–21, 1960/para. 14; and 879th Mtg./July 21–22, 1960/para. 108.
161 ECOSOC Res. 363(XII), Mar. 14, 1951.

parties to international arrangements should "seek to obtain . . . in and through such bodies and arrangements, all possible support for collective measures undertaken by the United Nations." [162]

In its second report, the Collective Measures Committee dealt in more detail with the specific kinds of support the various agencies might be in a position to render. In its conclusions, the Committee stated that "members of the United Nations which are also members of the specialized agencies have an essential part to play in assuring ready co-operation and assistance on the part of those agencies in United Nations collective measures." In this connection, the Committee stressed "that the mobilization for collective-security purposes of the resources of the individual agencies depends fundamentally on the collective will of their respective memberships" and expressed its confidence that, in the event collective measures were undertaken, members would give "effect" to the provisions of Article 48 of the Charter.[163]

Article 49

The Members of the United Nations shall join in affording mutual assistance in carrying out the measures decided upon by the Security Council.

The obligation of mutual assistance as set forth in Article 49 is in essence a reaffirmation and extension of the principle of assistance stated in Article 2(5) and the general obligations assumed by members under Article 25. It corresponds in a general way with Article 16(3) of the Covenant of the League of Nations, under which members agreed to "mutually support one another" in the event sanctions were decided upon.

Article 49 clearly applies to the furnishing of both military assistance and economic and financial assistance, the latter being further particularized in Article 50. As the United States Secretary of State pointed out in his report on the San Francisco Conference, "these two articles provide for a world-wide adjustment, by equitable distribution of the economic burden of sanctions, to the accidents of geography and international trade." [164]

The principle of mutual assistance was accepted at Dumbarton Oaks, despite Soviet skepticism as to the possibilities of devising practical methods for its implementation.[165] The text of Article 49 as adopted at San Francisco is virtually identical with the text agreed upon at

[162] GA Res. 503A(VI), Jan. 12, 1952.
[163] GAOR/7th Sess./1952/*Supp. 17*(A/2215)/pp. 7–10.
[164] State Dept., *Report to the President*, p. 99.   [165] Russell, p. 466.

Dumbarton Oaks. The only aspect of the matter that was discussed at any length at the Conference concerned the expenses of enforcement measures. The Union of South Africa sought to include in Article 49 a provision requiring the party against which measures were taken "to pay the costs of such enforcement action and to make reparation for losses and damage sustained thereby." Under this scheme, the Security Council would approve claims and be responsible for the "action required to ensure recovery." Although this proposal was defeated, it was agreed to include in the rapporteur's report a mention of the "desire" that the Organization "should, in the future, seek to promote a system aiming at the fairest possible distribution of expenses incurred as a result of enforcement action." [166]

Aside from the exchange of views on the costs of enforcement action, there was no discussion at San Francisco concerning the extent of the obligations of members under Article 49. Nor has this matter been discussed in the Security Council. The report of the Military Staff Committee contained a reference to Article 49 in the chapter on "Logistical Support of Armed Forces." China, the United Kingdom, and the United States favored the inclusion of a provision whereby a member might invoke the aid of the Security Council in seeking assistance from other members, if it found itself unable effectively to discharge its responsibilities under Article 43.[167] This was one of the articles in the report on which agreement was not reached.

The concept of mutual assistance was discussed at some length in the Collective Measures Committee. The Committee paid particular attention to economic and financial measures and in this connection reviewed past experience, especially of the League of Nations and World War II. In its first report, the Committee included the following among the "guiding principles" it recommended:

The application of economic and financial measures, whether to weaken the aggressor or to assist the victim State and co-operating States, should, as a matter of mutual assistance, be equitably shared as far as possible among the co-operating States, taking into account the total burden borne by them in relation to the collective action and their abilities.[168]

The Committee also recommended that the United Nations should assume responsibility for the coordination of such measures.

In its second report, the Committee again emphasized "the impor-

---

[166] UNCIO, *Documents*, XII, 613, 513. See also statement by delegate of Canada, *ibid.*, p. 443. For problems the UN has faced in financing peace-keeping operations, see commentary on Art. 17.

[167] The importance of mutual assistance under Art. 49 was particularly stressed by China. SCOR/2d Yr./1947/*Special Supp. 1*/pp. 6 and 24–25.

[168] GAOR/6th Sess./1951/*Supp. 13*(A/1891), pp. 16–19, 33.

tance of mutual assistance in the application of collective measures."
After drawing attention to Articles 49 and 50, the report stated that
"the same principles should apply" whenever collective action is undertaken by the General Assembly in conformity with the Uniting for
Peace resolution.[169]

It is not at all unusual for the Security Council and the General
Assembly to include in their resolutions a provision "requesting," "recommending," or "calling upon" members to render assistance in actions
taken by those organs for the maintenance of international peace and
security. In some cases, the measures to be taken by members are
specified, but often the resolutions are couched in the general language
of Article 2(5) of the Charter.

Only in connection with the situation in the Congo has Article 49
been specifically invoked. As pointed out in the commentary on Article
25, the Security Council in its resolution of August 9, 1960, called upon
all members "in accordance with Articles 25 and 49 of the Charter of
the United Nations, to accept and carry out the decisions of the Security Council and to afford mutual assistance in carrying out measures
decided upon by the Council." Subsequently, the General Assembly
adopted a similar resolution couched in the form of a "request" to all
member states. Aside from one comment stressing that Article 49 required not merely compliance with but "positive" assistance in the
implementation of the Council's resolutions,[170] neither in the Security
Council nor in the General Assembly was there any discussion concerning the obligations of members under Article 49 or the specific measures they were expected to undertake.

Some light upon the relationship between these obligations and
United Nations actions in the Congo is provided by various statements
by the Secretary-General. While stating that none of these actions
could be construed as enforcement measures within the meaning of
Articles 41 and 42, he repeatedly stressed the "mandatory character" of
the Council's decisions and the "legal obligations" thereby imposed
upon members. In these statements, he frequently referred to the invocation of Articles 25 and 49 in the Council's resolution of August 9,
1960.

Immediately following the adoption of this resolution, the Secretary-
General asked for and received assurance from the Republic of the
Congo that it would "apply the rules of co-operation" which derive
from Article 49 of the Charter.[171] It should be noted that the Republic

[169] GAOR/7th Sess./1952/*Supp. 17*(A/2215), p. 6.
[170] Delegate of Ecuador, SCOR/15th Yr./886th Mtg./Aug. 8–9, 1960/pars.
47–49.
[171] SCOR/15th Yr./*Supp.* for July, Aug., and Sept., 1960/p. 57.

of the Congo (Leopoldville) at that time had not been admitted to membership in the United Nations. Although Article 49 specifically refers only to "Members" of the Organization, the Secretary-General considered that the principles of that article were nevertheless applicable. Furthermore, with regard to Katanga, the Secretary-General expressed the view that Articles 25 and 49 "confer on the Security Council an authority applicable directly to Governments, and a fortiori to subordinate territorial non-governmental authorities." [172]

With regard to the importation of Belgian weapons into Katanga, the Secretary-General emphasized that this action was contrary to the resolutions of the Security Council, which were "binding under Articles 25 and 49." [173] He also cited the Council's resolution invoking these two articles in protesting attacks by Congolese troops against United Nations forces. In this case, he stressed that members were "under the obligation positively and actively to assist" the United Nations operations and were precluded from taking any actions that might hamper those operations or render them ineffective.[174]

Two further references by the Secretary-General to Article 49 deserve note. In expressing grave concern over the conduct of Ghanaian troops in the Congo, he asked that Ghana give assurances of "unreserved support in keeping with Article 49 of the Charter" to the actions decided upon by the Security Council.[175] On another occasion, in protesting a decision by the Republic of the Congo (Brazzaville) to forbid landing and overfly rights to aircraft transporting men and supplies for ONUC, the Secretary-General stated that these measures constituted a "clear violation" of United Nations resolutions and "flagrantly" contradicted the provisions of Articles 25 and 49 of the Charter.[176]

Article 50

If preventive or enforcement measures against any state are taken by the Security Council, any other state, whether a Member of the United Nations or not, which finds itself confronted with special economic problems arising from the carrying out of those measures shall have the right to consult the Security Council with regard to a solution of those problems.

[172] *Ibid.*, pp. 48–49.

[173] See his letter of Sept. 8, 1960 to Belgium, *ibid.*, p. 139.

[174] See his letter of Mar. 8, 1961. SCOR/16th Yr./*Supp.* for Jan., Feb., and Mar., 1961/pp. 262–63.

[175] See his note of Aug. 18, 1960. SCOR/15th Yr./*Supp.* for July, Aug., and Sept., 1960/pp. 99–100.

[176] See SCOR/16th Yr./*Supp.* for Oct., Nov., and Dec., 1961/pp. 211–12.

As a corollary to the obligation of mutual assistance under Article 49, the Charter provides in Article 50 for specific recourse to the Security Council for any state confronted with "special economic problems" as the result of measures decided upon by the Security Council. The two articles differ somewhat in scope. While Article 49 refers to "measures decided upon by the Security Council," Article 50 is more specific in referring to "preventive or enforcement measures." Moreover, under Article 50 any state, whether a member of the United Nations or not, has the right to consult the Council. The obligation of mutual assistance, however, specifically applies only to members of the Organization. Thus, although a nonmember may bring its problem to the Council's attention, United Nations members are not under the same obligation to assist in the solution of the problem as they would be in the case of another member of the Organization.

The principle embodied in Article 50 was readily accepted at the San Francisco Conference. The draft agreed upon at Dumbarton Oaks, however, was modified to make it clear that a state against which preventive or enforcement measures were being taken was not entitled to assistance in the solution of its economic problems.[177]

The provisions of Article 50 have never been discussed in the Security Council. They were, however, considered at some length by the Collective Measures Committee in connection with the equitable sharing of the burdens involved in collective measures. In the Committee's view, the principles of Articles 49 and 50 are applicable not only to action decided upon by the Security Council but also to collective measures instituted by the General Assembly.

The Committee noted that collective economic measures "are not without cost to those employing them" and that these costs are "almost certain, in the absence of careful planning to the contrary, to fall very unevenly on the co-operating countries." [178] Some states will suffer unduly for geographic reasons or because of their special economic and financial relationships with the victim state or the state against which measures are directed. Conceding that each situation would have to be dealt with in the light of circumstances, the Committee stressed the need for consultative machinery and suggested some means of alleviation that might be useful, such as "direct assistance in cash or kind, provision of alternative sources of supply and alternative markets, specific commodity purchase agreements, compensatory adjustments of international tariffs," and so forth.[179] Noting the failure of the League of Nations to solve this problem in connection with the sanctions

[177] UNCIO, *Documents*, XVII, 207.
[178] GAOR/6th Sess./1951/*Supp. 13*(A/1891), p. 8.
[179] GAOR/7th Sess./1952/*Supp. 17*(A/2215), p. 6.

against Italy, the Committee emphasized the direct relationship between the readiness of members to take collective measures and the establishment of arrangements to distribute the burdens thereof in an equitable manner.

Article 51

Nothing in the present Charter shall impair the inherent right of individual or collective self-defense if an armed attack occurs against a Member of the United Nations, until the Security Council has taken measures necessary to maintain international peace and security. Measures taken by Members in the exercise of this right of self-defense shall be immediately reported to the Security Council and shall not in any way affect the authority and responsibility of the Security Council under the present Charter to take at any time such action as it deems necessary in order to maintain or restore international peace and security.

The genesis of Article 51 is to be found in discussions and proposals at San Francisco and earlier, which reflected a concern over giving the Security Council complete control over enforcement measures taken under regional arrangements or other special agreements.[180]

The Dumbarton Oaks Proposals had provided that the Security Council should, when appropriate, utilize regional arrangements or agencies for enforcement action, but that no enforcement action should be taken under such arrangements or by such agencies without the Council's authorization.[181] While the Proposals contained no provision with regard to the vote by which the Council's decision was to be taken, it was generally understood, and later confirmed at Yalta, that a decision on a substantive question of this importance would require the concurrence of the permanent members of the Council, thus giving to any one permanent member a right of veto.

Considerable progress had been made before Dumbarton Oaks in the development of an inter-American system for the maintenance of peace and security.[182] The Latin American republics were anxious to preserve the autonomy of these regional arrangements and were concerned about certain features of the emerging plan for a global organization regarding which they had not been consulted. The United States government, seeing the need to have the support of the Latin American republics and their participation in the future organization when

---

[180] See Russell, chs. XXII and XXVII.   [181] Cr. VIII, sec. C, para. 2.
[182] Notably by the Conventions of the Inter-American Conference for the Maintenance of Peace of 1936, the Declaration of Lima of 1938, and Declaration XV of the Second Meeting of Ministers of Foreign Affairs of 1940.

established, agreed to the holding of an inter-American Conference at Mexico City in early 1945 to discuss urgent and postwar problems, including proposals for the new world organization.[183]

At this Conference, agreement was reached on the Act of Chapultepec, which constituted the fullest development up to that time of a system of hemispheric collective security.[184] While the act provided for specific collective measures for meeting threats or acts of aggression only for the duration of the war then in progress, it envisaged, following the establishment of peace, the conclusion of a treaty providing for similar collective security arrangements for peacetime. This action of the American republics brought to the fore the issue of how such a regional system was to be fitted into a global system with sufficient assurance that its operation would not be thwarted by states outside the hemisphere.

In the consultations at San Francisco among the Sponsoring Powers and France, the consideration of this demand for the autonomy of the inter-American security system supported by the United States was merged with the consideration of two proposals to exempt security arrangements against aggression by enemy states from the requirement of Security Council authorization. One of these, a French proposal, provided that an exception to the Security Council's exclusive authority should be made in the case of "the application of measures of an urgent nature provided for in treaties of assistance concluded between members of the Organization and of which the Security Council has been advised." [185] The other, a Soviet proposal, provided that a similar exception be made in the case of treaties directed at any then current enemy state.

Various suggested drafts were objected to on the ground that they would weaken the global organization by unduly emphasizing the regional approach to security or unduly extending the period of time when enemy states would be subject to special security arrangements. Finally agreement was reached on a British proposal which omitted all reference to regional arrangements as such, emphasized the inherent right of individual or collective self-defense in case of armed attack in the event of failure of the Security Council to act, and provided that measures taken in the exercise of this right should be immediately reported to the Council and should not affect in any way its responsibility. To emphasize that the measures taken were in the exercise of a reserved right of members and not by virtue of special exemption from Security Council authority over regional arrangements, it was also agreed that the new proposal should be included in the chapter en-

[183] On the work of the Conference, see State Dept., *Inter-American Conference.*
[184] For text, see *ibid.,* pp. 72–75.   [185] Russell, p. 690.

titled "Action with Respect to Threats to the Peace, Breaches of the Peace, and Acts of Aggression" instead of being added to the chapter on "Regional Arrangements." The Sponsoring Governments and France also agreed to amend the Dumbarton Oaks Proposals to emphasize the obligation of members to resort to regional agencies or arrangements for the settlement of disputes.[186] With respect to the requirement of Security Council authorization of enforcement action under regional arrangements, they agreed to make an exception of measures taken against any enemy state under transitional or regional security arrangements.[187]

These agreements were ratified by the San Francisco Conference. The effect was to open the door to the independent functioning of regional and other special security arrangements in the exercise of "the inherent right of individual and collective self-defense" without explicitly granting to such arrangements the measure of autonomy from Security Council control that the Latin American republics had initially demanded. In addition the article as approved provided the legal basis for special security arrangements, not necessarily strictly regional in nature, which might appear necessary if the global security system failed to materialize due to lack of agreement of the permanent members of the Security Council.

The Right of Individual Self-Defense

The right of self-defense is referred to as being "inherent." [188] The effect of the article is not to create the right but explicitly to recognize its existence. Under previous international agreements relating to peace and security, this right has more commonly been tacitly reserved. During the negotiation of the Kellogg-Briand Pact of 1928, Secretary of State Kellogg observed that the right was inherent and that there was no necessity of stating it expressly.[189]

The effectiveness of an international organization for the maintenance of peace and security requires that some restriction be placed on the right of states to use force.[190] Since states frequently justify the use of armed force on the ground of legitimate self-defense, it is clear that the limitation of the right of any state to use force involves in part a

[186] See Arts. 33 and 52(2) and commentary.
[187] See Art. 53 and commentary.
[188] In testimony before the Committee on Foreign Relations, Secretary of State Acheson referred to the right as inherent "in the very existence of nationhood." *North Atlantic Treaty*, Hears./USS CFR/81C1/1949/Part I, p. 15.
[189] The Secretary of State to the Ambassador in France (Herrick), Apr. 23, 1928, in State Dept., *Foreign Relations of the United States, 1928*, I, 36–37.
[190] See Arts. 12, 13, and 15 of the Convenant and Art. 2(4) of the Charter and commentary.

definition of the limits of the right of self-defense. One approach to the problem is to define specifically those acts which constitute the unjustified use of force and to require that states immediately take collective measures against the state using force illegally. The architects of the Charter chose a more flexible system by first establishing general principles in accordance with which the Organization and its members should act, and then placing on the Security Council the primary responsibility for deciding whether in a particular case a threat to the peace, breach of the peace, or act of aggression existed and what collective measures should be taken to maintain or restore peace. By requiring that the Council's decision could be taken only with the concurrence of the permanent members, they created the certainty that no decision would be taken in many critical situations.[191] Until the Security Council has taken the measures necessary for the maintenance of international peace and security, exercise of the right of self-defense is explicitly recognized as legitimate in the case of an armed attack against a member.

If the right of self-defense is inherent, the question arises whether Article 51, taken together with other articles of the Charter, limits the exercise of the right to the case of an armed attack. Practice does not provide a very satisfactory answer to this question. If the right of self defense is inherent, it must exist in case of an armed attack against a nonmember as well as a member state. More debatable is the question whether the right may be exercised under other circumstances than an armed attack. The development of atomic and hydrogen bombs and methods of delivery, creating the possibility that the initial armed attack will be decisive, make it highly unlikely that states will wait for such an attack to occur before exercising the right of self-defense. However, the restraint shown by the United States government in the Cuban missile crisis, and its use of Article 52 of the Charter to justify quarantine measures instead of invoking the right of self-defense under Article 51, are evidence of recognition of the dangers inherent in relying upon a claim to the right of self-defense going beyond the Charter text.

The right of self-defense has been many times invoked by members in justification of their actions and on numerous occasions has been referred to in the discussions of United Nations organs. Egypt invoked the right in justification of restrictions imposed on the passage through the Suez Canal of goods destined for Israel. It claimed that though an armistice agreement had been concluded, a state of belligerency contin-

---

[191] Absence of the Soviet representative permitted the Security Council to adopt its resolution of June 25, 1950, declaring that North Korea had committed "a breach of peace."

ued to exist. Most members of the Council took the view that with hostilities suspended and no evidence that Israel was preparing an armed attack, the right of self-defense could not be invoked.[192] By a vote of 8 to 0 with 3 abstentions, the Council adopted a resolution finding that the Egyptian practice "cannot in the prevailing circumstances be justified on the ground that it is necessary for self-defense." [193]

On a number of occasions, a distinction has been made between legitimate acts of self-defense and acts of retaliation or reprisal. Following repeated incidents in the Middle East in late 1955 and early 1956 involving alleged violations of the General Armistice Agreements, the Security Council authorized the Secretary-General to survey enforcement and compliance, and arrange with the parties for the adoption of remedial measures.[194] In *aide-memoire* and letters exchanged with the Secretary-General, the Egyptian and Israeli governments, while affirming the unconditional acceptance of the cease-fire clause of the armistice agreement, reserved the right of self-defense.[195] In reporting to the Security Council, the Secretary-General stated that his interpretation of the armistice agreement "makes it clear that the reservation as to self-defense does not permit acts of retaliation, which repeatedly have been condemned by the Security Council." [196] Although the Security Council did not specifically confirm this interpretation, it commended the Secretary-General and declared that the parties should cooperate with him in putting into effect his proposals for full compliance.[197]

In 1964 a somewhat similar case was presented to the Security Council on the complaint of the Yemeni government that British forces had attacked Yemeni towns and villages, killing and injuring many persons. The British representative justified these actions under Article 51 as measures of defense "in the case of attacks on a territory for whose defense we are by treaty responsible." [198] He stated explicitly that "this action was not a retaliation or a reprisal," and continued: "There is, in existing law, a clear distinction to be drawn between two forms of self-help. One, which is of a retributive or punitive nature, is termed

---

[192] SCOR/6th Yr./550th–552d Mtgs./Aug. 1–16, 1951.

[193] UN Doc. S/2322, Sept. 1, 1951. In January, 1955, in concluding discussion of the Bat Galim affair, the President of the Council declared that most members of the Council considered this resolution to have continuing validity and effect. See SCOR/10th Yr./687th and 688th Mtgs./Jan. 4 and 13, 1955/p. 20.

[194] UN Doc. S/3575, Apr. 4, 1956.

[195] UN Doc. S/3584, Apr. 12, 1956/Parts III and IV.

[196] UN Doc. S/3596, May 9, 1956. This view was repeated by him in connection with new incidents in the Negev and Gaza Strip. UN Doc. S/3638, Aug. 21, 1956, *Annex IIB*.

[197] UN Doc. S/3605, June 4, 1956.

[198] SCOR/19th Yr./1106th Mtg./Apr. 2, 1964/p. 13.

'retaliation' or 'reprisal'; the other, which is expressly contemplated and authorized by the Charter, is self-defense against armed attack." [199]

The Security Council, by a vote of 9 to 0 with 2 abstentions, condemned "reprisals as incompatible with the purposes and principles of the United Nations and deplored the British military action." [200]

In seeking to justify the United States aerial strikes against North Vietnamese torpedo boats following attacks on United States naval ships in the Gulf of Tonkin in August, 1964, the United States representative to the Security Council invoked Article 51 and emphasized that the response was proportionate to the provocation. The Soviet representative distinguished between the right of retaliation and that of self-defense. Quoting Secretary of Defense McNamara as characterizing the action as retaliation, he condemned it as contrary to the Charter.[201]

In the course of General Assembly discussion in 1965 of the principles of international law governing friendly relations and cooperation among members, the Mexican delegate said: "For the use of force in self-defense to be permissible under the Charter, such force must . . . be immediately subsequent to and proportional to the armed attack to which it was an answer. If excessively delayed or excessively severe it ceased to be self-defense and became a reprisal which was an action inconsistent with the purposes of the United Nations." [202]

The question of whether the right of self-defense extends to an anticipated armed attack was considered initially by the Atomic Energy Commission in connection with its efforts to prepare a system of atomic energy control. In its report to the Security Council, the Commission stated: "In consideration of the problem of violation of the terms of the treaty or convention, it should also be borne in mind that a violation might be of so grave a character as to give rise to the inherent right of self-defense recognized in Article 51 of the Charter of the United Nations." [203]

The question of whether the threat of an armed attack justifies recourse to measures of self-defense was considered by the Special Committee on the Question of Defining Aggression without any conclusion being reached.[204] The question was discussed in the Sixth Committee of the Assembly during consideration of the report of the Special Committee but again with inconclusive results.[205] The United States did

199 *Ibid.*, 1109th Mtg./Apr. 7, 1964/pp. 4–5.
200 UN Doc. S/5649, Apr. 8, 1964.
201 SCOR/19th Yr./1140th Mtg./Aug. 5, 1964/paras. 44–46, 77–84.
202 GAOR/20th Sess., 6th Ctte./886th Mtg./Dec. 1, 1965/para. 42.
203 AEC, *Special Supp.*, 1946, pp. 109–10.
204 See GAOR/9th Sess./1954/*Supp. 11*(A/2638).
205 See GAOR/9th Sess., 6th Ctte./403d–420th Mtgs./Oct. 14–Nov. 10, 1954.

not seek to justify its action in the Cuban missile crisis as coming under the right to meet an anticipated attack or threat to its security by measures of self-defense; the justification that it did advance was based on Article 52 and provisions of the Rio Treaty.[206]

The Right of Collective Self-Defense

While there is general agreement among legal commentators that international law recognizes a right of individual self-defense, there is not the same measure of agreement on the existence and nature of a right of collective self-defense.[207] This right may be conceived in principle in two distinct ways: as the right of states to exercise collectively their individual rights of self-defense; [208] and as the right of one state to come to the assistance of another state that is exercising the right of self-defense, not on the basis of a special substantive interest, but rather on the basis of a general interest in peace and security.

It is not easy in practice to distinguish between these two conceptions, as much depends on how the proper limits of the individual right of self-defense are defined. Nevertheless, it is clear from the discussions at San Francisco and the practice of member states since then that the right of collective self-defense is interpreted to justify collective measures taken by some states in support of another state that is the sole victim of an armed attack. As we have seen, one principal reason for the inclusion of Article 51 was to provide a legal basis for an inter-American security system under which an attack upon one would be regarded as an attack upon all.

When the North Atlantic Treaty was under consideration by the Committee on Foreign Relations of the United State Senate, the view was expressed and generally accepted that the right of collective self-defense antedated the treaty and permitted a state to come to the assistance of another which was a victim of armed attack.[209] In sup-

---

[206] Arts. 6 and 8. See Abraham Chayes, "The Legal Case for U.S. Action in Cuba," State Dept., *Bulletin,* XLVIII (Nov. 19, 1962), 963–65.

[207] For discussion of nature of this right, see Derek W. Bowett, *Self-Defense in International Law* (New York, Praeger, 1958), ch. x; and Rosalyn Higgins, *The Development of International Law Through Political Organs of the United Nations* (London, Oxford University Press, 1963), pp. 208–10.

[208] Bowett would so limit the right by requiring that each participating state exercise "an individual right of self-defense, based on violation of its own substantive interests." Bowett, p. 245. This violation, however, need not take the form of an armed attack on the state itself.

[209] *North Atlantic Treaty,* Hears./USS CFR/81C1/1949/Part I, pp. 14–15. The intervention of the U.S. in World War II was cited as an example. The inclusion of Italy and Portugal (not at the time UN members) in the North Atlantic Treaty was justified on the ground that the right of collective self-defense existed independently of the Charter. *Ibid.,* p. 93.

port of the landing of United States armed forces in Lebanon in 1958, Ambassador Lodge claimed that the United States was acting "pursuant to what the United Nations Charter regards as an inherent right, the right of all nations to work together to preserve their independence." [210]

Article 51 was not specifically invoked by the United States to justify military measures taken in support of the Republic of Korea, even though the measures antedated the adoption of the Security Council's resolution of June 27, 1950. Instead the principles and purposes of the Charter were cited, the fact that the Republic of Korea was in a sense the creation of the United Nations was emphasized, and the Security Council's resolution was viewed as legitimizing the earlier action taken.[211] One possible reason for this failure to rely on Article 51 may have been that the Republic of Korea was not a member of the United Nations. In the debate leading up to the adoption of the Uniting for Peace resolution, the point was made that the military measures the General Assembly would be authorized to recommend would be measures members could take in the exercise of the right of collective self-defense under Article 51.[212]

Collective Self-Defense Arrangements

While Article 51 explicitly recognizes only the right of collective self-defense in case of armed attack, it clearly was not intended by the drafters that this right was limited to the taking of collective measures only after an armed attack occurred. The history of the article conclusively shows that it was intended to provide the basis for advance arrangements for meeting such an attack. It is also clear that one contingency very much in the minds of some at San Francisco was the possibility that the Security Council would not be able to function as intended because of disagreement among its permanent members. Article 51 was viewed as providing a basis for collective action to maintain peace and security in that situation.

Since the Charter entered into force, the following treaties, providing for collective self-defense explicitly or inferentially in accordance with the provisions of Article 51, have been concluded: the Inter-American Treaty of Reciprocal Assistance of September 2, 1947, to which the twenty-one American republics were signatories; [213] the Brussels Treaty of March 17, 1948, to which Belgium, France, Luxem-

[210] SCOR/13th Yr./827th Mtg./July 15, 1958/para. 44.
[211] See State Dept., *American Foreign Policy, 1950–1955*, II, 2556.
[212] See, for example, statements by delegates of the U.K. and Colombia. GAOR/5th Sess./360th Mtg./Oct. 12, 1950/paras. 4, 71–73.
[213] 21 UNTS, 77.

bourg, the Netherlands, and the United Kingdom were parties, as modified by the Protocol signed at Paris, October 23, 1954, by which the Federal Republic of Germany and Italy became parties; [214] the North Atlantic Treaty of April 4, 1949, to which fifteen states bordering on the Atlantic and the Mediterranean are parties; [215] the Mutual Defense Treaty between the United States and the Philippines of August 30, 1951; [216] the Security Treaty between Australia, New Zealand, and the United States of September 1, 1951; [217] the Security Treaty between the United States and Japan of September 8, 1951; [218] the Mutual Defense Treaty between the United States and Korea of October 1, 1953; [219] the Mutual Defense Treaty between the United States and the Republic of China of December 2, 1954; [220] the South-East Asia Collective Defense Treaty of September 8, 1954, to which the United States, the United Kingdom, France, Australia, New Zealand, the Philippines, Thailand, and Pakistan are parties; [221] the Bagdad Pact of February 24, 1955, to which Turkey, Iraq, the United Kingdom, Iran, and Pakistan were parties; [222] the Joint Defense and Economic Co-operation Treaty between the States of the Arab League of June 17, 1950; [223] and the Treaty of Friendship, Co-operation and Mutual Assistance (The Warsaw Pact) of May 14, 1955.[224]

Some of the treaties contain elements which bring them into the category of regional arrangements covered by the provisions of Chapter VIII, but all explicitly or by implication rely on Article 51 to justify the use of collective measures to meet an armed attack on one or more of the signatories.[225] The treaties generally recognize the superiority of rights and obligations under the Charter. They define the *casus belli* in the language of Article 51, though some provide for consultation in the case of threats of armed attack or aggressive actions short of armed attack with a view to agreement on measures to be taken.[226] They limit their application to armed attacks within defined geographical areas.

The treaties vary in the language used to define the commitment to

---

[214] 19 UNTS, 51; 211 UNTS, 342.   [215] 34 UNTS, 243.
[216] 177 UNTS, 133.   [217] 131 UNTS, 83.
[218] 136 UNTS, 211. Superseded by treaty of Jan. 20, 1960. 373 UNTS, 179–205.
[219] 238 UNTS, 199.   [220] 248 UNTS, 213.
[221] 209 UNTS, 28.   [222] 233 UNTS, 199.
[223] *Middle East Journal* (Spring, 1952), p. 238.   [224] 219 UNTS, 24.

[225] In testifying in support of the North Atlantic Treaty before the Committee on Foreign Relations, Secretary of State Acheson and Ambassador Austin emphasized that Art. 51 provided the basis for the treaty, although Ambassador Austin observed that in certain of its aspects it was a regional arrangement. *North Atlantic Treaty*, Hears./USS CFR/81C1/1949/Part I, p. 96.

[226] See Art. 6 of the Rio Treaty and Art. IV, para. 2 of the South-East Asia Treaty. Presumably, measures agreed to would be in conformity with Charter provisions.

give assistance in case of armed attack. In the case of treaties to which the United States is a party, the language has been dictated to a large extent by constitutional considerations. By the terms of the Rio Treaty, the parties agree that an armed attack against "any American State shall be considered as an attack against all the American States," and each undertakes to assist in meeting the attack in the exercise of the inherent right of individual or collective self-defense (Article 3[1]). Decisions of the Organ of Consultation with respect to the measures to be applied, taken by a two-thirds vote, are binding except that no state can be required to use armed force without its consent (Article 20). The North Atlantic Treaty also provides that an attack on one is an attack on all, and obligates the parties to "assist the Party or Parties so attacked by taking forthwith, individually, and in concert with the other Parties, such action as it deems necessary, including the use of armed force, to restore and maintain the security of the North Atlantic area" (Article 5[1]). The language of the South-East Asia Treaty is more cautious. Each party recognizes that an armed attack "would endanger its own peace and safety" and agrees that it will "act to meet the common danger in accordance with its constitutional processes." [227] The Warsaw Pact provides that the signatory shall afford the state or states attacked "immediate assistance individually and in agreement with other States Parties to the Treaty, by all the means it considers necessary, including the use of armed force" (Article 4).

Most of the treaties provide for consultations in case of any threat to peace and security within the area of the treaty. Some, particularly the North Atlantic Treaty and the Warsaw Pact, provide for detailed advanced preparations for implementation. In conformity with Article 51, they require that any armed attack and measures taken in the exercise of the right of self-defense shall be immediately reported to the Security Council and that these measures be terminated when the Council has taken the measures necessary to restore international peace and security.[228] However, this obligation has not been interpreted to require reports to the Security Council on preparations for exercising the right of self-defense.[229] Were these to be treated as regional arrangements subject to the provisions of Article 54, there would be an obligation to keep the Security Council "fully informed of activities undertaken or in contemplation."

[227] Art. 4. The other treaties concluded by the U.S. with countries in the Pacific area use similar language.
[228] See North Atlantic Treaty, Art. 5(2); South-East Asia Treaty, Art. 4; Warsaw Pact, Art. 4.
[229] See statement by Ambassador Austin, *North Atlantic Treaty*, Hears./USS CFR/81C1/1949/Part I, p. 138.

Effect on Authority of the Security Council

Article 51 explicitly provides that the exercise by members of the right of self-defense under the conditions indicated does not "in any way" affect the authority and responsibility of the Security Council to take necessary measures to maintain or restore international peace and security. Treaties that have been concluded emphasize this point, and officials of member governments explaining and seeking to justify such treaties or specific actions of member states emphasize that measures taken are to achieve the purposes of the Charter and are always subject to the authority of the Council.

On the other hand, Article 51 does open the door to arrangements and specific actions by some members of the Organization which, though professedly in accordance with the purposes and principles of the Charter, are not subject to the built-in assurances of the Charter that important interests of members will not be disregarded. Nor does Article 51 or the treaties concluded under it provide any assurance that emergency measures of self-help will be restricted to the circumstances justifying them and will be subjected to effective control by the responsible organs of the United Nations. The very nature of the Organization, and more importantly the requirement that the major powers be in agreement before a substantive decision of the Security Council can be taken, make it unlikely that in any situation where the important security interests of major powers are involved, any effective control of measures taken under Article 51 will be exercised by the Security Council. In testifying before the Committee on Foreign Relations of the United States Senate on the Mutual Defense Treaty with Korea, Secretary of State Dulles, when questioned about who decides when the Council has taken necessary measures for the maintenance of peace and security, agreed that "the determination as to that adequacy . . . would be ours to make." [230] It is not clear whether he meant that every nation had that right, or that as a practical matter, the veto power would not permit the Security Council to take a decision with which the United States disagreed.

It is inaccurate to say that Article 51 by itself has weakened the authority of the Security Council. To many of the architects of the Charter, Article 51 seemed necessary to provide the basis for measures of self-defense in case the Security Council was unable to discharge its responsibilities because of disagreements among major powers. It has been the fact of such disagreements, particularly between the Soviet

[230] "Mutual Defense Treaty with Korea," Hears., USS CFR/83C2/1954, pp. 22–23.

Union and the Western powers, that has seemed to justify the extensive resort to the right which Article 51 recognizes. If this article had not been introduced into the Charter, some member states would no doubt have invoked the inherent right of self-defense in the presence of a world organization incapable of providing the necessary security for its members. At least, Article 51, by expressly recognizing the right only in case of armed attack, may have had some restraining influence on members in the exercise of it.

CHAPTER VIII

Regional Arrangements

The role of regional arrangements in the maintenance of international peace and security and their relation to organizations of a global nature figured prominently in the discussions leading up to the approval of the Charter at San Francisco.[1] This was not surprising: regional security arrangements had been developed during the League period, professedly to strengthen the League system of collective security. Furthermore, regional considerations had long played a prominent part in national security policies—witness the Monroe Doctrine of the United States.

During the early years of World War II, allied statesmen emphasized the regional approach to the organization of security. Prime Minister Churchill stressed the regional principle because he believed that the League experience demonstrated that "it was only the countries whose interests were directly affected by a dispute who could be expected to apply themselves with sufficient vigour to secure a settlement."[2] Within the Roosevelt Administration there were differences of opinion regarding the emphasis to be placed on regionalism. Under-Secretary of State Sumner Welles, presumably because of his concern with Latin-American affairs, favored the regional principle, while Secretary of State Hull was an advocate of the global emphasis.[3] Hull's view prevailed in Washington and was accepted by the other conferees at the Moscow Conference of Allied Foreign Ministers in October, 1943.

The United States Tentative Proposals, submitted at Dumbarton Oaks, contained no separate section on regional arrangements. On the one hand, they provided for regional organizations or arrangements not inconsistent with the purposes of the general organization and able to function either on their own initiative or by reference from the general organization. On the other hand, the use of such arrangements

[1] As explained in the commentary on Art. 51, that article was a central part of the agreement finally reached, although it was not included in the chapter dealing specifically with regional arrangements.
[2] As quoted in Ruth B. Russell, *A History of the United Nations Charter* (Washington, Brookings Institution, 1958), p. 107.
[3] See Sumner Welles, *The Time for Decision* (New York, Harper, 1944); and Cordell Hull, *The Memoirs of Cordell Hull* (New York, Macmillan, 1948).

by the general organization was made subject to the discretion of the executive council.[4] At Dumbarton Oaks, the conference agreed to include a separate section on regional arrangements. This provided that the Security Council should encourage the settlement of local disputes through regional agencies, that it should use these agencies "where appropriate" for enforcement action under its authority, but that enforcement action should not be undertaken by regional agencies except with Security Council authorization.[5]

Article 52

1. Nothing in the present Charter precludes the existence of regional arrangements or agencies for dealing with such matters relating to the maintenance of international peace and security as are appropriate for regional action, provided that such arrangements or agencies and their activities are consistent with the Purposes and Principles of the United Nations.

2. The Members of the United Nations entering into such arrangements or constituting such agencies shall make every effort to achieve pacific settlement of local disputes through such regional arrangements or by such regional agencies before referring them to the Security Council.

3. The Security Council shall encourage the development of pacific settlement of local disputes through such regional arrangements or by such regional agencies either on the initiative of the states concerned or by reference from the Security Council.

4. This Article in no way impairs the application of Articles 34 and 35.

Article 52 recognizes the right of member states to establish regional arrangements or agencies for dealing with matters relating to the maintenance of international peace and security. The only explicit limitations imposed are that the matters dealt with must be "appropriate for regional action," and that the arrangements and agencies and their activities must be "consistent with the Purposes and Principles of the United Nations." The article goes beyond legitimizing such arrangements or constituting such agencies; it requires members to make every effort to achieve pacific settlement of local disputes by these means before referring them to the Security Council. Such procedure is consistent with the obligation members assume under Article 33 to seek, first of all, the settlement of their disputes by means of their own

[4] See chs. I(A), para. 4; V, paras. 3 and 10; and VI(D), para. 2, in State Dept., *Postwar Foreign Policy Preparation, 1939–1945,* pp. 600–2.

[5] See Russell, pp. 398–400, 472–73.

choice before appealing to the Council. Article 52 also requires the Security Council to encourage the use of regional arrangements and agencies for the settlement of "local disputes" either on the initiative of the states concerned or by reference from the Council itself. However, paragraph 4 states that the effect of the first three paragraphs is to leave the application of Articles 34 and 35 unimpaired.

The first paragraph has a broader scope than the other three since it legitimizes the existence and use of regional arrangements and agencies for the maintenance of international peace and security by all appropriate means, while the second and third paragraphs are only concerned with peaceful settlement of disputes.

Regional Arrangements and Agencies

From the discussions leading up to the approval of the Charter, it would appear that regionalism was considered primarily in connection with the maintenance of international peace and security. The question of including in the Charter a provision for regional arrangements with regard to economic and social matters was posed at San Francisco, and decided in the negative.[6] Also the question of what constitutes a regional arrangement was considered. A proposal by the Egyptian delegation to introduce a definition into the Charter that would emphasize as requirements such factors as permanent organization, geographical proximity, community of interest, and cultural and historical affinities was rejected on the ground that while it "clearly defined obvious legitimate and eligible factors," it failed to cover all possible cases.[7]

Neither the General Assembly nor the Security Council has found it necessary or desirable to attempt to define what constitutes regional arrangements and agencies. When the Assembly considered proposals to invite the chief administrative officers of the Organization of American States, the League of Arab States, and the Organization of African Unity to attend its meetings, views were advanced in the course of committee discussions regarding factors that should be taken into account in determining whether a particular organization qualified under Article 52.[8] In each case, it was decided to request the Secretary-General to invite the chief administrative office to attend as an observer.[9] It was understood that the invitation was extended as an act of courtesy and not on the basis of any right of a regional organization to

---

[6] UNCIO, *Documents*, X, 196.   [7] *Ibid.*, XII, 673, 833, 850.

[8] For Organization of American States, see for example, GAOR/3d Sess., 6th Ctte./70th and 71st Mtgs./Oct. 9 and 11, 1948; for League of Arab States, see *ibid.*, 5th Sess., 6th Ctte./215th–217th Mtgs./Oct. 2–5, 1950.

[9] GA Res. 253(III), Oct. 16, 1948; 477(V), Nov. 1, 1950; and 2011(XX), Oct. 11, 1965.

be represented. Furthermore, it was emphasized in discussions in one case that the invitation did not in any way imply that the organization was or was not a regional agency in the meaning of Article 52.[10]

In the course of debate in the sixth session of the General Assembly on various proposals for strengthening international peace and averting the dangers of a new world war, the North Atlantic Treaty was attacked by the Soviet Union on the grounds that it included states without geographical connection and without a common language, culture, and history, and that no regional action was therefore involved. Other members maintained that geographical propinquity was not a prerequisite to a regional arrangement, and that in any case the Charter basis of the treaty was Article 51.[11] The fact is, however, that the Charter basis of collective self-defense arrangements in Article 51 does not exclude the possibility that other provisions of the treaties and activities of the agencies in question come under Article 52.[12]

Appropriateness for Regional Action

The question whether a particular matter is appropriate for regional action has been discussed many times. While it is generally recognized that disputes between parties to regional arrangements are appropriate for settlement or adjustment by regional agencies, this does not necessarily exclude the possibility of Security Council consideration at the request of one of the parties, particularly where the possibility exists that a powerful state uses a regional agency for coercing a smaller state.[13] There is not always agreement, however, as to whether questions which the regional agencies are asked to consider are in the nature of disputes or situations requiring peaceful settlement or adjustment or are of a more serious nature requiring preventive or enforcement action. In 1954, Guatemala addressed a complaint to the Security Council under Articles 34, 35, and 39, claiming aggression, and argued

[10] Report of the Sixth Committee on invitation to the Secretary-General of the League of Arab States. GAOR/5th Sess./1950/*Annexes* 2, agenda item 58(A/1442), p. 6.

[11] For discussion, see GAOR/6th Sess., 1st Ctte./488th–493d Mtgs./Jan. 14–17, 1952; 7th Sess., 1st Ctte./596th–603d Mtgs./Apr. 10–16, 1953; 8th Sess., 1st Ctte./671st and 673d–676th Mtgs./Nov. 23–26, 1953. See also statements of Secretary Acheson and Ambassador Austin, *North Atlantic Treaty*, Hears./USS CFR/81C1/1949/I, 15, 30–31, 139–42.

[12] For example, Art. 1 of the North Atlantic Treaty obligates the parties to settle their disputes by peaceful means, as does Art. 1 of the treaty between the states of the Arab League, Art. 1 of the South-East Asia Treaty, Art. 2 of the Rio Treaty, and Art. 1 of the Warsaw Pact. See commentary on Art. 51.

[13] This was the argument of Cuba and the Soviet Union with respect to the decisions of the Punta del Este Conference of June 21–31, 1962. See SCOR/17th Yr./991st–998th Mtgs./Feb. 27–Mar. 23, 1962.

that the Organization of American States could not deal with the matter; this was allegedly not a dispute, but a situation calling for Council action under Chapter VII.[14]

There is wide agreement that certain matters relating to the organization and procedures of regional agencies are clearly appropriate for regional action. Thus, regional organizations are able to determine their own membership and stipulate qualifications of membership. This proposition was challenged by Cuba in questioning the validity of the Punta del Este resolutions of the Organization of American States. However, the majority of members of the Security Council and the General Assembly upheld the right of the OAS to establish conditions of membership and active participation as long as these were consistent with the purposes and principles of the Charter.[15]

There is considerable support for the view that regional action under Article 52 is not appropriate in a matter involving a state not a party to the regional arrangement. During Council consideration of economic measures taken against the Dominican Republic by the OAS, the Tunisian representative suggested that the case for requiring Security Council authorization of these nonmilitary measures would have been stronger had the Dominican Republic not been a member of the regional organization.[16] In another instance, Cyprus refused to accept an international peace-keeping force proposed by NATO members and appealed to the Security Council,[17] which decided to establish such a force. The Organization of African Unity considered itself competent to deal with the unsettled Congo situation in 1963, but when Belgium and the United States carried out a military operation to rescue white hostages at Stanleyville, OAU members joined in asking the Security Council to consider the action as a violation of the Charter.[18]

In the Cuban missile crisis, although the United States chose to go to the OAS to get legitimation of the quarantine measures, it requested simultaneously that the Security Council meet "to deal with the dangerous threat to the peace and security of the world which had been caused by the secret establishment in Cuba by the Soviet Union of launching bases and the installation of long-range ballistic missiles capable of carrying thermonuclear warheads to most of North and

[14] SCOR/9th Yr./675th Mtg./June 20, 1954, and *Supp.* for April, May, and June, pp. 11–13.

[15] The decision of the Security Council to recommend Kuwait for membership followed upon, and was made possible by, an earlier decision of the Council of the League of Arab States to admit Kuwait to membership in the regional organization. SCOR/16th Yr./985th Mtg./Nov. 30, 1961.

[16] SCOR/15th Yr./894th Mtg./Sept. 9, 1960/para. 37.

[17] UN Doc. S/5545, Feb. 15, 1964.

[18] See SCOR/19th Yr./1170th–1178th Mtgs./Dec. 9–17, 1964; 1181st and 1183d–1189th Mtgs./Dec. 22–30, 1964; and SC Res. 199, Dec. 30, 1964.

South America." [19] When the Council met, the United States presented a draft resolution by which the Council would call for the immediate dismantling and withdrawal of missiles, authorize the Secretary-General to dispatch a United Nations observer corps to assure and report on compliance, call for the termination of the quarantine on United Nations certification of compliance, and urgently recommend that the United States and the USSR confer to remove the threat of the missiles to peace and security.[20] Thus, Washington implicitly recognized that, for the settlement of its dispute with Moscow, the regional organization was not the appropriate organ, even though it might be used to give an appearance of legitimacy to measures that otherwise would require justification under Article 51.

Consistency with Purposes and Principles

The requirement that such arrangements and agencies and their activities should be consistent with "the Purposes and Principles of the United Nations" is in line with the general principle that Charter obligations prevail over obligations of other international agreements entered into by members.[21] It also respects the view that prevailed at Dumbarton Oaks and was accepted at San Francisco: that the global organization for peace and security is the basic one and that regional organizations and agencies function within that framework and subject to the same overriding purposes and principles.[22]

The consistency issue was raised by Israel with respect to the League of Arab States when the question of inviting its chief administrative officer to be present at meetings of the General Assembly was being considered. Israel maintained that the League was based on the principle of racial exclusiveness and that its activities in Palestine had been directed against the United Nations and had not been consistent with the purposes and principles of the Charter.[23] The Assembly took no decision on the question.

The question of consistency was again raised in 1962 in Cuba's contention that certain of the Punta del Este resolutions were inconsistent with the purposes and principles of the Charter. Particular attention was called to the declaration that the principles of communism were inconsistent with those of the inter-American system, to the recommendation of free elections for governments that fail to practice representative democracy, and to the declaration that the government of Cuba had voluntarily placed itself outside the inter-American system.

[19] UN Doc. S/5181, Oct. 22, 1962.   [20] UN Doc. S/5182, Oct. 23, 1962.
[21] See commentary on Art. 103.   [22] Russell, pp. 472–73.
[23] GAOR/5th Sess./*Annexes,* agenda item 58(A/C.6/336), pp. 1–2.

Cuba and the Soviet Union argued that these resolutions violated the principles of peaceful coexistence, nonintervention, and sovereign equality contained in the Charter; other members countered that the resolutions were adopted by the OAS to carry out its purposes and principles, and that these were fully consistent with those of the Charter. This view appeared to predominate in both the Assembly and the Security Council, although no resolution was adopted by either organ.[24]

Priority of the Use of Regional Arrangements for Peaceful Settlement

Article 52(2) places upon the parties to regional arrangements the obligation "to make every effort to achieve peaceful settlement of local disputes" under these arrangements before referring them to the Security Council, while paragraph 3 places on the Council the duty to "encourage the development" of peaceful settlement of local disputes through regional arrangements either by the states concerned or "by reference" from the Council. These provisions are in harmony with the general approach of the Charter to the peaceful settlement of disputes which is to encourage states, first of all, to seek to settle their disputes by means of their own choice.[25] Paragraph 4 provides that this article in no way impairs the application of Articles 34 and 35. The only regional arrangements that explicitly obligate parties to seek settlement of disputes by regional procedures before referring them to the Security Council are the Rio Treaty (Article 2), the Charter of the Organization of American States (Article 20), and the American Treaty of Peaceful Settlement (Article 2).[26]

In 1954, Guatemala requested a meeting of the Security Council in accordance with Articles 34, 35, and 39 of the Charter to put a stop to aggression against it from the direction of Nicaragua and Honduras. Guatemala, supported by the Soviet Union, argued that this was not a dispute but an act of aggression, and that therefore the Security Council was required to act. Other members, while admitting Guatemala's right to appeal to the Council and that organ's overriding concern with the maintenance of peace, nevertheless felt that the regional organization was in the best position to ascertain the facts and recommend measures. A draft resolution, introduced by Brazil and Colombia, provided for referring the complaint to the OAS "for urgent consideration"

[24] See GAOR/16th Sess., 1st Ctte./1230th–1243d Mtgs., Dec. 20, 1961—Feb. 15, 1962; UN Docs. A/4882, Sept. 22, 1961; and A/5090, Feb. 16, 1962; and SCOR/17th Yr./991st–998th Mtgs./Feb. 27–Mar. 23, 1962.

[25] See commentary on Arts. 33 and 36.

[26] 21 UNTS, 77; 119 UNTS, 3; and 30 UNTS, 55, respectively.

and requested it to inform the Council "as soon as possible, as appropriate, on the measures it has been able to take on the matter." [27] The draft resolution was defeated by a Soviet veto and a French proposal was adopted by which the Council called for the immediate termination of any action likely to cause bloodshed and requested members to abstain from giving assistance to such action. When the Guatemalan government renewed its request for Council action, the Council, by a vote of 4 to 5 with 2 abstentions, refused to place the item on its agenda, the prevailing argument being that the matter was under consideration by the OAS.[28]

In July, 1960, Cuba requested that the Security Council consider a grave situation it claimed had arisen as the result of United States threats, reprisals, and aggressive acts. Cuba maintained that it had the right to submit its complaint to the Security Council instead of first appealing to the OAS. The United States representative denied the charge, pointing out that in any case the whole situation was about to be considered by a Meeting of Consultation of the Foreign Ministers of the American Republics. Claiming that there was no question of replacing United Nations action, he argued that the regional organization should act first and that the Security Council should act only as a last resort. The Council, by a vote of 9 to 0 with 2 abstentions, adopted a resolution adjourning consideration of the question pending receipt of a report from the OAS, and inviting OAS members to assist in achieving a peaceful solution in accordance with the purposes and principles of the Charter.[29] Members of the Council supported the resolution on the following grounds: the OAS had already been seized of the matter; under the Charter it is mandatory that regional arrangements should be used first, though use of such arrangements does not preclude recourse to competent United Nations organs; and in the absence of more complete information the Council could not take a decision on substance until the conclusions of the OAS were known.[30]

Subsequently, the General Assembly was asked to consider renewed Cuban charges of United States aggression, and in the course of its discussions the Bay of Pigs incident was brought to its attention. It was not possible to achieve the necessary two-thirds majority for a proposal containing a special appeal to "member states which belong to the Organization of American States" to assist in achieving a settlement and to report to the United Nations as soon as possible within the year on the measures taken. The resolution finally adopted, by a vote of 59

[27] UN Doc. S/3236/Rev. 1, June 20, 1954.
[28] See SCOR/9th Yr./675th and 676th Mtgs./June 20 and 25, 1954; also, *Repertory*, II, 448–58.
[29] UN Doc. S/4395, July 19, 1960.
[30] For discussion, see SCOR/15th Yr./874th–876th Mtgs./July 18–19, 1960.

to 13 with 24 absentions, recalled earlier decisions of the Security Council and the OAS, reminded members of their obligations under the Charter, and exhorted "all Member States to take such peaceful action as is open to them to remove existing tension." [31] This resolution reflected the view that the competent United Nations organ could take appropriate action without requiring that the parties first make use of a regional agency or waiting for such agency to act.

The question of the priority of the United Nations or regional agencies came up for further discussion in connection with the Haitian complaint against the Dominican Republic in May, 1963. Some members of the Security Council maintained that, while any member of the OAS had the right to bring a controversy to the Council, action should be taken by the Council only when efforts to achieve a peaceful settlement at the regional level had failed. Others took the view that the Council could deal with the matter without waiting for the regional agency to act. The President of the Council noted that the majority felt it preferable, for the time being, to leave the initiative to the OAS. The parties raised no objection to this procedure.[32]

Although the majority of cases in which the priority of the use of regional arrangements has been raised have involved the OAS, the question has also come up in connection with the League of Arab States and the Organization of African Unity. In 1958, Lebanon agreed to Council deferment of consideration of its complaint of intervention by the United Arab Republic in its affairs until the League of Arab States had had an opportunity to examine the matter. It reserved, however, its right to request immediate convocation of the Security Council.[33] After the failure of the League of Arab States to take a decision and on the request of Lebanon, the Security Council resumed consideration of the matter and decided to send an observation group to ensure against "illegal infiltration." [34]

In February, 1964, Somalia in like manner agreed not to press its complaint against Ethiopia until the Organization of African Unity had concluded consideration of the matter; it later notified the Council that the OAU had taken satisfactory action.[35] The priority of the use of

[31] GA Res. 1616(XV), Apr. 21, 1961. For debate, see GAOR/15th Sess., 1st Ctte./1100th, 1106th, and 1107th Mtgs./Nov. 2, Nov. 8, and Nov. 10, 1960; and 909th and 910th Plen. Mtgs./Oct. 31 and Nov. 1, 1960.

[32] For discussion, see SCOR/18th Yr./1035th and 1036th Mtgs./May 8 and 9, 1963. During consideration of Panama's complaint over U.S. acts in the Canal Zone, similar views were expressed in favor of allowing the Inter-American Peace Committee to deal with the matter. SCOR/19th Yr./1086th Mtg./Jan. 10, 1964.

[33] SCOR/13th Yr./818th Mtg./May 25, 1958.

[34] UN Docs. S/4018, June 2, 1958 and S/4023, June 11, 1958.

[35] UN Doc. S/5542, Feb. 14, 1964; and Docs. S/5557 and S/5558, Feb. 18, 1964.

regional measures received strong support from African members and clear recognition by the Security Council during its consideration of the complaint of illegal intervention by the United States and Belgium in carrying out military intervention to rescue white hostages in Stanleyville. The resolution adopted by the Council expressed in its preamble the conviction that the Organization of African Unity should be able "in the context of Article 52 of the Charter to help find a peaceful solution to all the problems and disputes affecting peace and security in the continent of Africa." In its substantive provisions, the resolution supported and encouraged the OAU in its efforts to achieve national conciliation in the Congo. It requested the Secretary-General to follow the situation in the Congo and to report to the Council at an appropriate time.[36]

From this review of practice, it would appear that questions of priority to be accorded regional arrangements in the settlement of international differences have arisen primarily, though not exclusively, in connection with disputes and situations involving the American republics. This is not surprising considering the extent to which they have developed institutions and procedures for peaceful settlement, and the strength of the commitment of these countries to the use of their institutions and procedures. In addition, the United States has generally found it expedient to support regional action and thus avoid having non-American states exploit situations of tension and conflict.

In principle, there has been general agreement that the party to a regional arrangement has the right to have its complaint considered by the Security Council or the General Assembly; at the same time, there is general agreement that, consistent with the general philosophy of the Charter, an attempt should be made to achieve a settlement through regional arrangements and other means of the parties' own choice before appealing to the United Nations organ. Failure to do so, however, is not necessarily a reason for denial of a hearing or even a refusal by the Security Council or the General Assembly to adopt substantive measures. Political considerations weigh heavily in determining to what extent the United Nations organ will make use of or defer to regional agencies and procedures. One argument which usually carries weight is that the regional agency, being closer to the situation and in a better position to evaluate it, should be given the first opportunity to achieve an arrangement acceptable to the parties.

At the time the Security Council was considering the question of economic measures ordered by the Ministers of Foreign Affairs of the American republics against the Dominican Republic, the representative of Ecuador proposed that the Security Council should pursue a course:

[36] See SCOR/19th Yr./1170th–1178th, 1181st, 1183d–1189th Mtgs./Dec. 9–17, 1964; and UN Doc. S/6128, Dec. 30, 1964.

which will protect and guarantee the autonomy, the individuality, the structure, and the proper and effective working of regional agencies, so that they may deal with situations and disputes which are appropriate for regional action—provided there is no undermining of authority of the Security Council or of the Member States' right to appeal to it whenever they consider that the defense of their rights or interests requires such an appeal, or that a particular situation or dispute, even if appropriate for regional action, might endanger international peace and security.[37]

This is a fair statement of the view generally accepted with respect to the priorities to be accorded regional arrangements and the authority that the Security Council retains under Article 52.

Article 53

1. The Security Council shall, where appropriate, utilize such regional arrangements or agencies for enforcement action under its authority. But no enforcement action shall be taken under regional arrangements or by regional agencies without the authorization of the Security Council, with the exception of measures against any enemy state, as defined in paragraph 2 of this Article, provided for pursuant to Article 107 or in regional arrangements directed against renewal of aggressive policy on the part of any such state, until such time as the Organization may, on request of the Governments concerned, be charged with the responsibility for preventing further aggression by such a state.

2. The term enemy state as used in paragraph 1 of this Article applies to any state which during the Second World War has been an enemy of any signatory of the present Charter.

The general principle that regional arrangements shall only be used for enforcement action under the authority and by authorization of the Security Council was accepted at Dumbarton Oaks on United States initiative and reflected a view strongly held by most members of the State Department—especially Secretary of State Hull—that central Security Council control was essential to prevent return to a system of rival military alliances. At San Francisco, Article 51 was introduced to allow a measure of autonomy for regional and other groupings in case of an armed attack, and the exception contained in Article 53 was adopted to permit collective measures without Security Council authorization against an "enemy state."

[37] SCOR/893d Mtg./Sept. 8, 1960/para. 63. See also statement by the Secretary-General in his ninth annual report. GAOR/9th Sess./1954/*Supp.* 1(A/2663), p. xi.

Meaning of "Enforcement Action"

This term appears in identical or slightly modified form in other articles of the Charter.[38] The *procès verbaux* of the San Francisco Conference give strong support to the view that "enforcement action" was intended to mean any and all measures the Security Council was authorized to take under Articles 41 and 42.[39]

In practice, the term "enforcement action" has been given a more restricted interpretation by some members. The question of the interpretation of "enforcement action" in the context of Article 53 has come up in connection with complaints addressed to the Security Council regarding measures taken by the Organization of American States or proposals that the Council take specific action to approve such measures, thereby confirming its power to authorize.

In 1960, the Soviet Union requested a meeting of the Security Council to consider and endorse the resolution of the Sixth Meeting of Consultation of the Ministers of Foreign Affairs requiring the application of collective economic measures against the Dominican Republic. The Soviet Union argued that the Security Council must approve the resolution "so as to give it legal force and render it more effective,"[40] since it provided for the application of measures of the kind described in Article 41. Other members argued that approval was not necessary, and that the report to the Council on the action taken by the Meeting of Consultation was made in conformity with Article 54. The reasons given for opposing the Soviet position were that the measures taken collectively by members of the OAS could have been taken individually by members in the exercise of their national sovereignty; that "enforcement action" contemplates the exercise of force in a manner that would normally not be legitimate except with Security Council authorization; and that Article 53 does not apply to nonmilitary measures of the kind indicated in Article 41.[41] The Council adopted, by a vote of 9 to 0 with 2 abstentions, a resolution proposed by Argentina and Ecuador taking note of the report on the achieve-

[38] Art. 2(5) speaks of "preventive or enforcement action" as does Art. 5. Art. 2(7) refers to "enforcement measures" under ch. VII. Art. 50 uses the words "preventive or enforcement measures." Art. 11(2) uses the word "action," which has been interpreted to mean "enforcement action." See commentary on Art. 11.

[39] See report of committee dealing with Security Council action to meet threats to peace and acts of aggression. UNCIO, *Documents*, X, 507–8.

[40] SCOR/15th Yr./893d Mtg./Sept. 8, 1960/paras. 24–25.

[41] *Ibid.*, 894th and 895th Mtgs./Sept. 9, 1960. See supporting statements in Security Council at time of consideration of Cuban complaint in 1962. SCOR/17th Yr./994th Mtg./Mar. 16, 1962.

ments of the Meeting of Consultation and especially of the resolution adopted by it.[42]

Two years later, Cuba raised a similar question in asking that the Security Council condemn measures taken by the Meeting of Consultation of American Foreign Ministers at Punta del Este as being in violation of the United Nations Charter. The Council initially refused to include the item in its agenda on the ground that the matter had already been fully considered by the General Assembly and that the question of infringement of the Council's authority under Article 53 had been decided in the earlier case of the Dominican Republic.[43] Later, Cuba asked the Council to request the International Court of Justice to give an advisory opinion on certain legal questions, including the question whether "enforcement action" included measures provided for in Article 41.[44] The Council voted not to request an advisory opinion on this question. Among the reasons advanced were the following: the question was political, it had previously been decided by the Council that economic measures did not constitute enforcement action, and exclusion from participation in OAS meetings did not constitute enforcement action.[45]

The question of the meaning of "enforcement action" came up again during Security Council consideration of the Dominican crisis in May and June, 1965, specifically in connection with the report received of the establishment of an Inter-American Force by the resolution of May 6 of the Tenth Meeting of Consultation of Ministers of Foreign Affairs.[46] The resolution provided that the Force should cooperate in the establishment of normal conditions in the Dominican Republic. The Soviet representative took the position that this constituted enforcement action in violation of Article 53. The United States held that the action being taken by the OAS in the Dominican Republic was "most certainly not enforcement action," any more than action taken by the United Nations in Cyprus, Congo, or the Middle East.[47] In the Council discussion, one representative pointed out that the expression "enforcement action" presupposed the existence of something to be enforced, and that consequently enforcement of a recommendation, as contained in the OAS resolution, was a contradiction in terms. He also stressed that the OAS was carrying out a conciliatory mission, its forces

[42] UN Doc. S/4491, Sept. 9, 1960.
[43] SCOR/17th Yr./991st Mtg./Feb. 27, 1962/p. 28.
[44] UN Doc. S/5095, Mar. 20, 1962.
[45] For discussion, see SCOR/17th Yr./992d–998th Mtgs./Mar. 14–23, 1962.
[46] UN Doc. S/6333, May 7, 1965.
[47] SCOR/20th Yr./1222d Mtg./June 9, 1965/pp. 21–22. The ICJ has taken the position that peace-keeping operations of the nature of UNEF and ONUC do not constitute enforcement action. "Certain Expenses" case, *ICJ Reports,* 1962, pp. 164–65.

were not there in support of any claim against the state, and its function was that of pacific settlement under Article 52 and not that of enforcement under Article 53.[48] This appears to have been the view of the majority of Council members.

Exception of Measures Taken Against Enemy States

The measures that are excepted from the requirement of Security Council authorization in this article fall into two categories: measures against any enemy state as defined in paragraph 2 of this article, provided for pursuant to Article 107; and measures against such enemy states provided for in regional arrangements directed against the renewal of aggressive policy on the part of any such state. In respect to both kinds of measures, the exception holds until such time as the Organization may, "on request of the Governments concerned," be charged with responsibility for preventing further aggression.

The phraseology of this exception was the subject of extended and confused discussions at San Francisco. It was not easy to find language that would give equal satisfaction to those deeply concerned with the danger of renewed enemy aggression (France and the Soviet Union) and those whose interest was in having an effective general security organization with suitable provision for the autonomy of regional arrangements and who were opposed to unduly prolonging the period of treating the enemy states as a special security problem. In particular, some objected to relating the exception to regional arrangements, while others were unconvinced that mutual-assistance arrangements strictly conforming to Article 51 would give adequate security. The price of final agreement was a phraseology unsatisfactory to many states since it allowed the exception to remain operative as long as any "Government concerned" desired, and described as an exception to the principle of Article 53 measures which might, and in all likelihood would, be taken under arrangements that were in no real sense regional at all, but rather military alliances of the traditional nature.[49]

In the early postwar period, a number of treaties were concluded which implicitly or explicitly invoked the exception of "regional arrangements directed against renewal of enemy aggression," or at least could be regarded as coming under its terms. These included the Treaty of Alliance between the Soviet Union and the United Kingdom, signed May 26, 1942; [50] the Treaty of Alliance and Mutual Assistance

[48] Statement of representative of Malaysia. SCOR/20th Yr./1222d Mtg./June 9, 1965/pp. 66–68.
[49] See Russell, pp. 706–12; also commentary on Art. 107.
[50] U.K., *Parliamentary Papers,* Russia No. 1 (1942), Cmd. 6368.

between the Soviet Union and France, signed December 10, 1944; [51] the Treaty of Friendship and Alliance between the Soviet Union and the Republic of China, signed August 14, 1945; [52] the Treaty of Friendship and Alliance between France and the United Kingdom, signed March 4, 1947; [53] the network of bilateral mutual-assistance treaties concluded by the Soviet Union and East European states during the years 1943–48; [54] and the Treaty of Friendship, Alliance, and Mutual Assistance between the Government of the USSR and the Government of the People's Republic of China, signed February 14, 1950.[55]

Article 54

The Security Council shall at all times be kept fully informed of activities undertaken or in contemplation under regional arrangements or by regional agencies for the maintenance of international peace and security.

Article 54 was in substance included in the Dumbarton Oaks Proposals and was adopted at San Francisco without dissent. It places an obligation upon members of the Organization and upon regional agencies. The obligation is more extensive than that assumed under Article 51 in that it extends to activities "in contemplation" as well as to those "undertaken." Its obvious purpose is to provide the Security Council with the information it needs to discharge its "primary obligation" under Article 24, and to exercise the degree of control over the activities of regional organizations in the maintenance of international security that Articles 52 and 53 in particular envisage.

It would seem that the purpose of the article has not, in practice, been fully carried out. Information supplied to the Security Council has been largely limited to texts of resolutions and other documentary materials. The Organization of American States has regularly provided this kind of information. The language of Article 54, however, suggests that much more detailed reporting was envisaged; clearly, such would be necessary if the information is fully to serve the purpose of keeping the Security Council informed of what the regional agencies are doing and what can be expected of them in the maintenance of international peace and security.

[51] State Dept. *Bulletin,* XII, No. 289 (Jan. 7, 1945), p. 39.
[52] *Ibid.,* XIV, No. 345 (Feb. 10, 1946), 201.   [53] 9 UNTS, 187.
[54] For analysis and texts, see State Dept., *Documents and State Papers,* I, No. 4 (July, 1948). These bilateral treaties based on the exception contained in Art. 53 were superseded for most of the signatories by the Warsaw Pact of May 14, 1955, based on Art. 51. See commentary on Art. 51.
[55] 226 UNTS, 3.

Article 5 of the Inter-American Treaty of Reciprocal Assistance (the Rio Treaty) provides that

[the] High Contracting Parties shall immediately send to the Security Council of the United Nations, in conformity with Articles 51 and 54 of the Charter of the United Nations, complete information concerning the activities undertaken or in contemplation in the exercise of the right of self-defense or for the purpose of maintaining inter-American peace and security.

Neither the Pact of the League of Arab States nor the Charter of the Organization of African Unity contains a comparable provision.[56]

Information provided by the Organization of American States, primarily in the form of texts of resolutions and documents, comes from a variety of sources. Communications have been received from the Chairman of the OAS Council, from the Secretary-General, from the Chairman of the Inter-American Peace Committee, and from states parties to the disputes or directly involved in the situation. Communications have been addressed to the President of the Council and to the Secretary-General.[57] The communications are circulated as Security Council documents, and the Council's reports to the General Assembly customarily include summary accounts of the matters to which these documents refer.

The reports have in some instances been the occasion for Security Council discussion, particularly regarding the competence of the regional agency to take the action reported. In the case of the collective measures reported to have been taken against the Dominican Republic in 1960,[58] the Council after discussion adopted a resolution taking note of the report. In a few instances, the Security Council has specifically requested that the regional organization keep it informed of any action that it might take.[59]

[56] Art. 2 of the Treaty for Joint Defense and Economic Cooperation between the States of the Arab League of April 13, 1950, contains a provision in conformity with Art. 51, for notifying the Security Council of any acts of aggression and means and procedures to check it.

[57] For a list of such communications, see *Repertory*, II, 463–67; *Supp. 1*, I, 369–70; and *Supp. 2*, II, 479–80.

[58] See commentary on Art. 53.

[59] See, for example, resolution adopted apropos of the Stanleyville incident, UN Doc. S/6129, Dec. 30, 1964.

CHAPTER IX

International Economic and Social Cooperation

In drafting the Covenant of the League of Nations, little attention was given to the economic and social foundations of peace; almost exclusive emphasis was placed upon the direct means by which war might be prevented. Only two articles of the Covenant were expressly concerned with economic and social cooperation.[1] Other provisions of the Covenant, including the preamble, were interpreted as providing the basis for action in this area. Notwithstanding the paucity of Covenant provisions, a substantial part of the League's activity lay in the field of international economic and social cooperation.[2]

Officials of the U.S. State Department, when drafting proposals for a "general international organization" following the Moscow Conference, recognized the need for creating economic and social conditions in the postwar world favorable to peace and security and generally favored a single global organization that would combine "the negative function of preventing or punishing aggression with the positive function of promoting conditions conducive to peaceful relations among nations." [3] They favored arrangements that would make the new organization more effective in this respect than the League had been.[4] The Council of the League had recognized the weakness of the League's structure and procedures by creating in 1939 the Bruce Committee, which in its report made recommendations to a considerable extent anticipating the thinking that went into the establishment of the United Nations system.[5] The Tentative Proposals submitted by the United States govern-

[1] Arts. 23 and 24.
[2] See LN Secretariat, *Ten Years of World Cooperation;* Martin Hill, *The Economic and Financial Organization of the League of Nations* (Washington, Carnegie Endowment for International Peace, 1946); and Harriet E. Davis, ed., *Pioneers in World Order: An American Appraisal of the League of Nations* (New York, Columbia University Press, 1944).
[3] Ruth B. Russell, *A History of the United Nations Charter* (Washington, Brookings Institution, 1958), p. 206.
[4] See *ibid.,* pp. 303–29.
[5] LN Special Committee, The Development of International Co-operation in Economic and Social Affairs (A.23.1939).

ment to the Dumbarton Oaks conferees, contained detailed provisions for economic and social cooperation, including a provision for an economic and social council which would have important quasi-executive responsibilities.[6] After initial objections by the Soviet Union to broadening the scope of the proposed international organization to include economic and social cooperation had been overcome, the Dumbarton Oaks conferees accepted in substance the United States proposals. At San Francisco, partly because of pressures brought to bear by the smaller states and by nongovernmental organizations in a consultative relationship to the United States delegation, the provisions of the Dumbarton Oaks Proposals were considerably expanded.[7]

Article 55

With a view to the creation of conditions of stability and well-being which are necessary for peaceful and friendly relations among nations based on respect for the principle of equal rights and self-determination of peoples, the United Nations shall promote:

a. higher standards of living, full employment, and conditions of economic and social progress and development;

b. solutions of international economic, social, health, and related problems; and international cultural and educational cooperation; and

c. universal respect for, and observance of, human rights and fundamental freedoms for all without distinction as to race, sex, language, or religion.

Article 55 represents a substantial redrafting of the corresponding Dumbarton Oaks Proposal, which had provided that with "a view to the creation of conditions of stability and well-being which are necessary for peaceful and friendly relations, the Organization should facilitate solutions of international economic, social and other humanitarian problems and promote respect for human rights and fundamental freedoms." This phraseology had reflected a twofold preoccupation of United States leaders in particular: first, a belief resulting from the circumstances leading to World War II that it was necessary to take effective measures by international cooperation to restore and maintain conditions of economic stability and general well-being if war was to be avoided in the future; second, a conviction that respect for basic human rights and fundamental freedoms should be achieved not only

[6] Especially sec. viii. See State Dept., *Postwar Foreign Policy Preparation, 1939–1945*, pp. 595–606.

[7] In addition to chs. ix and x, these include Art. 1(3) and Art. 13(1b). See Russell, pp. 777–807.

as an end in itself but also as a condition favorable to the maintenance of international peace and respect for law.[8] At San Francisco, however, the Dumbarton Oaks text came under criticism for a variety of reasons. Many believed that it did not go far enough in stating what must be the objectives of international action in the postwar period in the economic and social fields. Others felt that it was desirable to state in greater detail the matters with which the Organization should be concerned, for fear that the general phraseology of the Dumbarton Oaks Proposals might provide an excuse for inaction. Last, there were those who believed that the obligations of members should be stated more explicitly and affirmatively to give assurance of achieving the purposes set forth in the article.

In drafting the present article, no serious difficulty was encountered except with respect to the inclusion of "full employment" as an objective of United Nations action.[9] The United States delegation in particular objected to the use of this term, preferring some such phrase as "high and stable levels of employment" on the ground that "full employment" was unrealistic and would provide the basis for United Nations intervention in matters of domestic jurisdiction. This latter fear was strengthened by another proposal that members should pledge themselves to take "separate" as well as "joint" action to carry out the objectives set forth.[10]

To reassure the United States delegation and others with similar fears, it was decided to include in the technical committee report a statement that the members were "in full agreement that nothing contained in the economic and social provisions of the Charter could be construed as giving authority to the Organization to intervene in the domestic affairs of Member States." [11] Additional reassurance was provided by the action of the Conference in broadening the domestic jurisdiction limitation of the Dumbarton Oaks Proposals and by transferring it to its present place in the Charter.[12]

The inclusion of human rights provisions in an article dealing primarily with economic and social cooperation requires some explanation, since international protection of human rights has usually been treated as a highly political matter, often involving considerations of peace and security; [13] it has also been considered as impinging on the domestic jurisdiction of states. The initiative for the inclusion of a human rights provision in the Charter came from the United States.

[8] See President Roosevelt's *Annual Message to Congress,* H. Doc. 1/77C1/1941; *The Atlantic Charter,* H. Doc. 358/77C1/1941; and *Declaration by United Nations,* U.S. Exec. Agreement Ser. 236, Jan. 1, 1942.
    [9] See Russell, pp. 781–89.   [10] See commentary on Art. 56.
    [11] UNCIO, *Documents,* X, 271–72.   [12] See commentary on Art. 2(7).
    [13] For example, the protection of minorities in the interwar period.

That country's Tentative Proposals to the Dumbarton Oaks conferees, gave the General Assembly the power to "initiate studies and make recommendations" for "the promotion of the observance of basic human rights in accordance with principles or undertakings agreed upon by the states members of the international organization." [14] This reflected United States thinking as expressed in President Roosevelt's State of the Union message of January 6, 1941.

At Dumbarton Oaks, there was strong opposition by the British and Soviet delegations to the inclusion of any provision on human rights. Ultimately, a compromise was effected in the form of a provision that the Organization should "promote respect for human rights and fundamental freedoms." [15] At San Francisco, there were widely supported demands for human rights provisions, not only in the article declaring the purposes of international economic and social cooperation but also in the articles on the purposes of the Organization and on the powers of the General Assembly. Furthermore, the Soviet position appeared to have changed since Dumbarton Oaks; at San Francisco the Soviet Union was not only prepared to support the above demands but it also proposed—as did other governments—a specific provision covering discrimination on the basis of race, language, religion, or sex. An amendment incorporating this provision was proposed by the Sponsoring Governments and was readily accepted. Insertion of the words "universal" and "and observance of" was made on committee recommendation and attracted no particular attention at the time. [16]

Article 55 has a central place in the total scheme of the Charter for promoting economic and social cooperation and respect for human rights. It is not the only article, however, relating to the scope of the responsibilities of the Organization and the range of its functions and powers. [17]

Nonetheless, in the discussions and decisions of United Nations organs, Article 55 has been most commonly invoked, largely because it is more specific than Article 1 in defining the responsibilities of the United Nations, and also because, taken together with Article 56, it creates a firmer commitment of members as well as of the Organization to take necessary measures to achieve the declared purposes. Article 1 emphasizes "international cooperation" while Article 55 stresses United Nations action. Article 1 refers to the solution of problems of an "economic, social, cultural, or humanitarian character." Article 55 commits the Organization, if not to specific solutions, at least

[14] State Dept., *Postwar Foreign Policy Preparation, 1939–1945*, p. 597.
[15] *Dumbarton Oaks Proposals*, ch. IX, sec. A, para. 1. See Russell, pp. 423–24.
[16] See *ibid.*, pp. 778–85.
[17] See also Arts. 1(3), 13(1b), and 62 in particular.

to achieving specific objectives. Article 1 envisages "international co-operation . . . in promoting and encouraging respect for human rights and fundamental freedoms," while Article 55 declares that the United Nations shall "promote . . . universal respect for, and observance of" these rights and freedoms.

United Nations Practice in Economic and Social Fields

In promoting the purposes set forth in Article 55 and related articles of the Charter, the United Nations has operated primarily through the General Assembly, the Economic and Social Council, and the Secretariat; through subsidiary organs established under the terms of Articles 7, 22, and 68; and through the specialized agencies provided for in Article 57. The work of United Nations organs in these areas has taken a variety of forms.[18] Subject to the requirements of the rules of procedure of the organ involved, any question falling within this broad area may be brought before the General Assembly or ECOSOC for discussion and possible action. The action taken may vary widely, being dependent on the nature of the consensus that emerges and the powers of the particular organ under the Charter. Possible alternatives include a study and report by the Secretariat, the preparation and publication by the Secretariat of information and analyses, the holding of an expert conference, the drafting of a convention to be submitted to members, a policy recommendation to governments, a recommendation of action to another organ or to one or more specialized agencies, and the establishment of programs to be carried out on a voluntary basis.[19]

From the beginning, great emphasis has been placed on United Nations responsibility for promoting economic and social progress and development. This has become a matter of mounting concern as successive volumes of the *World Economic Report* and the *Report on the World Social Situation* have revealed the existence of wide and growing divergences between the more advanced and the less-developed nations. Also, with the expansion of membership, the proportion of members falling in the category of "economically less developed countries" has become very large.[20] As an expression of its concern with developing and strengthening United Nations activity in this field, the

[18] See Robert E. Asher et al., *The United Nations and Promotion of the General Welfare* (Washington, Brookings Institution, 1957), pp. 108–49.

[19] For detailed summaries of action taken in the economic and social fields, see *Repertory*, Vol. III; *Supp. 1*, Vol. II; *Supp. 2*, Vol. III; and current *Y.U.N.* under the heading "Economic and Social Questions."

[20] For indication by the General Assembly of members falling within this category for purposes of reduction of assessments for peace-keeping operations, see GA Res. 1875(S–IV), June 27, 1963, para. 5.

General Assembly in 1961, following a proposal by the President of the United States in the course of the general debate, adopted a resolution designating "the current decade as the United Nations Development Decade." [21]

In its third session, the General Assembly took note of the need for action to improve conditions in those countries where "low standards of living" exist.[22] It also established a technical assistance program on a continuing basis to be financed under the regular budget.[23] The following year, ECOSOC adopted a resolution embodying the details of the Expanded Program of Technical Assistance (involving cooperation with the specialized agencies) [24] which the General Assembly subsequently approved.[25] In 1958, the General Assembly authorized the Secretary-General to supplement these programs by assisting governments to secure the temporary services of qualified personnel to perform administrative and executive functions (the OPEX program).[26]

In addition to providing technical assistance, the United Nations has through its responsible organs devoted much attention to the matter of financial assistance. One of the specialized agencies, the International Bank for Reconstruction and Development, has as its primary responsibility the provision of financial assistance for development purposes. Its policy has been to give assistance according to sound banking principles, which has limited the kinds of need it has been able to meet. As a result of constant pressure in ECOSOC and the General Assembly, the cooperation of the major financial powers was obtained in the establishment of 1) the International Finance Corporation, established as an affiliate of the Bank; [27] 2) the Special Fund, established as a subsidiary organ of the General Assembly; [28] and 3) the International Development Association, established as an affiliate of the Bank.[29] At its twentieth session, the General Assembly, on the recommendation of ECOSOC, established a new United Nations Development Programme, which combined the Expanded Program of Technical Assistance and the Special Fund.[30]

[21] GA Res. 1710(XVI), Dec. 19, 1961.   [22] GA Res. 198(III), Dec. 4, 1948.

[23] GA Res. 200(III), Dec. 4, 1948.

[24] ECOSOC Res. 222A(IX), Aug. 15, 1949.

[25] GA Res. 304(IV), Nov. 16, 1949.

[26] GA Res. 1256(XIII), Nov. 14, 1958.

[27] GA Res. 823(IX), Dec. 11, 1954; 922(X), Nov. 3, 1955; and UN Doc. E/2770, June 17, 1955.

[28] GA Res. 1240(XIII), Oct. 14, 1958.

[29] GA Res. 1420(XIV), Dec. 5, 1959; and Y.U.N., 1960, pp. 641–53.

[30] ECOSOC Res. 1020(XXXVII), Aug. 11, 1964; and GA Res. 2029(XX), Nov. 22, 1965. On Dec. 13, 1966, the Assembly established the United Nations Capital Development Fund "as an organ of the General Assembly" functioning "as an autonomous organization." GA Res. 2186 (XXI).

In response to the interest of the economically less-developed countries in promoting the growth of their own industries as ways of achieving diversification of their economic structures and overall advancement of their economies, the General Assembly and ECOSOC have taken a number of decisions to stimulate cooperative activity in this field. These have included the establishment by the Council of the Committee for Industrial Development; [31] the creation of the Industrial Development Center in the Secretariat; and finally, in December, 1965, the establishment by the General Assembly of the United Nations Organization for Industrial Development (UNOID) as an autonomous organization within the United Nations.[32]

While, in the early postwar years, problems of international trade were viewed primarily in terms of the avoidance of recessions and the maintenance of full employment, from 1960 on, increased emphasis was placed on the relation of the terms of trade to economic development. Responding to pressures from the underdeveloped countries and in the face of objections raised by some of the developed countries that considered the General Agreement on Tariffs and Trade the appropriate forum for discussion and negotiation, ECOSOC, with General Assembly endorsement, decided in 1962 to convene a United Nations conference on trade and development.[33] The conference met in Geneva from March 23 to June 16, 1964. It recommended that the General Assembly establish "continuing machinery" to keep world trade problems under continuous review; this was to consist of a conference to be convened at intervals of not more than three years, a trade and development board of fifty-five members, and a permanent secretariat. Other recommendations included a set of "general principles" to govern international trade relations and policies conducive to development.[34] On December 30, 1964, the United Nations Conference on Trade and Development (UNCTAD) was established as a subsidiary organ of the General Assembly.[35]

Discussions and decisions of United Nations organs have many times emphasized the close relationship between economic and social development. Thus, the General Assembly in its sixth session adopted a

[31] ECOSOC Res. 751(XXIX), Apr. 12, 1960.

[32] See ECOSOC Res. 1030B(XXXVI), Dec. 11, 1963; UN Doc. A/5826, Dec. 4, 1964; and GA Res. 2089(XX), Dec. 20, 1965. For structure and operating arrangements, see GA Res. 2152(XXI), Nov. 17, 1966.

[33] ECOSOC Res. 917(XXXIV), Aug. 3, 1962; GA Res. 1785(XVII), Dec. 8, 1962. See also ECOSOC Res. 944(XXXV), Apr. 18, 1963; and 963(XXXVI), July 18, 1963; and GA Res. 1897(XVIII), Nov. 11, 1963.

[34] For Final Act, see UN Doc. E/Conf.46/L. 28, June 16, 1964. For Report of Dr. Raoul Prebisch, Secretary-General of the Conference to the Secretary-General, see UN Doc. E/Conf.46/140, July 9, 1964.

[35] GA Res. 1995(XIX), Dec. 30, 1964.

resolution expressing the view that "action to promote social development and technical assistance in social matters should go hand in hand
with action to promote economic development and technical assistance
in economic matters." [36] The importance of balanced economic and
social development—with special attention to social problems that
arise in connection with implementing programs of economic development—was emphasized in resolutions adopted by ECOSOC and the
General Assembly in 1959.[37]

Promotion of Universal Respect for, and Observance of, Human Rights and Fundamental Freedoms

The United Nations has proceeded in a variety of ways to achieve
this result.[38] To assist in the Organization's work, the General Assembly and ECOSOC have established a number of subsidiary organs.[39]
Techniques used by these bodies have included: 1) the adoption of
resolutions designed to exercise persuasive influence on governments,
groups, and public opinion at large; 2) the drafting of conventions and
other international instruments for submission to and ratification by
states; 3) the convening of international conferences for the drafting of
such agreements; 4) the performance of special services, including the
rendering of technical assistance; 5) the preparation and dissemination
of information on the observance of human rights; and 6) measures
adopted with respect to specific allegations that human rights have
been violated to achieve remedial action by the governments concerned.

The most important single United Nations action under the
first heading was the General Assembly's approval on December 10,
1948, by a vote of 48 to 0 with 8 abstentions, of the Universal Declaration of Human Rights.[40] In the preamble to its resolution, the General
Assembly, after recalling the pledge of members "to achieve, in cooperation with the United Nations, the promotion of universal respect
for and observance of human rights and fundamental freedoms," asserted that "a common understanding of these rights and freedoms is of

[36] GA Res. 535(VI), Feb. 2, 1952.
[37] See ECOSOC Res. 723(XXVIII), July 17, 1959; 731(XXVIII), July 30, 1959;
and GA Res. 1329(XIV), Nov. 20, 1959.
[38] See *Repertory*, III, 55–110; *Supp. 1*, II, 24–32; and *Supp. 2*, III, 32–43.
[39] These include the Commission on Human Rights, with its Sub-Commission
on Prevention of Discrimination and Protection of Minorities, and bodies of a
temporary character, such as the UN Commission to Study the Racial Situation in
the Union of South Africa. GA Res. 616B(VII), Dec. 5, 1952.
[40] GA Res. 217(III), Dec. 10, 1948. For analysis of provisions of Declaration
and relevant decisions, see *Repertory*, III, 73–93; *Supp. 1*, II, 27–30; and *Supp. 2*,
III, 38–41.

the greatest importance for the full realization of this pledge." That the Declaration was a statement of objectives to be achieved was emphasized by the words of the document itself:

The General Assembly Proclaims this Universal Declaration of Human Rights as a common standard of achievement for all peoples and all nations, to the end that every individual and every organ of society, keeping this Declaration constantly in mind, shall strive by teaching and education to promote respect for these rights and freedoms and by progressive measures, national and international, to secure their universal and effective recognition and observance, both among the peoples of Member States themselves and among the peoples of territories under their jurisdiction.

Furthermore, the Commission on Human Rights pointed out in its report that the Declaration was only a first step in the elaboration of a human rights program, that it was not a treaty, and that it did not impose legal obligations.[41] It recommended that this should be followed by a covenant on human rights drafted in the form of a treaty creating legal obligations. Many governments have taken the position that the Declaration defines human rights and fundamental freedoms which members of the United Nations are legally obligated to respect; and some Assembly resolutions clearly accept this point of view.[42]

The General Assembly has adopted and opened for signature and ratification or accession a number of conventions relating in whole or in part to human rights, for example, the Convention on the Prevention and Punishment of the Crime of Genocide, and the Convention on the Political Rights of Women.[43] The major activity of the United Nations, however, has been in connection with the drafting of covenants on human rights. The Commission on Human Rights early decided— when it undertook, on the instruction of the Economic and Social Council, the preparation of an International Bill of Human Rights— that it would prepare a draft declaration setting forth general principles (which became the Universal Declaration of Human Rights), a draft convention setting forth binding legal obligations, and draft measures for implementation.[44] After adopting the Universal Declaration, the General Assembly requested ECOSOC to ask the Commission to continue to give priority to the preparation of a convention; it further decided that the draft covenant on human rights should include "eco-

[41] UN Doc. E/800, June 28, 1948.

[42] See, for example, GA Res. 1663(XVI), Nov. 28, 1961, on the question of race conflict in the Republic of South Africa in which the Assembly reaffirms "that the racial policies being pursued by the Government of South Africa are a flagrant violation of the Charter of the United Nations and the Universal Declaration of Human Rights and are totally inconsistent with South Africa's obligations as a Member State."

[43] GA Res. 260A(III), Dec. 9, 1948; 640(VII), Dec. 20, 1952.

[44] UN Doc. E/600, Dec. 17, 1947.

nomic, social and cultural rights"; and later, on the recommendation of ECOSOC, that the Commission on Human Rights should be instructed to draft two covenants, "one to contain civil and political rights and the other to contain economic, social and cultural rights." [45] At its tenth session, the Commission completed the two draft covenants, which ECOSOC considered and transmitted to the General Assembly.[46] They were on the agenda of each session of the General Assembly from 1954 to 1966. In its twenty-first session, the Assembly approved the two draft covenants, as revised by its Third Committee, and an optional protocol relating to implementation.[47]

The rendering of special services to governments in the field of human rights has received particular attention since 1954 after it appeared that full participation by some of the more important members in drafting and implementing the covenants would not be forthcoming. At its tenth session, the General Assembly adopted a proposal consolidating already approved technical assistance programs relating to the protection of the rights of women, the rights of minorities, and freedom of information with a broad program of assistance in the field of human rights—the entire program to be known as "advisory services in the field of human rights." [48] Assistance takes the form of advisory services of experts, fellowships and scholarships, and seminars, and is rendered at the request of governments.

The United Nations, chiefly through the Assembly, has dealt with a number of instances of alleged violation of human rights and fundamental freedoms. Included are the question of treatment of persons of Indian and Indo-Pakistan origin in South Africa; the question of racial discrimination in South Africa resulting from the policies of apartheid; the question of the observance by Bulgaria, Hungary, and Romania of the human rights provisions of the peace treaties; and the question of infringement of trade-union rights. In addition, the observance of human rights and fundamental freedoms has been an important factor in the consideration of many so-called colonial issues as, for example, the questions of Tunisia, Morocco, Algeria, and Angola. In dealing with these questions, United Nations organs have been faced with objections to their competence based on Article 2(7) of the Charter. Not-

[45] GA Res. 421(V), Dec. 4, 1950; 543(VI), Feb. 5, 1952. See also ECOSOC Res. 348(XIII), Aug. 29, 1951.

[46] Commission on Human Rights, Report of the Tenth Session, Feb. 23–April 16, 1954; ESCOR/18th Sess./1954/Supp. 7 (E/2573), and ECOSOC Res. 545B 1 and II (XVIII), July 29, 1954.

[47] GAOR/21st Sess./1966/Annexes, agenda item 62 (A/6546); and GA Res. 2200(XXI), Dec. 16, 1966.

[48] GA Res. 926(X), Dec. 14, 1955. See also UN Doc. E/2731, and Corr. 1, May 20, 1955; UN Doc. E/2781, July 27, 1955; and ECOSOC Res. 586E(XX), July 29, 1955.

withstanding objections raised, a wide range of decisions has been taken with a view to promoting respect for the rights in question.[49] These decisions have involved varying degrees of pressure and persuasion, such as reminding states of their international obligations, urging them to act in accordance with their Charter obligations, requesting states in conflict over questions of human rights to confer and to reach a peaceful settlement, setting up a committee of inquiry, affirming that continuation of policies of racial discrimination endangers international peace, and requesting members to take collective measures to bring about abandonment of such policies. At its seventeenth session, the General Assembly requested members to take the following measures against South Africa "to bring about the abandonment" of its apartheid policies:

(a) breaking off diplomatic relations with the Government of the Republic of South Africa or refraining from establishing such relations;

(b) closing their ports to all vessels flying the South African flag;

(c) enacting legislation prohibiting their ships from entering South African ports;

(d) boycotting all South African goods and refraining from exporting goods, including all arms and ammunition, to South Africa;

(e) refusing landing and passage facilities to all aircraft belonging to the Government and companies registered under the laws of South Africa.[50]

Article 56

All members pledge themselves to take joint and separate action in cooperation with the Organization for the achievement of the purposes set forth in Article 55.

The Dumbarton Oaks Proposals contained no comparable provision regarding action by members in the field of economic and social cooperation. At San Francisco, however, during the consideration by a drafting subcommittee of the equivalent of Article 55, a Canadian amendment was offered stating that "Members agree to cooperate fully with each other and with the United Nations with the object of" attaining the agreed purposes. In the course of discussion, the Australian delegate proposed a broader and more elaborate text, much of which was incorporated in a version, finally approved by the subcommittee, which read as follows: "All Members pledge themselves to take separate and joint action and to cooperate with the Organization and

[49] See *Repertory*, III, 63–65; *Supp. 1*, II, 26–27; and *Supp. 2*, III, 35–36.

[50] GA Res. 1761(XVII), Nov. 6, 1962. See also GA Res. 1881(XVIII), Nov. 6, 1963.

with each other to achieve these purposes." [51] In the full committee the United States reserved its position on the question of phraseology, and, on reference back to it, the subcommittee then recommended the following phraseology: "All Members undertake to cooperate jointly and severally with the Organization for the achievement of these purposes." Several delegates, including the Australian delegate, objected to this phraseology on the ground that it did not contain the threefold pledge to take separate action, to take joint action, and to cooperate with the Organization. It was decided to refer the matter to a subcommittee consisting of Australia, the Soviet Union, and the United States, which came up with the present wording. The United States delegate thought that this wording was somewhat vague but that it met the basic requirement of confining the provision to international action; the Australian delegate was able to reconcile the new phraseology with the position his government had taken.[52]

From this abbreviated history of Article 56, it is clear that two opposing points of view existed at San Francisco: one, that each member should pledge itself to take independent, separate, national action to achieve the purposes set forth in Article 55, and the other, that such a pledge of separate national action went beyond the proper scope of the Charter—the encouragement of international cooperation—and might infringe upon the domestic jurisdiction of members. The phraseology finally agreed upon was a compromise and clearly is capable of more than one interpretation. The problem of interpretation arises primarily with respect to the significance of the qualifying words "in cooperation with the Organization." They presumably refer to the Organization as a separate entity functioning through the appropriate organs, and not to its individual members; otherwise, "joint and separate action in cooperation with the Organization" becomes repetitious. If this is the proper interpretation, it would then appear that members pledge themselves not only to cooperate with each other, but also to cooperate with the appropriate organs of the United Nations with a view to achieving the purposes in question. It does not mean that recommendations of these organs become binding, but it does mean that members are obligated to refrain from obstructionist tactics and to cooperate in good faith to achieve the goals specified in Article 55.

Most of the references to Article 56 in the discussions of the General Assembly and ECOSOC have been in connection with the human rights provisions of Article 55. In some instances, the article has been mentioned specifically, while in others only the language has been

---

[51] Russell, pp. 786–88; UNCIO, *Documents,* X, 99.
[52] UNCIO, *Documents,* X, 130, 139–41, 161.

used. In a few cases, there has been reference to the article in the operative part of resolutions; in most cases it appears in the preamble only.[53]

In a number of resolutions, the General Assembly has made it clear that it considers that Article 56 imposes on members the definite obligation to follow or refrain from certain courses of action in the promotion of respect for human rights. Thus, the General Assembly at its seventh session, in considering the racial situation in the Union of South Africa, affirmed that governmental policies of member states not directed toward goals defined in an earlier paragraph of the resolution "but which are designed to perpetuate or increase discrimination, are inconsistent with the pledges of the Members under Article 56 of the Charter." [54] This declaration was repeated or reaffirmed in resolutions subsequently adopted dealing with the question of race conflict in the Union of South Africa and calling upon that country to abandon policies of racial discrimination.[55] The provisions of Article 56 appear to have been invoked by inference in calling upon members to take measures "separately or collectively, in conformity with the Charter, to bring about the abandonment of those policies." [56]

Article 57

1. The various specialized agencies, established by intergovernmental agreement and having wide international responsibilities, as defined in their basic instruments, in economic, social, cultural, educational, health, and related fields, shall be brought into relationship with the United Nations in accordance with the provisions of Article 63.

2. Such agencies thus brought into relationship with the United Nations are hereinafter referred to as specialized agencies.

In State Department discussions on postwar international organization, the initial thinking was in the direction of stressing the need for closer coordination of economic and social activities within the general structure. There was, however, another point of view which gained strength and then prevailed, to the effect that the actual existence of specialized international organizations in numerous fields made it necessary to tailor the machinery of the general organization to fit these facts.

[53] *Repertory*, III, 113–24; *Supp. 1*, II, 33–36; and *Supp. 2*, III, 45–48.
[54] GA Res. 616B(VII), Dec. 5, 1952.
[55] Notably, GA Res. 917(X), Dec. 6, 1955; 1016(XI), Jan. 30, 1957; 1248(XIII), Oct. 30, 1958; and 1663(XVI), Nov. 28, 1961.
[56] GA Res. 1761(XVII), Nov. 9, 1962.

In the United States Tentative Proposals, submitted as a basis for discussion at Dumbarton Oaks, there was full acceptance of the principle that responsibilities in the economic and social field should be assumed by a number of autonomous intergovernmental agencies brought into relationship with one another by agreements freely concluded.[57] This proposal, in somewhat simplified form, was incorporated into the Dumbarton Oaks Proposals without serious discussion and was accepted at San Francisco without any substantial impairment of the basic principle, though with considerable elaboration of detail.

Article 57 enunciates a basic principle governing the United Nations approach to economic and social cooperation: that in the economic and social fields the objectives of the general international organization should in large measure be achieved through autonomous specialized organizations created by intergovernmental agreement and brought into relationship with the United Nations by agreements freely entered into on both sides.

The Preparatory Commission in its report distinguished between intergovernmental agencies, using the term in its widest sense to indicate all agencies established by intergovernmental agreement, and specialized agencies as defined in Article 57. Following the view expressed by the technical committee of UNCIO,[58] the Commission concluded that ECOSOC might negotiate with the competent authorities "bringing into relationship such other inter-governmental agencies, including those of a regional character, as are not considered as being within the definition of Article 57 but which it is considered desirable to bring into relationship." [59] It thus recognized by implication that a regional organization or agency is not to be regarded as a specialized agency having "wide international responsibilities" within the meaning of Article 57.

With regard to international bureaus and agencies having highly specialized but global functions, such as the Universal Postal Union and the International Institute of Agriculture, which were in operation before World War II and which were never brought within the League system, the Commission suggested that, while it might be desirable for some to continue to function and "be brought into relationship with the United Nations," "more suitable organizational arrangements could be made for the exercise of the functions hitherto entrusted to many of them." It suggested three possible alternatives for reducing the number of agencies and bringing them into "a more rational and more unified structure": 1) liquidation and transfer of functions to a specialized agency; 2) liquidation and assumption of functions by an appropriate

[57] Russell, pp. 306–9.   [58] UNCIO, *Documents*, X, 281.
[59] *Report of the Preparatory Commission*, p. 401.

United Nations commission or committee; and 3) merger with another intergovernmental agency.

By the end of 1965, fifteen specialized intergovernmental organizations had been brought into a relationship with the United Nations. Of these, one, the International Refugee Organization, was established as a temporary specialized agency to solve the problem of refugees created by World War II and its aftermath, and passed out of existence in 1952.[60] A second, the International Atomic Energy Agency (IAEA), has not been formally designated a specialized agency but has the essential characteristics of one, including a formal relationship with the United Nations.

The intergovernmental organizations already in operation and brought into relationship with the United Nations by the end of 1965 were the following.

The International Labour Organisation (ILO)

This agency was initially established at the end of World War I as part of the League system of international cooperation. Its constitution provided for the establishment of a permanent organization for the improvement of labor conditions throughout the world, consisting of the General Conference, the Governing Body, and an International Labour Office.[61] The organization continued to function on a limited basis during World War II with headquarters in Montreal. At the twenty-sixth meeting of its General Conference, held in Philadelphia in June, 1944, a declaration of aims and purposes known as the "Philadelphia Charter" was adopted, setting forth the broad purposes of the organization for the future.[62]

The establishment of the United Nations and the termination of the League of Nations made necessary a revision of the original constitution. This work was completed at the twenty-seventh and twenty-ninth sessions of the International Labour Conference, meeting in Paris, October 5 to November 5, 1945, and in Montreal, September 19 to October 10, 1946.[63] The ILO was brought into relationship with the United Nations by an agreement approved by the International Labour Conference on October 2, 1946, and by the General Assembly on December 14, 1946.[64] The headquarters of the organization is in Geneva.[65]

[60] See Y.U.N., 1951, pp. 939–42.   [61] Part XIII of the Treaty of Versailles.
[62] International Labour Office, Official Bulletin, XXVI, No. 1, June 1, 1944.
[63] Ibid., XXVII, Nos. 1 and 2, Dec. 1, 1945; XXVIII, No. 3, Dec. 15, 1946; 38 UNTS, 3–15.
[64] UN Doc. A/72, Sept. 30, 1946; 1 UNTS, 184–205.
[65] For activities of the organization, see the annual reports of the Director-General.

The Food and Agriculture Organization
of the United Nations (FAO)

This was the first of the specialized organizations of a permanent character to be established during and after World War II. Agreement was reached at the United Nations Conference on Food and Agriculture, meeting in Hot Springs, Virginia, May 18 to June 3, 1943, to establish an interim commission to draft the constitution of the proposed organization. The constitution as drafted entered into force on October 6, 1945.[66] The work of organization was completed at a conference held in Quebec, October 16 to November 1, 1945. The headquarters of the organization is in Rome.

The purposes of the organization include raising levels of nutrition and standards of living, achieving greater efficiency in production and distribution of food and agricultural products, and improving living conditions of rural populations. The functions of the organization are to collect, analyze, interpret, and disseminate information; to promote and, where appropriate, to recommend national and international action; and to furnish such technical assistance as governments may require.

The principal organs of the organization are the Conference, in which all members are equally represented; the Council, consisting of representatives of twenty-seven members; and the Director-General and his staff. The organization was brought into relationship with the United Nations by an agreement approved by the second session of the conference in September, 1946, and by the General Assembly on December 14, 1946.[67]

The International Monetary Fund

This organization is provided for by the Articles of Agreement of the International Monetary Fund, which is Annex A of the Final Act of the United Nations Monetary and Financial Conference, held at Bretton Woods, July 1 to 22, 1944.[68] The Agreement entered into force on December 27, 1945, following the deposit of the instruments of acceptance by twenty-nine governments, signatories of the Final Act, whose subscriptions to the Fund amounted to 65 percent of the total. The headquarters of the Fund is in Washington.

The principal purposes of the Fund are to promote international monetary cooperation, to facilitate the expansion and balanced growth

[66] *Y.U.N.*, 1946–47, pp. 693–98.
[67] UN Doc. A/78, Sept. 30, 1946; 1 UNTS, 208–31.   [68] 2 UNTS, 40–133.

of international trade, "to promote exchange stability," and "to assist in the establishment of a multilateral system of payments in respect of current transactions between members and in the elimination of foreign exchange restrictions which hamper the growth of world trade." Except where otherwise provided, operations of the Fund are limited to transactions with the purpose of supplying a member with the currency of another member in exchange for gold or for the currency of the member desiring to make the purchase.

The functions of the Fund are performed by the Board of Governors, on which the members are equally represented; by the Executive Directors, currently twenty in number (of whom five are appointed by the five members with the largest quotas); and by the Managing Director and his staff. Voting power is related to the size of the contribution to the Fund's resources. The Fund was brought into relationship with the United Nations by an agreement approved by the Board of Governors in September, 1947, and by the General Assembly on November 15, 1947.[69]

The International Bank for Reconstruction and Development

The Bank functions under the terms of the Articles of Agreement, which constitute Annex B of the Bretton Woods Final Act.[70] The Articles of Agreement entered into force on December 3, 1945, following the deposit of the instruments of acceptance by twenty-nine signatories, governments whose subscriptions amounted to 65 percent of the total authorized capital. The headquarters of the organization is in Washington.

The primary purposes of the Bank are to assist in the reconstruction and development of territories of members by facilitating productive capital investment; to promote private foreign investment; to encourage public investment, when private capital is not available for productive purposes on reasonable terms; and "to promote the long-range balanced growth of international trade and the maintenance of equilibrium in balances of payments by encouraging international investment for the development of the productive resources of members." The operations of the Bank consist of making or facilitating loans.

The Bank performs its functions through its Board of Governors, on which each member is represented; twenty Executive Directors, of whom five are appointed by members having the largest number of shares; and the President, selected by the Executive Directors. Voting is based upon the number of shares of stock held by members. The organization was brought into relationship with the United Nations by

[69] UN Doc. A/349, Sept. 2, 1947; 16 UNTS, 326–39.   [70] 2 UNTS, 134–205.

an agreement approved by the Board of Governors in September, 1947, and by the General Assembly on November 15, 1947.[71]

The International Civil Aviation Organization (ICAO)

This organization was established by and operates under the terms of the Convention on International Civil Aviation, signed in Chicago on December 7, 1944.[72] It came into existence on April 4, 1947, thirty days after the Convention had been ratified or adhered to by twenty-six states. The headquarters of the organization is in Montreal.

The objectives of the organization have to do principally with the safety and development of international civil aviation. The functions vested in the organization include investigation and research, collection and publication of information, reporting on infractions of the Convention, the adoption of international standards and recommended practices, and the making of recommendations to members.

The organs include the Assembly, with equal representation and voting power for all members; the Council, composed of twenty-seven members elected by the Assembly, with adequate representation of states important for the purposes of transport and of different geographic areas; the Air Navigation Commission; and the Secretariat. The organization was brought into relationship with the United Nations by an agreement approved by the General Assembly on December 14, 1946, and subsequently by the first session of the ICAO Assembly.[73]

The United Nations Educational, Scientific and Cultural Organization (UNESCO)

This organization was established by and operates under the terms of the Constitution signed in London on November 16, 1945,[74] which entered into force on November 4, 1946, when, pursuant to its terms, the instruments of acceptance of twenty signatories had been deposited with the United Kingdom. The headquarters of the organization is in Paris.

The purposes of the organization are "to contribute to peace and security by promoting collaboration among the nations through education, science and culture in order to further universal respect for justice, for the rule of law and for the human rights and fundamental

[71] UN Doc. A/349, Sept. 2, 1947 and Add. 1, Sept. 24, 1947; 16 UNTS, 346–57.

[72] 15 UNTS, 295–375.

[73] UN Doc. A/106 and Corr. 1, Sept. 30, 1946; 8 UNTS, 324–42.

[74] UN Doc. E/CONF/29, Nov. 16, 1945; 4 UNTS, 275–301.

freedoms which are affirmed for the peoples of the world, without distinction of race, sex, language or religion, by the Charter of the United Nations"; to collaborate in the work of advancing the mutual knowledge and understanding of peoples through mass communication and to recommend such international agreements as may be necessary to promote the free flow of ideas; to encourage popular education and the spread of culture; and to maintain, increase, and diffuse knowledge by encouraging cooperation in all branches of intellectual activity.

The functions of the organization are performed by the General Conference, on which members are equally represented; the Executive Board of 30 members, elected by the Conference; and the Director-General and his staff. The organization was brought into relationship with the United Nations by an agreement approved by the first session of the Conference in 1946 and by the General Assembly on December 14, 1946.[75]

The World Health Organization (WHO)

The initiative in establishing this organization was taken by the Economic and Social Council under Articles 59 and 62. On February 15, 1946, the Council set up a Technical Preparatory Commission to prepare for an international health conference.[76] The Commission met in Paris from March 8 to April 5 and agreed on a draft constitution for a World Health Organization.[77] On the basis of this preliminary work, the World Health Conference, called by the Economic and Social Council and meeting in New York, June 19 to July 22, 1946, drafted and approved the constitution of the World Health Organization.[78] This instrument entered into force on April 7, 1948, following ratification by twenty-six members of the United Nations. The headquarters of the organization is in Geneva.

The object of the organization is "the attainment by all peoples of the highest possible level of health." Its functions include the promotion of cooperation among intergovernmental agencies, governments, and private groups; the rendering of technical assistance to governments and special groups; the drafting of conventions and other forms of international agreements; the promotion and conduct of research; the promotion of improved standards of teaching and training in medi-

[75] UN Doc. A/77 and Corr. 1 and 2, Sept. 30 and Dec. 12, 1946; 1 UNTS, 236–58.
[76] ESCOR/1st Yr./1st Sess./10th Mtg./Feb. 15, 1946/p. 89; and *Annex 8*, pp. 159–60.
[77] *Ibid.*, 2d Sess./Apr. 5, 1946/pp. 143–61.
[78] ECOSOC, "Final Act of the International Health Conference. . . . " UN Doc. E/155; ECOSOC/3d Sess./1946; 14 UNTS, 185–285.

cal and related programs; and the development of international standards with respect to food, biological, pharmaceutical, and similar products.

The work of the organization is carried out through the World Health Assembly composed of delegates of all members; the Executive Board, consisting of persons designated by twenty-four members chosen by the Assembly; and the Secretariat, headed by the Director-General. The constitution also provides for regional organizations to be integrated into the world organization.

The organization has taken over the functions in the health field of the League of Nations, the Office International d'Hygiène Public in Paris, the United Nations Relief and Rehabilitation Administration, and various other intergovernmental health organizations. The agreement defining the relationship of the organization to the United Nations was approved by the General Assembly on November 15, 1947.[79]

The Intergovernmental Maritime Consultative Organization (IMCO)

The Convention providing for the establishment of this organization was drafted and signed at the United Nations Maritime Conference which met in Geneva, February 19 to March 6, 1948.[80] The Conference was convened by the Economic and Social Council and was instructed "to consider the establishment of an inter-governmental maritime organization."[81] The Convention entered into force on March 17, 1958, when twenty-one states, of which seven had a total tonnage of not less than one million gross tons of shipping, had deposited ratifications.[82] The headquarters of the organization is in London.

The purposes of the organization are to provide for cooperation between governments in technical matters relating to shipping, to encourage the highest practical standards of safety and efficiency in operations, to encourage ending discriminatory action and unnecessary restrictions by governments, and to provide for the consideration of unfair shipping practices by shipping companies, and any other matters concerning shipping referred to it by any organ or specialized agency of the United Nations. The functions of the organization are consultative and advisory.

The organization consists of the Assembly, the Council, the Maritime Safety Committee, and the Secretariat. The Council has ten members

[79] UN Doc. A/348, Sept. 2, 1947 and Add. 1, Sept. 27, 1947; and Add. 2, Oct. 2, 1947; 19 UNTS, 194–213.

[80] ECOSOC, "Final Act of the United Nations Maritime Conference." UN Doc. E/CONF.4/62, Mar. 8, 1948 Corr. 1, Mar. 9, 1948; 289 UNTS, 48–109.

[81] ECOSOC Res. 35(IV), Mar. 28, 1947.   [82] Art. 60 of the Convention.

and is constituted so as to give representation to states with the largest interest in providing international shipping services and in international seaborne trade. The Maritime Safety Committee assumes functions in connection with the administration of the Convention on Safety at Sea, as revised at the London Conference of April 23, 1948.[83] It consists of fourteen members, of whom eight "shall be the largest ship-owning nations."[84] In an opinion given on June 8, 1960, at the request of IMCO, the International Court of Justice held that "the determination of the largest ship-owning nations depends solely upon the tonnage registered in the countries in question."[85] An agreement bringing the organization into relation with the United Nations was approved by the General Assembly on June 13, 1959.[86]

The Universal Postal Union (UPU)

The Union was founded under the terms of a Convention signed in Berne on October 9, 1874,[87] and revised at successive Postal Congresses—notably in Paris in 1947, when provision was made for the Executive and Liaison Committee, and in Ottawa in 1957, when the Consultative Committee on Postal Studies was established.[88] The Union includes countries and certain specified colonial administrations which have rights of participation as defined in Article 4 of the Convention.

The purpose of the Union is to promote and facilitate postal communications between states. Its work is carried out by the General Congress, which meets at least every five years; the Executive and Liaison Commission of twenty-five members; the Consultative Committee on Postal Studies; and the International Bureau. The headquarters of the organization is in Berne.

The Union is one of the prewar "bureaux and agencies" brought into relationship with the United Nations. This relationship was established by an agreement approved by the Twelfth Congress of the Universal Postal Union and by the United Nations General Assembly on November 16, 1947.[89]

[83] 164 UNTS, 113–357.   [84] Art. 28 of the Convention.
[85] *ICJ Reports*, 1960, p. 171.   [86] 324 UNTS, 274–91.
[87] *British and Foreign State Papers*, LXV, 13.
[88] On history and constitution of the UPU, see George A. Codding, Jr., *The Universal Postal Union* (New York, New York University Press, 1964). For text of Convention, see *Documents du Congrès d'Ottawa*, 1957 (Berne, 1958); 169 UNTS, 3–359.
[89] UN Doc A/347, Sept. 2, 1947; 19 UNTS, 220–30.

International Telecommunication Union (ITU)

The Union evolved from the International Telegraph Union, established under the terms of the Paris Convention of May 17, 1865.[90] Beginning in 1906, the Bureau of the Union was charged with certain responsibilities under the terms of conventions and regulations adopted by the Berlin Radiotelegraph Conference of 1906 and its successors. By resolutions adopted by the International Telegraph Conference in Paris in 1925 and by the International Radiotelegraph Conference in Washington in 1927, the two Conferences met in Madrid in 1932 and adopted a single Convention covering both radio and telegraph and providing for the establishment of the International Telecommunication Union. The Convention was extensively revised at the Atlantic City Conference of 1947 and again in 1959 and 1965.[91]

The Convention provides for a Plenipotentiary Conference, meeting every five years (with administrative conferences meeting at the same time to revise radio, telephone, and telegraph regulations); an Administrative Council, consisting of twenty-five members, responsible for the management of the affairs of the Union; three international consultative committees dealing with technical matters; and the General Secretariat. The headquarters of the Union is in Geneva. The Union was brought into relationship with the United Nations by an agreement approved by the General Assembly on November 15, 1947.[92]

The World Meteorological Organization (WMO)

Provision for the establishment of the World Meteorological Organization was made in a Convention adopted by the Conference of Directors of the International Meteorological Organization held in Washington, September 22 to October 11, 1947.[93] The Convention entered into force on March 23, 1953, thirty days after the deposit of the thirtieth instrument of accession.

The Convention declares the basic purpose of the organization to be the coordination, standardization, and improvement of world meteorological activities and the exchange of meteorological information.

The functions of the organization are performed by the Congress, the Executive Committee of eighteen members, the Secretariat, Regional Associations, and Technical Commissions. An agreement defin-

[90] *British and Foreign State Papers*, LVI, 294.
[91] ITU, International Telecommunication Convention (Montreux, 1965).
[92] UN Doc. A/370, Sept. 2, 1947, and Add. 1, Oct. 11, 1947; 30 UNTS, 316–30.
[93] See IMO, Final Report, Twelfth Conference of Directors (Washington, Sept. 22–Oct. 11, 1947); 77 UNTS, 143–83.

ing the relation of the organization to the United Nations was approved by the General Assembly on December 20, 1951.[94]

The International Finance Corporation (IFC)

The International Finance Corporation was established under Articles of Agreement drawn up in Washington on May 25, 1955; [95] it became operative July 20, 1956, when instruments of acceptance had been deposited by signatories whose subscriptions amounted to not less than 75 percent of the total capital. The International Finance Corporation is an affiliate of the International Bank for Reconstruction and Development but, at the same time, has a separate corporate personality and maintains its own accounts.

The purpose of the Corporation is to further economic development by encouraging productive private enterprise, particularly in the less developed areas, thus supplementing the activities of the Bank. Investments are made without government guarantees.

Its organs are the Board of Governors, the Board of Directors, and the President and his staff. The Corporation was brought into relationship with the United Nations by an agreement approved by the General Assembly on February 20, 1957.[96]

The International Development Association (IDA)

The International Development Association was established under Articles of Agreement, drawn up by the Bank, which entered into force on September 24, 1960, when accepted by governments whose subscriptions comprised not less than 65 percent of the total capital.[97] The Association, though an affiliate of the Bank, is a separate and distinct institution. The headquarters of the Association is in Washington.

The purposes of the Association are to promote economic development, increase production, and thus raise standards of living by providing financial assistance on terms more flexible than conventional loans and that bear less heavily upon the balance of payments of recipient countries.

Its organization consists of the Board of Governors, the Executive Directors, and the President and his staff. The Association was brought into relationship with the United Nations by an agreement approved by the General Assembly on March 27, 1961.[98]

[94] GA Res. 531(VI); 123 UNTS, 246–64.
[95] IBRD, Articles of Agreement of the International Finance Corporation (Washington, July 20, 1956); 264 UNTS, 117–61.
[96] UN Doc. A/3529/Rev. 1, Annex, Feb. 14, 1957; 265 UNTS, 314–20.
[97] 394 UNTS, 221–29.
[98] GA Res. 1594(XVI); ECOSOC Res. 805(XXX), Dec. 21, 1960.

The International Atomic Energy Agency (IAEA)

This organization operates under a Statute drawn up at a Conference held at United Nations headquarters in New York, September 20 to October 26, 1956.[99] It entered into force on July 29, 1957, following the deposit of the instruments of ratification by eighteen signatories, including at least three of the following: Canada, France, the Soviet Union, the United Kingdom, and the United States.

The Agency's main objectives are: to accelerate and enlarge the contribution of atomic energy to peace, health, and prosperity throughout the world, and to assure that the assistance it provides is not used to further any military purposes. In carrying out these functions, it may encourage and assist research and perform any operation or service likely to be aided by the peaceful application of atomic energy. The Agency is required to conduct its activities in accordance with the purposes and principles of the United Nations and is required to submit reports on its activities to the General Assembly, and—where these relate to the maintenance of peace and security—to the Security Council.

The main organs of the Agency are the General Conference, the Board of Governors, and the Director-General and his staff.

The relationship of the Agency to the United Nations assumed a special character because of the inability of the principal sponsors to agree upon the exact status of the Agency and because the extent to which its activities bear upon the maintenance of international peace and security have placed the Agency in a special relationship to the Security Council. Unlike the agreements concluded by the intergovernmental organizations referred to above, the Agreement determining the relationship of the United Nations to the International Atomic Energy Agency does not provide explicitly that the Agency shall be regarded as a "specialized agency." [100] Under the terms of the Agreement, the United Nations recognizes that the Agency "by virtue of its intergovernmental character and international responsibilities, will function under its statute as an autonomous international organization in the working relationship with the United Nations established by this Agreement." Article 1 of the Agreement provides that the United Nations recognizes the Agency "as the agency, under the aegis of the United Nations as specified in the present Agreement, responsible for international activities concerned with the peaceful uses of atomic energy in accordance with its statute, without prejudice to the rights

[99] For text, see 276 UNTS, 3–125.
[100] GA Res. 1145(XVII), Nov. 14, 1957; 281 UNTS, 370–87.

and responsibilities of the United Nations in this field under the Charter of the United Nations."

While the Agreement withholds from the Agency explicit recognition as a "specialized agency," its terms are in most respects similar to those of agreements concluded with specialized agencies. In fact, the Agreement directs the General Assembly to authorize the Agency to seek advisory opinions from the International Court of Justice. This is of particular significance since under the terms of Article 96(2) of the Charter, only "specialized agencies," in addition to "other organs of the United Nations," may request advisory opinions of the Court when authorized by the Assembly.[101]

The Preparatory Commission assumed that a specialized agency would be established to deal with trade policies. ECOSOC decided early in 1946 to convene a conference for this purpose.[102] The United Nations Conference on Trade and Development which met in Havana, November, 1947, to March, 1948, drew up a charter for the International Trade Organization which has not entered into force because of an insufficient number of ratifications. To facilitate tariff negotiations, the General Agreement on Tariffs and Trade (GATT) was concluded and entered into force January 1, 1948.[103] A series of negotiating conferences have been held. The headquarters of the Agreement is in Geneva.

Article 58

The Organization shall make recommendations for the coordination of the policies and activities of the specialized agencies.

The decision that the economic and social purposes of the United Nations should be sought, not only through the appropriate organs of the Organization, but also through autonomous intergovernmental organizations brought into relationship with the United Nations, made it essential that effective coordination of policies and activities should be achieved. The Dumbarton Oaks Proposals distinguished between the responsibility of the General Assembly for coordinating policies and the responsibility of ECOSOC for coordinating activities. In the Charter as finally adopted, this distinction is somewhat blurred. Under Articles 58 and 60, responsibility for the coordination of policies and activities is vested in the General Assembly and "under the authority of the General Assembly, in the Economic and Social Council." Article 63(2) authorizes ECOSOC to "coordinate the activities of the special-

[101] See commentary on Art. 96.   [102] ECOSOC Res. 1/13, Feb. 18, 1946.
[103] 324 UNTS, 300–33.

ized agencies" through consultation with and recommendations to such agencies and through recommendations to the General Assembly and to the Members of the United Nations." [104] The Preparatory Commission emphasized that the objectives of the United Nations in the economic and social fields would be more fully achieved if "a close relationship and coordination is established between the United Nations and the agencies." After making numerous specific proposals for achieving effective coordination through United Nations organs, the Commission concluded, however, that the basic responsibility rested with members.[105]

The difficulty of the task of coordination was magnified from the beginning, not only by the autonomy of the specialized agencies, but also by the divergencies among the agencies with respect to membership, structure of organs, and voting arrangements. Differences between the membership of the United Nations and that of the specialized agencies have tended to decrease with the wider participation in the work of the specialized agencies. Significant differences still remain, however, as the result of the continuing nonparticipation of some United Nations members, especially in the financial agencies, and the participation in the specialized agencies of a limited number of states that are not members of the United Nations. Differences of structure and voting arrangements in the specialized agencies, as compared to the United Nations, include the separate representation of governments, workers, and employers in the ILO; arrangements for the representation of states with special interests in the executive organs of IAEA, IMCO, and ICAO; and provisions for weighted voting in the constitutions of the financial agencies. These divergences may result in a lack of coordination even if individual members fully coordinate their policies and activities in the organizations of which they are members. Furthermore, they increase the difficulties faced by United Nations organs in obtaining the cooperation of the specialized agencies.

Approaches to Coordination

The Charter does not define in detail how the General Assembly is to discharge its general responsibility under Articles 58 and 60. It has the general power vested in it by Articles 10 and 13 to discuss, initiate studies, and make recommendations for achieving the purposes of the Organization in the economic and social field. Furthermore, the General Assembly has some specially enumerated powers it may use. These

---

[104] Other articles concerned with coordination are 13, 15, 57, 62, 63, 64, 66, 68, and 70.

[105] *Report of the Preparatory Commission,* pp. 40, 48.

include: 1) the power to consider and approve financial and budgetary arrangements with the specialized agencies and to examine and make recommendations with respect to their administrative budgets (Article 17[3]); 2) the approval of agreements concluded by ECOSOC with the agencies referred to in Article 57 (Article 63[1]); and 3) the approval of ECOSOC's rendering services at the request of members and of the specialized agencies (Article 66[2]).

The Charter is more specific in its enumeration of ECOSOC's powers. It may initiate studies and reports, make recommendations to the General Assembly and to members, and consult with and make recommendations to the specialized agencies. It may prepare draft conventions and call international conferences on matters within its competence. It may conclude agreements with agencies referred to in Article 57. It may take appropriate steps to obtain regular reports from the specialized agencies, and make arrangements with members and with the specialized agencies to obtain reports on the steps taken by them to give effect to its recommendations and those of the General Assembly. It may perform such functions as are assigned to it by the General Assembly.

The General Assembly and ECOSOC have developed and used a variety of methods for achieving better coordination. These include the following:

CONCLUSION OF AGREEMENTS. This is dealt with in some detail in the commentary on Article 63. The Preparatory Commission emphasized the importance of these arrangements in facilitating the achievement of economic and social objectives and enabling the United Nations and the specialized agencies to discharge their responsibilities.[106] Generally, these agreements recognize the responsibility of the United Nations, under Articles 58 and 63, to make recommendations and to engage the specialized agencies to arrange for the submission of such recommendations to the appropriate organs. The agreements rely upon methods of information, discussion, and persuasion for achieving coordination. They do not give the United Nations organs control over the budgets and programs of the specialized agencies; rather, they treat the specialized agencies as equals in their power to take independent decisions regarding policies and programs.

DEVELOPMENT OF MACHINERY OF COORDINATION. The performance of the coordination function requires much work of a technical and administrative character, which organs such as the General Assembly and ECOSOC find it impossible to do satisfactorily without assistance by specially constituted and qualified bodies. Consequently, they have established a number of committees, commissions, and special bodies

[106] *Report of the Preparatory Commission*, p. 40.

to assist them in the work.[107] In addition, they have relied heavily on the Secretariat. Both organs have on numerous occasions called upon the Secretary-General to assist in achieving better coordination by undertaking studies and reporting, by consulting with the administrative officers of the specialized agencies, and by assuming overall responsibility for the administration of programs involving cooperation between the United Nations and the specialized agencies.[108]

The General Assembly has made extensive use of the Advisory Committee on Administrative and Budgetary Questions in the review of financial and budgetary arrangements with the specialized agencies and in the examination of their administrative budgets.[109] At the Assembly's request, the Committee has also made special studies of other questions involved in administrative and budgetary coordination, such as common services and a common salary system. It has also advised ECOSOC, at the Assembly's request, on administrative and financial aspects of program coordination and better use of resources.

ECOSOC, which itself serves in a sense as a subsidiary organ of the General Assembly, has a wide variety of special aids at its disposal. For instance, one of its sessional committees, the Coordination Committee, meets during sessions to examine questions of coordination referred to it, and to report thereon. One of its major instruments is the Administrative Committee on Coordination, established by Council resolution in 1946, on the recommendation of the Preparatory Commission.[110] Under this resolution, the Secretary-General was requested "to establish a standing committee of administrative officers consisting of himself as chairman, and the corresponding officers of the specialized agencies brought into relationship with the United Nations, for the purpose of taking all appropriate steps, under the leadership of the Secretary-General, to insure the fullest and most effective implementation of the agreements entered into between the United Nations and the specialized agencies." The Committee is assisted by a preparatory committee of deputies and a number of ad hoc working bodies. To assist it in program appraisal and in more effectively achieving the goals of the United Nations Development Decade, ECOSOC established in 1960 an ad hoc working group and in 1962 a special committee on coordination.[111]

[107] See *Repertory*, III, 135–41; *Supp. 1*, II, 51–52; and *Supp. 2*, III, 62–66.

[108] Arts. 97 and 98 provide the constitutional basis for such assignments.

[109] On composition and functions of ACABQ, see GA *Rules of Procedure*, A/520/Rev.8, Mar. 1966, Rules 156–58.

[110] ECOSOC Res. 13(III), Sept. 21, 1946. Originally called the Coordination Committee, and later known as the Secretary-General's Committee on Coordination, the Committee was given its present name by ECOSOC in its seventh session.

[111] ECOSOC Res. 798(XXX), Aug. 3, 1960; 920(XXXIV), Aug. 3, 1962; and 1090G(XXXIX), July 31, 1965.

The functional and regional commissions established by the Council under Article 68 have played roles of varying importance in the performance of the coordination function. Some of the functional commissions have given valuable assistance to the Council through advice on matters in their respective fields of competence. The regional economic commissions, however, in addition to advising the Council, have been authorized to make direct recommendations on matters within their competence to specialized agencies as well as to governments. Liaison arrangements have been entered into between the commissions and the specialized agencies in the form of joint secretariat units, inter-secretariat working groups, and reciprocal representation.

COORDINATION OF ADMINISTRATIVE AND BUDGETARY PRACTICES.[112] While the General Assembly and ECOSOC have adopted numerous resolutions containing specific recommendations to this end, the major results have been achieved by cooperation at the administrative level, particularly through the Administrative Committee on Coordination. This Committee has concerned itself with such matters as personnel recruitment, budgetary and financial arrangements, information programs and publications, procedures for providing technical information, coordination of conference calendars, submission of agency reports, and privileges and immunities.

ESTABLISHMENT OF OPERATIONAL PROGRAMS. Operational programs, initially established under General Assembly resolutions and involving a number of specialized agencies as well as the United Nations, have required close coordination for their success. It has been found desirable and possible to institutionalize this coordination to a considerable degree. Programs under which coordination of this kind has been achieved include the Expanded Programme of Technical Assistance (EPTA) and the Special Fund (now combined into the United Nations Development Programme), the United Nations Children's Fund (UNICEF), the relief and works program for Palestine refugees, and the Korean reconstruction program. In the case of EPTA,[113] for example, the coordinating organs were the Technical Assistance Committee of ECOSOC, and the Technical Assistance Board, consisting of its Executive Chairman appointed by the Secretary-General, and representatives of participating agencies. The Board had responsibility for preparing programs, and establishing administrative and financial policies and procedures for the program as a whole, subject to review and

[112] See commentary on Art. 17(3).
[113] Established under ECOSOC Res. 222A(IX), Aug. 15, 1949, and GA Res. 304(IV), Nov. 16, 1949, and revised, especially as to programing procedure by ECOSOC Res. 542B(XVIII), July 29, 1954, and GA Res. 831(IX), Nov. 26, 1954. It was merged with the Special Fund to form the United Nations Development Programme by GA Res. 2029(XX), Nov. 22, 1965.

approval by the Technical Assistance Committee.[114] The Board was assisted in the preparation of programs by the Resident Technical Assistance Representatives who cooperated with governments and representatives of agencies in the preparation of programs at the country level. The regional economic commissions of ECOSOC have taken on important coordinating roles, particularly in connection with field programing.[115]

ESTABLISHMENT OF PRIORITIES. The effort has been made to establish priorities to achieve the most effective use of available resources in meeting the most pressing needs. In 1952, ECOSOC recommended priorities to be given programs in the economic and social fields, subject to the overriding objective of the economic and social development of underdeveloped areas.[116] Secretary-General Hammarskjöld in 1954 reminded the Council of this "overriding objective" of the Organization's economic and social program and emphasized the need to reduce work of lesser importance to avoid overburdening the Organization and in particular the Secretariat.[117] In his 1957 report to ECOSOC, the Secretary-General reiterated the need to assure the best use of limited resources and the desirability of concentrating on matters of first priority.[118] The Council responded by inviting the specialized agencies to include in their annual reports passages specifically indicating further concentration achieved, and to consider the extent to which they might apply "the general guiding principles in the field of cooperation and coordination of activities" set forth in the annex to the report of the Committee on Coordination.[119]

The desirability of giving priority to the economic and social development of underdeveloped territories was stressed in *Five-Year Perspective, 1959–1964*,[120] the program appraisal that had been requested by the General Assembly and the Economic and Social Council, and in resolutions adopted by those organs on the basis of the appraisal.

CONCERTED ACTION. In a resolution adopted on August 1, 1957,[121] the Economic and Social Council, after reaffirming its reliance on the

[114] For details of program and the role of the Board, see annual reports of the Technical Assistance Board to TAC.
[115] On work of Resident Technical Assistance Representatives, as well as other aspects of coordination at local level, see Walter A. Sharp, *Field Administration in the United Nations* (New York, Praeger, 1961), especially pp. 295–366.
[116] ECOSOC Res. 451A(XIV), July 28, 1952. See also "Report of the Coordination Committee of the Council," UN Doc. E/2306, July 25, 1952.
[117] UN Doc. E/2598, May 13, 1954.
[118] UN Doc. E/3011 and Corr. 1, June 6, 1957, and Add. 1, 2, June 14, 1957.
[119] ECOSOC Res. 664A and B(XXIV), Aug. 1, 1957; UN Doc. E/3034, *Annex*, July 20, 1957.
[120] UN Doc. E/3347/Rev. 1, June 20, 1960.
[121] ECOSOC Res. 665A(XXIV), Aug. 1, 1957.

Administrative Committee on Coordination (ACC) "to continue to develop and improve arrangements for the fullest consultations between the secretariats in all stages of planning and execution of programs of common interest," recognized "the need for establishing, on a regular basis, consultations of the governing bodies of competent organizations in all cases of major programs calling for the participation of several organizations within the framework of a plan of concerted action." In response to this resolution, ACC prepared a report on the possibilities of concerted action in various fields.[122] The following criteria were established for determining the suitability of a program for concerted action: 1) it should be sufficiently complex to call for efforts from different directions; 2) it should be sufficiently specific to allow the combination of these efforts within a definite area; and 3) it should be capable of a definition which the parties concerned would agree to accept as the framework for their joint efforts. Concerted action was differentiated from the regular coordination of activities, the former implying unified action under a jointly conceived and unified plan with a broad common objective, and the latter implying efforts to harmonize actions undertaken by different agencies within the framework of different programs. ECOSOC has given support to the preparation of programs of concerted action in a number of fields, including housing, water resources development, industrialization, urbanization, and oceanography.[123]

COMPREHENSIVE APPRAISAL OF PROGRAMS. In its report to the eleventh session of the General Assembly, the Advisory Committee on Administrative and Budgetary Questions suggested that ECOSOC arrange a comprehensive appraisal of the activities of the United Nations and the specialized agencies in the economic and social fields.[124] In its twenty-fourth session, ECOSOC requested the Secretary-General to make an appraisal of the scope, trend, and cost of the regular United Nations programs in these fields for the period 1959–64, and invited the specialized agencies most directly concerned to consider the most appropriate and practical methods of making similar appraisals of their programs.[125] The Council appointed a committee of individuals to prepare a consolidated report showing the extent to which the programs responded to basic needs and the interrelation of the activities

[122] ESCOR/26th Sess./1958/*Annexes*, agenda item 3. UN Doc. E/3108, *Annex 1*, Add. 1, May 9, 1958.

[123] See ECOSOC Res. 731B(XXVIII), July 30, 1959, and 792(XXX), Aug. 3, 1960.

[124] GAOR/11th Sess./*Annexes*, Vol. II, agenda item 49; UN Doc. A/3489, para. 17, Jan. 10, 1957.

[125] ILO, FAO, UNESCO, WHO, and WMO; ECOSOC Res. 665C(XXIV), Aug. 1, 1957. IAEA was subsequently invited to participate in the appraisal. ECOSOC Res. 743D(XXVIII), July 31, 1959.

designed to meet these needs.[126] In its resolution of August 3, 1960, the Council invited the specialized agencies and the IAEA to submit the report, "for consideration and comment, to their respective governing bodies or conferences, as appropriate," and "to include in their annual reports a section indicating the extent to which the trends and emphases of their programs, as outlined in their individual appraisals, are developing as anticipated." [127]

Article 59

The Organization shall, where appropriate, initiate negotiations among the states concerned for the creation of any new specialized agencies required for the accomplishment of the purposes set forth in Article 55.

The Preparatory Commission, in its 1945 Report, recognized that there might be certain fields in which organization for international cooperation was not adequately developed or in the process of development. The Commission listed the following alternatives as available to the United Nations in filling these gaps:

(a) the initiation of negotiations among the states concerned for the creation of a new specialized agency, in accordance with Article 59 of the Charter;

(b) the establishment of a commission or committee by the Economic and Social Council;

(c) the creation of a subsidiary organ of the General Assembly, in accordance with Article 22 of the Charter; or

(d) a recommendation by the Economic and Social Council to an existing specialized or other intergovernmental agency to undertake additional functions.[128]

The Commission assumed that the following subjects would fall within the responsibility of specialized agencies "to be brought in due course into relationship with the United Nations":

(a) relief and rehabilitation

(b) monetary cooperation and international investment

---

[126] ECOSOC Res. 694D(XXVI), July 31, 1958. The report of the Committee on Programme Appraisals was made under the title "Five-Year Perspective, 1959–1964." UN Doc. E/3347/Rev. 1, June 20, 1960. For separate UN and specialized agency appraisals, see UN Docs. E/3260/Rev. 1, Dec. 21, 1959 (UN); E/3341, Apr. 7, 1960 (ILO); E/3342, Apr. 7, 1960 (FAO); E/3343, May 17, 1960 (UNESCO); E/3344, Apr. 7, 1960 (WHO); E/3345, Apr. 3, 1960 (WMO); and E/3346, and Add. 1, Apr. 1, 1960 (IAEA).

[127] ECOSOC Res. 791(XXX), Aug. 3, 1960.

[128] *Report of the Preparatory Commission*, p. 41.

(c) trade policies (including commodity problems and restrictive practices of private international agreements)
(d) food and agricultural policies
(e) labor standards, labor welfare and related social questions
(f) education and cultural cooperation
(g) health
(h) some aspects of transport
(i) some aspects of communication [129]

At the time the United Nations began its operations, these areas of activity were to a considerable extent covered by intergovernmental agencies established or in the process of being established. Relief and rehabilitation, regarded at the time as a temporary field of activity, was the concern of the United Nations Relief and Rehabilitation Administration (UNRRA), established under an agreement signed in Washington, November 9, 1943.[130] Monetary cooperation and international investment were to be the responsibilities of the Bank and the Fund, established under the Bretton Woods Articles of Agreement. Trade policy was an open field, though basic principles had been laid down in the Lend-Lease Agreements. Food and agricultural policies were to be the concern of the Food and Agriculture Organization, planned at the Hot Springs Conference in 1943. The improvement of labor conditions had been the responsibility of the International Labour Organisation since its establishment in 1920. Educational and cultural cooperation, the responsibility during the interwar period of the International Institute of Intellectual Cooperation (a technical organization of the League), was to be the concern of UNESCO, whose constitution had just been drafted in London in November, 1945. Health, long a matter of international concern, and during the interwar period the responsibility of the League, was an area where the form of organization for the postwar period was yet to be determined. The fields of transport and communication were under the aegis of a variety of highly technical and regional agencies whose future had yet to be determined. It was established, however, that one important area—civil air transport —would be the responsibility of ICAO, for which provision was made in the Convention drafted at Chicago in November–December, 1944.

During the first session of the General Assembly, a joint subcommittee of the Second and Third Committees suggested that ECOSOC should propose "any form of international machinery which it considers the most effective for coordinating action in economic and social problems." [131] Among the considerations that have apparently influ-

---

[129] *Ibid.*, p. 35.   [130] U.S. Exec. Agreement Ser. 352.
[131] GAOR/1st Sess., 1st Part/19th Plen. Mtg./Jan. 19, 1946/p. 573, *Annex 3* (A/17).

enced decisions on the need for new agencies have been the importance of the field,[132] the nature of responsibilities envisaged for the international agency, the kind of participation and active support envisaged, the need of special organizational arrangements regarding such matters as financing and voting, and the desirability of further proliferation of autonomous international agencies.

The methods by which the Organization has performed its function under Article 59 have varied greatly. While in some instances it has directly initiated action, in other instances its role has been that of approval or support. Though ECOSOC has explicit powers under the Charter to prepare draft conventions and call conferences,[133] the General Assembly has on occasion acted on its own initiative as well as approving and supporting initiatives of ECOSOC.

In anticipation of the termination of UNRRA's activities, ECOSOC recommended the establishment of a nonpermanent specialized agency to be called the International Refugee Organization (IRO), and submitted a draft constitution for the General Assembly's approval, which after such action was opened for signature.[134] In the case of the World Health Organization (WHO), ECOSOC appointed a technical preparatory committee to prepare documentation, including a draft constitution, for submission to the International Health Conference, at which the Constitution of the new organization was approved. Similar procedures were adopted with a view to the establishment of the International Trade Organization (ITO) and the Intergovernmental Maritime Consultative Organization (IMCO).[135]

This pattern has not been consistently followed, however. In the cases of the International Finance Corporation (IFC) and the International Development Association (IDA), the procedure reflected the reluctance of the principal financial powers to agree to institutional arrangements for financing economic development favored by a majority of United Nations members. After the United States and the United Kingdom had—under considerable pressure—indicated their willingness to participate in an international finance corporation, set up by the Bank as an affiliate to assist in the financing of private enterprise in underdeveloped countries, the General Assembly requested the Bank to prepare a draft statute, to present the draft to the Bank's members, and to take steps to achieve agreement. In the case of the International Development Association, the Bank's Board of Governors decided in principle to establish the Association, after insistent demands had been made in the General Assembly and ECOSOC for a United Nations

---

[132] See commentary on Art. 57.   [133] Art. 62(3) and (4).
[134] See ECOSOC Res. 2/12, June 21, 1946; GA Res. 62(I), Dec. 16, 1946.
[135] *Y.U.N.*, 1946–47, pp. 492–95 and 500–1.

capital development fund. The General Assembly welcomed the decision and requested the Secretary-General to forward the record of its discussion to the President of the Bank for communication to the Executive Directors.[136]

The initiative for the establishment of the International Atomic Energy Agency, an intergovernmental organization related to the United Nations but not strictly speaking a specialized agency, was taken by the United States in negotiations outside the United Nations, though the idea was first broached by President Eisenhower in his address to the General Assembly, December 8, 1953. Negotiations were influenced by General Assembly discussions and in deference to its sentiments, a conference was held in New York September 20 to October 26, 1956, for the drafting of the statute.[137]

Article 60

Responsibility for the discharge of the functions of the Organization set forth in this Chapter shall be vested in the General Assembly and, under the authority of the General Assembly, in the Economic and Social Council, which shall have for this purpose the powers set forth in Chapter X.

Article 60 differs in two important respects from the corresponding provisions of the Covenant of the League of Nations. First, it vests the primary responsibility for the discharge of the economic and social functions of the United Nations in the General Assembly. The Covenant did not expressly differentiate between the responsibilities of Assembly and Council in the economic and social fields, except in so far as budgetary approval was involved. Second, the Charter provides for an Economic and Social Council separate from the Security Council, whereas the Covenant provided for one Council with responsibilities in the political, economic, and social fields.

In the practice of the League of Nations, a differentiation did develop between the responsibilities of the Assembly and the Council. The latter assumed the character of a quasi-executive organ, while the activities of the Assembly took on a quasi-legislative character. The fact that the Council was organized primarily to discharge responsibilities in the maintenance of international peace and security reduced its acceptability to many as an organ with important responsibilities in the economic and social fields. To strengthen the League in this area, the Council appointed the Bruce Committee on May 27, 1939, to make

---

[136] GA Res. 1420(XIV), Dec. 5, 1959.
[137] For detailed account, see Bernard G. Beehhoefer, "Negotiating the Statute of the International Atomic Energy Agency," *International Organization*, XII (1959), 38–59.

recommendations. In its report of August 22, the Committee recommended that the Assembly set up a new organ to be known as the Central Committee for Economic and Social Questions, to which would be entrusted the direction and supervision of the work of the League in these areas.[138] The report was adopted by the Assembly, but the outbreak of war prevented its implementation.

In the preparation of the United Nations Charter, the League experience and the conclusions of the Bruce Committee were given great weight. The Bruce Committee had concluded that the establishment of a Central Committee on Economic and Social Questions, elected by and responsible to the Assembly, would increase the efficiency of the League's work in the economic and social fields. The United States Tentative Proposals provided that responsibility for the discharge of functions in these areas "should be vested in the general assembly, and under the authority of the general assembly, in an economic and social council, established in the basic instrument of the organization." [139] This provision was in substance incorporated into the Dumbarton Oaks Proposals. The subordinate position of the Economic and Social Council was emphasized by the fact that it was not originally included among the principal organs of the Organization.[140]

At San Francisco, the granting to it of additional powers, combined with the desire to emphasize the importance of the work of the Organization in the economic and social fields, appears to have been the reason for elevating the Council to the level of a principal organ. Notwithstanding, the language of the Dumbarton Oaks Proposals defining the relation of the General Assembly and the Economic and Social Council was, in substance, retained.[141]

The Relationship between the General Assembly and ECOSOC

While Article 60 has been mentioned on several occasions in the discussions and decisions of United Nations organs, no decision has ever been adopted with the specific purpose of elaborating its meaning. However, both the General Assembly and the Council have made deci-

[138] LN Special Committee, The Development of International Co-operation in Economic and Social Affairs (A.23.1939). Hill, *Economic and Financial Organization*, pp. 106–19.

[139] State Dept., *Postwar Foreign Policy Preparation, 1939–1945*, p. 603. See also Russell, ch. xii.

[140] Ch. iv of the Dumbarton Oaks Proposals.

[141] In State Dept., *Report to the President*, p. 64, the following description is given: "The relationship of the Economic and Social Council to the Assembly in these matters is a subordinate one. Although the Economic and Social Council is itself one of the principal organs of the Organization and is intended to carry on the bulk of the work of the Organization in regard to such matters, it acts always under the authority of the General Assembly."

sions on procedural and substantive questions that bear on the practical application of the Article and the further definition of the relationship between the two organs.

The text of Article 60, taken in the context of other Charter provisions, leaves some room for uncertainty regarding the practical relationship between the two organs. ECOSOC clearly does not have the same kind of responsibility for promoting/economic and social cooperation that the Security Council has for the maintenance of international peace and security, since its responsibility in the economic and social fields is qualified by the words "under the authority of the General Assembly," while responsibility is vested in the Security Council without qualification and with substantial powers to implement it.[142] However, ECOSOC was not conceived by those who wrote the Charter as being simply a subsidiary organ of the General Assembly, responsible only for carrying out its decisions and acting only in accordance with its expressed desires. That ECOSOC is listed as a "principal organ" of the Organization (Article 7), and that it is given independent powers in Chapter X in addition to those which the Assembly may confer upon it, support the view that ECOSOC was conceived as an organ with important responsibilities and powers in its own right.[143]

In the first month of its existence, the General Assembly formally accepted the view that "the Economic and Social Council should be allowed the widest possible freedom to carry out its work." [144] This was consistent with the principle that the Assembly's authority under which ECOSOC discharged its responsibility was a continuing authority of a general nature. However, in practice since that time, for a variety of reasons not unrelated to the expansion and change in character of the Organization's membership, there has been a pronounced development in the direction of subordination in respect to detailed decisions as well as general authority.

Decisions of ECOSOC in the exercise of Charter powers have on a number of occasions been initially taken or subsequently revised on the Assembly's recommendation or request. After the Council decided to discontinue the Subcommission on the Prevention of Discrimination and the Protection of Minorities, the General Assembly invited the Council to authorize the Subcommission to continue its work, and the Council conformed.[145] Similarly, the Council revised its decision that

142 For the Assembly's powers, see Arts. 10, 13, 15(2), 17, 63(1), and 66.
143 This view finds support in the discussions and decisions at San Francisco. See UNCIO, *Documents*, X, 269–98.
144 GA Res. 5(1), Jan. 29, 1946, adopting report of the Second Committee; GAOR/1st Sess., 1st Part/19th Plen. Mtg./Jan. 19, 1946/pp. 297–99(A/16).
145 GA Res. 532B(VI), Feb. 4, 1952.

the Commission on the Status of Women meet once every two years to conform to the Assembly's request that it meet annually.[146] In 1959, the General Assembly recommended that the Council give consideration to the "prompt establishment" of a commission for industrial development, in accordance with Article 68 of the Charter, and the following year the Council conformed by establishing "a standing Committee for Industrial Development." [147]

On some occasions, the Assembly has addressed subsidiary organs of ECOSOC both directly and through the Council. Thus, the General Assembly in its sixth session requested that the Commission on Human Rights submit to it at its seventh session "recommendations concerning international respect for the self-determination of peoples" and requested the Council to instruct the Commission on Human Rights to give priority to the question.[148] In addition to giving directions to subsidiary organs of ECOSOC, the Assembly has recommended or requested specific organizational structures for subsidiary organs of ECOSOC. In this vein the Assembly in 1957 adopted a resolution recommending the expansion of the membership of the Technical Assistance Committee of ECOSOC by the election of six additional members from among members of the United Nations and the specialized agencies to give better representation to countries active in technical assistance matters.[149] In the discussion preceding this action, some delegates doubted the competence of the Assembly to make such a recommendation.[150]

Generally speaking, the General Assembly has viewed its relations to ECOSOC as permitting detailed review of the acts of that organ and free revision of its recommendations. One commentator has characterized the result as "endless repetition by the Assembly of discussions of issues that have already been given careful consideration by the Council" and as demonstrating the futility "of reasonable compromises by the Council . . . if they are regularly reconsidered by the General Assembly and reversed or changed beyond recognition." [151] However one views the result in terms of the efficiency of the Organization's work, it was probably inevitable from the beginning that the General Assembly should assume the role it has in view of its more representative character and the extent of its Charter powers.

[146] ECOSOC Res. 445 I (XIV), June 13, 1952.
[147] GA Res./1431(XIV), Dec. 5, 1959; and ECOSOC Res. 751(XXIX), Apr. 12, 1960.
[148] GA Res. 545(VI), Feb. 5, 1952; and 549(VI), Feb. 5, 1952. See also *Repertory*, III, 174–75.
[149] GA Res. 1036(XI), Feb. 26, 1957.
[150] GAOR/11th Sess., 2d Ctte./446th Mtg./Feb. 18, 1957. See *Repertory*, *Supp.* 2, III, 72–74.
[151] Asher, pp. 41–42.

CHAPTER X

The Economic and Social Council

COMPOSITION

Article 61

1. The Economic and Social Council shall consist of *twenty-seven Members* of the United Nations elected by the General Assembly.[1]

2. Subject to the provisions of paragraph 3, *nine* members of the Economic and Social Council shall be elected each year for a term of three years. A retiring member shall be eligible for immediate re-election.

3. *At the first election after the increase in the membership of the Economic and Social Council from eighteen to twenty-seven members, in addition to the members elected in place of the six members whose term of office expires at the end of that year, nine additional members shall be elected. Of these nine additional members, the term of office of three members so elected shall expire at the end of one year, and of three other members at the end of two years, in accordance with arrangements made by the General Assembly.*

4. Each member of the Economic and Social Council shall have one representative.

Size

The United States Tentative Proposals provided for a twenty-four member Council, but during the Dumbarton Oaks Conversations, British arguments prevailed to the effect that such a body would be too large for effective action.[2] Agreement was reached on a body of eighteen members. At San Francisco, various proposals for a larger council were introduced but were not accepted.

The campaign for a larger Council continued, however. Proposals of

[1] Italics indicate amendment that entered into force August 31, 1965, increasing the number of members from eighteen to twenty-seven. For text of the original article, see p. 687.

[2] See Ruth B. Russell, *A History of the United Nations Charter* (Washington, Brookings Institution, 1958), pp. 321 and 428.

this nature were pressed unsuccessfully at the first few sessions of the General Assembly.[3] From 1955 on, as the number of United Nations members increased, pressure for enlarging ECOSOC mounted. Support came not only from those groups of members who considered themselves inadequately represented on the Council but also from other members who recognized that to make the Council more broadly representative of regions within the existing structure of the Council would diminish their chances of election to ECOSOC. Originally, close to one-third of the members of the United Nations were members of ECOSOC; by 1960 this percentage had been cut almost in half.

In 1958, the General Assembly and the Council itself went on record in favor of enlarging ECOSOC, but Soviet opposition—on the ground that the question of Chinese representation must first be satisfactorily resolved—was an obstacle to action.[4] In 1960, though a majority of the General Assembly voted in favor of increasing the size of ECOSOC from eighteen to twenty-four members, the resolution failed of adoption, in part because of the insistence of the African and Asian states that the resolution also call for "immediate steps" for the redistribution of the existing seats on ECOSOC.[5] Finally, in 1963, the General Assembly adopted an amendment to the Charter increasing the membership of ECOSOC to twenty-seven,[6] which became effective in August, 1965.

Composition

Although the Charter does not provide for permanent members of ECOSOC, as it does in the case of the Security Council, and while it contains no criteria for the election of members, in practice a pattern of selection has emerged. The permanent members of the Security Council (except for China) have in effect been permanent members of ECOSOC as the result of their repeated reelection, which is expressly permitted by Article 61. The larger and economically more advanced countries have been represented with far greater frequency than have the smaller powers.

Even more striking has been the consistency of the pattern of representation of the regional and political groupings within the Organization during the first decade and a half (see Table 5). The great increase in the number of Asian and African members in the United Nations after 1960 produced pressures for changes in the general

[3] See commentary on Art. 108.

[4] ECOSOC Res. 690B(XXVI), July 31, 1958, and GA Res. 1300(XIII), Dec. 10, 1958. Also see commentary on Art. 108.

[5] GAOR/15th Sess., Special Pol. Ctte./217th Mtg./Dec. 5, 1960.

[6] GA Res. 1991(XVIII), Dec. 17, 1963.

Table 5
COMPOSITION OF ECOSOC BY GEOGRAPHICAL REGIONS *

	W. Europe	E. Europe	Africa	L. America	Asia	Common-wealth **
1946	3	3	0	4	3	1
1947	2	2	0	4	4	2
1948	2	2	0	4	3	3
1949	2	2	0	4	4	2
1950	2	2	—	4	4	2
1951	2	2	—	4	5	1
1952	2	2	1	4	4	1
1953	2	2	1	4	4	1
1954	2	2	1	4	4	1
1955	2	2	1	4	4	1
1956	3	2	1	4	3	1
1957	3	2	1	4	3	1
1958	3	2	1	4	3	1
1959	3	2	1	4	3	1
1960	3	2	1	4	3	1
1961	3	2	1	4	3	1
1962	2	2	2	4	3	1
1963	2	2	2	4	3	1
1964	2	2	2	4	3	1
1965	2	2	2	4	3	1

* Table does not include France, the United Kingdom, the United States, and the USSR, which have been consistently reelected when their terms have expired.
** Not including Asian and African members.
Source: *Yearbook of the United Nations.*

pattern of representation and intensified the competition for election. Threats to reduce the representation of regions and groups whose numbers remained constant in order to give more seats to the Asian and African members were a factor in inducing the former to agree to the Council's enlargement. In deciding that the size of ECOSOC should be increased to twenty-seven members, the General Assembly further decided that, "without prejudice to the present distribution of seats in the Economic and Social Council, the nine additional members shall be elected according to the following pattern: (a) Seven from African and Asian States; (b) One from Latin American States; (c) One from Western European and other States." [7]

Term of Office

Members of ECOSOC are elected by the Assembly for a term of three years. To assure greater continuity of membership than was offered by the provision for immediate reelection, it was decided at San Francisco that the members' terms of office should overlap. Thus, in

[7] *Ibid.* In UN parlance, "other States" are those generally considered "Western," although not "European."

accordance with Article 61(2), one-third of the members of ECOSOC are elected at each regular session of the General Assembly. To carry out this concept of overlapping membership, it was necessary to devise special procedures for the first election. The Assembly elected the original eighteen members of the Council by the required two-thirds vote; then by a simple majority vote it chose six of the eighteen to serve three-year terms, six for two-year terms, and six for one-year terms. After the amendment to Article 61 entered into force in August, 1965, the Assembly followed a similar procedure with respect to the nine additional members.

For filling unexpired terms, the General Assembly's Rules of Procedure provide that "Should a member cease to belong to a Council before its term of office expires, a by-election shall be held separately at the next session of the General Assembly to elect a member for the unexpired term" (Rule 141).

The terms of office of ECOSOC members begin on January 1 of the year following their election (Rule 140). At its fifteenth session, however, the Assembly was unable to complete elections by the required date. When the final vacancy was filled in mid-April, 1961, it was decided that the term of office of the newly elected member should be regarded as dating from January 1, 1961.[8] Because of this difficulty, the Council was short one member when it convened on April 4, 1961. At the outset of the session, it was alleged that a meeting with only seventeen members would be in violation of the Charter and that the Council's decisions might successfully be challenged. Those who considered that the Council was "legally constituted," and could proceed with its work, pointed out that under the Rules of Procedure a majority of members constituted a quorum (Rule 47). The discussion gave rise to an exchange of views on the relation of the Council vis-à-vis the Assembly. One group held that the Council itself could decide whether it was "legally constituted"; another, that this was a matter solely within the competence of the Assembly by virtue of its responsibilities under Articles 60 and 61 of the Charter. Eventually, it was decided to adjourn the meeting and request the President of the Assembly to expedite the election of the remaining member.[9] By the time the Council next met, election had been completed.

Representation on the Council.

For all of the United Nations Councils, the Charter stipulates that each member shall have one representative. ECOSOC's Rules of Proce-

[8] GAOR/15th Sess./987th Mtg./Apr. 18, 1961.
[9] ESCOR/31st Sess./1137 Mtg./Apr. 4, 1961/pp. 69 ff.

dure (Chapter III) provide that each representative may be accompanied by such alternate representatives and advisers as may be required. The credentials of representatives and the names of alternates must be submitted to the Secretary-General twenty-four hours before the opening of a Council session. The President and the Vice-Presidents examine the credentials and submit a report thereon to the Council. These are, in general, routine procedures. From 1950 to 1960, however, the issue of Chinese representation was raised at the beginning of each session, either as a point of order, or in connection with the report on credentials.

Article 62

1. **The Economic and Social Council may make or initiate studies and reports with respect to international economic, social, cultural, educational, health, and related matters and may make recommendations with respect to any such matters to the General Assembly, to the Members of the United Nations, and to the specialized agencies concerned.**

2. **It may make recommendations for the purpose of promoting respect for, and observance of, human rights and fundamental freedoms for all.**

3. **It may prepare draft conventions for submission to the General Assembly, with respect to matters falling within its competence.**

4. **It may call, in accordance with the rules prescribed by the United Nations, international conferences on matters falling within its competence.**

Studies, Reports, and Recommendations under Paragraph 1

By the terms of the Dumbarton Oaks Proposals, the Economic and Social Council was to be empowered "to make recommendations on its own initiative, with respect to international economic, social and other humanitarian matters." [10] At San Francisco this provision was expanded in three respects: 1) the Council was empowered to "make or initiate studies and reports" with respect to such matters; 2) the matters with which the Council might deal were specified in greater detail, in line with the provisions of Articles 1(3), 13(1), and 55; and 3) it was specified in greater detail to whom recommendations might be addressed. While these changes did not add powers that could not have been reasonably implied from the shorter Dumbarton Oaks text, they did reflect a widespread desire at San Francisco to strengthen the

[10] Ch. IX, sec. C, para. 1(b). See p. 671.

role of the Organization in economic and social fields, and, more particularly, to make ECOSOC an effective instrument in achieving its declared purposes.

The power granted under Article 62(1) to make studies and reports has been used most extensively.[11] In most instances, the Council has called upon the Secretary-General to organize the study and prepare the report. Use has also been made of the regional economic commissions, ad hoc committees and working parties, selected experts, and the specialized agencies. When outside experts have been used, their selection and appointment has in the majority of cases been left to the Secretary-General.[12] Action taken by the Council on studies and reports has varied greatly: it has approved or merely taken note of them; it has sometimes requested that further studies be made; it has brought them to the attention of governments, the General Assembly, the specialized agencies, and other bodies. In most cases, studies and reports have formed the basis of recommendations by the Council or its subsidiary organs.

In making recommendations the Council has seldom made a direct reference to Article 62(1), and it does not appear to have followed any uniform practice in the use of terminology. Differences in terminology appear to have no great significance, though the use of a particular phraseology may have been considered especially appropriate to the circumstances of the case at hand.[13] Among the terms most commonly used in Council resolutions of recommendation are "recommends," "requests," "invites," "urges," and "expresses its hope."

Recommendations have been addressed to member states in general, to particular categories or groups of member states, and to individual member states, depending upon the degree of their involvement in a particular problem.[14] Recommendations to the General Assembly have related for the most part to matters requiring action by the Assembly under the Charter or to Assembly decisions. Recommendations to the specialized agencies have been variously addressed to them in general, or to particular agencies.[15]

The Council has recognized from the beginning that studies or reports involving field surveys or investigations within the territories of individual states can only be undertaken with the concurrence of the governments concerned or upon their request. While the studies and

11 For the nature and subjects of these reports, see *Repertory*, III, 198–203; *Supp. 1*, II, 72; and *Supp. 2*, III, 86.

12 *Repertory*, III, 203–8; *Supp. 1*, II, 72–74; and *Supp. 2*, III, 86–90.

13 For list of terms used, see *Repertory*, III, 210–11.

14 For a detailed analysis with references to specific resolutions, see *ibid.*, 210–40.

15 For analysis of recommendations to the General Assembly and the specialized agencies, see *ibid.*

recommendations of the Council may be made with respect to particular groups of territories such as those within one geographical area or presenting common economic or social problems, they cannot be made with respect to trust territories as a distinct category except with the concurrence of the Trusteeship Council.[16]

The power of ECOSOC to consider disputes between states was called into question in connection with the dispute over alleged damage caused to the Federal People's Republic of Yugoslavia by the United States withholding of Yugoslav gold. The Council took the position that since it could not examine the substance of the matter without being led into consideration of the different aspects of the dispute, and since it could not take cognizance of such aspects because of the juridical issues involved, the matter did not fall within its competence.[17] The question was also raised in this case of the Council's power to make recommendations to individual states, but the Council did not take a position on this issue. It has in a number of instances, however, made recommendations to individual states.

The powers granted the Council under Article 62(1) can be delegated to a subsidiary organ. This has been done notably in the case of the regional economic commissions, established under Article 68, which have been empowered to make recommendations to member governments, governments admitted in a consultative capacity, and the specialized agencies.

Recommendations with Respect to Human Rights and Fundamental Freedoms

The language of Article 62(2) differs from that of Article 13(1b), which defines the powers of the General Assembly with respect to human rights and fundamental freedoms. It also differs from that of Article 62(1) in that no mention is made of the power to "make or initiate studies and reports." Furthermore, it does not specify to whom recommendations are to be made. There is nothing in the record of the San Francisco discussions to indicate any intention to distinguish between ECOSOC's powers under the two paragraphs.

In practice, the Council has made or initiated studies and reports on a wide range of subjects in the field of human rights, including freedom of information, status of women, slavery and servitude, forced labor, prevention of discrimination, and protection of minorities. It has

[16] See Report of the Joint Committee of ECOSOC and the Trusteeship Council: ESCOR/5th Sess./p. 477, *Annex 20* (Doc. E AND T/C.1/2, Aug. 13, 1947); and ECOSOC Res. 216(VIII), Feb. 10, 1949.

[17] ECOSOC Res. 11(VI), Mar. 9, 1948. See also *Repertory*, III, 235–38, 240.

established commissions and subcommissions for the purpose (Article 68); it has appointed ad hoc bodies and rapporteurs; and it has requested specialized agencies and the Secretary-General to make studies and reports. In many instances, a combination of methods has been used,[18] the implication being that the power to recommend carries with it the power to initiate studies and reports.

ECOSOC, in the exercise of its power to make recommendations on human rights, has followed the same varied practice as under paragraph 1 in the choice of phraseology and addressees. Its recommendations have been addressed to the General Assembly, to the Trusteeship Council, to members and nonmembers of the United Nations, to specialized agencies, and to nongovernmental bodies. It has been argued in ECOSOC that the very fact that paragraph 2 does not indicate the addressees of ECOSOC's recommendations gives the Council greater latitude than under paragraph 1.[19] In practice, the Council has interpreted its powers liberally in each case.

While the power of ECOSOC to make or initiate studies in the field of human rights has not been challenged, questions have arisen whether, to what extent, and under what conditions the Council may conduct direct inquiries or field investigations in matters relating to human rights. In those instances where the question has come up—as in connection with proposals to investigate conditions regarding refugees and displaced persons, existence of forced labor, and violation of trade-union rights—it has been fully recognized that such inquiries cannot be carried out except with the consent of the governments concerned.[20]

ECOSOC has been asked in a number of instances to evaluate allegations or reports concerning violations of human rights in specific states or territories and to recommend remedial action. For example, in 1949 the Council considered allegations of violations of trade-union rights by a number of member and nonmember states. The Council rejected a draft proposal recommending that the specific states named in the complaints "take effective measures at the earliest possible date to implement the principles" proclaimed by the United Nations.[21] In the discussion on the proposal, the view was expressed that the Council did not have juridical functions, that it was an organ of international cooperation with the duty to encourage solution of problems but with no power to enforce a solution, and that it could not act to redress

18 For further details see *Repertory*, III, 210–30; *Supp. 1*, II, 74–75; and *Supp. 2*, III, 90–91.
19 ESCOR/16th Sess./720th and 722d Mtgs./July 10 and 11, 1953.
20 See *Repertory*, III, 258–60.
21 ESCOR/8th Sess./266th Mtg./Mar. 8, 1949/p. 504.

particular violations.[22] The Council has in such cases limited itself to stating its evaluations and making its recommendations in general terms without naming individual states. It has been argued that to do otherwise would constitute a violation of the domestic jurisdiction principle.[23]

The Council has been faced with the necessity of establishing a procedure for dealing with the large number of communications received by the United Nations concerning alleged violations of human rights. This matter was dealt with in the report of the first session of the Commission on Human Rights.[24] Approving the statement of the Commission recognizing "that it has no power to take any action in regard to any complaints concerning human rights," the Council requested the Secretary-General to follow a prescribed procedure in handling communications received and in making available under certain conditions the contents thereof.[25] Complaints emanating from, or relating to, conditions in any trust territory, are dealt with by the Trusteeship Council in accordance with Article 87(b) of the Charter.[26] Complaints regarding the violation of trade-union rights are forwarded to the Governing Body of the International Labour Organisation, for its consideration "as to referral" to the Fact-Finding and Conciliation Commission on Freedom of Association, established by the Governing Body at the request of ECOSOC.[27]

The Preparation and Submission of Draft Conventions

No such provision as contained in Article 62(3) was included in the Dumbarton Oaks Proposals. At San Francisco, a proposal to give the General Assembly the express authority to initiate conventions was defeated. Notwithstanding, a proposal to empower ECOSOC to prepare draft conventions for submission to the General Assembly was approved, even though attention was called to a contrary decision regarding the Assembly; apparently, delegates reasoned that while such a prerogative was implicit in other powers accorded to the Assembly, it had to be explicitly stated in the case of the Council.

This power has been extensively used. Draft conventions, protocols,

22 For discussion, see *ibid.*, 252d Mtg./Feb. 25, 1949/p. 313; 256th Mtg./Mar. 1, 1949/pp. 364–65; 264th Mtg./Mar. 7, 1949/pp. 471–72; 265th Mtg./Mar. 8, 1949/p. 495; 266th Mtg./Mar. 8, 1949/p. 499. For other instances where discussion has arisen, see *Repertory*, III, 260–64.

23 See commentary on Art. 2(7).   24 UN Doc. E/259, Feb. 11, 1947.

25 ECOSOC Res. 75(V), Aug. 5, 1947, as amended by Res. 116A(VI), Mar. 1, 1948; 192A(VIII), Feb. 9, 1949; and 275B(X), Feb. 17, 1950.

26 See TCOR/2d Sess./31st Mtg./Mar. 5, 1948; and ECOSOC Res. 216(VIII), Feb. 10, 1949. Also ESCOR/5th Sess./*Annex 20* (E AND T/C.1/2), pp. 483–84.

27 See ECOSOC Res. 239(IX), Aug. 2, 1949; and 277(X), Feb. 15, 1950.

and agreements prepared by ECOSOC have related to a wide range of matters, including narcotic drugs, transport and communication, traffic in persons, human rights, status of refugees and stateless persons, freedom of information, political rights of women, and slavery.[28] The preparation of draft conventions has been undertaken on the initiative of the Council or on recommendation of its functional commissions, its ad hoc committees, conferences convened by it, specialized agencies or nongovernmental organizations having consultative relationship.

The Council has also undertaken the preparation of draft conventions and protocols at the request of the General Assembly. Various methods and procedures have been used in the case of draft conventions. In some cases, the Secretary-General has prepared preliminary drafts at the request of the Council or of its commissions. In other cases, the commissions have prepared drafts, as in the case of the draft covenants on human rights. In still other instances, the Council has set up ad hoc committees. In a number of instances, a combination of methods has been used.[29] In the preparation of all draft conventions, member states have been invited at some stage to submit their comments and observations, and on occasion the invitation has been extended to nonmembers, specialized agencies, and nongovernmental organizations. In submitting draft conventions to the General Assembly, the Council has usually made recommendations with regard to adoption, opening for signature, the states to be invited to sign and ratify, and, in some instances, the territorial application of the conventions.

The question of the applicability of Article 2(7) has been raised in connection with the preparation of draft conventions. It has been argued that the phrase "with respect to matters falling within its competence" denies to the Council the right to prepare and submit a draft convention that encroaches on the reserved domestic jurisdiction of states. This view does not appear to have had majority support, either in the Council or in the General Assembly.[30] The reasons for not submitting such proposals would appear to be of a practical rather than legal nature.

While Article 62(3) authorizes ECOSOC to prepare draft conventions for submission to the General Assembly, Article 62(4) empowers it to call international conferences on matters within its competence. Although the Council has submitted most of its draft conventions and protocols to the Assembly, it has called a number of conferences to

---

[28] See *Repertory*, III, 290–92, for list of draft conventions and protocols submitted to the General Assembly or to international conferences, or under preparation as of Aug. 31, 1954.

[29] For examples, see *ibid.*, pp. 277–79.   [30] See *ibid.*, pp. 281–82.

consider drafts it has prepared.[31] On July 28, 1958, for instance, ECOSOC decided to convene a conference of states for the adoption of a draft single convention on narcotic drugs, the preliminary draft having been prepared by the Commission on Narcotic Drugs at the request of the Council.[32]

Calling of International Conferences

Article 62(4) was approved at San Francisco following a proposal by the Australian delegation that the Economic and Social Council be empowered to call a conference in case of an emergency to consider and recommend action for safeguarding and promoting the economic and social purposes of the Charter.[33] The view prevailed that there existed no good reason for limiting this grant of power to an emergency. It was decided that such a grant should extend to all matters falling within the competence of the Council, but that the power should be exercised according to rules "prescribed by the United Nations."

The Council has used the authority conferred by this paragraph to call international conferences dealing with the whole range of matters within its competence.[34] Its practice has varied with regard to preparatory arrangements. In some instances, the Council has appointed committees to prepare draft annotated agenda and other material. In other cases, it has relied on a functional commission, subcommission, or the Secretariat. The Council customarily recommends the provisional agenda and draft rules of procedure.

The question of the meaning of "international conference" has been extensively discussed. One view is that the Council can only convene a conference of states under this paragraph. Another is that an "international conference" under this paragraph need not be limited to states but can include experts and representatives of nongovernmental organizations.[35] At its fourth session, the Assembly adopted a resolution establishing rules applicable only to a conference of states, though provision was made for the limited participation of specialized agencies and nongovernmental organizations enjoying consultative status.[36]

[31] For examples, see *ibid.*, pp. 288–89.

[32] The request was made in ECOSOC Res. 159 II(VII), Aug. 3, 1948, and 246D(IX), July 6, 1949. The decision to convene the Conference was taken in Res. 689J(XXVI), July 28, 1958. See Adolf Lande, "The Single Convention on Narcotic Drugs," *International Organization*, XVI (Autumn, 1962), pp. 776–97.

[33] UNCIO, *Documents*, X, 319.

[34] See *Repertory*, III, 296–98 and 319–20; *Supp. 1*, II, 88, 90; and *Supp. 2*, III, 102–4.

[35] For summary of discussion, see *Repertory*, III, 305–9.

[36] GA Res. 366(IV), Dec. 3, 1949.

The next year, the General Assembly adopted rules governing the calling of nongovernmental conferences by ECOSOC, without, however, clarifying the Charter basis for this action.[37] The view had been expressed that Articles 68 and 71, in addition to Article 62(4), provided the legal basis.

The rules for calling international conferences of states provide that the Council "shall decide what States shall be invited to the conference" (Rule 3). Though it was contended in the Sixth Committee that the Council could only call conferences open to all members, the above provision admits the contrary possibility, and this has occurred in the case of regional conferences.

A proposal to authorize ECOSOC to convene a conference of representatives of the peoples of non-self-governing territories was opposed on the ground that the Council had no competence in political affairs and that to give it the power to call such a conference would constitute a violation of Article 2(7).[38] The resolution finally adopted by the Assembly omitted all reference to the Council and recommended the calling of regional conferences of representatives of non-self-governing territories by the administering authorities concerned.[39]

Article 63

1. The Economic and Social Council may enter into agreements with any of the agencies referred to in Article 57, defining the terms on which the agency concerned shall be brought into relationship with the United Nations. Such agreements shall be subject to approval by the General Assembly.

2. It may coordinate the activities of the specialized agencies through consultation with and recommendations to such agencies and through recommendations to the General Assembly and to the Members of the United Nations.

Under the United Nations system of a general organization with overall responsibilities and a number of specialized organizations with responsibilities in defined areas,[40] the problem of coordination of policies and activities inevitably becomes important. Article 60 places on ECOSOC, acting "under the authority of the General Assembly," a significant part of the overall responsibility for coordination. Other articles of the Charter authorize ECOSOC to perform specific functions. That of concluding agreements with the specialized agencies

[37] GA Res. 479(V), Dec. 12, 1950.
[38] GAOR/1st Sess., 2d Part/64th Plen. Mtg./Dec. 14, 1946/pp. 1333–37, 1346–48.
[39] GA Res. 67(I), Dec. 14, 1946.   [40] See commentary on Art. 57.

subject to General Assembly approval is of primary importance, since these agreements define the legal framework within which the coordinating function is performed. Without such agreements, the various agencies would technically be free to pursue their own independent ways subject only to their own constitutional instruments, although presumably the fact of substantial overlapping of memberships would by itself result in some measure of coordination of policies and activities.

The Dumbarton Oaks Proposals contained provisions for giving ECOSOC the functions of concluding relationship agreements, subject to General Assembly approval, and coordinating activities through consultations and recommendations. The provisions were accepted by the technical committee at San Francisco. In its report, the committee emphasized that its purpose was "to provide for agreements sufficiently flexible to enable satisfactory arrangements to be worked out on the basis of need and experience." [41]

The Conclusion of Agreements with the Specialized Agencies

The Preparatory Commission emphasized the importance of bringing existing specialized agencies into relationship with the United Nations "at the earliest practicable moment" and of bringing agencies whose establishment is contemplated "into relationship immediately upon their establishment." [42] At its first session, ECOSOC established the Committee on Negotiations with Inter-Governmental Organizations, and directed it to enter into negotiations as soon as possible with FAO, ILO, the Fund, the Bank, and UNESCO. [43]

The procedure followed in the conclusion of agreements has normally consisted of the following stages: 1) adoption of a resolution by ECOSOC directing the Committee on Negotiations to enter into negotiations with the appropriate authority of the specialized agency; 2) completion of a draft agreement as the result of such negotiations and submission to ECOSOC for consideration and approval; 3) submission of the draft agreement to the General Assembly and to the appropriate ratifying organ of the specialized agency; and 4) approval by the General Assembly and the ratifying organ of the specialized agency. [44]

[41] UNCIO, *Documents*, X, 272–73.
[42] *Report of the Preparatory Commission*, p. 40.
[43] ECOSOC Res. 1/11, Feb. 16, 1946.
[44] The agreement normally enters into force on approval by the General Assembly, though there have been exceptions. In the case of IMCO, the draft agreement was approved by the General Assembly in 1948, but did not enter into force until 1959 when, the Convention having entered into force in March, 1958, the Assembly of IMCO in its first session in January, 1959, gave its approval. The agreements with UPU and ITU did not enter into force until new conventions had received the necessary number of ratifications.

In each case, the Secretary-General and the corresponding official of the specialized agency sign a protocol concerning the agreement's entrance into force. The agreements are registered with the Secretariat in accordance with the provisions of Article 102(1).

The Content of the Agreements

The question of the content of the agreements was considered by the Preparatory Commission. In its Report, the Commission listed items it considered appropriate for inclusion in the agreements.[45] Some of these were derived from provisions of the Charter; others, though not emanating from it directly, were considered important to the general plan of relationship. ECOSOC, in its resolution initiating the first set of negotiations, gave instructions to include in the preliminary draft agreements appropriate provisions on the items mentioned by the Preparatory Commission.

Agreements thus far concluded with the specialized agencies fall into three general categories, with some variations of detail: 1) agreements with ILO, FAO, ICAO, IMCO, UNESCO, WHO, and WMO contain in general the most detailed and, from the point of view of effective coordination, the most satisfactory definition of relationship; 2) agreements with ITU and UPU differ primarily from the first group in the generality of their provisions; and 3) agreements defining relationships with the Bank, the Fund, IFC, and IDA contain special provisions asserting the independence of the agencies and thereby weakening the legal basis for coordination.[46] In general, the agreements do not have the effect of subjecting the specialized agencies to effective United Nations control or of placing them in a subordinate legal position. They are in the nature of agreements between sovereign equals.

The substantive provisions of the agreements concluded may be summarized as follows:

STATUS OF AGENCY. In each agreement, the intergovernmental agency is recognized by the United Nations as the specialized agency responsible for taking action "as may be appropriate under its basic instrument." The agreement with each financial institution recognizes that the agency is required to function as "an independent international organization" and to provide for the safeguarding of confidential material.

MEMBERSHIP. The agreements with UNESCO and ICAO originally provided for limited United Nations control over the admission of new

---

[45] Report of the Preparatory Commission, pp. 40–48.
[46] For references to the texts of the agreements, see commentary on Art. 57, where references to basic documents for each agency are given.

members to the agencies. The agreement with UNESCO provided that applications for membership by states not members of the United Nations should be transmitted to ECOSOC and that its recommendation of rejection would be binding.[47] The agreement with ICAO contained a provision in effect giving the General Assembly a veto over the admission of any state that was an enemy in World War II.

RECIPROCAL REPRESENTATION. Each agreement provides for reciprocal representation without vote at meetings of organs where matters of concern to the agency in question are being considered. Article 70 of the Charter authorizes ECOSOC to make such arrangements on behalf of the United Nations.

PROPOSAL OF AGENDA ITEMS. Each agreement provides for the reciprocal proposal of agenda items, the right of the specialized agencies being limited to proposing agenda items for ECOSOC and its commissions and for the Trusteeship Council.

RECOMMENDATIONS. Under most of the agreements, the agency undertakes to arrange for "the submission, as soon as possible" to the appropriate organ of the agency, of all formal recommendations which the United Nations may make to it, special reference being made to Articles 55, 58, 62, and 63. Also, the agency agrees to enter into consultations on request, and to report on action taken. Furthermore, it agrees to cooperate fully in measures taken to achieve effective coordination, and to furnish such information as may be required. Under the agreement with the Bank, the United Nations recognizes that "it would be sound policy" to refrain from making recommendations regarding the terms of a Bank loan or financing. The agreement with the Fund provides for "reasonable prior consultation."

EXCHANGE OF INFORMATION AND DOCUMENTS. Subject to such arrangements as may be necessary for safeguarding confidential material, "the fullest and promptest" exchange of information and documents is provided for. Each agency also undertakes to transmit regular reports to the United Nations, and, subject to conditions, special reports as well. The agreements with the financial agencies stress the safeguarding of confidential materials.

ASSISTANCE TO THE SECURITY COUNCIL. The majority of agencies agree to cooperate with ECOSOC in giving the Security Council such information and assistance as it may request. The financial agencies agree to take note of the obligations assumed by their members under Article 48(2) and to "have due regard" for decisions of the Security Council under Articles 41 and 42. Articles in the agreements with UPU, ITU,

---

[47] Article II of the Agreement. This limitation on UNESCO's freedom of action was removed by an amendment to the Agreement approved by the General Assembly on Dec. 8, 1962. GA Res. 1786(XVII), Dec. 8, 1962.

and WMO safeguard the constitutional position of the agency by referring to the basic instrument and reserving the position of states that are not members of the United Nations. With a view to implementing the "Uniting for Peace" resolution,[48] ECOSOC requested the Secretary-General to consult with the specialized agencies regarding arrangements they might make to provide information and assistance in the maintenance of peace.[49] Resolutions adopted by the specialized agencies ranged from a general pledge "to render all appropriate assistance" to an indication of willingness to show "due regard" for recommendations of the General Assembly.[50]

ASSISTANCE IN TRUSTEESHIP AND NON-SELF-GOVERNING TERRITORY MATTERS. In general, the agencies undertake to cooperate with the Trusteeship Council. A substantial number also agree to cooperate in giving effect to the principles and obligations set forth in Chapter XI of the Charter.

RELATIONS WITH THE INTERNATIONAL COURT OF JUSTICE. With slight variations, all agreements (except that with UPU) provide that the agencies shall furnish the Court with such information as it may request under Article 34 of its Statute. Each agreement provides that the agency may request an advisory opinion on legal questions within the scope of its activities, other than questions relating to its relationship with the United Nations or other agencies.

HEADQUARTERS AND REGIONAL OFFICES. In a number of agreements, no provision regarding headquarters appears since the decision had already been taken by the responsible organ of the agency. In a few instances, there is a qualified commitment to establish headquarters of the agency at United Nations headquarters, or at least to consult before a final decision is taken.[51] With regard to regional offices of agencies, most agreements provide that, "so far as practicable," they shall be "closely associated" with such offices as the United Nations may establish.

PERSONNEL ARRANGEMENTS. The standard article of agreements recognizes "the desirability of a single unified international civil service." The United Nations and these agencies agree in general to develop "common personnel standards, methods and arrangements designed to avoid serious discrepancies in terms and conditions of employment, to avoid competition in recruitment of personnel, and to facilitate exchange of personnel in order to obtain the maximum benefit from their

[48] GA Res. 377(V), Nov. 3, 1950.
[49] ECOSOC Res. 363(XII), Mar. 14, 1951.
[50] See Report of the Secretary-General on Particular Coordination Matters, UN Doc. E/2060, July 28, 1951, and Add. 1, July 30, 1951; and Report of the Collective Measures Committee, GAOR/7th Sess./1952/*Supp. 17*, para. 56.
[51] See, for example, agreements with FAO and ILO.

services." They agree to consult for these purposes, and specifically to establish an International Civil Service Commission to advise on common standards of recruitment.[52] The agreements with UPU, ITU, and the financial agencies provide only for consultation with a view to achieving as much uniformity as is practicable.

STATISTICS. All agreements provide for maximum cooperation in the development of statistical services, the elimination of undesirable duplication, and free access to and exchange of statistical information. There are variations in the extent to which these provisions are spelled out.

ADMINISTRATIVE AND TECHNICAL SERVICES. All agreements recognize the desirability of avoiding wherever possible the establishment and operation of competitive or overlapping facilities and services. Provision is made for consultation to this end.

BUDGETARY AND FINANCIAL ARRANGEMENTS. All agreements, except those with ITU, UPU, and the financial agencies, recognize the desirability of establishing close budgetary and financial relationships to carry out efficiently and economically the administrative operations of the United Nations and the agencies and to obtain the maximum measure of coordination and uniformity. Consultation to achieve these ends is provided for, especially concerning the desirability of making appropriate arrangements for including the budget of the agency in that of the United Nations.[53] Pending an agreement on such arrangements, a number of detailed arrangements are specified to govern budgetary and financial relations between the United Nations and the agency in question.[54] These provide specifically for the submission of agency budgets to the United Nations and for agency participation in their examination by the General Assembly. The agreements with ITU and UPU provide that the agencies shall transmit annual budgets and that the General Assembly may make recommendations. The agreements defining relationships with the Bank, the Fund, IFC, and IDA require only the transmission of annual reports and quarterly financial statements. Furthermore, the United Nations agrees that in the interpretation of Article 17(3), it will take into consideration that the agency does not rely for its annual budget upon contributions of members and that the appropriate authorities "enjoy full autonomy in deciding the form and content of such budget."

[52] The General Assembly instructed the Secretary-General in 1946 to establish the Commission in consultation with executive heads of agencies. The title of the body was later changed to International Civil Service Advisory Board. ESCOR/6th Sess./1948/*Supp. 6*, para. 38.

[53] The Agreements with FAO and UNESCO provide for consultation "concerning appropriate arrangements."

[54] For example, see Art. XIV of Agreement between the United Nations and FAO.

IMPLEMENTATION AND REVISION. All agreements contain provisions authorizing the Secretary-General of the United Nations and the chief administrative officer of the agency to enter into such supplementary agreements as may be found necessary for the implementation of the agreement in question. All agreements are subject to revision by agreement of the parties.

Recommendations to, and Consultations with, Specialized Agencies

A major method of exercising ECOSOC's coordination function has been that of addressing recommendations to and carrying out consultations with the specialized agencies.[55] These recommendations and consultations have been primarily concerned with avoiding duplication of the activities of the United Nations and the specialized agencies and the establishment of priorities within their programs.[56] The Council has taken these steps both on its own initiative and at the request of the General Assembly.[57]

Rule 80 of ECOSOC's Rules of Procedure provides that where an item proposed for the provisional agenda or the supplementary list "contains a proposal for new activities to be undertaken by the United Nations relating to matters which are of direct concern to one or more specialized agencies, the Secretary-General shall enter into consultation with the agency concerned and report to the Council on the means of achieving coordinated use of the resources of the respective agencies." [58] Where a similar proposal is put forward in the course of a meeting of ECOSOC, the Secretary-General, after such consultations as are possible, is required to draw attention to the implications of the proposal. Before deciding on such proposal, the Council must satisfy itself that "adequate consultations have taken place with the agencies concerned."

Recommendations to Members

The question of the responsibility of members for coordination was considered by the Preparatory Commission in its report. The Commission observed:

---

[55] On coordination of policies and activities of specialized agencies, see Art. 58 and commentary thereon.

[56] See, for example, ECOSOC Res. 664A and B(XXIV), Aug. 1, 1957, with *Annex* containing general principles to guide future work. See commentary on Art. 58.

[57] For summary of actions taken during early years of UN, see *Repertory*, III, 365–76.

[58] UN Doc. E/3063.

While the United Nations, and particularly its Economic and Social Council, has the task of coordinating the policies and activities of the specialized agencies, this task can be performed only if Members will individually assist in making coordination possible. The acceptance by each Member of this responsibility for harmonizing its policies and activities in different fields covered by the specialized agencies and the United Nations will prevent confusion and conflict and enable the United Nations to achieve the purposes of Chapter IX of the Charter.[59]

The General Assembly and ECOSOC have urged members to coordinate their policies and activities and have recommended specific steps to this end.[60]

Article 64

1. The Economic and Social Council may take appropriate steps to obtain regular reports from the specialized agencies. It may make arrangements with the Members of the United Nations and with the specialized agencies to obtain reports on the steps taken to give effect to its own recommendations and to recommendations on matters falling within its competence made by the General Assembly.

2. It may communicate its observations on these reports to the General Assembly.

Article 64 has a twofold importance: 1) it provides for obtaining information from the specialized agencies upon which ECOSOC recommendations may be based; and 2) it envisages arrangements by which ECOSOC may perform a quasi-executive function by obtaining information regarding the extent to which its recommendations and those of the General Assembly are being carried out by the specialized agencies and by member states, and permits ECOSOC to make observations to the General Assembly on the situation as regards compliance. While these approaches to the problem of compliance are modest, they reflect the limited powers of the Organization in the economic and social fields and more particularly the basic principle of the Charter that the economic and social objectives are to be achieved by cooperation and not by forceful interjection of the authority of the Organization into areas which states have been accustomed to regard as subject to their domestic jurisdiction. Furthermore, in so far as the specialized agencies are concerned, this article reflects the principle that the specialized agencies, within the areas of their competence under their respective charters, enjoy a measure of autonomy which

[59] *Report of the Preparatory Commission*, p. 48.
[60] See GA Res. 125(II), Nov. 20, 1947, and ECOSOC Res. 590A II(XX), Aug. 5, 1955. For further discussion, see commentary on Article 58.

requires respect for their independence comparable to that shown for member states.

Reports from the Specialized Agencies

Steps taken to obtain "regular reports" from the specialized agencies include the insertion in agreements concluded under Article 63 of undertakings to submit regular reports and the adoption of various resolutions by ECOSOC reaffirming this undertaking and suggesting the content and timing of such reports. The standard agreement with the specialized agencies provides for the transmission to the United Nations of "regular reports on the activities of the Organization" and compliance "to the fullest extent practicable" with any request for "special reports, studies or information." [61]

In its second session, the General Assembly called upon the specialized agencies "to present each year, to the session of the Economic and Social Council preceding the opening of the General Assembly, their reports on past activities and their programmes of operations for the subsequent fiscal year." [62] Early in the following year, the Economic and Social Council requested the specialized agencies to submit to it, not later than May 15 of each year, reports on the organization of the agency, the activities of the past year, and activities and programs of the current year with an indication of priorities and proposed activities and work programs for the following year.[63] The Council subsequently gave the specialized agencies more detailed indications of matters which it desired them to cover in their reports.[64]

Reports on Effect Given to Recommendations

For the purposes of analysis, it is necessary to distinguish between arrangements made with specialized agencies and those made with member states. In the case of the former, the standard agreement contains a provision under which the specialized agency "agrees to enter into consultation with the United Nations upon request with respect to such recommendations or on the results of their consideration." [65] The Economic and Social Council has requested that reports submitted

[61] Art. V(2) of the Agreement with FAO.

[62] GA Res. 125(II), Nov. 20, 1947.

[63] ECOSOC Res. 128A(VI), Mar. 10, 1948.

[64] See ECOSOC Res. 497D(XVI), July 29, 1953; and 664A and B(XXIV), Aug. 1, 1957.

[65] Art. IV(2) of Agreement with FAO. The agreements with financial agencies provide for recommendations only after prior consultation. See commentary on Art. 63.

each year by the specialized agencies should note "particularly actions taken pursuant to recommendations of the General Assembly and the Council." [66] It has also on numerous occasions requested the agencies to submit special reports.

The question of members' implementation of recommendations by the General Assembly and ECOSOC on economic and social matters was considered by the Assembly in its second session. A resolution was adopted calling upon member states to carry out such resolutions of the General Assembly, and recommending that the Secretary-General report annually to ECOSOC, and that the latter report annually to the General Assembly "on steps taken by the Member Governments to give effect to the recommendations of the Economic and Social Council as well as to the recommendations made by the General Assembly on matters falling within the Council's competence." [67] When the matter was subsequently further considered by ECOSOC, a question was raised regarding the obligation of members to submit such reports. On this point the Legal Department of the Secretariat expressed the view that while Article 64(1) did not on the one hand imply "a legal obligation" of members to furnish the reports, on the other hand there was no intention "to detract from the general obligation of cooperation contained in Article 56." [68] A question was also raised regarding the meaning of the term "arrangements," and whether it implied that there must be a negotiated agreement with the governments concerned. The Legal Department in its memorandum interpreted the term as not requiring a formal agreement.

The Council has adopted two methods to obtain reports from members. It has requested governments to supply reports with respect to individual resolutions and to make reports with respect to lists of recommendations. The first method was initially followed until March, 1949, when the Council, after consideration of information from member governments,[69] and reports by the Secretary-General,[70] adopted a resolution making use of the second method.[71] By this resolution the Council requested the Secretary-General to transmit to member governments not later than October 1 of each year three lists of recommendations of the General Assembly and ECOSOC: 1) a list of those adopted during the year ending September 1 and requiring specific action by governments; 2) a list of previous recommendations on

66 ECOSOC Res. 128A(VI), Mar. 10, 1948.
67 GA Res. 119(II), Oct. 31, 1947.
68 ESCOR/10th Sess./1949/*Annexes*, agenda item 23 (E/1567), p. 15.
69 UN Doc. E/963 and Adds. 1–19, Aug. 24–Oct. 12, 1948; Adds. 20–48, Dec. 10, 1948—Sept. 26, 1949.
70 UN Docs. E/393/Rev. 1, Mar. 29, 1947 and E/1117, Feb. 3, 1949.
71 ECOSOC Res. 210(VIII), Mar. 18, 1949.

which further reports on continuing action are necessary; and 3)   a list of previous recommendations still to be implemented or requiring further action by particular governments. It requested member governments to report on steps taken to give effect to these recommendations and requested the Secretary-General to circulate the reports and to transmit to the Council not later than May 1 a fully annotated list and a factual statement showing the extent of implementation. The following year, on the basis of a report by an ad hoc committee, the Council voted to adopt a biennial system of reporting with a two-year cycle.[72] After a period of trial with this system, which was found to be unsatisfactory, the Council returned to its earlier method, and decided that each resolution should contain an indication of the timing of the report expected from the member government and that its annual report to the General Assembly should contain information on replies received.[73]

Action Taken by ECOSOC on Reports

Observations of the Council on the reports received from the specialized agencies and from members are included in the annual reports to the General Assembly made under Article 15(2) of the Charter. The annual report customarily includes sections dealing with questions of coordination and relations with specialized agencies and the implementation of recommendations by member governments.

Article 65

The Economic and Social Council may furnish information to the Security Council and shall assist the Security Council upon its request.

By way of implementing Article 65, ECOSOC has included in its Rules of Procedure provisions for the holding of special sessions at the request of the Security Council and for the inclusion on its provisional agenda of all items proposed by the Security Council.[74] Moreover, the agreements negotiated by ECOSOC with the specialized agencies all include some provision for rendering assistance to the Security Council.[75] The question of arrangements for a working relationship be-

[72] ESCOR/10th Sess./*Annexes*, agenda item 23 (E/1585), p. 15; and ECOSOC Res. 283(X), Feb. 8, 1950.

[73] ECOSOC Res. 450(XIV), July 29, 1952.

[74] Rules 4 and 10. For other rules bearing upon the relations of the two Councils, see Rules 7, 12, and 13.

[75] For further comment on the relations between the Security Council and the specialized agencies, see commentary on Arts. 48 and 63.

tween the two Councils was considered during the early sessions of both ECOSOC and the General Assembly, but no action was taken.[76]

Under Article 65, ECOSOC is clearly obligated to assist the Security Council in any matter within its competence. The article is open to the interpretation that ECOSOC may also on its own initiative "furnish information" to the Security Council, but it should be noted that the latter's rules do not provide for the consideration of items proposed by ECOSOC. On one occasion, ECOSOC requested the Secretary-General to transmit to the Security Council a record of its discussions on the observance of fundamental human rights in Palestine.[77] Although brought to the Council's attention, the matter was not discussed. Conversely, the Security Council transmitted to ECOSOC, "for any action" the latter might be able to take, the record of one of its discussions on the question of Palestine refugees,[78] but the matter was not discussed in ECOSOC.

In only one instance has the Security Council formally requested assistance from ECOSOC. In the early stages of the Korean conflict, the Security Council requested all organs of the United Nations, the specialized agencies, and appropriate nongovernmental organizations to provide assistance to the Unified Command, in particular such assistance as might be requested for the relief and support of the civilian population of Korea.[79] With regard to ECOSOC, the resolution specifically cited Article 65 of the Charter. ECOSOC in turn adopted a resolution declaring its readiness to provide such assistance and added its request for support from the specialized agencies and other bodies.[80]

It is not entirely clear what specific role the drafters of the Charter envisaged for ECOSOC with regard to measures for the maintenance or restoration of international peace and security. In practice, little use has been made of ECOSOC in this connection. The "Uniting for Peace" resolution, which was designed to mobilize the resources of the Organization for the taking of collective measures, contains no reference to ECOSOC; nonetheless, following the adoption of the resolution, ECOSOC asked the Secretary-General to consult with the specialized agencies concerning the information and assistance they might render to the Security Council or the General Assembly in any actions taken under the resolution.[81]

[76] Cf. commentary on Art. 91 regarding the relationship between ECOSOC and the Trusteeship Council.
[77] ECOSOC Res. 214B(VIII), Feb. 16, 1949.
[78] SCOR/3d Yr./354th Mtg./Aug. 19, 1948.
[79] SCOR/5th Yr./479th Mtg./July 31, 1950/p. 7.
[80] ECOSOC Res. 323(XI), Aug. 14, 1950.
[81] GA Res. 377(V), Nov. 3, 1950; ECOSOC Res. 363(XII), Mar. 14, 1951.

The Collective Measures Committee, established under the "Uniting for Peace" resolution, made no requests for assistance to ECOSOC, though it devoted considerable attention to the part ECOSOC and the specialized agencies might play in future collective measures. The Committee's first report mentions the possibility of ECOSOC's coordinating the activities of the specialized agencies and subsidiary organs of the United Nations in the collective measures field, citing as examples post-hostilities planning and the organization of postwar relief and rehabilitation.[82] When the Security Council called for assistance from the specialized agencies in connection with the situation in the Congo, it addressed its request through the Secretary-General rather than ECOSOC.[83]

Article 66

1. **The Economic and Social Council shall perform such functions as fall within its competence in connection with the carrying out of the recommendations of the General Assembly.**

2. **It may, with the approval of the General Assembly, perform services at the request of Members of the United Nations and at the request of specialized agencies.**

3. **It shall perform such other functions as are specified elsewhere in the present Charter or may be assigned to it by the General Assembly.**

The reason for the first paragraph of Article 66 is not clear, nor is its wording well chosen. That it has not in practice been regarded as having importance as a basis for action is indicated by the fact that it has never been referred to in a decision of the General Assembly or ECOSOC. In view of the relationship of ECOSOC to the General Assembly established by Article 60, it would seem obvious that the Council is to perform functions in connection with the carrying out of the recommendations of the General Assembly.

It would appear that Article 66(1) does not fully reflect the intent of the technical committee at San Francisco. The committee's recommendation, following closely the original Dumbarton Oaks text as to arrangement, placed this general grant of authority at the beginning of the enumeration of the Council's functions and powers. Besides, both in the original Dumbarton Oaks text and in the committee draft, the power conferred was "to carry out, within the scope of its functions, recommendations of the General Assembly." [84] The present text and

---

[82] GAOR/6th Sess./1951/*Supp. 13* (A/1891), p. 19.
[83] UN Doc. S/4405, July 22, 1960.
[84] Ch. ix, sec. c; UNCIO, *Documents*, X, 281.

its place in the listing of ECOSOC functions and powers were the result of last-minute changes by the coordination committee and suggests a more limited purpose than the technical committee had in mind.

The second paragraph establishes a method of action available to the United Nations for furthering the objectives set forth in Articles 1(3) and 55. The rendering of specific services to member states in the form of technical assistance and other kinds of aid was an activity of the League of Nations and the International Labour Organisation but it never achieved the importance that it has under the Charter of the United Nations. With the emphasis that has come to be placed on the economic and social development of less developed countries, the rendering of specific services has come to be one of the most important single activities of the Organization in the economic and social fields.

Various decisions providing for technical assistance services have expressly stated that these services are available only to "Member Nations," or that they are provided at the request of "Member Governments," or "Members of the United Nations." [85] There is, however, no express provision in the Charter either authorizing or prohibiting the rendering of services at the request of nonmembers. A number of General Assembly resolutions contain no provisions making eligibility dependent on membership in the United Nations.[86]

While ECOSOC, in providing for the establishment and functioning of the Expanded Programme of Technical Assistance, did not deal explicitly with the question of eligibility, in practice the services have been made available to nonmembers of the United Nations that are members of participating specialized agencies.[87] The General Assembly, in establishing the Special Fund, provided that participation shall be open "to any States Members of the United Nations or members of the specialized agencies or of the International Atomic Energy Agency." [88] In a few cases, the General Assembly has declared particular states that are members neither of the United Nations nor of specialized agencies eligible for services.[89] Non-self-governing or trust

[85] For example, see GA Res. 200(III), Dec. 4, 1948, establishing the Technical Assistance Programme. For references to other resolutions of the Assembly and ECOSOC where this practice is followed, see *Repertory*, III, 450–51.

[86] For example, GA Res. 57(I), Dec. 11, 1946, on the establishment of UNICEF; and 58(I), Dec. 14, 1946, on the transfer to the UN of the advisory social welfare functions of UNRRA.

[87] See ECOSOC Res. 222A(IX), Aug. 14, 1949, and *Repertory*, III, 452.

[88] GA Res. 1240(XIII), Oct. 14, 1958. Under the OPEX program, assistance can be given to governments participating in "the United Nations technical assistance programmes in the field of public administration." GA Res. 1256(XIII), Nov. 14, 1958.

[89] The Republic of Korea was declared eligible to receive technical assistance before it became a member of any specialized agency. GA Res. 410(V), Dec. 1, 1950.

territories receive services on the request of the administering state or authority.

The matter of services to specialized agencies is covered in certain of its aspects in the agreements concluded between the United Nations and the agencies.[90] There have been no decisions of ECOSOC or the General Assembly that have expressly invoked the provisions of Article 66(2) as they relate to specialized agencies. There have been a few instances where the Council has requested the Secretary-General to offer assistance to, or collaborate as appropriate with, a specialized agency in a matter of common concern.

The Council has not itself performed the services referred to in the second paragraph. It has arranged for the services to be performed through such machinery as it has considered most appropriate. Further, it has discharged its responsibility largely by recommending to the General Assembly the establishment of machinery and procedures for providing various categories of services, by implementing recommendations and directives originating with the Assembly, by prescribing the scope and the principles of operation of programs relating to such services, by authorizing the administrative action required, and by reviewing reports on the actual implementation of decisions taken.[91] With respect to administrative action, the usual procedure has been to request the Secretary-General to provide the services decided upon by the Council and the General Assembly. The Council has used its functional and regional economic commission in preparing programs of assistance and has authorized the latter to render services directly to governments.[92]

The services rendered under the terms of Article 66(2) cover a wide range of activities and have assumed various forms. To continue the emergency supplementary child-feeding carried on by UNRRA, UNICEF was established, and later was given permanent form as a special body.[93] To provide assistance to governments in matters relating to the repatriation and assimilation of refugees, the Office of the High Commissioner of Refugees was established.[94] The Expanded Programme of Technical Assistance, proposed by ECOSOC and approved by the General Assembly,[95] provides for the cooperation of the United Nations and certain specialized agencies within an administrative framework supervised by ECOSOC. To enlarge the scope of technical assistance operations, the Special Fund was established as "an

[90] See commentary on Art. 63.
[91] For illustrations, see *Repertory*, III, 442–44.
[92] See, for example, ECOSOC Res. 434I(XIV), July 28, 1952.
[93] GA Res. 57(I), Dec. 11, 1946.   [94] GA Res. 428(V), Dec. 14, 1950.
[95] See ECOSOC Res. 222(IX), Aug. 5, 1949; and GA Res. 304(IV), Nov. 16, 1949.

organ of the United Nations administered under the authority of the Economic and Social Council and of the General Assembly." [96] To combine in one agency the activities of the Expanded Programme and the Special Fund, the United Nations Development Programme was established, effective January 1, 1966.[97]

The conditions under which the services are to be rendered, including the responsibilities, financial and other, assumed by the recipients, are determined by resolutions of ECOSOC and the General Assembly and by agreement with the recipient governments. Since the United Nations has no authority to impose its services upon a state, and since no state, member or not, has the right to demand a service on its own terms, the conditions on which the service is rendered must be a matter of agreement, express or implied.

VOTING

Article 67

1. Each member of the Economic and Social Council shall have one vote.

2. Decisions of the Economic and Social Council shall be made by a majority of members present and voting.

The principle that each member shall have one vote is followed in all organs of the United Nations.[98] In stipulating that all decisions of ECOSOC "shall be made by a majority of the members present and voting," Article 67 is identical with Article 89 relating to voting in the Trusteeship Council, and differs from Charter provisions governing voting in the General Assembly and the Security Council, which require special majorities for certain decisions.[99]

The voting procedures of ECOSOC are further spelled out in Chapter XI of the Council's Rules of Procedure.[100] As in the case of other United Nations organs, ECOSOC in many instances adopts "decisions" without a formal vote. For example, despite the Rules of Procedure, it is normal for the officers of the Council to be elected by acclamation.[101]

Concern over the possibility that under the Rules decisions could be taken by the affirmative vote of a very few members led to a proposal that no decision be considered valid unless it received at least nine

[96] GA Res. 1240(XIII), Oct. 14, 1958.
[97] GA Res. 2029(XX), Nov. 22, 1965.   [98] See Arts. 18, 27, 67, and 89.
[99] See Arts. 27 and 18(2). It should be noted that decisions on economic and social questions are not included in the list of "important questions" requiring a two-thirds vote in the General Assembly. Art. 18(2).
[100] UN Doc. E/3063.   [101] For other instances see *Repertory,* III, 467.

votes.[102] The proposal was withdrawn in the face of arguments that it was contrary to the Charter. During the discussion the point was made that members were protected to some extent by the requirement that a majority of members constitutes a quorum (Rule 47).

The voting procedure of the Council's commissions, established under Article 68, is identical with that of the Council with a few minor exceptions,[103] the main one being that a two-thirds vote is required in the commissions for the inclusion on the agenda of any item proposed by a nongovernmental organization.

PROCEDURE

Article 68

The Economic and Social Council shall set up commissions in economic and social fields and for the promotion of human rights, and such other commissions as may be required for the performance of its functions.

The Dumbarton Oaks Proposals provided that ECOSOC "should set up an economic commission, a social commission, and such other commissions as may be required" and that these commissions "should consist of experts." [104] These proposals were based in large part on the experience of the League of Nations with technical committees and commissions in its economic and social work.[105] At San Francisco, there was considerable pressure to add to the number of commissions specifically required under the Dumbarton Oaks Proposals; at the same time there was recognition of the desirability of leaving the Council freedom of decision. As a compromise, it was decided to add the requirement of a commission on human rights and leave to the Council the decision whether other commissions were necessary for the performance of its functions. The provision regarding composition was dropped.[106]

In its report on the organization of ECOSOC, the Preparatory Commission listed five considerations it had taken into account in making its recommendations for the establishment of commissions under Article 68.[107] These considerations were: 1) the specific fields requiring

[102] See ESCOR/7th Sess./1948/*Annexes*, p. 330.

[103] See *Repertory*, III, 468–69; and *Supp. 1*, II, 118 and rules of procedure of the various commissions.

[104] Ch. IX, sec. D, para. 1.

[105] See H. R. G. Greaves, *League Committees and World Order* (London, Oxford University Press, 1931); and Felix Morley, *The Society of Nations* (Washington, Brookings Institution, 1932), pp. 227–60.

[106] See Russell, pp. 791–94.

[107] *Report of the Preparatory Commission*, pp. 34–36.

international economic and social cooperation would be diverse and call for treatment by more-or-less specialized bodies, the exact nature of the subordinate structure of the Council being largely dependent upon the extent to which specialized agencies would occupy the field; 2) complex economic and social problems of the greatest urgency arising out of the war would demand immediate attention; 3) certain functions and activities of the League of Nations would have to be continued; 4) there would be need for flexibility in the number of commissions, the scope of their activities, the powers delegated to them, the method of selecting their personnel, and the duration of their sessions; and 5) due regard must be given to the importance of the coordination of activities in closely related fields.

The Preparatory Commission recommended immediate establishment of a commission on human rights, an economic and employment commission, a temporary social commission, a statistical commission, and a commission on narcotic drugs. It recommended the establishment at an early date of a demographic commission, a temporary transport and communications commission, and a fiscal commission.[108] It also recommended the establishment of a commission to coordinate the activities of the various organs of the Council and of the specialized agencies. The Preparatory Commission also took note of the Council's need for a variety of committees to assist it in its work of organization and operation, and recommended that these be established at its first session, without, however, expressing any view regarding the Charter basis of such committees.

While Article 68 empowers and directs the Council to establish "commissions" to assist it in its work, no constitutional question has been raised regarding the type of subsidiary organ that can be established. This may be due in part to the fact that the Council's power under the Charter need not be based on Article 68 alone. Article 7, after listing the principal organs of the United Nations, authorizes the establishment of "such subsidiary organs as may be found necessary" "in accordance with the present Charter." Furthermore, Article 72, by empowering the Council to adopt its own rules of procedure, implicitly authorizes it to establish such committees and other subsidiary organs as may be necessary for its effective operation.

Types of Organs Set Up

In determining its subordinate structure, the Council was at the outset guided by the recommendations of the Preparatory Commission. As the overall pattern of intergovernmental arrangements for coopera-

108 *Ibid.*, pp. 36–39.

tion in the economic and social fields developed, and as the nature and scope of ECOSOC's responsibilities became more clearly defined, the Council found it necessary to modify the original substructure of commissions and committees in order to meet new situations and needs.[109]

The Council has used the word "commission" to designate two types of organs: 1) functional commissions, which undertake studies and make recommendations to the Council with respect to the fields of activity defined in their terms of reference; and 2) regional economic commissions, which are entrusted with broad responsibilities for economic and social problems of a regional character in specific areas of the world. "Commission" has been used at times, however, to describe ad hoc bodies, usually with investigatory functions.[110]

ECOSOC has established four regional economic commissions. These were not recommended by the Preparatory Commission, but were the result of the needs of war-devastated areas and underdeveloped countries which it was thought lent themselves particularly to regional treatment. The first two commissions established, the Economic Commission for Europe (ECE) and the Economic Commission for Asia and the Far East (ECAFE), were responses to demands for assistance in the reconstruction of war-devastated areas.[111] The Economic Commission for Latin America (ECLA) was established as a result of the demand for a regional approach to the economic needs of that area; the same was true of the Economic Commission for Africa, established in 1958.[112] An attempt to establish an economic commission for the Middle East failed, largely because of the Arab states' refusal to accept the inclusion of Israel.

Composition of Commissions

In regard to the functional commissions, the Preparatory Commission recommended that most of them should contain "a majority of highly-qualified governmental representatives," and argued that "[where] the work of a commission is likely to result in recommendations for special action by governments, acceptance of this principle would add realism and responsibility to the advice of the commission and improve the prospects of implementation by governments." It

[109] For list of functional and regional commissions, with memberships at end of 1965, see *Y.U.N.*, 1965, pp. 842–47.

[110] For example, the Commission of Enquiry into the Effects of Chewing the Coca Leaf.

[111] For summary and references to documents, see *Repertory*, III, Art. 68, para. 31. The commissions were established by ECOSOC Res. 36(IV), Mar. 28, 1947 and 37(IV), Mar. 28, 1947.

[112] ECOSOC Res. 106(V), Feb. 25, 1948; ECOSOC Res. 671A(XXV), Apr. 29, 1958.

added that nongovernmental members "with appropriate qualifications" might be chosen by the Council from among nationals of member states, such members to include "government officials chosen by the Council in their personal capacity after the Council had obtained the consent of the government concerned." [113]

ECOSOC, accepting the recommendation of a joint committee on composition of commissions, decided in its resolution of June 21, 1946, that the commissions should consist of members of the United Nations selected by the Council.[114] ECOSOC agreed, however, that governments elected to membership had the option to nominate persons either as government representatives or as experts in an individual capacity.

The number of members and the length of their terms are specified in the resolutions establishing the commissions. Changes have been made by subsequent resolutions. Except for the Commission on Narcotic Drugs and the Commission on International Commodity Trade, the selection of members of the functional commissions has occurred in three stages: 1) the Council selects, by secret ballot, members of the United Nations who are to appoint representatives to serve on the commission; 2) "[with] a view to securing a balanced representation in the various fields covered by the Commission," the Secretary-General consults with the states so selected before their representatives are nominated; and 3) the representatives nominated by the selected states are confirmed by the Council. By its resolution of August 3, 1961, the Council increased the membership of the functional commissions, in view of the increased membership of the United Nations.[115] Furthermore, in the case of the Commission on Narcotic Drugs, it provided that members should be elected from "Members of the United Nations and of the specialized agencies and the Parties to the Single Convention on Narcotic Drugs, 1961," "with due regard to the adequate representation of countries that are important producers of opium or coca leaves, of countries that are important in the field of the manufacture of narcotic drugs, and of countries in which drug addiction or the illicit traffic in narcotic drugs constitutes an important problem." The resolution also gave explicit recognition to "the importance of ensuring an equitable geographical distribution in the membership of the functional commissions."

With regard to regional economic commissions, the principles governing membership and participation have been first, that all countries or territories within a given region should be able to participate in the

[113] *Report of the Preparatory Commission*, p. 39.
[114] UN Doc. E/JC/1, June 17, 1946; ESCOR/1st Yr., 2d Sess./*Annexes*, Res. 2/12, June 21, 1946, pp. 406–9.
[115] ECOSOC Res. 845(XXXII), Aug. 3, 1961.

economic commission for that area, and second, that countries outside a particular region may nevertheless have a special interest that justifies participation in the work or some aspect of the work of the commission of that area. Membership and participation are not determined by election but rather by the terms of the relevant resolution of ECOSOC. Where a commission has sought to exclude members from participation, ECOSOC action has been necessary. In the case of the Economic Commission for Africa, ECOSOC decided that the Republic of South Africa should not "take part in the work of the Economic Commission for Africa until the Council, on the recommendation of the Economic Commission for Africa, shall find that conditions for constructive cooperation have been restored by a change in its racial policy." The Council also decided to expel Portugal from the Commission because of its refusal to accept its obligations under General Assembly and Commission resolutions.[116]

Under the first principle, the Council has provided initially in the case of all regional commissions that members of the United Nations within the geographical scope of a commission are members of that commission, and, in the case of ECAFE, ECLA, and ECA, that nonmembers of the United Nations and territories not responsible for their own international relations within the geographical scope of a commission may become associate members. In the case of ECE, nonmembers of the United Nations may have consultative status.

Under the second principle, the United States is a member of ECE, and the membership of ECAFE and ECLA includes several United Nations members situated outside those geographic areas. In the case of ECA, membership is limited to member states within the area or to those having "territorial responsibilities" in the area. A territory may be admitted to membership when it has become responsible for its own international relations. In the case of all commissions, provision is made for consultative participation by nonmembers under defined circumstances.

Functions and Powers

The functional commissions assist, advise, and make recommendations and reports to the Council on matters within their competence. They have been empowered to make studies and recommendations on their own initiative. The Commission on Narcotic Drugs is authorized to perform certain supervisory functions in connection with the carrying out of international conventions on narcotic drugs. The Commission on International Commodity Trade was authorized to bring to the

---

[116] ECOSOC Res. 974DIII and IV(XXXVI), July 24 and 30, 1963.

attention of member governments, as well as the Council, its views and recommendations "as to the need for governmental or intergovernmental action to deal with problems or emerging problems which its studies may disclose." [117] The Commission on Human Rights has had responsibility for the preparation of the draft universal declaration on human rights and draft covenants on human rights, and has also had a unique relationship to the General Assembly in that it has advised and performed services for that organ at its direct request.

The functions and powers of the regional economic commissions have extended beyond the rendering of advisory services to ECOSOC. Their terms of reference include initiating and participating in measures "for facilitating concerted action" within the area in the defined fields of activities. In these fields the commissions make or sponsor investigations and studies; undertake or sponsor the collection, evaluation, and dissemination of information; and perform advisory services to governments. In the resolutions establishing ECE, ECAFE, and ECLA, the fields of activity were defined as "economic, and technological problems and developments" within the geographical area. The resolution establishing ECA in 1958 provided that in carrying out its functions, it should "deal as appropriate with the social aspects of economic development and the interrelationship of economic and social factors." [118] The resolution also provided that ECA should "establish appropriate liaison and cooperation with other regional commissions in accordance with the resolutions and directives of the Economic and Social Council and the General Assembly." The directives of ECAFE and ECLA were amended in the following year to include these provisions.[119] In the case of all regional economic commissions, the directives provide that they shall act "within the framework of the policies of the United Nations and subject to the general supervision of the Economic and Social Council" and that they shall "take no action with respect to any country without the agreement of the government of that country."

Within recent years, there has been a definite trend in the direction of greater decentralization of the United Nations' work in economic and social development. This has taken the form of greater emphasis on the role of the regional economic commissions and the building up of their staffs to permit the discharge of increased responsibilities. This trend was noted in the consolidated report on appraisals of United Nations and specialized agency programs.[120] By its resolution of December 15, 1960, the General Assembly noted "with satisfaction"

---

[117] ECOSOC Res. 691A(XXVI), July 31, 1958.
[118] ECOSOC Res. 671A(XXV), Apr. 29, 1958.
[119] ECOSOC Res. 723B II and C II(XXVIII), July 17, 1959.
[120] Five Year Perspective, 1960–1964, UN Doc. E/3327/Rev. 1, June 20, 1960.

that the regional economic commissions were playing an increasingly important role in the preparation and carrying out of programs in the economic and social fields, invited members to take further advantage of their facilities and services, urged the commissions to strengthen cooperation among themselves, and requested the Secretary-General to strengthen their secretariats.[121]

Article 69

The Economic and Social Council shall invite any Member of the United Nations to participate, without vote, in its deliberations on any matter of particular concern to that Member.

Article 69 may be compared with Article 31, which deals with a comparable aspect of Security Council procedure.

At its first session, ECOSOC had occasion to establish the principle that it should "decide whether a matter is of particular concern to a Member State not a member of the Council." [122] This was subsequently embodied in the Council's Rules of Procedure.[123] It has been the practice of the Council to invite members to participate in the discussion of particular items or subitems on its agenda. Rule 75 provides that a member thus invited "shall not have the right to vote, but may submit proposals which may be put to the vote by request of any member of the Council." It was argued at the time the Council considered its Rules of Procedure that the last clause was unduly restrictive and contrary to Article 69, but this view did not prevail.[124] In addition, a member thus invited is allowed to participate in the work of drafting committees or working groups set up for the consideration of particular items. Similar rules have been applied to the commissions and committees of ECOSOC.

It has been suggested that Article 69 by inference does not permit ECOSOC to accord membership and voting rights in regional economic commissions to states not members of the United Nations. The Secretary-General presented to ECOSOC a memorandum supporting its right to do this.[125] The majority of members of the Council supported this view, and subsequently the Council adopted a resolution according full membership in ECAFE and ECE to certain nonmem-

[121] GA Res. 1518(XV). ECOSOC had on Aug. 3, 1960, adopted a resolution, welcomed by the General Assembly, specifically requesting the Secretary-General to draw on the services of the regional commissions, especially in the planning and execution of programs for advancing regional development. For details on the work of the commissions, see their annual reports.

[122] ESCOR/1st Sess./8th Mtg./Feb. 12, 1946/p. 77.

[123] UN Doc. E/3063, Rule 75.

[124] See ESCOR/8th Sess./278th Mtg./Mar. 16, 1949/pp. 620–23, and 630.

[125] UN Doc. E/2458, June 8, 1953.

bers of the United Nations on condition that they apply, and agree to contribute annually such amounts as the General Assembly shall assess.[126]

Article 70

The Economic and Social Council may make arrangements for representatives of the specialized agencies to participate, without vote, in its deliberations and in those of the commissions established by it, and for its representatives to participate in the deliberations of the specialized agencies.

The arrangements for reciprocal representation envisaged in Article 70 have been provided in specific articles of the agreements defining the relationship of the specialized agencies with the United Nations (Article 57) which the Economic and Social Council is authorized to enter into by the terms of Article 63. When the terms of these agreements were originally being discussed by ECOSOC's Committee on Negotiations with the specialized agencies, the majority were of the opinion that the language of the Charter and the terms of reference of the Committee contemplated relations between the United Nations as a whole and Specialized Agencies, and not just between ECOSOC and the agencies.[127] Consequently, in the agreements drafted by the Committee and finally approved, the right of representation and the obligation to accept specialized agency participation are not limited to ECOSOC.

The standard agreement provides that representatives of the United Nations shall be invited to attend meetings of the conference of an agency, its committees, its executive organs, and general, regional, and other special meetings, "and to participate, without vote, in the deliberations of these bodies." [128] It provides that representatives of the specialized agency shall be invited to attend meetings of ECOSOC, its commissions and committees, and the Trusteeship Council, "and to participate, without vote, in the deliberations of these bodies with respect to items on their agenda relating to matters within the scope of its activities." It provides that representatives of the agency shall be invited to attend meetings of the General Assembly "for purposes of consultation on matters within the scope of its activities," and of its main committees "when matters within the scope of its activities are under discussion and to participate, without vote, in such

[126] ECOSOC Res. 517A and B(XVII), Apr. 22, 1954.
[127] UN Doc. E/NSA/8, May 31, 1946.
[128] See, for example, Agreement with the FAO. Art. II, para. 1, UN Doc. A/78, Sept. 30, 1946.

discussion." [129] The agreements with the financial agencies restrict the right of attendance and participation of representatives of the United Nations to the organs of general representation, and to other meetings to which they may be specially invited. Representatives of these agencies have rights of representation and participation in United Nations organs similar to those of other agencies.

Rule 78 of ECOSOC's Rules of Procedure provides for representation and participation of the specialized agencies in accordance with the terms of the agreements. It further provides that they may submit proposals regarding items of concern to them "which may be put to the vote on request of any member of the Council or the committee concerned." The rules of procedure of the functional and regional commissions contain similar provisions.

Article 71

The Economic and Social Council may make suitable arrangements for consultation with non-governmental organizations which are concerned with matters within its competence. Such arrangements may be made with international organizations and, where appropriate, with national organizations after consultation with the Member of the United Nations concerned.

The question of the relation of nongovernmental organizations to intergovernmental organizations has arisen in the past. The International Association for Labor Legislation, organized in Paris in 1900, included representatives of nongovernmental organizations as well as those of governments. Under the constitution of the International Labour Organisation, adopted at the end of World War I, employer and employee organizations, as well as governments, were given representation in the Governing Body and Conference. In the preliminary discussions in the U.S. State Department and at Dumbarton Oaks, the question of the relation of nongovernmental organizations to the proposed "general international organization" was not considered.

At San Francisco, the question came up in connection with that of the relation of intergovernmental organizations such as ILO to the Conference and to the proposed organization. More specifically, the issue arose as the result of the insistence of the Soviet Union that the World Trade Union Conference (WTUC), a nongovernmental labor organization formed in February, 1945, with strong Soviet backing, should be given the same observer status at San Francisco as the ILO and other intergovernmental organizations, and the same relationship to the proposed "general international organization" under the terms of

[129] *Ibid.*, paras. 2–5.

the Charter. The steering committee of the Conference decided against giving nongovernmental organizations observer status. The issue as regards future relationship was sharpened by the effort of the United Kingdom to get assurance in the Charter that the ILO would be recognized as the organization responsible for securing improved labor standards, and the unwillingness of many delegations, including the United States, to give a nongovernmental organization an official relationship to the proposed organization.

The situation threatened to reach an impasse until agreement was achieved in a compromise solution under which the Council could arrange with intergovernmental agencies for reciprocal exchange of nonvoting participation in meetings and for "suitable" consultation with nongovernmental organizations "concerned with matters within its competence." [130] The United States delegation readily supported this proposal, since it was consistent with the practice it had followed at the Conference of giving its national nongovernmental organizations consultative status and responded to the desires of these groups.[131]

Arrangements for Consultation

The relationship of nongovernmental organizations to the United Nations was discussed at length during the first part of the General Assembly's first session in London. The Soviet Union, Belgium, and France had proposed that the World Federation of Trade Unions (WFTU) and the International Cooperative Alliance be given an "advisory capacity," while the United States sought equal status for the American Federation of Labor, which was not a member of the WFTU.[132] The General Assembly finally approved a resolution on February 14, 1946, recommending that ECOSOC "should, as soon as possible," adopt suitable arrangements enabling these organizations as well as other international, national, and regional nongovernmental organizations "whose experience the Economic and Social Council will find necessary to use, to collaborate for purposes of consultation with the Economic and Social Council." [133]

Taking note of the resolution of the General Assembly, ECOSOC in its first session created a temporary committee on arrangements for consultation with nongovernmental organizations, which was instructed to submit detailed proposals concerning consultation with international, national, and regional nongovernmental organiza-

[130] See commentary on Art. 70.
[131] See Russell, pp. 798–802 for further detail.
[132] GAOR/1st Sess., 1st Part/22d Plen. Mtg./Feb. 2, 1946/pp. 326–28; 29th Plen. Mtg./Feb. 12, 1946/pp. 402–12; 33d Plen. Mtg./Feb. 14, 1946/pp. 501–35.
[133] GA Res. 4(I), Feb. 14, 1946.

tions.[134] The report of the committee was approved by the Council on June 12, 1946.[135] In so doing, the Council determined the principles to be applied in establishing a list of nongovernmental organizations eligible for consultation and the procedures to be followed. It also established a standing committee with the same name as the old one, composed of the President of the Council and five members, to "review applications for consultative status submitted by non-governmental organizations, and to make recommendations to the Council." [136]

At its eighth session, the Council requested the Secretary-General to report on the activities of nongovernmental organizations and their work in support of the Council, and requested its NGO committee to make recommendations for the improvement of arrangements on the basis of this report.[137] Taking account of these recommendations, the Council adopted the basic resolution governing arrangements for consultation.[138] In addition to the provisions of this resolution, Rules 10(2), 12, 13, 14(3), and 82 to 86 of the Rules of Procedure of ECOSOC and Rules 6, 7, 37, 41, 74, and 75 of the rules of procedure of the functional commissions govern consultation with nongovernmental organizations.

Any international organization not established by intergovernmental agreement is considered a nongovernmental organization for the purposes of Article 71. The NGO Committee has in practice considered a nongovernmental organization to be international if it has affiliates in at least three countries. National nongovernmental organizations must have the national character of a member state and its consent to be accepted for consultative status. Normally, national organizations are expected to present their views through the nongovernmental international organization to which they belong.

Consultative arrangements are designed for the purpose of obtaining information and advice from nongovernmental organizations and for enabling them to express the views of the groups they represent. Three categories of nongovernmental organizations have been established: 1) Category A for organizations having a basic interest in most of the activities of the Council; 2) Category B for organizations interested in

[134] ESCOR/1st Yr./2d Sess./*Annexes 8* and *8a,* Doc. E/43 and E/43/Rev. 1, May 23 and June 19, 1946, pp. 314–23.

[135] ESCOR/1st Yr./2d Sess./*Annex 14,* Res. 2/3, June 21, 1946, pp. 360–65.

[136] The Committee, known as the NGO Committee, became in 1949 the Council Committee on Non-Governmental Organizations. Its membership was subsequently increased in 1950 to seven, and in 1966 to thirteen. See ECOSOC Res. 288B(X), Feb. 27, 1950 and 1099(XL), Mar. 4, 1966.

[137] ECOSOC Res. 214E(VIII), Feb. 16, 1949.

[138] UN Doc. E/1619, Feb. 21, 1950, Corr. 1, Feb. 24, and 2, Feb. 27, and Add. 1, Feb. 24; the Report of the Secretary-General is contained in UN Doc. E/C.2/231, Nov. 25, 1949, and Adds. 1–4, Dec. 6 and 13, 1949, Jan. 17 and 20, 1950; ECOSOC Res. 288B(X), Feb. 27, 1950.

some particular aspect of the Council's work and 3) the register which includes other organizations that have significant contributions to make to the work of the Council.[139]

Organizations in all three categories may send representatives to sessions of the Council and its commissions. Those in Categories A and B may submit written statements to the Council and its commissions, and may make oral statements to the Council's NGO Committee and to the commissions. Organizations in Category A may ask the committee to request that an item be placed on the provisional agenda of the Council; they may make oral statements on items proposed by them and, on the recommendations of the committee, on items not proposed by them. They may also propose items for the provisional agenda of the commissions. Organizations on the register may be invited by the Secretary-General to submit written statements to the Council and its commissions and may be heard by the Council on the recommendation of the Secretary-General and at the request of a commission.[140]

Article 72

1. The Economic and Social Council shall adopt its own rules of procedure, including the method of selecting its President.

2. The Economic and Social Council shall meet as required in accordance with its rules, which shall include provision for the convening of meetings on the request of a majority of its members.

The Economic and Social Council at its first session on January 23, 1946, adopted as its provisional rules of procedure the rules recommended by the Preparatory Commission.[141] These provisional rules had been considered and approved by the Joint Sub-Committee of the Second and Third Committees of the General Assembly and by the General Assembly in plenary session.[142] At its twelfth meeting, the Council adopted the provisional rules, slightly amended, as its permanent rules. These Rules of Procedure have been subsequently

[139] See *Y.U.N.*, 1965, pp. 513–16, for list. At the end of 1965, there were 10 NGOs in Category A, 131 in Category B, and over 200 on the register. NGOs in Category A were the International Chamber of Commerce, the International Federation of Free Trade Unions, the International Co-operative Alliance, the International Federation of Agricultural Producers, the International Federation of Christian Trade Unions, the International Organization of Employers, the Inter-Parliamentary Union, the World Federation of Trade Unions, the World Federation of United Nations Associations, and the World Veterans Association.

[140] See Rules 82–86 of ECOSOC, *Rules of Procedure* (Doc. E/3063). On problems that have arisen in connection with access of representatives of NGOs to Headquarters under the Headquarters Agreement, see commentary on Art. 105.

[141] *Report of the Preparatory Commission*, pp. 29–34.

[142] GA Res. 5(I) and 7(I), Jan. 29, 1946.

amended many times. In 1949 there was a comprehensive revision.[143] In 1952, the Council amended its Rules relating to sessions and agenda in accordance with provisions of a previous resolution on the organization and operation of the Council and its commissions.[144] At its eighteenth session, the Council adopted a resolution on "Organization and operation of the Council and its commissions" which involved some revision of the Rules of Procedure.[145] Other revisions of less importance have been made.[146]

The Rules of Procedure provide for their amendment and suspension. According to Rule 8, the Rules may not be amended until the Council has received a report on the proposed amendment from a committee. The Council has not always required prior receipt of a report before an amendment is adopted. Thus, in its fifteenth session, when the Council adopted Spanish as a working language in accordance with a General Assembly resolution, it revised its Rules on languages on the recommendation of the Secretary-General. In a number of instances the Council has adopted provisions rejected by its committee. Furthermore, the Council has adopted many provisions on procedural matters which have taken effect without necessarily being incorporated into the Rules of Procedure. Sometimes, the Rules have been amended by incorporating the provisions in question, but at other times, provisions relating to procedural matters contained in such resolutions have taken effect by virtue of Council adoption and have never been formally incorporated into the Rules of Procedure.[147]

In several instances, the Council has suspended or amended its Rules of Procedure as the result of resolutions or decisions adopted by the General Assembly. For the most part these have been concerned with financial matters.

[143] ECOSOC Res. 217(VIII), Mar. 18, 1949. See also Report of Committee on Procedure, UN Doc. E/1130, Feb. 9, 1949; and ESCOR/8th Sess./268th Mtg./Mar. 9, 1949/pp. 522–28; 272d Mtg./Mar. 11, 1949; 282d Mtg./Mar. 18, 1949/pp. 625–36 and 663–64.

[144] ECOSOC Res. 456A(XIV), July 29, 1952 and 414(XIII), Sept. 19, 1951.

[145] ECOSOC Res. 557(XVIII), Aug. 5, 1954.

[146] For current Rules of Procedure, see UN Doc. E/3063. For details on interpretation and application of the Rules of Procedure, see *Repertory*, III, 573–96.

[147] See, for example, provisions of ECOSOC Res. 101(V), Aug. 14 and 16, 1947, and 174(VII), Aug. 28, 1948, relating to preparation of annual programs of conferences, and provisions of ECOSOC Res. 288(X), Feb. 27, 1950, Mar. 3 and 6, 1950, relating to proceedings of Council Committee on Non-Governmental Organizations.

CHAPTER XI

Declaration Regarding Non-Self-Governing Territories

The adoption by the San Francisco Conference of the "Declaration Regarding Non-Self-Governing Territories" was a significant milestone in the effort to establish the principle of the international accountability of states for the administration of dependent territories under their jurisdiction. By the terms of Article 73 of the Charter, members of the United Nations recognize the principle that the interests of the inhabitants of the non-self-governing territories which they administer are "paramount," and they further accept as a "sacred trust" the obligation "to promote to the utmost . . . the well-being of the inhabitants" of those territories. To this end, they accept the more specific commitments listed in the article. This undertaking goes far beyond any previous international agreement in the definite character and broad scope of its provisions. In comparison, under Article 23 of the Covenant, members of the League of Nations merely undertook "to secure just treatment of the native inhabitants of territories under their control."

Chapter XI is to be sharply distinguished from Chapters XII and XIII, which relate to the trusteeship system and provide in detail for international accountability and international supervision, but only for those territories placed under trusteeship by special agreement. Chapter XI, by contrast, makes no specific provision for international supervisory machinery; however, it applies to all non-self-governing territories from the time the Charter entered into force.[1]

Article 73

Members of the United Nations which have or assume responsibilities for the administration of territories whose peoples have not yet attained a full measure of self-government recognize the principle that the interests of the inhabitants of these territories are paramount, and accept as a sacred trust the obligation to promote to the utmost, within the system of international peace and security established by

[1] GA Res. 9(I), Feb. 9, 1946.

the present Charter, the well-being of the inhabitants of these territories, and, to this end:

a. to ensure, with due respect for the culture of the peoples concerned, their political, economic, social, and educational advancement, their just treatment, and their protection against abuses;

b. to develop self-government, to take due account of the political aspirations of the peoples, and to assist them in the progressive development of their free political institutions, according to the particular circumstances of each territory and its peoples and their varying stages of advancement;

c. to further international peace and security;

d. to promote constructive measures of development, to encourage research, and to cooperate with one another and, when and where appropriate, with specialized international bodies with a view to the practical achievement of the social, economic, and scientific purposes set forth in this Article; and

e. to transmit regularly to the Secretary-General for information purposes, subject to such limitation as security and constitutional considerations may require, statistical and other information of a technical nature relating to economic, social, and educational conditions in the territories for which they are respectively responsible other than those territories to which Chapters XII and XIII apply.

Drafting the Article

As early as 1942, the postwar planners in the U.S. Department of State were working on proposals for an international system, applicable to all dependent territories, which they hoped could be set in motion immediately. These proposals encompassed: 1) a general declaration of principles applicable to all dependent territories; 2) an international trusteeship system applicable to certain categories of territories; and 3) the development of regional agencies through which the general principles could be indirectly applied to other territories.[2] Objections by the War and Navy Departments and the Joint Chiefs of Staff that proposals along these lines did not sufficiently protect United States security interests in the Pacific and that their discussion might lead to dissension among the Allies prevented their consideration at Dumbarton Oaks.

At the Yalta Conference, the foreign ministers of the Soviet Union, the United Kingdom, and the United States agreed that "consultations"

[2] For an account of early U.S. plans and the effort to work out a joint declaration, see Ruth B. Russell, A *History of the United Nations Charter* (Washington, Brookings Institution, 1958), pp. 84 ff., 175–76, 336–48, and 573–74.

would be held with a view to providing machinery in the Charter "for dealing with territorial trusteeship and dependent areas." In the final Protocol of the Conference, however, the reference to "dependent areas" was dropped, apparently as a concession to Prime Minister Churchill.[3]

During the period between the Yalta and San Francisco Conferences, those in charge of United States planning were so preoccupied with the effort to get agreement throughout the government on a proposed trusteeship system that the United States "temporarily lost sight of its previous interest in an accompanying declaration of general principles for the administration of dependent territories." [4] The idea was included, however, in both Australian and United Kingdom proposals,[5] and these provided the basis for the initial discussions at San Francisco. When it became apparent that agreement would not be easily reached in the Consultative Group composed of the five major powers, a highly unusual procedure was adopted. A working paper was prepared on the basis of the various proposals submitted, consisting of the declaration of general policy and specific provisions for an international trusteeship system.[6] This was presented to the Conference as tentative and binding on no one. Discussion of the working paper then continued concurrently in the Conference committee and in the Consultative Group. As a result of these discussions, the text of the working paper was considerably expanded and modified.[7]

Its opening section, as originally drafted, incorporated the phraseology of the British proposal which in turn reflected the language of the Covenant of the League of Nations (Article 22). It referred to "territories inhabited by peoples not yet able to stand by themselves under the strenuous conditions of the modern world." This language was criticized as outmoded by some delegates, who pointed out that in the economic and military conditions of the "modern world" there were, indeed, few states that could "stand by themselves." [8] It was agreed that the territories covered by the declaration should be characterized as "territories whose peoples have not yet attained a full measure of self-government."

The discussions also resulted in expanding the obligation to ensure

---

[3] Russell, pp. 541–42.   [4] *Ibid.*, p. 808.

[5] UNCIO, *Documents*, III, 548 ff. and 609–14. For the background of these proposals, see Norman Harper and David Sissons, *Australia and the United Nations* (New York, Carnegie Endowment for International Peace, 1959), pp. 69–78; Geoffrey L. Goodwin, *Britain and the United Nations* (New York, Carnegie Endowment for International Peace, 1958), pp. 341–53.

[6] UNCIO, *Documents*, X, 677–78.

[7] For a fuller account of these discussions, see Russell, ch. xxxi.

[8] UNCIO, *Documents*, X, 497–98. The use of the term "sacred trust of civilization" was also considered objectionable and therefore deleted.

the "economic and social advancement" of the peoples concerned to include "political" and "educational" advancement as well. Furthermore, the members administering non-self-governing territories undertook to ensure the "just treatment" of the inhabitants and "their protection against abuses," language that again reflected the League Covenant (Articles 22 and 23). An exchange between the United States and the Netherlands established that these "abuses" included grievances concerning protection of land rights, forced labor, and racial discrimination.[9]

The most controversial issue that arose during the discussions centered on the provision for the development of "self-government appropriate to the varying circumstances of each territory." Within the five-power Consultative Group, China and the Soviet Union sought to add "independence" as a policy objective and in this they had considerable support, especially from former dependent territories such as Iraq and the Philippines. The British and the French were strongly opposed to the inclusion of a reference to "independence." The United States position, though in general favorable, was complicated by disagreement in Washington where concern for congressional reaction and the opinions of the military with regard to future security needs tended to work in favor of a cautious approach.[10] In the end, it was agreed that there would be no reference to "independence" in the declaration regarding non-self-governing territories, but that it would be included among the objectives of the trusteeship system (Article 76). Moreover, the United Kingdom delegate gave assurances that his government did not rule out independence as a possible goal in appropriate cases.[11]

The third subparagraph, with its reference to furthering "international peace and security," was adopted without comment and is another example of the emphasis throughout the Charter upon this primary objective of the Organization. Two additional subparagraphs were added, largely as a result of Australia's desire to provide means by which the general principles could be put into effect.[12] These also reflected some of the ideas that had been developed earlier in the State Department. Subparagraph (d) obligates the administering members "to promote constructive measures of development, to encourage research, and to co-operate with one another and . . . with specialized international bodies with a view to the practical achievement of the social, economic, and scientific purposes" set forth in the article. The reference to "specialized international bodies" covered regional com-

---

[9] UNCIO, *Documents*, X, 619.   [10] See Russell, pp. 817 and 819.

[11] UNCIO, *Documents*, X, 562. See also the statement by the U.S. delegation that "self-government" included the possibility of "independence." U.S. State Department *Bulletin*, XII, No. 308 (May 20, 1945), 930.

[12] For the Australian proposal, see UNCIO, *Documents*, X, 695.

missions, such as the Caribbean Commission. The further development of such commissions had been a significant part of Anglo-American thinking concerning the postwar development of dependent territories.

Finally, under subparagraph (e), the administering states agree to "transmit regularly to the Secretary-General for information purposes . . . statistical and other information of a technical nature relating to economic, social, and educational conditions" in their non-self-governing territories. This obligation is subject to several important limitations. First, the transmission of information is "subject to such limitation as security and constitutional considerations may require." Second, the subparagraph does not apply to trust territories for which international supervisory machinery is established in Chapters XII and XIII of the Charter. Last, the obligation does not extend to information on "political" conditions in the territories.[13]

Application

The interpretation of this article has given rise to extensive controversy, generally revolving around efforts by a majority of members to develop a system of accountability and supervision comparable to that provided for in Chapters XII and XIII. In these efforts, nonadministering members have relied upon: 1) the provisions of Chapter XI of the Charter; 2) the principle of "equal rights and self-determination of peoples" recognized in Article 1 of the Charter; 3) the various Charter provisions concerning "human rights and fundamental freedoms"; 4) the broad powers of the General Assembly under Article 10 to discuss and make recommendations on "any questions or any matters within the scope" of the Charter (occasionally powers under Article 14 have also been cited); and 5) the right of the General Assembly to establish "such subsidiary organs as it deems necessary for the performance of its functions" (Article 22).

Those members of the United Nations administering non-self-governing territories have generally insisted upon a narrower construction of Chapter XI and have invoked the provisions of Article 2(7) prohibiting United Nations intervention in "matters which are essentially within the domestic jurisdiction of any state." Some administering members have also on occasion threatened to withdraw their cooperation. The lines of division between administering and nonadministering members have not in all cases been sharply drawn, for there has been considerable variation in attitude within both groups, and in

---

[13] Inclusion of political information was favored by some, including the Soviet Union. Russell, pp. 819–23.

many instances it has been possible to work out mutually satisfactory accommodations of interests.

From 1946 to 1960, the bulk of the discussion on conditions in non-self-governing territories took place in the Fourth Committee of the General Assembly and the special committees established to assist it.[14] The adoption by the General Assembly in 1960 of the Declaration on the Granting of Independence to Colonial Countries and Peoples marked the beginning of a new United Nations role with regard to non-self-governing territories, a change that was solidified the next year when the Assembly established a special committee having broad responsibility for implementation of the declaration.[15] Since that time, issues concerning non-self-governing territories have been considered primarily by that committee and by the General Assembly itself. With this development, the emphasis has tended to shift away from controversies over the interpretation of Chapter XI of the Charter.

There have been frequent occasions when members administering non-self-governing territories have been accused of not fulfilling their obligations under Article 73, especially the obligation to develop self-government, but the most extensive debates have centered on the interpretation of Article 73(e), and in particular, on the extent of the obligation to transmit information, the way in which that information is to be treated, and the related and basic question of what is a non-self governing territory and on what grounds and by what means this determination is to be made.

Transmission of Information

Article 73(e) establishes the obligation of members administering non-self-governing territories to transmit specific types of information to the Secretary-General "for information purposes." At its first session, the General Assembly invited the Secretary-General to include in his annual report on the work of the Organization a summary of the information transmitted under this article.[16] The Secretary-General thereupon addressed a letter to all members which, among other things, asked them to enumerate the non-self-governing territories under their jurisdiction. In accordance with the replies, a list was drawn up covering seventy-four territories administered by eight

[14] For a fuller account of these discussions through 1955, see Sady, "General Assembly and Non-Self-Governing Territories," ch. xxi in Robert E. Asher et al., *The United Nations and Promotion of the General Welfare* (Washington, Brookings Institution, 1957).

[15] GA Res. 1514(XV), Dec. 14, 1960; 1654(XVI), Nov. 27, 1961.

[16] GA Res. 9(I), Feb. 9, 1946.

United Nations members—Australia, Belgium, Denmark, France, the Netherlands, New Zealand, the United Kingdom, and the United States. This list was tacitly accepted by the Assembly and the administering members were invited to transmit the most recent information at their disposal to the Secretary-General by June 30 of each year.[17]

It was recognized that the usefulness of the information transmitted would be enhanced if some standard form of reporting were adopted. At its second session, the Assembly considered a standard form for the guidance of members in preparing information to be transmitted under Article 73(e). It recommended that members transmitting information "be invited to undertake the necessary steps to render the information as complete and up to date as possible" and to "ensure" that specified items in the standard form were "covered" in so far as they applied to the territories concerned.[18]

The standard form was revised in 1951 and again in 1955.[19] It consists of four parts. A general part covering such items as geography, history, and government is followed by three separate parts on economic, social, and educational conditions. Some of the items were categorized as "optional," but in fact there is nothing mandatory about the document, as it was clearly intended for the "guidance" of the administering members. In addition, the Assembly adopted a number of resolutions indicating its views concerning the methods for transmitting information and the kinds of information the members should submit.[20] Concern over the burden that annual reporting would impose on administrative officials in small territories led to agreement that information on "long range governmental policies" need be provided only once every three years.[21]

One of the most controversial issues concerned the transmission of information on political matters. The question first arose in 1947 when it was noted that some members were submitting such information, while others were not. Three views were expressed. One, held strongly by some of the administering members, was that the legal obligation extends only to the transmission of technical information relating to economic, social, and educational conditions and that the term "political" was intentionally omitted. A second group stressed that Article 73(e) cannot be considered separately from the other subparagraphs of that article, and that the obligation of administering members to

---

[17] GA Res. 66(I), Dec. 14, 1946.   [18] GA Res. 142(II), Nov. 3, 1947.

[19] GA Res. 551(VI), Dec. 7, 1951, and 930(X), Nov. 8, 1955. The 1951 revision was comprehensive; the 1955 revision consisted of the addition of a section on community development.

[20] For more details see *Repertory*, IV, 16–21; *Supp. 1*, II, 154; and *Supp. 2*, III, 181–82.

[21] GA Res. 551(VI), Dec. 7, 1951.

promote political advancement and to develop self-government carries with it a clear obligation to transmit information on political matters. The third view, which largely prevailed, was that while the administering members are under no legal obligation to transmit political information, they should be encouraged to do so in order that the General Assembly can effectively fulfill its functions.

In 1947, the Assembly rejected a proposal "recommending" that states transmit information on local government and instead adopted a resolution stating that "the voluntary transmission" of such information and its summarization by the Secretary-General were "entirely in conformity with the spirit of Article 73 of the Charter and should therefore be duly noted and encouraged." [22] In 1954 the General Assembly, emphasizing that its responsibilities under Article 73 related to political as well as economic, social, and educational advancement, reiterated its view that "the voluntary submission of information" on political developments was "fully in accord with the spirit of Article 73" and invited administering members to give "their utmost co-operation in this regard." [23]

In 1960, in connection with the report that it had asked the Secretary-General to make on the progress of non-self-governing territories,[24] the Assembly "once again" urged the administering members "to extend their full co-operation to the General Assembly in the performance of its functions by transmitting information of a political and constitutional character on development" in the territories they administered.[25] While opposition to this request by most of the administering members had earlier been manifested by negative votes, by 1960 it took the form of abstentions. In September, 1961, the United Kingdom announced that it would in the future send information on political and constitutional progress in its non-self-governing territories.[26]

The voluntary transmission of political information by some administering members was in a sense dependent initially upon the observance of certain ground rules. The information was summarized by the Secretary-General but not analyzed, nor was it discussed or made the subject of a resolution in the General Assembly or its committees.[27] Other members accepted these limitations, it would seem, only because they recognized that otherwise no political information at all would be transmitted. The first step in removing these restraints came in 1961

---

[22] GA Res. 144(II), Nov. 3, 1947.   [23] GA Res. 848(IX), Nov. 22, 1954.

[24] *Progress of the Non-Self-Governing Territories under the Charter.* UN Doc. ST/TRI/SER.A/15/Vols. 1–5.

[25] GA Res. 1535(XV), Dec. 15, 1960.

[26] GAOR/16th Sess./1017th Plen. Mtg./Sept. 27, 1961/p. 118.

[27] Cases involving cessation of the transmission of information were exceptions to these rules. See below, pp. 459–61.

when the Committee on Information from Non-Self-Governing Territories was authorized to examine political and constitutional information transmitted under Article 73(e).[28]

One further question that arose at an early stage was whether the summaries prepared by the Secretary-General must be based solely on information transmitted under Article 73(e). The General Assembly decided that the Secretary-General might use documents published by intergovernmental or scientific bodies and such other official publications as the administering members might transmit.[29] The Secretary-General was further authorized to use "all relevant and comparable official statistical information . . . which had been communicated to the United Nations or to the specialized agencies." [30] In both instances the authorizations were limited to the kinds of information listed in Article 73(e) and the use of "comparable" information required the consent of the member concerned.[31]

Examination of Information

The question of what was to be done with the information transmitted under Article 73(e) was raised early in the first session of the General Assembly. At that time, it rejected a proposal that the Secretary-General report on how the United Nations should exercise its functions under Chapter XI. As already pointed out, the Assembly merely asked the Secretary-General to include a summary of the information transmitted in his annual report.[32] Nonetheless, the Secretary-General submitted to the second part of the session a report in which he suggested the need for an expert body to assist him in preparing the summary and to assist the Assembly in giving it "the attention which it may merit." [33] This suggestion touched off the first of a long series of debates concerning the proper method for handling information transmitted under Article 73.

In general, those members administering non-self-governing territories took the position that there was no need for any special committee; and indeed, they raised doubts concerning the legality of establishing such a body. They stressed that the information was transmitted "for information purposes" only and that the Secretariat was the proper agency to deal with it.

[28] GA Res. 1700(XVI), Dec. 19, 1961.

[29] GA Res. 143(II), Nov. 3, 1947. See also GA Res. 1053(XI), Feb. 20, 1957.

[30] GA Res. 218(III), Nov. 3, 1948. See also GA Res. 1053(XI), Feb. 20, 1957, inviting the Secretary-General to prepare a report on progress in non-self-governing territories.

[31] GA Res. 447(V), Dec. 12, 1950.   [32] GA Res. 9(I), Feb. 9, 1946.

[33] GAOR/1st Sess., 2d Part, 4th Ctte., Part I/Annex 14, pp. 245–47.

This view was not accepted by the majority of members, and it was decided to establish an ad hoc committee on the transmission of information under Article 73(e) to examine the Secretary-General's summary and analysis, to aid the Assembly in considering this information, and to make recommendations regarding future procedure.[34] At the next session, a special committee, set up to examine the information, was authorized to make "procedural" recommendations to the Assembly and "substantive" recommendations on economic, social, and educational conditions in general, but it was not empowered to make recommendations with respect to individual territories; a similar decision was taken the next year.[35] It should be noted that the Assembly, in considering the reports of this and subsequent committees on information from non-self-governing territories, itself refrained from making recommendations regarding individual territories, except in connection with the cessation of the transmission of information.

At the 1949 session of the Assembly, when the special committee was reestablished for a three-year period, it was decided that the committee would each year concentrate its attention in rotation on economic, social, and educational conditions in the territories.[36] The committee's mandate was subsequently renewed for three-year periods in 1952, 1955, and 1958, and for an indefinite period in 1961; in 1963, the committee was "dissolved" and its functions transferred to a special committee established to implement the 1960 Declaration on Granting Independence to Colonial Countries and Peoples.[37]

The principle governing the composition of the various committees on information was established in 1947, when it was decided that the ad hoc committee would be composed of an equal number of administering and nonadministering states. This principle of "parity" was essential in order to obtain the cooperation of the administering members, but the disparity between the membership of the committee and that of the General Assembly itself led to some distrust and by-passing of the committee. The nonadministering members were elected by the Fourth Committee of the General Assembly;[38] the administering members, anxious to limit the role of the committee, insisted that it be

[34] GA Res. 66(I), Dec. 14, 1946. A proposal that the information be examined by the Trusteeship Council was rejected.

[35] GA Res. 146(II), Nov. 3, 1947; 219(III), Nov. 3, 1948.

[36] GA Res. 332(IV), Dec. 2, 1949. In 1951, the name was changed to the Committee on Information from Non-Self-Governing Territories. GA Res. 569(VI), Jan. 18, 1952.

[37] GA Res. 646(VII), Dec. 10, 1952; 933(X), Nov. 8, 1955; 1332(XIII), Dec. 12, 1958; and 1700(XVI), Dec. 19, 1961; 1973(XVIII), Dec. 16, 1963.

[38] The composition of the original ad hoc committee was decided by the Assembly itself. In 1949, procedures were adopted for staggering the terms of office of the nonadministering members.

a subcommittee of the Fourth Committee rather than a subsidiary organ of the Assembly itself.

Whenever the role of the committee on non-self-governing territories was discussed, the debate followed much the same general pattern. A majority of members obviously favored the establishment of a permanent organ with broad terms of reference. A number wished to set up machinery that would subject the administration of the non-self-governing territories to the same degree of international supervision that the Charter provides for trust territories. The administering members opposed the creation of a permanent organ and in general sought to restrict the committee's activities to a minimum. They were successful in large part because of the recognition by other members of the importance of their continuing cooperation.

From time to time, there were changes in the terms of reference of the committee and occasionally it was assigned special tasks. A substantial change occurred in 1961 when the committee was authorized to examine political and constitutional information transmitted under Article 73(e).[39] By that time, the mood of the General Assembly had changed considerably, primarily because many formerly non-self-governing territories had become independent and had also become members of the Organization. Dissatisfaction with the limitations imposed upon discussion of conditions in the non-self-governing territories grew, as did reluctance to make concessions in order to obtain the cooperation of the administering members. This led to the dissolution of the committee on non-self-governing territories and the transfer of its functions to the special committee charged with implementing the Declaration on Granting Independence to Colonial Countries and Peoples.[40] In this body, the principle of parity does not exist, nor does the committee feel itself in any way bound by the restraints that formerly governed the United Nations role with respect to non-self-governing territories. It hears petitioners, makes recommendations on specific territories, and, in fact, has attempted in every way to apply to all non-self-governing territories a system of international supervision no less far-reaching than that which the Charter provides for trust territories.

What Is a Non-Self-Governing Territory?

The Charter does not define a non-self-governing territory, nor do the records of the San Francisco Conference shed much light on what

[39] GA Res. 1700(XVI), Dec. 19, 1961.
[40] GA Res. 1973(XVIII), Dec. 16, 1963.

the drafters of the Charter had in mind. The letter the Secretary-General sent out pursuant to the Assembly's initial resolution in 1946 invited all members to express their opinions on the factors to be taken into account in determining which territories should be considered non-self-governing. In response, some members suggested definitions or criteria, while others expressed the view that it was for the states administering such territories to decide whether they should be considered non-self-governing territories within the meaning of Chapter XI of the Charter.

For the next several years, controversy centered on the decisions by the administering authorities that, because of changes in the status of some of the territories under their administration, they were no longer obligated to transmit the information required under Article 73(e). In some cases, these claims were challenged. Moreover, a majority of members believed that the decision to cease transmitting information was not one to be taken by the administering member alone, but that the United Nations had the right to examine the circumstances and to reach its own conclusions as to whether the obligation to transmit information should continue.

In its third session, the Assembly declared that it was "essential" that the United Nations be "informed" in cases where a member ceased to transmit information because of changes in the constitutional position and status of a non-self-governing territory. Members were requested to communicate the necessary information to the Secretary-General within six months.[41] While not objecting to making the information available informally—since it was a matter of public record—administering members took exception to the implication that the General Assembly could question a decision by an administering member that a territory had ceased to be non-self-governing.

When the responses of the administering members were discussed in 1949, both the United Kingdom and France, in defending their positions, drew attention to the clause in Article 73(e) subjecting the transmission of information to "such limitation" as "constitutional considerations may require." Thus, the United Kingdom explained that Malta, although not fully self-governing, had a government fully responsible for economic, social, and educational matters, and that the United Kingdom was precluded from transmitting information on these subjects.[42] Other members insisted that once a territory had been listed as non-self-governing, the administering member no longer held

[41] GA Res. 222(III), Nov. 3, 1948.
[42] Subsequently, when the constitution of Malta was suspended, the U.K. resumed transmitting information.

sole responsibility for deciding whether there was an obligation to transmit information. A resolution was adopted stating that it was "within the responsibility of the General Assembly to express its opinion on the principles which have guided or which may in the future guide the Members concerned in enumerating the territories for which the obligation exists to transmit information under Article 73(e)." [43] At the same time, the Assembly established a special committee to examine the "factors which should be taken into account in deciding whether any territory is or is not a territory whose people have not yet attained a full measure of self-government."

In 1953, having authorized successive studies, the Assembly recommended that the "list of factors" developed as a result of these studies should be used by the Assembly and the administering members "as a guide in determining whether any Territory, due to changes in its constitutional status, is or is no longer within the scope of Chapter XI of the Charter, in order that . . . a decision may be taken by the General Assembly on the continuation or cessation of the transmission of information required by Chapter XI of the Charter." [44]

The list was divided into three groups of factors, indicative of: 1) independence; 2) other separate systems of self-government; and 3) free association of a territory on an equal basis with the metropolitan or another country. The Assembly asserted that the manner in which a territory could become fully self-governing was "primarily" through the attainment of independence; yet it recognized that self-government could be achieved by a form of association with one or more states if done on the basis of absolute equality and the freely expressed will of the people. The Committee on Information was instructed to study documentation transmitted by administering members concerning the cessation of the transmission of information in the light of the list of factors.

At this same session, in a resolution agreeing that Chapter XI no longer applied to Puerto Rico, the Assembly asserted its "competence" to decide whether a non-self-governing territory "has or has not attained a full measure of self-government." [45] This was the first time this claim had been formally asserted, and the provision gave rise to an extensive debate.[46] Subsequently, similar resolutions were adopted

[43] GA Res. 334(IV), Dec. 2, 1949.
[44] GA Res. 742(VIII), Nov. 27, 1953. See also GA Res. 567(VI), Jan. 18, 1952; 648(VII), Dec. 10, 1952.
[45] GA Res. 748(VIII), Nov. 27, 1953.
[46] Adoption of this resolution was possible only because of the Assembly's decision that resolutions on non-self-governing territories could be adopted by majority vote. For further comments, see Art. 18. The Assembly had previously "noted" that Indonesia had become independent and that the Netherlands had ceased to transmit information. GA Res. 448(V), Dec. 12, 1950.

with respect to Greenland, Surinam and the Netherlands Antilles, Alaska, and Hawaii.[47] From discussions in and resolutions adopted by the General Assembly, it is clear that the majority of members welcome the evolution of a non-self-governing territory to independence and are willing to accept the complete integration of a territory (as in the case of Greenland, Alaska, and Hawaii), but are reluctant to approve any other status as permitting cessation of the transmission of information under Article 73(e).

Portugal and Spain, following their admission to United Nations membership, asserted that they did not administer any territories covered by Chapter XI. Eventually, Spain agreed to transmit information on "all those provinces of Spain which could be of interest to the United Nations."[48] Portugal's continuing refusal to transmit information on its overseas territories brought forth a series of progressively more harshly worded resolutions by the General Assembly.

In 1960, the Assembly declared that the territories were non-self-governing "within the meaning of Chapter XI of the Charter" and that Portugal was under an obligation to transmit information thereon.[49] The following year, the Assembly condemned Portugal for "continuing non-compliance" with its obligations under Chapter XI and for its refusal to cooperate with the Committee on Information from Non-Self-Governing Territories.[50] The Assembly, asserting that it "must . . . continue to discharge its own obligations and responsibilities towards the inhabitants of the territories," established a special committee and authorized it to receive petitions and hear petitioners. The Secretary-General was requested to prepare background papers on the conditions in the territories.

The outbreak of rebellion in some of the territories and the repressive measures taken by Portugal moved the question of the future of the territories far beyond the confines of Chapter XI of the Charter. The situation was considered as "a serious threat to international peace and security," immediate steps toward the granting of independence to the territories were called for, and the Security Council was asked to take appropriate measures.[51]

Displeasure over the attitudes of certain colonial powers with re-

[47] See GA Res. 849(IX), Nov. 22, 1954; 945(X), Dec. 15, 1955; and 1469(XIV), Dec. 12, 1959.

[48] GAOR/14th Sess., 4th Ctte./981st Mtg./Dec. 2, 1959.

[49] GA Res. 1542(XV), Dec. 15, 1960.

[50] GA Res. 1699(XVI), Dec. 19, 1961.

[51] See GA Res. 1807(XVII), Dec. 14, 1962. See also GA Res. 1913(XVIII), Dec. 3, 1963; SC Res., July 31, 1963(S/5380); and SCOR/18th Yr./1963/*Supp.* for July, Aug., and Sept., pp. 63–64. For a full account of the development of this issue see Patricia Wohlgemuth, "The Portuguese Territories and the United Nations," *International Conciliation,* No. 545 (November, 1963).

spect to the transmission of information on territories which many members regarded as non-self-governing gave rise to pressures for a further study of the obligations of members under Chapter XI of the Charter. The proposal, first made in 1956, enjoyed the backing of the increasing number of formerly dependent territories that had become members of the Organization.

Not until 1959, however, could agreement be reached. A special committee was set up, and the following year, on the basis of its report, the General Assembly adopted a set of "principles which should guide members in determining whether or not an obligation exists to transmit the information called for under Article 73(e) of the Charter." [52] This document stated that "*prima facie* there is an obligation to transmit information in respect of a territory which is geographically separate and is distinct ethnically and/or culturally from the country administering it." It recognized that "other elements" may enter into consideration. With regard to the limitation in Article 73(e) concerning security and constitutional considerations, it was stated that the limitation "cannot relieve" a member of its obligations under Chapter XI but can only relate "to the quantum of information" to be transmitted. However, in some circumstances the transmission of information might be precluded.

Three methods by which a non-self-governing territory can be said to have achieved a full measure of self-government are set out: 1) emergence as a sovereign independent state; 2) free association with an independent state; or 3) integration with an independent state. With regard to the last of these, new principles were introduced to the effect that "the integration should be the result of the freely expressed wishes of the territory's peoples . . . through democratic processes . . . impartially conducted and based on universal adult suffrage," and that "the United Nations could, when it deems it necessary, supervise these processes."

Article 74

Members of the United Nations also agree that their policy in respect of the territories to which this Chapter applies, no less than in respect of their metropolitan areas, must be based on the general principle of good-neighbourliness, due account being taken of the interests and well-being of the rest of the world, in social, economic, and commercial matters.

While Article 73 obligates members to recognize the interests of the inhabitants of non-self-governing territories as paramount and to pro-

52 GA Res. 1541(XV), Dec. 15, 1960.

mote their well-being, Article 74 commits them in respect of these territories to the "general principle of good neighbourliness." Obviously, this is at most a guiding principle of policy without any specific legal content. The language recognizes in a general way that other countries have interests in these territories which, if adversely affected by the policies of the administering state, would give them legitimate ground for complaint. It requires members to take these interests into account in formulating policies for the territories in question, but it does not give to other countries any legal protection against policies and practices that might be generally regarded as unneighborly. The article was, apparently, directed in particular against such policies as the closed-door in commercial relations, discriminatory immigration restrictions, and exclusion of or discrimination against nationals of countries other than the administering state in the granting of concessions.

Article 74 "has been the source of little difficulty and little interest." [53] It was adopted without discussion at San Francisco, and has been infrequently cited in discussions in the United Nations, and then usually in connection with the operation of Chapter XI as a whole.

[53] Sady, in Asher, p. 837.

CHAPTER XII

International Trusteeship System

The international trusteeship system is the successor to the mandates system of the League of Nations, but there are significant differences between the two. The mandates system applied only to specific territories detached from the Turkish empire and to Germany's former overseas possessions. The Covenant and the mandates agreements gave the League limited authority to supervise the administration of these territories.[1] The trusteeship system was designed to cover a wider range of territories and gave the United Nations much greater powers.

Some of the early plans considered by the U.S. State Department during World War II envisaged a trusteeship system applicable to *all* dependent territories; one in fact gave the United Nations power to designate the administering authorities, set the terms of the trusteeship, modify those terms, and terminate the trust status of a territory.[2] As planning progressed and conversations were held with the British,[3] a much more modest system evolved.

Provisions for an international trusteeship system were not discussed during the Dumbarton Oaks Conversations primarily because of the opposition of United States military leaders, who argued that such discussion would open up a divisive debate among the Allies concerning the postwar disposition of specific territories.[4] At the Yalta Conference, however, it was agreed that the Charter should provide for a system of trusteeship and that the five major powers would consult on this matter prior to the San Francisco Conference.[5] There was also agreement on the categories of territories to be placed under the system.[6]

It proved impossible for the major powers to consult prior to the conference. The United States continued to encounter difficulties in

---

[1] Quincy Wright, *Mandates under the League of Nations* (Chicago, University of Chicago Press, 1930); Hessel Duncan Hall, *Mandates, Dependencies, and Trusteeships* (New York, Carnegie Endowment for International Peace, 1948).

[2] Ruth B. Russell, *A History of the United Nations Charter* (Washington, Brookings Institution, 1958), especially chs. IV and XIII.

[3] See Geoffrey L. Goodwin, *Britain and the United Nations* (New York, Carnegie Endowment for International Peace, 1958), ch. XIV.

[4] Russell, pp. 343–48.   [5] State Dept., *Malta and Yalta Documents*, p. 844.

[6] See commentary on Art. 77.

devising a plan that satisfied the views of its military leaders concerning the protection of United States security interests in the Pacific.[7] Not until the very eve of the conference was the United States prepared to put forward its proposals.[8] Thus, consultations among the major powers had to proceed concurrently with the discussion in the conference committee; this resulted in considerable confusion and delay.[9]

To expedite matters, it was agreed that a "working paper," based on Australian, British, and United States drafts, should be prepared by the United States delegate, it being understood that the paper was "tentative," binding on no one, and that it in no way affected any positions taken by the various delegations.[10]

The working paper was the subject of extensive debate, with vigorous efforts by some delegations to expand the powers of the Organization in the trusteeship field. As a result of the debate, some additions and modifications were made, but the provisions finally approved by the Conference essentially followed the lines of the original United States proposals.

Article 75

The United Nations shall establish under its authority an international trusteeship system for the administration and supervision of such territories as may be placed thereunder by subsequent individual agreements. These territories are hereinafter referred to as trust territories.

Article 75 commits the United Nations to the establishment of an international trusteeship system. However, the system could come into being only after some territories had been placed under trusteeship and this, as Article 75 makes clear, was to be accomplished by "subsequent individual agreements."

The Preparatory Commission devoted considerable attention to setting up the trusteeship system. Concerned over the possible serious consequences of undue delay, it considered the idea of establishing a temporary trusteeship committee to function until a sufficient number of trusteeship agreements had been concluded. This suggestion was rejected, and the Commission confined itself to recommending that the General Assembly call upon states administering territories under the

[7] See Russell, ch. XXIII; and commentary on Art. 82.

[8] For the text of the proposals, see State Dept., *Postwar Foreign Policy Preparation, 1939–1945*, pp. 686–87.

[9] See Russell, ch. XXXI.

[10] UNCIO, *Documents*, X, 447 and 677–83. See commentary on Art. 73.

League of Nations mandates system to undertake steps for the conclusion of trusteeship agreements.[11] At the first part of the first session of the General Assembly, most of these states declared their intention to place these territories under the trusteeship system. The Assembly welcomed these declarations and invited the states "administering territories now under mandate to undertake practical steps, in concert with the other States directly concerned" to conclude trusteeship agreements and submit them for approval, "preferably not later than the second part of the first session of the General Assembly." [12]

Accordingly, draft agreements for eight former mandated territories were submitted to the Assembly, which after careful consideration approved them on December 13, 1946.[13] The following day, the Assembly proceeded to constitute the Trusteeship Council, which met for the first time on March 26, 1947.

Article 76

The basic objectives of the trusteeship system, in accordance with the Purposes of the United Nations laid down in Article 1 of the present Charter, shall be:

a. to further international peace and security;

b. to promote the political, economic, social, and educational advancement of the inhabitants of the trust territories, and their progressive development towards self-government or independence as may be appropriate to the particular circumstances of each territory and its peoples and the freely expressed wishes of the peoples concerned, and as may be provided by the terms of each trusteeship agreement;

c. to encourage respect for human rights and for fundamental freedoms for all without distinction as to race, sex, language, or religion, and to encourage recognition of the interdependence of the peoples of the world; and

d. to ensure equal treatment in social, economic, and commercial matters for all Members of the United Nations and their nationals, and also equal treatment for the latter in the administration of justice, without prejudice to the attainment of the foregoing objectives and subject to the provisions of Article 80.

The above statement of basic objectives follows closely the statement of fundamental obligations set forth in the Declaration Regarding Non-Self-Governing Territories (Chapter XI). There are, however, important differences, due in large measure to the fact that Article 76 applies

[11] *Report of the Preparatory Commission*, p. 49.
[12] GA Res. 9(I), Feb. 9, 1946.   [13] See commentary on Arts. 77 and 79.

to territories which are by agreement placed under international supervision, with the administering authorities exercising only the powers of a trustee as defined in the trusteeship agreements.

In defining the basic purposes of the trusteeship system, the Charter goes far beyond the provisions in the Covenant of the League of Nations. The purposes of the League mandates system were not brought together in one place or stated in generalized terms. The well-being and development of "peoples not yet able to stand by themselves under the strenuous conditions of the modern world" were recognized as general overall purposes in Article 22 of the Covenant. And, in Article 23(b), League members further undertook "to secure just treatment of the native inhabitants of territories under their control." The attainment of independence was a principal objective in so far as the Class A mandates were concerned. Other objectives were set forth with respect to the Class B mandates: "freedom of conscience and religion"; prohibition of abuses such as the slave trade, the arms traffic, and the liquor traffic; prohibition of fortifications and military training of natives for other than police purposes and the defense of the territory; and "equal opportunity for the trade and commerce of other members of the League." In the case of territories placed under Class C mandates, only those purposes relating to the interests of the indigenous population were recognized. The more specific statement of basic objectives of the trusteeship system, as incorporated in the Charter, is yet another reflection of the wider acceptance of the principle of international accountability.

International Peace and Security

Article 76 states that a basic objective of the trusteeship system, "in accordance with the Purposes of the United Nations laid down in Article 1" of the Charter,[14] is to further international peace and security. This view that the trust territories should play their part in the maintenance of international peace and security finds further expression in Article 84 of the Charter and calls for no detailed comment here.

Political, Economic, Social, and Educational Advancement

Article 76(b) was the subject of considerable controversy during the drafting of the Charter and later in the United Nations, especially in the General Assembly. As pointed out in the commentary on Article 73,

[14] This reference to Art. 1 was included on the initiative of the Soviet Union. See Russell, p. 831.

the exclusion of any reference to "independence" in that article was accepted at San Francisco on condition that "independence" would be included in the statement of the objectives of the trusteeship system. In Article 76(b) the basic objective of the trusteeship system is declared to be the "progressive development towards self-government or independence." Thus, "self-government" and "independence" become alternative goals. The factors determining the choice of alternatives as stated in Article 76(b) are: "the particular circumstances of each territory and its peoples"; the "freely expressed wishes of the peoples"; and the terms of each trusteeship agreement.

At the San Francisco Conference, Egypt sought to eliminate the reference to "the terms of each trusteeship agreement." Without this phrase, the provision was unacceptable to France and the United Kingdom, and the Egyptian amendment was defeated because of the realization that "if the objectives were considered too flagrantly objectionable by the metropolitan governments, few territories would be put under trusteeship." The reference in Article 76(b) to the "freely expressed wishes of the peoples concerned" stemmed from a proposal by the Soviet Union to include a specific reference to the right of self-determination. To this, Britain and France raised objections, and the final wording was in the nature of a compromise suggested by the United States.[15]

ECONOMIC ADVANCEMENT. In addition to a general statement of the obligation to administer a trust territory in such manner as to achieve the basic objectives laid down in Article 76, all the trusteeship agreements contained specific articles concerning such matters as the provision of public services, and the protection of land rights and natural resources. Because the economies of most of the trust territories are basically agricultural, the Trusteeship Council and the General Assembly have paid particular attention to such matters as the protection of land rights of the inhabitants and the improvement of agricultural productivity. In this connection, the Council, at the Assembly's request, established in 1951 a committee on rural economic development to study prevailing policies, laws, and practices relating to land utilization and alienation in the trust territories.[16] Other subjects in which the Assembly and the Council have shown special concern include long-range planning for economic development; diversification of the economy; improvement in transit, communications, and fiscal systems; and the fuller participation of the indigenous inhabitants in the economic life of the territory.[17] The economic future of certain territories after

[15] Russell, pp. 831–33.
[16] See GA Res. 438(V), Dec. 2, 1950; and 561(VI), Jan. 18, 1952.
[17] For details see *Repertory*, IV, 112–22; *Supp. 1*, II, 182–86; and *Supp. 2*, III, 216–17.

the termination of their trusteeship status has also been a matter of special concern (particularly Somalia and Ruanda-Urundi).

SOCIAL ADVANCEMENT. The elimination of such abuses as slavery, forced labor, and traffic in liquor, drugs, and arms received major emphasis in the League mandates system. The trusteeship system substitutes the more general but positive objective of "social advancement." Only three of the trusteeship agreements contained specific provisions for the elimination of abuses such as those listed above.[18] Most of the discussion in the General Assembly and the Trusteeship Council relating to social advancement in the trust territories has centered on the promotion of human rights and fundamental freedoms as specifically provided for in Article 76(c). Subjects of special concern to the two organs have included abolition of corporal punishment, improvement in the status of women, improvement in medical and health facilities and training, and labor conditions in the trust territories.[19]

EDUCATIONAL ADVANCEMENT. Recognizing the close relationship between education and the progress of the trust territories toward self-government or independence, both the General Assembly and the Trusteeship Council have attached special importance to the educational advancement of the inhabitants of the trust territories. Most recommendations in this area have concerned the improvement of educational facilities and the training of teachers. Under the program initiated by the General Assembly in 1952, member states have made a number of scholarships available to students from the trust territories.

Progressive Development Toward Self-Government or Independence

None of the Charter provisions concerning the international trusteeship system has raised more controversy than those concerning the "political advancement" of the inhabitants of trust territories and "their progressive development towards self-government or independence." It has taken the form of constant pressures on the administering authorities to accelerate the pace of political development and of repeated criticism of any measures taken by the administering authorities which might impede that development. The administering authorities have generally maintained that the long-range interests of the inhabitants are best served by an orderly and more slowly paced rate of development.

[18] The three were those for Western Samoa, Italian Somaliland, and the Pacific Islands strategic trusteeship. The exclusion of such provisions from the agreements for the other African trust territories was justified on the ground that such matters were already covered by existing treaties and conventions.

[19] For details, see *Repertory*, IV, 123–31; *Supp. 1*, II, 186–87; and *Supp. 2*, III, 216–17.

All the trusteeship agreements contain special provisions concerning the political advancement of the inhabitants of the trust territories. Under them, the administering authorities undertake to promote the development of free political institutions suitable to the territory, to assure the inhabitants a progressively increasing share in the administration and other services of the territory, and to develop the participation of the inhabitants in the various branches of government. In line with these undertakings, the General Assembly and the Trusteeship Council have adopted numerous recommendations on such matters as extension of suffrage, development of legislative institutions, and preparation of the inhabitants for governmental responsibilities.[20]

None of the trusteeship agreements, except the one for Somaliland,[21] contains a specific reference to the goal of "self-government or independence" or a specific date by which the objectives of Article 76(b) are to be achieved. When the first eight draft trusteeship agreements were considered by the General Assembly, it was proposed that each agreement set a specific date when the trust territory would be declared "fully self-governing or independent." It was argued that experience had shown that colonial powers hindered the advancement of peoples under their control on the ground that they were not prepared to exercise a greater degree of self-government. The administering powers in turn stressed that it was impossible to fix in advance a date when the people of a trust territory would be in a position to exercise such powers. The proposal was defeated, as was another proposal that specific dates be fixed after the trusteeship system had been in operation for five years.[22]

In subsequent discussions on the operations of the trusteeship system, the Assembly has constantly sought specific information as to when and how each of the trust territories is to attain self-government or independence, the "ultimate objective" of the trusteeship system.[23] At its sixth session, the Assembly invited each administering authority to include in its annual report information as to the timing and the manner in which the territories could expect to attain this objective.[24] Dissatisfied with the responses, the Assembly further requested the Trusteeship Council to include in its annual report to the Assembly a separate section on this matter, specifying in particular the measures taken with respect to consultations with the inhabitants, development

[20] See *Repertory*, IV, 108–12; *Supp. 1*, II, 180–82; and *Supp. 2*, III, 216–17.
[21] For the special circumstances surrounding the conclusion of this agreement, see commentary on Arts. 77 and 79.
[22] GAOR/1st Sess., 2d Part, 4th Ctte./23d Mtg./Dec. 9, 1946/p. 147.
[23] See GA Res. 226(III), Nov. 18, 1948.
[24] GA Res. 558(VI), Jan. 18, 1952. See also GA Res. 321(IV), Nov. 15, 1949, regarding instructions to visiting missions to report on the steps taken toward self-government or independence.

of organs of government and of universal suffrage, training and selection of indigenous persons for administrative responsibility, and development of adequate public revenue.[25] Subsequently, the Assembly recommended that the administering authorities intensify their efforts to develop representative organs of government and administration in the territories, and the increased participation of the indigenous inhabitants therein as a means of facilitating an appropriate determination of the date on which the peoples of the territories would be prepared for self-government or independence.[26]

The implementation of these resolutions ran into some resistance from the administering authorities, most of which shared the view that it was neither possible nor desirable to determine the period by which the territory might attain self-government or independence.[27] By 1956, however, the Trusteeship Council had accepted the idea of giving special consideration to the measures taken in each trust territory for attaining the objective of self-government or independence, and particularly of establishing intermediate target dates.[28] By this time, it had become clear that a number of trusteeship agreements would soon be terminated as the result of the attainment of the objectives set forth in Article 76(b). Thus, the issue of fixing target dates and special measures for their achievement lost most of its urgency.

Another center of controversy, especially during the early history of the trusteeship system, has been the issue of "administrative unions." With three exceptions (Western Samoa, Nauru, and Italian Somaliland), trusteeship agreements have authorized the administering authorities to constitute "a customs, fiscal or administrative union or federation with adjacent territories" under their sovereignty or control.

When the first draft trusteeship agreements were examined by the General Assembly, many members saw in these provisions evidence of "annexationist" designs by the administering authorities. They expressed fear that the special status of the trust territories would be endangered and the advancement of the inhabitants slowed. Proposals to delete the provisions from the trusteeship agreements were rejected, but only after the administering authorities had given assurance that they did not consider that these provisions empowered them to "establish any form of political association" between the trust territory and an adjacent territory that would involve annexation of the trust territory in any sense or have the effect of modifying its status.[29]

[25] GA Res. 752(VIII), Dec. 9, 1953.
[26] GA Res. 858(IX), Dec. 14, 1954.
[27] See, in particular, the debate in TCOR/17th Sess./687th Mtg./Mar. 16, 1956/pp. 267 ff.
[28] This change was largely due to a change in the position taken by the U.S.
[29] GAOR/1st Sess., 2d Part, 4th Ctte./1946/*Annex* 72 (UN Doc. A/258 and Add. 1), pp. 1544–45.

Following the entry into force of the trusteeship agreements, all arrangements and proposals for administrative unions were subject to particularly close scrutiny by both the General Assembly and the Trusteeship Council. In 1949, the Assembly adopted a set of principles concerning administrative unions which included provisions that the Council be notified before new unions were established or old ones extended, that a separate judicial organ and a separate legislative body be established for each territory, and that the freely expressed wishes of the peoples of the territory be taken into account.[30] The Assembly also reaffirmed the principle, previously endorsed by it and the Council, that any such union must not in any way hamper the free evolution of each trust territory toward self-government or independence. The Trusteeship Council subsequently established a standing committee on administrative unions and listed four "safeguards" it considered necessary to preclude the possibility of prejudicing the attainment of the objectives of the trusteeship system.[31]

In considering the progress of trust territories toward self-government or independence, the Trusteeship Council and, to an even greater extent, the General Assembly have paid particular attention to the provision in Article 76(b) concerning the "freely expressed wishes of the peoples" of the trust territories. The principle of consultation[32] with the inhabitants concerning the achievement of the objectives of Article 76(b) has been frequently endorsed both explicitly and implicitly in the actions taken by the Assembly and the Council.

The General Assembly, for example, invited the administering authorities to submit information on the manner in which the freely expressed wishes of the peoples concerned were being taken into account.[33] It asked the Trusteeship Council to specify in its reports the measures taken with respect to "consultations with the inhabitants"[34] and recommended that the visiting missions seek out public opinion on important problems in the trust territories, undertake popular consultations, and encourage public discussion on the annual reports of the administering authorities.[35]

Concern over the proper method of consultation mounted as many of the trust territories reached a point where independence or self-government appeared imminent. Since the trusteeship agreement for

[30] GA Res. 326(IV), Nov. 15, 1949. See also GA Res. 224(III), Nov. 18, 1948.
[31] TC Res. 293(VII), July 17, 1950.
[32] Only the trusteeship agreements for French Togoland and French Cameroons contained specific provisions. See Art. 5 of respective trusteeship agreements, *Y.U.N.*, 1946–47, pp. 197 and 200, respectively.
[33] GA Res. 558(VI), Jan. 18, 1952.   [34] GA Res. 752(VIII), Dec. 9, 1953.
[35] GA Res. 853(IX), Dec. 14, 1954. The resolution also made recommendations concerning the handling of petitions that might have a special bearing on public opinion in the trust territories.

British Togoland was the first to be terminated and set the general pattern for other cases, the process in this first case will be described in some detail.

British Togoland had been administered under the trusteeship agreement as an integral part of the adjacent territory of the Gold Coast. At its ninth session (1954), the Assembly had before it a memorandum from the administering authority stating that, since the Gold Coast would soon become independent, it would be necessary to amend, replace, or terminate the trusteeship agreement for British Togoland. The administering authority posed the question whether the objectives set forth in Article 76(b) could be considered as having been attained if the trust territory were to become an integral part of a fully self-governing Gold Coast. Noting that any change in the agreement must be arrived at by agreement between the Assembly and the administering authority, the memorandum suggested that the United Nations arrange to ascertain, by whatever means it considered desirable and appropriate, the freely expressed wishes of the inhabitants of the territory.[36]

The situation was complicated by the fact that the Assembly had previously declared that the unification of British Togoland and the neighboring trust territory under French administration was "the manifest aspiration of the majority of the peoples,"[37] a view which the administering authorities considered highly dubious. In adopting the course favored by the United Kingdom, the Assembly would in effect be reversing itself. It nonetheless decided:

. . . in view of the eventual revision or termination of the Trusteeship Agreement, that steps should be taken, in the light of the particular circumstances of the Trust Territory, to ascertain the wishes of the inhabitants as to their future, without prejudice to the eventual solution they may choose whether it be independence, unification of an independent Togoland under British administration with an independent Togoland under French administration, unification with an independent Gold Coast, or some other self-governing or independent status.[38]

The Trusteeship Council was asked to consider what arrangements should be made for implementing this decision.

The Council's visiting mission to the two Togolands favored a plebiscite under United Nations supervision in British Togoland on the following questions:

[36] GAOR/9th Sess./1954/*Annexes*, agenda items 35 and 52.
[37] GA Res. 750C(VIII), Dec. 8, 1953. Continuing sentiment in favor of unification complicated the process of terminating not only the trusteeship agreement for British Togoland, but also the agreement for French Togoland.
[38] GA Res. 860(IX), Dec. 14, 1954.

1. Do you want the integration of Togoland under British administration with an independent Gold Coast?

2. Do you want the separation of Togoland under British administration from the Gold Coast and its continuance under trusteeship, pending the ultimate determination of its political future? [39]

The mission considered that full United Nations observation and supervision at all stages of arrangements for conducting the plebiscite were essential.

The mission's report was transmitted by the Council to the Assembly, which in turn appointed a United Nations Plebiscite Commissioner to organize and conduct a plebiscite to ascertain the wishes of the inhabitants of the territory concerning the two questions posed in the visiting mission's report.[40]

Following the plebiscite on May 9, 1956, the Council adopted a resolution noting that the "will of the majority of the inhabitants, as expressed at the plebiscite . . . is in favour of union of the Territory with an independent Gold Coast." [41]

On the basis of the Council's recommendations, the Assembly expressed its "approval" of the union of British Togoland with an independent Gold Coast. At the same time, it "resolved," with the agreement of the administering authority, that, "on the date on which the Gold Coast becomes independent and the union with it of the Territory of Togoland under British administration takes place, the Trusteeship Agreement approved by the General Assembly in resolution 63(I) of December 13, 1946 shall cease to be in force, the objectives of trusteeship having been attained." [42]

The termination of other trusteeship agreements followed much the same pattern of interrelationships between the administering authority and the organs of the United Nations—that is, the visiting missions, the Trusteeship Council, the General Assembly, and, in a majority of cases, the special bodies established by the Assembly to assist in ascertaining the wishes of the inhabitants in the trust territories.

The General Assembly has never considered that it was for the administering authority alone to determine when and how a trusteeship agreement was to be terminated. The Assembly has at every stage asserted its right to review the actions taken or contemplated by the administering authorites in order to ascertain whether they are in the best interests of the inhabitants of the trust territories. While not always successful in getting the administering authorities to accept its

[39] TCOR/5th Special Sess./1955/*Supp.* 2.
[40] GA Res. 944(X), Dec. 15, 1955.
[41] TC Res. 1496(XVIII), July 31, 1956.
[42] GA Res. 1045(XI), Dec. 13, 1956.

views, the Assembly has by no means merely gone along with whatever proposals the administering authority has put forward.

Human Rights and Fundamental Freedoms

The phraseology used in the first part of Article 76(c) is taken from the statement of purposes in Article 1(3) of the Charter.[43] The trusteeship agreements, without exception, contain provisions intended to give effect to this clause. Most of the agreements specifically obligate the administering authority to guarantee to the inhabitants of the trust territory freedom of conscience, speech, press, assembly, petition, worship and religious training, and migration and movement, subject only to the requirements of public order and morality.

"Human rights and fundamental freedoms" in the trust territories have for the most part been discussed in the Trusteeship Council and the General Assembly in conjunction with the attainment of the objectives listed in Article 76(b) of the Charter. Among the specific subjects with which the two organs have concerned themselves are the following: [44] Any evidence of racial discrimination in the trust territory has been carefully scrutinized. The General Assembly has recommended the abolition of discriminatory laws and practices as contrary to the principles of the Charter and the trusteeship agreements, and the Council has also urged the administering authorities to ensure that no such laws or practices exist in the territories.[45] The elimination of disparities, based on racial grounds, in such matters as wages and the availability of educational and health facilities, improving the generally inferior status of women in the trust territories, and the abolition of corporal punishment, which the Trusteeship Council declared inconsistent with the Universal Declaration of Human Rights, have also been the subjects of recommendations to the administering authorities. In general, the administering authorities have sought to carry out these recommendations, although considerations of order, security, and native customs have sometimes hindered prompt or full compliance.

The Trusteeship Council and, even more, the General Assembly have been especially concerned over any actions by the administering authority that might interfere with the political rights of the inhabitants of the trust territories, in particular their freedom to engage in political activities. In this area the recommendations of the two organs have come most frequently into conflict with the views of the adminis-

[43] For comment on the meaning of the terms "human rights" and "fundamental freedoms," see Art. 1(3).

[44] For further examples, see *Repertory,* IV, 148–54; *Supp. 1,* II, 212–14; and *Supp. 2,* III, 263–66.

[45] GA Res. 323(IV), Nov. 15, 1949; TC Res. 127(VI), Mar. 28, 1950.

tering authorities concerning the requirements of public order and security.

Equality of Treatment

Article 76(d) lists objectives that relate to the interests of members of the United Nations, as distinguished from the interests of the indigenous population of the trust territory. It seeks to ensure in the trust territories "equal treatment in social, economic, and commercial matters" and "in the administration of justice" to all the United Nations members and their nationals.

The principle of equality of opportunity has a long history. It was applied to the Congo Basin by the Berlin Convention of 1885.[46] It was recognized in Article 22 of the Covenant in so far as Class B mandates were concerned, and was also applied in Class A mandates, although not specifically required by the provisions of the Covenant. As for Class C mandates, this clause was omitted, with the result that they were in this respect assimilated into colonial areas. This had long been an issue between the mandatory powers and the United States, which sought the extension of nondiscriminatory open-door policies to all the mandates.[47]

In the discussions among the five major powers at San Francisco, the United States proposed general nondiscriminatory policies in all trust areas to cover "economic and other civil activities of nationals of all member states." France and Britain objected that the application of such policies in the Class B mandates had benefited outsiders and worked to the disadvantage of the native populations.[48] To meet this point, it was agreed that the statement of the principle of equality of treatment would be subject to the qualification that it should not prejudice the advancement of the inhabitants, and it was in this form that the principle was finally included in the Charter.

Application of the principle of equality of treatment to all trust territories represented an advance over previous practice. However, the "qualification" included in Article 76(d) virtually permitted the administering authorities to ignore the principle if they so chose. The objectives of the article are "subject to the provisions of Article 80," which conserves existing rights pending the conclusion of a trusteeship agreement. This reservation had the effect that, only to the extent agreed upon in the individual trusteeship agreements, were existing rights affected by the provisions of Article 76(d). Thus, it protected the position of states administering Class C mandates, which were not

[46] *British and Foreign State Papers*, LXXVI, 4–20.
[47] See Russell, p. 333.   [48] *Ibid.*, p. 827.

required under the mandate agreements to apply the principle of equal treatment. Moreover, by stating that the objectives in Article 76(d) were to be sought "without prejudice to the attainment" of other objectives listed in the article, the Charter, in effect, gave the administering authorities considerable leeway in deciding the manner of application of the principle.

To carry out the objectives listed in Article 76(d), all the agreements for the African trust territories obligated the administering authorities to take "all necessary steps to ensure equal treatment in social, economic, industrial, and commercial matters" for all United Nations members and their nationals. They agreed to ensure the same rights to all nationals of United Nations members as to their own nationals in respect of entry and residence, freedom of transit and navigation, acquisition of property, the protection of person and property, and the exercise of professions and trades; not to discriminate on grounds of nationality against nationals of any United Nations member in matters relating to the grant of concessions for the development of natural resources and not to grant concessions having the character of a general monopoly; and to ensure equal treatment in the administration of justice to the nationals of all United Nations members. The rights conferred on nationals of United Nations members apply also to companies and associations controlled by such nationals.

These agreements further provided that measures to give effect to the above would be subject "to the over-riding duty" of the administering authority, "to promote the political, economic, social, and educational advancement of the inhabitants" of the trust territory, to carry out the other basic objectives of the international trusteeship system, and to maintain peace, order, and good government.

The relevant provisions in the strategic trusteeship agreement for the Pacific Islands are quite different in that the United States grants "most-favored nation" treatment only to other United Nations members and their nationals, that is, treatment "no less favorable" than that accorded to the national companies and associations of any other member "except the Administering Authority." [49]

It should be noted that these islands, under the League system, were classified as Class C mandates, in which the open-door policy did not apply. This was also true of the territories of Western Samoa, New Guinea, and Nauru. When these territories were placed under the trusteeship system, no specific provisions concerning equality of treatment were included in the trusteeship agreements, although in each case, the agreement contained a general statement by which the administering authority undertook to administer the territory in accor-

[49] For further comment, see Art. 83.

dance with the provisions of the Charter, and in such manner as to achieve the basic objectives of the international trusteeship system, set forth in Article 76 of the Charter.[50] When the agreements were considered by the General Assembly, efforts to include in them provisions similar to those mentioned above for the African trust territories were unsuccessful. The administering authorities (Australia and New Zealand) objected, stressing the paramountcy of the interests of the inhabitants.

During the discussions in the General Assembly on the first trusteeship agreements, there were objections to the inclusion in some of them of provisions expressly permitting the creation of monopolies under certain circumstances. Considerable skepticism was expressed as to the wisdom and propriety of permitting such monopolies, both because of possible violation of the equality principle and because of adverse effects they might have on the economic development of the territories. Opposition was somewhat abated by statements made by the administering authorities that they had no intention of using the granting of private monopolies as normal instruments of policy, that such monopolies would be granted only when essential to economic development in the interests of the inhabitants, and that in these special cases they would be granted for limited periods and promptly reported to the Trusteeship Council.[51]

Article 77

1. The trusteeship system shall apply to such territories in the following categories as may be placed thereunder by means of trusteeship agreements:

   a. territories now held under mandate;

   b. territories which may be detached from enemy states as a result of the Second World War; and

   c. territories voluntarily placed under the system by states responsible for their administration.

2. It will be a matter for subsequent agreement as to which territories in the foregoing categories will be brought under the trusteeship system and upon what terms.

The territories to be covered by the international trusteeship system and the means of bringing such territories into that system were the subject of extensive consideration during the entire period of planning

---

[50] The trusteeship agreement for Western Samoa also quotes Art. 76 in its entirety.

[51] GAOR/1st Sess., 2d Part, 4th Ctte./22d Mtg./Dec. 4, 1946, pp. 166–67.

for a postwar international organization. At the time of the Dumbarton Oaks Conversations, the U.S. State Department favored provisions along the following lines: "subject to such exceptions as may be made by common agreement in the interest of international peace and security," a system of international trusteeship should be established by which the international organization would "(a) succeed to the rights, titles, and interest of the Principal Allied and Associated Powers . . . and the rights and responsibilities of the League of Nations" with respect to mandated territories and "(b) acquire authority over certain territories" that might be detached from the enemy states following World War II. The General Assembly might extend the system "to any territories for which assistance is requested by member states having control over such territories." [52]

As already noted, proposals for a trusteeship system were not discussed during the Dumbarton Oaks Conversations, primarily because of objections by United Sates military leaders. At the Yalta Conference, however, it was agreed that the trusteeship system would apply to territories in the following categories: "(a) existing mandates of the League of Nations; (b) territories detached from the enemy as a result of the present war; (c) any other territory which might voluntarily be placed under trusteeship." It was further agreed that "it will be a matter for subsequent agreement which territories within the above categories will be placed under trusteeship." [53]

As a result of discussions within the United States government, its proposals for a trusteeship system were further refined. In particular, the voluntary nature of the system was emphasized by providing that the system would apply only to areas covered by the terms of trusteeship agreements.[54]

During the discussions at San Francisco, France proposed the elimination of any mention of "territories voluntarily placed" under the system.[55] Australia and the Philippines suggested the application of the trusteeship system to all dependent territories.[56] Egypt proposed the elimination of all references to "subsequent agreements"; this by implication would have permitted the Organization to decide what territories should come under the system. Guatemala, safeguarding its claims regarding British Honduras, proposed that the trusteeship system be declared inapplicable to "any territory in dispute between members of the Organization." None of these proposals was accepted,

[52] Russell, p. 345.   [53] State Dept., *Malta and Yalta Documents*, p. 977.
[54] Russell, p. 579.   [55] *Ibid.*, p. 824.
[56] For background of the Australian proposal, see Norman Harper and David Sissons, *Australia and the United Nations* (New York, Carnegie Endowment for International Peace, 1959), pp. 69 ff. For early U.S. plans for an all-inclusive system, see Russell, pp. 85–89 and 321 ff.

and the text finally agreed upon followed the lines of the decision reached at Yalta.

The Mandated Territories

Despite hopes that the trusteeship system would have wide application, it has been restricted, with one exception, to the former mandated territories, and not all of those were brought within the system.

None of the Class A mandated territories was placed under United Nations trusteeship. Article 78 declares the trusteeship system inapplicable to territories that have become United Nations members; three original members of the Organization had previously been mandated territories. One of these, Iraq, had become independent in October, 1932, and was a member of the League and an original member of the United Nations. Syria and Lebanon were also original members of the United Nations, despite the fact that final arrangements with the mandatory power, France, had not yet been concluded. As for Transjordan, the United Kingdom announced at the first part of the first session of the General Assembly its intention of terminating the mandate.[57] In March, 1946, a treaty formalizing the independence of Transjordan was concluded, and the League Assembly at its final session in April adopted a resolution welcoming the termination of the mandate.[58]

The only remaining territory in the Class A category was Palestine. The United Kingdom, as the mandatory power, having failed to work out arrangements satisfactory to the Jewish and Arab populations in the territory, brought the question of the future of Palestine to the General Assembly in the spring of 1947. While there was general agreement that the mandate should be terminated, there were highly conflicting views regarding the future of Palestine. Nevertheless, the General Assembly adopted a resolution calling for the termination of the mandate, and the establishment of separate Jewish and Arab states, with Jerusalem being placed under an international regime with the Trusteeship Council as the administering authority.[59] When it became clear that this plan could not be implemented by peaceful means, the United States proposed that the territory be placed under temporary United Nations trusteeship, but this proposal failed to gain wide support. Proclamation of the independence of the state of Israel on May 14, 1948, preceded by a few hours the relinquishment of the mandate by the United Kingdom. Subsequently on May 11, 1949, Israel was

[57] GAOR/1st Sess., 1st Part/11th Plen. Mtg./Jan. 17, 1946, p. 167.
[58] LN, *Official Journal, Special Supp. 194,* 7th Plen. Mtg., Apr. 18, 1946, p. 58.
[59] GA Res. 181(II), Nov. 29, 1947.

admitted to United Nations membership. No separate Arab state was established, and, because of opposition from both sides, the international regime for Jerusalem never came into force.

All the territories classified as Class B mandates under the League of Nations were placed under the trusteeship system when the General Assembly, on December 13, 1946, approved trusteeship agreements for the British Cameroons, the French Cameroons, British Togoland, French Togoland, Tanganyika (under British administration), and Ruanda-Urundi (under Belgian administration).

Of the Class C mandates, all but one were brought into the United Nations trusteeship system. The trusteeship agreements submitted by Australia for New Guinea and by New Zealand for Western Samoa were approved by the General Assembly on December 13, 1946.[60] At its second session, the Assembly approved the trusteeship agreement for Nauru to be administered by Australia on behalf of itself, New Zealand, and the United Kingdom.[61]

In these cases, as well as in the cases of the Class B mandates mentioned above, the transfer from the mandates system to the trusteeship system was accomplished without any change in the administering authority. The Pacific Islands, which Japan had held under the League mandates system, presented a different situation. This mandate was never regarded by the League as terminated or in any way affected by Japan's withdrawal from the League in March, 1935, or by the outbreak of World War II. In signing the Instrument of Surrender of September 2, 1945, Japan accepted the terms of the Potsdam Proclamation and the Cairo Declaration with regard to the disposition of the Islands. In February, 1947, the United States, which had occupied the Islands during the course of the war, submitted a draft trusteeship agreement to the Security Council, designating the Islands as a strategic area under the terms of Article 82 of the Charter, with the United States as the administering authority. Although there was some feeling that action should be postponed until a peace treaty with Japan came into force, the United States took the position that the Islands had never belonged to Japan and that the approval of the agreement would be in accordance with the General Assembly's resolution inviting members "now administering territories held under mandate" to undertake practical steps to bring such territories within the trusteeship system.[62] The draft agreement was thereupon approved by the Security Council on April 2, 1947.[63]

Of all the territories mandated under the League of Nations, only

60 GA Res. 63(I), Dec. 13, 1946.   61 GA Res. 140(II), Nov. 1, 1947.
62 GA Res. 9(1), Feb. 9, 1946.   63 For further comment, see Arts. 82 and 83.

Table 6

TERRITORIES UNDER UNITED NATIONS TRUSTEESHIP

Territory	Administering Authority	Previous Mandate Status	Approval of Trusteeship Agreement	Termination of Trusteeship Agreement	Admitted to United Nations
Cameroons (Br.)	United Kingdom	Class B (United Kingdom)	GA Res. 63(I), Dec. 13, 1946	North section joined to Nigeria; south section to Cameroons. GA Res. 1608(XV), Apr. 21, 1961	
Cameroons (Fr.)	France	Class B (France)	GA Res. 63(I), Dec. 13, 1946	Became independent Jan. 1, 1960. GA Res. 1349(XIII), March 13, 1959	GA Res. 1467(XV), Sept. 20, 1960
Marianas, Caroline, and Marshall Islands	United States	Class C (Japan)	SC Res., Apr. 2, 1947		
Nauru	Australia (on behalf of Australia, New Zealand, and United Kingdom)	Class C (Australia)	GA Res. 140(II), Nov. 1, 1947	Became independent Jan. 31, 1968. GA Res. 2111(XX), Dec. 21, 1965	
New Guinea	Australia	Class C (Australia)	GA Res. 63(I), Dec. 13, 1946		
Ruanda-Urundi	Belgium	Class B (Belgium)	GA Res. 63(I), Dec. 13, 1946	Became independent states of Rwanda and Burundi. GA Res. 1746(XVI), June 27, 1962	GA Res. 1748 and 1749 (XVII), Sept. 18, 1962

Territory	Administering Authority	Classification	Trusteeship Agreement	Status	Termination
Samoa (Western)	New Zealand	Class C (New Zealand)	GA Res. 63(I), Dec. 13, 1946	Became independent Jan. 1, 1962. GA Res. 1626(XVI), Oct. 18, 1961	GA Res. 1479(XV), Sept. 20, 1960
Somalia	Italy	Italian colony	GA Res. 442(V), Dec. 2, 1950	Became independent July 1, 1960. GA Res. 1418(XIV), Dec. 5, 1959	GA Res. 1667(XVI), Dec. 14, 1961
Tanganyika	United Kingdom	Class B (United Kingdom)	GA Res. 63(I), Dec. 13, 1946	Became independent Dec. 9, 1961. GA Res. 1642(XVI), Nov. 6, 1961	GA Res. 1118(XI), March 8, 1957
Togoland (Br.)	United Kingdom	Class B (United Kingdom)	GA Res. 63(I), Dec. 13, 1946	Joined with Gold Coast to form Ghana March 6, 1957. GA Res. 1044(XI), Dec. 13, 1956	GA Res. 1477(XV), Sept. 20, 1960
Togoland (Fr.)	France	Class B (France)	GA Res. 63(I), Dec. 13, 1946	Became independent as Togo, April 27, 1960. GA Res. 1253(XIII), Nov. 14, 1958 and 1416(XIV), Dec. 15, 1959	

one, South West Africa, was neither placed under the international trusteeship system nor transformed into an independent state. As early as the San Francisco Conference, South Africa, the mandatory power, had indicated its intention of annexing the territory.[64] When the question was first considered by the Assembly, South Africa's plan for incorporation of the territory met with strong protests from other members. The Assembly refused to accede to the plan, recommended that the territory be placed under the trusteeship system, and invited South Africa to propose a draft agreement for its consideration. Although South Africa did not proceed with the annexation, it refused to accept this and subsequent recommendations [65] that the territory be placed under trusteeship. South Africa argued that it was under no obligation to do so and supported its position by referring to the phrase "as may be placed thereunder" in Articles 75 and 77 of the Charter and to the permissive language of Article 77(2). Other members contended that South Africa was under a legal, or at the least a moral, obligation to propose a trusteeship agreement for the territory. When the matter was discussed by the Assembly at its second session, a majority of members favored a draft resolution to the effect that it was "the clear intention of Chapter XII of the Charter of the United Nations that all territories previously held under mandate" should "until granted self-government or independence, be brought under the international trusteeship system." [66] This section of the resolution was, however, deleted when the proposal was voted upon in plenary.

As the disagreement over the status of the territory continued, the Assembly decided in 1949 to request an advisory opinion from the International Court of Justice.[67] The Court was unanimously of the opinion that the "provisions of Chapter XII of the Charter are applicable to the Territory of South West Africa in the sense that they provide a means by which the Territory may be brought under the Trusteeship System." But a majority of the judges held that Chapter XII did "not impose on the Union of South Africa a legal obligation to place the Territory under the Trusteeship System." Six members of the Court dissented, holding that the Charter did impose such an obligation. The majority of the judges, while conceding that it was "expected" that the mandatory powers would follow the normal course of placing the mandated territories under trusteeship, considered that the language of Articles 75, 77, and 79 was permissive and that had the

[64] UNCIO, *Documents*, X, 434 and 439. See also statement in GAOR/1st Sess., 1st Part, 4th Ctte./3d Mtg./Jan. 22, 1946/p. 11.

[65] GA Res. 65(1), Dec. 14, 1946; Res. 141(II), Nov. 1, 1947; 227(III), Nov. 26, 1948; 337(IV), Dec. 6, 1949.

[66] GAOR/2d Sess., 4th Ctte./45th Mtg./Oct. 15, 1947/p. 96.

[67] GA Res. 338(IV), Dec. 6, 1949.

authors of the Charter intended to create an obligation, they would have done so in positive terms.[68]

At its next session, the General Assembly "accepted" the Court's opinion. At this and subsequent sessions, the Assembly reiterated its view that the territory should be placed under the trusteeship system, but South Africa has continued to refuse to do so.[69]

In 1958, it was suggested that the territory might be partitioned: the northern part to be administered as an integral part of South Africa under a United Nations trusteeship, the rest of the territory to be annexed by South Africa. Some members felt that the United Nations should consider any plan that might extend the benefits of trusteeship to some of the inhabitants, even if the trusteeship system could not be applied in full. The overwhelming majority of members, however, were strongly opposed to the plan, considering it tantamount to an abandonment by the United Nations of its responsibilities and a repudiation of previous Assembly resolutions.[70]

Subsequently, pressures on South Africa to place the territory under trusteeship virtually ceased, and instead, emphasis shifted to proposals for transferring the administration of the territory to an authority to be appointed by the United Nations.[71]

Territories Detached from Enemy States

During World War II there were many, including President Roosevelt, who saw the international trusteeship system as a means for dealing with territories detached from the enemy states. It should be noted that Article 77(b) is not expressly limited to territories that were non-self-governing before the war. After the war ended, however, relatively little consideration was given to placing under the United Nations trusteeship system territories formerly held by enemy states, partly due to the difficulties the major powers encountered in agreeing upon the peace treaties.

The action taken concerning the former Japanese mandated islands has already been mentioned. The only other proposal for placing territories detached from Japan under the trusteeship system was made with respect to Korea. The Cairo Declaration of 1943 had stated that

[68] *ICJ Reports*, 1950, pp. 144, 138–40. On the continuing obligations of South Africa and the role of the General Assembly, see commentary on Art. 80.

[69] GA Res. 449(V), Dec. 13, 1950; 852(IX), Nov. 23, 1954; 940(X), Dec. 3, 1955; 1141(XII), Oct. 25, 1957; 1246(XIII), Oct. 30, 1958; 1360(XIV), Nov. 17, 1959.

[70] The suggestion arose as a result of negotiations between South Africa and a committee of good offices appointed by the Assembly.

[71] See below, pp. 496–500.

Korea "in due course" would become "free and independent." [72] At the Moscow meeting of the Council of Foreign Ministers in December, 1945, a joint commission was established to prepare possible proposals "for the working out of an agreement concerning a four-power trusteeship of Korea for a period of up to five years." [73] The joint commission failed to reach agreement and the United States withdrew its support for a trusteeship, largely on the ground that it was not acceptable to the Koreans. At the initiative of the United States, the problem of Korea was subsequently considered by the General Assembly, but no proposal for trusteeship was considered.

Only in connection with the former Italian colonies in Africa was there any discussion in the General Assembly of the possibility of placing former enemy territories under United Nations trusteeship. The territories involved were Eritrea, Italian Somaliland, and Libya. By the terms of the Italian peace treaty, Italy renounced all claim to the territories and, in accordance with the terms of the treaty, the question of the disposal of colonies was placed before the General Assembly after the four powers had failed to reach agreement. When the matter was discussed in the spring of 1949, a majority of members supported a plan that would have placed Somaliland under Italian trusteeship and would have placed the three regions of Libya—Fezzan, Tripolitania, and Cyrenaica—under separate trusteeships with France, Italy, and the United Kingdom as the respective administering authorities. The plan failed to receive the necessary two-thirds vote, largely because of opposition to the proposal for Tripolitania. At the next session of the Assembly, agreement was reached on independence for Libya and a ten-year trusteeship for Somaliland, with Italy as the administering authority.[74]

Territories Voluntarily Placed Under Trusteeship

Early hopes that the United Nations trusteeship system could be expanded to cover a great many dependent territories failed to materialize. None of the states responsible for the administration of non-self-governing territories chose to take advantage of the provisions of Article 77(c) by "voluntarily" placing such territories under the trusteeship system.

At the second session of the General Assembly, India took the lead in urging that members place territories not ready for self-government under the trusteeship system. A draft resolution was introduced stating

[72] State Dept., *Cairo and Tehran*, pp. 448–49.
[73] State Dept., *Treaties and Other International Acts Series 1555*.
[74] GA Res. 289A(IV), Nov. 21, 1949.

that "at the time of the creation of the United Nations it was intended that Non-Self-Governing Territories be voluntarily placed" under the international trusteeship system, and that the system provides "the surest and quickest means of enabling the peoples of dependent territories to secure self-government and independence under the collective guidance and supervision of the United Nations." Although the proposal was adopted in committee, it failed to pass in plenary.[75] The rejection of this resolution further emphasized the purely voluntary character of the process by which territories were to be placed under the trusteeship system.

Article 78

The trusteeship system shall not apply to territories which have become Members of the United Nations, relationship among which shall be based on respect for the principle of sovereign equality.

Since the first principle of the Charter states that the "Organization is based on the principle of the sovereign equality of its Members" (Article 2[1]), it hardly seems necessary to stipulate that the trusteeship system is not applicable to territories which had become members of the Organization. At the time of the San Francisco Conference, however, the international status of some of the participants had not been completely clarified.[76] Article 78 was, therefore, included in the Charter to reassure these members that the trusteeship system would not apply to them. Of particular relevance was the situation of Syria and Lebanon, both of which had been Class A mandated territories under the League of Nations. They had been declared "independent" in 1941, subject to the conclusion of treaties redefining French rights in the area. At the time of the San Francisco Conference, these treaties had not yet been concluded; nonetheless, both countries were invited to participate in the Conference and became original members of the United Nations.

Article 78 is applicable not only to the original members of the United Nations but also to states subsequently admitted to membership. In those cases where trust territories have achieved independence, all aspects of the trusteeship system have come to an end. Thus, it has been the general practice of the Trusteeship Council not to consider further petitions or communications concerning former trust territories once the trusteeship agreement has been terminated.[77]

[75] GAOR/2d Sess./106th Plen. Mtg./Nov. 1, 1947/p. 666; and 4th Ctte./43d and 44th Mtgs./Oct. 13 and 14, 1947/pp. 78–92.

[76] See commentary on Art. 3.

[77] See, for example, GAOR/17th Sess./1962/*Supp. 4*, p. 3.

Article 79

The terms of trusteeship for each territory to be placed under the trusteeship system, including any alteration or amendment, shall be agreed upon by the states directly concerned, including the mandatory power in the case of territories held under mandate by a Member of the United Nations, and shall be approved as provided for in Articles 83 and 85.

Under the provisions of the Charter, the terms of any trusteeship agreement must be: 1) agreed upon by the "states directly concerned" in accordance with Article 79; and 2) approved by the General Assembly under Article 85, or by the Security Council under Article 83 in the case of territories designated as strategic. Article 79 is therefore of basic importance in determining the way individual territories are brought under the international trusteeship system. It also establishes the important principle that any alteration or amendment of the terms of trusteeship must be agreed to by the states directly concerned as well as by the relevant organs of the United Nations.

"States Directly Concerned"

The introduction of the ambiguous phrase "states directly concerned" resulted from the discussions within the United States government during the period when plans for the Charter were being made. Objecting to the State Department's plan, representatives of the War and Navy Departments insisted that before any territory was placed under trusteeship, the "states concerned" should have the right to approve the terms of the trusteeship and the designation of the administering authority. To meet these objections, the State Department proposed that "the placing of any territory under the trusteeship system should be effected by means of trusteeship arrangements entered into by the Organization and the state or states possessing title or the prerogatives of title to the territory, as well as the state immediately responsible for its administration." [78] It was later decided, however, to delete any reference to the matter of title in view of the controversy it was likely to invoke.[79]

At the San Francisco Conference, it was agreed that, in the case of the mandated territories, the "states directly concerned" would include the mandatory powers; this provision was added to Article 79. The

[78] See Russell, pp. 577–81.
[79] The question of sovereignty over the mandates was the subject of heated and unresolved controversy in the League of Nations. See Wright, esp. Part III.

Soviet proposal that the phrase include states "which are or were concerned," was not accepted.[80] In reply to Soviet questions, the United States emphasized that the trusteeship system was not designed to settle territorial claims. Rather, territories would be placed under trusteeship only after such claims had been resolved and the states concerned had agreed among themselves on a trusteeship arrangement which would then be presented to the international organization for approval.

As was to be expected, the question of which states should be considered as "directly concerned" raised problems when the conclusion of trusteeship agreements came up for consideration. With regard to the mandated territories, the mandatory powers generally favored a restrictive interpretation, while certain other states, notably the Soviet Union, argued for a wider one. No agreement on the meaning of the phrase was reached during the discussions in the Preparatory Commission or at the first part of the first session of the General Assembly. During these initial discussions, various conflicting views were expressed concerning the criteria for defining "states directly concerned," the organ competent to make the definition, and the need for a definition. On the last point, there were those who considered an early definition essential to the establishment of the trusteeship system. Others felt there was no need to define the term at that juncture and that to attempt to do so might impede the prompt establishment of the system.

The resolution adopted by the General Assembly invited "the states administering territories now held under mandate to undertake practical steps, in concert with the other states directly concerned, for the implementation of Article 79 of the Charter." [81] The Assembly did not, however, indicate how in its judgment the phrase "states directly concerned" should be interpreted. As a result, each of the mandatory powers made its own decision. Australia exchanged views regarding the terms of the trusteeship agreement for New Guinea with France, New Zealand, the United Kingdom, and the United States. New Zealand followed the same procedure for Western Samoa. Belgium submitted its draft agreement for Ruanda-Urundi to the United Kingdom as a "state directly concerned" and communicated the text to China, France, the Soviet Union, and the United States "for their information." France submitted its texts for Togoland and the Cameroons to the United Kingdom as a state directly concerned and communicated it "for information purposes" to the other permanent members of the Security Council and to other states holding mandated territories in Africa. The United Kingdom submitted its texts for Tanganyika, Togo-

[80] Russell, pp. 834–35.   [81] GA Res. 9(I), Feb. 9, 1946.

land, and the Cameroons to France, Belgium, and South Africa for comment and to the other permanent members for information.[82]

When these draft agreements were discussed in the General Assembly, the procedure of consultation that had been followed was criticized by several members as contrary to the provisions of Article 79. A few members entered claims to be considered as "states directly concerned" with regard to specific territories.[83] A more controversial issue was raised by the insistence of the Soviet Union that all the permanent members of the Security Council be considered as "states directly concerned" for all the trusteeship agreements. The opposition argued that this would be tantamount to granting them a veto power over the terms of the trusteeship agreements. An impasse that threatened to block the establishment of the trusteeship system seemed imminent, but a way out was found through a formula put forward by the United States. Under its terms, the trusteeship agreements would be approved by the General Assembly with the following understanding:

All Members of the United Nations have had an opportunity to present their views with reference to the terms of Trusteeship now proposed to the General Assembly for approval. There has, however, been no specification by the General Assembly of "states directly concerned" in relation to the proposed Trust Territories. Accordingly, the General Assembly in approving the terms of Trusteeship does not prejudge the question of what states are or are not "directly concerned" within the meaning of Article 79. It recognizes that no state has waived or prejudiced its right hereafter to claim to be such a "state directly concerned" in relation to approval of subsequently proposed Trusteeship agreements and any alteration or amendment of those now approved, and that the procedure to be followed in the future with reference to such matters may be subject to later determination.[84]

In line with this understanding, it was decided not to include in the preambles to the trusteeship agreements statements to the effect that the General Assembly had satisfied itself that the requirements of Article 79 of the Charter had been "complied with." The Soviet Union, however, maintaining its position with regard to the interpretation of Article 79, continued to insist that the agreements had been drafted contrary to the fundamental requirements of the Charter. When the Soviet proposal that the General Assembly reject the agree-

[82] GAOR/1st Sess., 2d Part, 4th Ctte./1946/Part II/*Annex 14.*

[83] See India's statement regarding Tanganyika. GAOR/1st Sess., 2d Part, 4th Ctte./28th Mtg./Dec. 10, 1946/pp. 210–11; and statement by the Arab countries regarding any territory with an Arab population, *ibid.*, 24th Mtg./Dec. 5, 1946/p. 179; and *Annexes,* pp. 1553–56.

[84] GAOR/1st Sess., 2d Part, 4th Ctte./1946/Part I, *Annex 22a.*

ments was defeated, and the eight agreements were approved, it challenged the validity of this action,[85] and initially refused to take part in the work of the Trusteeship Council. It was not until 1948 that it reversed its position and occupied its seat on the Council.

In the above cases the initiative was taken by the mandatory power, which submitted a draft trusteeship agreement to the General Assembly. Clearly, the Assembly had the power to approve or disapprove these agreements, but its power to alter the terms set out by the mandatory powers was in practice very limited. A considerable number of amendments to the drafts submitted by the mandatory powers were introduced. Some modifications resulted. But in no case did the Assembly approve an amendment unacceptable to the mandatory power concerned. Obviously, other members, anxious to see the trusteeship system established, were generally unwilling to press their views to a point where any mandatory power might feel impelled to withdraw its proposal for placing a territory under the trusteeship system. In effect, the mandatory power and it alone had a practical veto over the terms of the agreements.

In the Security Council, which has the responsibility for approving trusteeship agreements for strategic areas, each permanent member, of course, has a veto. But the preeminent position of the country in actual control of the proposed trust territory was clearly demonstrated when the Council considered the draft agreement for the Pacific Islands that Japan formerly held under League of Nations mandate. The draft agreement was submitted by the United States as the state in control of the territory. While accepting some suggestions for modifications of the terms of the agreement, the United States made it clear that it might be obliged to withdraw its tender of an agreement if the Security Council approved any amendments unacceptable to it.[86] The final terms were mutually acceptable to the Council and to the United States.

In these discussions, the United States stated that it had met the requirements of Article 79 by submitting the draft agreement to the Council for approval and by transmitting copies of the draft to all members of the United Nations which, in its view, might have a special interest in the Islands. Moreover, in this case, those members of the Far Eastern Commission not represented on the Council were invited to participate in the discussion on the draft agreement. There was very little discussion in the Council regarding the application of Article 79,

[85] See also the similar position taken by the Soviet Union when the agreement for the territory of Nauru was approved. GAOR/2d Sess./104th Plen. Mtg./Nov. 1, 1947/p. 570.

[86] SCOR/2d Yr., No. 31/124th Mtg./Apr. 2, 1947, p. 665. For further comment, see Art. 83.

and the agreement was approved without any effort having been made to reach a determination as to the "states directly concerned."

The issue of "states directly concerned" was raised again when the former Italian colony of Somaliland was brought into the trusteeship system. This case was unique in that the decision to place the territory under trusteeship was taken by the General Assembly itself on the basis of the previous agreement of France, the Soviet Union, the United Kingdom, and the United States that had been incorporated in the Italian Peace Treaty. The Assembly asked the Trusteeship Council to negotiate with Italy, which was designated the administering authority, a draft trusteeship agreement for submission to the Assembly.[87] When the Trusteeship Council took up this question, the President ruled that Italy be invited to participate, without vote, in its work. A number of other United Nations members not represented on the Council were also invited to participate "in an advisory capacity and without the right to vote" in the negotiation of the agreement, in view of their particular concern and without prejudice to the interpretation of Article 79.[88]

It is important to note that the controversy over defining the term "states directly concerned" had a significance beyond the immediate issue of the conclusion of the agreements bringing territories into the trusteeship system. Under the provision of Article 79, any alteration or amendment of a trusteeship agreement has to be agreed upon by the states directly concerned. The administering authorities have generally sought to protect their positions in this respect by stipulating in the trusteeship agreement that the terms of the agreement cannot be altered or amended except as provided in Article 79. The agreement for the Pacific Islands trust territory is even more explicit in stating that the terms of the agreement cannot be "altered, amended, or terminated without the consent of the administering authority."

Entry into Force of Agreements

Article 79 provides for the approval of the trusteeship agreements by the General Assembly or the Security Council, as the case may be. The Charter says nothing about the entry into force of the agreements. In practice, the agreements have been considered as coming into force immediately upon approval by the General Assembly.

One exception was the strategic trusteeship agreement for the Pacific Islands, which contained a special provision that the agreement would come into force "when approved by the Security Council of the United

[87] GA Res. 289A(IV), Nov. 21, 1949.
[88] TCOR/2d Special Sess./2d Mtg./Dec. 9, 1949/p. 16.

Nations and by the Government of the United States after due constitutional process."

Termination of Agreements

There are no provisions in the Charter concerning the termination of trusteeship agreements. Early United States plans authorized the Organization to determine the conditions under which trust status might be terminated and also empowered the Organization to remove any administering authority that failed to fulfill either the terms of the trusteeship agreement or the provisions of the Charter. These provisions were later dropped, and the United States proposals submitted at the San Francisco Conference were "silent on the question of criteria or methods for terminating a trust or transferring it from one administering authority to another." [89] In the United States view such changes constituted "alterations" in the agreement. They would, therefore, in accordance with Article 79, require agreement by the states directly concerned and approval by the General Assembly or the Security Council, as the case might be.

Egypt, however, introduced an amendment that would have empowered the General Assembly, in the case of trust territories within its competence, "to terminate the status of trusteeship and declare the territory to be fit for full independence, either at the instance of the Administering Authority or upon the recommendation of any member of the Assembly." Under this amendment, the General Assembly would have been authorized to take the necessary steps for the transfer of a territory under trusteeship in the event the administering authority violated the terms of the trusteeship, ceased to be a member of the United Nations, or was suspended from membership.[90] In this connection, attention was drawn to the inability of the League of Nations to act when Japan violated the terms of the mandate and withdrew from the League.

In opposition to this proposal, it was argued that provisions for the termination or transfer of a trusteeship without the consent of the administering authority would be contrary to the voluntary basis upon which the trusteeship system was to rest. The practical difficulties of taking a territory away from a state were also pointed out. It was further argued that, even if a member withdrew from the United Nations, it might not be necessary to change its status as an administering authority.[91] These views prevailed.

[89] See Russell, pp. 332–35, 342, 346, 577, 580, and 837.
[90] UNCIO, *Documents*, X, 510.
[91] On the issue of possible withdrawal of an administering authority from UN membership, see *ibid.*, pp. 620–21.

With regard to the trusteeship agreements themselves, only the agreement for Somaliland contained specific provisions for termination. Proposals that specific dates for the termination of trusteeship be included in other agreements were defeated. In practice, the termination of agreements has taken place with the approval of the General Assembly and the administering authorities concerned. In none of the cases where agreements have been terminated has the issue of "states directly concerned" been raised.[92]

Article 80

1. Except as may be agreed upon in individual trusteeship agreements, made under Articles 77, 79, and 81, placing each territory under the trusteeship system, and until such agreements have been concluded, nothing in this Chapter shall be construed in or of itself to alter in any manner the rights whatsoever of any states or any peoples or the terms of existing international instruments to which Members of the United Nations may respectively be parties.
2. Paragraph 1 of this Article shall not be interpreted as giving grounds for delay or postponement of the negotiation and conclusion of agreements for placing mandated and other territories under the trusteeship system as provided for in Article 77.

Known as the "conservatory clause," Article 80 was included in the Charter for the purpose of safeguarding existing rights pending the entry into force of the trusteeship agreements provided for in Articles 77, 79, and 81 of the Charter. The issue of protecting existing rights first arose in the discussions among the five major powers at San Francisco, when the United States proposed a general commitment to non-discriminatory policies in trust territories with regard to economic, commercial, and other such matters.[93] France objected that such a general commitment would alter the terms of some of the mandate agreements. To meet this point, it was decided to add a provision that, "except as may be agreed upon in individual trusteeship arrangements," nothing in the Charter provisions on trusteeship should be "construed in and of itself to alter in any manner the rights of any state or any peoples in any territory, or the terms of any mandate." [94]

This provision was criticized by others on the ground that it protected the position of the mandatory powers but did not go far enough

[92] For more detailed comment on the procedure by which trusteeship agreements have been terminated, see Art. 76.

[93] The "equal treatment" provision was incorporated in Article 76(d) of the Charter.

[94] UNCIO, *Documents*, X, 477. See also Russell, pp. 827 ff.

in safeguarding the rights of the inhabitants of the territories. Egypt proposed a more limited text that would have protected against alteration "the rights of the people of any territory or the terms of any mandate." [95] This proposal reflected the desire of all the Arab states to ensure that Palestine, then a Class A mandate, would not be placed under the trusteeship system on terms less advantageous to the Arabs. Zionist groups, also active at the Conference, were equally concerned with protecting Jewish rights in Palestine. One writer has commented that "as most of these factors had to remain unspoken . . . the result was a good deal of discursive indirection in the committee discussions." [96]

The United States sought to clarify the situation by making a statement that under its interpretation of the provision, "all rights, whatever they may be, remain exactly the same as they exist—that they are neither increased nor diminished by the adoption of this Charter. Any change is left as a matter for subsequent agreements." [97] Later, the United States said that among those rights were those set forth in Article 22(4) of the Covenant which covers the Class A mandates.[98]

In the final text, the reference to the "terms of the mandate" was changed to "terms of existing international instruments to which Members of the United Nations may respectively be parties." As adopted, Article 80 covers not only the rights of the mandatory powers and the peoples of the territories, but also the rights of other states and other peoples.

A further problem arose when the Soviet Union proposed the deletion of the first paragraph on the ground that it might permit the existing mandatory powers to extend their control indefinitely. To meet this point, another paragraph, 80(2), was added, to the effect that the conservatory clause should not be so interpreted as to give "grounds for delay or postponement of the negotiation and conclusion of the agreements placing mandated and other territories under the trusteeship system."

Article 80 was cited with some frequency during the debates in the General Assembly over the future of Palestine, primarily by the Arab states in challenging the legality of the partition resolution endorsed by the General Assembly in 1947. The most extensive discussion of the terms of Article 80, however, has occurred in connection with the question of South West Africa.

[95] UNCIO, *Documents*, X, 477.   [96] Russell, p. 828.
[97] UNCIO, *Documents*, X, 486.
[98] A British proposal to include a specific reference to this provision of the Covenant was opposed by the U.S. Russell, p. 829.

At the first session of the General Assembly, when South Africa announced that it did not intend to place South West Africa under the trusteeship system, it gave assurances that, pending agreement regarding the future status of the territory, it would continue to administer the territory in the spirit of the League of Nations mandate.[99] When the League Assembly met in its final session, it took note of the "expressed intentions" of the mandatory powers to continue to administer the territories under mandate in accordance with the obligations contained in the mandate agreements "until other arrangements have been agreed between the United Nations and the respective mandatory Powers." [100]

In 1946 and 1947, South Africa submitted reports on the territory that were examined by the Trusteeship Council at the request of the General Assembly.[101] During the discussion in the Assembly, reference was made to Article 80 as the basis for maintaining that supervisory powers over the territory were vested in the United Nations. In 1948 South Africa took the position that the United Nations had no supervisory jurisdiction over the territory, that it was under no legal obligation to submit reports, and the previous reports had been submitted on a purely voluntary basis with the stipulation that this act should not be considered as a precedent or a commitment to further action, or as in any way recognizing any measure of accountability to the United Nations. In the Assembly, there was considerable support for the view that South Africa was under a legal obligation to report to the Assembly on its administration of the territory. It was contended that the terms of Article 80 made it clear that the situation that had prevailed in South West Africa under the mandate system should not be changed pending the conclusion of a trusteeship agreement; that the rights of the people were clearly compromised when the international community did not receive information upon the administration of the territory; and that the refusal of South Africa to submit reports was a flagrant violation of Article 80. It was in these circumstances that the General Assembly requested an advisory opinion from the International Court of Justice concerning the international status of South West Africa, the obligations of South Africa, and the competence to modify the status of the territory.[102]

With regard to the status of the territory, the Court was unanimously of the opinion that South West Africa was "a territory under the international Mandate assumed by the Union of South Africa on December 17th, 1920," [103] and that South Africa "acting alone" was not compe-

[99] GAOR/1st Sess., 1st Part, 4th Ctte./3d Mtg./Jan. 22, 1946/p. 10.
[100] LN, *Official Journal, Special Supp. 194,* 1946, *Annex* 27, pp. 278–79.
[101] See GA Res. 65(I), Dec. 14, 1946; and 141(II), Nov. 1, 1947.
[102] GA Res. 338(IV), Dec. 6, 1949.   [103] *ICJ Reports,* 1950, p. 128.

tent to modify the international status of the territory. It could do so only "with the consent of the United Nations."

With regard to South Africa's obligations,[104] the Court stated that South Africa continued to have "the international obligations stated in Article 22 of the Covenant of the League of Nations and in the Mandate for South-West Africa." In the Court's opinion, Article 7 of the mandate agreement concerning the submission of disputes with regard to its interpretation to the Permanent Court of International Justice was "still in force" and, therefore, in accordance with Article 80 of the Charter and Article 37 of the Statute of the International Court of Justice, South Africa was under an obligation to accept the compulsory jurisdiction of the Court with regard to such matters.

Again citing Article 80 of the Charter, the majority of the judges held that: 1) its provisions presupposed "that the rights of States and peoples" shall not lapse automatically on the dissolution of the League of Nations"; 2) it was obviously intended to "safeguard the rights of States and peoples under all circumstances and in all respects, until each territory should be placed under the Trusteeship System"; and 3) the purpose of the article "must have been to provide a real protection for those rights; but no such rights of the peoples could be effectively safeguarded without international supervision and a duty to render reports to a supervisory organ." In the Court's opinion, it could not be admitted that "the obligation to submit to supervision" had disappeared "merely because the supervisory organ has ceased to exist, when the United Nations has another international organ performing similar, though not identical, supervisory functions." The Court thus considered that South Africa was under an obligation to submit annual reports and transmit petitions from the inhabitants of the territory to the United Nations. The Court further concluded that

. . . the General Assembly of the United Nations is legally qualified to exercise the supervisory functions previously exercised by the League of Nations with regard to the administration of the territory, and that the Union of South Africa is under an obligation to submit to supervision and control of the General Assembly and to render annual reports to it.

By way of guidance, the Court stated that the degree of supervision to be exercised by the General Assembly should not "exceed that which applied under the Mandates System, and should conform as far as possible to the procedure followed in this respect by the Council of the League of Nations."

Following its acceptance of the opinion of the Court,[105] the General

[104] For the Court's view on the obligation to place the territory under the trusteeship system, see commentary on Art. 77.

[105] GA Res. 449A(V), Dec. 13, 1950.

Assembly continued to urge South Africa to negotiate a trusteeship agreement for South West Africa, but its principal focus of attention shifted to efforts to establish some system of international supervision over the administration of the territory. South Africa, however, continued to maintain that the mandate had lapsed with the demise of the League of Nations and that it was under no obligation to submit to the supervision of the United Nations. South Africa challenged the Court's interpretation of Article 80, contending that it could only safeguard the rights of states and peoples from being altered by the terms of Chapter XII of the Charter; it could not safeguard rights under the terms of other international instruments if the parties to those instruments wished to change them. In this connection, South Africa at various times indicated that it would be willing to enter into negotiations regarding the territory with France, the United Kingdom, and the United States as the remaining Principal Allied and Associated Powers of World War I, a course which was unacceptable to the General Assembly.

From 1953 through 1961, the General Assembly's Committee on South West Africa undertook most of the detailed work in connection with the United Nations effort to exercise supervisory functions over the administration of the territory.[106] Initially, the Committee was asked to prepare for the Assembly "a procedure for the examination of reports and petitions" which would "conform as far as possible to the procedure followed in this respect by the Assembly, the Council and the Permanent Mandates Commission of the League of Nations." [107] Accordingly, the Committee submitted a set of proposed rules but also concluded that "alternative procedures" would be necessary if South Africa refused to submit reports and petitions with respect to South West Africa.[108] Since South Africa did so refuse, the Committee operated under these "alternative procedures"; thus, its examination of conditions in the territory was based primarily on information and documents prepared by the Secretariat of the United Nations.

Two issues that arose in connection with the Committee's work deserve special mention: 1) the question of the appropriate voting procedure in the General Assembly; and 2) the hearing of petitions concerning South West Africa.

The Committee recommended that questions relating to reports and

[106] The Committee was replaced by the Special Committee for South West Africa, GA Res. 1702(XVI), Dec. 19, 1961, which was in turn dissolved the next year, and its responsibilities were transferred to the Special Committee on the Implementation of the Declaration on the Granting of Independence to Colonial Countries and Peoples, GA Res. 1805(XVII), Dec. 14, 1962.

[107] GA Res. 749A(VIII), Nov. 28, 1953.

[108] GAOR/9th Sess./1954/*Supp. 14.*

petitions concerning the territory be considered by the General Assembly as "important questions" within the meaning of Article 18(2); thus the adoption of decisions on such matters would require only a two-thirds majority of the members present and voting. South Africa contended that the principle of unanimity which applied in the Council and the Assembly of the League of Nations should also be applicable to any decisions on South West Africa taken by the United Nations and that any other procedure would deprive it of rights it possessed under the League system. The Assembly's decision to adopt the contested rule was upheld by the International Court as a "correct interpretation" of the Court's previous advisory opinion of July 11, 1950.[109]

In its 1950 opinion, the Court had held that the right of petition which the inhabitants of South West Africa had acquired under the practices of the League of Nations was "maintained" by Article 80 and that South Africa was under an obligation to transmit such petitions to the United Nations. The question arose whether the Committee on South West Africa should grant hearings to petitioners. While this is an accepted practice under the United Nations trusteeship system, no such procedure had been followed under the mandates system. The Court was again asked for an advisory opinion and a majority of judges held that "it would not be inconsistent" with the Court's initial opinion of July 11, 1950, "for the General Assembly to authorize a procedure for the grant of oral hearings . . . provided that the General Assembly was satisfied that such a course was necessary for the maintenance of effective international supervision of the administration of the Mandated Territory." [110]

While the General Assembly sought to discharge its supervisory responsibilities through the Committee on South West Africa, it also made various efforts to work out a system acceptable to South Africa. These included authorization to the Committee on South West Africa to enter into negotiations with South Africa, a request to the Secretary-General to explore the possibilities of a solution, and the appointment in 1958 of a good offices committee. None of these efforts was successful, for South Africa continued to deny the competence of the United Nations.

In 1960 a new approach to the problem was initiated when Liberia and Ethiopia instituted proceedings against South Africa before the International Court of Justice. They asked the Court to declare that: 1) the mandate is a treaty in force and that South Africa remains subject to its obligations under the League mandates system; 2) the General Assembly is legally qualified to take over the League's supervisory

[109] *ICJ Reports*, 1955, pp. 67–68.   [110] *ICJ Reports*, 1956, p. 32.

functions and that South Africa is obligated to submit to its supervision and control; 3) South Africa had modified the terms of the mandate without United Nations consent; and 4) South Africa had violated the terms of the mandate and the League Covenant by its practice of apartheid, by failing to promote the well-being and social progress of the inhabitants of the territory, and by refusing to transmit to the United Nations reports and petitions concerning the territory.

While some members considered that further action should be postponed until the Court had rendered its judgment, the Assembly continued to adopt increasingly strong resolutions with regard to the situation in South West Africa.

By its judgment of December 21, 1962, the Court found that it had "jurisdiction to adjudicate upon the merits of the dispute." However, after considering arguments on the merits, the Court on July 18, 1966, rejected the claims of Ethiopia and Liberia on the ground that the applicants "cannot be considered to have established any legal right or interest appertaining to them in the subject matter of the present claims." [111] After considering the question of South West Africa in the light of the Court's final judgment, the General Assembly adopted a resolution declaring that South Africa had failed to fulfill its obligations in respect to the administration of the mandated territory, that it had in fact "disavowed the mandate," and that the mandate was, therefore, "terminated." The Assembly established an ad hoc committee to recommend practical measures for the administration of the territory with a view to achieving its independence.[112]

Article 81

The trusteeship agreement shall in each case include the terms under which the trust territory will be administered and designate the authority which will exercise the administration of the trust territory. Such authority, hereinafter called the administering authority, may be one or more states or the Organization itself.

The individual trusteeship agreements constitute the essential basis of the trusteeship system. The provisions of Article 81 contrast with some of the earlier United States plans, under which the Organization would have set the terms of administration and designated the administering authority.[113] Under the Charter, these matters are covered in

[111] *ICJ Reports*, 1966, p. 6. See also *ibid.*, 1962, p. 319.
[112] GA Res. 2145(XXI), Oct. 28, 1966.
[113] See Russell, pp. 332, 589. The Organization would also have been authorized to remove the administering authority if it failed to live up to its obligations. *Ibid.*, pp. 346 and 580.

the individual trusteeship agreements themselves and must be agreed upon by the states directly concerned (Article 79) as well as approved by the Organization.

The Nature of the Administering Authority

Article 81 provides that the administering authority for a trust territory may be "one or more states or the Organization itself." The idea of direct administration by the Organization itself or by a specially constituted international commission had been included in most of the early United States plans and was a feature that particularly appealed to President Roosevelt. But the proposals originally submitted by the United States at the time of the San Francisco Conference made no mention of this feature. The provision making it possible to designate the United Nations itself as an administering authority was suggested by China, and the proposal for joint trusteeships came from Egypt. Despite some doubts as to the effectiveness of such arrangements, both proposals were adopted.[114]

When the General Assembly considered the first draft trusteeship agreements, a proposal was made that, as a rule, the United Nations should be the administering authority for trust territories. In the case of the draft agreement for Western Samoa, for example, an amendment was submitted to the effect that New Zealand should act on behalf of the United Nations, which would itself be the administering authority within the meaning of Article 81. In favor of this course, it was argued that the Organization would be "more impartial," that it would have a "broader outlook," and that the inhabitants of the territories would make more rapid strides toward self-government and independence under the international organization. This approach was not accepted, largely because of the unanimous opposition of the mandatory powers.[115]

In practice, all but one of the trusteeship agreements have designated a single state as the administering authority. The trusteeship agreement for Nauru designates the governments of Australia, New Zealand, and the United Kingdom as the "administering authority," but Article 4 of the agreement provides that Australia, on their behalf, will exercise full powers of legislation, administration, and jurisdiction in and over the territory.

There have been other proposals for joint trusteeships. The plan agreed upon at the Moscow meeting of the Council of Foreign Minis-

[114] See Russell, pp. 835–36.
[115] GAOR/1st Sess., 2d Part, 4th Ctte., Part 2/2d Mtg./Nov. 18, 1946, p. 6; and 6th Mtg./Nov. 23, 1946/pp. 32–42.

ters in December, 1945, envisaged a trusteeship for Korea with China, the Soviet Union, the United Kingdom, and the United States as administering authorities, but this plan was later abandoned. The General Assembly proposed in November, 1947, that Jerusalem be placed under an international regime with the Trusteeship Council as administering authority; and in 1948, the United States proposed that the whole of Palestine be placed under a temporary United Nations trusteeship. Various proposals were introduced in the United Nations for placing Somaliland and Libya under a collective trusteeship, but none was accepted. Both in the Council of Foreign Ministers and in the United Nations, there were proposals to place the former Italian colonies under direct United Nations trusteeship. These also were rejected, and in the end the Assembly decided that Libya should become independent and that Somaliland should be placed under a ten-year trusteeship with Italy as the administering authority. This last decision is of some interest in that Italy was not at the time a member of the United Nations, but Article 81 does not specify that the administering authority must be a United Nations member.

Terms of the Trusteeship Agreements

The Charter establishes the general principles to govern the administration of the trust territories and defines the functions that the various organs of the United Nations are to perform. The obligations and responsibilities of the administering authorities, however, are not set out in detail in the Charter but are covered by the terms of the individual trusteeship agreements. All of these have followed the same general pattern, with some variations to take into account the special circumstances of particular territories. There are a number of special features in the trusteeship agreement for the Pacific Islands, arising mainly from the fact that this is the only trust territory that has been designated a "strategic area." [116] The trusteeship agreement for Somaliland, while closely following the general pattern of the other agreements, dealt in considerably more detail with the obligations of the administering authority. This is accounted for primarily by the special circumstances surrounding the negotiation of this trusteeship agreement.[117]

Leaving aside the variations in particular cases, the general pattern of the trusteeship agreements was as follows:[118]

Each trusteeship agreement defined the boundaries of the territory

[116] See commentary on Art. 83.　　　[117] See commentary on Arts. 77 and 79.
[118] For texts of first eight trusteeship agreements, see GAOR/1st Sess., 2d Part/Supp. 5; for analysis of the constitutional basis of their provisions, see *Repertory*, IV, 231–34.

and designated the administering authority. Most stipulated that the agreement could not be altered or amended except as provided in the Charter. Most provided that disputes between the administering authority and another member of the United Nations relating to the interpretation or application of the provisions of the agreement were to be settled by the International Court of Justice.[119] At the time the first trusteeship agreements were considered in the General Assembly, it was proposed that disputes be settled by the Trusteeship Council, which could if necessary refer the question to the Court for an advisory opinion, but this proposal was defeated.[120]

Most of the trusteeship agreements provided for "full collaboration" by the administering authority with the General Assembly and the Trusteeship Council to facilitate the discharge by those organs of the functions specified in Article 87 of the Charter. Each trusteeship agreement contained a general undertaking by the administering authority to administer the territory in accordance with the provisions of the Charter and in such manner as to achieve the basic purposes of the international trusteeship system as set forth in Article 76. The bulk of the provisions of the trusteeship agreements related to the attainment of these purposes.

The administering authorities accepted the responsibility for ensuring that their respective trust territories played their part in the maintenance of international peace and security; to this end, they were authorized to establish bases, erect fortifications, station armed forces, and raise volunteer contingents in the territories, subject to the provisions of the Charter and the individual agreements.[121] All the agreements recognized by reference to Article 76(d) that one of the purposes of administration was to ensure for other United Nations members equal treatment in social, economic, and commercial matters and in the application of justice. As to the promotion of human rights and fundamental freedoms (Article 76c), the administering authorities were obligated to guarantee freedom of speech, of the press, of assembly, and of petition, subject only to the requirements of public order. Most of the agreements also obligated the administering authority to ensure freedom of thought and free exercise of all forms of religious worship, consistent with public order and morality. With regard to the "political, economic, social, and educational advancement of the inhabitants" of the trust territories as set out in Article 76(b), all the agreements contained specific provisions concerning education and most had

[119] This provision is absent from the agreements for New Guinea and Nauru.
[120] GAOR/1st Sess., 2d Part, 4th Ctte., Part 2/12th Mtg./Nov. 29, 1946/pp. 86–88.
[121] See commentary on Art. 84.

specific provisions for the protection of the rights of the inhabitants with respect to land ownership and natural resources.

All the agreements granted the administering authority "full powers of legislation, administration, and jurisdiction." In most of the agreements, this grant of power also included the right to administer the territory "as an integral part" of the territory of the administering power. Most of them also authorized the administering authority to constitute "a customs, fiscal or administrative union or federation with adjacent territories" under its sovereignty or control. These provisions provoked considerable controversy when the first trusteeship agreements were considered by the General Assembly, and their implementation continued to be the subject of heated and extensive debate in subsequent years.

Article 82

There may be designated, in any trusteeship agreement, a strategic area or areas which may include part or all of the trust territory to which the agreement applies, without prejudice to any special agreement or agreements made under Article 43.

The idea that certain areas of strategic importance might be placed under some kind of international trusteeship was one President Roosevelt found especially appealing.[122] The inclusion in the Charter of special provisions for strategic trusteeships, however, stemmed from a different source.

When the proposals for a trusteeship system were discussed within the United States government in February, 1945, the War and Navy Departments objected strongly to the plan put forward by the State Department on the ground that it would not adequately protect United States security interests in the Pacific. Conscious of the United States commitment to the principle of "no territorial aggrandizement" as set out in the Atlantic Charter and the Cairo Declaration, and aware of the decision taken at the Yalta Conference that proposals for an international trusteeship system would be discussed by the major powers prior to the San Francisco Conference, the State Department was anxious that agreement be reached within the government as soon as possible. Although considering that its trusteeship plan sufficiently safeguarded United States interests, the State Department made a number of changes in its draft to meet the objections of the military.[123]

One principal objection to the plan was that all trust territories were treated alike, with no special arrangements for territories of strategic

[122] See Russell, pp. 90, 101–2, 156, 160–61, and 254.
[123] *Ibid.,* pp. 577–79.

importance.[124] The extent of the powers vested in the General Assembly was also criticized. The State Department, therefore, introduced the idea of classifying the trust territories into strategic and nonstrategic areas, the overriding authority in the former case to be exercised not by the General Assembly and the Trusteeship Council but by the Security Council where the United States would be protected by its right of veto. The President and the civilian officials considered that these special arrangements need apply only to limited areas of strategic importance, but the military representatives insisted that any trusteeship for the Pacific Islands, formerly under Japanese mandate, must include the entire territory as a strategic area with *all* the functions of the United Nations exercised by the Security Council. The military view prevailed, and the proposal submitted by the United States stipulated that the designation of a strategic area might include "part or all of the trust territory." [125]

When the United States proposal was subsequently discussed by the major powers at San Francisco, the United Kingdom objected to the concept of special treatment for strategic areas. In its view, the difficulties in drawing a line between strategic and nonstrategic areas could easily result in the designation of whole territories as strategic areas, thus removing them from the purview of the Trusteeship Council. The British favored a system based on a distinction between civil and security functions, with the administering authority reporting on the latter to the Security Council and on all other matters to the Trusteeship Council.[126] This proposal was unacceptable to the United States, as was a Soviet proposal that strategic areas be designated on the recommendation of the Security Council as the agency primarily responsible for the maintenance of peace and security. Although some changes were made in the provisions concerning the operation of the trusteeship system for strategic areas, as set out in Article 83, the concept as put forward by the United States was accepted by the major powers and subsequently by the San Francisco Conference. It was embodied in Article 82 in essentially the same form as originally proposed by the United States.

Since Articles 82 and 83 were included wholly because of the apprehensions of the United States armed services as to the future security of the Pacific, it is not surprising that the only area to be placed within the strategic trusteeship system has been the islands Japan formerly held under a League of Nations mandate. The location of these islands

[124] The League mandates had been divided into three classes, principally on the basis of their potentialities for self-government. Security considerations, however, did play an important part in the designation of the Class C mandates.
[125] Russell, pp. 582–89.
[126] *Ibid.*, pp. 833–34. See also UNCIO, *Documents,* III, 612–13.

across the lines of communication between the United States and Asia, the use made of them during World War II, and uncertainties as to their use in any future war, apparently led the United States to insist that the whole of the territory be treated as a strategic area.

The Charter specifies neither the procedure for designating a strategic area nor the criteria upon which to base such a designation. In the case of the former Japanese-mandated islands, the United States took the initiative by submitting to the Security Council a draft trusteeship agreement, Article 1 of which designated the trust territory as a strategic area. By adopting this article, the Council in effect approved the designation, although the appropriateness of the designation was never itself discussed in the Council.[127]

The question of what constitutes a "strategic area" was, however, discussed in the General Assembly when that body considered the first eight trusteeship agreements submitted to it. The matter arose in connection with certain amendments proposed by the Soviet Union. It was the Soviet view that the provisions in the agreements permitting the establishment of military bases and fortifications in the trust territories should be subject to approval by the Security Council under Article 82. This position was not accepted.[128] It should be noted that all of the trusteeship agreements for the former mandated territories in Africa contained specific provisions safeguarding the right of the administering authorities to propose at any future time the amendment of the agreements for the purpose of designating the whole or parts of the territories concerned as strategic areas. None of the administering authorities ever found it necessary to exercise this right.

Article 83

1. All functions of the United Nations relating to strategic areas, including the approval of the terms of the trusteeship agreements and of their alteration or amendment, shall be exercised by the Security Council.

2. The basic objectives set forth in Article 76 shall be applicable to the people of each strategic area.

3. The Security Council shall, subject to the provisions of the trusteeship agreements and without prejudice to security considerations, avail itself of the assistance of the Trusteeship Council to perform those functions of the United Nations under the trusteeship

---

[127] SCOR/2d Yr., No. 31/124th Mtg./Apr. 2, 1947/p. 658, and *Supp. 8, Annex 17.*

[128] GAOR/1st Sess., 2d Part/62d Plen. Mtg./Dec. 13, 1946 (delegate of USSR), pp. 1279–80. For further comment, see Art. 84.

system relating to political, economic, social, and educational matters in the strategic areas.

Article 83(1) is virtually identical with the original proposal submitted by the United States at San Francisco. Paragraphs 2 and 3 of that article, however, were added at the suggestion of other members. The reference to the objectives of the trusteeship system as set forth in Article 76 was suggested by China. China also felt that the Security Council should utilize the assistance of the Trusteeship Council, and Egypt considered that the Security Council should be required to do so in relation to the implementation of nonsecurity objectives in strategic trust areas.[129] This principle was accepted by the United States, subject to two safeguarding clauses: the obligation to utilize the Trusteeship Council is subject to the actual provisions of the trusteeship agreement and is "without prejudice" to security considerations.

Although the powers vested in the Security Council under Article 83(1) are identical with those given to the General Assembly under Article 85(1) with regard to nonstrategic territories, nowhere in the Charter are there any specific provisions concerning how the Security Council is to carry out its functions. At San Francisco, the United States objected to a Chinese suggestion for the application to strategic trusteeships of the obligations of Article 88 concerning annual reports by the administering authority. Nor is there any provision similar to that in Article 87 authorizing the Security Council to receive reports, accept petitions, or send visiting missions to strategic trust territories. The United States considered that the powers of the Security Council were adequate to cover such matters.[130] In practice, these functions have been performed by the Trusteeship Council, as agreed by the Security Council.

Approval of the Agreement for the Pacific Islands

Only once has the Security Council been called upon to exercise the functions vested in it under Article 83. In February, 1947, the United States submitted to the Security Council a draft trusteeship agreement for the Pacific Islands formerly held by Japan under a League of Nations mandate. The text followed the general pattern of the nonstrategic trusteeship agreements approved by the General Assembly at the second part of its first session, with two important differences. These concerned the application of the objectives set out in Article 76 of the Charter and the application of Articles 87 and 88 to strategic trusteeships.

[129] Russell, p. 834.   [130] Ibid., pp. 839 and 841.

During the discussion in the Security Council, several amendments to the United States draft were introduced, resulting in some relatively minor modifications. Other proposed amendments ran into strong United States opposition and were not adopted. The United States representative announced that he would "abstain" from voting on these amendments, thus not exercising any right of veto, but that, if the unacceptable amendments were adopted, the United States might be obliged "in view of its responsibilities, to withdraw the tender of an agreement." [131]

The provisions for the alteration, amendment, or termination of the agreement were the subject of a particularly extended debate. The Soviet Union proposed that these measures be taken "by decision of the Security Council." Poland proposed that no changes be made "except as provided by the Charter." After these proposals were rejected, the Security Council adopted the text, originally proposed by the United States, which provided that the terms of the agreement should not be "altered, amended, or terminated without the consent of the administering authority." [132]

This provision reinforces the veto the United States enjoys as a permanent member of the Security Council. Presumably, the United States is protected against any action the Council might take regarding the trust territory; this was the reason for the decision to designate the area as strategic and to place the territory under the Security Council rather than the General Assembly. It should be noted, however, that any other permanent member of the Security Council can exercise its veto and thus block measures or changes in the trusteeship agreement that the United States might favor.

The Application of Article 76

Article 83(2) provides that the basic objectives of the trusteeship system, as set forth in Article 76 of the Charter, shall be applicable to the people of each strategic area. During the discussion in the Security Council on the draft agreement for the Pacific Islands, the question was raised whether all the provisions of Article 76 were applicable. The draft agreement provided for the application of all the provisions of paragraphs (a), (b), and (c) of that article—and indeed went further than other trusteeship agreements in its detailed provisions for the political, economic, social, and educational advancement of the inhabitants. The agreement differs from the others in the application of

[131] SCOR/2d Yr., No. 31/124th Mtg./Apr. 2, 1947/p. 665.
[132] *Ibid.*, No. 20/113th Mtg./Feb. 26, 1947/p. 415, No. 23/116th Mtg./Mar. 7, 1947/p. 477; and No. 31/124th Mtg./Apr. 2, 1947/p. 676.

Article 76(d) ensuring "equal treatment in social, economic, and commercial matters for all Members of the United Nations and their nationals." The text of the relevant provisions as proposed by the United States reads as follows:

In discharging its obligations under Article 76(d) of the Charter . . . the administering authority, subject to the requirements of security and the obligation to promote the advancement of the inhabitants, shall accord to nationals of each Member of the United Nations and to companies and associations organized in conformity with the law of such Members, treatment in the Trust Territory no less favorable than that accorded therein to nationals, companies, and associations of any other United Nation except the administering authority.[133]

Thus the United States sought to apply "most-favored nation" treatment rather than full equality. Under the agreement, it would be permitted to discriminate in favor of its own nationals. The Soviet Union contended that this provision was incompatible with the Charter and proposed its deletion. The United States representative explained that the restriction on the application of Article 76(d) was based on considerations of security deemed essential by the administering authority and that in a strategic area the security objective must be an overriding consideration. He pointed out that Article 83(2) specifically referred to the "people" of the strategic area and that therefore there was no obligation to apply those provisions of Article 76(d) that did not relate to the people of the territory.

With regard to the Pacific Islands trusteeship, there is one special matter that deserves mention. During the discussions in the Trusteeship Council, the question was raised whether the use of a trust territory for the conduct of nuclear test explosions was compatible with the objectives of the trusteeship system.

Following the hydrogen bomb test in 1954, when the Council received a number of petitions requesting the cessation of tests, it recommended that, if other tests were necessary, precautions be taken to ensure that the inhabitants were not again endangered.[134] Two years later the subject was raised again, and the Council reaffirmed its position, taking note of the declaration by the United States that further tests were necessary for the maintenance of international peace and security. At that time, India indicated its intention to ask the General Assembly to request an advisory opinion from the International Court of Justice as to whether the conduct of nuclear tests was consistent

---

[133] Art. 8. It was also expressly stated that nothing in the article "shall be so construed as to accord traffic rights to aircraft flying into and out of the Trust Territory."

[134] TC Res. 1082(XIV), July 15, 1954.

with the terms of trusteeship. This step was not taken, but in 1958 India proposed that the Trusteeship Council request the United States not to conduct such tests in or in the proximity of the trust territory. This proposal was, however, rejected.[135]

Functions of the Trusteeship Council

Although Article 83(1) vests "all functions of the United Nations relating to strategic areas" in the Security Council, this provision is qualified by the statement in Article 83(3) that the Security Council is to "avail itself of the assistance of the Trusteeship Council." The specific functions the latter is expected to perform are spelled out in Articles 87 and 88 of the Charter. Article 13 of the trusteeship agreement for the Pacific Islands states that the provisions of these two articles "shall be applicable" to that trust territory "provided that the administering authority may determine the extent of their applicability to any area which may from time to time be specified as closed for security reasons." The United States considered their application to the trust territory went beyond the requirements of the Charter, which contains no provisions on this point.[136] Nonetheless, when the Security Council subsequently considered the question of its relations with the Trusteeship Council, it decided in effect that Articles 87 and 88 applied to all strategic areas under trusteeship.

In November, 1947, the Secretary-General notified the Security Council that "procedures should now be formulated" to govern the detailed application of Articles 87 and 88 to the Pacific Islands trust territory.[137] The matter was referred to the Council's Committee of Experts; when it reported in January, 1948, there was a clear division among the members.[138] On the one hand, the representatives of the Soviet Union and the Ukrainian SSR contended that Article 83(3) was "permissive"; that the Security Council was required to exercise all functions relating to strategic areas itself. Other members supported a resolution whereby the Security Council, while reserving to itself the discussion of security matters, would request the Trusteeship Council to exercise the functions specified in Articles 87 and 88. Following consultations with the Trusteeship Council, the Security Council, on

[135] TCOR/17th Sess./674th Mtg./Mar. 2, 1956/p. 165; 22d Sess./904th Mtg./ June 26, 1958/p. 103.

[136] SCOR/2d Yr., No. 20/113th Mtg./Feb. 26, 1947/p. 412.

[137] When the Trusteeship Council adopted its Rules of Procedure, it had considered the question of its functions in relation to strategic areas but did not define its relations with the Security Council or the precise scope of its powers. See Repertory, IV, 248–49.

[138] SCOR/3d Yr./Supp. for June, 1948/p. 5.

March 7, 1949, adopted a resolution along these lines. At the same time, it endorsed an "interpretation" of the resolution given by the Trusteeship Council. Shortly thereafter, the Trusteeship Council formally decided it would undertake these functions "in accordance with Article 83(3) of the Charter and in the light of the Security Council's resolution and the interpretation given to it by the Trusteeship Council." [139]

Under the terms of the Security Council's resolution, the Trusteeship Council was requested, subject to the provisions of the strategic trusteeship agreement and to the decisions the Security Council might take regarding security considerations, "to perform in accordance with its own procedures, on behalf of the Security Council the functions specified in Articles 87 and 88 of the Charter relating to the political, economic, social, and educational advancement of the inhabitants" of the strategic areas. The Trusteeship Council was requested to submit to the Security Council its reports and recommendations on these matters, and the Secretary-General was requested to advise the Security Council of all reports and petitions relating to strategic areas under trusteeship. Under the interpretation agreed upon by the two Councils, it is the duty of the Trusteeship Council to examine such reports and petitions that do not involve security considerations in accordance with its normal procedures and to report thereon to the Security Council. Since the latter is to be advised immediately of all reports and petitions, it has ample opportunity to forestall any action by the Trusteeship Council, if security considerations are involved. In practice, the Security Council has never taken any action with regard to any reports or petitions concerning the Pacific Islands trust territory.

The Security Council in its resolution also requested the Trusteeship Council to submit to it a copy of the questionnaire formulated in accordance with Article 88 and any amendments thereof that might later be adopted. Under the agreed interpretation, the Security Council may alter or amend the questionnaire only for security reasons, and the Trusteeship Council is not obligated to accept amendments based on any other considerations. In practice, the Security Council never discussed the provisional questionnaire or the later revisions the Trusteeship Council submitted to it.

The Trusteeship Council, in performance of its functions under Articles 87 and 88, has examined the reports submitted by the United States as the administering authority for the territory, it has dispatched visiting missions to the area, and it has examined a number of petitions and adopted resolutions thereon. The only restrictions that have been

[139] For the texts of the resolutions, see TC Res. 46(IV), Mar. 24, 1949; and SCOR/4th Yr., No. 18/415th Mtg./Mar. 7, 1949/pp. 10–11.

imposed upon the Trusteeship Council occurred when the United States invoked security considerations to declare the atolls of Bikini and Eniwetok "closed" to the periodic visiting missions of the Council. Thus, the Pacific Islands trust territory has been supervised by the Trusteeship Council in much the same manner as other areas under trusteeship.

Each year the Trusteeship Council reports to the Security Council, but neither these reports [140] nor any other matters concerning the Pacific Islands have been discussed in the Security Council. The main distinction between strategic and other trusteeships, therefore, has been that the developments in the Pacific Islands territory and the actions of the Trusteeship Council have not been subject to further review by any other United Nations organ. Some resolutions adopted by the General Assembly have been relevant to all trust territories, but none has been directed specifically to the Pacific Islands trust territory. There is some question whether the General Assembly is competent to adopt resolutions concerning strategic trust territories.[141] Some members have argued that Assembly resolutions are generally applicable to strategic as well as other trusteeships; others have considered that only the Security Council is competent to adopt such resolutions. In the one instance when this matter was discussed in the Trusteeship Council, the latter view prevailed.[142]

Article 84

It shall be the duty of the administering authority to ensure that the trust territory shall play its part in the maintenance of international peace and security. To this end the administering authority may make use of volunteer forces, facilities, and assistance from the trust territory in carrying out the obligations towards the Security Council undertaken in this regard by the administering authority, as well as for local defense and the maintenance of law and order within the trust territory.

The provisions of Article 84 represent a considerable departure from the League system which, in so far as Class B and C mandates were concerned, obligated the mandatory powers to prevent "the establish-

[140] The reports were not even printed in the *Official Records* of the Security Council until 1956, when a special supplement was issued covering the reports for the years 1949–1954. SCOR/11th Yr./1956/*Special Supp. 1.*

[141] Art. 13 of the trusteeship agreement can be viewed as empowering the Assembly to do so. See Sady, in Robert E. Asher et al., *The United Nations and Promotion of the General Welfare* (Washington, Brookings Institution, 1957), p. 990.

[142] See TCOR/26th Sess./1130th Mtg./June 29, 1960/pp. 529–30; and 1134th Mtg./June 30, 1960/p. 556.

ment of fortifications of military and naval bases" and the "military training of natives for other than police purposes and defense of the territory." [143] The desire of Australia and the United Kingdom to remove these restrictions upon the mandatory power was responsible for the inclusion of Article 84 in the Charter.[144] In accepting these provisions, the San Francisco Conference rejected a proposal by Egypt that would have made the utilization of such forces and facilities subject to the "control of the Security Council." [145] The principal objection to this proposal was that it would have given the Security Council a share in the supervisory jurisdiction over all trust territories, not merely those designated as "strategic trusteeships." [146]

The implementation of Article 84 provoked heated controversy when the General Assembly considered the first eight draft trusteeship agreements. All but one contained a provision expressly authorizing the administering authority to establish naval, military, and air bases, to erect fortifications, and to station and employ armed forces in the trust territory. Some members, including China, India, and the Soviet Union, strongly opposed these provisions on the ground that they went beyond the terms of Article 84. They sought to delete the provisions or to amend them in order to subject the actions of the administering authorities to the approval of the Security Council. The Soviet Union argued that, if forces and bases were needed, the territories should be designated as "strategic" areas and the agreements then approved by the Security Council in accordance with Article 83.

Those favoring the retention of the above-mentioned provisions in the trusteeship agreements stressed that Article 84 made it not merely the right but the duty of the administering authority to ensure that the trust territories play their part in the maintenance of international peace and security. The authorities had the corresponding right to the means for discharging this duty. The only limitation imposed by Article 84 was that the forces to be used must be volunteer, not conscripted, forces. Furthermore, it was argued, the Charter does not require that all trust territories on which military installations are established be designated strategic areas; indeed, the decision whether they are to be so designated is left to the discretion of the administering authority, subject to approval by the Security Council.

At the end of the lengthy debate, all the amendments were defeated and the eight trusteeship agreements approved. The Soviet Union continued to insist that the agreements should be rejected as inconsistent with the Charter, arguing in particular that the provisions for the

[143] Whether such natives could be used for the defense of the territory of the mandatory power itself was never resolved in the League. See Wright, pp. 39 and 115.

[144] Russell, p. 836.   [145] UNCIO, *Documents*, X, 485.

[146] Russell, p. 836, fn. 48. See also commentary on Art. 83.

establishment of military, naval, and air bases without the consent of the Security Council were contrary to Article 83 of the Charter.[147]

The application of Article 84 was again discussed at the next session when the Assembly considered the draft trusteeship agreement for Nauru, which included a provision authorizing the administering authority to "take all measures in the Territory which it considers desirable to provide for the defence of the Territory and for the maintenance of international peace and security." A reference to the duties of the administering authority under Article 84 was added but proposals to refer to Article 83 or to restrict the measures to be taken to those necessary for local defense and the maintenance of law and order in the territory were defeated.[148]

A brief discussion bearing upon Article 84 also occurred in the Trusteeship Council when it was considering the questionnaire it is required to formulate in accordance with Article 88 of the Charter. On that occasion, it decided to include questions concerning local defense and the maintenance of law and order in the trust territories, but not to include questions concerning forces and bases or expenditures thereon.[149]

The only other discussion of Article 84 occurred in 1960 when protests were raised that Belgium was permitting certain elements in the Congo to use facilities in the adjoining trust territory of Ruanda-Urundi. The General Assembly called upon Belgium as the administering authority "to refrain from using the territory as a base whether for internal or external purposes for the accumulation of armaments and armed forces not strictly required for the purposes of maintaining public order in the territory." [150] Even stronger action was subsequently proposed in the Security Council when a draft resolution was unsuccessfully introduced recommending that the General Assembly consider Belgium's action as a "violation of the trusteeship agreement." [151]

Article 85

1. The functions of the United Nations with regard to trusteeship agreements for all areas not designated as strategic, including the approval of the terms of the trusteeship agreements and of their alteration or amendment, shall be exercised by the General Assembly.

2. The Trusteeship Council, operating under the authority of the

[147] GAOR/1st Sess., 2d Part/62d Plen. Mtg./Dec. 13, 1946/pp. 1279–83.
[148] GAOR/2d Sess., 4th Ctte./Annex 2, pp. 130 ff.
[149] TCOR/1st Sess./24th–25th Mtgs./Apr. 25–26, 1947/pp. 614 ff.
[150] GA Res. 1579(XV), Dec. 20, 1960.
[151] SCOR/16th Yr./924th–927th Mtgs./Jan. 12–14, 1961. See also SCOR/16th Yr./Supp. for Jan., Feb., and Mar. 1961; UN Doc. S/4606, Jan. 1, 1961; and S/4621, Jan. 11, 1961.

General Assembly, shall assist the General Assembly in carrying out these functions.

Article 85 establishes a system quite different from that of the Covenant of the League of Nations, which made the Council responsible for the performance of League functions concerning the mandated territories. It was assisted by the Permanent Mandates Commission, a body of experts appointed by it. The Covenant assigned no role to the League Assembly, but in practice the Assembly reviewed the administration of the mandates in connection with its consideration of the Secretary-General's report, and it did not hesitate to raise criticisms and make recommendations.[152]

The idea of giving the General Assembly the overall responsibility for discharging the functions of the United Nations with regard to trusteeship (except for strategic trusteeship) originated with the United States.[153] It was readily accepted at the San Francisco Conference. Australia and Britain, however, preferred, in place of the Trusteeship Council, an expert commission similar to the Permanent Mandates Commission that would have reported to the General Assembly through the Economic and Social Council. This reflected a view that the United Nations would be primarily concerned with economic, social, and humanitarian matters in the trust territories. The United States maintained that the trusteeship organ should have a higher status with political representation and should report directly to the Assembly.[154]

The operation of the trusteeship system has been profoundly different from that of the mandates system, and the decision to entrust the functions of supervision to the General Assembly and the Trusteeship Council has apparently been a major, although by no means the only, reason for the difference. One writer has commented upon the differences between the two systems as follows:

The broad powers of the General Assembly in trusteeship matters, its relationship to the Trusteeship Council, and the governmental character of the membership of the Council contrast sharply with the limited powers of the Assembly under the League of Nations mandates system, the subordination of the Permanent Mandates Commission to the Council of the League, and the independent status and technical competence of the members of the Mandates Commission.[155]

It has been generally agreed that the functions of the Trusteeship Council are not limited to those specifically assigned to it under Arti-

[152] Wright, pp. 133–35.
[153] For the development of the U.S. position on this matter, see Russell, pp. 335–36, 341–43, 577, and 580.
[154] *Ibid.*, pp. 838–39. [155] Sady, in Asher, p. 840.

cles 87 and 88 of the Charter. This is reflected in the Council's Rules of Procedure.[156] Moreover, the Council has, on occasion, undertaken special assignments for the General Assembly, as requested by it: 1) to examine the reports initially submitted by South Africa concerning the mandated territory of South West Africa; 2) to negotiate the draft trusteeship for Somaliland with the designated administering authority, Italy; and 3) to draft the statute for a special international regime for Jerusalem which, had it come into force, would have required the Trusteeship Council to assume certain responsibilities for the operation of the regime.[157]

The relations between the General Assembly and the Trusteeship Council have been complicated by the fact that, while each is listed as a "principal organ of the United Nations" (Art. 7), the Charter grants both organs concurrent functions with respect to the supervision of developments in the trust territories. It also specifies that the Council in carrying out these functions operates "under the authority of the General Assembly" (Arts. 85[2] and 87).

It was clearly intended that the General Assembly would exercise an overall supervision, with the Trusteeship Council undertaking the detailed consideration of conditions in the trust territories. The Assembly would not itself exercise the specific functions listed in Article 87 but would consider developments in the trust territories on the basis of the annual reports that the Trusteeship Council is required to submit to it (Arts. 15[2] and 88).

Since the Trusteeship Council is equally divided between administering and nonadministering members (Art. 86), the administering authorities, acting together, can prevent the Council from taking any action they oppose. In the General Assembly, on the other hand, they are very much in the minority. Their position is protected to some extent by the requirement that decisions on trusteeship matters must be approved by two-thirds of the members present and voting (Art. 18). But the administering authorities have frequently been unable to muster sufficient support to block measures of which they disapprove.

As many members came increasingly to view the Trusteeship Council as too subservient to the interests of the administering authorities, the General Assembly exercised more directly the functions of the United Nations under the trusteeship system, "by-passing the Council or attempting to use the Council solely as its agent, somewhat as it would use one of its own subsidiary organs." [158]

[156] See comment on Rule 104 under Art. 87(d).
[157] See GA Res. 181(II)A, Nov. 29, 1947; and 303(IV), Dec. 9, 1949. See also commentary on Arts. 79 and 80.
[158] Sady, in Asher, p. 987.

The most controversial action in the General Assembly was the Fourth Committee's decision to grant hearings to petitioners. Protests that this was a confusion of the functions of the Trusteeship Council and the Assembly and that at the least the petitioners should be heard first in the Council were unavailing.[159] The kinds of requests the General Assembly should address to the administering authorities have also been the subject of debate. Thus, for example, at its fourth session, the Fourth Committee had before it a proposal that the Assembly call upon the administering authorities to furnish it with information on the development of the trust territories toward self-determination, self-government, or independence. The opposition argued that it was the function of the Council to exercise supervision over the trust territories, to obtain such information, and to report to the General Assembly. As a result, the proposal was amended to provide that the information be submitted to the Trusteeship Council.[160]

The area in which the greatest amount of friction has developed concerns the kinds of requests and recommendations that the General Assembly would or should address to the Trusteeship Council and the extent to which the Council is required to comply with them.[161]

The General Assembly has made recommendations to the Council concerning the form and content of its annual report to the Assembly, and on general procedures of the Council and its procedures with regard to visiting missions and the examination of petitions. These latter have often been challenged on the grounds that under Article 90 the Council has sole competence to adopt its rules of procedure and that the General Assembly should not seek to impose a particular procedure on the Council or make detailed recommendations to it. But the majority of members have not considered that the Assembly is barred from making recommendations concerning the Council's procedures.

As to the attitude of the Trusteeship Council toward the recommendations of the General Assembly, the *Repertory of United Nations Practice* states:

In cases in which these recommendations have been formulated in general terms, the Council has considered itself free to use its discretion in any subsequent action it might take upon them. In cases in which the General Assembly has made specific recommendations, or has indicated that it would desire the Council to take a certain course of action, debate has occurred, in some instances, on the question whether the Council was required, under Article 85(2) and Article 87, to carry out these recommendations.[162]

[159] See commentary on Art. 87.
[160] GAOR/4th Sess., 4th Ctte./100th Mtg./Oct. 14, 1949/pp. 54–55.
[161] For details, see *Repertory*, IV, 283–300; *Supp. 1*, II, 256–63; *Supp. 2*, III, 322–24.
[162] *Repertory*, IV, 295.

While the nonadministering members have in general taken the position that under Article 85 the Trusteeship Council is required to assist the General Assembly in carrying out its functions, the administering authorities have argued that the Council was not merely an executive organ of the General Assembly but a "principal" organ under the Charter, that an Assembly recommendation was only a request that should be discussed by the Council and not an instruction to be followed, and that the Council should follow it only in so far as the recommendation did not conflict with those provisions of the Charter relating to the Trusteeship Council.[163]

The resistance of the administering authorities to the implementation by the Trusteeship Council of recommendations which they had previously opposed in the General Assembly led in a number of instances to delays in the Council's taking action, and to the adoption of resolutions which at the most could be described as "quasi-compliance" with the Assembly's requests.[164]

[163] See, in particular, the debate in the Council on the Assembly's recommendation that the Council direct its visiting missions to report fully on the steps taken toward attaining the objectives set out in Art. 76(b). TCOR/6th Sess./9th–10th Mtgs./Jan. 30–31, 1950/pp. 56 ff.

[164] See, in particular, the debate in the Council on the Assembly's recommendations concerning the flying of the UN flag in the trust territories: TCOR/6th Sess./76th–77th Mtgs./Mar. 30, 1950/pp. 603 ff.; 7th Sess./30th Mtg./July 21, 1950/pp. 265 ff.; and the closer association of the indigenous inhabitants with the work of the Council: TCOR/13th Sess./523d–524th Mtgs./Mar. 23–24, 1954/pp. 319 ff.

CHAPTER XIII

The Trusteeship Council

COMPOSITION

Article 86

1. The Trusteeship Council shall consist of the following Members of the United Nations:
   a. those Members administering trust territories;
   b. such of those Members mentioned by name in Article 23 as are not administering trust territories; and
   c. as many other Members elected for three-year terms by the General Assembly as may be necessary to ensure that the total number of members of the Trusteeship Council is equally divided between those Members of the United Nations which administer trust territories and those which do not.
2. Each member of the Trusteeship Council shall designate one specially qualified person to represent it therein.

Membership

The Trusteeship Council is composed of three categories of members: (a) those members of the United Nations that administer trust territories; (b) the permanent members of the Security Council not included in category (a); and (c) members elected for three-year terms by a two-thirds vote of the General Assembly. Article 86 provides for "balanced" representation in the Council between administering and nonadministering members. Thus, the size of the Council and the number of members to be elected by the General Assembly vary in accordance with the number of administering members.

At the San Francisco Conference, the United States originally proposed a Council divided equally between administering and elected members. The Soviet Union insisted that all the permanent members of the Security Council be guaranteed membership on the Trusteeship Council. There also was a proposal to constitute the Trusteeship Council on the basis of an equal number of elected and nonelected members, on the ground that the permanent members in their interests closely resembled the administering authorities and that the interests of the inhabitants would be better protected if half the members of the Council were elected by the General Assembly. This would have placed the administering members in a minority and for that reason the proposal was defeated.[1]

The first elections to the Trusteeship Council took place at the second part of the first session of the General Assembly, immediately after it had approved the first eight trusteeship agreements. The original composition of the Council included five administering members (Australia, Belgium, France, New Zealand, and the United Kingdom); two members (Mexico and Iraq) elected by the General Assembly; and the three permanent members of the Security Council (China, the Soviet Union, and the United States) that did not administer trust territories.

When the strategic trusteeship agreement for the Pacific Islands came into force on July 18, 1947, the United States became an "administering member." To correct the imbalance in representation, the Assembly elected two additional members to the Council. From 1948 to 1955, the composition of the Trusteeship Council remained the same: six administering members, four elected members, plus China and the Soviet Union.

The trusteeship agreement for Somaliland was concluded in 1950, with Italy designated as the administering authority. Since Article 86 restricts membership on the Trusteeship Council to members of the United Nations and since Italy was not then a member, it was necessary to devise special rules to permit Italy's participation in the Council's deliberations. Italy was not, however, given the right to vote and therefore it was not considered necessary to elect an additional member to the Council to maintain the balance between administering and nonadministering members. When Italy was admitted to United Nations membership at the end of 1955, it became a full member of the Trusteeship Council and the Assembly consequently elected an additional member to the Council. From 1956 to 1960, the Council was thus composed of seven administering members, five elected members, plus China and the Soviet Union.

The elected members of the Trusteeship Council have been drawn from two groups within the United Nations: the Latin American states and the Afro-Asian group.

The Charter provides for a three-year term for the elected members of the Trusteeship Council. As in other Councils, the term of office

[1] For discussion at San Francisco, see Ruth B. Russell, *A History of the United Nations Charter* (Washington, Brookings Institution, 1958), pp. 839 and 841; and UNCIO, *Documents*, X, 516–17.

begins on January 1 following the election.[2] However, the Rules of Procedure of the General Assembly make an exception in the case where a member is elected to the Trusteeship Council because a new trusteeship agreement has been concluded and the number of administering authorities thereby increased. Under these special circumstances, the newly elected members take office immediately upon election. The three-year term of office, however, dates from January 1 of the year following the election.[3] As in the other Councils, if an elected member of the Trusteeship Council retires before its term of office has expired, the Assembly holds a by-election to fill the unexpired terms. The Charter neither specifically prohibits nor expressly permits the reelection of members; reelection has, however, been very common.

Since 1960, the composition of the Trusteeship Council has presented a dilemma which the drafters of the Charter failed to foresee. This has been due to the success of the trusteeship system in achieving the objectives of independence for the trust territories.

At the time of the Assembly's 1959 session, the Council was composed of seven administering members: two "permanent" nonadministering members (China and the Soviet Union) and five elected members, three of which had been elected at the previous session for terms running from 1959 through 1961. The terms of the other two elected members were to end on December 31, 1959. The issue before the Assembly was whether two new members should be elected in view of the fact that the number of administering members was soon to be reduced. The two territories under French administration, the Cameroons and Togoland, were scheduled to become independent in 1960, and the date for the termination of Italy's trusteeship over Somaliland had been set for July 1, 1960. The number of administering members would thus be reduced from seven to five. At the same time, the number of nonadministering members would be augmented, since France as a permanent member of the Security Council would retain a seat on the Trusteeship Council even after it ceased to be an administering member.

There was considerable divergence of opinion, cutting across the normal pattern of Assembly alignments, on the action to be taken.[4] The difficulty lay in reconciling the principle of parity with the requirement of the three-year term. When none of the various proposals received the required two-thirds vote, the Assembly proceeded to elect two members, leaving the future to take care of itself.

[2] See GA Rules of Procedure, Rule 140.   [3] *Ibid.*, Rule 148.

[4] For a detailed account of these proceedings, see Sydney Bailey, *The General Assembly of the United Nations* (New York, Praeger, 1960), pp. 187 ff. For record of discussion, see GAOR/14th Sess./857th Plen. Mtg./Dec. 12, 1959/pp. 780 ff.

As of July, 1960, the Trusteeship Council was thus composed of five administering and eight nonadministering members. Despite this imbalance, the General Assembly at its next session accepted the suggestion that the Council continue to function with this membership until the end of 1960, at which time the terms of three elected members would expire and balance would be restored.[5]

By the end of 1961, however there had been further progress in the liquidation of the trusteeship system. When Tanganyika and Western Samoa became independent on December 9, 1961, and January 1, 1962, respectively, New Zealand and the United Kingdom ceased to be "members administering trust territories," the terminology used in Article 86. However, they are jointly designated with Australia as the "administering authority" for the trust territory of Nauru. Although Australia is, in fact, the member "administering" the territory, it was agreed that all three should be considered as administering members. Under this interpretation, the Trusteeship Council at the beginning of 1962 was composed of an equal number of administering and nonadministering members. However, when Ruanda and Urundi became independent in July, 1962, Belgium ceased to be a member of the Council and the balance was again upset until the terms of two elected members expired at the end of the year. Liberia was then elected to the Council, the first country from sub-Saharan Africa to be so chosen. With the termination of all the African trusteeships, the size of the Trusteeship Council thus became much reduced, with four administering members (Australia, New Zealand, the United Kingdom, and the United States); three permanent nonadministering members (China, France, and the Soviet Union); and a single elected member (Liberia). Independence for Nauru by January 31, 1968, in accordance with the General Assembly resolution of December 21, 1965, by reducing the number of administering authorities to two, creates a situation in which under the provisions of Article 86 it is impossible to achieve the equal division "between those members of the United Nations which administer trust territories and those which do not" except by the creation of new trust territories.

Representation on the Council

The Charter provides that each member of the Trusteeship Council shall have one representative. Its Rules of Procedure concerning alternate representatives and advisers, and the rules governing the submission and examination of credentials, are essentially the same as

[5] GAOR/15th Sess./979th Mtg./Apr. 7, 1961/pp. 235–36.

those of the other Councils. The Trusteeship Council has followed the practice of other Councils in rejecting the argument that actions taken in the absence of a member of the Council are invalid.[6] In protest against the trusteeship agreements, the Soviet Union refused to take part in the Council sessions until April, 1948. Also, the Trusteeship Council, like other United Nations organs, has been confronted with the problem of China's representation. The Soviet Union again boycotted the Council, from January to November, 1950, in protest against the continued seating of the Chinese Nationalists.

Two features relevant to representation on the Trusteeship Council call for special comment. In the first place, the Charter states that each member shall designate one "specially qualified person" to represent it on the Council. The inclusion of this phrase was a carry-over from the League of Nations, where the main burden of overseeing the operation of the mandates system had rested with the Permanent Mandates Commission, a body of individual experts appointed by the Council to assist it. Although under the United Nations system, a body composed of member states was accepted, there was still a desire to stress the concept of technical competence. Since the members of the Council are sovereign states and can designate whomsoever they please to represent them, the inclusion of this provision in the Charter was more in the nature of a hope than a requirement. In practice, the administering members have generally been represented by persons with previous experience in colonial administration and, whenever a particular territory is under discussion in the Council, experts are available to give information and answer questions. As for the nonadministering members, many of their delegates have acquired considerable expertise through long service on the Assembly's Fourth Committee, on the Trusteeship Council, and through participation in the visiting missions and other bodies concerned with the trusteeship system.

A second unique feature of representation on the Trusteeship Council stems from the repeated recommendations by the General Assembly and by the Council itself that the administering authorities associate the peoples of the trust territories more closely with the work of the Council. As a result, it has become a relatively common practice for the administering authorities to include on their delegations representatives of the inhabitants of the trust territories.

[6] For comment on the quorum rule, see Art. 89.

FUNCTIONS AND POWERS

Article 87

The General Assembly and, under its authority, the Trusteeship Council, in carrying out their functions, may:

a. consider reports submitted by the administering authority;
b. accept petitions and examine them in consultation with the administering authority;
c. provide for periodic visits to the respective trust territories at times agreed upon with the administering authority; and
d. take these and other actions in conformity with the terms of the trusteeship agreements.

One of the most significant distinctions between the United Nations trusteeship system and the League of Nations mandates system is the more extensive power of supervision entrusted to United Nations organs under the Charter. The only specific function of supervision mentioned in the Covenant was the examination of the annual reports the mandatory powers were required to submit to the Council. From the beginning it was taken for granted that the United Nations would be similarly authorized to examine the annual reports submitted by administering authorities on territories placed under the trusteeship system. The powers of the United Nations in this respect are further enhanced by the requirement that the annual reports be based upon a questionnaire formulated by the Trusteeship Council in accordance with Article 88 of the Charter. These provisions were included in the Charter without difficulty.

In all the United States plans, the rights to accept petitions and to institute investigations in the trust territories were considered essential elements of any trusteeship system.[7] Although not mentioned in the Covenant, a rudimentary system for handling petitions had been developed in the League.[8] The Council adopted a procedure by which petitions from the inhabitants of the mandated territories were received if submitted through the mandatory power, which was required to append its comments. Petitions from other sources, if considered of sufficient importance, could also be brought to the attention of the Council. There was, however, no procedure for carrying out investigations in the mandated territories. It was the contention of the manda-

[7] See Russell, pp. 334, 342, 580.
[8] Quincy Wright, *Mandates under the League of Nations* (Chicago, University of Chicago Press, 1930), p. 170.

tory powers that inquiries on the spot under the direction of the Permanent Mandates Commission would undermine the authority of the mandatory powers. During the discussions among the five powers at San Francisco, France and the United Kingdom raised this same objection to the United States proposal to authorize the United Nations to accept petitions and institute investigations. A compromise was reached whereby the General Assembly and, under its authority, the Trusteeship Council were authorized to examine petitions "in consultation with the administering authority" and further authorized to carry out periodic visits, albeit "at times agreed upon with the administering authority." [9] These formulas were accepted by the San Francisco Conference and incorporated in Article 87.

All the trusteeship agreements contain provisions by which the administering authority undertakes to facilitate the performance by the Trusteeship Council and the General Assembly of the functions enumerated in Article 87.[10] The one exception is the strategic agreement for the Pacific Islands: Article 87 does not specifically apply to strategic trusteeships. Nonetheless, the strategic trusteeship agreement states that the provisions of Article 87 and 88 shall be applicable and the Trusteeship Council is entrusted with the performance of the tasks listed in Article 87. In practice, there has been no significant difference in the way the Trusteeship Council has carried out its functions with regard to strategic and other trusteeships. The following comments upon the operations of the Trusteeship Council thus apply to both types, but the comments concerning the General Assembly are not relevant to strategic trusteeships.

Reports by Administering Authorities

Article 87(a) empowers the General Assembly and the Trusteeship Council to consider reports submitted by the administering authorities. Although Article 88 stipulates that the annual reports of the administering authority shall be submitted to the General Assembly, the Trusteeship Council undertakes the detailed consideration of the reports. The annual reports and their examination by the Council "constitute the backbone of the system of international supervision." They provide the basis for review by the Council of conditions in the trust territories and of the manner in which the administering authorities are fulfilling their obligations. It is through the examination of reports that the Council "follows up on general questions raised in petitions, on the findings of

[9] Russell, pp. 839–40.

[10] See "Comparative Survey of Individual Trusteeship Agreements Showing the Formulation of the Terms Bearing upon the Application of Article 87" in *Repertory*, IV, 394–99.

its visiting missions, and on the steps taken by the administering authorities to carry out recommendations of the Council and the Assembly." [11]

A large part of each session of the Trusteeship Council is devoted to examining the annual reports of the administering authorities. In accordance with the Council's Rules of Procedure and the terms of the trusteeship agreements, a "special representative," usually an official from the territory, is present to answer questions by other Council members.[12]

The reports are considered by the Council in conjunction with petitions concerning the territory and, when available, the reports of visiting missions to the territories. Together these provide the basis for the Council's report to the General Assembly. Although the Assembly itself has never directly considered the annual reports of the administering authorities, it has made recommendations concerning their content and on a few occasions requested the administering authorities to report directly to it on particular subjects. To proposals of this kind, it has sometimes been objected that the Assembly is interfering with functions that should be performed by the Trusteeship Council, but in general the Assembly has tended to assert and protect its own authority.

Petitions

The importance attached to the examination of petitions as an element in the supervision of trust territories is reflected in the fact that the handling of petitions became a major source of friction within the Trusteeship Council and between the Council and the General Assembly. Within the Council, the administering members had some success in placing restrictions upon the right of petition, but in the Assembly, where they are in the minority, their efforts have been unavailing.

In general, the Trusteeship Council has followed a liberal policy with respect to the acceptance and examination of petitions. Under the Rules of Procedure, petitions may concern "the affairs of one or more Trust Territories or the operation of the International Trusteeship System" (Rule 76). They may be from the "inhabitants of Trust Territories or other parties" (Rule 77). They may be presented in writing or orally (Rule 78). A written petition may be in the form of a letter, telegram, or other document and may be addressed directly to the Secretary-General or transmitted to him through the administering

---

[11] Sady, in Robert E. Asher et al., *The United Nations and Promotion of the General Welfare* (Washington, Brookings Institution, 1957), p. 946.
[12] See TC, Rules of Procedure, XIV, "Examination of Annual Reports." See also XIII, on the submission of reports, UN Doc. T/1/Rev. 6, 1962.

authority. Representatives of the Trusteeship Council engaged on visiting missions are also authorized to accept petitions; such missions decide "which of the communications are intended for its own information and which . . . are to be transmitted to the Secretary-General" (Rule 84).

Normally, petitions are considered inadmissible if they are directed against judgments of competent courts of the administering authority, but this does not preclude the consideration of petitions against legislation on the ground of incompatibility with the Charter of the United Nations or the trusteeship agreement.

Over the years, the rules concerning the submission and circulation of petitions, as well as the rules governing their examination, have been subject to numerous changes prompted largely by the volume of work to be performed, but also by proddings from the General Assembly. At its early sessions, the Council created an ad hoc committee which met during each session to advise on the admissibility of petitions and to group them for more expeditious examination by the Council. The task of examining petitions proved much greater than had been anticipated and the backlog of unexamined petitions became a matter of serious concern, especially to the nonadministering members. As a result, in 1950 the General Assembly adopted a resolution stressing that the right of petition was one of the fundamental human rights and one of the most important features of the trusteeship system. It made a number of recommendations to the Trusteeship Council for improving the procedure for handling petitions, including a request that the Council consider the advisability of constituting a special committee on petitions to meet if necessary between sessions.[13] Some administering authorities objected to a standing committee, and it was not until 1952 that such a committee was established.

The revised Rules of Procedure provided for a standing committee composed of three administering and three nonadministering members, appointed at the end of each regular session.[14] The work of the committee has been described as follows:

The Standing Committee screens the petitions and performs a variety of other tasks in connection with them. . . . Between sessions of the Council, the Standing Committee conducts, in consultation with representatives of the administering authority concerned, a preliminary examination of those petitions on which written observations by the administering authority are available. It attempts to complete its preliminary examination of those petitions that the administering authority agrees to have examined without the

[13] GA Res. 435(V), Dec. 12, 1950. See also GA Res. 321(IV), Nov. 15, 1949; and 552(VI), Jan. 18, 1952.
[14] TC, Rules of Procedure, XV, Rule 90.

presence of the special representative. It formulates questions for submission to the administering authority or its special representative, when necessary, and instructs the Secretariat to make such studies as may be needed. The committee prepares a report to the Council on each petition to which the established petition procedure should be applied together with recommendations for action by the Council in each case.[15]

The Trusteeship Council may decide to take no action on a petition or merely to direct the attention of the petitioner to the observations of the administering authority. It has referred petitioners to local courts or called their attention to their legal and political rights. On occasion, it has requested the administering authority to look into the complaint and to inform the Council of the results of its inquiries. In some cases, the Council has recommended special measures or action to be taken by the administering authority or has suggested that the administering authority reconsider its decisions.[16] Under the Rules, the Secretary-General is entrusted with the task of informing the administering authorities and the petitioners of the actions taken by the Council and of transmitting to them the official records of the public meetings at which the petitions were examined.[17]

The establishment of the Standing Committee and the revisions in the Rules that accompanied this action brought a considerable improvement in the examination of petitions. The acute political problems that arose as many of the trust territories moved toward independence, however, brought a flood of petitions that could not be handled under the existing procedures.[18] As a special measure, the Council at its seventeenth session appointed a committee on communications from the French Cameroons, where the situation was further complicated by the receipt of numerous petitions from political organizations outlawed by the administering authority and upon which that authority refused to submit observations.[19] In 1957, the continued increase in the quantity of petitions, as well as the large backlog of unexamined petitions, led the Trusteeship Council to reconsider its procedures. It established a committee on classification of communications, consisting of two members, to determine with the assistance of the Secretariat the provisional classification of all communications received. The committee was also given broad powers to summarize petitions when confronted with a large number of them on the same subject.[20]

[15] Sady, in Asher, p. 952.   [16] *Repertory*, IV, 347.
[17] TC, Rules of Procedure, XVI, Rule 92.
[18] On the growth of the number of petitions, see *Repertory*, IV, 390; *Supp. 1*, II, 287; *Supp. 2*, III, 345.
[19] See *Repertory, Supp. 1*, II, 280–81; and *Supp. 2*, III, 339, for similar situation in the British Cameroons.
[20] TC Res. 1713(XX), July 8, 1957. See also TCOR/19th Sess./759th Mtg./ Mar. 25, 1957/pp. 47 ff., with regard to the temporary committee set up at the previous session.

As more trust territories achieved independence, the load of petitions naturally decreased. In 1961, the Trusteeship Council decided to discontinue the special procedures adopted in 1957 and to disband the committee on classification.[21] The following year, the Council decided to revise its Rules and to disband the standing committee on petitions since, with only three South Pacific territories under the trusteeship system, the Council could itself undertake all of the functions of examining petitions.[22]

The preceding comments are concerned primarily with the handling of written petitions; nevertheless, Article 87(b) has been interpreted as authorizing oral petitions as well. The handling of these provoked sharp controversy in the Trusteeship Council and the General Assembly. Under its Rules of Procedure, the Trusteeship Council "may hear oral presentations in support or elaboration of a previously submitted written petition" and, "in exceptional cases," it may hear oral petitions that have not been previously submitted in writing, provided the Council and the administering authority have been previously informed of the subject matter. The Council President is authorized between sessions to inform any petitioner when and where the Council will grant him a hearing. But if the administering authority is of the opinion that there are "substantial reasons" why the matter should first be discussed in the Council, the action of the President is deferred (Rule 80). Representatives on visiting missions and other official missions are also authorized to receive oral petitions subject to instructions they may receive from the Council.

In the General Assembly, there are no rules covering the hearing of petitioners. The subject did not come up during the first few sessions of the Assembly, apparently because it had not occurred to anyone that the Assembly could itself exercise directly the functions listed in Article 87. In 1951 the Assembly's Fourth Committee decide to grant hearings to petitioners from trust territories. At that and subsequent sessions, a number of members expressed the view that petitioners should be heard first by the Trusteeship Council, but this view did not prevail. Concern over the indiscriminate granting of requests for hearings and the tendency of the Fourth Committee to usurp the functions of the Trusteeship Council led to efforts to establish some criteria for determining what kinds of petitions the committee should consider. But these efforts were unsuccessful.

Despite repeated protests, usually by the administering authorities— that certain petitioners should be heard by the Trusteeship Council rather than the Fourth Committee, that the Committee should not normally hear petitioners not residents of the trust territories or repre-

[21] TCOR/27th Sess./1171st Mtg./July 13, 1961/pp. 199 ff.
[22] TC Res. 2134(XXIX), June 4, 1962.

sentatives of organizations declared illegal in the territories, and that the Committee should not grant hearings without foreknowledge of the status of petitioners and the subject matter they wish to raise—the Fourth Committee continued to follow a liberal policy in granting requests and, indeed, adopted many resolutions designed to facilitate the access of petitioners to the Committee.[23]

Visiting Missions

The authority given to the United Nations under Article 87(c) to dispatch visiting missions to territories under trusteeship was a significant innovation in the procedures of international supervision. The missions permit representatives of the Trusteeship Council to check on the spot information supplied by the administering authorities in their annual reports and to look into issues raised in the petitions received by the Council. They place the United Nations in direct contact with the people of the territory and to some degree acquaint them with the Organization and its interest in their problems.

When the Trusteeship Council first considered the composition of visiting missions, some members, including the Soviet Union, contended that, as the Council was composed of states, the visiting missions should be similarly constituted. On the other hand, it was argued that the missions represented the Council and not individual governments, that the Council must be assured of the competence and integrity of the members of the mission, and that it should thus designate specific individuals to serve as members of the missions. It was finally decided that the "Trusteeship Council shall select the members of each visiting mission who shall preferably be one or more of the representatives on the Council." The general practice has been for the Council to select states that are members of the Council; they in turn nominate persons to serve on the missions, and the individual nominations are then approved by the Council. The Rules of Procedure also state that "a mission and the individual members thereof shall, while engaged in a visit, act only on the basis of the instructions of the Council and shall be responsible exclusively to it." [24]

Most of the individuals who have served on the visiting missions have been either representatives or alternate representatives of members of the Trusteeship Council. The desirability of having such representatives participate in the visiting missions was recognized from the beginning by the Council. This principle was reaffirmed by the General Assembly which, however, recommended that other members be in-

[23] For a summary of the Assembly practice in hearing petitioners from the trust territories, see *Repertory*, IV, 278–82; *Supp. 1*, II, 249–56; *Supp. 2*, III, 308–21.
[24] TC, Rules of Procedure, XVI, Rule 95.

vited to nominate persons to serve on the missions if the appointment of representatives on the Council was not possible.[25]

The size of the visiting missions is not specified in the Council's Rules of Procedure. In practice, missions have been composed of four representatives: two selected from states that are administering authorities, and two from nonadministering states. The administering authority of the territory being visited, however, never has one of its nationals on the mission. Initially, there was some support for larger missions, but four-member teams have been accepted, largely because of the difficulty of finding qualified representatives to serve and also because of transportation and cost factors.[26]

The Rules of Procedure also provide that "acting in conformity with the terms of the respective Trusteeship agreements," the Council shall define the terms of reference of each mission and issue "such special instructions as it may consider appropriate" (Rule 94). The Council may, "in agreement with the administering authority," conduct "special investigations or inquiries when it considers that conditions in a Trust Territory make such action desirable" (Rule 96).[27]

Each mission is required to report on its visit to the Trusteeship Council. Generally, representatives of the administering authority are consulted during the drafting of the report. The reports, while differing substantially in tone, follow the same general pattern, with chapters on political, economic, social, and educational conditions, and separate chapters on special problems. The reports, including the comments and observations of the missions, are discussed by the Trusteeship Council, usually in conjunction with the annual reports of the administering authorities and the petitions concerning the territory. The reports of the missions are usually not discussed directly in the General Assembly, which generally bases its debate on the report of the Trusteeship Council itself.

Although the Rules of Procedure say nothing about the frequency of visits to the trust territory, the practice developed of sending a mission to each territory every three years. In the Preparatory Commission, annual visits were suggested and some members favored biennial visits. At the other extreme, France and the United Kingdom suggested in the Trusteeship Council that visits every four or five years would be sufficient. One practical reason for accepting the three-year cycle was that the territories to be visited fell into three geographic groups, i.e. West Africa, East Africa, and the South Pacific.

[25] GA Res. 553(VI), Jan. 18, 1952. See also GA Res. 434(V), Dec. 2, 1950.
[26] All expenses of the missions are borne by the UN. See Rules of Procedure, XVI, Rule 97.
[27] There is no mention of "special investigations" in the Charter or the trusteeship agreements.

The General Assembly has been critical of the time spent by the missions in the territories. In 1950 and again in 1951, it recommended that the Council review its procedures, particularly with a view to increasing the duration of the visits and limiting the number of territories visited by any single mission.[28] The Council, however, did not change its procedures. The situation subsequently became more critical with the increased tempo of activities in the trust territories as progress toward independence accelerated.

In 1954, the General Assembly requested the Council to send a special mission to the territories of British and French Togoland.[29] No such mission was sent, but the Council did depart from its usual procedure by sending out two missions, one to the two Togolands and another to the British and French Cameroons. The Council followed a similar procedure in 1959 and in 1960 with missions to the South Pacific territories.

When the above-mentioned Assembly request for a special mission to the Togolands was discussed in the Trusteeship Council, the French representative objected that the only missions the Council was authorized to dispatch under Article 87(c) were the regular periodic visiting missions. Any special inquiry would require the agreement of the administering authority.[30] Subsequently, when France asked the Council to "appoint a mission of observers to observe the referendum" France intended to conduct in French Togoland, the proposal was defeated by a tie vote in the Council. A number of members were not satisfied with the conditions under which the observation would be undertaken, but it was also argued that in acceding to France's request, the Council would be going beyond the role assigned to it under the Charter.[31] None of the missions dispatched by the Trusteeship Council can therefore be considered as "special missions," with the exception of the first mission to Western Samoa, which was sent out in 1947 before the procedures of the Trusteeship Council had been fully established.

While all the "periodic visits," as this phrase in Article 87(c) has been interpreted, have been undertaken under the direction of the Trusteeship Council, the General Assembly has felt free to express its opinion on the organization and procedures of the visiting missions. From time to time, the Assembly has singled out particular tasks it has felt the visiting missions should be asked to perform. In particular, as certain trust territories have progressed toward independence, the visiting missions have been asked to assist in ascertaining the wishes of the

[28] GA Res. 434(V), Dec. 2, 1950; and 553(VI), Jan. 18, 1952.
[29] GA Res. 860(IX), Dec. 14, 1954.
[30] TCOR/15th Sess./597th Mtg./Mar. 11, 1955/p. 258. See above comments on Rule 96.
[31] TCOR/18th Sess./737th–745th Mtgs./Aug. 2–14, 1956/pp. 299–348.

population. In this connection, the Assembly in a number of instances has itself established its own subsidiary bodies to investigate and observe events in the trust territories.[32]

Other Council Functions

After setting out the powers of the General Assembly and, under its authority, the Trusteeship Council with regard to the reports of the administering authorities, petitions, and visiting missions, Article 87(d) goes on to state that the two organs may "take these and other actions in conformity with the terms of the trusteeship agreements." This paragraph allows the powers of the two organs to be extended by the terms of the trusteeship agreement, but it also has a restrictive effect by stipulating that the actions of the two organs must conform to the terms of the individual trusteeship agreements.[33]

The provisional rules of procedure drafted by the Preparatory Commission stated that "the Council shall perform such other functions as may be provided for in the Trusteeship Agreements or as may be assigned to it by the General Assembly or the Security Council." [34] In the Trusteeship Council, objections were raised that this rule was too broad. By authorizing the Trusteeship Council to undertake any functions assigned to it by the other two organs, the essential basis of the trusteeship system—that is, the trusteeship agreements—would be undermined. The rule as finally approved provided that:

The Trusteeship Council shall perform such other functions as may be provided for in the Trusteeship Agreements, and, in pursuance of the duty imposed upon it by Article 85 of the Charter, may submit to the General Assembly recommendations concerning the functions of the United Nations with regard to Trusteeship Agreements, including the approval of the terms of the Trusteeship Agreements and of their alteration or amendment. With regard to strategic areas, the Trusteeship Council may similarly perform such functions in so far as it may be requested to do so by the Security Council. [Rule 103]

Under this rule, actions taken by the Trusteeship Council under Article 87 "must" be provided for in the trusteeship agreements,[35] but the Council may also take action under Articles 83 and 85 in the general field of trusteeship.

None of the trusteeship agreements have called for the Trusteeship Council or the General Assembly to take actions other than those specified in paragraphs (a), (b), and (c) of Article 87. None of the

[32] See commentary on Art. 76(b).   [33] See UNCIO, *Documents,* X, 679.
[34] *Report of the Preparatory Commission,* ch. IV, sec. 2.
[35] *Repertory,* IV, 386.

actions of the two organs relating to the supervision of the administration of trust territories "has ever been explicitly based" on paragraph (d) of that article.[36]

Article 88

The Trusteeship Council shall formulate a questionnaire on the political, economic, social, and educational advancement of the inhabitants of each trust territory, and the administering authority for each trust territory within the competence of the General Assembly shall make an annual report to the General Assembly upon the basis of such questionnaire.

Annual Reports

In requiring the administering authorities to render annual reports upon their administration of the trust territories for which they are responsible, the United Nations Charter follows the practice established in the League of Nations Covenant. Under the League system, the mandatory powers reported to the Council (Article 22[7]), whereas Article 88 of the Charter calls for annual reports to the General Assembly on each trust territory within its competence. There is no mention in the article of reports on trust territories designated as strategic areas and thus, under the Charter, within the competence of the Security Council rather than the Assembly. At the San Francisco Conference, a proposal to require administering authorities to report on such territories to the Security Council was rejected because of United States opposition.[37] Nevertheless, the only strategic trusteeship agreement that has been approved by the Security Council provides for the application of the provisions of Article 88 to the Pacific Islands trust territory. Under the arrangements worked out between the Security Council and the Trusteeship Council pursuant to Article 83, the United States, as the administering authority for the territory, submits an annual report that is essentially no different from the reports on other trust territories.

Within the Trusteeship Council, there was initially considerable divergence concerning the form and content of the annual reports to be submitted by the administering authorities. In general, the administering authorities preferred the "narrative" form. They objected to including in each annual report full information on matters on which there had been no change. Furthermore, they objected to preparing separate reports for the Trusteeship Council covering subjects already reported

---

[36] *Ibid.,* p. 328.   [37] See Russell, pp. 839 and 589.

on in full to the specialized agencies. Other members insisted on the inclusion of full information in each report. They also argued that the reports should be in the form of specific replies to the questions in the questionnaire, for only in that way could the obligation of Article 88 be fulfilled. With the revision of the questionnaire in 1956, this ceased to be a matter of concern.

The timing of the annual reports also caused some concern during the first decade of the Trusteeship Council's operations. In general, the administering authorities stressed the need for sufficient time, both for the preparation and study of the reports. Other members were disturbed by the time lag between the end of the period covered by the annual report and its examination by the Council, a lag sometimes as long as eighteen months. This problem was met partly by changes in the Council's procedures.[38]

The Questionnaire

The requirement in Article 88 that the annual reports of the administering authorities be based upon a questionnaire formulated by the Trusteeship Council represents an advance over the League system. The Permanent Mandates Commission of the League sought to achieve a measure of uniformity and greater completeness in the reports of the mandatory powers through the use of a questionnaire but achieved only partial success since the mandatory powers were under no obligation to use the questionnaire.[39] Article 88 requires the Trusteeship Council to formulate a questionnaire on the "political, economic, social, and educational advancement of the inhabitants of each trust territory." The listing of the matters to be covered was added to Article 88 at San Francisco on the insistence of some members as a guarantee of full publicity of the record of each administering authority.

Both the form and the content of the questionnaire have been the subject of disagreement, not only in the Trusteeship Council but also in the General Assembly. When the formulation of the questionnaire was first discussed in the Council, there were divergent views as to whether the questionnaire should be in the form of specific questions or in the form of topics upon which the administering authorities were to report. The provisional questionnaire, as approved by the Council, consisted mainly of specific questions. However, the administering authorities were also requested to include in their reports descriptive material on the territory and its inhabitants, a summary of progress made in various fields during the year, and an appendix providing statistical infor-

[38] See TC, Rules of Procedure, XIII, Rule 72.
[39] See Wright, pp. 160–61.

mation. The Council emphasized the provisional character of the questionnaire and invited the administering authorities, ECOSOC, and the specialized agencies to submit comments and suggestions for improvement.[40]

In 1952, a revised questionnaire was adopted by the Trusteeship Council. The "direct question" form was abandoned and the administering authorities were asked to supply descriptive information on the matters covered by this basic questionnaire.[41]

Another point regarding the interpretation of Article 88, discussed at some length in both the Trusteeship Council and the General Assembly, was whether a single questionnaire covering all trust territories was adequate or whether separate questionnaires should be prepared for each territory. Those favoring the latter stressed that the language of Article 88 called for a questionnaire "for each trust territory."

After considering the question of separate questionnaires adapted to the particular circumstances of each trust territory, the Assembly adopted a resolution drawing attention to the terms of Article 88 and stating that the basic questionnaire as revised by the Trusteeship Council in 1952 was "not applicable" in its entirety to all trust territories. It also established a special subcommittee to study the changes necessary to adapt the questionnaire to the special conditions of each territory.[42] There was some opposition to this resolution on the ground that Article 88 expressly conferred upon the Trusteeship Council the right to formulate the questionnaire and that the General Assembly should not usurp this function.[43]

In its 1956 report, the subcommittee stated that separate questionnaires were not necessary for a number of territories in view of the expected early termination of the trusteeships. On the basis of the subcommittee's suggestions and the views of the administering authorities, separate questionnaires were eventually adopted for New Guinea, Nauru, and Tanganyika. In 1961, the General Assembly abolished the subcommittee,[44] and at the same time the Trusteeship Council, on the basis of the work of its own ad hoc committee, made a number of changes in the basic questionnaire.

[40] TC Res. 7(I), Apr. 28, 1947.   [41] TC Res. 463(XI), June 6, 1952.
[42] GA Res. 751(VIII), Dec. 8, 1953. See also GA Res. 656(VII), Dec. 2, 1952, requesting that the Trusteeship Council consider the desirability of a special questionnaire for Somaliland, and the Council's reply that a special questionnaire was "not necessary."
[43] In this respect, Art. 88 differs from Art. 87, which mentions both organs.
[44] GA Res. 1645(XVI), Nov. 6, 1961.

VOTING

Article 89

1. Each member of the Trusteeship Council shall have one vote.
2. Decisions of the Trusteeship Council shall be made by a majority of the members present and voting.

In the Trusteeship Council, as in the Assembly and the other two Councils, each member has one vote. Decisions are made by a majority of those "present and voting" and, as in the other organs, those who abstain are not counted as voting. Although Article 89(2) mentions only "decisions," the Rules of Procedure refer to "decisions and recommendations" and, as is customary United Nations practice, "decisions" has been interpreted to cover both forms of action.[45] Voting is usually by a show of hands, but a roll call is taken whenever any member so requests.

Although "questions relating to the operation of the trusteeship system" require a two-thirds majority of members present and voting in the General Assembly,[46] decisions in the Trusteeship Council are made by a simple majority. It should be noted, however, that the Council carries out its functions "under the authority" of the Assembly and that it is the latter which performs the essential function of approving the terms of the trusteeship agreements and any alterations or amendments thereof.[47]

The administering authorities are also protected by the terms of Article 86 of the Charter against the Trusteeship Council's taking actions of which they disapprove. This article stipulates that membership on the Council shall be divided equally between administering and nonadministering members. The members in these two groups have not invariably voted together on every issue, but the split between the two groups has been apparent on a number of significant questions. Partly because of the composition of the Trusteeship Council, "tie" votes are by no means uncommon. The *Repertory of Practice* records over ninety tie votes during the first ten years of the Council's history. To deal with this situation, the Council included in its Rules of Procedure a unique provision. In the Assembly and in ECOSOC, if the votes

[45] TC, Rules of Procedure, VII, Rule 37. The procedures for elections in the TC are similar to those followed in other UN organs. TC, Rules of Procedure, VII, Rules 41–43.

[46] See commentary on Art. 18.　　　[47] See commentary on Art. 85.

are equally divided, a proposal is considered "rejected." [48] If a vote is equally divided in the Trusteeship Council, however, a second vote is taken "at the next meeting . . . or following a brief recess." [49] In a few cases, the second vote has resulted in a clear rejection of the proposal; occasionally the proposal has been adopted; generally, however, the Council has remained divided on the second vote as well and the proposal is "deemed to be lost." Because of this provision and the tendency toward tie votes, the members of the Trusteeship Council have been particularly sensitive to the manner in which a question is put to the vote. [50]

Recognition of the effect of "absences" upon the voting pattern in the Trusteeship Council has led to the inclusion of a second unique feature in the Council's Rules. In ECOSOC and in the plenary meetings of the General Assembly, a majority of members constitute a quorum. [51] In the Trusteeship Council, the presence of two-thirds of the members is required for a quorum, [52] thus protecting members from the possibility of action being taken by a "rump" Council.

Over the years, the practice developed whereby much of the work of the Trusteeship Council was based upon a "consensus," usually expressed by the President. To a much greater extent than in other organs, the Council has tended to avoid recourse to voting, particularly on matters that are procedural or not highly controversial. In line with this approach, the Council records its conclusions and recommendations in its reports to the General Assembly without any indication of voting but with ample opportunity for all members to have their individual opinions clearly stated. The split between the administering and nonadministering members in the Council, while resulting in a number of tie votes, has not paralyzed the Trusteeship Council to the extent that the veto has prevented action by the Security Council. Still, this split has often been cited as the chief reason why the General Assembly has taken over the direction of the operations of the trusteeship system to a greater extent than was originally anticipated. [53]

[48] Except in the case of elections, which are handled by special rules in all UN organs.

[49] TC, Rules of Procedure, VII, Rule 38.

[50] See, for example, the debate in TCOR/16th Sess./134th Mtg./June 30, 1960/p. 557.

[51] In Assembly committees, the presence of only one-third of the members is required, except when a vote is taken.

[52] TC, Rules of Procedure, X, Rule 50.   [53] See commentary on Art. 85.

PROCEDURE

Article 90

1. The Trusteeship Council shall adopt its own rules of procedure, including the method of selecting its President.

2. The Trusteeship Council shall meet as required in accordance with its rules, which shall include provision for the convening of meetings on the request of a majority of its members.

When the Council first met in April, 1947, it had before it the provisional rules formulated by the Preparatory Commission and referred to the Council by the General Assembly.[54] The Secretariat had also prepared a set of provisional rules based upon the experience of other United Nations organs. These formed the basis for the Rules as finally adopted. Over the years, they have been frequently amended, usually in minor respects.[55] The most important addition was the chapter containing "supplementary" rules to deal with the special problem of the Somaliland trusteeship.

Article 90(1) has not been interpreted to preclude the General Assembly's considering the Council's procedures. From time to time, the Assembly has made both specific and general recommendations to the Council, and in some cases this has led to changes in the Council's Rules. For example, the Rules concerning petitions (Rules 76–93) were changed largely as the result of recommendations by the Assembly, which was dissatisfied with the way the Council was handling this matter.[56]

Numerous objections have been raised to the effect that the Assembly should not give directives to the Council regarding its Rules, since under Article 90 this matter falls solely within its competence.[57] While such views have resulted in the defeat or modification of some proposals, in general the Assembly has refused to consider itself barred from making specific recommendations to the Council. The wisdom of the Assembly's attempting to direct the operations of another "principal organ" may be questioned, but its authority to do so seems to be established by both the broad powers of the Assembly under Article 10 of the Charter and the specific provisions of the Charter concerning the relationship of the Assembly and the Trusteeship Council (Articles 15, 85, and 88).

[54] *Report of the Preparatory Commission*, pp. 50–56.
[55] See UN Doc. T/1/Rev. 6, Oct. 6, 1962.
[56] GA Res. 435(V), Dec. 2, 1950; and 522(VI), Jan. 18, 1952.
[57] See commentary on Art. 85.

The Presidency

Under the Council's Rules of Procedure, the President and the Vice-President are elected by secret ballot at the beginning of the Council's regular annual session.[58] Although not specified in the Rules, the practice grew up of alternating the presidency and the vice-presidency between members that are administering authorities and those that are not. Neither officer is eligible for reelection,[59] although it is not uncommon for the Vice-President to accede to the presidency.

In normal Council practice, the President designates an alternate in his delegation to represent his government in the Council, in which case the President does not have the right to vote (Rule 22). Moreover, the President is expected to turn the chair over to the Vice-President whenever the Council is considering a question in which his government is directly concerned, particularly the consideration of petitions and reports on a trust territory administered by the President's government.

The Vice-President acts as President during the temporary absence of the latter. In the event the President is no longer able to fill his office, the Council elects a new President for the unexpired term.

Sessions

Until 1962, the Rules of Procedure provided for two regular sessions of the Trusteeship Council each year. With the decline in the number of trust territories, one annual session was deemed sufficient to discharge the Council's responsibilities. Therefore, at its June, 1962, session, the Council decided to amend its Rules to provide for one regular session to be convened during May of each year. The members of the Council have generally taken a flexible attitude as to when—and sometimes even whether—a regular session shall be held. This has been necessary in part because of the need to coordinate the Council's work with that of other bodies, especially the Assembly's.[60]

In fulfillment of Article 90(2), the Council's rules specify that special sessions shall be held by decision of the Trusteeship Council itself, at the request of the General Assembly or the Security Council, or at the

[58] From 1957 to 1962 when the Rules provided for two sessions each year, elections were held at the January session. Prior to 1957, elections were held at the beginning of the June session.

[59] Compare TC, Rules of Procedure, IV, Rule 20, with Rule 21 of ECOSOC Rules of Procedure.

[60] Originally, regular sessions were held in June and November. The decision in 1949 to change from November to January was made in the light of the increased length of Assembly sessions.

request of a majority of members of the Trusteeship Council. ECOSOC may also request a special session, which is held if the request is acceded to by a majority of members of the Trusteeship Council.

Article 91

The Trusteeship Council shall, when appropriate, avail itself of the assistance of the Economic and Social Council and of the specialized agencies in regard to matters with which they are respectively concerned.

Article 91 is one of several provisions in the Charter designed to facilitate the proper coordination of activities of the organs and agencies within the United Nations system. The article states that the Trusteeship Council shall avail itself of the assistance of ECOSOC and the specialized agencies, but the inclusion of the phrase "when appropriate" leaves a considerable measure of discretion to the Trusteeship Council.

Means of cooperation with ECOSOC and the specialized agencies are spelled out in the Trusteeship Council Rules of Procedure. These reflect the recommendations of a joint committee established by the two Councils in 1947 "to discuss arrangements for co-operation in dealing with matters of common concern." [61] Accordingly, ECOSOC may request a special session of the Trusteeship Council (Rule 3); it is entitled to receive notification of the meetings of the Trusteeship Council and of its provisional agenda (Rules 4 and 8); it may propose items for inclusion on the provisional agenda (Rule 9); and it receives copies of the annual reports of the administering authorities "and such reports and other documents" as may be of special concern to it (Rule 105). [62]

These rights (except the right to request a special session) apply to the specialized agencies. In addition, the Rules provide that representatives of the specialized agencies shall be invited to attend meetings of the Trusteeship Council and to participate, without vote, in its deliberations in the circumstances indicated in the respective agreements between the United Nations and the specialized agencies (Rule 13). ECOSOC's Rules of Procedure and the agreements with the specialized agencies also contain provisions for rendering assistance to the Trusteeship Council. The latter's interest in the agreements with the specialized agencies has been recognized, and representatives of

[61] TC Res. 1, Apr. 23, 1947.
[62] ECOSOC's Rules of Procedure accord similar privileges to the Trusteeship Council.

that Council have been represented in the negotiation of such agreements.

The report of the above-mentioned joint committee covered a number of other areas of cooperation between the two Councils.[63] It recommended conferences between the Presidents and the possible appointment of joint ad hoc committees on matters of mutual concern. In practice, no such committees have been established.

Another subject dealt with in the report was the delimitation of the responsibilities of the two Councils, particularly with regard to "studies" and "recommendations." It recommended that ECOSOC should not single out trust territories for specific recommendations, except with the concurrence of the Trusteeship Council, and that ECOSOC commissions should address all requests for inquiries and studies to be made in the trust territories through ECOSOC to the Trusteeship Council. The report, however, recognized ECOSOC's authority to initiate studies and to make recommendations of general application on economic and social problems, and that it would be useful for ECOSOC to call the attention of the Trusteeship Council to the desirability of undertaking certain studies in the trust territories. The report of the joint committee recommended that all petitions, such as those on human rights or the status of women, emanating from or relating to conditions in any of the trust territories, should be dealt with by the Trusteeship Council in accordance with Article 87(b).

In practice, contacts between ECOSOC and the Trusteeship Council have been neither frequent nor of particular significance.[64] They have been mainly confined to an exchange of resolutions. In the Trusteeship Council, whenever any matter concerning ECOSOC has been discussed, there has been a tendency for members to stress the independence of the Trusteeship Council.

In contrast, contacts between the Trusteeship Council and the specialized agencies have been more fruitful. In 1949, the Trusteeship Council recommended that the "specialized agencies study the annual reports on the administration of Trust Territories with a view to making such observations and suggestions as they may consider proper in order to facilitate the work of the Trusteeship Council." [65] Almost from the beginning, UNESCO has submitted observations on the sections on education in the reports by the administering authorities. Collaboration with the International Labour Organisation was initiated in 1950 when the Trusteeship Council requested "expert advice" from that organization on problems of migrant labor and penal sanctions for

[63] UN Doc. E & T/C.1/2/Rev. 1, Nov. 10, 1947.
[64] For a few examples, see *Repertory,* IV, 459–60.
[65] TC Res. 47(IV), Mar. 1, 1949.

breach of labor contracts.[66] For some time, the World Health Organization has submitted observations on those sections in the annual reports concerning public health. Noting the valuable cooperation of these three agencies, the Trusteeship Council expressed the hope that the Food and Agriculture Organization would also submit observations.[67] The organization subsequently did so on matters of land tenure and land use.

[66] TC Res. 127(VI), Mar. 28, 1950.   [67] TC Res. 1370(XVII), Apr. 4, 1956.

CHAPTER XIV

The International Court of Justice

In all the planning for a postwar system to maintain international peace and security, it was accepted that there should be an international court. The participants in the Dumbarton Oaks Conversations readily agreed that it should be the "principal judicial organ" of the Organization; that all members would automatically be parties to the court's statute; and that other states might, under certain conditions, also become parties to the statute. No decision was taken, however, as to whether the Statute of the Permanent Court of International Justice (PCIJ) should continue in force, with some modifications, or whether a new statute should be prepared. In either case, it was agreed that the statute should be annexed to, and be considered a part of, the Charter. No attempt was made at Dumbarton Oaks to draft such a statute; instead, this task was to be undertaken by a special committee of jurists to be convened in advance of the projected conference to consider the Charter.[1]

The Committee of Jurists met in Washington April 9–20, 1945, with representatives from forty-three countries in attendance.[2] Some twenty-four of these submitted proposals for changes in the Statute of the Permanent Court of International Justice. The Committee also had before it recommendations by the Informal Inter-Allied Committee on the Future of the PCIJ and by the Inter-American Juridical Committee.[3]

Working on the basis of a proposed revision of the Statute of the PCIJ submitted by the United States, the Committee reached agreement on all but a few points. The changes made in the Statute were of two kinds: 1) those "rendered necessary by the substitution of the

[1] On the Dumbarton Oaks Conversations, see Ruth B. Russell, A History of the United Nations Charter, (Washington, Brookings Institution, 1958), pp. 429–30.

[2] This included all those invited to attend the forthcoming San Francisco Conference with the following exceptions: India, Lebanon, and the Union of South Africa.

[3] The first was a group that met in London on the initiative of the British from May, 1943, to February, 1944. It was composed of experts from certain European and Commonwealth countries. For a compilation of the various suggestions, see UNCIO, Documents, XIV, 387–452.

United Nations for the League of Nations," [4] and 2) other changes deemed desirable in the light of experience. With regard to the second category, the Committee adopted an essentially conservative course. Despite numerous proposals, relatively few changes were endorsed. This was a reflection of the generally accepted view that the PCIJ had "functioned for twenty years to the satisfaction of the litigants and that, if violence had suspended its activities, at least this institution had not failed in its task." [5]

The Committee was divided on the method of nominating judges. Some delegates felt that the cumbersome system of the PCIJ should be changed to require nominations by governments rather than by national groups. In the absence of agreement, alternative texts were included in the Committee's report. A much more serious difference arose over the question of the jurisdiction of the Court. A large majority (which included neither the United States nor the Soviet Union) clearly favored giving the Court compulsory jurisdiction over legal disputes. "In spite of this predominant sentiment," as the Committee's report stated, "it did not seem certain, nor even probable, that all of the nations whose participation in the proposed International Organization appears to be necessary, were now in a position to accept the rule of compulsory jurisdiction." [6] In this case, too, the Committee presented alternative drafts, one providing for compulsory jurisdiction and the other maintaining the "optional clause" of the Statute of the PCIJ under which states could, if they so chose, accept the Court's compulsory jurisdiction. Finally, the Committee decided that it was for the San Francisco Conference itself to determine whether a new court should be established, and, if so, what its relationship to the United Nations should be.

The San Francisco Conference accepted the draft statute as prepared by the Committee with only a few, mostly minor, modifications. Discussion at the Conference centered on those points that had not been resolved by the Committee of Jurists. In addition, the Conference had the task of giving further substance to the Charter provisions concerning a new court, for the Dumbarton Oaks Proposals contained only a bare outline.

Status of the Court

The Conference decided to establish a new court which would be designated the "principal judicial organ" of the United Nations. This decision, together with the decision that the Statute of the Court would

---

[4] See *ibid.,* p. 823.   [5] *Ibid.,* p. 822.   [6] *Ibid.,* p. 840.

be "annexed" to and form "an integral part" of the Charter, was incorporated into Article 92.

Many delegates were of the opinion that the PCIJ should be continued. This attitude reflected not only a high regard for the record of the Permanent Court but also a desire to maintain the continuity of international judicial institutions. It was pointed out that hundreds of international conventions referred to the PCIJ and recognized it as the tribunal to which parties were to refer their disputes. Continuing the Permanent Court, however, raised a number of problems. The most important was the status of those countries that were parties to the Statute of the PCIJ but would not be original members of the United Nations. These included some of the enemy states and also a number of neutrals. Another problem was the lack of any provision for revision of the Statute of the PCIJ. In the past whenever changes were considered desirable, a new conference had been held and the changes went into effect when ratified by all the participants. It was felt that, while the rights of the enemy states could be terminated as a part of the conditions of peace, the exclusion of the neutral states could "probably not be accomplished without some breach of the accepted rules of international law." [7] Some countries, especially the Soviet Union, were strongly opposed to including these neutral states as parties to the Statute. Under the circumstances, it was decided that a new court should be established.

The creation of the new Court would not necessarily "break the chain of continuity with the past." [8] Its Statute would be based on that of the PCIJ, a fact expressly stated in the Charter (Article 92). Moreover, whenever a treaty or convention in force provided for reference of a matter to the PCIJ, "as between the parties to the present Statute," the matter was to be referred to the new Court (Article 37 of the Statute). Finally, declarations still in force accepting the compulsory jurisdiction of the PCIJ were to be deemed as between the parties to the present Statute to be acceptances of the compulsory jurisdiction of the ICJ (Article 36[5] of the Statute).

Compulsory Jurisdiction

The controversy at San Francisco concerning the Court's jurisdiction followed lines that had already become apparent in the Committee of Jurists. The discussions showed "the existence of a great volume of support for extending the international legal order by recognizing immediately throughout the membership of the new Organization the

7 *Ibid.*, XIII, 524–25.   8 *Ibid.*, p. 384.

compulsory jurisdiction of the Court." This view, however, encountered powerful opposition; both the Soviet Union and the United States made it clear that they could not accept the Statute if such a clause were included.[9]

Various efforts at compromise were made. The main proposal was that the compulsory jurisdiction of the Court be accepted in principle, but with liberal provision for reservations.[10] This also was unacceptable. Eventually, it was decided to retain the "optional" clause in essentially the same form as it had appeared in the PCIJ Statute. Many delegates, however, continued strongly to support the principle of compulsory jurisdiction and voted for the text only to achieve agreement.[11]

Selection of Judges

Those who had sought in the Committee of Jurists to change the method of nomination of judges did not press their view at San Francisco. With little debate, it was decided to retain the system of nomination by national groups, largely on the ground that this method had worked satisfactorily in the past.

A new controversy arose over the procedure for the election of judges. Alternate methods were considered: 1) election by the General Assembly and the Security Council voting concurrently, or 2) election by the Assembly alone. Those favoring the latter method objected to the possibility of a "double" vote for some members. The method of concurrent election was defended, partly because of the special responsibility of the Security Council, but mainly on the ground that the system had worked well in past elections of PCIJ judges. The old system was retained, but only after agreement that the veto would not apply in Security Council voting on the election of judges.[12] The Statute provides that judges shall be elected by an "absolute majority" of votes in the General Assembly and in the Security Council, and that in the Council the vote "shall be taken without any distinction between permanent and non-permanent members." [13]

[9] *Ibid.*, pp. 226, 390. For U.S. views on this point, see Russell, pp. 877–78 and 886–88.

[10] See especially the proposal by New Zealand, UNCIO, *Documents*, XIII, 487 and 557.

[11] For the discussion and the statements of reservations, see *ibid.*, pp. 246–55 and 391–92; and Russell, pp. 884–90.

[12] See Russell, pp. 882–84.

[13] Art. 10 of the Statute. Note that this system departs from the normal procedure for voting in both the General Assembly and the Security Council. See commentary on Arts. 18 and 27.

Termination of the Permanent Court

No specific action was taken at the San Francisco Conference to terminate the PCIJ, that matter being left to those members who were parties to its Statute. The Permanent Court held its final session in October, 1945, at which time it adopted a number of decisions to "preserve continuity in international justice." [14] On January 31, 1946, the judges submitted their resignations and at the final meeting of the Assembly of the League of Nations on April 18, 1946, the Permanent Court was formally "dissolved." On February 6, the judges of the new Court were elected by the General Assembly and the Security Council, and the Court held its first meeting on April 3, 1946.

Article 92

The International Court of Justice shall be the principal judicial organ of the United Nations. It shall function in accordance with the annexed Statute, which is based upon the Statute of the Permanent Court of Justice and forms an integral part of the present Charter.

The Court as a Principal Organ

Although more closely integrated into the United Nations system than the Permanent Court was into the League system, the International Court functions with a considerable degree of independence. It is the only principal organ not located at the Organization's headquarters; the Court continues to occupy the Peace Palace at The Hague, which had been the seat of the Permanent Court. The Court appoints its Registrar and other officers. States not members of the United Nations may be parties to the Statute of the Court.

The Court's unique character as a principal organ of the United Nations stems primarily from the fact that it is a "judicial" rather than a "political" organ. While the General Assembly and the three Councils are composed of representatives of member states, the Court is composed of fifteen "independent" judges, elected "regardless of nationality" from among qualified persons of "high moral character." [15] Moreover, the Court functions on the basis of rules that are more precisely

---

[14] For an account of the measures taken to terminate the PCIJ and to establish the new Court, see *ICJ Yearbook,* 1946–1947, pp. 25 ff.

[15] Art. 2 of the Statute. No two judges, however, may be nationals of the same state (Art. 3), and the Statute further states that "the representation of the main forms of civilization and the principal legal systems of the world should be assured" (Art. 9). Regarding ad hoc judges, see Art. 31 of the Statute.

stated and more strictly adhered to than is the case with the other organs.

From the organizational point of view, the ties between the Court and the other organs are that the judges are elected by the General Assembly and the Security Council voting concurrently, and that the budget of the Court is subject to approval by the General Assembly.[16]

As the principal judicial organ, the Court has two major functions: first, it renders advisory opinions on legal questions at the request of the Security Council, the General Assembly, and other organs or agencies authorized by the latter to request opinions; second, it decides contentious cases between states.[17]

The Court and the Peaceful Settlement of Disputes

As the "principal judicial organ of the United Nations," the International Court is the chosen instrument for the judicial settlement of disputes between states. The Charter does not oblige members to submit disputes to the Court; indeed, it emphasizes the freedom of the parties to utilize whatever peaceful means they choose for settling their disputes.[18] Nonetheless, the special role of the Court is recognized in the Charter. Under Article 36(3), the Security Council, in recommending procedures of settlement, is to "take into consideration that legal disputes should as a general rule be referred by the parties" to the International Court. There is no similar provision with regard to the General Assembly; but that body, in urging greater use of the Court, recommended that "as a general rule . . . States should submit their legal disputes" to the Court.[19]

In both organs there have been frequent statements to the effect that a particular dispute was suitable for referral to the Court. Seldom, however, has either organ recommended this course. In dealing with the dispute between the United Kingdom and Albania over incidents in the Corfu Channel, the Security Council recommended that the parties immediately refer the matter to the Court, in accordance with the provisions of the Statute.[20] But this is the only time the Council has made such a recommendation. In recommending that Austria and Italy seek a solution of their dispute concerning the status of the

[16] The budget of the Court is one chapter in the UN budget.

[17] The President of the Court is frequently requested to perform tasks outside the judicial work of the Court, such as the appointment of arbitrators. See *ICJ Yearbook*, 1963–1964, pp. 49–50, 255–321.

[18] See commentary on Arts. 33 and 95; and Art. 13 of the Covenant of the League of Nations.

[19] GA Res. 171(II), Nov. 14, 1947.

[20] SCOR/2d Yr., No. 32/127th Mtg./Apr. 9, 1947/p. 727.

German-speaking element in Bolzano, the General Assembly listed recourse to the International Court as one of the means the parties should consider favorably.[21] This is the only such recommendation the Assembly has ever made with respect to an actual dispute. It should be emphasized that neither the Security Council nor the General Assembly is empowered under the Charter to refer a dispute to the Court. In the Corfu Channel case, the United Kingdom argued that the Security Council resolution recommending submission of the dispute by the parties conferred jurisdiction on the Court. The Court found it unnecessary to express an opinion on this point since it established jurisdiction on other grounds. However, seven judges in a separate opinion explicitly denied that a recommendation could have that effect.[22]

The jurisdiction of the Court is limited to disputes between states (Article 34[2]). Disputes between individuals or corporations and states can only be brought before the Court if the cause of the individual or corporation is taken up by a state and treated as a matter of state interest. International organizations as such cannot be parties in cases before the Court. In the meetings of the Committee of Jurists prior to the San Francisco Conference, it was suggested that public international organizations should be permitted to become parties to cases before the Court. The Committee, however, was unwilling to go further than to propose that public international organizations might, either on their own initiative or on request, supply the Court with information. The Conference accepted this solution (Article 34[2]). International organizations are also entitled to submit oral or written statements whenever the Court is considering a request for an advisory opinion on a subject in which they have some concern (Article 66).

The contentious jurisdiction of the Court is based upon the consent of the states which are parties to the dispute. This consent can be given in various ways: 1) by a special agreement concluded by the parties for the specific purpose of submitting their dispute to the Court; 2) by application by one party requesting that the Court give judgment, followed by acceptance by the other party of the Court's jurisdiction; [23] and 3) by agreement in advance to accept the Court's jurisdiction in certain categories of disputes (the basis of the compulsory jurisdiction of the Court). In most instances where the second method

---

[21] GA Res. 1487(XV), Oct. 31, 1960.

[22] *ICJ Reports,* 1948, p. 15. See also commentary on Art. 36(3).

[23] In the Corfu Channel case, the U.K. filed an application for a judgment on its behalf, and after notification to it by the Registrar of the Court, Albania sent a communication which the Court interpreted as an acceptance of its jurisdiction. See *ICJ Reports,* 1948, p. 15. After the Court's decision upholding its competence, the parties signed a special agreement.

has been attempted, as for example in complaints brought by the United States against Eastern European states over aerial incidents, the defendant has refused to accept the Court's jurisdiction and the case has been "removed" by the Court from its list for lack of jurisdiction.

Advance acceptance of the Court's jurisdiction may take either of two forms: 1) international agreements, bipartite or multipartite, to refer particular categories of disputes, often disputes relating to the interpretation of the particular agreement, to the Court;[24] and 2) declarations made under Article 36 of the Statute of the Court. Paragraphs 2 and 3 of the article provide:

2. The states parties to the present Statute may at any time declare that they recognize as compulsory *ipso facto* and without special agreement, in relation to any other state accepting the same obligation, the jurisidiction of the Court in all legal disputes concerning:
   a. the interpretation of a treaty;
   b. any question of international law;
   c. the existence of any fact which, if established, would constitute a breach of an international obligation;
   d. the nature or extent of the reparation to be made for the breach of an international obligation.
3. The declarations referred to above may be made unconditionally or on condition of reciprocity on the part of several or certain states, or for a certain time.

This article also provides that declarations made under Article 36 of the PCIJ Statute "which are still in force" shall be deemed acceptances of the Court's compulsory jurisdiction "as between the parties to the present Statute."

The San Francisco Conference unanimously recommended that members proceed as soon as possible to "make declarations recognizing the obligatory jurisdiction" of the Court.[25] Subsequently, the General Assembly called to the attention of its members the "desirability of the greatest possible number of States accepting this jurisdiction with as few reservations as possible."[26] The increase in the number of declarations accepting the compulsory jurisdiction of the Court has not kept pace with the increase in membership, nor does it represent as high a proportion of the total membership as accepted the compulsory jurisdiction of the PCIJ. Furthermore, many of the declarations contain reservations that seriously curtail the extent of the Court's jurisdiction.

[24] A chronological list of such agreements is given in the *ICJ Yearbook*.
[25] UNCIO, *Documents*, I, 627; and XIII, 413.
[26] GA Res. 171(II), Nov. 14, 1947.

For example, the United States declaration excludes disputes "with regard to matters which are essentially within the domestic jurisdiction" of the United States "as determined by the United States." [27]

An essential element of the concept of compulsory jurisdiction is that the Court determines its own competence. Thus, if one party to the dispute invokes the compulsory jurisdiction of the Court by requesting a decision, and if the other party denies the Court's jurisdiction, the Court can take a binding decision on the preliminary question of competence and proceed to final judgment on the merits.

In deciding cases submitted to it, the Court shall apply:

a. international conventions, whether general or particular, establishing rules expressly recognized by the contesting parties;
b. international custom, as evidence of a general practice accepted as law;
c. the general principles of law recognized by civilized nations;
d. subject to the provisions of Article 59 [of the Statute], judicial decisions and the teachings of the most highly qualified publicists of the various nations as subsidiary means for the determination of rules of law. [Article 38]

The Court may also decide disputes *ex aequo et bono* if the parties so agree.

The Statute as an "Integral" Part of the Charter

Although the Statute of the International Court differs in only minor ways from the Statute of the PCIJ, it occupies quite a different position. In the words of Article 92, it "forms an integral part" of the Charter. Thus, the Statute enjoys the same primacy over other international agreements accorded to the Charter itself in Article 103.

The provisions for amendment underline the fact that the Statute is an integral part of the Charter. Amendment of the Statute "shall be effected by the same procedure" as is provided for the amendment of the Charter itself. The General Assembly, acting upon the recommendation of the Security Council, provides means for participation in the amendment process of those parties to the Statute that are not members of the United Nations (Article 69).

The Statute empowers the Court itself to propose amendments (Article 70). It has thus far never chosen to do so. Only one proposal for changing the Statute has been put forward in the General Assembly. In 1956, a group of Latin American states proposed that the Court

[27] Whereas in 1948, out of a total of 58 states parties to the Statute, 34 had made declarations under Art. 36, in 1966, 41 out of 120 had done so. For texts of declarations in force as of July 31, 1966, see *ICJ Yearbook*, 1965–1966, pp. 41–68.

be enlarged from fifteen to nineteen judges; this proposal was never voted upon.[28]

Article 93

1. All Members of the United Nations are *ipso facto* parties to the Statute of the International Court of Justice.

2. A state which is not a Member of the United Nations may become a party to the Statute of the International Court of Justice on conditions to be determined in each case by the General Assembly upon the recommendation of the Security Council.

In making all members of the United Nations automatically parties to the Statute of the International Court of Justice, the Charter differs from the League Covenant, under which a state could become a member of the League without adhering to the Statute of the PCIJ. When the Soviet Union, for example, joined the League, it did not become a party to the Court's Statute. By requiring all members to be parties to the Statute of the new Court, the Charter again emphasizes the more intimate relationship of the Court to the United Nations system.

Article 93(2) establishes the procedure by which a state not a member of the United Nations may become a party to the Statute of the Court. This provision recognizes the desirability of extending as widely as possible the specific commitments of the Statute and the utilization of the procedures set forth therein for the pacific settlement of disputes. It recognizes, too, in its requirement that the General Assembly act upon the recommendation of the Security Council, the special responsibility of the latter body for the maintenance of international peace and security.

The "conditions" under which a nonmember can become a party to the Statute were first set down by the Security Council and the General Assembly in 1946. The Swiss government requested information on the conditions it would be required to meet. The Council referred the matter to its Committee of Experts; the recommendations of the Committee were adopted by the Council and subsequently by the General Assembly. They provide that:

Switzerland will become a party to the Statute of the Court on the date of the deposit with the Secretary-General of the United Nations of an instrument, signed on behalf of the Government of Switzerland and ratified as may be required by Swiss constitutional law, containing:

(a) Acceptance of the provisions of the Statute of the International Court of Justice;

[28] See commentary on Art. 108.

(b) Acceptance of all the obligations of a Member of the United Nations under Article 94 of the Charter;

(c) An undertaking to contribute to the expenses of the Court such equitable amount as the General Assembly shall assess from time to time after consultation with the Swiss Government.[29]

Despite statements that the conditions recognized as appropriate in this case were not intended to constitute a precedent, the same conditions were subsequently applied in each case where a nonmember wished to become a party to the Statute. Liechtenstein became a party to the Statute in 1950; San Marino in 1954; and, before being admitted to membership in the United Nations, Japan also became a party to the Statute under the same conditions.[30]

Under the Statute of the Court, the General Assembly, on the recommendation of the Security Council, establishes the conditions under which states that are parties to the Statute but not members of the United Nations may participate in the process of amending the Statute (Article 69) and of electing judges (Article 4[3]). The Assembly in 1948 adopted the recommendation of the Council that nonmembers, parties to the Statute, should be "on an equal footing with members of the United Nations" with respect to the nomination and election of judges. Under this resolution, "equal footing" specifically includes the possibility of denying the right to vote to states in default of their contributions to the expenses of the Court.[31]

The Statute of the International Court of Justice provides that the Court "shall be open" to states other than parties to the Statute on conditions to be laid down by the Security Council (Article 35). The resolution that the Security Council adopted on this matter follows the general pattern established by the Council of the League of Nations regarding access to the PCIJ.[32]

Under this resolution, the Court is "open to a state" which is not a party to the Statute on condition that it deposit with the Registrar of the Court a declaration in which it: 1) accepts the jurisdiction of the Court "in accordance with the Charter of the United Nations and with the terms and subject to the conditions of the Statute and Rules of the Court"; 2) undertakes to comply "in good faith" with the decision or decisions of the Court; and 3) accepts all the obligations of a United

---

[29] GA Res. 91(I), Dec. 11, 1946; and SCOR/1st Yr., 2d Ser./80th Mtg./Nov. 15, 1946/pp. 501–2.

[30] See GA Res. 363(IV), Dec. 1, 1949; 806(VII), Dec. 9, 1953; and 805(VII), Dec. 9, 1953.

[31] GA Res. 264(III), Oct. 8, 1948; and SCOR/3d Yr./360th Mtg./Sept. 28, 1948/p. 30.

[32] For an explanation of the modifications required by the differences between the Charter and the Covenant, see the report of the Committee of Experts in SCOR/1st Yr., 2d Ser./1946/*Supp. 6*/pp. 153–56.

Nations member under Article 94 of the Charter.[33] A state may make either a "particular" or a "general" declaration. A "particular" declaration is one "accepting the jurisdiction of the Court in respect only of a particular dispute or disputes which have already arisen"; a "general" declaration is one "accepting the jurisdiction generally in respect of all disputes or of a particular class or classes of disputes which have already arisen, or which may arise in the future." Under the general declaration, a state may, in accordance with Article 36(2) of the Statute, "recognize the compulsory jurisdiction of the Court," but it cannot rely upon this acceptance of jurisdiction, without explicit agreement, vis-à-vis states that are parties to the Statute.

As of July, 1966, "general declarations" were on file with the International Court from two states—the Federal Republic of Germany and the Republic of Vietnam.[34] Prior to their admission to United Nations membership in 1955, Cambodia, Ceylon, Finland, Italy, Japan, and Laos had also filed general declarations. Particular declarations had been made by Albania in connection with the Corfu Channel case and by Italy in connection with the Monetary Gold case.

Article 94

1. Each Member of the United Nations undertakes to comply with the decision of the International Court of Justice in any case to which it is a party.

2. If any party to a case fails to perform the obligations incumbent upon it under a judgment rendered by the Court, the other party may have recourse to the Security Council, which may, if it deems necessary, make recommendations or decide upon measures to be taken to give effect to the judgment.

It is an established principle of international law that the decision of an international court is binding upon the parties. Article 94(1) is a specific application of that principle and of the general principle laid down in Article 2(2), under which all members of the United Nations pledge themselves to "fulfill in good faith the obligations assumed by them" under the Charter. The binding effect of the Court's decisions is also set out in Article 60 of the Statute, which declares that the judgment of the Court "is final and without appeal." Only the discovery of new facts of a decisive nature is considered sufficient ground for an application for revision of the judgment (Article 61 of the Statute). Under decisions by the Security Council and the General Assembly for carrying out the provisions of Article 93, nonmembers wishing to be-

[33] SCOR/1st Yr., 2d Ser./76th Mtg./Oct. 15, 1946/p. 468.
[34] *ICJ Yearbook*, 1965–1966, pp. 30–31.

come parties to the Court Statute are required to accept these obligations.

The inclusion in the Charter of a specific provision obligating parties to comply with the decisions of the Court did not satisfy a number of delegates at San Francisco who were especially concerned with building up the authority of the International Court. Thus, several proposals were introduced to associate the Security Council with the implementation of the Court's judgments in somewhat the same manner as under the League system. The Covenant empowered the League Council to propose steps to give effect to the decisions of the Permanent Court in the event of any failure by the parties to carry them out.[35]

In its report to the San Francisco Conference, the Committee of Jurists called attention to this provision and to the "great importance" of "formulating rules on this point in the Charter." [36] Proposals to empower the Council to enforce the decisions of the Court were opposed by those states, the United States and the Soviet Union included, that were against authorizing the Organization to "impose" a settlement of a dispute upon the parties. Moreover, there were objections to conferring on the Security Council the power to act in any matter unless international peace and security were endangered. The failure of a state to comply with a decision of the Court would not necessarily result in a threat to the peace by either party. A proposal that any refusal to comply with a decision of the Court be considered an act of aggression was not accepted by the Conference.

The formula finally agreed upon for Article 94(2) is considerably weaker than the corresponding provision in the Covenant in that the latter placed an obligation on the Council to act, whereas the Charter emphasizes the discretionary authority of the Security Council. In effect, Article 94(2) merely assures the aggrieved party of recourse to the Security Council in the event the other party fails to perform its obligations under a judgment of the Court. The initiative rests with the aggrieved party, although there is, of course, no bar to the Council's considering the matter under Chapters VI or VII of the Charter in the absence of such an initiative.

The phraseology of Article 94(2) raises the question whether it confers on the Security Council powers in addition to those conferred on it under Chapters VI and VII of the Charter. Does it empower the Council to make recommendations even though international peace and security are not endangered? Even more important, may the Council take a "decision," binding upon members, in the absence of a "threat to

[35] Art. 13(4). Under this provision, League members also pledged themselves not to resort to war against any member that complied with the Court's decisions.
[36] See Russell, p. 891.

the peace"? The interpretation given by United States experts shortly after the signing of the Charter was that the Council would call upon the parties concerned to carry out the judgment of the Court "only if the peace of the world is threatened, and if the Council has made a determination to that effect." In this view, the Council is simply handling "a political situation" which might arise from the failure of one of the parties to carry out the Court's judgment.[37] The records of the San Francisco discussions present no evidence to support this interpretation. Indeed, from the text of the article, it appears that the intent was to provide a possible means for giving effect to the Court's judgment irrespective of whether peace and security were endangered.[38]

Very rarely have states refused to implement the decisions of an international tribunal. In no case did parties refuse to carry out a judgment of the Permanent Court of International Justice. The difficulty has always been in getting states to submit their disputes to international tribunals; having done so, they have generally been willing to accept an adverse judgment. The record of acceptance of judgments of the International Court has also been good; the notable exception has been the refusal of Albania to comply with the Court's decision setting the amount of compensation due the United Kingdom for damages in the Corfu Channel case. The United Kingdom has sought through various means to collect the amount due, but no attempt has been made to invoke Article 94(2) by bringing the matter before the Security Council.

On only one occasion has the Security Council been asked to consider its role in relation to the execution of decisions of the International Court. Because of the special circumstances of the case, however, the Council's discussions shed little light on the interpretation of Article 94(2). At the end of September, 1951, the United Kingdom submitted to the Council a complaint concerning Iran's failure to comply with the provisional measures previously indicated by the Court in connection with the dispute over the Anglo-Iranian Oil Company.[39] Neither in the complaint nor in the draft resolution introduced by the United Kingdom was there any reference to Article 94 of the Charter. In his presentation, the United Kingdom representative referred to Articles 34 and 35 of the Charter as the "formal basis" for the submission of the complaint. He did, however, draw attention to the "special

[37] See testimony by Leo Pasvolsky, *The Charter of the United Nations,* Hears./USS CFR/79C1/1945/p. 287. See also article by Green Hackworth in State Dept. *Bulletin,* XII, No. 320 (Aug. 12, 1945), pp. 216–19.

[38] On this point, see Oscar Schachter, "Enforcement of International Judicial and Arbitral Decisions," *American Journal of International Law,* XLIV (1960), pp. 216–24.

[39] *ICJ Reports,* 1951, p. 89.

functions" of the Council in relation to decisions of the Court and contended that interim measures indicated by the Court were no less binding upon the parties than a final judgment. Iran put forward the opposite interpretation of Article 94, arguing that only final judgments were binding.[40] It furthermore argued that the matter was one of domestic jurisdiction, and that neither the Council nor the Court was competent to deal with the dispute. After discussion, the Council decided to adjourn its debate until the Court ruled on the question of its own competence.[41] The Court subsequently upheld Iran's contention that it lacked jurisdiction in the case, at which time the provisional measures previously indicated "lapsed" and no further action was taken by the Security Council.[42]

The action, or more accurately the inaction, of the Security Council in the Anglo-Iranian case gives little indication of what the attitude of the members of the Council might be if faced with a more clear-cut situation—that is, one in which the Court's own competence was not in doubt and in which the Council was dealing with a failure to comply with a final judgment. The question of institutional enforcement of the Court's decisions has not, however, received a great deal of attention. In bringing its case to the Security Council, the British representative commented that "when this kind of situation arose in the past, it was commonly settled by resort to force." [43] Acceptance of the obligations of United Nations membership has, of course, placed restraints upon the kinds of unilateral actions a member may take. The extent of these limitations has been variously interpreted.[44]

Article 95

Nothing in the present Charter shall prevent Members of the United Nations from entrusting the solution of their differences to other tribunals by virtue of agreements already in existence or which may be concluded in the future.

Underlying the United Nations Charter is the principle that parties to a dispute should be left to solve their problems by means "of their own choice" as long as international peace and security are not endangered (Article 33). Article 95 is one manifestation of this principle. It is also a carry-over from the League period. To avoid undermining the

---

[40] SCOR/6th Yr./559th Mtg./Oct. 10, 1951/pp. 4 and 20; 560th Mtg./Oct. 15, 1951/pp. 10–12. See also the statement by Ecuador, *ibid.*, 562d Mtg./Oct. 17, 1951/pp. 8–9.
[41] *Ibid.*, 565th Mtg./Oct. 19, 1951/p. 12.   [42] *ICJ Reports,* 1952, p. 93.
[43] SCOR/6th Yr./559th Mtg./Oct. 1, 1951/p. 12.
[44] See commentary on Arts. 2(4) and 51.

then-existing complex of treaties of pacific settlement, the Statute of
the PCIJ specifically stated that the Court was established "in addition
to the Court of Arbitration organized by the Conventions of The
Hague of 1899 and 1907, and to the special Tribunals of Arbitration to
which States are always at liberty to submit their disputes for settlement." [45] While this provision was not retained in the Statute of the
new Court, the point is adequately covered in the present article.

Clearly, the designation of the International Court as the "principal
judicial organ of the United Nations" (Article 92) was not intended to
preclude the establishment of other judicial organs under the auspices
of the United Nations or outside the framework of the Organization.[46]

Since World War II there has been a general decline in the use of
arbitral tribunals, in contrast to the interwar period when thousands of
claims were arbitrated. Nevertheless, there have been some significant
developments in the creation of intergovernmental judicial organs. One
example is the Court of Justice established by the treaty creating the
European Economic Community.[47] Another is the European Court of
Human Rights.[48] The United Nations has considered the possibility
of establishing an international court of human rights,[49] and an international criminal court for the trial of genocide and certain other
crimes. The need for a judicial organ of the latter type was first
noted by the General Assembly in 1948. The matter was discussed over
the next five years, and then was postponed indefinitely.[50]

Article 96

**1. The General Assembly or the Security Council may request the
International Court of Justice to give an advisory opinion on any
legal question.**

**2. Other organs of the United Nations and specialized agencies,
which may at any time be so authorized by the General Assembly,**

[45] See Art. 1 of the Statute of the PCIJ and also Art. 13(3) of the Covenant of
the League which provided for the submission of legal disputes to the Permanent
Court or "any tribunal agreed on by the parties to the dispute or stipulated in any
convention existing between them."

[46] The United Nations created two special tribunals to deal with economic and
financial problems connected with the former Italian colonies; GA Res. 383A(V),
Dec. 15, 1950; and 530(VI), Jan. 23, 1952.

[47] 298 UNTS, 11, especially 73–78 and 147–56.

[48] Convention for the Protection of Human Rights and Fundamental Freedoms,
213 UNTS, 221–71.

[49] Australia was the leading advocate.

[50] See GA Res. 260(III), Dec. 9, 1948; and 989(IX), Dec. 14, 1954. See also
ILC Yearbook, 1950, II, 1–23 and 378–79; and reports of the two special committees established by GA Res. 489(V), Dec. 12, 1950; and 687(VII), Dec. 5,
1952.

may also request advisory opinions of the Court on legal questions arising within the scope of their activities.

In authorizing the General Assembly and the Security Council to request advisory opinions from the International Court of Justice, the Charter continued a practice that had proved useful under the League system. Under the Dumbarton Oaks Proposals, only the Security Council was authorized to request opinions, and then only in connection with disputes before it. The San Francisco Conference, accepting the recommendations of the Committee of Jurists, decided that both the Council and the Assembly should be authorized to request opinions, as had been the situation under the League Covenant.

In a departure from previous arrangements, Article 96(2) also empowers the General Assembly to authorize other organs and specialized agencies to request opinions. Both in the Committee of Jurists and again at San Francisco, it was suggested that under certain circumstances individual states should also be permitted to request advisory opinions. This was opposed on the ground that it might overload the Court and might also interfere with the operations of other United Nations organs.[51] Thus, a state can obtain an advisory opinion from the Court only if its proposal is adopted by one of the organs or agencies authorized to make such a request.

Authorizations to Request Opinions

The General Assembly has adopted a relatively liberal policy in the application of Article 96(2). Authorizations to request opinions from the Court have been given to two principal organs of the United Nations, to two subsidiary organs, and to all but one of the specialized agencies.[52] Under the League system, the Council in many cases acted as go-between in requesting opinions from the Court on questions of concern to the International Labour Organisation. Under the United Nations system, specialized agencies, such as the ILO, have been given direct access to the Court. When the General Assembly first considered this question, it decided that authorizations to the specialized agencies should be general rather than specific. Thus, an agency is not required to obtain an authorization each time it wishes to approach the Court. Authorizations have been given, however, with the understanding that they can be revoked by the Assembly at any time.

Each agreement concluded with a specialized agency (except the Universal Postal Union) contains a provision authorizing the agency to request advisory opinions from the Court. Although the phraseology

---

[51] UNCIO, *Documents*, XIII, 445–47 and 850; XIV, 234–35 and 496–97.
[52] Term used here to include International Atomic Energy Agency (IAEA).

varies somewhat, generally the agency is authorized to request opinions on legal questions arising within the scope of its competence or activities.[53] Questions concerning the relationship of the agencies to the United Nations and to other agencies are, however, specifically excluded. Moreover, the agencies (except for IAEA) are required to inform ECOSOC whenever a request is made.

The authorization to ECOSOC is similarly general in character. To enable the Council to discharge its responsibilities for coordinating the activities of the specialized agencies, ECOSOC is specially authorized to request opinions on legal questions "concerning mutual relationships of the United Nations and the specialized agencies." [54] The Assembly has given similar general authorizations to the Trusteeship Council, the Interim Committee of the General Assembly (despite some objections that it was inappropriate to confer this power upon a "subsidiary" organ),[55] and the Committee on Applications for Review of Administrative Tribunal Judgments.

During the discussion on a covenant of human rights, the question was raised of the propriety of authorizing a body which was neither a principal organ of the United Nations nor a specialized agency to request opinions from the Court. In light of the opinion given by the Secretary-General that the proposed human rights committee did not come within the terms of Article 96(2) of the Charter and therefore could not be authorized to request opinions from the Court either directly or indirectly through other United Nations organs, it was decided that the committee should be authorized to "recommend" that ECOSOC request an advisory opinion on "any legal question connected with a matter of which the Committee is seized." [56]

The question of authorizing a subsidiary organ to request advisory opinions from the Court was considered again by the General Assembly in connection with the decision to establish some kind of judicial review of the judgments of the United Nations Administrative Tribunal. Discussion centered on a review procedure that would utilize advisory opinions of the Court. In a memorandum to the special committee considering this matter, the Secretary-General pointed out that it would "appear to be too cumbersome a procedure for the General Assembly, itself, to request an advisory opinion in each case." [57] He

[53] See chart in Shabtai Rosenne, *The International Court of Justice* (Leyden, Sijthoff, 1957), pp. 450 ff.

[54] GA Res. 89(I), Dec. 11, 1946.

[55] GA Res. 171B(II), Nov. 14, 1947; 196(III), Dec. 3, 1948.

[56] See *Repertory*, V, 91–92.

[57] For text of the memorandum, see GAOR/10th Sess./1955/*Annexes*, agenda item 49.

drew attention to the possibility of the Assembly's authorizing the Secretary-General to make the request. Although there was some support for this approach, the Assembly decided to establish a special committee which it authorized, under certain limited circumstances, to request advisory opinions from the Court.[58]

Of the principal organs of the United Nations, only the Secretariat is not authorized to request advisory opinions. It has been suggested from time to time that the Secretary-General be authorized to do so. He may, of course, suggest that one of the other organs request an opinion.

Circumstances Under Which Requests Have Been Made

In the period through 1965, twelve requests for advisory opinions have been addressed to the Court (see Table 7). Of these, two originated with specialized agencies—UNESCO and IMCO—and ten with the General Assembly. None of the Councils has availed itself of the opportunity.

The failure of the Security Council to request an advisory opinion contrasts sharply with the practice of the League Council, which was responsible for all advisory opinion requests to the PCIJ. Only three proposals for requesting advisory opinions have advanced to the voting stage in the Security Council and these were all defeated.[59]

There has been a marked difference in the nature of questions submitted to the ICJ in comparison with those submitted to the PCIJ. Of the twelve questions submitted to the former, only one has dealt with a legal question arising in connection with consideration of an actual dispute or situation. A considerable number of PCIJ opinions dealt with such questions, especially those arising in connection with the application of minorities treaties. In the only instance in which the ICJ has been asked to deal with such a question, the General Assembly asked the Court for an opinion whether the diplomatic exchanges between "Bulgaria, Hungary, and Romania, on the one hand, and certain Allied and Associated Powers signatories to the Treaties of Peace, on the other," concerning the implementation of human rights provisions, "disclose disputes subject to the provisions for the settlement of disputes" contained in the Treaty, and if so, what were the obligations of

---

[58] GA Res. 957(X), Nov. 8, 1955. The Committee is composed of those states represented on the General Committee of the last regular session of the Assembly.

[59] A Belgian proposal concerning the competence of the Council to deal with the Indonesian question, a Syrian proposal on the competence of the United Nations with regard to Palestine, and a Cuban proposal concerning certain decisions taken by the Organization of American States at the Punta del Este Conference.

Table 7
CASES SUBMITTED TO THE COURT FOR ADVISORY OPINION

REQUESTS BY THE GENERAL ASSEMBLY

Subject	Submitted by	Date of Opinion	Subsequent Action
1. Conditions for the Admission of a State to UN Membership	GA Res. 113A(II), Nov. 17, 1947	May 28, 1948	GA Res. 197A(III), Dec. 8, 1948
2. Reparation for Injuries Suffered in UN Service	GA Res. 258(III), Dec. 3, 1948	April 11, 1949	GA Res. 365(IV), Dec. 1, 1949
3. Interpretation of Peace Treaties with Bulgaria, Hungary, and Romania	GA Res. 294(IV), Oct. 22, 1949	Mar. 30, 1950 July 18, 1950	GA Res. 385(V), Nov. 3, 1950
4. Competence of General Assembly for Admission of a State to UN	GA Res. 296(IV), Nov. 22, 1949	Mar. 3, 1950	GA Res. 495(V), Dec. 4, 1950
5. International Status of S. W. Africa	GA Res. 338(IV), Dec. 6, 1949	July 11, 1950	GA Res. 449 (V), Dec. 13, 1950
6. Reservations to Genocide Convention	GA Res. 478(V), Nov. 16, 1950	May 28, 1951	GA Res. 598 (VI), Jan. 12, 1952
7. Effect of Awards of UN Administrative Tribunal	GA Res. 785A(VIII), Dec. 9, 1953	July 13, 1954	GA Res. 888(IX), Dec. 17, 1954 and 957(X), Nov. 8, 1955
8. Voting Procedure regarding Reports and Petitions on S. W. Africa	GA Res. 904(IX), Nov. 23, 1954	June 7, 1955	GA Res. 934(X), Dec. 3, 1955
9. Hearing of Petitioners by the Committee on S. W. Africa	GA Res. 942(X), Dec. 3, 1955	June 1, 1956	GA Res. 1047(XI), Jan. 23, 1957
10. Certain Expenses of the UN	GA Res. 1731(XVI), Dec. 20, 1961	July 20, 1962	GA Res. 1854A(XVII), Dec. 19, 1962

REQUESTS BY SPECIALIZED AGENCIES

Judgments of ILO Administrative Tribunal on Complaints against UNESCO	UNESCO Executive Board, Nov. 25, 1955	Oct. 23, 1956
Constitution of the IMCO Maritime Safety Committee	IMCO Assembly, Jan. 19, 1959	June 8, 1960

the three governments and the responsibilities of the Secretary-General in relation thereto.[60]

On a number of other occasions, there have been proposals that the Court be asked for an advisory opinion on an issue central to a dispute or situation being considered by the Assembly. Generally, these proposals have concerned the Assembly's competence to take certain actions. The first such proposal was made during the debate on a complaint by India concerning the treatment of persons of Indian origin in the Union of South Africa. South Africa asked the Assembly to request an advisory opinion as to whether the matters raised in the Indian complaint were, "under Article 2, paragraph 7 of the Charter, essentially within the domestic jurisdiction of the Union." The proposal was rejected by a vote of 31 to 21 with 2 abstentions.[61] The competence of the Assembly to deal with this question and the question of South Africa's apartheid policies has been challenged repeatedly at subsequent sessions of the Assembly. A number of statements have been made to the effect that the issue "should" be referred to the Court, but no concrete proposals to that effect have been introduced.

At three different points during the Assembly's consideration of the Palestine question, proposals for requesting advisory opinions from the Court were submitted. Proposals to request opinions on questions dealing with the international status of Palestine, and the power of the United Nations to partition it, were narrowly defeated in committee in 1947 and again in 1948. In 1952, the Assembly rejected a proposal to request an opinion from the Court on the status of the Palestine Arab refugees by a vote of 26 to 13 with 19 abstentions.[62]

The principal arguments against requesting advisory opinions from the Court have been much the same in the General Assembly and in the Security Council. They have included the following: 1) that the matter is "political" and therefore not suitable for reference to the Court since under Article 96 opinions may be requested only on "legal" questions; 2) that the Court should not be asked to interpret the Charter, that being the function of each organ with respect to its own powers; 3) that the subject matter is essentially within the domestic jurisdiction of a state; 4) that there is no need for an opinion from the

---

[60] For text of GA resolution and opinion of Court, see *ICJ Reports*, 1950, p. 65.

[61] GAOR/1st Sess., 2d Part/52d Plen. Mtg./Dec. 8, 1946/p. 1061. A second proposal, couched in more general terms, requested an opinion on the obligations of members and the authority of the Assembly with regard to legislation on racial discrimination. It was not put to the vote. See *ibid.*, Jt. 1st and 6th Ctte./4th Mtg./Nov. 27, 1946/pp. 33–34.

[62] For discussion see GAOR/2d Sess., Ad Hoc Ctte. on the Palestinian Question/31st Mtg./Nov. 24, 1947/pp. 203 and 299; GAOR/3d Sess., 1st Ctte./227th Mtg./Dec. 4, 1948/pp. 931–33; and GAOR/6th Sess., Ad Hoc Pol. Ctte./39th Mtg./Dec. 11, 1952/pp. 236–37.

Court since the issue is perfectly clear or should be decided by the Assembly or Council itself; 5) that other procedures for settling a disputed issue have been agreed upon; and 6) that the request would unduly delay the work of the Assembly or the Council or cast doubt upon their previous actions.

With regard to the last point, the Assembly and the Security Council have generally not considered it proper to request the Court to give an opinion as to the validity of resolutions previously adopted. This was the principal reason for defeat of the proposals to request an advisory opinion on the status of Palestine.[63] The same attitude was expressed during the discussion prior to the request for an opinion on "Certain Expenses of the United Nations," when the Assembly rejected an amendment that would have asked the Court to give an opinion whether the various resolutions adopted with regard to UNEF and the United Nations operations in the Congo "were . . . in conformity with the provisions of the Charter." [64]

The Procedure for Making Requests

Proposals to request opinions from the Court have at times lacked the desired degree of precision.[65] In this regard, the United Kingdom took the lead in an attempt to improve the Assembly's practices. In 1952, a special committee established to consider this matter recommended that, whenever a request by the Assembly was being considered, the question should at some appropriate stage be referred to the Sixth (Legal) Committee or to an ad hoc subcommittee for advice on the legal aspects and on the drafting of the request.[66] The Assembly decided against making such a procedure mandatory; instead, the resolution states that "the matter may" be referred to the Sixth Committee or that it might be considered jointly with the Sixth Committee.[67] In practice, this resolution has had no effect on Assembly procedure.

For both the General Assembly and the Security Council there is a question of the vote necessary to adopt a request for an advisory opinion. Since no such proposal in the Security Council has ever received seven affirmative votes, the question of the application of the veto has not arisen. In its report on voting procedures in the Security Council, the Interim Committee expressed the view that such a proposal should

[63] See above, p. 564.

[64] GAOR/16th Sess./1086th Plen. Mtg./Dec. 20, 1961/pp. 1150–54.

[65] Art. 65(2) of the Statute requires that the request contain "an exact statement of the question upon which an opinion is required." For difficulties the Court has encountered in dealing with some of the Assembly's ambiguous phraseology, see Rosenne, pp. 474 ff.

[66] GAOR/7th Sess./1952/*Annexes*, agenda item 53, p. 2.

[67] GA Res. 684(VII), Nov. 6, 1952.

be treated as procedural; [68] this was one of the few conclusions of the Committee not endorsed by the General Assembly. While a request for an advisory opinion may be viewed as a "procedure" by which the Council seeks clarification of a legal issue, the view may also be taken that since an opinion of the Court can have the practical effect of determining the question of substance, the decision to ask it should be treated as a matter of substance.

For the most part, the General Assembly has not found it necessary to consider the question of voting procedure. Proposals to request opinions have either failed to receive the support of a simple majority or have been adopted by a vote of two-thirds or more of those present and voting. In 1946, the General Assembly, when considering the question of the treatment of persons of Indian origin in South Africa, decided that a proposal to request an opinion, submitted as an amendment to the main draft resolution, required a two-thirds vote for adoption.[69] The amendment failed to receive a simple majority. At a subsequent session of the General Assembly when the question was raised of voting procedure on a request for an advisory opinion on the international status of South West Africa, the President referred to the action taken by the Assembly in 1946 as "an exceptional decision . . . reached on the specific understanding that no precedent was to be established," [70] and he ruled that the request required only a simple majority for adoption. The ruling was not challenged, but the proposal was adopted by more than a two-thirds vote.

The Procedure of the International Court

Requests for advisory opinions from United Nations organs are submitted to the International Court by means of a letter from the Secretary-General of the United Nations containing the text of the resolution adopted.[71] The Court Statute requires that the written request contain "an exact statement of the question upon which an opinion is required" and that it be "accompanied by all documents likely to throw light upon the question" (Article 65[2]). Occasionally, the Assembly has specified the documents to be submitted to the Court, but generally this matter has been left to the Secretary-General. He has

[68] GAOR/3d Sess./1948/*Supp. 10*/p. 14.

[69] For discussion, see GAOR/1st Sess., 2d Part/52d Plen. Mtg./Dec. 8, 1946/pp. 1048–61.

[70] GAOR/4th Sess./269th Plen. Mtg./Dec. 6, 1949/pp. 536–37. See Art. 18 and commentary.

[71] The two requests from specialized agencies were submitted by the Director General of UNESCO forwarding the resolution of the Executive Board, and by the Secretary-General of IMCO forwarding the resolution of the IMCO Assembly.

played a significant role in the advisory opinion proceedings; this has been characterized as "an *amicus curiae* function." [72] It is customary for the Secretary-General, or his representative, to present both written and oral statements to the Court.

The Statute of the Court requires that the Registrar give notice of the request to all states entitled to appear before the Court (Article 66[1]). The Registrar is also required, "by means of special and direct communication," to notify any state entitled to appear before the Court or any international organization considered "as likely to be able to furnish information on the question" that the Court will receive written statements and hear oral statements (Article 66[2]). In connection with the request for an opinion on "Certain Expenses of the United Nations," for example, twenty members submitted written statements and nine participated in the oral hearings.[73] Both the Statute (Article 68) and the Rules of the Court (Articles 82 and 83) stress that the Court shall be guided in the exercise of its advisory functions by provisions applying in contentious cases to the extent that they are applicable.

The Court's Obligation to Give Opinions

The power of the Court to give an advisory opinion is discretionary. This discretionary character was spelled out in the opinion on "Certain Expenses of the United Nations":

. . . the Court can give an advisory opinion only on a legal question. If a question is not a legal one, the Court has no discretion in the matter; it must decline to give the opinion requested. But even if the question is a legal one, which the Court is undoubtedly competent to answer, it may nonetheless decline to do so.[74]

In an earlier opinion, "Interpretation of the Peace Treaties," the Court affirmed its power "to examine whether the circumstances of the case are of such a character as should lead it to decline" to give an opinion. In fact, the Court has never refused to comply with a request for an opinion. It has stated that "the reply of the Court, itself an 'organ of the United Nations,' represents its participation in the activities of the Organization, and, in principle, should not be refused," [75] and that "only compelling reasons" [76] should lead the Court to refuse to give the requested opinion.

The argument most frequently made against the Court's giving an advisory opinion has been that the question is "political." The Court

---

[72] Rosenne, p. 484.
[73] *ICJ Reports,* 1962, pp. 153–54.
[74] *ICJ Reports,* 1962, p. 155.
[75] *ICJ Reports,* 1950, pp. 71, 72.
[76] "Judgments of the Administrative Tribunal of the ILO," *ICJ Reports,* 1956, p. 86.

has consistently rejected this argument. In each instance, it has found that the question, being one of interpreting a treaty provision, is a "legal" one and has refused to "attribute a political character" to the request.[77]

Another frequent objection has been that the Court lacks the authority to give an advisory opinion on questions involving interpretation of the Charter.[78] The Court itself has consistently overridden these objections. In its first opinion, the Court stated: "Nowhere is any provision to be found forbidding the Court, 'the principal judicial organ of the United Nations,' to exercise in regard to Article 4 of the Charter, a multilateral treaty, an interpretative function which falls within the normal exercise of its judicial powers." [79] The Court has reaffirmed this position on subsequent occasions when it has been asked to give an advisory opinion concerning a provision of the United Nations Charter.[80]

Nor has the Court considered that the absence of consent by the parties to a dispute precludes it from giving an opinion on a legal question involved in the dispute. This was a central issue in the "Interpretation of the Peace Treaties" case. The three countries directly concerned—Bulgaria, Hungary, and Romania—objected to the Court's rendering an opinion, contending that in doing so, the Court would violate "the well-established principle of international law according to which no judicial proceedings relating to a legal question pending between States can take place without their consent." [81] In the Eastern Carelia case, the PCIJ had declined to give an advisory opinion on the ground that to answer the question put to it "would be substantially equivalent to deciding the dispute" between Finland and the Soviet Union over the objections of the latter.[82] In the Interpretation of the Peace Treaties case, the International Court referred to this opinion, noted the "large amount of discretion" the Court possesses regarding the application of the provisions governing contentious cases, and concluded that the circumstances in the two cases were "profoundly different." The "sole object" of the request was to "enlighten the General Assembly"; the legal positions of the parties would be in no way compromised by the answers the Court might give; the Court's reply was "only of an advisory character" having "no binding force." The Court

---

[77] "Admission of a State to the United Nations," *ICJ Reports,* 1948, p. 61. Cited in a number of subsequent opinions.

[78] The controversy over authorizing the Court to interpret the Charter goes back to the San Francisco Conference, see above, p. 14.

[79] *ICJ Reports,* 1948, p. 61.

[80] "Competence of Assembly regarding Admission to the United Nations," *ICJ Reports,* 1950. p. 6; "Certain Expenses of the United Nations," *ICJ Reports,* 1962, p. 156.

[81] *ICJ Reports,* 1950, p. 71.   [82] *Publications of the PCIJ,* Ser. B, No. 5.

stated that "no State, whether a Member of the United Nations or not, can prevent the giving of an Advisory Opinion which the United Nations considers to be desirable." It therefore found "no reason why it should abstain from replying" to the Assembly's request.

The Effect of Advisory Opinions

In the General Assembly and in the opinions of the Court itself, there have been frequent references to the fact that the Court's opinions are purely "advisory." Nonetheless, they are expected to have, and have indeed been accorded, great weight. Although the Court's opinions are advisory, there is nothing to preclude the parties concerned from agreeing in advance to consider themselves bound thereby. Numerous agreements regulating relationships within the United Nations system rely upon advisory opinions of the Court for deciding disputed issues.

The Convention on the Privileges and Immunities of the United Nations, for example, sets out a procedure for requesting advisory opinions from the Court on any legal question arising from differences between the United Nations on the one hand and a member on the other. This provision specifically states that "the opinion given by the Court shall be accepted as decisive by the parties" (Section 30). There is a similar provision in the Convention on the Privileges and Immunities of the Specialized Agencies (Section 32). The Headquarters Agreement between the United Nations and the United States also provides for recourse to the Court in case of differences over interpretation or application of the Agreement. Under the Agreement, however, the final decision is rendered by an arbitral tribunal "having regard to the opinion of the Court" (Section 21).

The Statute of the Administrative Tribunal of the International Labour Organisation provides that under certain circumstances the question of the validity of the decisions of the tribunal "shall be submitted" to the International Court for an advisory opinion and that "the opinion given by the Court shall be binding" (Article XII).[83] On the one occasion when the Court was asked to give an opinion on judgments of the Tribunal, it noted that this provision of the Statute "goes beyond the scope attributed by the Charter and by the Statute of the Court to an Advisory Opinion." But the Court concluded that this was "a rule of conduct" for the agencies concerned and "in no wise affected the way in which the Court functions." [84]

The Statute of the Administrative Tribunal of the United Nations, as

[83] This tribunal serves not only the ILO but a number of other specialized agencies.
[84] *ICJ Reports*, 1956, p. 84.

revised in 1955, also provides for possible resort to the International Court for advisory opinions on the judgments of the tribunal. Some members objected, however, "to saying expressly that an 'advisory opinion' was 'binding.'"[85] The Statute, therefore, states that "the Secretary-General shall either give effect to the opinion of the Court, or request the Tribunal to convene especially in order that it shall confirm its original judgment, or give a new judgment, in conformity with the opinion of the Court."[86]

Action by the General Assembly

The actions taken by the General Assembly upon receipt of advisory opinions from the Court have necessarily differed from case to case. In all but one instance, the Assembly has adopted a resolution either noting or endorsing the Court's opinion. The exception was the opinion on the "Competence of the General Assembly for the Admission of a State to the United Nations." In this case, the subsequent action of the Assembly implied acceptance of the Court's opinion.

With regard to the three advisory opinions on South West Africa, the Assembly either "accepted" or "accepted and endorsed" the opinions by unanimous or nearly unanimous votes.[87] In a number of other cases, the Assembly has "taken note" of the Court's opinions.[88]

Following the receipt of the Court's opinion on "Certain Expenses of the United Nations," there was a debate whether the Assembly should "accept" or "take note" of the opinion. It was argued that the Assembly could accept or reject the opinion, but that it could not "consider, approve, or criticize" the reasoning behind the opinion or voice its agreement or disagreement with the Court's advice. There were frequent statements to the effect that not to "accept" the opinion would be a "blow" to the prestige of the Court and the rule of law. On the other hand, it was proposed that the Assembly should merely "take note" of the opinion, and that to "accept" it would be to confer a "binding" effect upon an opinion that was "advisory" in character.[89]

[85] See report of the special committee established to consider the revision of the Statute. GAOR/10th Sess./1955/*Annexes*, agenda item 49, pp. 12–13.

[86] See GA Res. 956(X), Nov. 8, 1955. See Statute of the Administrative Tribunal of the United Nations, Art. 11, in UN Doc. AT/11/Rev., Feb. 1, 1959.

[87] GA Res. 449(V), Dec. 13, 1950; 934(X), Dec. 3, 1955; and 1047(XI), Jan. 23, 1957.

[88] See GA Res. 197A(III), Dec. 8, 1948, on the admission of new members; 385(V), Nov. 3, 1950, on the interpretation of the peace treaties with Bulgaria, Hungary, and Romania; and 888(IX), Dec. 17, 1954, on the awards of the UN Administrative Tribunal.

[89] France and Jordan were the principal advocates of the "take note" formula. For the discussion, see GAOR/17th Sess., 5th Ctte./especially 961st–62d Mtgs./ Dec. 6, 1962, and 972d–73d Mtgs./Dec. 14 and 17, 1962. See also the debate as to

This proposal was defeated, however, and the Assembly decided by a vote of 76 to 17 with 8 abstentions to "accept" the opinion.[90]

In addition to "accepting" or "noting" the opinions of the Court, the Assembly has frequently used the opinions as a basis for further action. To cite examples: The Assembly "recommended" that members "act in accordance" with the opinion of the Court on the "Conditions for the Admission of a State to the United Nations." [91] It "urged" South Africa "to take the necessary steps to give effect to the opinion" of the Court on the international status of South West Africa and at the same time established a special committee to assist in "implementing" the opinion.[92] In the "Reparations" case and in the case concerning awards of the United Nations Administrative Tribunal, the opinions of the Court were cited by the Assembly in authorizing the Secretary-General to take action—in the first case to press claims and in the second to pay the amounts awarded by the Tribunal.[93] After the Court rendered its opinion on "Reservations to the Genocide Convention," the Assembly recommended that states "be guided" by the opinion and requested the Secretary-General "to conform his practice" to the opinion. The Assembly also made recommendations to organs of the United Nations, the specialized agencies, states, and the Secretary-General regarding future multilateral conventions.[94]

---

whether the Assembly should accept as an "authoritative statement of law" the Court's opinion in the Reparations case. GAOR/4th Sess./262d Plen. Mtg./Dec. 1, 1949/pp. 440–49; Annex, agenda item 51, pp. 200–1; and 6th Ctte./183d–184th Mtgs./Nov. 3 and 4, 1949/pp. 273–88.

[90] GA Res. 1854A(XVII), Dec. 19, 1962.
[91] GA Res. 197A(III), Dec. 8, 1948.
[92] GA Res. 449(V), Dec. 13, 1950. For the Assembly's actions on the two subsequent requests to the Court for advisory opinions in this case, see pp. 498 ff.
[93] GA Res. 365(IV), Dec. 1, 1949, and 888(IX), Dec. 17, 1954.
[94] GA Res. 598(VI), Jan. 12, 1952.

CHAPTER XV

The Secretariat

The authors of the Charter provisions relating to the Secretariat drew upon the extensive experience gained from the League period. Before the League was established, small permanent secretariats or bureaus existed to perform limited technical functions for public international unions such as the Universal Postal Union. It was not, however, until the establishment of the League of Nations and the International Labour Organisation that the necessity arose of establishing international secretariats composed of substantial numbers of persons, drawn from many nationalities, having a wide range of functions, and operating continuously. The League was also a pioneer in its acceptance of the concept of an international civil service.

The Covenant provided for a "permanent" secretariat to consist of "a Secretary-General and such secretaries and staff as may be required." It named the first Secretary-General—Sir James Eric Drummond—and provided that his successor should be appointed by the Council with the approval of "the majority of the Assembly." It directed that the Secretary-General should act "in that capacity" at all meetings of the Assembly and the Council. It empowered the Secretary-General "with the approval of the Council" to appoint "the secretaries and the staff of the Secretariat" and required that all Secretariat positions be "open equally to men and women." Nothing in the Covenant required that the Secretariat should be an international service instead of an intergovernmental one, that its members should be recruited directly with the obligation to serve the League, and that they should be subject to the exclusive authority of the Secretary-General. It was Sir Eric Drummond who, with the support of the Council and the Assembly, decided that the career civil service model, to which he had been accustomed as a British civil servant, should be followed in so far as was practicable.[1]

[1] For detailed description and analysis of League experience, see Egon F. Ranshofen-Wertheimer, *The International Secretariat* (Washington, Carnegie Endowment for International Peace, 1945).

History of the Charter Provisions

Experts in the United States State Department engaged in preparing proposals for a postwar international organization readily agreed that its secretariat should be modeled on that of the League. The only question causing some difference of opinion was that of the organization and functions of the top direction.[2] One suggestion was that the chief administrative officer—called General Secretary in early drafts—should combine secretarial and administrative functions with the nonvoting chairmanship of the Council and its executive committee. Another suggestion, advanced by President Roosevelt, was that there should be a political head, a person of "eminent attainment" who would preside at meetings of the Council and act as "moderator" of differences, and an administrative head who would perform secretarial and administrative functions. The President's suggestion raised what were thought to be insuperable difficulties and was dropped.

The proposals submitted by the United States to the other Dumbarton Oaks conferees provided for a director-general "elected by the General Assembly with the concurrence of the executive council," with administrative and secretarial responsibilities comparable to those the League Secretary-General had in practice assumed. No specific mention was made of political responsibilities or powers.[3]

At Dumbarton Oaks, it was agreed, following British and Chinese suggestions, that the chief administrative officer—now called the Secretary-General—should have the right to bring to the attention of the Security Council any matter "which in his opinion may threaten international peace and security." This appears to have reflected a feeling that the League system suffered from the fact that only a member state could bring an alleged threat to the peace to the Council's attention.[4]

The only serious disagreements at San Francisco concerned the method of election of the Secretary-General and the manner of selecting his deputies. On the first question, there were strong arguments by the smaller states that the General Assembly alone should elect, and that if the Security Council participated, the veto should not apply. The view that finally prevailed, however, was that the Assembly should appoint on the recommendation of the Security Council, the concurrence of the permanent members being required.[5] No provision was

[2] Ruth B. Russell, A History of the United Nations Charter (Washington, Brookings Institution, 1958), pp. 370–77.
[3] State Dept., Post-War Foreign Policy Preparation, 1939–1945, p. 605.
[4] Russell, p. 432.   [5] Ibid., p. 859.

made regarding the terms of office or reeligibility. On the question of appointing deputy secretaries-general, it was finally decided, the Soviet Union reluctantly agreeing, that the Secretary-General should have the power to select his staff, including his principal assistants. In addition to resolving these two controversial issues, the Conference decided to incorporate into the Charter provisions for assuring the independence and individual qualification of staff members (Articles 100 and 101).

Functions and Powers as Defined by the Charter

The Secretariat's importance is emphasized by the fact that it is listed in Article 7 as one of the "principal organs" of the United Nations. The functions and powers of the Secretary-General and his staff are set forth in various articles of the Charter, including the Statute of the International Court of Justice. Articles 97, 98, 99, and 101 are of central importance in this respect. Other articles assign specific responsibilities to the Secretary-General. Article 12 requires him, with the consent of the Security Council, to notify the General Assembly of matters relating to the maintenance of international peace and security that are being dealt with by the Council. Article 20 makes him the instrumentality through which special sessions of the General Assembly are called. By the terms of Article 73(e), he receives certain information from members on conditions in non-self-governing territories they administer. Article 102 provides for registration with and publication by the Secretariat of treaties and other international agreements. The Statute of the International Court of Justice gives the Secretary-General certain specific functions in connection with the election of judges, the establishment of the Court's compulsory jurisdiction, the advisory-opinion procedure, and communication of proposals by the Court for the amendment of the Statute.[6]

The Preparatory Commission grouped the principal functions assigned to the Secretary-General, "explicitly or by inference," under six headings: 1) general administrative and executive functions; 2) technical functions; 3) financial functions; 4) organization and administration of the International Secretariat; 5) political functions; and 6) representational functions.[7] Another way of classifying his functions so as to emphasize his responsibilities as they have developed in practice would distinguish his executive functions (including political), his administrative or managerial functions, and his functions as coordinator

[6] See Arts. 5, 7, 14, 36, 67, and 70 of the Statute.
[7] *Report of the Preparatory Commission,* p. 86. This grouping has been substantially followed by the authors of the *Repertory* except that functions and powers coming under the fourth heading are considered under Art. 101 instead of Art. 98. See *Repertory,* V, 122.

of the policies and activities of the United Nations and the specialized agencies.[8]

The Preparatory Commission showed considerable appreciation of the role the Secretary-General would have:

> While the responsibility for the framing and adoption of agreed international policies rests with the organs representative of the members—the General Assembly, the Security Council, the Economic and Social Council and the Trusteeship Council—the essential tasks of preparing the ground for those decisions and of executing them in co-operation with the Members will devolve largely upon the Secretariat. The manner in which the Secretariat performs these tasks will largely determine the degree in which the objectives of the Charter will be realized. . . .
>
> The United Nations cannot prosper, nor can its aims be realized without the active and steadfast support of the peoples of the world. The aims and activities of the General Assembly, the Security Council, the Economic and Social Council and the Trusteeship Council will, no doubt, be represented before the public primarily by the Chairmen of these organs. But the Secretary-General, more than anyone else, will stand for the United Nations as a whole. In the eyes of the world, no less than in the eyes of his own staff, he must embody the principles and ideals of the Charter to which the Organization seeks to give effect.[9]

The Commission could not foresee how the "special power" given to the Secretary-General by Article 99 would be exercised, nor did it foresee the possibilities inherent in the Secretary-General's position as head of a principal organ committed to achieving the purposes and principles of the Charter.

THE SECRETARY-GENERAL AS CHIEF EXECUTIVE. One aspect of the Secretary-General's position, the full implications of which could only be appreciated with time and experience, is his role as chief executive of the Organization. Dag Hammarskjöld observed that the initial United States proposal of a single officer combining executive and administrative functions was "a reflection, in some measure, of the American political system, which places authority in a chief executive officer who is not simply subordinated to the legislative organs but who is constitutionally responsible for carrying out the authority derived from the constitutional instrument directly." [10] While this analogy has value only within carefully defined limits, in broad terms it can be said that the Secretary-General performs, within the context of an international organization, the functions normally associated with a chief execu-

[8] See "The United Nations Secretariat," *United Nations Studies,* No. 4 (New York, Carnegie Endowment for International Peace, 1950), p. 19.

[9] *Report of the Preparatory Commission,* pp. 84, 87.

[10] "The International Civil Servant in Law and in Fact," in Wilder Foote, ed., *Dag Hammarskjöld: Servant of Peace* (New York, Harpers, 1962), pp. 335–36.

tive.[11] The development of his executive powers has been one of the most important aspects of his evolving position and has been particularly responsive to the changes in international political relations, to the changing roles of the Security Council and the General Assembly, and to the personalities of successive Secretaries-General.

The executive functions and powers of the Secretary-General are extensive in scope. A number of factors have contributed to their progressive enlargement. These include: 1) the natural advantages the Secretary-General enjoys, as a permanent full-time official with a knowledgeable staff, in his relations with the General Assembly and the Councils; 2) the limited effectiveness of the Security Council, because of the inability of the permanent members to agree; 3) the inherent inability of the General Assembly to perform executive functions; and 4) the confidence that occupants of the office have inspired by their ability to discharge executive tasks satisfactorily. The Secretary-General has certain obvious advantages as a claimant to executive power; the degree to which he has succeeded in establishing his position as chief executive is in no small degree due to his personal qualities.

The Secretary-General has used his annual report to the General Assembly to discuss controversial issues and to make specific suggestions for the consideration of governments and the interested public. Although he has used his "special right" under Article 99 sparingly, the possibility of its use has been an important influence, and it has also served as the basis for important fact-finding and exploratory activities. While the Charter does not explicitly give the Secretary-General the same right to bring matters to the attention of the Assembly and the other Councils, the rules of procedure of these organs empower him to do so.[12] This right the Secretary-General has used repeatedly to exercise an important influence on the work of these organs. He may also intervene in the discussions of the General Assembly and the Councils to make statements on any matter under consideration.[13] This right he has used on many occasions to clarify his own position, to call attention to special aspects that need consideration, and to encourage action.

The General Assembly and the Councils have entrusted the Secretary-General with a variety of functions of an executive nature involving the exercise of discretion,[14] for example, in connection with the UNEF and ONUC peace-keeping operations. Especially in matters of finance, the Secretary-General has been given important executive responsibilities. According to the Financial Regulations adopted by the

[11] "The United Nations Secretariat," pp. 19–30.
[12] GA Rule 13; TC Rule 9; ECOSOC Rule 10.
[13] GA Rule 72; SC Rule 22; ECOSOC Rule 21; TC Rule 26.
[14] See commentary on Art. 98.

General Assembly, the Secretary-General prepares the annual budget estimates, reports to the Fifth Committee of the General Assembly on the financial implications of proposed resolutions, and has a qualified veto over proposed expenditures in that they cannot be incurred until he certifies that they can be covered either by existing appropriations or under the resolution on unforeseen and extraordinary expenses.[15] The Secretary-General's financial powers provide him with a means of guiding, and in some measure controlling, the activities authorized by the Assembly and Council.

In the discharge of executive responsibilities for the maintenance of international peace and security, the Secretary-General has by no means been limited to the exercise of authority explicitly given by Article 99 or conferred upon him under Article 98. In the exercise of the authority conferred by Article 99, he has asserted the right to carry out field investigations on his own responsibility and to establish United Nations "presences" for the purpose of informing himself and providing a channel of influence. In performing functions entrusted to him by the Assembly or the Security Council under Article 98, Hammarskjöld expressed the view that he was under obligation to carry out the general policies adopted by those organs even though the detailed directives might be inadequate to provide guidance in a given situation, and even though his decisions might involve him in political controversy.[16]

The Secretary-General has found a source of executive authority in his position as head of one of the principal organs of the United Nations committed to upholding the purposes and principles of the Organization. In his statement to the General Assembly on his reelection to a second term, Dag Hammarskjöld forcefully stated this concept of the inherent responsibility of the Secretary-General. After indicating that in his view the Secretary-General should not be asked to act if no guidance for his action is to be found in the Charter or in the decisions of the main organs, he continued:

On the other hand, I believe that it is in keeping with the philosophy of the Charter that the Secretary-General should be expected to act also without such guidance, should this appear to him necessary, in order to help in filling any vacuum that may appear in the system which the Charter and traditional diplomacy provide for the safeguarding of peace and security.[17]

As the chief executive officer of the United Nations, the Secretary-General represents the Organization in relations with members and

[15] UN Doc. ST/SGB/Financial Rules/Jan. 1, 1960, Regulations 13.1 and 13.2.
[16] Foote, p. 346. For further discussion, see commentary on Art. 98.
[17] GAOR/12th Sess./690th Plen. Mtg./Sept. 26, 1957. For further discussion see commentary on Art. 99.

other states and with other international organizations. Through his personal statements and writings and through the activities of his information staff, he has a major responsibility for seeing that the Organization is presented favorably to world opinion, and he has been the most important single influence in determining the view of itself that the Organization presents to the world.

Central to the Secretary-General's executive power is his right to select and appoint the members of his staff (Article 101). Without this ability to appoint those who are to advise and assist him in carrying out his responsibilities, he would be in a weak position indeed in performing his other executive functions. While the Charter does specify certain criteria to be applied in the selection of staff, it clearly establishes the principle that the Secretary-General himself decides how these criteria are best satisfied. The insistence of successive Secretaries-General on their responsibility for the selection of personnel and the accountability of staff to them and to them alone has been an important factor in the development of the executive authority of the office.

THE SECRETARY-GENERAL AS CHIEF ADMINISTRATOR. As "chief administrative officer" (Article 97), the Secretary-General has functions and powers in line with and similar to those of his precursor, the Secretary-General of the League of Nations. The functions and powers coming under this head are essentially of a managerial nature. He must direct the Secretariat in the rendering of services, essentially of a secretarial nature, to the General Assembly, the Security Council, ECOSOC, the Trusteeship Council, and the large number of subsidiary organs and special bodies set up to do the work of the United Nations. These services consist of providing meeting places for these bodies, arranging for necessary facilities, preparing and circulating documentation, and seeing that records are prepared. The large number of meetings to be serviced, the expanding membership of the organization, and the number of official and working languages used place heavy demands upon the staff.

In addition to servicing meetings in this strict sense, there are technical services to be performed such as the preparation of background papers, the preparation of reports and periodical publications, and a multitude of specific technical tasks which the Secretariat may be asked to perform by the General Assembly and the Councils. Further, there are the tasks of personnel and financial administration which must be performed well if the Organization is to function smoothly.

These essentially administrative tasks do not necessarily involve to any great extent the personal attention of the Secretary-General, as they may be delegated to his department heads. However, the responsibility for their proper discharge is his.

THE SECRETARY-GENERAL AS CHIEF COORDINATOR. In addition to being chief executive and administrator of the United Nations, the Secretary-General has important functions and powers as coordinator of the policies and activities of the United Nations and the specialized agencies. The responsibilities of the Secretary-General result from the fact that the General Assembly and ECOSOC, the organs which have specific coordination responsibilities under the Charter,[18] need assistance in obtaining information and in formulating and implementing their recommendations.

The Secretary-General's responsibilities for coordination are nowhere explicitly stated in the Charter. They derive from resolutions passed by the General Assembly and ECOSOC requesting him to undertake various tasks in this area. The agreements concluded under authority of Article 63 to define relationships under Article 57, either explicitly or implicitly, indicate a number of functions the Secretary-General is to perform. At its third session in 1946, ECOSOC requested that the Secretary-General establish a standing committee of the top administrative officers of the United Nations and the specialized agencies, with himself as chairman, to take appropriate steps to give the fullest effect to these agreements.[19] The annual report of ECOSOC on economic and social programs, prepared by the Secretariat, serves as a basis for coordination discussions, as do special reports prepared by the Secretary-General at ECOSOC's request. The Secretary-General has been frequently entrusted with coordinating responsibilities in connection with particular projects and activities.[20]

His position as coordinator of policies and activities of the United Nations and the specialized agencies is essentially weak, not because of lack of a basis in the Charter or lack of willingness on the part of ECOSOC and the General Assembly to delegate authority to him, but because, in his relations with other administrative heads, he is one among equals. His success, and indeed that of the General Assembly and ECOSOC, is primarily dependent on the willingness of states as members of these organizations to follow consistent policies and to support coordination efforts in all organizations of which they are members.

[18] See Arts. 57, 58, 60, 63, 64 and commentary.
[19] ECOSOC Res. 13(III), Sept. 21, 1946. This committee was later named the Administrative Committee on Coordination (ACC).
[20] See, for example, ECOSOC Res. 417(XIV), Apr. 14, 1953, on international cooperation on water control and utilization; and GA Res. 2084(XX), Dec. 29, 1965, on attaining the objectives of the Development Decade.

Article 97

The Secretariat shall comprise a Secretary-General and such staff as the Organization may require. The Secretary-General shall be appointed by the General Assembly upon the recommendation of the Security Council. He shall be the chief administrative officer of the Organization.

The Nature of the Secretariat

The Charter, in describing the nature and composition of the Secretariat, follows quite closely the phraseology of the Covenant. The phrase "such staff as the Organization may require" suggests a group of persons engaged in the administrative service of an organization with defined responsibilities and functions. Furthermore, the word "Secretariat" suggests an integrated group, an impression confirmed by the last sentence, which declares that the Secretary-General is the chief administrative officer. This concept of an integrated secretariat had validity in the case of the League of Nations, since the numerous activities undertaken to carry out the purposes of the League were under the control of the main organs and their administration was largely centralized. In the case of the United Nations, for a variety of reasons, a considerable amount of administrative decentralization has occurred, beyond that inherent in the establishment of specialized agencies enjoying administrative autonomy.[21] As a result, it becomes necessary, for particular purposes, to distinguish among different kinds of staff.

The *Repertory* lists under the heading "The Staff of the Organization": "Staff of the Secretariat," "Staff of Certain Organs," and "Staff of the Office of the Registry of the International Court of Justice." While it is not explicit as to the basis of the distinctions, analysis permits the inference that degree of subjection to Staff Regulations and Staff Rules is an important consideration. The *Repertory* states that "[members] of the staff appointed by the Secretary-General to perform, under his direction, functions required by United Nations organs or other functions within the area of responsibility of the Secretary-General, whether at Headquarters or at duty stations away from Headquarters," are governed by Staff Regulations and Staff Rules, but it recognizes

[21] See Art. 57 and commentary. For examples of administrative decentralization, see GA Res. 2089(XX), Dec. 20, 1965, establishing the United Nations Organization for Industrial Development as an autonomous organization with a secretariat headed by an executive director appointed by the Secretary-General with confirmation by the General Assembly.

that there are members of the "regular staff" that are subject to special staff rules.

To clarify the somewhat confused situation that has developed, particularly from the point of view of the budget, the Secretary-General in his annual report for 1964–65 distinguished between those staff members appointed for service within the establishment approved under the budget, and staff members specifically appointed for service with United Nations programs financed by voluntary contributions, such as the United Nations Children's Fund, the Technical Assistance Board and the Special Fund (United Nations Development Programme), and the Office of the High Commissioner for Refugees.[22]

The Secretary-General: Method of Appointment and Term of Office

The Charter provision on the method of appointing the Secretary-General was approved at San Francisco following insistence by the major powers that the vesting of important political responsibilities in the Secretary-General required that the Security Council be given a decisive part in the choice of a person to fill the office. It was emphasized that if the Secretary-General were to be effective in this political role, he would need to have the confidence of the major powers. Furthermore, the League Secretary-General had been appointed by the Council with Assembly approval; consequently, the Charter provision was in line with League practice. The use of the word "appointed" instead of "elected" was suggested by the fact that the office of Secretary-General was conceived at the time as being primarily—though not exclusively—an administrative office.[23]

The Preparatory Commission, recognizing the heavy responsibilities that would rest upon the Secretary-General and the need of his being a man of eminence and possessing the confidence of members, recommended that the General Assembly and the Security Council should discuss both his nomination and his appointment at private meetings, and that the vote in either body should be by secret ballot.[24] This recommendation was accepted by the General Assembly. Rule 142 of its Rules of Procedure provides that "[when] the Security Council has submitted its recommendation on the appointment of the Secretary-General, the General Assembly shall consider the recommendation and vote upon it by secret ballot in private meeting." All Security Council meetings to consider recommendations in this regard have been held in private. The General Assembly in its first session accepted the view of

[22] GAOR/20th Sess./1965/Supp. 1/p. 173. [23] See Russell, pp. 854–60.
[24] Report of the Preparatory Commission, p. 81.

the Preparatory Commission that it was desirable for the Security Council "to proffer one candidate only," and that practice has been followed by the Council.[25] Appointment is by simple majority, unless the Assembly itself decides that a two-thirds majority is necessary (Article 18). The Secretary-General assumes his title and functions immediately upon taking the oath of office at a public meeting of the General Assembly.[26]

The Charter contains no provision on the term of office. The Dumbarton Oaks Proposals simply stated that the Secretary-General should serve "for such term and under such conditions as are specified in the Charter." [27] At San Francisco, the Sponsoring Governments proposed that the Secretary-General should be elected for a three-year term and be eligible for reelection. When the smaller states finally yielded on the method of appointment, accepting the requirement of Security Council recommendation and permanent-member concurrence, they insisted that the provision for a three-year term be dropped, on the ground that a short term would make the Secretary-General too dependent on the permanent members.[28]

The term of office of the first Secretary-General, Trygve Lie, was fixed by the General Assembly at five years, in accordance with the recommendation of the Preparatory Commission. Subsequent appointments have been for five-year terms.[29] This procedure has been accepted as a reasonable compromise between the requirement of accountability and that of effectiveness in the discharge of the responsibilities of office.

The problem of what to do in case of the interruption, threatened or actual, of the exercise of the functions vested in the office of the Secretary-General has twice arisen under differing circumstances and with differing solutions. The Preparatory Commission in its report and the General Assembly in its resolution on the administrative organization of the Secretariat anticipated the situation where the Secretary-General might be absent or unable to perform his duties by providing that there should always be one assistant secretary-general designated by the Secretary-General to deputize for him.[30]

[25] GA Res. 11(I), Feb. 1, 1946.
[26] For text of oath, see Staff Rules, UN Doc. ST/SGB/Staff Rules/1, Regulation 1.8.
[27] Ch. x, para. 1.   [28] Russell, pp. 854–60.
[29] Dag Hammarskjöld in 1953 and 1958. U Thant, initially appointed Acting Secretary-General in 1961, was subsequently appointed Secretary-General for a term of five years, to run from the time of his first appointment, Nov. 3, 1961. GA Res. 1771(XVII), Nov. 30, 1962.
[30] Report of the Preparatory Commission, p. 81; GA Res. 13(I), Feb. 13, 1946.

No provision, however, had been made for the situation that arose in 1950 when the office threatened to become vacant as the result of the expiration of Mr. Lie's term on February 2, 1951, and the failure of the permanent members of the Security Council to agree on a recommendation of an appointment. When the question of the appointment of a Secretary-General was placed on the agenda of the General Assembly, the Soviet Union objected to consideration of the matter on the ground that the Security Council had not made a recommendation; notwithstanding, the General Assembly adopted a resolution continuing Mr. Lie in office for a period of three years.[31] The majority based their action on "the necessity to ensure the uninterrupted exercise of the functions vested by the Charter in the office of Secretary-General." [32] The refusal of the Soviet Union and other communist states to recognize the validity of the General Assembly's action and their complete boycott of Mr. Lie led him to the conviction that he should resign,[33] in order that the full influence of the office might be exercised in the cause of peace.

The problem arose a second time when Dag Hammarskjöld died on September 18, 1961, in Africa. Since it was Mr. Hammarskjöld's custom to maintain close contact with his staff in New York when he was abroad, he had not designated a deputy when he left New York. Duties of the office were performed by the undersecretaries, with the Executive Assistant to the Secretary-General, Andrew Cordier, acting as coordinator, pending appointment of a successor. The United States took the view that the General Assembly had authority to make a provisional appointment, citing as precedents: 1) the action of the Assembly in January, 1946, in designating Sir Gladwyn Jebb, Executive Secretary of the Preparatory Commission, to perform the duties of Secretary-General pending a regular appointment; and 2) the Assembly's action in continuing Mr. Lie in office. The Soviet Union, in addition to insisting initially on the substitution of a triumvirate for a single person, argued that the matter must first be considered by the Security Council and that the General Assembly could act only on recommendation of that organ.[34] Agreement was finally reached between the United States and the USSR after extended private discussions on a formula under which the Security Council would recommend the appointment of U Thant as Acting Secretary-General for the remainder of Mr.

[31] GAOR/5th Sess./296th Plen. Mtg./Oct. 31, 1950/paras. 15–27; GA Res. 492(V), Nov. 1, 1950. The vote was 46 to 5, with 8 abstentions.

[32] For statements made in the General Assembly, see GAOR/5th Sess./296th and 298th Plen. Mtgs./Oct. 31 and Nov. 1, 1950.

[33] Trygve Lie, *In the Cause of Peace* (New York, Macmillan, 1954), pp. 406–13.

[34] State Dept., *U.S. Participation in the UN*, pp. 179, 180.

Hammarskjöld's term. On November 3, 1961, the Security Council unanimously recommended this appointment, which the General Assembly unanimously voted to make on the afternoon of the same day.

The concept of the Secretary-General as "chief administrative officer" was implied in the provisions of the League Covenant and was fully accepted and carried out in League practice. It was embodied in substance in the Tentative Proposals submitted by the United States government to the Dumbarton Oaks conferees, was incorporated into the Dumbarton Oaks Proposals, and was accepted without debate at San Francisco. It is spelled out in detail in other provisions of the Charter and in Staff Regulations approved by the General Assembly.[35]

Article 98

The Secretary-General shall act in that capacity in all meetings of the General Assembly, of the Security Council, of the Economic and Social Council, and of the Trusteeship Council, and shall perform such other functions as are entrusted to him by these organs. The Secretary-General shall make an annual report to the General Assembly on the work of the Organization.

Article 98 was approved at San Francisco without discussion or dissent. Only one substantive change was made in the Dumbarton Oaks text, the introduction of the last clause of the first sentence. The United States proposals had provided that the Secretary-General, then called "Director-General," should serve as Secretary-General of the General Assembly, the executive council, and such other organs as might be established, and that he should make an annual report on the work of the Organization. The Dumbarton Oaks Proposals incorporated the substance of these provisions.[36] At San Francisco, the substance was accepted without question, with changes in phraseology to take account of other decisions; but it was decided, without controversy, to add the words "and shall perform such other functions as are entrusted to him by these organs." The addition of these words made explicit what in any case would have been implied—that the Secretary-General might be authorized by the General Assembly or one of the Councils to perform certain functions in connection with the discharge of their responsibilities. This had been League of Nations practice and was considered essential to the smooth and efficient functioning of the Or-

---

[35] For further discussion, see pp. 578–79, and commentary on Arts. 98 to 101.
[36] Ch. x, para. 2.

ganization, since the Secretary-General and his staff would alone be in the position to provide the expertise and continuity essential to carrying out many of the decisions these organs might take.

Secretarial Functions

In providing that the Secretary-General "shall act in that capacity" at all meetings of the General Assembly and the Councils, Article 98 follows closely the phraseology of Article 6(4) of the Covenant. The functions here referred to are clearly those associated with the secretarial character of the office. The Rules of Procedure of the General Assembly and the Councils contain provisions based on this provision of Article 98, and either expressly provide or have been interpreted as providing that the Secretary-General shall act in a similar capacity at meetings of commissions, committees, and subcommittees,[37] the one exception being the Military Staff Committee. In all cases, it is provided that the Secretary-General may act through a deputy.

The secretarial functions of the Secretary-General and his staff are defined by the Rules of Procedure of the General Assembly and the Councils in varying detail. Rule 47 of the General Assembly's Rules of Procedure provides that:

[The] Secretariat shall receive, translate, print and distribute documents, reports and resolutions of the General Assembly, its committees and organs; interpret speeches made at the meetings; prepare, print and circulate the summary records of the session; have the custody and proper preservation of the documents in the archives of the General Assembly; publish the reports of the meetings; distribute all documents of the General Assembly to the Members of the United Nations, and, generally, perform all other work which the General Assembly may require.[38]

"Such Other Functions As Are Entrusted to Him"

These words, inclusive in purpose, do not exclude functions of a secretarial nature, but they do go beyond these and provide the basis for the Secretary-General's being entrusted with responsibilities involving the exercise of considerable discretion and political judgment. The General Assembly, in its second session, adopted a resolution in which

[37] See GA Rule 45; SC Provisional Rules of Procedure, Rule 21; ECOSOC Rule 28; TC Rule 23. The rules of procedure of the commissions of ECOSOC contain similar provisions.

[38] ECOSOC Rule 33 also describes the Secretary-General's secretarial duties in considerable detail, but the Rules of Procedure of the Security Council and the Trusteeship Council leave more to inference.

it drew the attention of the Councils and their commissions, as well as commissions appointed by the General Assembly, to the desirability of utilizing to the utmost the services of the Secretariat; [39] it also recommended "specifically to the organs of the United Nations to consider carefully, before the creation of special commissions and sub-commissions, whether the task to be carried out could not usefully be entrusted to the Secretariat."

In resolutions adopted by the General Assembly and the Councils, the Secretary-General is commonly requested to assume some measure of responsibility in connection with their implementation. The specific functions entrusted to him have included making preliminary studies, preparing drafts, assembling information on the attitudes of governments, summarizing reports received from governments, communicating decisions to governments, preparing plans for technical assistance, preparing estimates of expenditures, discussing with governments methods to achieve specified objectives, preparing plans for peace forces, recruiting and directing peace-keeping forces, soliciting voluntary contributions to United Nations programs, concluding truce agreements, and establishing observation groups. In fact, the range of functions the Secretary-General has been or may be intrusted with, by the General Assembly and the Councils, is limited only by the functions and powers of these organs. Practically, the extent to which functions are entrusted to the Secretary-General depends on the willingness of governments to allow decisions to pass from their immediate control, the confidence the particular occupant of the office inspires, and the advantages which member governments see in having functions performed and decisions taken by a knowledgeable, experienced, and objective international official and his staff.

The assignment of functions to the Secretary-General inevitably involves vesting in him some discretion with regard to the carrying out of his task. While the extent of this discretion varies with the nature and circumstances of the assignment, it may become of considerable importance and political significance in connection with tasks he is asked to perform in the peace and security field. Governments often find it easier to entrust such assignments to the Secretary-General than to subsidiary organs composed of representatives of member states. How broad the mandate may be is illustrated by the General Assembly's resolution in the Lebanon-Jordan case, by which the Secretary-General was requested to make—in consultation with governments concerned and in accordance with the Charter—"such practical arrangements as would adequately help in upholding the purposes and principles of the Charter in relation to Lebanon and Jordan in the

[39] GA Res. 183(II), Oct. 20, 1947.

present circumstances, and thereby facilitate the early withdrawal of the foreign troops from the two countries." [40]

The Secretary-General may find himself in the position where the directives provided by resolutions of the Security Council or General Assembly do not cover a new situation or are unclear in their application to it, while at the same time the organ or organs that have assigned functions to him are unable to redefine or clarify their assignment: the Congo experience provided striking examples. The Secretary-General's initial assignment from the Security Council, based upon his own recommendation, had been:

to take the necessary steps, in consultation with the Republic of the Congo, to provide the Government with such military assistance as may be necessary, until, through the efforts of the Congolese Government with the technical assistance of the United Nations, the national security forces may be able, in the opinion of the Government, to meet fully their tasks.[41]

The Secretary-General, in submitting his recommendation, indicated that his actions would be based on principles set forth in a report of 1958 on previous experience in this field.[42] Subsequent resolutions of the Security Council and the General Assembly reaffirmed, modified, and interpreted the directives under which the Secretary-General was to act.[43]

Disagreement arose over the Secretary-General's interpretation of his powers with respect to the introduction of United Nations forces into Katanga, the role of these forces in the civil war, and the extent to which support might be given to one or the other claimant to legitimate authority. The USSR challenged the Secretary-General's authority to act as he did, proposed a draft resolution envisaging the dismissal of Dag Hammarskjöld, subjected him to a boycott, and proposed that his office be reorganized according to the "troika" principle. Mr. Hammarskjöld's defense was that, in a situation where the authorizing organs were unable to clarify their directives, he was faced with the alternatives of refusing to proceed with his mission, which would mean chaos, or of undertaking to carry out his assignment on the basis of his international responsibility even though he had to deal with basically

[40] GA Res. 1237(ES-III), Aug. 12, 1958. Other examples are to be found in the Security Council resolution of Apr. 4, 1956 (S/3575), giving the Secretary-General a broad assignment to secure compliance with the General Armistice Agreements; and the Security Council Resolutions of July 13, 1960 (S/4387) and Nov. 24, 1961 (S/5002) relating to the Congo.

[41] UN Doc. S/4387, July 13, 1960.

[42] UNEF, Summary Study of Experience . . . Report of the Secretary-General. UN Doc. A/3943, Oct. 9, 1958.

[43] For the period to Apr. 1961, SC Resolutions of July 22, 1960 (S/4405), Aug. 9, 1960 (S/4426), and Feb. 21, 1961 (S/4741); and GA Res. 1474(ES-IV) Sept. 20, 1960, and 1599 and 1600(XV), Apr. 15, 1961.

controversial issues. In following the latter course, Mr. Hammarskjöld sought guidance in the purposes and principles of the Charter, the body of legal doctrine and precepts accepted by states generally, and the opinions of member states as expressed through their permanent representatives and through advisory committees.[44]

The Annual Report [45]

The requirement of an annual report is in line with the practice of the League of Nations Secretary-General. His report, however, was purely factual, covering the work of the Organization during the preceding year. It provided the basis for the general debate at the beginning of the annual Assembly session. The annual report of the United Nations Secretary-General, on the other hand, covering the year July 1 to June 30, while containing a factual review of accomplishments during that period, is accompanied by an introduction giving the views of the Secretary-General on achievements of the past year, the state of international affairs, and what the Organization and its members can do better to promote its purposes.

The General Assembly Rules of Procedure provide that the Secretary-General shall not only make an annual report, but also "such supplementary reports as are required" (Rule 38). He is required to communicate the annual report to members at least forty-five days before the opening of the regular session. The introduction may be, and usually is, submitted later. The provisional agenda of the General Assembly must include the report of the Secretary-General. The report has not been made the subject of discussion in the general debates at the beginning of each session of the General Assembly, as was the practice of the League of Nations, and no resolutions have been adopted concerning it.

Article 99

The Secretary-General may bring to the attention of the Security Council any matter which in his opinion may threaten the maintenance of international peace and security.

Article 99 had its initial official acceptance at the Dumbarton Oaks Conference, where it was apparently agreed that the League of Na-

---

[44] For a factual review of the Congo experience and documentary references on the question here discussed, see *Y.U.N.*, 1960, pp. 52–108. For Mr. Hammarskjöld's defense of the Secretary-General's position, see "The International Civil Servant in Law and Fact" in Foote, pp. 329–49.

[45] See also Art. 15 and commentary.

tions had suffered from the fact that such initiative could only be taken by a member state. The proposal was accepted at San Francisco, the only differences of opinion being whether the exercise of the power should be made obligatory or optional, and whether the Secretary-General should also be empowered to act similarly with respect to the General Assembly. On the first point, the majority agreed that the right should be exercised at the discretion of the Secretary-General and should not be made a duty.[46] On the second point, it was argued that applying the provision explicitly to the General Assembly would violate the principle of the primary responsibility of the Security Council.

The Preparatory Commission, referring to the Secretary-General's right under Article 99 as "a quite special right which goes beyond any power previously accorded to the head of an international organization," concluded that it was "impossible to foresee how this Article will be applied; but the responsibility it confers upon the Secretary-General will require the exercise of the highest qualities of political judgment, tact and integrity." [47]

Application

Under the Provisional Rules of Procedure of the Security Council, the President must call a meeting of the Council if "the Secretary-General brings to the attention of the Security Council any matter under Article 99" (Rule 3). In only one instance has a meeting of the Council been called at the request of the Secretary-General with a specific reference to Article 99. In a letter dated July 13, 1960, to the President of the Security Council,[48] the Secretary-General used the following words:

I want to inform you that I have to bring to the attention of the Security Council a matter which, in my opinion, may threaten the maintenance of international peace and security. Thus, I request that you call an urgent meeting of the Security Council to hear a report of the Secretary-General on a demand for United Nations action in relation to the Republic of the Congo.

When the Security Council met on the call of the President, the letter was listed on the provisional agenda as the second item. When the Soviet representative proposed that the telegrams received by the Secretary-General from the President and Prime Minister of the Republic of the Congo be added to the agenda item, Mr. Hammarskjöld commented that these were addressed to him and not to the Security

[46] UNCIO, *Documents*, VII, 392.
[47] *Report of the Preparatory Commission*, p. 87.
[48] UN Doc. S/4381, July 13, 1960.

Council, that they had been circulated as Security Council documents, but that the Council could of course add these to the item if it so desired. The Soviet representative did not press the matter to a vote.[49]

Secretary-General Lie's intervention in connection with the Korean question did not, strictly speaking, constitute a use of Article 99. The initial formal request for the calling of a meeting of the Security Council to consider the invasion of the territory of the Republic of Korea by North Korean forces came in the form of a letter from the representative of the United States to the Secretary-General transmitting a communication to the President of the Security Council. On the proposal of the President, the Council included in its agenda item, along with this letter, a cablegram received from the United Nations Commission on Korea addressed to the Secretary-General and suggesting that he exercise his right under Article 99.[50] The Secretary-General, recognized as the first speaker, said:

The present situation is a serious one and is a threat to international peace. The Security Council is, in my opinion, the competent organ to deal with it. I consider it the clear duty of the Security Council to take steps necessary to reestablish peace in that area.[51]

In July, 1961, the Security Council was considering, at the request of the Tunisian government, the situation resulting from French bombing of Tunisian territory and Tunisian counter-measures. Mr. Hammarskjöld, referring to the latest reports indicating the seriousness of developments and the risks of irreparable damage to international peace and security, and citing his right as Secretary-General under Article 99, stated that he considered it his duty to make an urgent appeal to the Council to take immediate action. Specifically, he asked the Council to take a decision requesting a cessation of hostilities, without in any way prejudging the final outcome of deliberations on the substantive issues.[52]

Earlier, in requesting the opportunity to report on a letter received from the Minister of Foreign Affairs of Laos soliciting United Nations assistance, Mr. Hammarskjöld made a distinction between a request that he be allowed to make a statement on a matter within the range of responsibility of the Council "as he considers called for under the terms of his own responsibilities," and an initiative taken under Article 99. In the first instance, under Rule 22 of the Council's Provisional Rules of Procedure, the Council could decide not to consider the matter; in the

[49] SCOR/15th Yr./873d Mtg./July 13, 1960/pp. 1–2.
[50] UN Docs. S/1495 and S/1496, June 25, 1950.
[51] SCOR/5th Yr./473d Mtg./June 25, 1950/p. 3. For Mr. Lie's account of his role in initiating UN action, see Lie, pp. 327–30.
[52] SCOR/16th Yr./962d Mtg./July 22, 1961/paras. 2–3.

second instance, the Council would be required to consider it. In this particular instance, the meeting of the Security Council was called by the President on the request of the Secretary-General to hear his report on the letter received. The Secretary-General expressly stated that he was not acting under Article 99. He explained that he did not as yet have the information that would enable him to make the judgment required.[53] The provisional agenda listed as the main item "Report by the Secretary-General on the Letter. . . ." The Soviet Representative questioned the propriety of the proposed procedure under the Provisional Rules of Procedure, arguing that Rule 22 applied only when a matter was already under consideration by the Council. That body, however, approved the provisional agenda as submitted, and proceeded to consider the matter covered by the Secretary-General's report.

The right of the Secretary-General to bring a matter which in his opinion threatens the maintenance of international peace and security to the attention of the Security Council has been generally recognized to carry with it the right to take preliminary steps necessary to determine whether he should act. During consideration by the Security Council in 1946 of a United States proposal to establish a commission to investigate facts relating to incidents along Greece's northern frontier, Secretary-General Lie stated that should the proposal not be carried, "I hope that the Council will understand that the Secretary-General must reserve his right to make such enquiries or investigations as he may think necessary in order to determine whether or not he should consider bringing any aspect of this matter to the attention of the Council under the provisions of the Charter." [54] The Soviet representative expressed his explicit approval of what the Secretary-General had said.

Following the submission in October, 1959, of the report of the Security Council's subcommittee on the situation in Laos,[55] the Secretary-General announced on November 8 that he had accepted an invitation to visit the country, and later explained that he had done so in order to provide himself with independent and full knowledge that would enable him to discharge his responsibilities. While the Security Council was considering the Tunisian complaint of French aggression in July, 1961, Mr. Hammarskjöld received an invitation from the President of Tunisia to visit the the country for an exchange of views.[56] In

[53] SCOR/14th Yr./847th Mtg./Sept. 7, 1959/pp. 2–3.
[54] SCOR/1st Yr., 2d Ser. No. 16/70th Mtg./Sept. 20, 1946/p. 404. Mr. Hammarskjöld interpreted his responsibilities with respect to observation in Lebanon in 1958 in similar terms without specifically relating them to Art. 99. SCOR/13th Yr./837th Mtg./July 22, 1958/paras. 12–14.
[55] UN Doc. S/4236, Nov. 5, 1959.　　　[56] UN Doc. S/4835, July 23, 1961.

reporting to the Security Council on his visit, Mr. Hammarskjöld justified his actions as follows:

Quite apart from the fact that it is naturally the duty of the Secretary-General to put himself at the disposal of the Government of a Member State, if that Government considers a personal contact necessary, my acceptance of the invitation falls within the framework of the rights and obligations of the Secretary-General, as Article 99 of the Charter authorizes him to draw to the attention of the Security Council what, in his view, may represent a threat to international peace and security, and as it is obvious that the duties following from the Article cannot be fulfilled unless the Secretary-General, in case of need, is in a position to form a personal opinion about the relevant facts of the situation which may represent such a threat.[57]

On a number of occasions, the Secretary-General has designated persons to represent him, with the consent of the receiving states, in situations of tension for the purpose of keeping him informed regarding developments.[58]

Inherent Powers of the Secretary-General

Many actions of the Secretary-General, particularly in the field of peace and security, can only be justified with the greatest difficulty under particular grants of authority by the provisions of the Charter or of resolutions of the principal organs. Secretaries-General have explicitly or by inference claimed that certain powers were inherent in their office.[59] In general, these powers can be characterized as diplomatic in nature and as justifying initiatives the Secretary-General may take in his relations with governments to achieve alleviation of conflicts. The activity in question has been characterized as "quiet diplomacy" and "preventive diplomacy." The Secretary-General is the sole judge as to whether an initiative on his part will be helpful. Naturally, he feels more secure if he has some indication from governments that his initiatives will be helpful, but this is a consideration relating to the expediency of his action and not to its legal justification.

When requested by the General Assembly in December, 1954, to seek the release of United States airmen in Communist China, Mr. Hammarskjöld, finding that the Peking government refused to recog-

---

[57] SCOR/16th Yr./964th Mtg./July 28, 1961/para. 86. Similar action was taken by the Secretary-General through an appointed representative on the invitation of the British Government when the General Assembly was considering the question of Oman. See *Y.U.N.*, 1963, pp. 70–73.

[58] Examples were Lebanon and Jordan in 1958, Laos in 1959, and Cyprus in 1964.

[59] See Mr. Hammarskjöld's statement on the occasion of his reappointment in 1957, GAOR/12th Sess./690th Plen. Mtg./Sept. 26, 1957/para. 72–73.

nize the validity of the General Assembly's resolution, invoked his general authority under the Charter in carrying out his mission.[60] When the Security Council requested him in April, 1956, to take steps in support of the Middle East armistice agreements, he stated that "[it] is obvious that the request neither detracts from nor adds to the authority of the Secretary-General under the Charter." [61] In October, 1956, the Secretary-General was present at exploratory conversations between the foreign ministers of Egypt, France, and the United Kingdom, and assisted in the formulation of principles to govern a Suez Canal settlement that were subsequently approved by the Security Council.[62]

On the invitation of the two governments and acting through designated representatives, the Secretary-General assisted in establishing normal relations between Cambodia and Thailand, first in 1958–59 and again in 1962–64.[63] Negotiations between Indonesia and the Netherlands for the settlement of the West Irian question, with Ellsworth Bunker acting as mediator, were undertaken following appeals by U Thant. In the Cuban missile crisis, U Thant's offer of services was welcomed by both parties and contributed significantly to the final settlement. In a situation of alleged military intervention by the United Arab Republic and Saudi Arabia in support of rival regimes in Yemen, U Thant on his own responsibility sent his personal representatives to the area, and through conversations obtained a disengagement agreement and made preliminary arrangements for a United Nations observation mission. Subsequently, the Security Council was called into session at the request of the Soviet Union to approve the action. Though the Council requested the Secretary-General to establish the observation mission "as defined by him" and to report, the action of the Council was in effect ratification of what the Secretary-General had already done.[64]

Article 100

1. In the performance of their duties the Secretary-General and the staff shall not seek or receive instructions from any government or from any other authority external to the Organization. They shall refrain from any action which might reflect on their position as international officials responsible only to the Organization.

2. Each Member of the United Nations undertakes to respect the

[60] GA Res. 906(IX), Dec. 10, 1954; *Repertory, Supp. 1*, II, 373–74; and Joseph P. Lash, "Hammarskjöld's Conception of His Office," *International Organization*, XVI (1962), p. 548.

[61] SCOR/11th Yr./722d Mtg./April 4, 1956/pp. 11–12.

[62] UN Doc. S/3675, Oct. 13, 1956.   [63] See *Y.U.N.* for these years.

[64] See *Y.U.N.*, 1963, pp. 63–69.

exclusively international character of the responsibilities of the Secretary-General and the staff and not to seek to influence them in the discharge of their responsibilities.

This article reflects the standards the first Secretary-General of the League sought to apply and which were accepted by the majority of its members, though the Covenant contained no express provisions to this effect.[65] The Dumbarton Oaks Proposals were silent on the matter, but at San Francisco the foreign ministers of the Sponsoring Governments agreed on an amendment in substance identical with the text finally approved. There was complete agreement that such provisions should be included in the Charter.[66]

The Preparatory Commission observed that "[if] it is to enjoy the confidence of all the Members of the United Nations, the Secretariat must be truly international in character." After quoting the provisions of Article 100, the Commission continued:

Such a Secretariat cannot be composed, even in part, of national representatives responsible to Governments. For the duration of their appointments, the Secretary-General and the staff will not be the servants of the state of which they are nationals, but the servants only of the United Nations. . . .

It is essential that officials should be inspired by a sense of loyalty to the United Nations and devotion to the ideal for which it stands, and that they should develop an *esprit de corps* and a habit of daily co-operation with persons of other countries and cultures. Loyalty to the Organization is in no way incompatible with an official's attachment to his own country, whose higher interest he is serving in serving the United Nations. It clearly involves, however, a broad international outlook and a detachment from narrow prejudices and narrow national interests.[67]

Regulation 1.1 of the Staff Regulations reads:

Members of the Secretariat are international civil servants. Their responsibilities are not national but exclusively international. By accepting appointment, they pledge themselves to discharge their functions and to regulate their conduct with the interests of the United Nations alone in view.[68]

They are required to subscribe to the following oath or declaration:

I solemnly swear (undertake, affirm, promise) to exercise in all loyalty, discretion and conscience the functions entrusted to me as an international civil servant of the United Nations, to discharge these functions and regulate my conduct with the interests of the United Nations only in view, and not to seek or accept instructions in regard to the performance of my duties from any government or other authority external to the Organization.[Regulation 1.9]

[65] See Ranshofen-Wertheimer, pp. 239–78.   [66] Russell, pp. 861–62.
[67] *Report of the Preparatory Commission*, p. 85.
[68] UN Doc. ST/SGB/Staff Rules, 1.

The concept of the Secretariat as an international career service has been many times affirmed by the General Assembly. In his report on personnel policy of January 30, 1953, Mr. Lie observed:

The concept of career service is at the heart of the organization of the Secretariat. This concept runs throughout the report of the Preparatory Commission and was explicitly and firmly stated in that report. The first staff regulations, though wisely approved on a provisional basis, also envisaged a career staff. While many organizational problems have been faced and much has been learned from experience during the first six or seven years of the Secretariat's existence, the career idea has been steadily strengthened and reaffirmed.[69]

In his first report as Secretary-General on personnel policy, Mr. Hammarskjöld reiterated this view.[70] In his Oxford University address of May 30, 1961, Mr. Hammarskjöld argued that the concept had special validity in the light of the development of the political functions of the Secretary-General and his staff. Speaking on this development, he said that it

. . . takes us beyond the concept of a non-political civil service into an area where the official, in the exercise of his functions, may be forced to take stands of a politically controversial nature. It does this, however, on an international basis and, thus, without departing from the basic concept of "neutrality"; in fact Article 98, as well as Article 99, would be unthinkable without the complement of Article 100 strictly observed both in letter and spirit.[71]

The concept of the Secretariat as an international civil service functioning independently of governments has not gone without challenge. The most severe challenge came at the time of the Congo crisis in 1960–61, when Mr. Khrushchev accused Mr. Hammarskjöld and his staff of "[partiality] in the implementation of practical measures" and claimed that "Mr. Hammarskjöld, the Secretary-General, in implementing the decisions of the Security Council, in effect sided with the colonialists." He proposed reorganization of the Secretariat, specifically by setting up in place of the Secretary-General "a collective executive body of the United Nations comprising three persons, each of whom would represent a certain group of states." [72] He held that this princi-

[69] UN Doc. A/2364, Jan. 30, 1953, para. 17.

[70] UN Doc. A/2533, Nov. 2, 1953, paras. 16–17.

[71] Foote, pp. 337–38. For Mr. Hammarskjöld's comments on what the concept of "neutrality" of the international civil servant involves, see *ibid.*, p. 348. See also his statement in the Security Council during consideration of the crisis resulting from invasion of Egypt, SCOR/11th Yr./751st Mtg./Oct. 31, 1956/para. 4.

[72] The groups would be states parties to Western military blocs, the socialist states, and the neutralist states. For main statements of Soviet position, see GAOR/15th Sess./869th, 882d, and 904th Plen. Mtgs./Sept. 23 and Oct. 3 and 13, 1960.

ple of equal representation of three groups should be applied to the staff as well.[73] This position was based on the premises that the concept of independence and neutrality are, in practice, impossible of realization, that the Secretariat should be regarded as essentially intergovernmental in character and function, and that to achieve maximum effectiveness it must reflect the world balance of forces. This position was not accepted by the great majority of members; they believed that implementation of the Soviet proposals would destroy the Secretariat's effectiveness.

The Obligations of Members of the Secretariat

By accepting appointment, staff members pledge themselves "to discharge their functions and to regulate their conduct with the interests of the United Nations only in view." They are subject to the authority of the Secretary-General and responsible to him in the exercise of their functions (Regulation 1.2). The requirement that they shall not seek or receive instructions from any government has been interpreted to permit technical assistance experts to collaborate closely with a government pursuant to an agreement between that government and the United Nations.[74] Staff members are required to exercise utmost discretion in all matters of official business (Regulation 1.5) and to act impartially in the performance of their duties.[75]

Secretariat officials have certain obligations regarding their personal conduct. They must act at all times "in a manner befitting their status as international civil servants." While they are not expected to give up their national sentiments or their political and religious convictions, they must always "bear in mind the reserve and tact incumbent upon them by reason of their international status" (Regulation 1.4). Staff members may not engage in "any continuous or recurring outside occupation or employment without the prior approval of the Secretary-General" (Regulation 101.6[a]); they are restricted as to their financial holdings (Regulation 101.6[b, c, d]); with certain exceptions they are prohibited from making public statements or publishing their writings on matters relating to the United Nations (Regulation 101.6[e]); and they may not use any information available to them only in their official position to private advantage (Regulation 1.5). A staff member may not accept "any honor, decoration, favour, gift or renumeration"

[73] See also separate opinion of Mr. A. Roschin, "Review of the Activities and Organization of the Secretariat," Report of the Committee of Experts . . . , UN Doc. A/4776, June 14, 1960, *Appendix*, p. 5.

[74] UN Doc. ST/HFS/SGB/94/Add. 3, Rule 201.5.

[75] UN Doc. A/2364, Jan. 30, 1953, para. 25. See Mr. Hammarskjöld's comments on what constitutes "neutrality," cited above, fn. 71.

from any government except for war service, or from any source external to the Organization without first obtaining the Secretary-General's approval, to be granted only in exceptional cases (Regulation 1.6).

With regard to political activities, the regulations in force until 1953 provided that any member of the Secretariat "who becomes a candidate for a public office of a political character shall resign from the Secretariat." [76] Otherwise, a member was subject only to the requirement that he conduct himself in a manner befitting his status as an international civil servant. Mr. Hammarskjöld, in his 1953 report on personnel policy, emphasized the need of clarification or amplification of the staff regulation, arguing that the Secretary-General, as the one responsible for maintaining "Charter standards and the impartiality of the staff," should have the right to exercise his judgment and to determine whether the official should continue particular activities and remain a member of the Staff. The Secretary-General's recommendation was accepted by the General Assembly in revised form.[77] The revised text, as approved by the General Assembly, reads:

Staff members may exercise the right to vote but shall not engage in any political activity which is inconsistent with or might reflect upon the independence and impartiality required by their status as international civil servants.[78]

On March 8, 1954, the Secretary-General promulgated Staff Rule 101.8 implementing the new text:

(a) Membership in a political party is permitted provided that such membership does not entail action, or obligation to action, contrary to Staff Regulation 1.7. The payment of normal financial contributions shall not be construed as an activity contrary to staff regulation 1.7.

(b) In any case of doubt as to the interpretation or application of Staff Regulation 1.7 and the present rule, the staff member concerned shall request a ruling from the Secretary-General.

While there is no question regarding the obligation of a staff member to refrain from subversive and criminal activities, the question has arisen concerning his obligation to disclose circumstances relating to such alleged activities to national investigatory agencies, and the obligation of the Secretary-General to take action requested by the member state as a consequence. In 1952, investigations were conducted by a

[76] GA Res. 13(I), Feb. 13, 1946, *Annex II*, Regulation 8, and GA Res. 590(VI), Feb. 2, 1952, Staff Regulation 1.7.

[77] UN Doc. A/2533, Nov. 2, 1953, paras. 23–27. For Secretary-General's proposed revision of Regulation 1.7 and comment, see *ibid.*, paras. 73–77. For comment of Advisory Committee on Administrative and Budgetary Questions, see GAOR/8th Sess./*Annexes*, agenda item 51, p. 21(A/2555), and for Report of Fifth Committee, see *ibid.*, A/2615.

[78] GA Res. 782(VIII), Dec. 9, 1953.

United States federal grand jury and by the Internal Security Sub-committee of the United States Senate Judiciary Committee of possible subversive activities by Secretariat officials of United States nationality. Some of these admitted membership in the Communist Party before joining the Secretariat; others invoked the Fifth Amendment protection against self-incrimination. On the basis of information provided by the United States government and an opinion rendered by a commission of jurists appointed by him, the Secretary-General dismissed, or terminated the employment of a number of staff members.[79] He based his action on the provisions of Staff Regulation 1.4 requiring staff members to avoid any action "which may adversely reflect on their status." In the General Assembly discussion, divergent views were expressed, including the opinion that purely national criteria could not be accepted as conclusive and that no evidence had been submitted of activity violating an obligation of a Secretariat official.[80] In reviewing cases appealed to it, the United Nations Administrative Tribunal found no grounds for misconduct charges.[81] Mr. Hammarskjöld, in reporting to the General Assembly, recommended modifications of the Staff Regulations that were subsequently approved.[82] These place officials under the positive obligation to avoid any action reflecting "on the integrity, independence and impartiality" required by their international status. They give the Secretary-General the right to terminate a permanent appointment on the ground of conduct not meeting "the high standards of integrity" required by the Charter, if facts "anterior to the appointment and relative to the administrative suitability" of the official come to the attention of the Secretary-General which, if known, would have precluded his appointment.[83] In his report, Mr. Hammarskjöld explicitly stated, however, that in exercising this power of termination, his decision would rest "upon established facts thoroughly evaluated by him" and that conclusions to be drawn from these facts "must reflect his own opinion as to their weight and their effect upon the requirements of good administration."[84]

[79] The Secretary-General's explanation of his action is given in UN Doc. A/2364, Jan. 30, 1953. The opinion of the Commission of Jurists is given as *Annex III.*

[80] For statements made, see GAOR/7th Sess., 416th–421st Plen. Mtgs./Mar. 28–Apr. 1, 1953.

[81] UN Administrative Tribunal, *Judgments,* Nos. 29–37.

[82] GA Res. 782(VIII), Dec. 19, 1953.

[83] UN Doc. A/2533, Nov. 2, 1953, paras. 28–35, 58–72. The modifications were approved by the General Assembly and incorporated in Staff Regulations 1.4 and 9.1(a).

[84] UN Doc. A/2533, Nov. 2, 1953, para. 34. See commentary on Art. 101.

The Obligations of Member States

Article 100(2) expresses the reverse of the principle of the first paragraph. The Secretary-General and his staff are required not to seek or receive instructions from any government. The natural and necessary complement is that members must agree to respect the exclusively international character of the responsibilities of the Secretary-General and his staff and not to seek to influence them in the discharge of their responsibilities.

A possibility that was clearly in the minds of those who drafted the Charter was that a staff member might be required, in the discharge of his responsibilities, to engage in activities which, under the laws of his state, were not only illegal but treasonable. Such might be the case if a staff member were engaged in preparation of plans for the taking of measures under Articles 41 and 42 against the state of his nationality.

The only express formulation of the obligations assumed by member states to respect the international character and independence of the Secretariat is to be found in the General Convention on the Privileges and Immunities of the United Nations and other similar agreements such as the Headquarters Agreement between the United States and the United Nations.[85]

The Preparatory Commission emphasized the connection between privileges and immunities and the independence of staff in these terms: "An adequate system of immunities and privileges as provided in Article 105 of the Charter is essential if officials are to be free from pressure by individual governments and to discharge their duties efficiently." [86]

Staff Regulation 1.8 states that the immunities and privileges attached to the United Nations by virtue of Article 105 "are conferred in the interest of the Organization." In any case where they are in question, the staff member is expected to report immediately to the Secretary-General "with whom alone it rests to decide whether they shall be waived."

Member states are obligated to refrain from certain kinds of action in connection with the appointment, tenure, and removal of staff members. The Secretary-General has asked governments to provide facts that are not readily available to him in connection with appointments and has invited them to recommend candidates. This form of assistance has not been regarded by him as derogating from his exclusive author-

[85] GA Res. 22A(I), Feb. 13, 1946 and 169(II), Oct. 31, 1947. See also commentary on Arts. 104 and 105.
[86] Report of the Preparatory Commission, p. 85.

ity to make the final decision.[87] Member governments may take the initiative in proposing candidates, usually their nationals, for particular posts; this is permissible so long as they recognize the Secretary-General's responsibility for selecting his staff. They may not, however, seek to influence the Secretary-General to promote their nationals, to designate them to specific posts, or to dismiss them in the event that they are out of favor with the regime in power.

Under an Executive Order of the United States government, dated January 9, 1953, United States nationals in the Secretariat were submitted to security investigation and clearance. Fingerprinting required by the investigation was carried out in the Secretariat building with the permission of the Secretary-General. These actions were regarded by the Secretary-General as not constituting violations of Article 100.[88] In the General Assembly discussion, however, these actions were viewed by some delegations as violating Article 100, but no condemnatory resolution was adopted.

The Relationship of National to International Loyalty

The Committee of Jurists, in their opinion referred to the above, expressed the view that "[membership on the United Nations] staff . . . in no way abrogates, limits or qualifies the loyalty a person owes to the state of which he is a citizen."[89] The possibility of conflict has been discounted in other statements. The Preparatory Commission took the view that in serving the United Nations, the international official was serving the highest interests of his country.[90] The International Civil Service Advisory Board has expressed a similar view, that legitimate national interests can only be served by the promotion of United Nations objectives.[91]

Article 101

1. The staff shall be appointed by the Secretary-General under regulations established by the General Assembly.

[87] Statement by Secretary-General Lie. GAOR/7th Sess./413th Plen. Mtg./Mar. 10, 1953/para. 17.

[88] UN Doc. A/2364, Jan. 30, 1953, paras. 54–56, 62–65. In a number of cases where the Director-General of UNESCO refused to renew fixed-term contracts of U.S. nationals because of their refusal to appear before a U.S. Loyalty Board, the Administrative Tribunal of the ILO ordered the Director-General's decisions rescinded on the ground that he could not thus associate himself with the carrying out of a national policy. See *Judgments of the Administrative Tribunal of the ILO*, Nos. 17, 18, and 19.

[89] UN Doc. A/2364, *Annex III*, p. 25.

[90] *Report of the Preparatory Commission*, p. 85.

[91] UN Doc. COORD/Civil Service/5, para. 22.

2. Appropriate staffs shall be permanently assigned to the Economic and Social Council, the Trusteeship Council, and, as required, to other organs of the United Nations. These staffs shall form a part of the Secretariat.

3. The paramount consideration in the employment of the staff and in the determination of the conditions of service shall be the necessity of securing the highest standards of efficiency, competence, and integrity. Due regard shall be paid to the importance of recruiting the staff on as wide a geographical basis as possible.

The first and third paragraphs of Article 101 are in substance a statement of the practice of the League of Nations.[92] The Dumbarton Oaks Proposals contained no such provisions. At San Francisco, there was a widespread feeling that principles governing the recruitment and employment of the staff should be included in the Charter. Though a couple of delegations thought the third paragraph dealt with minor technical details that should not be included in the Charter, no opposition was expressed to the ideas themselves.[93]

The Power of Appointment

The power of the Secretary-General to appoint staff members is unqualified. A proposal made at San Francisco that deputy secretaries-general be appointed in the same manner as the Secretary-General was opposed on the ground that this would weaken the authority of the Secretary-General, detract from the efficiency of the Secretariat, and lead to the political domination of the Secretariat by the great powers.[94]

During the discussions concerning the organization of the Secretariat in the Administrative and Budgetary Committee of the Preparatory Commission, a proposal was submitted under which appointments of officials of the Secretariat would require the concurrence of the governments of the candidates concerned.[95] In support of this proposal, it was argued that governments were in the best position to assess the qualifications of candidates, that persons appointed should command the confidence of their governments, and that once appointed their exclusively international responsibilities would be respected. The view prevailed that the suggested procedure would impinge on the exclusive responsibility of the Secretary-General under Article 101.

The provisions of paragraph 1 are restated in Staff Regulation 4.1. The power of appointment has been interpreted to carry with it the

---

[92] See Ranshofen-Wertheimer, Part IV.
[94] *Ibid.*, pp. 854–60.

[93] Russell, pp. 861–62.
[95] UN Doc. PC/AB/54.

power to terminate the appointment or dismiss the official under conditions set forth in the letter of appointment and the Staff Rules and Regulations.

The Power to Determine Administrative Structure

The Charter does not specifically define the respective powers of the Secretary-General and the General Assembly in determining the administrative structure of the Secretariat. However, the General Assembly's control of the budget gives practical assurance that the Secretary-General must have the approval of that organ for any organizational plans he may wish to carry out. The only other limitation imposed by the Charter is that appropriate staffs must be permanently assigned to ECOSOC, the Trusteeship Council, and, as required, to other organs. In the resolution outlining the initial organization of the Secretariat,[96] as recommended by the Preparatory Commission, the following language was used:

The Secretary-General shall take immediate steps to establish an administrative organization which will permit the effective discharge of his administrative and general responsibilities under the Charter and the efficient performance of those functions and services required to meet the needs of the several organs of the United Nations.

The next paragraph listed the principal units to be established. While stating that initially the departments and services "should, broadly speaking, conform" to the recommendations of the Preparatory Commission, the Assembly authorized the Secretary-General to "make such changes in the initial structure as may be required to the end that the most effective distribution of responsibilities and functions among the units of the Secretariat may be achieved."

When the Secretary-General made certain proposals for the reorganization of the Secretariat in 1953, the General Assembly took note and recommended that he prepare his 1955 budget estimates within the broad framework of these proposals; the following year, the Assembly "generally" approved the measures adopted and invited the Secretary-General to proceed with implementation, taking into account the comments of the Advisory Committee on Administrative and Budgetary Questions and observations made in the Fifth Committee.[97] It would appear that the Secretary-General was recognized as having the authority to propose and implement, subject to comment and final approval by the General Assembly.

[96] GA Res. 13(I), Feb. 13, 1946.
[97] GAOR/8th Sess./*Annexes,* agenda item 48 (A/2554), p. 1; GA Res. 784(VIII), Dec. 9, 1953; and 886(IX), Dec. 17, 1954.

Principles Governing Structure

As for the basic principle governing the Secretariat's structure, two different views were advanced in the Preparatory Commission: 1) that the Secretariat should be organized as a single working body with each department serving each organ within the limits of its particular responsibilities; and 2) that each organ should have its own separate secretariat. The Commission accepted the first view. Its reasons for favoring a unified Secretariat were: all organs have their responsibilities in the primary common task of maintaining international peace and security; duplication of work, overlapping and waste of time, and confusion would be avoided; and the second alternative would give rise to divided loyalties and undesirable rivalry. The Commission found no incompatibility between the principle of a unified secretariat and the provision of Article 101(2), interpreted to mean "that the Secretary-General has full authority to move staff at his discretion within the Secretariat but must always provide the Economic and Social Council, the Trusteeship Council, and other organs with adequate permanent specialized staffs forming part of the Secretariat." [98] The Staff Regulations provide that staff members are subject to his authority "and to assignment by him to any of the activities or offices of the United Nations" (Regulation 1.2).

Following the recommendations of the Preparatory Commission, the General Assembly recommended in 1946 that the Secretariat should consist of eight principal units or departments: Security Council Affairs, Economic Affairs, Social Affairs, Trusteeship and Information from Non-Self-Governing Territories, Public Information, Legal, Conference and General Services, and Administrative and Financial Services.[99]

Under the proposals submitted by Mr. Hammarskjöld in 1953, and approved by the General Assembly in 1954,[100] the structure of the Secretariat was modified in the following respects: 1) the Departments of Economic Affairs and Social Affairs were merged into one; 2) the Department of Conference and General Services was divided into two separate offices; 3) the Legal Department and the Department of Administrative and Financial Services became staff offices designated Office of Legal Affairs, Office of the Controller, and Office of Personnel; 4) the two highest levels of posts, Assistant-Secretary-General and Principal Director, were replaced by a single supervisory level.

[98] *Report of the Preparatory Commission,* p. 88.
[99] GA Res. 13(I), Feb. 13, 1946.
[100] GAOR/8th Sess./1953/*Annexes,* agenda item 48 (A/2554), p. 1.

Principles Governing Selection of Staff and Conditions of Service

Article 101(3) clearly states that the paramount consideration in the employment of staff and in the determination of conditions of service is the necessity of securing the highest standards of efficiency, competence, and integrity. Efficiency and competence have been described as primarily standards of performance, while integrity is a standard of personal conduct. In Mr. Hammarskjöld's view, the staff member "must not only be honest in fact, but his conduct must be beyond the suspicion of dishonesty; that is to say, he must perform all functions with scrupulous objectivity and must never permit himself to be placed in a situation where he might be suspected of using his position for private gain." [101]

The principle that staff should be recruited on "as wide a geographical basis as possible" is given a subordinate position in the third paragraph. Nevertheless, it has received wide support as essential to an international civil service both in the United Nations and in the League of Nations. The Preparatory Commission observed, referring to the two principles of Article 101(3), that "as experience has shown, [they] can in large measure be reconciled." [102] The General Assembly has not only affirmed that no conflict exists but has also stated that "in view of its international character, and in order to avoid undue predominance of national practices, the policies and administrative methods of the Secretariat should reflect, and profit to the highest degree from, assets of the various cultures and technical competence of all Member nations." [103]

Under great pressure to recruit a working staff quickly in the Organization's first year, Mr. Lie turned to persons most readily available; these happened to be predominantly nationals of North American and Western European countries. Geographical imbalance in the composition of the Secretariat resulted. In its second session, the General Assembly requested that the Secretary-General take steps to improve "the present geographical distribution of the staff." [104]

---

[101] Review of the Staff Regulations and of the principles and standards progressively applied thereto: Report of the Secretary-General. GAOR/12th Sess./ 1957/*Annexes,* agenda item 51 (A/C.5/726, Oct. 25, 1957), paras. 23 and 24. For further definition of integrity see report of ICSAB, Doc. COORD/Civil Service/5, para. 4. See also GAOR/8th Sess./1953/*Annexes,* agenda item 51(A/2533, Nov. 2, 1953), para. 59 where "integrity" is defined and distinguished from "loyalty."

[102] *Report of the Preparatory Commission,* p. 85.

[103] GA Res. 153(II), Nov. 15, 1947. This view was reaffirmed in GA Res. 1559(XV), Dec. 18, 1960.

[104] GA Res. 153(II), Nov. 15, 1947.

In reporting on the composition of the Secretariat to the third session of the General Assembly, Mr. Lie interpreted the principle of geographical distribution as follows:

Rightly understood, the cardinal principle of geographical distribution is not that nationals of a particular nation should have a specified number of posts at a particular grade or grades or that they should receive in salary as a group a particular percentage of the total outlay in salaries, but that, in the first place, the administration should be satisfied that the Secretariat is enriched by the experience and culture which each member nation can furnish and that each Member nation should in its turn, be satisfied that its own culture and philosophy make a full contribution to the Secretariat.[105]

He defined the problem of application as "that of establishing acceptable criteria that are administratively workable." He concluded that while no single criterion would be valid, "as financial contributions to the United Nations budget had been fixed in relation to a combination of pertinent criteria, it would be reasonable to take them as a basis for a flexible system," allowing an upward or downard variation of 25 percent, except that for a member contributing over 10 percent to the regular budget the downward variation alone would be allowed.

With membership of the Organization relatively stable during the first ten years, it was possible for the Secretary-General to achieve by orderly administrative methods a degree of geographical distribution generally satisfactory to the General Assembly. The rapid expansion of membership by 1955 and the years following, together with the recognition by some members of the increased importance of the Secretariat, created new discontents which could not be satisfied quickly without seriously departing from established practices of recruitment and promotion or without substantial expansion of staff. Under these circumstances, the application of the principle of wide geographical distribution was again considered at length during the years 1960–63.[106]

After extended discussion of the matter during the sixteenth session, the General Assembly requested the Secretary-General to present his views to the Assembly at its next session.[107] At that time, the Assembly recommended that the Secretary-General

be guided in his efforts to achieve a more equitable geographical distribution, within the general framework of his report, by the following principles and factors:

[105] GAOR/3d Sess., 1st Part/Plen./*Annexes* (A/652, Sept. 2, 1948), p. 157.

[106] The 15th Assembly referred the question to the Committee of Experts on the Activities and Organization of the Secretariat. GA Res. 1559(XV), Dec. 18, 1960. The Committee made recommendations in its report, UN Doc. A/4776, June 14, 1961, ch. IV, which were commented on by the Secretary-General. UN Doc. A/4794, June 30, 1961, paras. 31–40. The recommendations and comments were considered by the Fifth Committee of the General Assembly.

[107] UN Doc. A/5063, Dec. 18, 1961.

(a) In the recruitment of all staff, due regard shall be paid to securing as wide a geographical distribution as possible;

(b) In the Secretariat proper, an equitable geographical distribution should take into account the fact of membership, Members' contributions and their populations as outlined in the Secretary-General's report, particularly paragraph 69(b) thereof; no Member State should be considered "overrepresented" if it has no more than five of its nationals on the staff by virtue of its membership;

(c) The relative importance of posts at different levels;

(d) The need for a more balanced regional composition of the staff at levels of D-1 and above;

(e) In career appointments, particular account should be taken of the need to reduce "under-representation." [108]

To gauge the application of the principles set forth in the resolution to positions in the "Secretariat proper," the Secretary-General in 1963 developed a new formula for determining the desirable range of posts.[109]

Nature and Forms of Appointment

The letter of appointment states that "the appointment is subject to the provisions of the Staff Regulations and of the Staff Rules applicable to the category of appointment in question, and to changes which may be duly made in such regulations and rules from time to time" (Regulation 4.1, Annex II). The appointment creates a contractual relationship between the Organization and the person concerned. The International Court of Justice has expressed the opinion that when the Secretary-General concludes such a contract of service with a staff member, "he engages the legal responsibility of the Organization, which is the juridical person on whose behalf he acts." [110] The Administrative Tribunal has made a distinction between contractual and statutory elements of the relationship between the person and the Organization. All matters affecting the personal status of the staff member, such as the nature of his contract, salary, and grade, are contractual, while matters affecting the general organization of the international civil service—for example, general rules having no personal reference—are statutory.[111] Contractual elements cannot be changed without the agreement of the two parties, while statutory elements may be changed by regulations established by the General Assembly.

[108] See UN Doc. A/5270, Oct. 24, 1962, and GA Res. 1852(XVII), Dec. 19, 1962.

[109] See *Composition of the Secretariat,* UN Doc. A/C.5/987, Oct. 11, 1963. The formula applies to appointments of more than six months' duration to posts in the regular establishment at the professional level and above provided for in the regular budget, posts with special language requirements being excluded.

[110] *ICJ Reports,* 1954, p. 53.   [111] AT/DEC/20–25 and 27.

Appointments granted to staff members fall into three broad categories: temporary, permanent, and regular (Staff Regulation 4.5 and Staff Rules 104.12 and 104.13). Temporary appointments may be probationary appointments granted initially to persons recruited for the career service, fixed-term appointments granted for a period not exceeding five years and carrying no expectancy of renewal, and indefinite appointments granted to persons recruited for special missions or agency service. Permanent appointments may be granted to staff members who are holders of probationary appointments and who by qualification, performance, and conduct have demonstrated their suitability as international civil servants. Regular appointments are granted to staff members in the General Service and Manual Worker categories.

Conditions of Service

The authority to establish regulations concerning the Secretariat, vested in the General Assembly by Article 101(1), is restated in Rule 50 of the Assembly Rules of Procedure. Pursuant to these provisions, the Assembly adopts regulations laying down the conditions of service in the Secretariat. In the performance of this function, the Assembly is assisted by the Advisory Committee on Administrative and Budgetary Questions, which, however, is limited to dealing with personnel questions "only in their budgetary aspects." [112] Provision is also made for staff participation in the discussion of matters relating to their conditions of service. Staff Regulation 8.1 provides for a Staff Council, elected by the Staff and so composed as to afford equitable representation at all levels, to ensure "continuous contact between the staff and the Secretary-General." The Council may make proposals for the improvement of the situation of the staff members "both as regards conditions of work and their general conditions of life."

Disciplinary Measures and Termination of Appointments

The Charter contains no express provision regarding termination of the term of service, or dismissal, of a staff member. The power of appointment is commonly interpreted to carry with it the power of removal. Article 101 gives this power of appointment to the Secretary-General "under regulations established by the General Assembly"; however, the Staff Regulations adopted by the General Assembly place specific limitations on the power of the Secretary-General to put an end to an appointment once it has been made.

The Staff Regulations distinguish between the termination of an ap-

[112] GA Res. 14(I), Feb. 13, 1946.

pointment and various forms of disciplinary action, of which summary dismissal is the most extreme. Termination does not normally carry any implication of misconduct and requires the payment of an indemnity (Regulation 9.3). Until 1953, the appointment of a staff member holding a permanent appointment could be terminated "if the necessities of the service require abolition of the post or reduction of the staff, if the services of the individual concerned proved unsatisfactory, or if he is for reasons of health, incapacitated for further service" (Regulation 9.1[a]). The word "services" was interpreted by the United Nations Administrative Tribunal "solely to designate professional behavior within the Organization and not to cover all the obligations incumbent on a staff member." [113] In the light of experience in dealing with the cases of staff members of United States nationality who had been summarily dismissed for refusing to reply to certain questions put to them by a United States government agency and whose dismissal had subsequently been found illegal by the Administrative Tribunal, the Secretary-General recommended certain modifications of the Staff Regulation to bring them more fully into line with standards of the Charter.[114] According to the revised Regulation, the Secretary-General may also, "giving his reasons therefor," terminate a permanent appointment

(i) If the conduct of the staff member indicates that the staff member does not meet the highest standards of integrity required in Article 101, paragraph 3, of the Charter;

(ii) If facts anterior to the appointment of the staff member and relevant to his suitability come to light which, if they had been known at the time of his appointment, should, under the standards established in the Charter, have precluded his appointment.[115]

Finally, under the revised Regulation, the Secretary-General may terminate a permanent appointment "if such action would be in the interest of the good administration of the Organization and in accordance with the standards of the Charter, provided that the action is not contested by the staff member concerned."

The Secretary-General may impose disciplinary measures on staff members whose conduct is unsatisfactory; he may "summarily dismiss" a member for serious misconduct (Regulation 10). Disciplinary measures consist of written censure, suspension without pay, demotion, and summary dismissal. The Administrative Tribunal has defined conduct punishable under Staff Regulation 10 to be "either misconduct committed in the exercise of a staff member's professional duties or acts committed outside his professional activities but prohibited by provisions creating general obligations for staff members." [116]

---

[113] AT/DEC/37.   [114] UN Doc. A/2533, Nov. 2, 1953.
[115] GA Res. 782 A(VIII), Dec. 9, 1953; Staff Regulation 9.1(a), paras. 2–4.
[116] AT/DEC/37.

The Staff Regulations provide that the Secretary-General "shall establish administrative machinery with staff participation to advise him in case of any appeal by staff members against an administrative decision alleging the non-observance of their terms of appointment, including all pertinent regulations and rules, or against disciplinary action" (Regulation 11.1). Pursuant to this provision, a Joint Appeals Board was established (Rules 111.1–4). The Administrative Tribunal was established by the Assembly "to hear and pass judgment upon applications alleging non-observance of contracts of employment of staff members . . . or of the terms of appointment of such staff members." [117] It is composed of seven members appointed by the General Assembly, no two of whom may be nationals of the same state. An application will not be received by the Tribunal unless the person concerned has previously submitted the dispute to the Joint Appeals Board, except where the Secretary-General and the applicant agree to submit directly to the Tribunal. The Tribunal's decision is final and binding upon all parties concerned, except for possible appeal through a request for an advisory opinion to the International Court of Justice by a Committee of the General Assembly.[118] The Tribunal's decision commits the General Assembly to authorize payment of any compensation awarded.[119]

[117] Statute of the United Nations Administrative Tribunal. AT/111/Rev. 1, Feb. 1, 1959, Art. 2. See GA Res. 351 A(IV), Nov. 24, 1949 as amended by GA Res. 782 B(VIII), Dec. 9, 1953 and 957(X), Nov. 8, 1955.

[118] Arts. 11 and 12 of the Statute of the Tribunal. The Tribunal is required to revise its decisions to conform to the Court's opinion.

[119] *ICJ Reports,* 1954, p. 47.

CHAPTER XVI

Miscellaneous Provisions

Article 102

1. Every treaty and every international agreement entered into by any Member of the United Nations after the present Charter comes into force shall as soon as possible be registered with the Secretariat and published by it.

2. No party to any such treaty or international agreement which has not been registered in accordance with the provisions of paragraph 1 of this Article may invoke that treaty or agreement before any organ of the United Nations.

Registration and Publication

The requirement of registration of international agreements was provided for in Article 18 of the League Covenant as follows:

Every treaty or international engagement entered into hereafter by any Member of the League shall be forthwith registered with the Secretariat and shall as soon as possible be published by it. No such treaty or international engagement shall be binding until so registered.

The League system of treaty registration proved so satisfactory that its continuation in principle under the Charter was taken for granted by most governments at San Francisco. In the discussions, special consideration was given to two aspects of the matter: the sanction to be applied for nonregistration, and the range of agreements to be covered. Since the validity of agreements depends on the reciprocal action of the parties irrespective of registration, it was decided that the sanction should be inability to invoke an unregistered agreement before an international organ. There was some sentiment to the effect that certain types of agreements should be excluded because of their relative unimportance, temporary character, or international security considerations, but the final decision was that there should be no exceptions to the general requirement of registration.[1]

[1] Ruth B. Russell, *A History of the United Nations Charter* (Washington, Brookings Institution, 1958), pp. 923–25.

Acting in accordance with the recommendation of the Preparatory Commission, the General Assembly at its first session instructed the Secretary-General: 1) to invite members to transmit for filing and publication treaties and international agreements entered into before the date of entry into force of the Charter, and to transmit for registration and publication only those entered into after that date; 2) to receive from nonmember states treaties and international agreements, entered into both before and after that date which they might voluntarily submit for filing and publication; and 3) to submit to the General Assembly proposals for detailed regulations and other measures for giving effect to the provisions of Article 102.[2]

On the basis of recommendations submitted by the Secretary-General, the General Assembly adopted regulations which, as subsequently amended, provide for the registration and publication of treaties and international agreements.[3]

When the draft regulations proposed by the Secretary-General were being considered by the General Assembly in the second part of its first session, the possibility of defining more explicitly the categories of treaties and agreements requiring registration was discussed. It was decided, however, that the article defining the scope of the requirement should follow closely the language of Article 102(1), the only change being the insertion of the words "whatever its form and descriptive name" after "Every treaty or international agreement." In its report to the General Assembly, the Sixth Committee observed that its subcommittee had had regard to the "undesirability of attempting at this time to define in detail the kinds of treaty or agreement requiring registration under the Charter, it being recognized that experience and practice will in themselves aid in giving definition to the terms of the Charter."[4]

Article 102 places upon the Secretariat a special responsibility for the operation of the system of registration and publication, and, in so far as ex officio registration, filing, and recording are concerned, it is also responsible for initiating action. In determining whether instruments

[2] *Report of the Preparatory Commission*, p. 59; GA Res. 23(I), Feb. 10, 1946.
[3] GAOR/1st Sess., 2d Part, 6th Ctte./p. 189/*Annex 8* (UN Doc. A/C.6/56, Nov. 6, 1946). The draft regulations recommended by the Secretary-General were considered by the Sixth Committee, and by a subcommittee whose recommendations were accepted by the Sixth Committee and the General Assembly. See *ibid.*, 15th Mtg./Nov. 6, 1946/p. 68; and for summary of discussion in subcommittee, *ibid.*, p. 195, *Annex 8a* (UN Doc. A/C.6/124, Dec. 7, 1946). See also GA Res. 97(I), Feb. 10, 1946, as amended by GA Res. 364B(IV), Dec. 1, 1949; and 482(V), Dec. 12, 1950. For text of regulations as amended, see 76 UNTS, 18–29; and *Repertory*, V, 283–92.
[4] GAOR/1st Sess., 2d Part/Plen. Mtgs./*Annex 91* (UN Doc. A/266, Dec. 13, 1946), p. 1586.

fall within the category of treaties and agreements requiring registration or are susceptible to filing and recording, the Secretariat is guided by general principles of international law, established practice, and views expressed during discussions in the Sixth Committee.[5]

With regard to "unilateral engagements of an international character," the view of the technical committee at San Francisco that they should be treated as international agreements has been accepted.[6] Accordingly, the Secretariat has taken steps for the ex officio registration of declarations accepting the compulsory jurisdiction of the International Court of Justice pursuant to Article 36(2) of the Statute. The Egyptian Declaration of April 24, 1957, on the Suez Canal and its operation, elaborating principles set forth in an earlier memorandum of March 18, was submitted to the Secretariat for registration; the Secretary-General in accepting it stated his understanding that the government of Egypt considered the Declaration as an engagement of international character coming within the terms of Article 102.[7]

In the case of certain agreements registered by member states, the question has arisen as to the consequences of such registration for other members not recognizing some of the parties to such agreements. This question has arisen with respect to agreements to which the Democratic People's Republic of Korea, the German Democratic Republic, and the People's Republic of China have been parties, and which have been registered by members who are parties to them.

The position of the Secretariat has been formulated as follows:

[Since] the terms "treaty" and "international agreement" have not been defined either in the Charter or in the Regulations, the Secretariat, under the Charter and the Regulations, follows the principle that it acts in accordance with the position of the Member State submitting an instrument for registration that so far as that party is concerned the instrument is a treaty or an international agreement within the meaning of Article 102. Registration of an instrument submitted by a Member State, therefore, does not imply a judgment by the Secretariat on the nature of the instrument, the status of a party, or any similar question. It is the understanding of the Secretariat that its action does not confer on the instrument the status of a treaty or an international agreement if it does not already have that status and does not confer on a party a status which it would not otherwise have.[8]

[5] See *Repertory*, V, 295–96, for examples of cases that have arisen and positions taken.

[6] UNCIO, *Documents*, XIII, 705.

[7] See 285 UNTS, 299; and SCOR/12th Yr./*Supp.* for Apr.–June, 1957/pp. 8–12 (Docs. S/3818 and S/3819).

[8] From prefatory note to *Statement of Treaties and International Agreements Registered or Filed and Recorded with the Secretariat during November, 1955*, UN Doc. ST/LEG/SER.A/105, Nov., 1955.

The United States government informed the Secretary-General that it regarded registration of these instruments "as without significance because in its opinion the regimes in question do not possess international capacity and the instruments do not constitute treaties or international agreements within the meaning of Article 102 of the Charter."[9] The government of the United Kingdom expressed the view that it

. . . will not consider the registration or filing and recording of an instrument submitted by a Member State as conferring on the instrument or on a party to the instrument, or as constituting evidence of, any status which such instrument or party would not otherwise have.[10]

Article 102 does not apply to treaties and international agreements between nonmember states. The Regulations, however, provide for voluntary submission for purposes of filing and publication. In connection with agreements between members and nonmembers concluded after the entry into force of the Charter, the question arose at the time of the drafting of the Regulations whether a nonmember should have the right to register such a treaty in order to place it on a level of equality with the member in invoking it before an organ of the United Nations. It was decided that this right should be accorded and Article 1(3) of the Regulations permits it.[11]

Sanctions for Nonregistration

Article 18 of the League Covenant stated that no treaty or international agreement entered into by any member of the League "shall be binding" until registered as required. This article was never applied but it created certain theoretical difficulties. The second paragraph of Article 102 is more modest in its approach. It does not exclude the possibility that an unregistered treaty or agreement to which a member of the United Nations is a party may have considerable legal affect in a situation where it is not actually invoked before a United Nations organ. The paragraph does not exclude the possibility of the invocation of an unregistered agreement in the course of normal diplomatic exchanges or before specially constituted organs such as arbitral tribunals that are not organs of the United Nations.

The practice of United Nations organs is of little help in the interpretation of the paragraph. On several occasions the effect of nonregistration has been referred to in proceedings before the International Court of Justice, but the Court has never applied the sanction or con-

[9] *Repertory, Supp. 1,* II, 401.   [10] *Ibid.,* p. 402.
[11] On this point, see UNCIO, *Documents,* XIII, 796.

sidered its application.[12] In cases where the interpretation of treaties by other organs of the United Nations has been in issue, the question of the effect of nonregistration has not been raised. In practically all cases agreements involved have been duly registered or have not been subject to registration. One exception was the invocation by the USSR of the treaty of February, 1950, with the Central People's Government of China in partial answer to the claim of the Nationalist Government that the USSR had violated its obligations under the Treaty of Friendship and Alliance of August 14, 1945. At the time the 1950 treaty was invoked in January, 1952, it had not been registered, but no reference was made to this fact in the course of discussions in the Assembly's First Committee or in the resolution adopted.[13]

Article 103

In the event of a conflict between the obligations of the Members of the United Nations under the present Charter and their obligations under any other international agreement, their obligations under the present Charter shall prevail.

The situation envisaged by Article 103 may exist where: 1) there is conflict between the obligation of a member under the Charter and the obligation of that member under an agreement with another member contracted before the entry into force of the Charter; 2) there is conflict between the obligation of a member under the Charter and the obligation of that member under an agreement with another member contracted after the entry into force of the Charter; and 3) there is conflict between the obligation of a member under the Charter and the obligation of that member under an agreement contracted with a nonmember state, whether before or after the entry into force of the Charter.

Under the terms of Article 20(1) of the Covenant of the League of Nations, members agreed that the Covenant abrogated "all obligations or understandings *inter se*" that were inconsistent with its terms, and they undertook not to enter into any engagements in the future inconsistent with the terms thereof. This paragraph covered the first two situations referred to above where the parties concerned were members of the League. For the situation where one party to the agreement was

[12] Shabtai Rosenne, *The Law and Practice of the International Court of Justice* (Leyden, Sijthoff, 1965), I, 474–75; and Rosalyn Higgins, *The Development of International Law Through the Political Organs of the United Nations* (London, Oxford University Press, 1963), p. 334.

[13] See GAOR/6th Sess./502d–506th Mtgs./Jan. 26–29, 1952; and GA Res. 505(VI), Feb. 1, 1952.

not a member and therefore not bound by the Covenant, Article 20(2) provided that in case any member of the League had, before becoming a member, contracted obligations inconsistent with the terms of the Covenant, it was the duty of that member "to take immediate steps to procure its release from such obligations."

In the technical committee discussions at San Francisco, there was general willingness to accept "as evident the rule according to which all previous obligations inconsistent with the terms of the Charter should be superseded by the latter." However, it was thought inadvisable to provide for the automatic abrogation by the Charter of obligations inconsistent with the terms thereof. Rather, it was deemed preferable "to have the rule depend upon and be linked with the case of conflict between the two categories of obligations." While the nature of the conflict was not defined, it was considered sufficient that the conflict arise from the carrying out of the obligations of the Charter. The conflict might arise either

. . . because of intrinsic inconsistency between the two categories of obligations or as the result of the application of the provisions of the Charter under given circumstances: e.g., in the case where economic sanctions were applied against a state which derives benefits or advantages from previous agreements contrary to said sanctions.[14]

With respect to the Covenant rule that members should not enter into any engagement inconsistent with its terms, the Committee thought this was so evident as not to require express statement, all the more since it was stated in positive form in what is now Article 2 (2). With respect to obligations to nonmembers, while the Committee recognized that international law did not ordinarily recognize the possibility of an international agreement's affecting the rights of third parties, it felt that performance of members' obligations under the Charter should not be hindered by obligations assumed toward nonmember states.

The question of possible conflict between obligations of members under the Charter and obligations under other agreements was considered in connection with the drafting of recommendations by the Collective Measures Committee for strengthening the United Nations system of collective security. Specifically, the question discussed was that of the legal liabilities of member states under international agreements as a consequence of carrying out United Nations collective measures.[15] In the course of Committee consideration, the question was raised whether Article 103 had application to recommendations made by the

[14] UNCIO, *Documents*, XIII, 707.   [15] *Repertory*, V, 316–18.

General Assembly and the Security Council in contrast to binding decisions taken by the Council under Chapter VII. The text finally agreed upon by the Committee as one of the "Guiding Principles of General Application" was as follows: "It is of importance that States should not be subjected to legal liabilities under treaties or other international agreements as a consequence of carrying out United Nations collective measures." The General Assembly took note of the Report containing this statement.[16]

Only infrequently has Article 103 been discussed or invoked in connection with the consideration of specific questions by United Nations organs. In 1948, in the course of consideration of the Czechoslovak question by the Security Council, the question was raised of possible conflict between the obligations of certain members under the Charter and their obligations under the San Francisco Statement on Voting Procedure in the Security Council.[17] The view was expressed that obligations of members under the Charter took precedence over obligations under the Statement, assuming that this was to be regarded as an agreement among the permanent members. The Soviet representative, however, argued that the Statement was an interpretation of the Charter, not a separate international agreement, and that thus there could be no conflict under Article 103.[18]

The provisions of Article 103 have been cited most frequently when the Security Council has been asked to make a decision on a matter under consideration by the Organization of American States. In asking the Security Council to act in connection with the "invasion" of its territory in June, 1954, Guatemala, for example, cited Article 103 and asserted that there was a conflict between the obligations undertaken by member states under the Charter of the United Nations and those assumed under the Charter of the OAS.[19] Cuba referred to Article 103 both in its charges against the United States in July, 1960, and in its complaint about OAS action in relation to the situation in the Dominican Republic in November, 1961. In the first case, the Council itself, in deciding to adjourn the discussion, took note of Article 103.[20] In general, members of the Security Council, with the notable exception of the Soviet Union, have been reluctant to support action by the Council on any matter being handled by the OAS and have avoided discussion

[16] GAOR/6th Sess./1951/*Supp. 13* (A/1891), p. 33; GA Res. 503A(VI), Jan. 12, 1952.

[17] See commentary on Art. 27.

[18] See *Repertory*, V, 318–19 and SCOR/3d Yr., No. 63/288th Mtg./Apr. 29, 1948/pp. 19 ff.; and *ibid.*, No. 71/300th Mtg./May 21, 1948/pp. 18 ff. See also Art. 27 and commentary.

[19] SCOR/9th Yr./675th Mtg./June 20, 1954/paras. 189–91.

[20] UN Doc. S/4395, July 19, 1960.

of possible conflict between obligations under the Charter of the United Nations and obligations under the Charter of the OAS.[21]

Article 104

The Organization shall enjoy in the territory of each of its Members such legal capacity as may be necessary for the exercise of its functions and the fulfillment of its purposes.

Article 105

1. The Organization shall enjoy in the territory of each of its Members such privileges and immunities as are necessary for the fulfillment of its purposes.

2. Representatives of the Members of the United Nations and officials of the Organization shall similarly enjoy such privileges and immunities as are necessary for the independent exercise of their functions in connection with the Organization.

3. The General Assembly may make recommendations with a view to determining the details of the application of paragraphs 1 and 2 of this Article or may propose conventions to the Members of the United Nations for this purpose.

Articles 104 and 105 deal with related aspects of a single topic—the legal status of the United Nations within the territory of, and in its relations with, member states—and thus will be discussed together.[22]

The Covenant of the League of Nations contained the following provisions on the privileges and immunities of the Organization, its officials and the representatives of its members:

Representatives of the Members of the League and officials of the League when engaged on the business of the League shall enjoy diplomatic privileges and immunities.

The buildings and other property occupied by the League or its officials or by Representatives attending its meetings shall be inviolable.[23]

[21] See commentary on ch. VIII. Thus the Security Council rejected a Cuban proposal to ask the International Court of Justice for an advisory opinion on certain questions relating to decisions of the Punta del Este Conference of Jan. 23–31, 1962. One question Cuba wished to put to the Court was whether the provisions of the Charter of the OAS and the Inter-American Treaty of Mutual Assistance could "be considered to take precedence over the obligations of Member States under the United Nations Charter." UN Doc. S/5095. See also SCOR/17th Yr./998th Mtg./Mar. 23, 1962.

[22] See *Repertory*, V, 321–74, where the same practice is followed.

[23] Art. 7(4) and (5).

Detailed arrangements concerning privileges and immunities were worked out in agreements concluded between the Secretary-General and the Swiss Government.[24]

The drafting of the Charter provisions was influenced by two major considerations: the desirability of finding a more appropriate theoretical basis for privileges and immunities, and the desirability of formulating the provisions in general terms, leaving their detailed application to subsequent discussions and arrangements. In response to the first consideration, the decision was taken to substitute for the standard of "diplomatic privileges and immunities" used in the Covenant, a functional standard—what is necessary for the independent exercise of the functions of the Organization and the fulfillment of its purposes.[25]

On the basis of recommendations of the Preparatory Commission, the General Assembly at its first session approved the Convention on the Privileges and Immunities of the United Nations and submitted it to members for accession.[26] The Headquarters Agreement was signed on June 26, 1947, by the Secretary-General of the United Nations and the Secretary of State of the United States,[27] and was approved by the General Assembly on October 31. On December 11, 1946, the General Assembly had approved agreements concluded between the International Court of Justice and the Netherlands government on the privileges and immunities and facilities to be enjoyed by judges and others associated with the work of the Court.[28]

The General Assembly has stated that the Headquarters Agreement is complementary to the General Convention "since these instruments taken together are intended to define the status of the United Nations in the country where these headquarters are located." [29] The United States has not acceded to the General Convention, which raises certain problems of interpretation and application.[30]

In addition to the agreements mentioned above, a number of other agreements have been concluded for implementation of the provisions of Articles 104 and 105, including some agreements which confer privi-

[24] Martin Hill, *Immunities and Privileges of International Officials* (Washington, Carnegie Endowment for International Peace, 1947). The text of the provisional modus vivendi of 1921 is given as *Annex I* and that of 1926 as *Annex II*.

[25] See UNCIO, *Documents,* XIII, 704–5.

[26] *Report of the Preparatory Commission,* pp. 72–80; GA Res. 22A(I), Feb. 13, 1946; 1 UNTS, 15–33. Accession is effected by deposit of an instrument with the Secretary-General. At the end of 1965, 92 states had acceded to the Convention.

[27] Agreement between the United Nations and the United States of America. Regarding the Headquarters of the United Nations. For text, see UN Doc. A/427, Oct. 27, 1947, pp. 9–15; 11 UNTS, 11.

[28] GA Res. 90(I), Dec. 11, 1946.   [29] GA Res. 258(III), Dec. 8, 1948.

[30] See Leo Gross, "Immunities and Privileges of Delegations to the United Nations," *International Organization,* XVI(1962), 483–520, for a discussion of these problems.

leges and immunities in nonmember states.[31] Of special significance is the Interim Arrangement with Switzerland signed on July 1, 1946, and approved by the General Assembly on December 14.[32]

The International Personality of the Organization

Articles 104 and 105 do not expressly refer to the matter of international personality. Nevertheless, the attributes accorded the United Nations within the territories of member states assume the existence of international status, even though it need not be the full status of a sovereign state. Article I, Section 1, of the General Convention states that the United Nations "shall possess juridical personality." The Interim Arrangement with Switzerland contains an explicit recognition by the Swiss government of the international personality of the United Nations.

The question of international personality arose at the third session of the General Assembly, when consideration was being given to steps the Organization might take to obtain reparations for injuries incurred by agents of the United Nations while engaged in the performance of their duties.[33] The General Assembly requested the International Court of Justice to give an advisory opinion on whether the United Nations had "the capacity to bring an international claim" against the responsible government with a view to obtaining reparations for injuries. In maintaining the capacity of the Organization to bring a claim, the Court said:

In the opinion of the Court, the Organization was intended to exercise and enjoy, and is in fact exercising and enjoying, functions and rights which can only be explained on the basis of the possession of a large measure of international personality and the capacity to operate upon an international plane. It is at present the supreme type of international organization, and it could not carry out the intentions of its founders if it was devoid of international personality. It must be acknowledged that its Members, by entrusting certain functions to it, with the attendant duties and responsibilities, have clothed it with the competence required to enable those functions to be effectively discharged.[34]

Concrete evidence of the intent of the Charter to give the United Nations a personality independent of that of its members is to be found

[31] See *Repertory*, V, 327–28.

[32] GAOR/1st. Sess., 2d Part, 6th Ctte./*Annex 17* (A/175), *Appendix I*; 1 UNTS, 164–80.

[33] The occasion was the assassination of Count Bernadotte during his service as United Nations Mediator in Palestine.

[34] "Reparations for Injuries Suffered in the Service of the United Nations," *ICJ Reports*, 1949, p. 179.

in provisions requiring them to give every assistance to the Organization in any action it takes under the Charter (Article 2[5]), and to accept and carry out decisions of the Security Council (Article 25); authorizing the organs to perform specified functions and to exercise specific powers; giving the Organization legal capacity and privileges and immunities in the territory of members; and providing for the conclusion of agreements between the Organization and its members and between the Organization and other intergovernmental organizations. Practice has fully confirmed and further elaborated this concept.[35]

The Legal Capacity of the Organization within the Territory of a Member

Article 104 has been implemented by Article I, Section 1, of the General Convention, which defines the legal capacity of the United Nations as the capacity: "(a) to contract; (b) to acquire and dispose of immovable and movable property; and (c) to institute legal proceedings." The United Nations has entered into a variety of contracts of a private-law character, for example, contracts for maintenance of property, for the purchase of office equipment, for printing, and for the sale of its publications. It has acquired immovable property, for example, the tract of land for its permanent headquarters in New York, the Ariana site in Geneva, and the buildings erected on these sites. Movable property includes furniture, office equipment, books, and supplies. Special mention might be made in this connection of equipment and supplies acquired and used for UNEF and ONUC. The United Nations has brought a number of legal actions of a private-law character in the courts of member states. Though the United States is not a party of the General Convention, it has by national legislation accorded the United Nations a legal capacity.[36]

Privileges and Immunities of the Organization

Article 105(1) is concerned with the privileges and immunities which the Organization enjoys as a separate personality. Privileges and immunities are to be enjoyed to the extent that they "are necessary for the fulfillment of [the Organization's] purposes." They may be classified under two principal heads: 1) property, funds and assets; and 2) facilities in respect to communications. The specific provisions of the

[35] See, for example, Guenter Weissberg, *The International Status of the United Nations* (New York, Oceana, 1961).

[36] Section 2(a) of the International Organization Immunities Act of 1945 (US Public Law 291, 79th Cong.; 59 Stat. 669), and Executive Order 9698, Feb. 19, 1946.

General Convention dealing with these matters are contained in Articles II and III respectively. The privileges and immunities granted include—in principle and subject to some qualifications—immunity of property and assets from legal process; inviolability of premises and archives; the right to hold funds, open accounts, and transfer funds freely; exemption from direct taxes, customs duties, and restrictions on import and export of articles for official use; most-favored-nation treatment for its official communications; and the right to use codes and couriers.[37]

Under the terms of the Headquarters Agreement, the Organization is accorded additional privileges and immunities made necessary by the fact of the location of the United Nations facilities and staff within the territory of a member state. The Agreement provides, among other things, for the establishment and operation of adequate communication facilities, for placing the headquarters district under United Nations control and authority subject to certain accommodations to United States territorial juristiction, for the inviolability of the headquarters district, and for transit to and from the district of various categories of persons engaged in the business of the Organization.

Other privileges and immunities considered necessary to the implementation of particular programs or activities are specified in special agreements concluded in connection with their execution.[38]

Privileges and Immunities of Representatives of Members

Under Article 7(4) of the League Covenant, representatives of members, when engaged in the business of the League, enjoyed diplomatic privileges and immunities. Article 105(2) of the Charter provides that representatives of members shall enjoy "such privileges and immunities as are necessary to the independent exercise of their functions in connection with the Organization." Though Article IV of the General Convention adheres to this functional standard in the enumeration of privileges and immunities, most states, whether members or not, in their special agreements with the United Nations have extended full diplomatic privileges and immunities to the representatives of members attending meetings of United Nations organs in their territory.[39] Thus the change in the theoretical basis of privileges and immunities from the diplomatic standard to the functional standard has not had the practical consequence that might have been anticipated.

The General Convention, in Section 16, defines "representatives of Members of the United Nations," to include "all delegates, deputy

[37] See *Repertory*, V, 338–46.   [38] See, for example, *ibid.*, p. 339.
[39] *Ibid.*, p. 350.

delegates, advisers, technical experts and secretaries of delegations."[40] The Headquarters Agreement in Article V lists the following categories of persons as being "resident representatives to the United Nations":

1. Every person designated by a Member as the principal resident representative to the United Nations of such Member or as resident representative with the rank of ambassador or minister plenipotentiary.

2. Such resident members of their staffs as may be agreed upon between the Secretary-General, the Government of the United States and the Government of the Member concerned.[41]

The General Assembly has recommended to the Secretary-General and to the appropriate authorities of the United States that they use Section 16 of the General Convention as a guide in interpreting and applying the relevant provisions of Article V of the Headquarters Agreement.[42]

Article IV, Section 11, of the General Convention defines the privileges and immunities of representatives of members as follows:

Representatives of Members to the principal and subsidiary organs of the United Nations and to conferences convened by the United Nations shall, while exercising their functions and during their journey to and from the place of meeting, enjoy the following privileges and immunities:

(a) immunity from personal arrest or detention and from seizure of their personal baggage, and, in respect of words spoken or written and all acts done by them in their capacity as representatives, immunity from legal process of every kind;

(b) inviolability for all papers and documents;

(c) the right to use codes and to receive papers or correspondence by courier or in sealed bags;

(d) exemption in respect of themselves and their spouses from immigration restrictions, aliens registration or national service obligations in the state they are visiting or through which they are passing in the exercise of their functions;

(e) the same facilities in respect of currency or exchange restrictions as are accorded to representatives of foreign governments on temporary official missions;

(f) the same immunities and facilities in respect of their personal baggage as are accorded to diplomatic envoys, and also;

(g) such other privileges, immunities and facilities not inconsistent with the foregoing as diplomatic envoys enjoy, except that they shall have no right to claim exemption from customs duties on goods imported (otherwise than as part of their personal baggage) or from excise duties or sales taxes.

---

[40] GA Res. 22A(I), Feb. 13, 1946.

[41] Since the U.S. is not a party to the General Convention, the Headquarters Agreement provisions assume special importance. The procedure is for consultations to take place as prescribed and for the agreed list to be thereupon included in the "Bluebook" issued by the U.S. Mission to the UN in cooperation with the UN Protocol Division.

[42] GA Res. 169(II), Oct. 31, 1947.

In addition, the Convention provides that the privileges and immunities are accorded, "not for the personal benefit of the individuals themselves, but in order to safeguard the independent exercise of their functions in connection with the United Nations." Consequently, it is stated, the member "not only has the right but is under a duty to waive the immunity in any case where in the opinion of the Member the immunity would impede the course of justice" (Section 14).

The Headquarters Agreement, on the other hand, does not attempt to list specific privileges and immunities of representatives; rather, it states that they shall "[whether] residing inside or outside the headquarters district, be entitled in the territory of the United States to the same privileges and immunities, subject to corresponding conditions and obligations, as it accords to diplomatic envoys accredited to it." In the case of members whose governments are not recognized by the United States, such privileges and immunities "need be extended . . . only within the headquarters district, at their residences and offices outside the district, in transit between the district and such residences and offices, and in transit on official business to and from foreign countries" (Section 15[4]).

The main problems that have arisen in connection with the privileges and immunities of representatives have related to their right to travel in the United States and their right to enter and remain there. Washington has applied travel restrictions to representatives of certain members in retaliation for restrictions on the travel of United States diplomats in those countries. This action has been criticized on the ground that these representatives are in the United States not at the sufferance of the United States but in pursuance of rights enjoyed under international law. It is argued that under the Charter, the General Convention, and the Headquarters Agreement, there is no basis for retaliatory or discriminatory treatment.[43]

The issue of United States control of the entry and presence of representatives has been more troublesome than that of travel restrictions once the representative has entered. Washington rests its case for being able to determine whether representatives may be allowed in the country on two grounds: 1) a provision in the International Organizations Immunities Act which states that formal notification from the Secretary of State is required in order for a representative to enjoy the benefits of that act (Section 8); and 2) a Senate reservation to the Headquarters Agreement which states that "nothing in the agreement shall be construed as in any way diminishing, abridging, or weakening the right of the United States to safeguard its own security and completely to control the entrance of aliens into any territory." [44] The United Na-

---

[43] See Gross, pp. 483–520.   [44] U.S. Statutes-at-Large, LXI, sec. 6.

tions has never recognized this reservation and does not consider it to have any binding force.[45]

Privileges and Immunities of Officials

Article V, Section 17, of the General Convention provides that:

The Secretary-General will specify the categories of officials to which the provisions of this Article and Article VII shall apply. He shall submit these categories to the General Assembly. Thereafter these categories shall be communicated to the Governments of all Members. The names of the officials included in these categories shall from time to time be made known to the Governments of Members.

The Headquarters Agreement contains no provision defining the categories of officials enjoying privileges and immunities.

Following a report by the Secretary-General, the Assembly adopted a resolution in which it approved "the granting of the privileges and immunities referred to in Articles V and VI of the Convention on the Privileges and Immunities of the United Nations . . . to all Members of the staff of the United Nations, with the exception of those who are recruited locally and are assigned to hourly rates." [46] Other persons included in the category of officials are specialized personnel serving as consultants in the Secretariat and technical assistance experts.[47]

Article V of the General Convention defines the privileges and immunities of officials of the United Nations as follows:

Section 18. Officials of the United Nations shall:

(a) be immune from legal process in respect of words spoken or written and in all acts performed by them in their official capacity;

(b) be exempt from taxation on the salaries and emoluments paid to them by the United Nations;

(c) be immune from national service obligations;

(d) be immune, together with their spouses and relatives dependent on them, from immigration restrictions and alien registration;

(e) be accorded the same privileges in respect of exchange facilities as are accorded to the officials of comparable ranks forming part of diplomatic missions to the Government concerned;

(f) be given, together with their spouses and relatives dependent on them, the same repatriation facilities in time of international crises as diplomatic envoys;

(g) have the right to import free of duty their furniture and effects at the time of first taking up their post in the country in question.

45 See Gross, pp. 512–14.
46 UN Docs. A/116, Oct. 16, 1946; and A/116/Add. 1, Nov. 9, 1946; GA Res. 76(I), Dec. 7, 1946.
47 See Repertory, V, 352, and Supp. 1, II, 424–25.

Section 19. In addition to the immunities and privileges specified in section 18, the Secretary-General and all Assistant Secretaries-General shall be accorded in respect of themselves, their spouses and minor children, the privileges and immunities, exemptions and facilities accorded to diplomatic envoys, in accordance with international law.[48]

The specific privileges and immunities of United Nations officials as defined in the General Convention have, in some instances, been qualified or extended by special agreements, by reservations to the General Convention, or by national legislation.[49] In particular, the United States, having failed to ratify the General Convention, applies the provisions of the International Organizations Immunities Act of December 29, 1945, which does not accord exemption from taxation of salaries and immunity from national service to United States nationals.[50] The refusal of the United States to accord tax exemption placed its nationals in a disadvantageous position. To remedy this, the General Assembly on November 20, 1947, adopted a resolution authorizing the Secretary-General to reimburse them for national income taxes paid on salaries and allowances during 1946, 1947, and 1948; on November 18, 1948, the General Assembly approved a plan for staff assessments to provide the means for reimbursement.[51] With changes of detail, this arrangement has been continued. The Convention emphasizes that "privileges and immunities are granted to officials in the interests of the United Nations and not for the personal benefit of the individuals themselves." The Secretary-General is expected to waive the immunity of any official in any case where, in his opinion, immunity would impede the course of justice and where this can be done "without prejudice to the interests of the United Nations." In the case of the Secretary-General, the Security Council has the right of waiver.[52]

Experts performing missions for the United Nations enjoy such privileges and immunities "as are necessary for the independent exercise of their functions during the period of their missions, including the time spent on journeys in connection with their missions." [53]

The General Convention also provides for the issuance of United Nations *laissez-passer* to its officials, to be accepted by member authorities as valid documents. Such persons must be granted facilities for

[48] Similar provisions are contained in the Interim Arrangement between the UN and Switzerland.

[49] For summary, see *Repertory*, V, 353-55.

[50] U.S. Public Law 291, 79th Cong. For analysis of Act, see Lawrence Preuss, "The International Organizations Immunities Act," *American Journal of International Law*, XL (1946), 332-45.

[51] GA Res. 106(II), Nov. 20, 1947; 239(III), Nov. 18, 1948.

[52] General Convention, Art. V, sec. 20.

[53] *Ibid.*, Art. VI, sec. 22. Compare with privileges and immunities of representatives of members under sec. 11.

speedy travel. The Secretary-General, the assistant secretaries-general, and directors traveling on United Nations *laissez-passer* on United Nations business are entitled to the same facilities as diplomatic envoys.

Under the Statute of the International Court of Justice and the Agreement between the Court and the Netherlands, the Judges of the Court, the Registrar, and the Deputy Registrar, when acting for the Registrar, enjoy diplomatic privileges and immunities.[54] Agents, counsel, and advocates of the parties enjoy the privileges and immunities necessary to the independent exercise of their duties.[55]

[54] See *Repertory*, V, 362–65.   [55] Statute, Art. 42(3).

CHAPTER XVII

Transitional Security Arrangements

In reporting to the President of the United States on the results of the San Francisco Conference, the Secretary of State referred to Chapter XVII of the Charter as a manifestation of "the intelligent realism of the architects of the United Nations." It was realized, he stated,

. . . that the Charter could not create an Organization which would spring into being possessed from the start of full power to maintain international peace and security . . . that if it was to succeed it must not be burdened at the outset with responsibilities which it could not immediately fulfill . . . that it must be given time to become firmly established. Above all . . . that it would be not only an impossibility but a tragic mistake to throw upon the Organization the task of enforcing the peace against the enemy states.[1]

The mere fact that the United Nations Charter was signed while World War II was still in progress necessitated some kind of transitional arrangements. Those primarily responsible for prosecuting the war had no intention of tying their hands in any way, either with respect to the waging of the war or the making of the peace. The United Nations was to have no responsibilities for negotiating the peace settlements; nor was it intended "that the world organization to be created should be charged with control over the defeated enemy, at least for a considerable time." [2] Moreover, at the time the Charter was agreed upon, it was impossible to predict how chaotic the world situation might be when hostilities ceased, or how long it might take to establish a climate in which the new Organization would be able to exercise its assigned powers and functions. As a result of these reasonings and uncertainties, it was decided to include in the Charter a chapter on "transitional security arrangements" which in effect placed upon the great powers, for an interim period, the primary responsibility for enforcing security throughout the world, and most particularly in relation to the enemy states.

Among themselves, the major powers had no difficulty in agreeing on these provisions; they were included in the Dumbarton Oaks Proposals with little discussion. Moreover, despite the reservations about

---

[1] State Dept., *Report to the President*, p. 161.   [2] *Ibid.*, p. 163.

great-power domination that permeated the San Francisco Conference, other states accepted these arrangements as necessary. The Mexican delegate did voice the opinion that inclusion of these provisions in the Charter would involve "an original sin as great as or even greater than" that which had led to criticism of the Covenant of the League because of its connection with the Treaty of Versailles. He suggested that these provisions should not be included in the Charter but incorporated in a separate protocol.[3] The United States had earlier considered this possibility but rejected it, partly for domestic political reasons.[4] Opposition to the Mexican proposal came primarily from France and the Soviet Union, who, for understandable reasons, were especially concerned with arrangements to prevent any reemergence of German aggressive power.

Other delegates sought more precision in the wording of the two articles and clarification of the intentions of the major powers. How long would the "transitional" period last? What precisely would be the role of the United Nations Security Council during this period? What would be the responsibilities of other members under these transitional arrangements? These queries brought some slight modifications in the language of Chapter XVII, and some interpretative comments by the United States and the United Kingdom.

To the major question that perturbed the delegates at San Francisco —how long the transitional period would last—the answer obviously depended on the speed with which the major powers reached agreements on the terms of the peace treaties and on the means for supplying the Security Council with the forces necessary for it to assume its responsibilities.

The aim was, according to the United States Secretary of State, "to provide for the orderly growth of the Security Council's functions, to permit it to take successively larger bites of responsibility." He also echoed the hope that "the day is not many years off when Chapter XVII will become a dead letter."[5] Much of the chapter has indeed become so, but not for the expected reasons. Difficulties arose over the peace treaties, and a settlement for Germany has never been reached. Likewise, the agreements for supplying the Security Council with armed forces have never been concluded; the same factors that prevented agreement on this matter largely prevented the major powers from taking "joint action on behalf of the Organization" under Article 106. The "transition" from interim control by the major powers to full effectiveness of the United Nations system as envisaged in the Charter

---

[3] UNCIO, *Documents*, XII, 614.

[4] For the U.S. position, see Ruth B. Russell, *A History of the United Nations Charter* (Washington, Brookings Institution, 1958), pp. 475–76 and 683.

[5] State Dept., *Report to the President*, pp. 162, 163.

has never taken place. Instead, the Organization has developed along quite different lines.

Article 106

Pending the coming into force of such special agreements referred to in Article 43 as in the opinion of the Security Council enable it to begin the exercise of its responsibilities under Article 42, the parties to the Four-Nation Declaration, signed at Moscow, October 30, 1943, and France, shall, in accordance with the provisions of paragraph 5 of that Declaration, consult with one another and as occasion requires with other Members of the United Nations with a view to such joint action on behalf of the Organization as may be necessary for the purpose of maintaining international peace and security.

That the major powers would bear the primary responsibility for the maintenance of international peace and security in the immediate postwar period was regarded as axiomatic by those engaged in planning the peace. Indeed, in the initial planning stages, some, including President Roosevelt, favored a prolonged period during which the major powers would act on behalf of the international community.[6] As planning progressed, more emphasis was placed upon establishing the new Organization as soon as practicable, and on associating the other states more closely with the development of the postwar international security system.

It was realized that, even under the best of circumstances, it would be some time after the establishment of the Organization before it could discharge its responsibilities of maintaining peace. For this interim period, the Charter provided, in effect, for an extension, in somewhat modified form, of the commitment undertaken by China, the Soviet Union, the United Kingdom, and the United States in the Moscow Declaration of October 30, 1943. Paragraph 5 of that Declaration stated:

That for the purpose of maintaining international peace and security pending the re-establishment of law and order and the inauguration of a system of general security, they will consult with one another and as occasion requires with other members of the United Nations with a view to joint action on behalf of the community of nations.[7]

At the suggestion of the United States, it was agreed at Dumbarton Oaks to include in the Charter a provision for extending this commit-

[6] See Russell, pp. 96–97, 101–2, 123, and 227.
[7] The reference to "other members" was a British suggestion. *Ibid.*, p. 135.

ment to cover the period up to the coming into force of the special
agreements by which the Security Council would be supplied with
armed forces and facilities.[8]

This provision was accepted by the San Francisco Conference with a
few modifications. The inclusion of France with the four signatories of
the Moscow Declaration was accepted unanimously. Other proposals
for change, however, provoked debate. The language of the Dumbarton Oaks Proposals was open to the interpretation that *all* the
agreements under Article 43 would have to be concluded before the
"transitional" arrangements became inoperative. The transition period
might then be very long indeed, and could be prolonged by the recal-
citrance of any member. The Conference was assured that this was not
the intention of the article. It was decided to clarify the point by specifying that it was up to the Security Council to decide when the forces
and facilities at its disposal were sufficient to enable it to exercise its
responsibilities under Article 42 of the Charter. The Soviet view that
this matter should be decided by the "responsible powers" themselves
was not accepted, but obviously the Security Council would not be
able to make the decision that it was ready to assume its responsibilities unless the five permanent members concurred.[9]

A number of delegates, still dissatisfied with ambiguities in Article
106, sought a more precise definition of the phrase "joint action on behalf of the Organization." What would be the respective responsibilities of the Security Council and the five powers during the transitional
period, especially with regard to the pacific settlement of disputes?
The United Kingdom and United States delegates replied that the
Council would be responsible for pacific settlement; they opposed
a precise definition of the role of the Council on the ground
that flexibility was desirable. The United States, however, drew
attention to the reference in Article 106 to Article 42, and stated that
the Security Council "would refrain from the performance of its responsibilities only with respect to those functions the exercise of which
would be suspended until the conclusion of the special agreements." In
the United States view, "only the power to take military enforcement
action" was withheld from the Security Council, and that "only temporarily." [10]

The fact that Article 106 links Article 42 to Article 43 of the
Charter is of some significance. Clearly, it was intended that any "action" by the Security Council under Article 42 would be taken by
means of the forces made available to the Council under the special

---

[8] *Ibid.*, pp. 261 and 474–76.

[9] See *ibid.*, pp. 680 ff.; and UNCIO, *Documents,* XII, 401–3 and 558–59.

[10] UNCIO, *Documents,* XII, 509; see also Russell, p. 559; and State Dept.,
Report to the President, pp. 162–63.

agreements called for in Article 43. Nowhere in Chapter VII of the Charter, however, is this linkage specifically stated. Article 42 can be interpreted to permit the Council to take action with forces supplied to it in other ways, but the case for this interpretation is weakened by the phraseology of Article 106.

Nothing in Article 106 precludes the five powers from making forces available so that the Security Council can act despite the absence of the Article 43 agreements. It would not appear, however, that other United Nations members would be under any obligation to supply forces for such action or for action taken by the five powers themselves under Article 106. All members are obligated, according to Article 2(5), to give "every assistance" to the United Nations in any action it takes "in accordance with the present Charter" and not to assist "any state against which the United Nations is taking preventive or enforcement action." While this double obligation might be considered as applying in the case of "joint action" under this article, the specific obligations of Article 25 and Chapter VII referring to formal Council decisions cannot be considered as applicable.

Article 106 has not fulfilled its intended function. The special agreements called for in Article 43 have never been concluded because of disagreement among the permanent members, and this same inability to agree has rendered ineffective the provisions of Article 106.

During the early debates on the Palestine question in the Security Council, there was a tentative approach to invoking Article 106. The United Nations Palestine Commission had reported that it could not carry out its functions under the General Assembly's partition resolution unless "military forces in adequate strength" were made available to it.[11] The United States representative, without directly referring to Article 106, indicated that his government would be "ready to consult under the Charter with a view to such action as may be necessary to maintain international peace," pointing out that such consultation would be "required" in view of the nonexistence of the Article 43 agreements.[12] Thereupon, Colombia proposed that the Council "invite" the five permanent members "according to Article 106 . . . to consult with one another with a view to such joint action on behalf of the Organization" as might be necessary to prevent "any threat to the peace, breach of the peace, or act of aggression arising from the implementation" of the partition resolution.[13] The resolution as adopted made no reference to Article 106, but merely called upon the five members to "consult" and to make recommendations "regarding the guidance and instructions which the Council might usefully give to the Pal-

[11] SCOR/3d Yr./1948/*Special Supp. 2.*
[12] *Ibid.*, 253d Mtg./Feb. 24, 1948/p. 267.
[13] *Ibid.*, 254th Mtg./Feb. 24, 1948/p. 293.

estine Commission with a view of implementing" the partition resolution.[14] Given the divergent interests of the five permanent members, and especially the British refusal to cooperate in any attempt to impose the plan by force, it was not surprising that these consultations were unfruitful.

There was obviously no possibility of "joint action" by the major powers on such matters as the Greek civil war, Korea, or the Hungarian revolt, where the interests of the Soviet Union and the West were so diametrically opposed. Even in those situations where the differences between the policies of the United States and the Soviet Union were less obvious—such as Indonesia, Palestine, Suez, and various other issues with "colonial" overtones—"joint action" was equally impossible, partly because of British and French attitudes, but largely because the Western powers had no intention of supporting the introduction of Soviet troops into troubled areas even as part of a joint effort.

The situation as it gradually developed in the United Nations is in a sense a direct reversal of what the drafters of the Charter anticipated. It had been expected that the five major powers would supply the bulk of whatever forces might be needed for maintaining international peace and security, initially under Article 106 and eventually under the system outlined in Chapter VII of the Charter. Instead, in those instances where military or paramilitary forces have been considered necessary by the United Nations, the tendency has been to exclude the great powers from participating and to rely upon other members to provide the required forces.

This development has not gone unchallenged by the Soviet Union.[15] During the debate at the 1950 session of the General Assembly on the "Uniting for Peace" resolution, the Soviet Union introduced a number of proposals calling for the "implementation" of Article 106,[16] all of which were rejected. Subsequently, in its protests against the legality of those operations where armed forces have been supplied voluntarily by members (especially the Congo force and UNEF), the Soviet Union has cited Article 106 and the special responsibility thereunder of the permanent members of the Security Council. The Soviet Union has never, however, proposed that the five powers act jointly in these various situations.

[14] *Ibid.*, 263d Mtg./Mar. 4, 1948/p. 43.

[15] See, for example, Soviet protests over the composition of the Truce Supervision Organization in Palestine. SCOR/3d Yr./314th Mtg./June 7, 1948/p. 3; and 320th Mtg./June 15, 1948/p. 9.

[16] GAOR/5th Sess./1950/agenda item 68/pp. 9–10; 1st Ctte., Vol. I/368th–369th Mtgs./Oct. 18–19, 1950/pp. 156 ff.; and 302d Plen. Mtg./Nov. 3, 1950/pp. 345 ff.

Article 107

Nothing in the present Charter shall invalidate or preclude action, in relation to any state which during the Second World War has been an enemy of any signatory to the present Charter, taken or authorized as a result of that war by the Governments having responsibility for such action.

The purpose of Article 107 was to make it clear that the making of the peace following World War II would proceed as independently of the Charter as if that document did not exist. The terms of the peace were to be decided upon by those governments primarily responsible for the defeat of the enemy states. Nor was anything in the Charter to "invalidate or preclude" any action those governments considered necessary in their relations with the enemy states.

The need for inclusion in the Charter of some provision along these lines was first raised during the discussions at Dumbarton Oaks on "regional" enforcement action. The British asked whether the requirement of prior authorization of enforcement action by the Security Council would limit Allied freedom of action in enforcing surrender terms on the enemy states. At that time, the British were interested in a regional European organization to guard against resurgent German aggression and the Soviet Union was pursuing a policy of bilateral agreements aimed at blocking this same threat. The United States suggested that the provisions on regional arrangements be modified so that prior approval by the Security Council would not be required for any action concerning the enemy states "taken or authorized . . . by the governments having responsibility for such action." This proposal did not meet with Soviet approval. It was decided to leave the regional provisions unchanged but to add a paragraph to the chapter on "transitional" arrangements providing that nothing in the Charter should preclude action in relation to the enemy states by the governments responsible therefor.[17]

At San Francisco, the regional issue was again raised, and the Dumbarton Oaks provisions were substantially modified.[18] At the same time, the terms of Article 107 were accepted in essentially the same form as agreed upon at Dumbarton Oaks, but only after the draft proposal had been subject to criticism on two major grounds: the breadth of the exception and the lack of any indication as to how long the "transitional" period might last.[19] Attempts to redraft the paragraph

[17] Russell, pp. 473–74.   [18] See commentary on Arts. 51 and 53.
[19] UNCIO, *Documents*, XII, 403–4, and 419–22.

along more precise lines failed, but the debate did elicit the following explanation by the United Kingdom delegate as to the meaning of the various terms in the article.

Enemy States are those which, on the day of the signature of the Charter, are still at war with any one of the United Nations.

The present war is to be understood as a series of wars which began on or before September 3, 1939 and which are still in progress.

"Action taken or authorized" . . . As to the exact meaning of the expression . . . the distinction is made between "positive" and "negative" action; that is to say, between action with respect to enemy States by the governments responsible for this action, and the action which the responsible governments had authorized other governments to take.[20]

The San Francisco Conference adopted Article 107 with full realization that the action referred to therein would probably be taken, at least for an initial period of uncertain length, by the governments chiefly responsible for the military defeat of the enemy and without any limitations being placed upon them with respect to such action by the terms of the Charter. Other members are not bound in any way to support these actions for they are not, as is the case under Article 106, taken "on behalf of the Organization."

There is nothing in Article 107 to prevent the United Nations from accepting responsibilities regarding the former enemy states, should the governments responsible so agree. Such agreement was reached in three instances, and the United Nations was asked to undertake responsibilities in relation to certain territories detached from the defeated Axis powers. First, at the request of France, the Soviet Union, the United Kingdom, and the United States, the Security Council accepted various responsibilities for the Free Territory of Trieste in accordance with the provisions of the Italian peace treaty.[21] Second, under this same treaty, the General Assembly, at the request of the same four powers, made recommendations on the disposition of Italy's former African colonies.[22] Third, the Security Council "approved" a "strategic trusteeship" agreement, with the United States as the administering authority, for the Pacific Islands formerly held by Japan under League of Nations mandate.[23]

In other instances in which the United Nations has considered issues either directly or indirectly related to the peace settlements, the Soviet Union has objected on the ground that all such matters are outside the jurisdiction of the United Nations.

[20] *Ibid.*, p. 560.

[21] SCOR/2d Yr./89th and 91st Mtgs./Jan. 7 and 10, 1947/pp. 4 ff., and 44 ff.

[22] GA Res. 289(IV), Nov. 21, 1949; and 390(V), Dec. 2, 1950.

[23] SCOR/2d Yr./124th Mtg./Apr. 2, 1947/p. 687. See also commentary on Art. 83.

This issue first came up at the second session of the General Assembly when a number of Latin American members asked the Assembly to consider revision of the Italian peace treaty. The Soviet representative stated that the proposal contravened the Charter, which excludes from the competence of the United Nations all measures by the Allied powers in relation to countries with which they were at war. In his view, Article 107 left no doubt that such matters were not subject to discussion by the General Assembly. Most of the other delegates took a less restrictive view of the Assembly's competence. Nonetheless, the proposal was later withdrawn in the light of various objections it had raised. At this same session, however, the Assembly decided to consider and make recommendations on the "problem of the independence of Korea," a matter brought to the United Nations by the United States after negotiations had failed to produce an agreement with the Soviet Union on the means for establishing a unified, independent Korea. Soviet objections to the Assembly's considering the question were based largely on Article 107 of the Charter.[24]

The most extensive discussion on the application of Article 107 took place in the fall of 1948 when France, the United Kingdom, and the United States complained to the Security Council that the Soviet blockade in Berlin was a threat to the peace. The Soviet Union took the position that "the whole question of Germany, including the Berlin question" was to be settled by negotiations among the occupying powers in accordance with their various agreements, and that Article 107 clearly excluded "intervention" in this matter by the United Nations. The Western powers argued that Article 107 precluded "appeals to United Nations organs by defeated enemy states concerning action taken against them during the period of military occupation by the responsible Allied powers"; but that it was not "designed to prevent any dispute among the victorious powers from coming to the Security Council," much less to "preclude consideration by the Security Council of action by a Member of the United Nations constituting a threat to the peace." The Western position prevailed in so far as the Council decided to consider the question, but the Soviet Union refused to participate in the discussion and subsequently used its veto to prevent the Council's adopting any resolution.[25]

In 1951, France, the United Kingdom, and the United States asked the General Assembly to appoint an impartial international commission to investigate whether existing conditions throughout Germany made it

[24] GAOR/2d Sess./90th Plen. Mtg./Sept. 23, 1947/p. 277 and Gen. Ctte./37th–38th Mtgs./Sept. 20–21, 1947/pp. 15 ff.; 1st Ctte./116th Mtg./Nov. 19, 1947/p. 527.

[25] For the discussion on Art. 107, see SCOR/3d Yr./361st and 362d Mtgs./Oct. 4–5, 1948.

possible to hold genuinely free elections. Again, the members of the Soviet bloc protested that under Article 107 and under the Potsdam agreements, all matters pertaining to the peace settlement were to be dealt with by the Council of Foreign Ministers and were outside the competence of the United Nations.[26] The Assembly proceeded, over Soviet objections, to appoint the commission; but the refusal of the authorities in East Germany to cooperate meant that it could not carry out its mandate.

Other issues on which the Assembly has made recommendations—despite Soviet objections that it was barred by Article 107 from doing so—include the following: charges that Bulgaria, Hungary, and Romania had violated the provisions of the peace treaties regarding human rights and fundamental freedoms (1949–50); complaint of the failure of the Soviet Union to repatriate or otherwise account for prisoners of war (1950); and appeal for an early conclusion of the treaty for Austria (1952). The Soviet Union also cited Article 107 in its protests against the Assembly's considering the question of Formosa in 1950. Although the Assembly placed this question on its agenda, no action was taken.

Throughout these discussions, the position of the Soviet Union and the other members of the Soviet group has been that all problems concerning the postwar peace settlements are beyond the competence of the United Nations.[27] This included not only interpretation or implementation of the peace treaties, but all situations arising directly from the war. In the Soviet view, the consideration of such questions by the United Nations was a violation of the Charter, and the Western powers, in bringing them to the United Nations, were violating their agreements as to the way in which these issues were to be dealt with.

In general, the position of the Western powers has been that the purpose of Article 107 was merely to prevent former enemy states from contesting in the United Nations the decisions or actions of the Allied powers; it precluded complaints to the United Nations by those states that Allied actions in relation to them were contrary to the Charter. Article 107 did not rule out other questions arising from the peace treaties or from the failure of the governments responsible to conclude such treaties; nor did it prevent the United Nations from considering differences that might arise among those governments on questions concerning the former enemy states. In their statements, the Western powers have drawn attention to the General Assembly's competence with re-

[26] GAOR/6th Sess., Gen. Ctte./76th Mtg./Nov. 9, 1951/paras. 37–54. See also debate in the ad hoc Pol. Ctte./15th–26th Mtgs./Dec. 4–19, 1951/pp. 75 ff.

[27] For a summary of the discussions and actions taken, see *Repertory*, V, 387–96. It should be noted that in many cases Soviet objections were not based solely on Art. 107.

spect to human rights and its authority under Article 14 to consider and make recommendations on situations "regardless of origin." They have also stressed the responsibilities of the Assembly and the Security Council for the maintenance of international peace and security. In the Western view, none of the questions brought to the United Nations has fallen within that narrow range of issues on which the Organization is barred from taking action by reason of Article 107; this position has been supported by nearly all the other members of the United Nations.

None of the questions referred to above was brought to the United Nations by a former enemy state. In this connection, it is of interest to note the following unanimous agreement reached at San Francisco: "It is understood that the enemy states in this war shall not have the right of recourse to the Security Council or the General Assembly before the Security Council grants them this right." [28] There was no discussion at San Francisco or thereafter as to the conditions under which the Security Council should grant this right, but presumably it was intended that after the peace treaties had come into force the former enemy states would be admitted to the United Nations with full rights of membership.

With admission to the United Nations, the former enemy states acquire the same rights as other members to bring matters to the attention of the Security Council and the General Assembly.

[28] UNCIO, *Documents,* XII, 560. The statement is along the lines of an amendment to Art. 107 proposed by Greece.

CHAPTER XVIII

Amendments

It is usual for an instrument such as the Charter of the United Nations to contain provisions for its own amendment. The problem is to devise a formula that permits adaptation in the light of experience and at the same time protects the stability of the organization and the rights of its members.

The Charter sets out a two-step process for amendment. First, an amendment must be adopted by a two-thirds vote of the members of either the General Assembly (Article 108) or a general conference called to review the Charter (Article 109). It should be noted that, while the Assembly may adopt resolutions on important questions by two-thirds of the members *present and voting* (Article 18), approval by two-thirds of *all* the members is needed for the adoption of amendments to the Charter. Second, amendments come into force when ratified "in accordance with their respective constitutional processes by two thirds of the Members, including all the permanent members of the Security Council."

The process for the adoption of amendments was agreed upon with little difficulty at San Francisco, although there was considerable debate over the provision for a general conference to review the Charter.[1] A major controversy, however, developed with regard to the ratification of amendments. Three elements were involved: 1) the special position given to the permanent members of the Security Council; 2) the number of ratifications needed for an amendment to enter into force; and 3) the binding effect of amendments upon members that opposed them.

The Special Position of the Permanent Members

The requirement that no amendment to the Charter can come into force unless ratified by all the permanent members met with even stronger opposition at the San Francisco Conference than did the Charter provision giving the permanent members a veto power in the Security Council. Statements were made to the effect that the veto had

[1] See commentary on Art. 109.

been accepted with reluctance by many states and then only because the major powers had made it a condition for the establishment of the Organization. This acceptance had been tempered by the hope that the provision would later be reconsidered and possibly eliminated. It was, as one delegate stated, "particularly objectionable that the principle should be given permanent status by incorporating it in the amending process." [2] The major powers, however, were adamant on this matter, maintaining that they "could not enter upon the great responsibilities and obligations of membership which they were prepared to accept if forced to take the risk that these responsibilities might be increased without their consent." [3] They insisted that the requirement of the concurrence of the permanent members be written into both Articles 108 and 109 of the Charter, and their view prevailed. To allay some of the dissatisfaction, the major powers made a number of minor concessions on other points concerning the amendment process.

Entry into Force

The great powers were not alone in their anxiety to protect themselves from a situation in which they might be bound to accept amendments to the Charter that did not have their approval. During the Dumbarton Oaks Conversations, two positions developed. Considering that the adoption of amendments by the Assembly should be made easy but that entry into force should be more difficult, the United States favored a simple majority for adoption with requirement of ratification by two-thirds of the members, including the permanent members of the Security Council. The United Kingdom took the opposite view. Noting that ratification of amendments to the League Covenant was often long delayed, not for political reasons but because of inertia, the United Kingdom favored adoption of amendments to the Charter by two-thirds vote of the members of the Assembly, with ratification by the five permanent members and a majority of the other members.[4] The British position was accepted and incorporated into the Dumbarton Oaks Proposals.

The above-mentioned controversy over the requirement that amendments be ratified by all the permanent members highlighted the disparity between the positions of the major powers and the other members. While the former were fully protected, the latter were in fact endorsing a blank check, obligating themselves to accept in advance international

[2] Statement by New Zealand: UNCIO, *Documents,* VII, 242.
[3] *Ibid.,* p. 468.
[4] In early U.S. plans, even larger majorities were required: three-fourths and four-fifths. See Ruth B. Russell, *A History of the United Nations Charter* (Washington, Brookings Institution, 1958), pp. 388–89, 426–27.

commitments which their duly accredited representatives might vote against and which their constitutional authorities might refuse to ratify. To minimize the danger that members might be faced with amendments unacceptable to them, it was agreed at San Francisco to raise the requirement for ratification to two-thirds of the membership. Although there were some objections on the ground that this would make amendment more difficult,[5] it was decided that it was more important to give protection to possible dissident minorities.

Increasing the size of the majority to two-thirds raised an additional complication. Experience with other constitutional instruments has shown that there is often a long time lag between the adoption of an amendment and its final ratification. Any changes in the size of the membership of the United Nations during the period between these two steps would, presumably, affect the number of ratifications needed before the amendment could come into force. The drafters of the Charter were aware of this problem and some thought was given to including a time limit within which the necessary ratifications would have to take place. In the end, the matter was left unresolved.[6]

Withdrawal

The concession on the two-thirds requirement for entry into force was not sufficient to allay the fears of some states that they might be forced to accept new obligations of which they did not approve. Norway had proposed that dissenting members not be bound by amendments to key provisions of the Charter affecting their obligations.[7] The constitutional instruments of some of the specialized agencies draw a distinction between simple amendments and those involving new obligations or the alteration of key provisions, and make the latter subject to special procedures.[8] None of these alternatives was discussed at San Francisco. The only proposal seriously considered was to include in the Charter a statement that nothing should preclude the right of a member to withdraw from the Organization if its rights and obligations were changed by an amendment it was unable to accept. Under this proposal, a member would have a similar right to withdraw if an amendment accepted by the required majority failed to secure the necessary ratifications.[9]

[5] Australia, New Zealand, and the Soviet Union, for example. See *ibid.*, pp. 746–47.

[6] For subsequent comment on this point, see GAOR/8th Sess., 6th Ctte./375th Mtg./Oct. 26, 1953/paras. 35 ff. (Israel); and 10th Sess./542d Plen. Mtg./Nov. 17, 1955/paras. 127 ff. (Ecuador).

[7] UNCIO, *Documents*, VII, 140.

[8] See FAO, Art. 20; IMF, Art. 7; IBRD, Art. 8; and UNESCO, Art. 13.

[9] UNCIO, *Documents*, VII, 262–67.

As pointed out previously, it was decided not to include in the Charter any provision concerning withdrawal, but the declaration approved at San Francisco makes it clear that a member would be justified in withdrawing if either of these two situations obtained.[10]

Article 108

Amendments to the present Charter shall come into force for all Members of the United Nations when they have been adopted by a vote of two-thirds of the members of the General Assembly and ratified in accordance with their respective constitutional processes by two-thirds of the Members of the United Nations, including all the permanent members of the Security Council.

The years since the adoption of the United Nations Charter have brought profound changes in the Organization, but until 1965, none of these was brought about through formal amendment of the Charter. Indeed, despite numerous suggestions for change, relatively few concrete proposals have been made in the United Nations for amendment. The main reason for the lack of such proposals has been the realization that no amendments could come into effect over the objections of any of the permanent members of the Security Council.

During the first few sessions of the General Assembly, a few proposals were made to amend the Charter. A proposal to amend Article 27(3) to curtail the veto was introduced in 1946, and in 1947 there was a proposal to amend Article 61 in order to enlarge ECOSOC.[11] Both proposals were withdrawn for lack of support. Efforts during these years to call a conference to review the Charter were similarly unfruitful.[12]

In 1956, following the great influx of new members, further proposals to amend the Charter were brought up in the General Assembly. A group of Latin American states proposed amendment of Article 61 of the Charter to enlarge ECOSOC from eighteen to twenty-four members; and amendment of Articles 23 and 27 to increase by two the number of nonpermanent members on the Security Council, and, correspondingly, to increase to eight the number of affirmative votes needed for a decision by the Council. These states also proposed amending Article 3 of the Statute of the International Court of Justice to increase the number of judges on the Court.[13]

Although these proposals appeared on the agenda of subsequent ses-

[10] See commentary on ch. II.

[11] GAOR/1st Sess., 2d Part, 1st Ctte./1946/*Annex* 7A, pp. 323–24 (Philippines); and 2d Sess., Jt. 2d and 3d Cttes./1947/*Annex* 6/pp. 73–74 (Argentina).

[12] See commentary on Art. 109.

[13] For texts, see GAOR/11th Sess./1957/*Annexes*, agenda items 56, 57, and 58.

sions of the General Assembly and were discussed from time to time,[14] it was not until the fifteenth session that any direct vote was taken on them. There was general agreement on the desirability of enlarging the two Councils, especially ECOSOC. There was less support for enlarging the Court and as a result, this proposal was dropped in 1959. The principal obstacle to any amendment to the Charter was the position taken by the members of the Soviet group to the effect that, since modification of the Charter required the approval of all five permanent members, they would oppose any amendments until the People's Republic of China was represented in the Organization.

By 1960, however, the continued increase in the Organization's membership was making it more and more difficult to reach agreement on the distribution of seats in both Councils; pressure for enlarging them mounted to the point where it overcame much of the previous reluctance to vote for proposed amendments over Soviet opposition. In committee, the actual texts of the amendments were adopted by a vote far in excess of the two-thirds majority of all members required by Article 108.[15] However, by a slim majority, composed of Afro-Asian and Soviet states, the committee attached to the two draft resolutions a call for the immediate redistribution of seats in the two Councils. This was unsatisfactory to the other members; as a result, the draft resolutions as a whole were rejected.

The desire to enlarge the two Councils continued. At its eighteenth session in 1963, the Assembly "adopted" amendments to increase the size of ECOSOC to twenty-seven members and to increase the size of the Security Council to fifteen members, with a corresponding amendment to Article 27 to require nine affirmative votes for the adoption of a Security Council decision. At the same time, the Assembly called upon members to ratify the amendments in accordance with their constitutional processes by September 1, 1965.[16] The amendments entered into force on August 31, 1965, when the United States deposited its instrument of ratification.

[14] See GAOR/11th Sess./661st Plen. Mtg./Feb. 26, 1957/p. 1224; GA Res. 1190(XII), Dec. 12, 1957; 1299(XIII), Dec. 10, 1958; and 1404(XIV), Nov. 25, 1959.

[15] For the texts of the draft resolutions, see GAOR/15th Sess./1960/*Annexes,* agenda item 23. For the debate, see *ibid.,* Spec. Pol. Ctte./186th–219th Mtgs./Oct. 31–Dec. 7, 1960/pp. 52–206.

[16] GA Res. 1991(XVIII), Dec. 17, 1963. For the debate, see GAOR/18th Sess., Spec. Pol. Ctte./417th–429th Mtgs./Nov. 27–Dec. 16, 1963; and 1285th Plen. Mtg./Dec. 17, 1963. For discussion on the Assembly's decisions concerning the distribution of seats on the two Councils, see commentary on Arts. 23 and 61.

Article 109*

1. A General Conference of the Members of the United Nations for the purpose of reviewing the present Charter may be held at a date and place to be fixed by a two-thirds vote of the members of the General Assembly and by a vote of any *nine* members of the Security Council. Each Member of the United Nations shall have one vote in the conference.

2. Any alteration of the present Charter recommended by a two-thirds vote of the conference shall take effect when ratified in accordance with their respective constitutional processes by two-thirds of the Members of the United Nations including all the permanent members of the Security Council.

3. If such a conference has not been held before the tenth annual session of the General Assembly following the coming into force of the present Charter, the proposal to call such a conference shall be placed on the agenda of that session of the General Assembly, and the conference shall be held if so decided by a majority vote of the members of the General Assembly and by a vote of any seven members of the Security Council.

The decision to include specific provision for a general conference to review the Charter stemmed largely from the desire to assure those who were dissatisfied with certain provisions that there would be an opportunity for reconsidering the document at some future time. Although most delegates considered the San Francisco Conference a success, some were frankly disappointed. The special position of the major powers was particularly objectionable to many, and was accepted only because without it the Organization could not have been established. To some, the Charter was acceptable as a first step on the understanding that it would be reviewed within a reasonable time with the aim of eliminating its more objectionable features. Some delegates went so far as to state that, without some assurance along this line, it was doubtful that their countries would consent to the ratification of the Charter.

Drafting Article 109

The idea of a general conference to review the Charter in the light of experience was readily agreed upon at San Francisco. No such provision had been included in the Dumbarton Oaks Proposals, apparently

---

* Italics indicate amendment that entered into force June 12, 1968. For original text, see p. 667.

because of a desire to avoid reflecting upon the permanence of the Organization.[17]

After considering the reactions to the Dumbarton Oaks Proposals and to a Canadian proposal for a future conference to consider revising the Charter, the United States took the initiative in getting the Sponsoring Governments to introduce a provision for a general conference to review the Charter. Under this proposal, the decision to hold a conference was to be taken by a vote of three-fourths of the members of the General Assembly and any seven members of the Security Council; thus, the veto would not be applicable. Subsequently, as a concession to those who were most dissatisfied with the amendment procedure, the required majority in the Assembly was reduced to two-thirds. These provisions, together with the provision that at the conference each member would have one vote, were incorporated into Article 109(1) with little difficulty.

There was some opposition to the terms of paragraph 2 of the article. Mexico proposed that, in so far as the general conference was concerned, the question of procedure for the adoption and ratification of amendments should be left open. The major powers, however, successfully insisted upon including in Article 109 a specific provision making it clear that any alteration of the Charter recommended by the general conference could come into force only when ratified by all the permanent members of the Security Council. Thus, whether amendments are voted upon in the Assembly according to Article 108 or in a general conference according to Article 109, the process is substantially the same.

Article 109 does not guarantee that a general conference will be held. The desire of some states for a specific commitment on this latter point provoked another sharp debate. The majority clearly favored setting some time limit for the holding of a conference. A number of states, including the five permanent members, opposed fixing any date on the ground that it was impossible to know in advance when it would be wise to hold such a conference. Britain and the United States were willing to compromise to the extent of stipulating that the question of holding a conference would be placed on the agenda of the tenth session of the General Assembly, if no conference had been held before that time. In their view, this concession would head off the drive for setting a definite date and also discourage early efforts at amendment.[18] Despite Soviet opposition, this formula was eventually accepted. As an additional compromise, it was decided to stipulate in Article 109(3) that in this special case a conference could be called by a vote of any seven members of the Security Council and by a majority—rather than a two-thirds—vote in the General Assembly.

[17] See Russell, pp. 427 and 617.   [18] Ibid., p. 747.

In reality, the "concessions" incorporated into Article 109 were of no great significance. True, provision was made for a general conference. None of the permanent members could prevent the calling of such a conference, or block the adoption of recommendations by the conference; but each retained its right to prevent the entry into force of any amendments to the Charter. Since any member may at any time propose that the Assembly call a general conference to review the Charter, the special provision in Article 109(3) for placing the matter on the agenda of the tenth session was of minor importance, although some significance seems to have been attached to the special voting procedure that would be applicable in that particular case.

When Articles 23 and 27 were amended to increase the number of members of the Security Council to fifteen and the number of affirmative votes required for a decision to nine, the requirement of seven votes in Article 190(1) was not changed. The General Assembly on December 20, 1965, voted to amend this paragraph to conform to the new requirement of Article 27; it was agreed, however, that the amendment of Article 109(3) was not necessary since the only decision possible under that paragraph had been taken.[19]

During the first three sessions of the General Assembly, proposals were introduced for the calling of a general conference to review the Charter. None, however, was adopted. As early as the autumn of 1946, it was proposed that the Assembly call a conference "in order to eliminate the so called 'veto privilege.'" This proposal was withdrawn in favor of another that did not mention the veto but called for a conference to review the Charter.[20] The next year, it was proposed that the Assembly convoke a general conference "for the purpose of studying the privilege of the veto . . . with a view to its abolition." This draft was not put to the vote, after it was decided to refer the whole question of voting procedure in the Council to the newly created Interim Committee of the Assembly for study.[21] In its report, the Committee recommended that the Assembly consider "whether the time has come or not to call a general conference as provided for in Article 109 of the Charter." [22] At the next session of the Assembly, a proposal to call a conference was again defeated.[23]

These proposals not only ran into Soviet opposition but were also opposed by other members on the grounds that the time had not yet

[19] GA Res. 2101(XX), Dec. 20, 1965; GAOR/20th Sess., 6th Ctte./897th Mtg./Dec. 14, 1965/pp. 357–59.

[20] Both proposals were put forward by Cuba. GAOR/1st Sess., 2d Part, 1st Ctte./1946/Annex 7b, pp. 324 and 326.

[21] GA Res. 117(II), Nov. 21, 1947. For the Argentine proposal to call a conference, see GAOR/2d Sess., 1st Ctte./1947/Annex 2, p. 529.

[22] For the report, see GAOR/3d Sess./1947/Supp. 10, p. 16.

[23] Proposal by Argentina, GAOR/3d Sess., ad hoc Pol. Ctte./1948/Annex, pp. 13–14.

come to convene a general review conference and that to discuss amendments on which the great powers were obviously divided would be idle and might even widen the split among them.

Application of Article 109(3)

No general conference to review the Charter having been held prior to the tenth session of the General Assembly, the question of calling such a conference was automatically placed on the agenda of that session as required by Article 109(3). During the previous few years, there had been considerable discussion in both official and unofficial circles concerning the desirability of "reviewing" or "revising" the Charter. The General Assembly itself at its eighth session (1953) considered the matter of preparatory work for the possible holding of a general review conference and requested the Secretariat to undertake certain studies concerning the legislative history of the Charter and the practices of United Nations organs.[24] The caution with which many members approached the holding of a conference and the desire to avoid any prejudging of the decision to be taken at the tenth session were demonstrated by the lack of support given to other proposals to invite members to submit their views on the Charter and to establish a special committee to assist in the preparatory work by preparing and circulating a questionnaire to members.[25]

The leading advocate of convening a general review conference was the United States Secretary of State, John Foster Dulles, in whose view the Charter was a "pre-atomic" document. For the United States, it was "a matter of simple fulfillment of an obligation to lend its full support" to the calling of a Charter review conference.[26] The frequent references by United States spokesmen to "obligations" in connection with a review conference should be understood as expressions of the view that the United States considered itself morally obliged to support a conference. The terms of Article 109(3) make it very clear that the Assembly was under no obligation to call a conference but merely to place the matter on the agenda of its tenth session.

The debate at the tenth session revealed little enthusiasm for a review conference. Given the negative attitude of the Soviet Union and its ability to block any amendments to the Charter, it was scarcely likely that a conference would be fruitful. Moreover, greatly encouraged by signs of improvement in the relations between the Soviet Union and the West during the few years preceding the debate on a

[24] GA Res. 796(VIII), Nov. 27, 1953.
[25] For the debate, see GAOR/8th Sess., 6th Ctte./371st–380th Mtgs./Oct. 19–Nov. 4, 1953/pp. 55–105.
[26] GAOR/10th Sess./542d Plen. Mtg./Nov. 17, 1955/para. 45.

Charter review conference, many members were reluctant to give support to an undertaking that might hinder this development in any way.[27]

The course the Assembly decided upon was in effect a compromise, which like most compromises left a number of issues unsettled. The Assembly expressed the view that it would be "desirable to review the Charter in the light of experience gained in its operation," but that such a review "should be conducted under auspicious international circumstances." Thus, the resolution merely stated that "a general Conference . . . shall be held at an appropriate time." [28] A committee of the whole was established to consider "in consultation with the Secretary-General the question of fixing a time and place for the Conference, and its organization and procedure." Subsequently, the Security Council expressed "its concurrence with the Assembly's decision." [29]

Although the Assembly's resolution was adopted by a substantial majority (43 to 6 with 9 abstentions), the propriety of its actions was questioned.[30] Article 109(3), it was pointed out, conferred on the tenth session the special privilege of deciding to call a general conference by a majority vote. By failing to fix a time and place for the conference, the Assembly was in effect postponing an essential part of the decision. It was argued that the tenth session of the Assembly could not bind a future session or transfer its special authority to it. The propriety of the Assembly's entrusting to a committee the question of the time, place, organization, and procedure of the conference was also questioned. The Charter merely authorized the tenth session of the Assembly to call a conference; it made no provision for any procedure such as the Assembly was taking. Moreover, what vote would be required at a future Assembly session for the fixing of a time and place for the conference? Only the tenth session was authorized to act by majority vote. If a two-thirds vote were necessary, then there was little point in the Assembly's taking any action at the tenth session, since the Assembly could at any time call a conference under the terms of Article 109(1). A somewhat related point was raised in the Security Council as to whether a further vote by the Council would be needed when the question of actually convening the conference arose. For the most part, these various questions remained unanswered.

[27] For the debate, see GAOR/10th Sess./542d–547th Plen. Mtgs./Nov. 17–21, 1955/pp. 296–370.

[28] GA Res. 992(X), Nov. 21, 1955.

[29] SCOR/10th Yr./707th Mtg./Dec. 16, 1955/pp. 66 ff. The Soviet Union voted against; France abstained.

[30] See, in particular, statements made during the Assembly debate by Sweden, Yugoslavia, Pakistan, and Norway. GAOR/10th Sess./542d–547th Plen. Mtgs./Nov. 17–21, 1955/pp. 315, 325, 337, and 347.

CHAPTER XIX

Ratification and Signature

Article 110

1. The present Charter shall be ratified by the signatory states in accordance with their respective constitutional processes.

2. The ratifications shall be deposited with the Government of the United States of America, which shall notify all the signatory states of each deposit as well as the Secretary-General of the Organization when he has been appointed.

3. The present Charter shall come into force upon the deposit of ratifications by the Republic of China, France, the Union of Soviet Socialist Republics, the United Kingdom of Great Britain and Northern Ireland, and the United States of America, and by a majority of the other signatory states. A protocol of the ratifications deposited shall thereupon be drawn up by the Government of the United States of America which shall communicate copies thereof to all the signatory states.

4. The states signatory to the present Charter which ratify it after it has come into force will become original Members of the United Nations on the date of the deposit of their respective ratifications.

Ratification is the act by which the proper authority of the state sanctions an international agreement. The procedure is determined by the constitution of each state. The Charter expressly recognizes this. In the United States, for example, the ratification of all treaties is an executive act requiring approval by a two-thirds vote of the Senate.

The provisions concerning ratification of the Charter were adopted at San Francisco with little difficulty; the main question concerned how many states would have to deposit their ratifications before the Charter came into force. It was agreed that ratification by all five permanent members of the Security Council would be required. The desire to avoid delay in establishing the new Organization led to agreement that ratification by only a majority of the other states would be needed for the Charter to come into force.

President Truman urged swift ratification by the United States as a demonstration of support for the new Organization. Although the

United States was not the first to ratify the Charter (El Salvador, Nicaragua, and New Zealand preceded it), it was the first (August 8, 1945) to deposit its ratification. By October 22, four of the five permanent members of the Security Council and twenty additional states had done likewise. On October 24, with the deposit of ratifications by the Soviet Union, Byelorussian SSR, Ukrainian SSR, and Poland, the Charter came into force. In accordance with Article 110(3), a Protocol of Deposit of Ratification was signed by the Secretary of State of the United States on the same day.

Under Article 110(4), all the states that had signed the Charter became "original" members of the United Nations on the date of the deposit of their ratifications. At San Francisco, a "time limit" for ratifications had been suggested to stimulate early action, but the suggestion was turned down, partly because of the continued unsettled status of Poland, which all agreed should be permitted to sign and ratify the Charter and thus become an "original" member as soon as agreement was reached on a provisional government.[1]

It was not until December 27, 1945 (only two weeks before the opening of the first session of the Assembly) that the last of the "original" members (Belgium) deposited its ratification.

Article 111

The present Charter, of which the Chinese, French, Russian, English, and Spanish texts are equally authentic, shall remain deposited in the archives of the Government of the United States of America. Duly certified copies thereof shall be transmitted by that Government to the Governments of the other signatory states.

The League of Nations Covenant was drawn up in two languages. The two texts were declared to be equally authentic. In practice, certain discrepancies were found to exist between them. The United Nations Charter was drafted and signed in five languages. This article declares that the five texts are equally authentic. Considering the great pressure under which the work of translation was done in the closing days of the San Francisco Conference, as well as the inevitable difficulty of expressing identical meanings in different languages, it is indeed surprising that organs of the United Nations have not found it necessary to take decisions involving the interpretation and application of this article.

The Permanent Court of International Justice, in the Mavrommatis Case,[2] took the view that where there is more than one language text,

[1] See commentary on Art. 3.
[2] PCIJ, Series A, No. 2, p. 19.

RATIFICATION OF THE CHARTER

	Date Ratified	*Ratification Deposited*
Argentina	8 September	24 September
Australia	4 October	1 November
Belgium	19 December	27 December
Bolivia	17 October	14 November
Brazil	8 September	21 September
Byelorussian SSR	30 August	24 October
Canada	1 November	9 November
Chile	18 September	11 October
China	24 August	28 September
Colombia	24 October	5 November
Costa Rica	9 August	2 November
Cuba	13 October	15 October
Czechoslovakia	19 September	19 October
Denmark	11 September	9 October
Dominican Republic	24 August	4 September
Ecuador	14 December	21 December
Egypt	13 October	22 October
El Salvador	12 July	26 September
Ethiopia	11 October	13 November
France	14 August	31 August
Greece	28 September	25 October
Guatemala	15 October	21 November
Haiti	17 August	27 September
Honduras	13 December	17 December
India	18 October	30 October
Iran	23 September	16 October
Iraq	1 November	21 December
Lebanon	4 September	15 October
Liberia	17 October	2 November
Luxembourg	11 September	17 October
Mexico	17 October	7 November
Netherlands	16 November	10 December
New Zealand	16 August	19 September
Nicaragua	6 July	6 September
Norway	16 November	27 November
Panama	27 October	13 November
Paraguay	28 September	12 October
Peru	15 October	31 October
Philippines	21 September	11 October
Poland	16 October	24 October
Saudi Arabia	30 September	18 October
Syria	30 August	19 October
Turkey	24 August	28 September
Ukrainian SSR	22 August	24 October
Union of South Africa	19 October	7 November
Union of Soviet Socialist Republics	20 August	24 October
United Kingdom	20 September	20 October
United States	8 August	8 August
Uruguay	15 December	18 December
Venezuela	2 November	15 November
Yugoslavia	24 August	19 October

each possessing equal authority, and it is found that the different texts do not exactly correspond, the most restricted interpretation, that is to say, the one which can be made to harmonize with all the others, should be adopted.

This conclusion, however, would not seem entirely satisfactory in so far as the Charter is concerned. Though the five texts of the Charter are equally authentic, the languages in which the work of drafting was done were English and French. Accordingly, in the interpretation of the Charter, it would seem that more weight should be attached to the English and French texts and, in the event of any discrepancy between these two texts, the interpretation most likely to be correct would be that based on the language text which was originally adopted. It must of course be recognized that this method is, strictly speaking, inconsistent with the formal equality of all the official languages; but it is also a recognized principle of treaty interpretation that where the meaning of a treaty provision is not clear, resort may be had to the *travaux préparatoires* for the purpose of determining the intention of the parties. Considering that the English text of the Charter was the one first completed and that the other language texts were prepared from it, there would appear to be sound reasons for giving special weight to the English text in case of conflict.[3]

[3] This method of interpretation is not inconsistent with the views of the PCIJ and has been to some extent adopted by it. See, in particular, PCIJ, Series A/B, No. 50, p. 379.

IN FAITH WHEREOF the representatives of the Governments of the United Nations have signed the present Charter.

DONE at the city of San Francisco the twenty-sixth day of June, one thousand nine hundred and forty-five.

APPENDIX

Documents

COVENANT OF THE LEAGUE OF NATIONS [1]

THE HIGH CONTRACTING PARTIES,

In order to promote international cooperation and to achieve international peace and security

by the acceptance of obligations not to resort to war,

by the prescription of open, just and honorable relations between nations,

by the firm establishment of the understandings of international law as the actual rule of conduct among Governments, and

by the maintenance of justice and a scrupulous respect for all treaty obligations in the dealings of organized peoples with one another,

Agree to this Covenant of the League of Nations.

Article 1
MEMBERSHIP AND WITHDRAWAL

1. The original Members of the League of Nations shall be those of the Signatories which are named in the Annex to this Covenant and also such of those other States named in the Annex as shall accede without reservation to this Covenant. Such accessions shall be effected by a declaration deposited with the Secretariat within two months of the coming into force of the Covenant. Notice thereof shall be sent to all other Members of the League.

2. Any fully self-governing State, Dominion or Colony not named in the Annex may become a Member of the League if its admission is agreed to by two-thirds of the Assembly, provided that it shall give effective guaranties of its sincere intention to observe its international obligations, and shall accept such regulations as may be prescribed by the League in regard to its military, naval and air forces and armaments.

3. Any Member of the League may, after two years' notice of its intention so to do, withdraw from the League, provided that all its international obligations and all its obligations under this Covenant shall have been fulfilled at the time of its withdrawal.

[1] Entered into force on Jan. 10, 1920. The texts printed in italics indicate amendments in force June 26, 1945. Article 6 as amended went into force Aug. 13, 1924; Articles 12, 13 and 15 as amended, Sept. 26, 1924; and Article 4 as amended, July 29, 1926.

Article 2
EXECUTIVE ORGANS

The action of the League under this Covenant shall be effected through the instrumentality of an Assembly and of a Council, with a permanent Secretariat.

Article 3
ASSEMBLY

1. The Assembly shall consist of representatives of the Members of the League.

2. The Assembly shall meet at stated intervals and from time to time, as occasion may require, at the Seat of the League or at such other place as may be decided upon.

3. The Assembly may deal at its meetings with any matter within the sphere of action of the League or affecting the peace of the world.

4. At meetings of the Assembly each Member of the League shall have one vote and may have not more than three Representatives.

Article 4
COUNCIL

1. The Council shall consist of representatives of the Principal Allied and Associated Powers [United States of America, the British Empire, France, Italy and Japan], together with Representatives of four other Members of the League. These four Members of the League shall be selected by the Assembly from time to time in its discretion. Until the appointment of the Representatives of the four Members of the League first selected by the Assembly, Representatives of Belgium, Brazil, Greece and Spain shall be Members of the Council.

2. With the approval of the majority of the Assembly, the Council may name additional Members of the League, whose Representatives shall always be Members of the Council; the Council with like approval may increase the number of Members of the League to be selected by the Assembly for representation on the Council.

2. *bis. The Assembly shall fix by a two-thirds' majority the rules dealing with the election of the non-permanent Members of the Council, and particularly such regulations as relate to their term of office and the conditions of re-eligibility.*

3. The Council shall meet from time to time as occasion may require, and at least once a year, at the Seat of the League, or at such other place as may be decided upon.

4. The Council may deal at its meetings with any matter within the sphere of action of the League or affecting the peace of the world.

5. Any Member of the League not represented on the Council shall be invited to send a Representative to sit as a member at any meeting of the Council during the consideration of matters specially affecting the interests of that Member of the League.

6. At meetings of the Council, each Member of the League represented

on the Council shall have one vote, and may have not more than one representative.

Article 5
VOTING AND PROCEDURE

1. Except where otherwise expressly provided in this Covenant or by the terms of the present Treaty, decisions at any meeting of the Assembly or of the Council shall require the agreement of all the Members of the League represented at the meeting.

2. All matters of procedure at meetings of the Assembly or of the Council, including the appointment of Committees to investigate particular matters, shall be regulated by the Assembly or by the Council and may be decided by a majority of the Members of the League represented at the meeting.

3. The first meeting of the Assembly and the first meeting of the Council shall be summoned by the President of the United States of America.

Article 6
SECRETARIAT AND EXPENSES

1. The permanent Secretariat shall be established at the Seat of the League. The Secretariat shall comprise a Secretary-General and such secretaries and staffs as may be required.

2. The first Secretary-General shall be the person named in the Annex; thereafter the Secretary-General shall be appointed by the Council with the approval of the majority of the Assembly.

3. The secretaries and the staff of the Secretariat shall be appointed by the Secretary-General with the approval of the Council.

4. The Secretary-General shall act in that capacity at all meetings of the Assembly and of the Council.

5. *The expenses of the League shall be borne by the Members of the League in the proportion decided by the Assembly.*

Article 7
SEAT, QUALIFICATIONS OF OFFICIALS, IMMUNITIES

1. The Seat of the League is established at Geneva.

2. The Council may at any time decide that the Seat of the League shall shall be established elsewhere.

3. All positions under or in connection with the League, including the Secretariat, shall be open equally to men and women.

4. Representatives of the Members of the League and officials of the League when engaged on the business of the League shall enjoy diplomatic privileges and immunities.

5. The buildings and other property occupied by the League or its officials or by Representatives attending its meetings shall be inviolable.

Article 8
REDUCTION OF ARMAMENTS

1. The Members of the League recognize that the maintenance of peace requires the reduction of national armaments to the lowest point consistent

with national safety and the enforcement by common action of international obligations.

2. The Council, taking account of the geographical situation and circumstances of each State, shall formulate plans for such reduction for the consideration and action of the several Governments.

3. Such plans shall be subject to reconsideration and revision at least every 10 years.

4. After these plans shall have been adopted by the several Governments, the limits of armaments therein fixed shall not be exceeded without the concurrence of the Council.

5. The Members of the League agree that the manufacture by private enterprise of munitions and implements of war is open to grave objections. The Council shall advise how the evil effects attendant upon such manufacture can be prevented, due regard being had to the necessities of those Members of the League which are not able to manufacture the munitions and implements of war necessary for their safety.

6. The Members of the League undertake to interchange full and frank information as to the scale of their armaments, their military, naval and air programs and the condition of such of their industries as are adaptable to warlike purposes.

Article 9
PERMANENT MILITARY, NAVAL AND AIR COMMISSION

A permanent Commission shall be constituted to advise the Council on the execution of the provisions of Articles 1 and 8 and on military, naval and air questions generally.

Article 10
GUARANTIES AGAINST AGGRESSION

The Members of the League undertake to respect and preserve as against external aggression the territorial integrity and existing political independence of all Members of the League. In case of any such aggression or in case of any threat or danger of such aggression the Council shall advise upon the means by which this obligation shall be fulfilled.

Article 11
ACTION IN CASE OF WAR OR THREAT OF WAR

1. Any war or threat of war, whether immediately affecting any of the Members of the League or not, is hereby declared a matter of concern to the whole League, and the League shall take any action that may be deemed wise and effectual to safeguard the peace of nations. In case any such emergency should arise the Secretary-General shall on the request of any Member of the League forthwith summon a meeting of the Council.

2. It is also declared to be the friendly right of each Member of the League to bring to the attention of the Assembly or of the Council any circumstance whatever affecting international relations which threatens to

disturb international peace or the good understanding between nations upon which peace depends.

Article 12
DISPUTES TO BE SUBMITTED FOR SETTLEMENT

1. The Members of the League agree that, if there should arise between them any dispute likely to lead to a rupture, they will submit the matter either to arbitration *or judicial settlement* or to inquiry by the Council, and they agree in no case to resort to war until three months after the award by the arbitrators *or the judicial decision,* or the report by the Council.

2. In any case under this Article the award of the arbitrators *or the judicial decision* shall be made within a reasonable time, and the report of the Council shall be made within six months after the submission of the dispute.

Article 13
ARBITRATION OR JUDICIAL SETTLEMENT

1. The Members of the League agree that, whenever any dispute shall arise between them which they recognize to be suitable for submission to arbitration *or judicial settlement,* and which can not be satisfactorily settled by diplomacy, they will submit the whole subject-matter to arbitration *or judicial settlement.*

2. Disputes as to the interpretation of a treaty, as to any question of international law, as to the existence of any fact which, if established, would constitute a breach of any international obligation, or as to the extent and nature of the reparation to be made for any such breach, are declared to be among those which are generally suitable for submission to arbitration *or judicial settlement.*

3. *For the consideration of any such dispute, the court to which the case is referred shall be the Permanent Court of International Justice, established in accordance with Article 14, or any tribunal agreed on by the parties to the dispute or stipulated in any convention existing between them.*

4. The Members of the League agree that they will carry out in full good faith any award *or decision* that may be rendered, and that they will not resort to war against a Member of the League which complies therewith. In the event of any failure to carry out such an award *or decision,* the Council shall propose what steps should be taken to give effect thereto.

Article 14
PERMANENT COURT OF INTERNATIONAL JUSTICE

The Council shall formulate and submit to the Members of the League for adoption plans for the establishment of a Permanent Court of International Justice. The Court shall be competent to hear and determine any dispute of an international character which the parties thereto submit to it. The Court may also give an advisory opinion upon any dispute or question referred to it by the Council or by the Assembly.

Article 15
DISPUTES NOT SUBMITTED TO ARBITRATION OR JUDICIAL SETTLEMENT

1. If there should arise between Members of the League any dispute likely to lead to a rupture, which is not submitted to arbitration *or judicial settlement* in accordance with Article 13, the Members of the League agree that they will submit the matter to the Council. Any party to the dispute may effect such submission by giving notice of the existence of the dispute to the Secretary-General, who will make all necessary arrangements for a full investigation and consideration thereof.

2. For this purpose the parties to the dispute will communicate to the Secretary-General, as promptly as possible, statements of their case with all the relevant facts and papers, and the Council may forthwith direct the publication thereof.

3. The Council shall endeavor to effect a settlement of the dispute, and, if such efforts are successful, a statement shall be made public giving such facts and explanations regarding the dispute and the terms of settlement thereof as the Council may deem appropriate.

4. If the dispute is not thus settled, the Council either unanimously or by a majority vote shall make and publish a report containing a statement of the facts of the dispute and the recommendations which are deemed just and proper in regard thereto.

5. Any member of the League represented on the Council may make public a statement of the facts of the dispute and of its conclusions regarding the same.

6. If a report by the Council is unanimously agreed to by the Members thereof other than the Representatives of one or more of the parties to the dispute, the Members of the League agree that they will not go to war with any party to the dispute which complies with the recommendations of the report.

7. If the Council fails to reach a report which is unanimously agreed to by the members thereof, other than the Representatives of one or more of the parties to the dispute, the Members of the League reserve to themselves the right to take such action as they shall consider necessary for the maintenance of right and justice.

8. If the dispute between the parties is claimed by one of them, and is found by the Council, to arise out of a matter which by international law is solely within the domestic jurisdiction of that party, the Council shall so report, and shall make no recommendation as to its settlement.

9. The Council may in any case under this Article refer the dispute to the Assembly. The dispute shall be so referred at the request of either party to the dispute, provided that such request be made within 14 days after the submission of the dispute to the Council.

10. In any case referred to the Assembly, all the provisions of this Article and of Article 12 relating to the action and powers of the Council shall apply to the action and powers of the Assembly, provided that a report made by the Assembly, if concurred in by the Representatives of those Members of the League represented on the Council and of a majority of

the other Members of the League, exclusive in each case of the Representatives of the parties to the dispute, shall have the same force as a report by the Council concurred in by all the members thereof other than the Representatives of one or more of the parties to the dispute.

Article 16
SANCTIONS OF PACIFIC SETTLEMENT

1. Should any Member of the League resort to war in disregard of its covenants under Articles 12, 13 or 15, it shall *ipso facto* be deemed to have committed an act of war against all other Members of the League, which hereby undertake immediately to subject it to the severance of all trade or financial relations, the prohibition of all intercourse between their nationals and the nationals of the covenant-breaking State, and the prevention of all financial, commercial or personal intercourse between the nationals of the covenant-breaking State and the nationals of any other State, whether a Member of the League or not.

2. It shall be the duty of the Council in such case to recommend to the several Governments concerned what effective military, naval or air force the Members of the League shall severally contribute to the armed forces to be used to protect the covenants of the League.

3. The Members of the League agree, further, that they will mutually support one another in the financial and economic measures which are taken under this Article, in order to minimize the loss and inconvenience resulting from the above measures, and that they will mutually support one another in resisting any special measures aimed at one of their number by the covenant-breaking State, and that they will take the necessary steps to afford passage through their territory to the forces of any of the Members of the League which are cooperating to protect the covenants of the League.

4. Any Member of the League which has violated any covenant of the League may be declared to be no longer a Member of the League by a vote of the Council concurred in by the Representatives of all the other Members of the League represented thereon.

Article 17
DISPUTES INVOLVING NON-MEMBERS

1. In the event of a dispute between a Member of the League and a State which is not a Member of the League, or between States not Members of the League, the State or States not Members of the League shall be invited to accept the obligations of membership in the League for the purposes of such dispute, upon such conditions as the Council may deem just. If such invitation is accepted, the provisions of Articles 12 to 16, inclusive, shall be applied with such modifications as may be deemed necessary by the Council.

2. Upon such invitation being given, the Council shall immediately institute an inquiry into the circumstances of the dispute and recommend such action as may seem best and most effectual in the circumstances.

3. If a State so invited shall refuse to accept the obligations of mem-

bership in the League for the purposes of such dispute, and shall resort to war against a Member of the League, the provisions of Article 16 shall be applicable as against the State taking such action.

4. If both parties to the dispute when so invited refuse to accept the obligations of membership in the League for the purposes of such dispute, the Council may take such measures and make such recommendations as will prevent hostilities and will result in the settlement of the dispute.

Article 18
REGISTRATION AND PUBLICATION OF TREATIES

Every treaty or international engagement entered into hereafter by any Member of the League shall be forthwith registered with the Secretariat and shall as soon as possible be published by it. No such treaty or international engagement shall be binding until so registered.

Article 19
REVIEW OF TREATIES

The Assembly may from time to time advise the reconsideration by Members of the League of treaties which have become inapplicable, and the consideration of international conditions whose continuance might endanger the peace of the world.

Article 20
ABROGATION OF INCONSISTENT OBLIGATIONS

1. The Members of the League severally agree that this Covenant is accepted as abrogating all obligations or understandings *inter se* which are inconsistent with the terms thereof, and solemnly undertake that they will not hereafter enter into any engagements inconsistent with the terms thereof.

2. In case any Member of the League shall, before becoming a Member of the League, have undertaken any obligations inconsistent with the terms of this Covenant, it shall be the duty of such Member to take immediate steps to procure its release from such obligations.

Article 21
ENGAGEMENTS THAT REMAIN VALID

Nothing in this Covenant shall be deemed to affect the validity of international engagements, such as treaties of arbitration or regional understandings like the Monroe doctrine, for securing the maintenance of peace.

Article 22
MANDATORY SYSTEM

1. To those colonies and territories which as a consequence of the late war have ceased to be under the sovereignty of the States which formerly governed them and which are inhabited by peoples not yet able to stand by themselves under the strenuous conditions of the modern world, there should be applied the principle that the well-being and development of

such peoples form a sacred trust of civilization and that securities for the performance of this trust should be embodied in this Covenant.

2. The best method of giving practical effect to this principle is that the tutelage of such peoples should be intrusted to advanced nations who by reason of their resources, their experience or their geographical position can best undertake this responsibility, and who are willing to accept it, and that this tutelage should be exercised by them as Mandatories on behalf of the League.

3. The character of the mandate must differ according to the stage of the development of the people, the geographical situation of the territory, its economic conditions and other similar circumstances.

4. Certain communities formerly belonging to the Turkish Empire have reached a stage of development where their existence as independent nations can be provisionally recognized subject to the rendering of administrative advice and assistance by a Mandatory until such time as they are able to stand alone. The wishes of these communities must be a principal consideration in the selection of the Mandatory.

5. Other peoples, especially those of Central Africa, are at such a stage that the Mandatory must be responsible for the administration of the territory under conditions which will guarantee freedom of conscience and religion, subject only to the maintenance of public order and morals, the prohibition of abuses such as the slave trade, the arms traffic and the liquor traffic, and the prevention of the establishment of fortifications of military and naval bases and of military training of the natives for other than police purposes and the defense of territory, and will also secure equal opportunities for the trade and commerce of other Members of the League.

6. There are territories, such as Southwest Africa and certain of the South Pacific islands, which, owing to the sparseness of their population, or their small size, or their remoteness from the centers of civilization, or their geographical contiguity to the territory of the Mandatory, and other circumstances, can be best administered under the laws of the Mandatory as integral portions of its territory, subject to the safeguards above mentioned in the interests of the indigenous population.

7. In every case of mandate, the Mandatory shall render to the Council an annual report in reference to the territory committed to its charge.

8. The degree of authority, control or administration to be exercised by the Mandatory shall, if not previously agreed upon by the Members of the League, be explicitly defined in each case by the Council.

9. A permanent Commission shall be constituted to receive and examine the annual reports of the Mandatories and to advise the Council on all matters relating to the observance of the mandates.

Article 23
SOCIAL AND OTHER ACTIVITIES

Subject to and in accordance with the provisions of international conventions existing or hereafter to be agreed upon, the Members of the League:

(a) will endeavor to secure and maintain fair and humane conditions of labor for men, women and children, both in their own countries and in all countries to which their commercial and industrial relations extend, and for that purpose will establish and maintain the necessary international organizations;

(b) undertake to secure just treatment of the native inhabitants of territories under their control;

(c) will intrust the League with the general supervision over the execution of agreements with regard to traffic in women and children, and the traffic in opium and other dangerous drugs;

(d) will intrust the League with the general supervision of the trade in arms and ammunition with the countries in which the control of this traffic is necessary in the common interest;

(e) will make provision to secure and maintain freedom of communications and of transit and equitable treatment for the commerce of all Members of the League. In this connection, the special necessities of the regions devastated during the war of 1914–1918 shall be borne in mind;

(f) will endeavor to take steps in matters of international concern for the prevention and control of disease.

Article 24
INTERNATIONAL BUREAUS

1. There shall be placed under the direction of the League all international bureaus already established by general treaties if the parties to such treaties consent. All such international bureaus and all commissions for the regulation of matters of international interest hereafter constituted shall be placed under the direction of the League.

2. In all matters of international interest which are regulated by general conventions but which are not placed under the control of international bureaus or commissions, the Secretariat of the League shall, subject to the consent of the Council and if desired by the parties, collect and distribute all relevant information and shall render any other assistance which may be necessary or desirable.

3. The Council may include as part of the expenses of the Secretariat the expenses of any bureau or commission which is placed under the direction of the League.

Article 25
PROMOTION OF RED CROSS AND HEALTH

The Members of the League agree to encourage and promote the establishment and cooperation of duly authorized voluntary national Red Cross organizations having as purposes the improvement of health, the prevention of disease and the mitigation of suffering throughout the world.

Article 26
AMENDMENTS

1. Amendments to this Covenant will take effect when ratified by the Members of the League whose Representatives compose the Council and

by a majority of the Members of the League whose Representatives compose the Assembly.

2. No such amendment shall bind any Member of the League which signifies its dissent therefrom, but in that case it shall cease to be a Member of the League.

ANNEX

1. Original Members of the League of Nations, Signatories of the Treaty of Peace

*United States of America
Belgium
Bolivia
Brazil
British Empire
  Canada
  Australia
  South Africa
  New Zealand
  India
China
Cuba
†Ecuador
France
Greece
Guatemala
Haiti

*Hedjaz
Honduras
Italy
Japan
Liberia
Nicaragua
Panama
Peru
Poland
Portugal
Rumania
Serb-Croat-Slovene State [Yugoslavia]
Siam
Czechoslovakia
Uruguay

* Never accepted membership by ratification of treaty of peace.

† Did not accept membership by ratification of treaty of peace, but was admitted in 1934.

States Invited to Accede to the Covenant

Argentine Republic
Chile
Colombia
Denmark
Netherlands
Norway
Paraguay

Persia [now Iran]
Salvador
Spain
Sweden
Switzerland
Venezuela

2. First Secretary-General of the League of Nations, The Honorable Sir James Eric Drummond, K.C.M.G., C.B.

States Admitted to Membership

Afghanistan	Sept. 27, 1934	Egypt	May 26, 1937
Albania	Dec. 17, 1920	Estonia	Sept. 22, 1921
Austria	Dec. 15, 1920	Ethiopia	Sept. 28, 1923
Bulgaria	Dec. 16, 1920	Finland	Dec. 16, 1920
Costa Rica	Dec. 16, 1920	Germany	Sept. 8, 1926
Dominican Republic	Sept. 29, 1924	Hungary	Sept. 18, 1922
Ecuador	Sept. 28, 1934	Iraq	Oct. 3, 1932

Irish Free State	Sept. 10, 1923	Mexico	Sept. 12, 1931
Latvia	Sept. 22, 1921	Turkey	July 18, 1932
Lithuania	Sept. 22, 1921	Union of Soviet	
Luxembourg	Dec. 16, 1920	Socialist Republics	Sept. 18, 1934

WITHDRAWALS AND EXPULSIONS FROM MEMBERSHIP IN THE
LEAGUE OF NATIONS

Country	Notification of Withdrawal	Ceased to be a Member
Brazil	June 14, 1926	June 13, 1928
Chile	June 2, 1938	June 1, 1940
Costa Rica	Dec. 24, 1924	Jan. 1, 1927
Germany	Oct. 21, 1933	Oct. 20, 1935
Guatemala	May 26, 1936	May 25, 1938
Honduras	July 10, 1936	July 9, 1938
Hungary	Apr. 11, 1939	Apr. 10, 1941
Italy	Dec. 11, 1937	Dec. 10, 1939
Japan	Mar. 27, 1933	Mar. 26, 1935
Nicaragua	June 27, 1936	June 26, 1938
Paraguay	Feb. 24, 1937	Feb. 23, 1939
Peru	Apr. 9, 1939	Apr. 8, 1941
Rumania	July 11, 1940	July 10, 1942
Salvador	Aug. 10, 1937	Aug. 9, 1939
Spain	May 9, 1939	May 8, 1941
Union of Soviet Socialist Republics		Dec. 14, 1939
Venezuela	July 11, 1938	July 10, 1940

DUMBARTON OAKS PROPOSALS [2]

THERE SHOULD BE established an international organization under the title of The United Nations, the Charter of which should contain provisions necessary to give effect to the proposals which follow.

CHAPTER I. PURPOSES

The purposes of the Organization should be:

1. To maintain international peace and security; and to that end to take effective collective measures for the prevention and removal of threats to the peace and the suppression of acts of aggression or other breaches of the peace, and to bring about by peaceful means adjustment or settlement of international disputes which may lead to a breach of the peace;

2. To develop friendly relations among nations and to take other appropriate measures to strengthen universal peace;

3. To achieve international cooperation in the solution of international economic, social and other humanitarian problems; and

4. To afford a center for harmonizing the actions of nations in the achievement of these common ends.

CHAPTER II. PRINCIPLES

In pursuit of the purposes mentioned in Chapter I the Organization and its members should act in accordance with the following principles:

1. The Organization is based on the principle of the sovereign equality of all peace-loving states.

2. All members of the Organization undertake, in order to ensure to all of them the rights and benefits resulting from membership in the Organization, to fulfill the obligations assumed by them in accordance with the Charter.

3. All members of the Organization shall settle their disputes by peaceful means in such a manner that international peace and security are not endangered.

4. All members of the Organization shall refrain in their international

---

[2] Proposals for the establishment of a general international organization, Dumbarton Oaks, Washington, Oct. 7, 1944. State Dept., *Bulletin,* XI, 368. Ch. vi, sec. c was agreed upon at the Crimean Conference and subsequently included in the Proposals.

relations from the threat or use of force in any manner inconsistent with the purposes of the Organization.

5. All members of the Organization shall give every assistance to the Organization in any action undertaken by it in accordance with the provisions of the Charter.

6. All members of the Organization shall refrain from giving assistance to any state against which preventive or enforcement action is being undertaken by the Organization.

The Organization should ensure that states not members of the Organization act in accordance with these principles so far as may be necessary for the maintenance of international peace and security.

CHAPTER III. MEMBERSHIP

1. Membership of the Organization should be open to all peace-loving states.

CHAPTER IV. PRINCIPAL ORGANS

1. The Organization should have as its principal organs:
   a. A General Assembly;
   b. A Security Council;
   c. An international court of justice; and
   d. A Secretariat.

2. The Organization should have such subsidiary agencies as may be found necessary.

CHAPTER V. THE GENERAL ASSEMBLY

Section A. Composition. All members of the Organization should be members of the General Assembly and should have a number of representatives to be specified in the Charter.

Section B. Functions and Powers. 1. The General Assembly should have the right to consider the general principles of cooperation in the maintenance of international peace and security, including the principles governing disarmament and the regulation of armaments; to discuss any questions relating to the maintenance of international peace and security brought before it by any member or members of the Organization or by the Security Council; and to make recommendations with regard to any such principles or questions. Any such questions on which action is necessary should be referred to the Security Council by the General Assembly either before or after discussion. The General Assembly should not on its own initiative make recommendations on any matter relating to the maintenance of international peace and security which is being dealt with by the Security Council.

2. The General Assembly should be empowered to admit new members to the Organization upon recommendation of the Security Council.

3. The General Assembly should, upon recommendation of the Security Council, be empowered to suspend from the exercise of any rights or privileges of membership any member of the Organization against which preventive or enforcement action shall have been taken by the Security

Council. The exercise of the rights and privileges thus suspended may be restored by decision of the Security Council. The General Assembly should be empowered, upon recommendation of the Security Council, to expel from the Organization any member of the Organization which persistently violates the principles contained in the Charter.

4. The General Assembly should elect the non-permanent members of the Security Council and the members of the Economic and Social Council provided for in Chapter IX. It should be empowered to elect, upon recommendation of the Security Council, the Secretary-General of the Organization. It should perform such functions in relation to the election of the judges of the international court of justice as may be conferred upon it by the statute of the court.

5. The General Assembly should apportion the expenses among the members of the Organization and should be empowered to approve the budgets of the Organization.

6. The General Assembly should initiate studies and make recommendations for the purpose of promoting international cooperation in political, economic and social fields and of adjusting situations likely to impair the general welfare.

7. The General Assembly should make recommendations for the co-ordination of the policies of international economic, social, and other specialized agencies brought into relation with the Organization in accordance with agreements between such agencies and the Organization.

8. The General Assembly should receive and consider annual and special reports from the Security Council and reports from other bodies of the Organization.

Section C. Voting. 1. Each member of the Organization should have one vote in the General Assembly.

2. Important decisions of the General Assembly, including recommendations with respect to the maintenance of international peace and security; election of members of the Security Council; election of members of the Economic and Social Council; admission of members, suspension of the exercise of the rights and privileges of members, and expulsion of members; and budgetary questions, should be made by a two-thirds majority of those present and voting. On other questions, including the determination of additional categories of questions to be decided by a two-thirds majority, the decisions of the General Assembly should be made by a simple majority vote.

Section D. Procedure. 1. The General Assembly should meet in regular annual sessions and in such special sessions as occasion may require.

2. The General Assembly should adopt its own rules of procedure and elect its President for each session.

3. The General Assembly should be empowered to set up such bodies and agencies as it may deem necessary for the performance of its functions.

CHAPTER VI. THE SECURITY COUNCIL

Section A. Composition. The Security Council should consist of one representative of each of eleven members of the Organization. Representatives of the United States of America, the United Kingdom of Great Britain and Northern Ireland, the Union of Soviet Socialist Republics, the Republic of China, and, in due course, France, should have permanent seats. The General Assembly should elect six states to fill the non-permanent seats. These six states should be elected for a term of two years, three retiring each year. They should not be immediately eligible for re-election. In the first election of the non-permanent members three should be chosen by the General Assembly for one-year terms and three for two-year terms.

Section B. Principal Functions and Powers. 1. In order to ensure prompt and effective action by the Organization, members of the Organization should by the Charter confer on the Security Council primary responsibility for the maintenance of international peace and security and should agree that in carrying out these duties under this responsibility it should act on their behalf.

2. In discharging these duties the Security Council should act in accordance with the purposes and principles of the Organization.

3. The specific powers conferred on the Security Council in order to carry out these duties are laid down in Chapter VIII.

4. All members of the Organization should obligate themselves to accept the decisions of the Security Council and to carry them out in accordance with the provisions of the Charter.

5. In order to promote the establishment and maintenance of international peace and security with the least diversion of the world's human and economic resources for armaments, the Security Council, with the assistance of the Military Staff Committee referred to in Chapter VIII, Section B, paragraph 9, should have the responsibility for formulating plans for the establishment of a system of regulation of armaments for submission to the members of the Organization.

[*Section C. Voting.* 1. Each member of the Security Council should have one vote.

2. Decisions of the Security Council on procedural matters should be made by an affirmative vote of seven members.

3. Decisions of the Security Council on all other matters should be made by an affirmative vote of seven members including the concurring votes of the permanent members; provided that, in decisions under Chapter VIII, Section A, and under the second sentence of paragraph 1 of Chapter VIII, Section C, a party to a dispute should abstain from voting.]

Section D. Procedure. 1. The Security Council should be so organized as to be able to function continuously and each state member of the Security Council should be permanently represented at the headquarters of the Organization. It may hold meetings at such other places as in its judgment may best facilitate its work. There should be periodic meetings at which each state member of the Security Council could if it so desired be represented by a member of the government or some other special representative.

2. The Security Council should be empowered to set up such bodies or agencies as it may deem necessary for the performance of its functions including regional subcommittees of the Military Staff Committee.

3. The Security Council should adopt its own rules of procedure, including the method of selecting its President.

4. Any member of the Organization should participate in the discussion of any question brought before the Security Council whenever the Security Council considers that the interests of that member of the Organization are specially affected.

5. Any member of the Organization not having a seat on the Security Council and any state not a member of the Organization, if it is a party to a dispute under consideration by the Security Council, should be invited to participate in the discussion relating to the dispute.

CHAPTER VII. AN INTERNATIONAL COURT OF JUSTICE

1. There should be an international court of justice which should constitute the principal judicial organ of the Organization.

2. The court should be constituted and should function in accordance with a statute which should be annexed to and be a part of the Charter of the Organization.

3. The statute of the court of international justice should be either (a) the Statute of the Permanent Court of International Justice, continued in force with such modifications as may be desirable, or (b) a new statute in the preparation of which the Statute of the Permanent Court of International Justice should be used as a basis.

4. All members of the Organization should *ipso facto* be parties to the statute of the international court of justice.

5. Conditions under which states not members of the Organization may become parties to the statute of the international court of justice should be determined in each case by the General Assembly upon recommendation of the Security Council.

CHAPTER VIII. ARRANGEMENTS FOR THE MAINTENANCE OF INTERNATIONAL PEACE AND SECURITY INCLUDING PREVENTION AND SUPPRESSION OF AGGRESSION

Section A. Pacific Settlement of Disputes. 1. The Security Council should be empowered to investigate any dispute, or any situation which may lead to international friction or give rise to a dispute, in order to determine whether its continuance is likely to endanger the maintenance of international peace and security.

2. Any state, whether member of the Organization or not, may bring any such dispute or situation to the attention of the General Assembly or of the Security Council.

3. The parties to any dispute the continuance of which is likely to endanger the maintenance of international peace and security should obligate themselves, first of all, to seek a solution by negotiation, mediation, conciliation, arbitration or judicial settlement, or other peaceful means of their own choice. The Security Council should call upon the parties to settle their dispute by such means.

4. If, nevertheless, parties to a dispute of the nature referred to in para-

graph 3 above fail to settle it by the means indicated in that paragraph, they should obligate themselves to refer it to the Security Council. The Security Council should in each case decide whether or not the continuance of the particular dispute is in fact likely to endanger the maintenance of international peace and security, and, accordingly, whether the Security Council should deal with the dispute, and, if so, whether it should take action under paragraph 5.

5. The Security Council should be empowered, at any stage of a dispute of the nature referred to in paragraph 3 above, to recommend appropriate procedures or methods of adjustment.

6. Justiciable disputes should normally be referred to the international court of justice. The Security Council should be empowered to refer to the court, for advice, legal questions connected with other disputes.

7. The provisions of paragraphs 1 to 6 of Section A should not apply to situations or disputes arising out of matters which by international law are solely within the domestic jurisdiction of the state concerned.

Section B. Determination of Threats to the Peace or Acts of Aggression and Action With Respect Thereto. 1. Should the Security Council deem that a failure to settle a dispute in accordance with procedures indicated in paragraph 3 of Section A, or in accordance with its recommendations made under paragraph 5 of Section A, constitutes a threat to the maintenance of international peace and security, it should take any measures necessary for the maintenance of international peace and security in accordance with the purposes and principles of the Organization.

2. In general the Security Council should determine the existence of any threat to the peace, breach of the peace or act of aggression and should make recommendations or decide upon the measures to be taken to maintain or restore peace and security.

3. The Security Council should be empowered to determine what diplomatic, economic, or other measures not involving the use of armed force should be employed to give effect to its decisions, and to call upon members of the Organization to apply such measures. Such measures may include complete or partial interruption of rail, sea, air, postal, telegraphic, radio and other means of communication and the severance of diplomatic and economic relations.

4. Should the Security Council consider such measures to be inadequate, it should be empowered to take such action by air, naval or land forces as may be necessary to maintain or restore international peace and security. Such action may include demonstrations, blockade and other operations by air, sea or land forces of members of the Organization.

5. In order that all members of the Organization should contribute to the maintenance of international peace and security, they should undertake to make available to the Security Council, on its call and in accordance with a special agreement or agreements concluded among themselves, armed forces, facilities and assistance necessary for the purpose of maintaining international peace and security. Such agreement or agreements should govern the numbers and types of forces and the nature of the facilities and

assistance to be provided. The special agreement or agreements should be negotiated as soon as possible and should in each case be subject to approval by the Security Council and to ratification by the signatory states in accordance with their constitutional processes.

6. In order to enable urgent military measures to be taken by the Organization there should be held immediately available by the members of the Organization national air force contingents for combined international enforcement action. The strength and degree of readiness of these contingents and plans for their combined action should be determined by the Security Council with the assistance of the Military Staff Committee within the limits laid down in the special agreement or agreements referred to in paragraph 5 above.

7. The action required to carry out the decisions of the Security Council for the maintenance of international peace and security should be taken by all the members of the Organization in cooperation or by some of them as the Security Council may determine. This undertaking should be carried out by the members of the Organization by their own action and through action of the appropriate specialized organizations and agencies of which they are members.

8. Plans for the application of armed force should be made by the Security Council with the assistance of the Military Staff Committee referred to in paragraph 9 below.

9. There should be established a Military Staff Committee the functions of which should be to advise and assist the Security Council on all questions relating to the Security Council's military requirements for the maintenance of international peace and security, to the employment and command of forces placed at its disposal, to the regulation of armaments, and to possible disarmament. It should be responsible under the Security Council for the strategic direction of any armed forces placed at the disposal of the Security Council. The Committee should be composed of the Chiefs of Staff of the permanent members of the Security Council or their representatives. Any member of the Organization not permanently represented on the Committee should be invited by the Committee to be associated with it when the efficient discharge of the Committee's responsibilities requires that such a state should participate in its work. Questions of command of forces should be worked out subsequently.

10. The members of the Organization should join in affording mutual assistance in carrying out the measures decided upon by the Security Council.

11. Any state, whether a member of the Organization or not, which finds itself confronted with special economic problems arising from the carrying out of measures which have been decided upon by the Security Council should have the right to consult the Security Council in regard to a solution of those problems.

Section C. Regional Arrangements. 1. Nothing in the Charter should preclude the existence of regional arrangements or agencies for dealing with such matters relating to the maintenance of international peace and security as are appropriate for regional action, provided such arrangements or agencies and their activities are consistent with the purposes and principles of the Organization. The Security Council should encourage settlement of local disputes through such regional arrangements or by such regional agencies, either on the initiative of the states concerned or by reference from the Security Council.

2. The Security Council should, where appropriate, utilize such arrangements or agencies for enforcement action under its authority, but no enforcement action should be taken under regional arrangements or by regional agencies without the authorization of the Security Council.

3. The Security Council should at all times be kept fully informed of activities undertaken or in contemplation under regional arrangements or by regional agencies for the maintenance of international peace and security.

CHAPTER IX. ARRANGEMENTS FOR INTERNATIONAL ECONOMIC AND SOCIAL COOPERATION

Section A. Purpose and Relationships. 1. With a view to the creation of conditions of stability and well-being which are necessary for peaceful and friendly relations among nations, the Organization should facilitate solutions of international economic, social and other humanitarian problems and promote respect for human rights and fundamental freedoms. Responsibility for the discharge of this function should be vested in the General Assembly and, under the authority of the General Assembly, in an Economic and Social Council.

2. The various specialized economic, social and other organizations and agencies would have responsibilities in their respective fields as defined in their statutes. Each such organization or agency should be brought into relationship with the Organization on terms to be determined by agreement between the Economic and Social Council and the appropriate authorities of the specialized organization or agency, subject to approval by the General Assembly.

Section B. Composition and Voting. The Economic and Social Council should consist of representatives of eighteen members of the Organization. The states to be represented for this purpose should be elected by the General Assembly for terms of three years. Each such state should have one representative, who should have one vote. Decisions of the Economic and Social Council should be taken by simple majority vote of those present and voting.

Section C. Functions and Powers of the Economic and Social Council. 1. The Economic and Social Council should be empowered:

a. to carry out, within the scope of its functions, recommendations of the General Assembly;

b. to make recommendations, on its own initiative, with respect to international economic, social and other humanitarian matters;

c. to receive and consider reports from the economic, social and other organizations or agencies brought into relationship with the Organization, and to coordinate their activities through consultations with, and recommendations to, such organizations or agencies;

d. to examine the administrative budgets of such specialized organizations or agencies with a view to making recommendations to the organizations or agencies concerned;

e. to enable the Secretary-General to provide information to the Security Council;

f. to assist the Security Council upon its request; and

g. to perform such other functions within the general scope of its competence as may be assigned to it by the General Assembly.

Section D. Organization and Procedure. 1. The Economic and Social Council should set up an economic commission, a social commission, and such other commissions as may be required. These commissions should consist of experts. There should be a permanent staff which should constitute a part of the Secretariat of the Organization.

2. The Economic and Social Council should make suitable arrangements for representatives of the specialized organizations or agencies to participate without vote in its deliberations and in those of the commissions established by it.

3. The Economic and Social Council should adopt its own rules of procedure and the method of selecting its President.

CHAPTER X. THE SECRETARIAT

1. There should be a Secretariat comprising a Secretary-General and such staff as may be required. The Secretary-General should be the chief administrative officer of the Organization. He should be elected by the General Assembly, on recommendation of the Security Council, for such term and under such conditions as are specified in the Charter.

2. The Secretary-General should act in that capacity in all meetings of the General Assembly, of the Security Council, and of the Economic and Social Council and should make an annual report to the General Assembly on the work of the Organization.

3. The Secretary-General should have the right to bring to the attention of the Security Council any matter which in his opinion may threaten international peace and security.

CHAPTER XI. AMENDMENTS

Amendments should come into force for all members of the Organization, when they have been adopted by a vote of two-thirds of the members of the General Assembly and ratified in accordance with their respective constitutional processes by the members of the Organization having permanent membership on the Security Council and by a majority of the other members of the Organization.

CHAPTER XII. TRANSITIONAL ARRANGEMENTS

1. Pending the coming into force of the special agreement or agreements referred to in Chapter VIII, Section B, paragraph 5, and in accordance

with the provisions of paragraph 5 of the Four-Nation Declaration, signed at Moscow, October 30, 1943, the states parties to that Declaration should consult with one another and as occasion arises with other members of the Organization with a view to such joint action on behalf of the Organization as may be necessary for the purpose of maintaining international peace and security.

2. No provision of the Charter should preclude action taken or authorized in relation to enemy states as a result of the present war by the Governments having responsibility for such action.

NOTE

In addition to the question of voting procedure in the Security Council referred to in Chapter VI, several other questions are still under consideration.

CHARTER OF THE UNITED NATIONS [3]

WE THE PEOPLES OF THE UNITED NATIONS DETERMINED
to save succeeding generations from the scourge of war, which twice
in our lifetime has brought untold sorrow to mankind, and

to reaffirm faith in fundamental human rights, in the dignity and worth
of the human person, in the equal rights of men and women and of
nations large and small, and

to establish conditions under which justice and respect for the obligations arising from treaties and other sources of international law can
be maintained, and

to promote social progress and better standards of life in larger freedom,

AND FOR THESE ENDS
to practice tolerance and live together in peace with one another as
good neighbors, and

to unite our strength to maintain international peace and security, and

to ensure, by the acceptance of principles and the institution of methods,
that armed force shall not be used, save in the common interest, and

to employ international machinery for the promotion of the economic
and social advancement of all peoples,

HAVE RESOLVED TO COMBINE OUR EFFORTS TO ACCOMPLISH
THESE AIMS.

Accordingly, our respective Governments, through representatives assembled in the city of San Francisco, who have exhibited their full powers
found to be in good and due form, have agreed to the present Charter of
the United Nations and do hereby establish an international organization
to be known as the United Nations.

[3] Signed at the United Nations Conference on International Organization, San
Francisco, California, June 26, 1945.

CHAPTER I. PURPOSES AND PRINCIPLES

Article 1

The Purposes of the United Nations are:

1. To maintain international peace and security, and to that end: to take effective collective measures for the prevention and removal of threats to the peace, and for the suppression of acts of aggression or other breaches of the peace, and to bring about by peaceful means, and in conformity with the principles of justice and international law, adjustment or settlement of international disputes or situations which might lead to a breach of the peace;

2. To develop friendly relations among nations based on respect for the principle of equal rights and self-determination of peoples, and to take other appropriate measures to strengthen universal peace;

3. To achieve international cooperation in solving international problems of an economic, social, cultural, or humanitarian character, and in promoting and encouraging respect for human rights and for fundamental freedoms for all without distinction as to race, sex, language, or religion; and

4. To be a center for harmonizing the actions of nations in the attainment of these common ends.

Article 2

The Organization and its Members, in pursuit of the Purposes stated in Article 1, shall act in accordance with the following Principles.

1. The Organization is based on the principle of the sovereign equality of all its Members.

2. All Members, in order to ensure to all of them the rights and benefits resulting from membership, shall fulfil in good faith the obligations assumed by them in accordance with the present Charter.

3. All Members shall settle their international disputes by peaceful means in such a manner that international peace and security, and justice, are not endangered.

4. All Members shall refrain in their international relations from the threat or use of force against the territorial integrity or political independence of any state, or in any other manner inconsistent with the Purposes of the United Nations.

5. All Members shall give the United Nations every assistance in any action it takes in accordance with the present Charter, and shall refrain from giving assistance to any state against which the United Nations is taking preventive or enforcement action.

6. The Organization shall ensure that states which are not Members of the United Nations act in accordance with these Principles so far as may be necessary for the maintenance of international peace and security.

7. Nothing contained in the present Charter shall authorize the United Nations to intervene in matters which are essentially within the domestic jurisdiction of any state or shall require the Members to submit such mat-

ters to settlement under the present Charter; but this principle shall not prejudice the application of enforcement measures under Chapter VII.

CHAPTER II. MEMBERSHIP

Article 3

The original Members of the United Nations shall be the states which, having participated in the United Nations Conference on International Organization at San Francisco, or having previously signed the Declaration by United Nations of January 1, 1942, sign the present Charter and ratify it in accordance with Article 110.

Article 4

1. Membership in the United Nations is open to all other peace-loving states which accept the obligations contained in the present Charter and, in the judgment of the Organization, are able and willing to carry out these obligations.

2. The admission of any such state to membership in the United Nations will be effected by a decision of the General Assembly upon the recommendation of the Security Council.

Article 5

A Member of the United Nations against which preventive or enforcement action has been taken by the Security Council may be suspended from the exercise of the rights and privileges of membership by the General Assembly upon the recommendation of the Security Council. The exercise of these rights and privileges may be restored by the Security Council.

Article 6

A Member of the United Nations which has persistently violated the Principles contained in the present Charter may be expelled from the Organization by the General Assembly upon the recommendation of the Security Council.

CHAPTER III. ORGANS

Article 7

1. There are established as the principal organs of the United Nations: a General Assembly, a Security Council, an Economic and Social Council, a Trusteeship Council, an International Court of Justice, and a Secretariat.

2. Such subsidiary organs as may be found necessary may be established in accordance with the present Charter.

Article 8

The United Nations shall place no restrictions on the eligibility of men and women to participate in any capacity and under conditions of equality in its principal and subsidiary organs.

CHAPTER IV. THE GENERAL ASSEMBLY

COMPOSITION

Article 9

1. The General Assembly shall consist of all the Members of the United Nations.

2. Each Member shall have not more than five representatives in the General Assembly.

FUNCTIONS AND POWERS

Article 10

The General Assembly may discuss any questions or any matters within the scope of the present Charter or relating to the powers and functions of any organs provided for in the present Charter, and, except as provided in Article 12, may make recommendations to the Members of the United Nations or to the Security Council or to both on any such questions or matters.

Article 11

1. The General Assembly may consider the general principles of co-operation in the maintenance of international peace and security, including the principles governing disarmament and the regulation of armaments, and may make recommendations with regard to such principles to the Members or to the Security Council or to both.

2. The General Assembly may discuss any questions relating to the maintenance of international peace and security brought before it by any Member of the United Nations, or by the Security Council, or by a state which is not a Member of the United Nations in accordance with Article 35, paragraph 2, and, except as provided in Article 12, may make recommendations with regard to any such questions to the state or states concerned or to the Security Council or to both. Any such question on which action is necessary shall be referred to the Security Council by the General Assembly either before or after discussion.

3. The General Assembly may call the attention of the Security Council to situations which are likely to endanger international peace and security.

4. The powers of the General Assembly set forth in this Article shall not limit the general scope of Article 10.

Article 12

1. While the Security Council is exercising in respect of any dispute or situation the functions assigned to it in the present Charter, the General Assembly shall not make any recommendation with regard to that dispute or situation unless the Security Council so requests.

2. The Secretary-General, with the consent of the Security Council, shall

notify the General Assembly at each session of any matters relative to the maintenance of international peace and security which are being dealt with by the Security Council and shall similarly notify the General Assembly, or the Members of the United Nations if the General Assembly is not in session, immediately the Security Council ceases to deal with such matters.

Article 13

1. The General Assembly shall initiate studies and make recommendations for the purpose of:

a. promoting international cooperation in the political field and encouraging the progressive development of international law and its codification;

b. promoting international cooperation in the economic, social, cultural, educational, and health fields, and assisting in the realization of human rights and fundamental freedoms for all without distinction as to race, sex, language, or religion.

2. The further responsibilities, functions and powers of the General Assembly with respect to matters mentioned in paragraph 1 (*b*) above are set forth in Chapters IX and X.

Article 14

Subject to the provisions of Article 12, the General Assembly may recommend measures for the peaceful adjustment of any situation, regardless of origin, which it deems likely to impair the general welfare or friendly relations among nations, including situations resulting from a violation of the provisions of the present Charter setting forth the Purposes and Principles of the United Nations.

Article 15

1. The General Assembly shall receive and consider annual and special reports from the Security Council; these reports shall include an account of the measures that the Security Council has decided upon or taken to maintain international peace and security.

2. The General Assembly shall receive and consider reports from the other organs of the United Nations.

Article 16

The General Assembly shall perform such functions with respect to the international trusteeship system as are assigned to it under Chapters XII and XIII, including the approval of the trusteeship agreements for areas not designated as strategic.

Article 17

1. The General Assembly shall consider and approve the budget of the Organization.

2. The expenses of the Organization shall be borne by the Members as apportioned by the General Assembly.

3. The General Assembly shall consider and approve any financial and budgetary arrangements with specialized agencies referred to in Article 57 and shall examine the administrative budgets of such specialized agencies with a view to making recommendations to the agencies concerned.

VOTING

Article 18

1. Each member of the General Assembly shall have one vote.

2. Decisions of the General Assembly on important questions shall be made by a two-thirds majority of the members present and voting. These questions shall include: recommendations with respect to the maintenance of international peace and security, the election of the non-permanent members of the Security Council, the election of the members of the Economic and Social Council, the election of members of the Trusteeship Council in accordance with paragraph 1 (*c*) of Article 86, the admission of new Members to the United Nations, the suspension of the rights and privileges of membership, the expulsion of Members, questions relating to the operation of the trusteeship system, and budgetary questions.

3. Decisions on other questions, including the determination of additional categories of questions to be decided by a two-thirds majority, shall be made by a majority of the members present and voting.

Article 19

A Member of the United Nations which is in arrears in the payment of its financial contributions to the Organization shall have no vote in the General Assembly if the amount of its arrears equals or exceeds the amount of the contributions due from it for the preceding two full years. The General Assembly may, nevertheless, permit such a Member to vote if it is satisfied that the failure to pay is due to conditions beyond the control of the Member.

PROCEDURE

Article 20

The General Assembly shall meet in regular annual sessions and in such special sessions as occasion may require. Special sessions shall be convoked by the Secretary-General at the request of the Security Council or of a majority of the Members of the United Nations.

Article 21

The General Assembly shall adopt its own rules of procedure. It shall elect its President for each session.

Article 22

The General Assembly may establish such subsidiary organs as it deems necessary for the performance of its functions.

CHAPTER V. THE SECURITY COUNCIL

COMPOSITION

Article 23 *

1. The Security Council shall consist of eleven Members of the United Nations. The Republic of China, France, the Union of Soviet Socialist Republics, the United Kingdom of Great Britain and Northern Ireland, and the United States of America shall be permanent members of the Security Council. The General Assembly shall elect six other Members of the United Nations to be non-permanent members of the Security Council, due regard being specially paid, in the first instance to the contribution of Members of the United Nations to the maintenance of international peace and security and to the other purposes of the Organization, and also to equitable geographical distribution.

2. The non-permanent members of the Security Council shall be elected for a term of two years. In the first election of the non-permanent members, however, three shall be chosen for a term of one year. A retiring member shall not be eligible for immediate re-election.

3. Each member of the Security Council shall have one representative.

FUNCTIONS AND POWERS

Article 24

1. In order to ensure prompt and effective action by the United Nations, its Members confer on the Security Council primary responsibility for the maintenance of international peace and security, and agree that in carrying out its duties under this responsibility the Security Council acts on their behalf.

2. In discharging these duties the Security Council shall act in accordance with the Purposes and Principles of the United Nations. The specific powers granted to the Security Council for the discharge of these duties are laid down in Chapters VI, VII, VIII, and XII.

3. The Security Council shall submit annual and, when necessary, special reports to the General Assembly for its consideration.

Article 25

The Members of the United Nations agree to accept and carry out the decisions of the Security Council in accordance with the present Charter.

Article 26

In order to promote the establishment and maintenance of international peace and security with the least diversion for armaments of the world's human and economic resources, the Security Council shall be responsible for formulating, with the assistance of the Military Staff Committee referred to in Article 47, plans to be submitted to the Members of the United Nations for the establishment of a system for the regulation of armaments.

* For amendment effective Aug. 31, 1965, see p. 192.

Voting

Article 27 *

1. Each member of the Security Council shall have one vote.

2. Decisions of the Security Council on procedural matters shall be made by an affirmative vote of seven members.

3. Decisions of the Security Council on all other matters shall be made by an affirmative vote of seven members including the concurring votes of the permanent members; provided that, in decisions under Chapter VI, and under paragraph 3 of Article 52, a party to a dispute shall abstain from voting.

Procedure

Article 28

1. The Security Council shall be so organized as to be able to function continuously. Each member of the Security Council shall for this purpose be represented at all times at the seat of the Organization.

2. The Security Council shall hold periodic meetings at which each of its members may, if it so desires, be represented by a member of the government or by some other specially designated representative.

3. The Security Council may hold meetings at such places other than the seat of the Organization as in its judgment will best facilitate its work.

Article 29

The Security Council may establish such subsidiary organs as it deems necessary for the performance of its functions.

Article 30

The Security Council shall adopt its own rules of procedure, including the method of selecting its President.

Article 31

Any Member of the United Nations which is not a member of the Security Council may participate, without vote, in the discussion of any question brought before the Security Council whenever the latter considers that the interests of that Member are specially affected.

Article 32

Any Member of the United Nations which is not a member of the Security Council or any state which is not a Member of the United Nations, if it is a party to a dispute under consideration by the Security Council, shall be invited to participate, without vote, in the discussion relating to the dispute. The Security Council shall lay down such conditions as it deems just for the participation of a state which is not a Member of the United Nations.

* For amendment effective Aug. 31, 1965, see p. 215.

CHAPTER VI. PACIFIC SETTLEMENT OF DISPUTES

Article 33

1. The parties to any dispute, the continuance of which is likely to endanger the maintenance of international peace and security, shall, first of all, seek a solution by negotiation, enquiry, mediation, conciliation, arbitration, judicial settlement, resort to regional agencies or arrangements, or other peaceful means of their own choice.

2. The Security Council shall, when it deems necessary, call upon the parties to settle their dispute by such means.

Article 34

The Security Council may investigate any dispute, or any situation which might lead to international friction or give rise to a dispute, in order to determine whether the continuance of the dispute or situation is likely to endanger the maintenance of international peace and security.

Article 35

1. Any Member of the United Nations may bring any dispute, or any situation of the nature referred to in Article 34, to the attention of the Security Council or of the General Assembly.

2. A state which is not a Member of the United Nations may bring to the attention of the Security Council or of the General Assembly any dispute to which it is a party if it accepts in advance, for the purposes of the dispute, the obligations of pacific settlement provided in the present Charter.

3. The proceedings of the General Assembly in respect of matters brought to its attention under this Article will be subject to the provisions of Articles 11 and 12.

Article 36

1. The Security Council may, at any stage of a dispute of the nature referred to in Article 33 or of a situation of like nature, recommend appropriate procedures or methods of adjustment.

2. The Security Council should take into consideration any procedures for the settlement of the dispute which have already been adopted by the parties.

3. In making recommendations under this Article the Security Council should also take into consideration that legal disputes should as a general rule be referred by the parties to the International Court of Justice in accordance with the provisions of the Statute of the Court.

Article 37

1. Should the parties to a dispute of the nature referred to in Article 33 fail to settle it by the means indicated in that Article, they shall refer it to the Security Council.

2. If the Security Council deems that the continuance of the dispute

is in fact likely to endanger the maintenance of international peace and security, it shall decide whether to take action under Article 36 or to recommend such terms of settlement as it may consider appropriate.

Article 38
Without prejudice to the provisions of Articles 33 to 37, the Security Council may, if all the parties to any dispute so request, make recommendations to the parties with a view to a pacific settlement of the dispute.

CHAPTER VII. ACTION WITH RESPECT TO THREATS TO THE PEACE, BREACHES OF THE PEACE, AND ACTS OF AGGRESSION

Article 39
The Security Council shall determine the existence of any threat to the peace, breach of the peace, or act of aggression and shall make recommendations, or decide what measures shall be taken in accordance with Articles 41 and 42, to maintain or restore international peace and security.

Article 40
In order to prevent an aggravation of the situation, the Security Council may, before making the recommendations or deciding upon the measures provided for in Article 39, call upon the parties concerned to comply with such provisional measures as it deems necessary or desirable. Such provisional measures shall be without prejudice to the rights, claims, or position of the parties concerned. The Security Council shall duly take account of failure to comply with such provisional measures.

Article 41
The Security Council may decide what measures not involving the use of armed force are to be employed to give effect to its decisions, and it may call upon the Members of the United Nations to apply such measures. These may include complete or partial interruption of economic relations and of rail, sea, air, postal, telegraphic, radio, and other means of communication, and the severance of diplomatic relations.

Article 42
Should the Security Council consider that measures provided for in Article 41 would be inadequate or have proved to be inadequate, it may take such action by air, sea, or land forces as may be necessary to maintain or restore international peace and security. Such action may include demonstrations, blockade, and other operations by air, sea, or land forces of Members of the United Nations.

Article 43
1. All Members of the United Nations, in order to contribute to the maintenance of international peace and security, undertake to make available to the Security Council, on its call and in accordance with a special

agreement or agreements, armed forces, assistance, and facilities, including rights of passage, necessary for the purpose of maintaining international peace and security.

2. Such agreement or agreements shall govern the numbers and types of forces, their degree of readiness and general location, and the nature of the facilities and assistance to be provided.

3. The agreement or agreements shall be negotiated as soon as possible on the initiative of the Security Council. They shall be concluded between the Security Council and Members or between the Security Council and groups of Members and shall be subject to ratification by the signatory states in accordance with their respective constitutional processes.

Article 44

When the Security Council has decided to use force it shall, before calling upon a Member not represented on it to provide armed forces in fulfillment of the obligations assumed under Article 43, invite that Member, if the Member so desires, to participate in the decisions of the Security Council concerning the employment of contingents of that Member's armed forces.

Article 45

In order to enable the United Nations to take urgent military measures, Members shall hold immediately available national air-force contingents for combined international enforcement action. The strength and degree of readiness of these contingents and plans for their combined action shall be determined, within the limits laid down in the special agreement or agreements referred to in Article 43, by the Security Council with the assistance of the Military Staff Committee.

Article 46

Plans for the application of armed force shall be made by the Security Council with the assistance of the Military Staff Committee.

Article 47

1. There shall be established a Military Staff Committee to advise and assist the Security Council on all questions relating to the Security Council's military requirements for the maintenance of international peace and security, the employment and command of forces placed at its disposal, the regulation of armaments, and possible disarmament.

2. The Military Staff Committee shall consist of the Chiefs of Staff of the permanent members of the Security Council or their representatives. Any Member of the United Nations not permanently represented on the Committee shall be invited by the Committee to be associated with it when the efficient discharge of the Committee's responsibilities requires the participation of that Member in its work.

3. The Military Staff Committee shall be responsible under the Security Council for the strategic direction of any armed forces placed at the dis-

posal of the Security Council. Questions relating to the command of such forces shall be worked out subsequently.

4. The Military Staff Committee, with the authorization of the Security Council and after consultation with appropriate regional agencies, may establish regional subcommittees.

Article 48

1. The action required to carry out the decisions of the Security Council for the maintenance of international peace and security shall be taken by all the Members of the United Nations or by some of them, as the Security Council may determine.

2. Such decisions shall be carried out by the Members of the United Nations directly and through their action in the appropriate international agencies of which they are members.

Article 49

The Members of the United Nations shall join in affording mutual assistance in carrying out the measures decided upon by the Security Council.

Article 50

If preventive or enforcement measures against any state are taken by the Security Council, any other state, whether a Member of the United Nations or not, which finds itself confronted with special economic problems arising from the carrying out of those measures shall have the right to consult the Security Council with regard to a solution of those problems.

Article 51

Nothing in the present Charter shall impair the inherent right of individual or collective self-defense if an armed attack occurs against a Member of the United Nations, until the Security Council has taken the measures necessary to maintain international peace and security. Measures taken by Members in the exercise of this right of self-defense shall be immediately reported to the Security Council and shall not in any way affect the authority and responsibility of the Security Council under the present Charter to take at any time such action as it deems necessary in order to maintain or restore international peace and security.

CHAPTER VIII. REGIONAL ARRANGEMENTS

Article 52

1. Nothing in the present Charter precludes the existence of regional arrangements or agencies for dealing with such matters relating to the maintenance of international peace and security as are appropriate for regional action, provided that such arrangements or agencies and their activities are consistent with the Purposes and Principles of the United Nations.

2. The Members of the United Nations entering into such arrangements

or constituting such agencies shall make every effort to achieve pacific settlement of local disputes through such regional arrangements or by such regional agencies before referring them to the Security Council.

3. The Security Council shall encourage the development of pacific settlement of local disputes through such regional arrangements or by such regional agencies either on the initiative of the states concerned or by reference from the Security Council.

4. This Article in no way impairs the application of Articles 34 and 35.

Article 53

1. The Security Council shall, where appropriate, utilize such regional arrangements or agencies for enforcement action under its authority. But no enforcement action shall be taken under regional arrangements or by regional agencies without the authorization of the Security Council, with the exception of measures against any enemy state, as defined in paragraph 2 of this Article, provided for pursuant to Article 107 or in regional arrangements directed against renewal of aggressive policy on the part of any such state, until such time as the Organization may, on request of the Governments concerned, be charged with the responsibility for preventing further aggression by such a state.

2. The term enemy state as used in paragraph 1 of this Article applies to any state which during the Second World War has been an enemy of any signatory of the present Charter.

Article 54

The Security Council shall at all times be kept fully informed of activities undertaken or in contemplation under regional arrangements or by regional agencies for the maintenance of international peace and security.

CHAPTER IX. INTERNATIONAL ECONOMIC AND SOCIAL COOPERATION

Article 55

With a view to the creation of conditions of stability and well-being which are necessary for peaceful and friendly relations among nations based on respect for the principle of equal rights and self-determination of peoples, the United Nations shall promote:

a. higher standards of living, full employment, and conditions of economic and social progress and development;

b. solutions of international economic, social, health, and related problems; and international cultural and educational cooperation; and

c. universal respect for, and observance of, human rights and fundamental freedoms for all without distinction as to race, sex, language, or religion.

Article 56

All Members pledge themselves to take joint and separate action in cooperation with the Organization for the achievement of the purposes set forth in Article 55.

Article 57

1. The various specialized agencies, established by intergovernmental agreement and having wide international responsibilities, as defined in their basic instruments, in economic, social, cultural, educational, health, and related fields, shall be brought into relationship with the United Nations in accordance with the provisions of Article 63.

2. Such agencies thus brought into relationship with the United Nations are hereinafter referred to as specialized agencies.

Article 58

The Organization shall make recommendations for the coordination of the policies and activities of the specialized agencies.

Article 59

The Organization shall, where appropriate, initiate negotiations among the states concerned for the creation of any new specialized agencies required for the accomplishment of the purposes set forth in Article 55.

Article 60

Responsibility for the discharge of the functions of the Organization set forth in this Chapter shall be vested in the General Assembly and, under the authority of the General Assembly, in the Economic and Social Council, which shall have for this purpose the powers set forth in Chapter X.

CHAPTER X. THE ECONOMIC AND SOCIAL COUNCIL

COMPOSITION

Article 61 *

1. The Economic and Social Council shall consist of eighteen Members of the United Nations elected by the General Assembly.

2. Subject to the provisions of paragraph 3, six members of the Economic and Social Council shall be elected each year for a term of three years. A retiring member shall be eligible for immediate re-election.

3. At the first election, eighteen members of the Economic and Social Council shall be chosen. The term of office of six members so chosen shall expire at the end of one year, and of six other members at the end of two years, in accordance with arrangements made by the General Assembly.

4. Each member of the Economic and Social Council shall have one representative.

FUNCTIONS AND POWERS

Article 62

1. The Economic and Social Council may make or initiate studies and reports with respect to international economic, social, cultural, educational, health, and related matters and may make recommendations with respect to any such matters to the General Assembly, to the Members of the United Nations, and to the specialized agencies concerned.

* For amendment effective Aug. 31, 1965, see p. 408.

2. It may make recommendations for the purpose of promoting respect for, and observance of, human rights and fundamental freedoms for all.

3. It may prepare draft conventions for submission to the General Assembly, with respect to matters falling within its competence.

4. It may call, in accordance with the rules prescribed by the United Nations, international conferences on matters falling within its competence.

Article 63

1. The Economic and Social Council may enter into agreements with any of the agencies referred to in Article 57, defining the terms on which the agency concerned shall be brought into relationship with the United Nations. Such agreements shall be subject to approval by the General Assembly.

2. It may coordinate the activities of the specialized agencies through consultation with and recommendations to such agencies and through recommendations to the General Assembly and to the Members of the United Nations.

Article 64

1. The Economic and Social Council may take appropriate steps to obtain regular reports from the specialized agencies. It may make arrangements with the Members of the United Nations and with the specialized agencies to obtain reports on the steps taken to give effect to its own recommendations and to recommendations on matters falling within its competence made by the General Assembly.

2. It may communicate its observations on these reports to the General Assembly.

Article 65

The Economic and Social Council may furnish information to the Security Council and shall assist the Security Council upon its request.

Article 66

1. The Economic and Social Council shall perform such functions as fall within its competence in connection with the carrying out of the recommendations of the General Assembly.

2. It may, with the approval of the General Assembly, perform services at the request of Members of the United Nations and at the request of specialized agencies.

3. It shall perform such other functions as are specified elsewhere in the present Charter or as may be assigned to it by the General Assembly.

Voting

Article 67

1. Each member of the Economic and Social Council shall have one vote.

2. Decisions of the Economic and Social Council shall be made by a majority of the members present and voting.

PROCEDURE

Article 68

The Economic and Social Council shall set up commissions in economic and social fields and for the promotion of human rights, and such other commissions as may be required for the performance of its functions.

Article 69

The Economic and Social Council shall invite any Member of the United Nations to participate, without vote, in its deliberations on any matter of particular concern to that Member.

Article 70

The Economic and Social Council may make arrangements for representatives of the specialized agencies to participate, without vote, in its deliberations and in those of the commissions established by it, and for its representatives to participate in the deliberations of the specialized agencies.

Article 71

The Economic and Social Council may make suitable arrangements for consultation with non-governmental organizations which are concerned with matters within its competence. Such arrangements may be made with international organizations and, where appropriate, with national organizations after consultation with the Member of the United Nations concerned.

Article 72

1. The Economic and Social Council shall adopt its own rules of procedure, including the method of selecting its President.

2. The Economic and Social Council shall meet as required in accordance with its rules, which shall include provision for the convening of meetings on the request of a majority of its members.

CHAPTER XI. DECLARATION REGARDING NON-SELF-GOVERNING TERRITORIES

Article 73

Members of the United Nations which have or assume responsibilities for the administration of territories whose peoples have not yet attained a full measure of self-government recognize the principle that the interests of the inhabitants of these territories are paramount, and accept as a sacred trust the obligation to promote to the utmost, within the system of international peace and security established by the present Charter, the well-being of the inhabitants of these territories, and, to this end:

    a. to ensure, with due respect for the culture of the peoples concerned, their political, economic, social, and educational advancement, their just treatment, and their protection against abuses;

    b. to develop self-government, to take due account of the political aspirations of the peoples, and to assist them in the progressive development of their free political institutions, according to the particular circumstances of each territory and its peoples and their varying stages of advancement;

c. to further international peace and security;

d. to promote constructive measures of development, to encourage research, and to cooperate with one another and, when and where appropriate, with specialized international bodies with a view to the practical achievement of the social, economic, and scientific purposes set forth in this Article; and

e. to transmit regularly to the Secretary-General for information purposes, subject to such limitation as security and constitutional considerations may require, statistical and other information of a technical nature relating to economic, social, and educational conditions in the territories for which they are respectively responsible other than those territories to which Chapters XII and XIII apply.

Article 74

Members of the United Nations also agree that their policy in respect of the territories to which this Chapter applies, no less than in respect of their metropolitan areas, must be based on the general principle of good-neighbourliness, due account being taken of the interests and well-being of the rest of the world, in social, economic, and commercial matters.

CHAPTER XII. INTERNATIONAL TRUSTEESHIP SYSTEM

Article 75

The United Nations shall establish under its authority an international trusteeship system for the administration and supervision of such territories as may be placed thereunder by subsequent individual agreements. These territories are hereinafter referred to as trust territories.

Article 76

The basic objectives of the trusteeship system, in accordance with the Purposes of the United Nations laid down in Article 1 of the present Charter, shall be:

a. to further international peace and security;

b. to promote the political, economic, social, and educational advancement of the inhabitants of the trust territories, and their progressive development towards self-government or independence as may be appropriate to the particular circumstances of each territory and its peoples and the freely expressed wishes of the peoples concerned, and as may be provided by the terms of each trusteeship agreement;

c. to encourage respect for human rights and for fundamental freedoms for all without distinction as to race, sex, language, or religion, and to encourage recognition of the interdependence of the peoples of the world; and

d. to ensure equal treatment in social, economic, and commercial matters for all Members of the United Nations and their nationals, and also equal treatment for the latter in the administration of justice, without prejudice to the attainment of the foregoing objectives and subject to the provisions of Article 80.

Article 77

1. The trusteeship system shall apply to such territories in the following categories as may be placed thereunder by means of trusteeship agreements:

   a. territories now held under mandate;

   b. territories which may be detached from enemy states as a result of the Second World War; and

   c. territories voluntarily placed under the system by states responsible for their administration.

2. It will be a matter for subsequent agreement as to which territories in the foregoing categories will be brought under the trusteeship system and upon what terms.

Article 78

The trusteeship system shall not apply to territories which have become Members of the United Nations, relationship among which shall be based on respect for the principle of sovereign equality.

Article 79

The terms of trusteeship for each territory to be placed under the trusteeship system, including any alteration or amendment, shall be agreed upon by the states directly concerned, including the mandatory power in the case of territories held under mandate by a Member of the United Nations, and shall be approved as provided for in Articles 83 and 85.

Article 80

1. Except as may be agreed upon in individual trusteeship agreements, made under Articles 77, 79, and 81, placing each territory under the trusteeship system, and until such agreements have been concluded, nothing in this Chapter shall be construed in or of itself to alter in any manner the rights whatsoever of any states or any peoples or the terms of existing international instruments to which Members of the United Nations may respectively be parties.

2. Paragraph 1 of this Article shall not be interpreted as giving grounds for delay or postponement of the negotiation and conclusion of agreements for placing mandated and other territories under the trusteeship system as provided for in Article 77.

Article 81

The trusteeship agreement shall in each case include the terms under which the trust territory will be administered and designate the authority which will exercise the administration of the trust territory. Such authority, hereinafter called the administering authority, may be one or more states or the Organization itself.

Article 82

There may be designated, in any trusteeship agreement, a strategic area or areas which may include part or all of the trust territory to which the agreement applies, without prejudice to any special agreement or agreements made under Article 43.

Article 83

1. All functions of the United Nations relating to strategic areas, including the approval of the terms of the trusteeship agreements and of their alteration or amendment, shall be exercised by the Security Council.

2. The basic objectives set forth in Article 76 shall be applicable to the people of each strategic area.

3. The Security Council shall, subject to the provisions of the trusteeship agreements and without prejudice to security considerations, avail itself of the assistance of the Trusteeship Council to perform those functions of the United Nations under the trusteeship system relating to political, economic, social, and educational matters in the strategic areas.

Article 84

It shall be the duty of the administering authority to ensure that the trust territory shall play its part in the maintenance of international peace and security. To this end the administering authority may make use of volunteer forces, facilities, and assistance from the trust territory in carrying out the obligations towards the Security Council undertaken in this regard by the administering authority, as well as for local defense and the maintenance of law and order within the trust territory.

Article 85

1. The functions of the United Nations with regard to trusteeship agreements for all areas not designated as strategic, including the approval of the terms of the trusteeship agreements and of their alteration or amendment, shall be exercised by the General Assembly.

2. The Trusteeship Council, operating under the authority of the General Assembly, shall assist the General Assembly in carrying out these functions.

CHAPTER XIII. THE TRUSTEESHIP COUNCIL
COMPOSITION

Article 86

1. The Trusteeship Council shall consist of the following Members of the United Nations:

a. those Members administering trust territories;

b. such of those Members mentioned by name in Article 23 as are not administering trust territories; and

c. as many other Members elected for three-year terms by the General Assembly as may be necessary to ensure that the total number of members of the Trusteeship Council is equally divided between those Members of the United Nations which administer trust territories and those which do not.

2. Each member of the Trusteeship Council shall designate one specially qualified person to represent it therein.

FUNCTIONS AND POWERS

Article 87

The General Assembly and, under its authority, the Trusteeship Council, in carrying out their functions, may:

a. consider reports submitted by the administering authority;

b. accept petitions and examine them in consultation with the administering authority;

c. provide for periodic visits to the respective trust territories at times agreed upon with the administering authority; and

d. take these and other actions in conformity with the terms of the trusteeship agreements.

Article 88

The Trusteeship Council shall formulate a questionnaire on the political, economic, social, and educational advancement of the inhabitants of each trust territory, and the administering authority for each trust territory within the competence of the General Assembly shall make an annual report to the General Assembly upon the basis of such questionnaire.

VOTING

Article 89

1. Each member of the Trusteeship Council shall have one vote.

2. Decisions of the Trusteeship Council shall be made by a majority of the members present and voting.

PROCEDURE

Article 90

1. The Trusteeship Council shall adopt its own rules of procedure, including the method of selecting its President.

2. The Trusteeship Council shall meet as required in accordance with its rules, which shall include provision for the convening of meetings on the request of a majority of its members.

Article 91

The Trusteeship Council shall, when appropriate, avail itself of the assistance of the Economic and Social Council and of the specialized agencies in regard to matters with which they are respectively concerned.

CHAPTER XIV. THE INTERNATIONAL COURT OF JUSTICE

Article 92

The International Court of Justice shall be the principal judicial organ of the United Nations. It shall function in accordance with the annexed Statute, which is based upon the Statute of the Permanent Court of International Justice and forms an integral part of the present Charter.

Article 93

1. All Members of the United Nations are *ipso facto* parties to the Statute of the International Court of Justice.

2. A state which is not a Member of the United Nations may become a party to the Statute of the International Court of Justice on conditions to be determined in each case by the General Assembly upon the recommendation of the Security Council.

Article 94

1. Each Member of the United Nations undertakes to comply with the decision of the International Court of Justice in any case to which it is a party.

2. If any party to a case fails to perform the obligations incumbent upon it under a judgment rendered by the Court, the other party may have recourse to the Security Council, which may, if it deems necessary, make recommendations or decide upon measures to be taken to give effect to the judgment.

Article 95

Nothing in the present Charter shall prevent Members of the United Nations from entrusting the solution of their differences to other tribunals by virtue of agreements already in existence or which may be concluded in the future.

Article 96

1. The General Assembly or the Security Council may request the International Court of Justice to give an advisory opinion on any legal question.

2. Other organs of the United Nations and specialized agencies, which may at any time be so authorized by the General Assembly, may also request advisory opinions of the Court on legal questions arising within the scope of their activities.

CHAPTER XV. THE SECRETARIAT

Article 97

The Secretariat shall comprise a Secretary-General and such staff as the Organization may require. The Secretary-General shall be appointed by the General Assembly upon the recommendation of the Security Council. He shall be the chief administrative officer of the Organization.

Article 98

The Secretary-General shall act in that capacity in all meetings of the General Assembly, of the Security Council, of the Economic and Social Council, and of the Trusteeship Council, and shall perform such other functions as are entrusted to him by these organs. The Secretary-General shall make an annual report to the General Assembly on the work of the Organization.

Article 99

The Secretary-General may bring to the attention of the Security Council any matter which in his opinion may threaten the maintenance of international peace and security.

Article 100

1. In the performance of their duties the Secretary-General and the staff shall not seek or receive instructions from any government or from any other authority external to the Organization. They shall refrain from any action which might reflect on their position as international officials responsible only to the Organization.

2. Each Member of the United Nations undertakes to respect the exclusively international character of the responsibilities of the Secretary-General and the staff and not to seek to influence them in the discharge of their responsibilities.

Article 101

1. The staff shall be appointed by the Secretary-General under regulations established by the General Assembly.

2. Appropriate staffs shall be permanently assigned to the Economic and Social Council, the Trusteeship Council, and, as required, to other organs of the United Nations. These staffs shall form a part of the Secretariat.

3. The paramount consideration in the employment of the staff and in the determination of the conditions of service shall be the necessity of securing the highest standards of efficiency, competence, and integrity. Due regard shall be paid to the importance of recruiting the staff on as wide a geographical basis as possible.

CHAPTER XVI. MISCELLANEOUS PROVISIONS

Article 102

1. Every treaty and every international agreement entered into by any Member of the United Nations after the present Charter comes into force shall as soon as possible be registered with the Secretariat and published by it.

2. No party to any such treaty or international agreement which has

not been registered in accordance with the provisions of paragraph 1 of this Article may invoke that treaty or agreement before any organ of the United Nations.

Article 103

In the event of a conflict between the obligations of the Members of the United Nations under the present Charter and their obligations under any other international agreement, their obligations under the present Charter shall prevail.

Article 104

The Organization shall enjoy in the territory of each of its Members such legal capacity as may be necessary for the exercise of its functions and the fulfillment of its purposes.

Article 105

1. The Organization shall enjoy in the territory of each of its Members such privileges and immunities as are necessary for the fulfillment of its purposes.

2. Representatives of the Members of the United Nations and officials of the Organization shall similarly enjoy such privileges and immunities as are necessary for the independent exercise of their functions in connection with the Organization.

3. The General Assembly may make recommendations with a view to determining the details of the application of paragraphs 1 and 2 of this Article or may propose conventions to the Members of the United Nations for this purpose.

CHAPTER XVII. TRANSITIONAL SECURITY ARRANGEMENTS

Article 106

Pending the coming into force of such special agreements referred to in Article 43 as in the opinion of the Security Council enable it to begin the exercise of its responsibilities under Article 42, the parties to the Four-Nation Declaration, signed at Moscow, October 30, 1943, and France, shall, in accordance with the provisions of paragraph 5 of that Declaration, consult with one another and as occasion requires with other Members of the United Nations with a view to such joint action on behalf of the Organization as may be necessary for the purpose of maintaining international peace and security.

Article 107

Nothing in the present Charter shall invalidate or preclude action, in relation to any state which during the Second World War has been an enemy of any signatory to the present Charter, taken or authorized as a result of that war by the Governments having responsibility for such action.

CHAPTER XVIII. AMENDMENTS

Article 108

Amendments to the present Charter shall come into force for all Members of the United Nations when they have been adopted by a vote of two thirds of the members of the General Assembly and ratified in accordance with their respective constitutional processes by two thirds of the Members of the United Nations, including all the permanent members of the Security Council.

Article 109 *

1. A General Conference of the Members of the United Nations for the purpose of reviewing the present Charter may be held at a date and place to be fixed by a two-thirds vote of the members of the General Assembly and by a vote of any seven members of the Security Council. Each Member of the United Nations shall have one vote in the conference.

2. Any alteration of the present Charter recommended by a two-thirds vote of the conference shall take effect when ratified in accordance with their respective constitutional processes by two thirds of the Members of the United Nations including all the permanent members of the Security Council.

3. If such a conference has not been held before the tenth annual session of the General Assembly following the coming into force of the present Charter, the proposal to call such a conference shall be placed on the agenda of that session of the General Assembly, and the conference shall be held if so decided by a majority vote of the members of the General Assembly and by a vote of any seven members of the Security Council.

CHAPTER XIX. RATIFICATION AND SIGNATURE

Article 110

1. The present Charter shall be ratified by the signatory states in accordance with their respective constitutional processes.

2. The ratifications shall be deposited with the Government of the United States of America, which shall notify all the signatory states of each deposit as well as the Secretary-General of the Organization when he has been appointed.

3. The present Charter shall come into force upon the deposit of ratifications by the Republic of China, France, the Union of Soviet Socialist Republics, the United Kingdom of Great Britain and Northern Ireland, and the United States of America, and by a majority of the other signatory states. A protocol of the ratifications deposited shall thereupon be drawn up by the Government of the United States of America which shall communicate copies thereof to all the signatory states.

4. The states signatory to the present Charter which ratify it after it has

* For amendment effective June 12, 1968, see p. 643.

come into force will become original Members of the United Nations on the date of the deposit of their respective ratifications.

Article 111

The present Charter, of which the Chinese, French, Russian, English, and Spanish texts are equally authentic, shall remain deposited in the archives of the Government of the United States of America. Duly certified copies thereof shall be transmitted by that Government to the Governments of the other signatory states.

IN FAITH WHEREOF the representatives of the Governments of the United Nations have signed the present Charter.

DONE at the city of San Francisco the twenty-sixth day of June, one thousand nine hundred and forty-five.

STATUTE OF THE INTERNATIONAL COURT OF JUSTICE [4]

Article 1

THE INTERNATIONAL COURT OF JUSTICE established by the Charter of the United Nations as the principal judicial organ of the United Nations shall be constituted and shall function in accordance with the provisions of the present Statute.

CHAPTER I. ORGANIZATION OF THE COURT

Article 2

The Court shall be composed of a body of independent judges, elected regardless of their nationality from among persons of high moral character, who possess the qualifications required in their respective countries for appointment to the highest judicial offices, or are jurisconsults of recognized competence in international law.

Article 3

1. The Court shall consist of fifteen members, no two of whom may be nationals of the same state.

2. A person who for the purposes of membership in the Court could be regarded as a national of more than one state shall be deemed to be a national of the one in which he ordinarily exercises civil and political rights.

Article 4

1. The members of the Court shall be elected by the General Assembly and by the Security Council from a list of persons nominated by the national groups in the Permanent Court of Arbitration, in accordance with the following provisions.

2. In the case of Members of the United Nations not represented in the Permanent Court of Arbitration, candidates shall be nominated by national groups appointed for this purpose by their governments under the same

[4] Signed at the United Nations Conference on International Organization, San Francisco, California, June 26, 1945.

conditions as those prescribed for members of the Permanent Court of Arbitration by Article 44 of the Convention of The Hague of 1907 for the pacific settlement of international disputes.

3. The conditions under which a state which is a party to the present Statute but is not a Member of the United Nations may participate in electing the members of the Court shall, in the absence of a special agreement, be laid down by the General Assembly upon recommendation of the Security Council.

Article 5

1. At least three months before the date of the election, the Secretary-General of the United Nations shall address a written request to the members of the Permanent Court of Arbitration belonging to the states which are parties to the present Statute, and to the members of the national groups appointed under Article 4, paragraph 2, inviting them to undertake, within a given time, by national groups, the nomination of persons in a position to accept the duties of a member of the Court.

2. No group may nominate more than four persons, not more than two of whom shall be of their own nationality. In no case may the number of candidates nominated by a group be more than double the number of seats to be filled.

Article 6

Before making these nominations, each national group is recommended to consult its highest court of justice, its legal faculties and schools of law, and its national academies and national sections of international academies devoted to the study of law.

Article 7

1. The Secretary-General shall prepare a list in alphabetical order of all the persons thus nominated. Save as provided in Article 12, paragraph 2, these shall be the only persons eligible.

2. The Secretary-General shall submit this list to the General Assembly and to the Security Council.

Article 8

The General Assembly and the Security Council shall proceed independently of one another to elect the members of the Court.

Article 9

At every election, the electors shall bear in mind not only that the persons to be elected should individually possess the qualifications required, but also that in the body as a whole the representation of the main forms of civilization and of the principal legal systems of the world should be assured.

Article 10

1. Those candidates who obtain an absolute majority of votes in the General Assembly and in the Security Council shall be considered as elected.

2. Any vote of the Security Council, whether for the election of judges or for the appointment of members of the conference envisaged in Article 12, shall be taken without any distinction between permanent and non-permanent members of the Security Council.

3. In the event of more than one national of the same state obtaining an absolute majority of the votes both of the General Assembly and of the Security Council, the eldest of these only shall be considered as elected.

Article 11

If, after the first meeting held for the purpose of the election, one or more seats remain to be filled, a second and, if necessary, a third meeting shall take place.

Article 12

1. If, after the third meeting, one or more seats still remain unfilled, a joint conference consisting of six members, three appointed by the General Assembly and three by the Security Council, may be formed at any time at the request of either the General Assembly or the Security Council, for the purpose of choosing by the vote of an absolute majority one name for each seat still vacant, to submit to the General Assembly and the Security Council for their respective acceptance.

2. If the joint conference is unanimously agreed upon any person who fulfills the required conditions, he may be included in its list, even though he was not included in the list of nominations referred to in Article 7.

3. If the joint conference is satisfied that it will not be successful in procuring an election, those members of the Court who have already been elected shall, within a period to be fixed by the Security Council, proceed to fill the vacant seats by selection from among those candidates who have obtained votes either in the General Assembly or in the Security Council.

4. In the event of an equality of votes among the judges, the eldest judge shall have a casting vote.

Article 13

1. The members of the Court shall be elected for nine years and may be re-elected; provided, however, that of the judges elected at the first election, the terms of five judges shall expire at the end of three years and the terms of five more judges shall expire at the end of six years.

2. The judges whose terms are to expire at the end of the above-mentioned initial periods of three and six years shall be chosen by lot to be drawn by the Secretary-General immediately after the first election has been completed.

3. The members of the Court shall continue to discharge their duties until their places have been filled. Though replaced, they shall finish any cases which they may have begun.

4. In the case of the resignation of a member of the Court, the resignation shall be addressed to the President of the Court for transmission to the Secretary-General. This last notification makes the place vacant.

Article 14

Vacancies shall be filled by the same method as that laid down for the first election, subject to the following provision: the Secretary-General shall, within one month of the occurrence of the vacancy, proceed to issue the invitations provided for in Article 5, and the date of the election shall be fixed by the Security Council.

Article 15

A member of the Court elected to replace a member whose term of office has not expired shall hold office for the remainder of his predecessor's term.

Article 16

1. No member of the Court may exercise any political or administrative function, or engage in any other occupation of a professional nature.

2. Any doubt on this point shall be settled by the decision of the Court.

Article 17

1. No member of the Court may act as agent, counsel, or advocate in any case.

2. No member may participate in the decision of any case in which he has previously taken part as agent, counsel, or advocate for one of the parties, or as a member of a national or international court, or of a commission of enquiry, or in any other capacity.

3. Any doubt on this point shall be settled by the decision of the Court.

Article 18

1. No member of the Court can be dismissed unless, in the unanimous opinion of the other members, he has ceased to fulfill the required conditions.

2. Formal notification thereof shall be made to the Secretary-General by the Registrar.

3. This notification makes the place vacant.

Article 19

The members of the Court, when engaged on the business of the Court, shall enjoy diplomatic privileges and immunities.

Article 20

Every member of the Court shall, before taking up his duties, make a solemn declaration in open court that he will exercise his powers impartially and conscientiously.

Article 21

1. The Court shall elect its President and Vice-President for three years; they may be re-elected.

2. The Court shall appoint its Registrar and may provide for the appointment of such other officers as may be necessary.

Article 22

1. The seat of the Court shall be established at The Hague. This, however, shall not prevent the Court from sitting and exercising its functions elsewhere whenever the Court considers it desirable.

2. The President and the Registrar shall reside at the seat of the Court.

Article 23

1. The Court shall remain permanently in session, except during the judicial vacations, the dates and duration of which shall be fixed by the Court.

2. Members of the Court are entitled to periodic leave, the dates and duration of which shall be fixed by the Court, having in mind the distance between The Hague and the home of each judge.

3. Members of the Court shall be bound, unless they are on leave or prevented from attending by illness or other serious reasons duly explained to the President, to hold themselves permanently at the disposal of the Court.

Article 24

1. If, for some special reason, a member of the Court considers that he should not take part in the decision of a particular case, he shall so inform the President.

2. If the President considers that for some special reason one of the members of the Court should not sit in a particular case, he shall give him notice accordingly.

3. If in any such case the member of the Court and the President disagree, the matter shall be settled by the decision of the Court.

Article 25

1. The full Court shall sit except when it is expressly provided otherwise in the present Statute.

2. Subject to the condition that the number of judges available to constitute the Court is not thereby reduced below eleven, the Rules of the Court may provide for allowing one or more judges, according to circumstances and in rotation, to be dispensed from sitting.

3. A quorum of nine judges shall suffice to constitute the Court.

Article 26

1. The Court may from time to time form one or more chambers, composed of three or more judges as the Court may determine, for dealing with particular categories of cases; for example, labor cases and cases relating to transit and communications.

2. The Court may at any time form a chamber for dealing with a par-

ticular case. The number of judges to constitute such a chamber shall be determined by the Court with the approval of the parties.

3. Cases shall be heard and determined by the chambers provided for in this Article if the parties so request.

Article 27

A judgment given by any of the chambers provided for in Articles 26 and 29 shall be considered as rendered by the Court.

Article 28

The chambers provided for in Articles 26 and 29 may, with the consent of the parties, sit and exercise their functions elsewhere than at The Hague.

Article 29

With a view to the speedy despatch of business, the Court shall form annually a chamber composed of five judges which, at the request of the parties, may hear and determine cases by summary procedure. In addition, two judges shall be selected for the purpose of replacing judges who find it impossible to sit.

Article 30

1. The Court shall frame rules for carrying out its functions. In particular, it shall lay down rules of procedure.

2. The Rules of the Court may provide for assessors to sit with the Court or with any of its chambers, without the right to vote.

Article 31

1. Judges of the nationality of each of the parties shall retain their right to sit in the case before the Court.

2. If the Court includes upon the Bench a judge of the nationality of one of the parties, any other party may choose a person to sit as judge. Such person shall be chosen preferably from among those persons who have been nominated as candidates as provided in Articles 4 and 5.

3. If the Court includes upon the Bench no judge of the nationality of the parties, each of these parties may proceed to choose a judge as provided in paragraph 2 of this Article.

4. The provisions of this Article shall apply to the case of Articles 26 and 29. In such cases, the President shall request one or, if necessary, two of the members of the Court forming the chamber to give place to the members of the Court of the nationality of the parties concerned, and, failing such, or if they are unable to be present, to the judges specially chosen by the parties.

5. Should there be several parties in the same interest, they shall, for the purpose of the preceding provisions, be reckoned as one party only. Any doubt upon this point shall be settled by the decision of the Court.

6. Judges chosen as laid down in paragraphs 2, 3, and 4 of this Article shall fulfill the conditions required by Articles 2, 17 (paragraph 2), 20, and

24 of the present Statute. They shall take part in the decision on terms of complete equality with their colleagues.

Article 32

1. Each member of the Court shall receive an annual salary.

2. The President shall receive a special annual allowance.

3. The Vice-President shall receive a special allowance for every day on which he acts as President.

4. The judges chosen under Article 31, other than members of the Court, shall receive compensation for each day on which they exercise their functions.

5. These salaries, allowances, and compensation shall be fixed by the General Assembly. They may not be decreased during the term of office.

6. The salary of the Registrar shall be fixed by the General Assembly on the proposal of the Court.

7. Regulations made by the General Assembly shall fix the conditions under which retirement pensions may be given to members of the Court and to the Registrar, and the conditions under which members of the Court and the Registrar shall have their traveling expenses refunded.

8. The above salaries, allowances, and compensation shall be free of all taxation.

Article 33

The expenses of the Court shall be borne by the United Nations in such a manner as shall be decided by the General Assembly.

CHAPTER II. COMPETENCE OF THE COURT

Article 34

1. Only states may be parties in cases before the Court.

2. The Court, subject to and in conformity with its Rules, may request of public international organizations information relevant to cases before it, and shall receive such information presented by such organizations on their own initiative.

3. Whenever the construction of the constituent instrument of a public international organization or of an international convention adopted thereunder is in question in a case before the Court, the Registrar shall so notify the public international organization concerned and shall communicate to it copies of all the written proceedings.

Article 35

1. The Court shall be open to the states parties to the present Statute.

2. The conditions under which the Court shall be open to other states shall, subject to the special provisions contained in treaties in force, be laid down by the Security Council, but in no case shall such conditions place the parties in a position of inequality before the Court.

3. When a state which is not a Member of the United Nations is a party to a case, the Court shall fix the amount which that party is to

contribute towards the expenses of the Court. This provision shall not apply if such state is bearing a share of the expenses of the Court.

Article 36

1. The jurisdiction of the Court comprises all cases which the parties refer to it and all matters specially provided for in the Charter of the United Nations or in treaties and conventions in force.

2. The states parties to the present Statute may at any time declare that they recognize as compulsory *ipso facto* and without special agreement, in relation to any other state accepting the same obligation, the jurisdiction of the Court in all legal disputes concerning:

a. the interpretation of a treaty;

b. any question of international law;

c. the existence of any fact which, if established, would constitute a breach of an international obligation;

d. the nature or extent of the reparation to be made for the breach of an international obligation.

3. The declarations referred to above may be made unconditionally or on condition of reciprocity on the part of several or certain states, or for a certain time.

4. Such declarations shall be deposited with the Secretary-General of the United Nations, who shall transmit copies thereof to the parties to the Statute and to the Registrar of the Court.

5. Declarations made under Article 36 of the Statute of the Permanent Court of International Justice and which are still in force shall be deemed, as between the parties to the present Statute, to be acceptances of the compulsory jurisdiction of the International Court of Justice for the period which they still have to run and in accordance with their terms.

6. In the event of a dispute as to whether the Court has jurisdiction, the matter shall be settled by the decision of the Court.

Article 37

Whenever a treaty or convention in force provides for reference of a matter to a tribunal to have been instituted by the League of Nations, or to the Permanent Court of International Justice, the matter shall, as between the parties to the present Statute, be referred to the International Court of Justice.

Article 38

1. The Court, whose function is to decide in accordance with international law such disputes as are submitted to it, shall apply:

a. international conventions, whether general or particular, establishing rules expressly recognized by the contesting states;

b. international custom, as evidence of a general practice accepted as law;

c. the general principles of law recognized by civilized nations;

d. subject to the provisions of Article 59, judicial decisions and the teachings of the most highly qualified publicists of the various nations, as subsidiary means for the determination of rules of law.

2. This provision shall not prejudice the power of the Court to decide a case *ex aequo et bono,* if the parties agree thereto.

CHAPTER III. PROCEDURE

Article 39

1. The official languages of the Court shall be French and English. If the parties agree that the case shall be conducted in French, the judgment shall be delivered in French. If the parties agree that the case shall be conducted in English, the judgment shall be delivered in English.

2. In the absence of an agreement as to which language shall be employed, each party may, in the pleadings, use the language which it prefers; the decision of the Court shall be given in French and English. In this case the Court shall at the same time determine which of the two texts shall be considered as authoritative.

3. The Court shall, at the request of any party, authorize a language other than French or English to be used by that party.

Article 40

1. Cases are brought before the Court, as the case may be, either by the notification of the special agreement or by a written application addressed to the Registrar. In either case the subject of the dispute and the parties shall be indicated.

2. The Registrar shall forthwith communicate the application to all concerned.

3. He shall also notify the Members of the United Nations through the Secretary-General, and also any other states entitled to appear before the Court.

Article 41

1. The Court shall have the power to indicate, if it considers that circumstances so require, any provisional measures which ought to be taken to preserve the respective rights of either party.

2. Pending the final decision, notice of the measures suggested shall forthwith be given to the parties and to the Security Council.

Article 42

1. The parties shall be represented by agents.

2. They may have the assistance of counsel or advocates before the Court.

3. The agents, counsel, and advocates of parties before the Court shall enjoy the privileges and immunities necessary to the independent exercise of their duties.

Article 43

1. The procedure shall consist of two parts: written and oral.

2. The written proceedings shall consist of the communication to the

Court and to the parties of memorials, counter-memorials and, if necessary, replies; also all papers and documents in support.

3. These communications shall be made through the Registrar, in the order and within the time fixed by the Court.

4. A certified copy of every document produced by one party shall be communicated to the other party.

5. The oral proceedings shall consist of the hearing by the Court of witnesses, experts, agents, counsel, and advocates.

Article 44

1. For the service of all notices upon persons other than the agents, counsel, and advocates, the Court shall apply direct to the government of the state upon whose territory the notice has to be served.

2. The same provision shall apply whenever steps are to be taken to procure evidence on the spot.

Article 45

The hearing shall be under the control of the President or, if he is unable to preside, of the Vice-President; if neither is able to preside, the senior judge present shall preside.

Article 46

The hearing in Court shall be public, unless the Court shall decide otherwise, or unless the parties demand that the public be not admitted.

Article 47

1. Minutes shall be made at each hearing and signed by the Registrar and the President.

2. These minutes alone shall be authentic.

Article 48

The Court shall make orders for the conduct of the case, shall decide the form and time in which each party must conclude its arguments, and make all arrangements connected with the taking of evidence.

Article 49

The Court may, even before the hearing begins, call upon the agents to produce any document or to supply any explanations. Formal note shall be taken of any refusal.

Article 50

The Court may, at any time, entrust any individual, body, bureau, commission, or other organization that it may select, with the task of carrying out an enquiry or giving an expert opinion.

Article 51

During the hearing any relevant questions are to be put to the witnesses and experts under the conditions laid down by the Court in the rules of procedure referred to in Article 30.

Article 52

After the Court has received the proofs and evidence within the time specified for the purpose, it may refuse to accept any further oral or written evidence that one party may desire to present unless the other side consents.

Article 53

1. Whenever one of the parties does not appear before the Court, or fails to defend its case, the other party may call upon the Court to decide in favor of its claim.

2. The Court must, before doing so, satisfy itself, not only that it has jurisdiction in accordance with Articles 36 and 37, but also that the claim is well founded in fact and law.

Article 54

1. When, subject to the control of the Court, the agents, counsel, and advocates have completed their presentation of the case, the President shall declare the hearing closed.

2. The Court shall withdraw to consider the judgment.

3. The deliberations of the Court shall take place in private and remain secret.

Article 55

1. All questions shall be decided by a majority of the judges present.

2. In the event of an equality of votes, the President or the judge who acts in his place shall have a casting vote.

Article 56

1. The judgment shall state the reasons on which it is based.

2. It shall contain the names of the judges who have taken part in the decision.

Article 57

If the judgment does not represent in whole or in part the unanimous opinion of the judges, any judge shall be entitled to deliver a separate opinion.

Article 58

The judgment shall be signed by the President and by the Registrar. It shall be read in open court, due notice having been given to the agents.

Article 59

The decision of the Court has no binding force except between the parties and in respect of that particular case.

Article 60

The judgment is final and without appeal. In the event of dispute as to the meaning or scope of the judgment, the Court shall construe it upon the request of any party.

Article 61

1. An application for revision of a judgment may be made only when it is based upon the discovery of some fact of such a nature as to be a decisive factor, which fact was, when the judgment was given, unknown to the Court and also to the party claiming revision, always provided that such ignorance was not due to negligence.

2. The proceedings for revision shall be opened by a judgment of the Court expressly recording the existence of the new fact, recognizing that it has such a character as to lay the case open to revision, and declaring the application admissible on this ground.

3. The Court may require previous compliance with the terms of the judgment before it admits proceedings in revision.

4. The application for revision must be made at latest within six months of the discovery of the new fact.

5. No application for revision may be made after the lapse of ten years from the date of the judgment.

Article 62

1. Should a state consider that it has an interest of a legal nature which may be affected by the decision in the case, it may submit a request to the Court to be permitted to intervene.

2. It shall be for the Court to decide upon this request.

Article 63

1. Whenever the construction of a convention to which states other than those concerned in the case are parties is in question, the Registrar shall notify all such states forthwith.

2. Every state so notified has the right to intervene in the proceedings; but if it uses this right, the construction given by the judgment will be equally binding upon it.

Article 64

Unless otherwise decided by the Court, each party shall bear its own costs.

CHAPTER IV. ADVISORY OPINIONS

Article 65

1. The Court may give an advisory opinion on any legal question at the request of whatever body may be authorized by or in accordance with the Charter of the United Nations to make such a request.

2. Questions upon which the advisory opinion of the Court is asked shall be laid before the Court by means of a written request containing an exact statement of the question upon which an opinion is required, and accompanied by all documents likely to throw light upon the question.

Article 66

1. The Registrar shall forthwith give notice of the request for an advisory opinion to all states entitled to appear before the Court.

2. The Registrar shall also, by means of a special and direct communication, notify any state entitled to appear before the Court or international organization considered by the Court, or, should it not be sitting, by the President, as likely to be able to furnish information on the question, that the Court will be prepared to receive, within a time limit to be fixed by the President, written statements, or to hear, at a public sitting to be held for the purpose, oral statements relating to the question.

3. Should any such state entitled to appear before the Court have failed to receive the special communication referred to in paragraph 2 of this Article, such state may express a desire to submit a written statement or to be heard; and the Court will decide.

4. States and organizations having presented written or oral statements or both shall be permitted to comment on the statements made by other states or organizations in the form, to the extent, and within the time limits which the Court, or, should it not be sitting, the President, shall decide in each particular case. Accordingly, the Registrar shall in due time communicate any such written statements to states and organizations having submitted similar statements.

Article 67

The Court shall deliver its advisory opinions in open Court, notice having been given to the Secretary-General and to the representatives of Members of the United Nations, of other states and of international organizations immediately concerned.

Article 68

In the exercise of its advisory functions the Court shall further be guided by the provisions of the present Statute which apply in contentious cases to the extent to which it recognizes them to be applicable.

CHAPTER V. AMENDMENT

Article 69

Amendments to the present Statute shall be effected by the same procedure as is provided by the Charter of the United Nations for amendments to that Charter, subject however to any provisions which the General Assembly upon recommendation of the Security Council may adopt concerning the participation of states which are parties to the present Statute but are not Members of the United Nations.

Article 70

The Court shall have power to propose such amendments to the present Statute as it may deem necessary, through written communications to the Secretary-General, for consideration in conformity with the provisions of Article 69.

Index

Abbreviations
  Art. Article
  Ch. Chapter
  ECOSOC Economic and Social Council
  GA General Assembly
  ICJ International Court of Justice
  SC Security Council
  SG Secretary-General
  TC Trusteeship Council
  U.K. United Kingdom
  UN United Nations
  U.S. United States
  UNCIO United Nations Conference on International Organization